D1521349

Nat Turner and the Rising in Southampton County

NAT TURNER

AND THE RISING IN SOUTHAMPTON COUNTY

David F. Allmendinger Jr.

Johns Hopkins University Press *Baltimore*

Printed in the United States of America on acid-free paper
2 4 6 8 9 7 5 3 1

Johns Hopkins University Press
2715 North Charles Street
Baltimore, Maryland 21218-4363
www.press.jhu.edu

Library of Congress Cataloging-in-Publication Data

Allmendinger, David F.
Nat Turner and the rising in Southampton County / by David F. Allmendinger Jr.
pages cm
Includes bibliographical references and index.
ISBN-13: 978-1-4214-1479-9 (hardcover : alk. paper)
ISBN-13: 978-1-4214-1480-5 (electronic)
ISBN-10: 1-4214-1479-1 (hardcover : alk. paper)
ISBN-10: 1-4214-1480-5 (electronic)
1. Turner, Nat, 1800?–1831. 2. Southampton Insurrection, 1831. I. Title.
F232.S7A45 2014
975.5′552 —dc23 2013050171

A catalog record for this book is available from the British Library.

Special discounts are available for bulk purchases of this book. For more information, please contact Special Sales at 410-516-6936 or specialsales@press.jhu.edu.

Johns Hopkins University Press uses environmentally friendly book materials, including recycled text paper that is composed of at least 30 percent post-consumer waste, whenever possible.

CONTENTS

MAPS AND TABLES

MAPS

TABLES

ACKNOWLEDGMENTS

Three institutions generously supported the early research for this project: the Virginia Historical Society, through a Mellon Research Fellowship; the National Endowment for the Humanities, through grants for travel to collections; and the College of Arts and Science, University of Delaware, through supplemental funds grants for work in Virginia and Southampton. Portions of chapter 11 appeared in an earlier version in Kenneth S. Greenberg, ed., *Nat Turner: A Slave Rebellion in History and Memory* (New York: Oxford University Press, 2003), and are used here with permission.

NOTE ON SURNAMES

Authorities at the time of the uprising identified slaves by their given names and, in court records, usually provided the surnames of their owners. To avoid the confusion resulting from the use of given names only, in this study individual slaves have been assigned arbitrarily the surnames of those who held them in 1831 (in both notes and text), without enclosing brackets or parentheses. Individuals who chose surnames for themselves have been identified according to their choices.

Nat Turner and the Rising in Southampton County

The Key Account

> Public curiosity has been on the stretch to understand the origin and progress of this dreadful conspiracy, and the motives which influenced its diabolical actors.
>
> —Thomas R. Gray, *The Confessions of Nat Turner*

Reports from the field indicated that a rising of the slaves, long predicted in Virginia, had begun during the night of 21–22 August 1831 near the southeastern border of the state, in Southampton County. The rising proved to be the major outbreak of its kind between the Revolution and the Civil War. In one early account, a militiaman on duty in a neighboring county estimated that the insurgents had "butchered" between eighty and one hundred whites, severing heads from the victims' bodies. "These fellows commenced by murdering a family, taking their arms and horses," he said, "and pushing on to the next house with all possible speed, where they massacred every white, even to the infant in the cradle."[1] Alarmed, local officials appealed for help from state and U.S. forces, fearing, as one report said, "the local militia being in want of arms and ammunition, were unable of themselves, to put down the insurgents."[2] Within hours, witnesses across the lower half of the county had identified Nat Turner, a well-known figure in the vicinity of the violence, as a leader of the rebellion.[3]

Up to a point, the rising proceeded as Turner had planned. Starting on Sunday night, 21 August, and continuing all day on Monday, he and his men followed a winding route across St. Luke's Parish, stopping at sixteen chosen houses, putting to death every white man (twelve total), woman (nineteen), and child (twenty-four) they found at their various destinations. They headed generally east-northeast from Cabin Pond toward Jerusalem, the county seat (thirteen miles away, as the crow flies), but first moved south, then west-southwest, east, southeast, and north, before turning definitely east, toward the town (map 1). They seldom turned without purpose or stopped by chance. Turner later would claim that when they reached a point three miles south of the courthouse his men numbered "fifty or sixty, all mounted and armed with guns, axes, swords and clubs."[4]

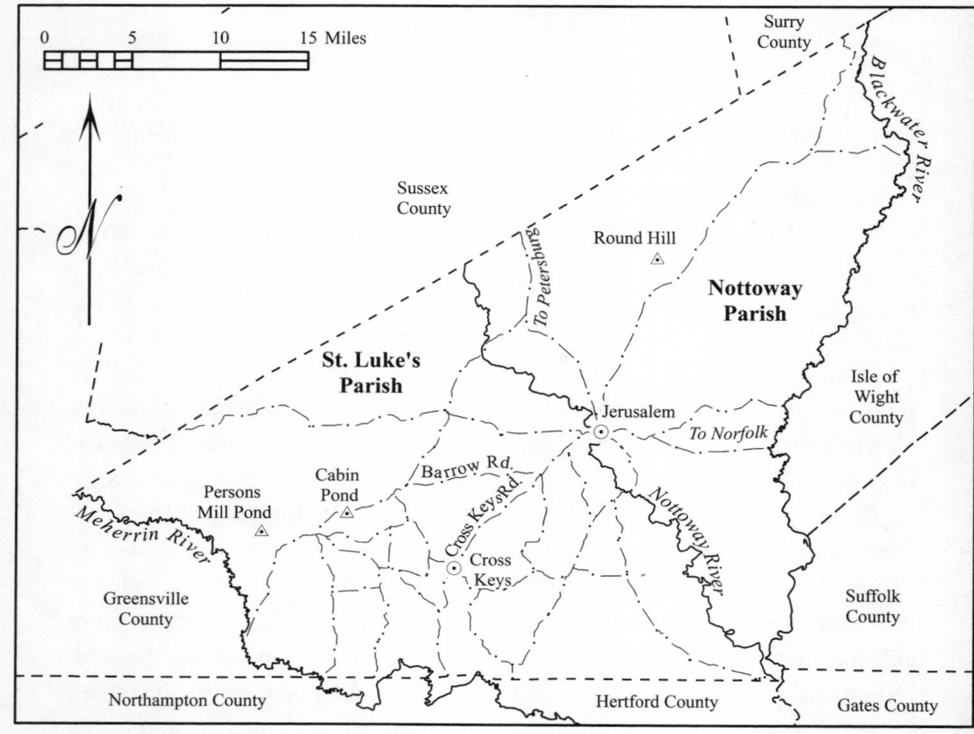

Map 1. Southampton County, 1831

They surprised and then shocked a complacent population. At house after house, the white residents displayed the same lack of vigilance, starting with Turner's master, Joseph Travis (rising in his bed, calling out, "Sally!"). Everywhere (with one exception), Turner observed their lack of preparedness, their inability to resist—young William Reese lying in bed in an unlocked house ("*Who is that?*"), the women hiding behind Elizabeth Turner's door, Rev. Whitehead staring from his mother's cotton patch, the Waller family running for their swamp. Turner witnessed as many as fifteen killings, took part in at least three, and claimed one himself. His men rode confidently to the very approaches of Jerusalem, but they were unable to enter the town. The ensuing suppression and executions in Southampton would take the lives of as many as forty-two slaves and two free black men (appendix F).

Evidence assembled over the next ten weeks would demonstrate that the rebellion originated entirely within the parish and that its plan was Turner's creation, influenced only by what he may have heard about failed conspiracies in Richmond (1800) and Charleston (1822). Turner derived little or no inspiration from the Northern abolition movement, which was only beginning to organize on a regional scale, or from the two central antislavery publications of the day, David Walker's *Appeal* (1829 and 1830) and William Lloyd Garrison's *Liberator* (beginning 1 January 1831). Turner's November confession, if credible, revealed that his thinking had turned toward violent resistance by the spring of 1828, antedating any influence from New England.[5] And though the confession contained a few passages with words that might have come from Walker's tract, it shared none of Walker's emphasis on spreading knowledge in the black population.[6] The violence of the rising was the product of Turner's own thought.

Other evidence, accumulating in the county clerk's office over the next thirty years, would indicate why slaveholding in Southampton persisted as long as it did. Immune to both suasion and terror, the white survivors of 1831 would suggest in their resistance to emancipation exactly how slavery would end and how it would not. That evidence, however, drew little attention. In the aftermath of 21–23 August, public curiosity focused understandably on the rebellion, its leader, and his motives.

Nat Turner went into hiding on Tuesday evening, 23 August, the second day of the rebellion, taking refuge for the night in woods near Cabin Pond, a short walk from the house of his murdered master. The next afternoon, in the distance, he said, he saw a company of white men "riding around the place as though they were looking for some one." On Thursday night he moved to a more permanent hiding place under a pile of fence rails in a field not more than a mile west of the old Benjamin Turner II plantation, his birthplace, where he remained for most of the time he was at large.[7] He spent all of September and October in seclusion, marking the days on a stick, knowing there would be intense interest in what he might say if taken alive.[8]

The weather, hot through September, did not turn cold until the end of October. In Norfolk, where editors of the *American Beacon* had been dreading the onset of hurricane season, there were signs on Thursday, 6 October, of an approaching storm. "On Sunday night, about 7 o'clock," the editors reported, "a heavy cloud arose in the N.W. which very speedily spread over the whole canopy, and poured out a torrent of rain accompanied by wind, exceeding what mariners term 'blowing a little fresh.'" The rain continued on Monday, 10 October, but temperatures remained warm.[9] Three weeks later, on Friday, 28 October, the *Norfolk Herald* reported a "remarkable change," starting at two o'clock on Thursday afternoon, brought on by a northeast wind that blew freshly into the evening. "The transition was almost instantaneous," the editors said, "from oppressive heat to a degree of cold which rendered it comfortable to be near a fire."[10]

Rumors had circulated in mid-September, first that Turner had been jailed in Baltimore (180 miles north as the crow flies), then that he had been seen in a swamp near Jerusalem (two miles south), and then that he had drowned in the New River (230 miles west).[11] On Saturday, 15 October, five days after the first storm passed over Norfolk, a slave named Nelson, identified as "a fellow-servant of the leader of the late insurrection," brought word to Jerusalem that "on that day he had seen *Nat Turner* in the woods, who hailed him, but that he, Nelson, seeing Nat armed, was afraid and ran from the villain."[12] Nelson must have been "Red Nelson," who formerly belonged to Salathiel Francis, a young farmer killed in the uprising. Nelson now was living at the nearby farm of his dead master's brother, Nathaniel Francis. Capt. Alexander P. Peete of the Southampton militia verified Red Nelson's report in a letter to the governor on 20 October. "I take the liberty to inform you," Peete wrote, "that Nat Turner the leader of the late insurrection in this county is certainly in the neighborhood where his master lived." A resident of the town later confirmed that Turner had been sighted "several times" by slaves during the last fifteen days of October.[13]

Nathaniel Francis, who had grown up with Turner, spotted him emerging from what one informant called a "den" on Thursday, 27 October.[14] Another source, a longtime neighbor, reported that Francis was inspecting fodder stacks in his fields when, to his astonishment, "Nat stepped out from between two of the stacks, which stood almost touching each other, with a smiling countenance, and without showing any hostile intention." Francis drew his pistol, Turner his sword. Francis fired; the shot passed through the crown of Turner's hat. "Nat ran off," the neighbor said, "carrying with him a ham of bacon, and leaving another together with some sweet potatoes and his shoes in the den."[15] (Francis, though armed, did not pursue.) The encounter led to a "general turn out" in the neighborhood, but after three days the parties had not caught sight of him.[16] On Sunday morning, 30 October, fifty men with dogs began searching the area within a two-mile radius of the Francis farm.[17] A young man named Benjamin Phipps, who held one taxable slave and owned fifty-five acres near the western edge of the county, went out alone that morning with his shotgun. Phipps, who did not know

Turner, was walking in Francis's woods when he came face to face with the fugitive, whose head suddenly appeared from a hole or "cave" dug beneath the branches of a freshly fallen pine.[18]

"Who are you?" Phipps asked, according to one account.

"*I am Nat Turner*," the man said.[19]

Phipps took aim, according to another account.

"Don't shoot, and I will give up," Turner said, throwing out his sword.[20]

"The prisoner, as his captor came up, submissively laid himself on the ground," said yet another source, "and was thus securely tied—not making the least resistance," a point made in virtually every report of the incident.[21] In fact, the prisoner seemed willing to give himself up. Thomas R. Gray, the young attorney who soon would take down Turner's confession, derided one notion about the surrender. "As to his being a coward, his reason as given for not resisting Mr. Phipps, shews the decision of his character," Gray said. "When he saw Mr. Phipps present his gun, he said he knew it was impossible for him to escape as the woods were full of men; he therefore thought it was better to surrender, and trust to fortune for his escape."[22] Turner's behavior over the next two days would suggest another motive: he had determined to make a statement.[23]

Phipps fired into the air to call for help, and after considerable delay other searchers arrived.[24] There could be no mistaking the prisoner's identity, the longtime neighbor said. "I have lived near him for years, I know him well, and had the gratification of seeing him yesterday carried from house to house in the neighborhood, where the females, who made such narrow escapes from him and his gang, expressed a curiosity to see him."[25] A witness from Petersburg who happened to be visiting the county that Sunday described Turner as "dejected, emaciated and ragged."[26] Reports gave conflicting details about the route of the procession, but the captors apparently secured their prisoner on the property of Peter Edwards, one mile north of the old Turner plantation.

In less than an hour, a crowd gathered. "The firing and rejoicing was so great," the neighbor reported, "as very soon to collect a great concourse of people from the surrounding country, who joined in the general expression of joy." (The reception betrayed their relief.) Turner exhibited his hat with holes in its crown "to shew how narrowly he had escaped being shot," according to one report, and seemed willing to answer questions. "I heard him speak more than an hour," said the neighbor, who added that Turner seemed to believe that even if he could live his life over again "he must necessarily act in the same way."[27] John Boykin, a St. Luke's Parish resident who joined the crowd at the Edwards place, gave an account of the assembly to Dr. Isaac Pipkin, of nearby Murfreesboro, North Carolina. "Nat pretends to have been destined by a Superior power to perform the part which he did in the late bloody tragedy," Boykin told Pipkin, "and affirms that since 1826, he has constantly acted from a Divine impulse."[28] (Boykin was the first of two witnesses within twenty-four hours to note a reference by Turner to the year 1826.) By nine o'clock that evening, word of the capture reached Jerusalem; two travelers who stayed in the town that night reported that on their arrival "the people were firing guns by way of rejoicing for the capture of Nat."[29]

The procession resumed on Monday morning, 31 October, and made its way across St. Luke's Parish to the courthouse in Jerusalem. Editors in Norfolk heard reports that the prisoner was "conveyed alive to Jerusalem" only "with difficulty."[30] But an eyewitness (the man visiting from Petersburg) claimed that "not the least personal violence was offered to Nat," and he praised citizens for their forbearance.[31] John Wheeler, the postmaster in Murfreesboro, followed the Southampton news with interest. "No doubt public curiosity is on tiptoe to hear his confession," he observed.[32] Thomas R. Gray, making the same point, said curiosity was "on the stretch." In one brief comment, editors at the *Norfolk Herald* caught the gist of the prisoner's purpose: "He is said to be very free in his confessions."[33]

He arrived with his guards at 1:15 P.M. and was taken to the courthouse, where magistrates James Trezvant and James W. Parker examined him for an hour and a half or two hours. In demeanor, he remained expansive; his remarks in the courthouse resembled those he had addressed to the crowd the previous day, making this, in effect, his second confession. Afterward, Trezvant gave the prosecutor an account of the examination; he too noted the prisoner's "opinions about his communications with god, his command over the clouds, &c &c which he had been entertaining as far back as 1826."[34] Trezvant's brother Theodore, the town's postmaster, reported that Turner answered every question "without confusion or prevarication."[35] William C. Parker, the leading local attorney (and soon to be named Turner's counsel), took part in the examination; the sheriff, his deputies, and the jailer also may have been in the courtroom.[36] There is no indication that Gray was present.

At around three o'clock the proceedings adjourned, and Nat Turner was committed to the jail—or, as Parker put it, to "the four walls." There he continued to talk. Someone asked him, in the presence of five other prisoners, what he had done with the money taken from the white victims. His response was recorded by an unidentified resident of the town who made a rare, if awkward, attempt—like those Gray soon would make—to capture the prisoner's voice in direct quotation: "He answered that he only received 4s. 6d., and turning to one of the prisoners (a free negro) who stands over for further trial, said to him you know that money was not my object."[37]

At some point between midafternoon and early evening, Thomas R. Gray appeared at the jail.[38] He may have been waiting there, in fact, when the prisoner arrived. With the jailer's permission, Gray gained access to the "condemned hole," the cell for prisoners being held for execution, and arranged with Turner to return the next day, "agreeable to his own appointment," to begin hearing his statement. The two men would meet on Tuesday, again on Wednesday, and again on Thursday. By Saturday morning, 5 November, six days after the arrest and in time for the trial, Gray had completed the manuscript of the famous confession.

Published later that month in Baltimore in a pamphlet bearing the title *The Confessions of Nat Turner*, Turner's statement became at once the key account of the Southampton affair, though its authenticity was in doubt from the day it appeared. Modern critics of Gray, noting his evident proslavery sympathies, have expressed skepticism about his work, sometimes placing its title in quotation marks. One such critic even referred to it as "Thomas Gray's so-called *Confessions*."[39] Still, the middle portion of the pamphlet, beginning at the bold, centered heading "CONFESSION," remains the authoritative original source. There, purportedly in his own words, the prisoner presented a memoir of his life and motives, followed by his own narrative of the rising. In commentaries preceding and following the confession, Gray offered his own theory that Turner was a fanatic, perhaps mad, driven by religious enthusiasm to foment the rebellion, which Gray insisted had been "entirely local" in origin and scope. Gray's theory—often disputed—established an interpretation that would have a lasting influence, though there was much the young attorney did not know.

Research for the following work has delved more deeply into local history than Thomas R. Gray could have done. It focuses on certain families in St. Luke's Parish who lived in the neighborhoods (between Cross Keys, Cabin Pond, and Jerusalem) where the rebellion took place. It draws upon the *Confessions*, but also upon evidence that Gray, who had just four days to work after meeting Nat Turner, could not have consulted. According to the

Confessions, Turner mentioned briefly just two of his former masters; and though he named all of the families he had targeted, house by house, the document says little about their histories. A Richmond Dragoon on his way to Southampton in August had declared that none of the targeted families were "much known."[40] There he let the matter drop; and there, for the most part, it remained. Gray did not press Turner for information about the individuals who had held him in slavery, or about the lives and motives of his followers and their masters. Nor did Gray have time to make inquiries at the county clerk's office, where volumes of evidence about those people were available. That evidence makes it possible to verify details in Turner's memoir and, in tracing the origins of the rising, to see the motives underlying his hatred of slavery and the causes beyond fanaticism.

Nor could Gray have consulted records for all forty-one slaves tried in Jerusalem (or for the five free blacks examined there) before Turner's capture on 30 October. He was familiar, however, with crucial portions of the evidence through his role as counsel for two of the most important defendant-witnesses, Jack Reese and Moses Moore.[41] More than one hundred other witnesses survived the rebellion and gave evidence concerning incidents along its route. Fifty-one different individuals testified in court, and more than fifty others gave statements to Meriwether B. Brodnax, the prosecutor, who kept notes on what they told him. Together, the hundred-plus witnesses became an almost-omniscient observer, verifying isolated facts and offering details that would not appear in the prisoner's narrative. Their collective testimony would establish an independent chronology, a means of checking Turner's narrative. Similarly, reports by those who heard Turner speak while on his way to jail would verify the character of his discourse.

Nor, finally, could Gray have examined closely his own manuscript, whose syntax and composition bear the marks of a hurried work. He did say that on the evening of his third day with Turner he conducted a "cross examination" that corroborated the prisoner's statement. But Gray had not grasped the full meaning of Turner's design, either in the rebellion or in the confession. As a consequence, for decades the key account would continue to yield new information.

PART ONE

MASTERS

I have been diligent in my inquiries to obtain information that can be relied on. The result is, about two hundred and fifty negroes from a Camp Meeting about the Dismal Swamp set out on a marauding excursion, and have for the sake of plunder, murdered about sixty persons, none of them families much known.

—Richmond Dragoon, letter, 23 August 1831

A History of Motives

I must go back to the days of my infancy, and even before I was born.

—Nat Turner, *The Confessions of Nat Turner*

Of all the accounts that appeared in 1831, only the memoir within *The Confessions of Nat Turner* advanced the notion that the rebellion leader's motives had a history. No previous account had linked so many events in Nat Turner's life to specific points in the past: 2 October 1800; the year 1803 or 1804; around 1809; about 1821; exactly 1825; around 1826; 12 May 1828; and early 1830. The level of detail in itself suggested authenticity. Not every incident was dated or placed in proper sequence, but an emphasis on the importance of time infused the account and the sensibility that produced it.

Turner dictated this portion of his confession in the jail on 1 November, during his first long interview with Thomas R. Gray. In the pamphlet's introduction, Gray claimed that the prisoner had spoken voluntarily, even expansively. He claimed, moreover, to have recorded the statement in Turner's voice (except for material in parentheses, footnotes, or clearly marked exchanges) "with little or no variation from his own words." But Gray was a novice at such devices. He intruded as early as the fourth sentence of the memoir, coloring the prisoner's remarks about the "enthusiasm" that had "terminated so fatally to many," for which he, the prisoner, was about to "atone at the gallows." The intrusions raised doubt. And there were other difficulties: Gray was the sole witness to the statement and the sole keeper of the document, much of whose content would prove difficult to verify; by late November, when *The Confessions of Nat Turner* was published, the source had been hanged. Still, there are signs that Gray managed to convey more fully than he realized the substance of what the chief insurgent said.[1]

Early History

The account begins with a stilted salutation. "SIR," says the prisoner, "You have asked me to give a history of the motives which induced me to undertake the late insurrection, as you call it—To do so I must go back to the days of my infancy, and even before I was born." In that voice, according to the only record of what was said, Turner commenced a review of events that had occurred long before August 1831. The memoir proper, 2,055 words in length, covered five full pages in the original pamphlet. Turner told Gray he had been born "the property of Benj. Turner of this county," and that he was thirty-one years old on 2 October, thereby establishing the year of his birth. His father, mother, and grandmother (whose names he did not provide) appeared in his earliest memories of childhood, when all three had lived at Benjamin Turner's plantation, before his father ran away.[2]

Nat Turner recalled three incidents that must have occurred between 1803 and 1808 at his master's house in the Cross Keys neighborhood of St. Luke's Parish. Together, these incidents gave rise at the time to a belief that he was exceptional, destined for "some great purpose," he said, and later to a feeling that destiny had been thwarted. The first incident, in 1803 or 1804, involved his telling other children about "something" that his mother, overhearing, said had happened before he was born. This feat astonished other adults (not identified), he recalled, causing them to say that he "surely would be a prophet," as the Lord had shown him things that had happened before his birth. His parents, citing as evidence some marks on his head and breast, concurred, saying in his presence that he was intended for a great purpose. Even as he met with Gray in that "dungeon," Turner said, he could not "divest" himself of this belief.[3]

The next incident, which must have occurred between 1803 and 1808, involved some unnamed "religious persons" he often saw at prayer in the house of Benjamin Turner. The boy's master, "who belonged to the church," his grandmother, "who was very religious," and others in attendance remarked at the "singularity" of his manners and his "uncommon intelligence." Those persons, betraying perhaps a vestige of an earlier Methodism, remarked that he had "too much sense" to be raised a slave, "and if I was, I would never be of any service to any one as a slave."[4]

A similar theme appeared in the third incident, which concerned his ability to read and write. These gifts he had acquired with "the most perfect ease"—such ease, in fact, that he had "no recollection whatever" of learning the alphabet. He did recall, however, a scene that must have occurred in Benjamin Turner's house around 1805. He had been shown a book to keep him from crying, whereupon, to the astonishment of "the family" (including everyone in the house), he began to spell the names of different objects. His performance became "a source of wonder to all in the neighborhood, particularly the blacks." Thereafter, in glancing at books belonging to the schoolchildren, he would see things (not specified) his imagination already had depicted.[5] This gift of seeing he never lost.

Between 1809 and 1822, from youth to early manhood, he was the property of Benjamin Turner's eldest son, Samuel G. Turner. Though he did not refer in the memoir to this second master, the sequence of his recollections indicates that around 1809 he began to work in Samuel's fields. After that year he recalled no scenes like those inside the house of Benjamin Turner, though he did say that he continued to find opportunities to look at books being read by schoolchildren in the family. In free moments he prayed and, apparently before 1821, conducted experiments, attempting to make earthen molds, paper, and gunpowder. He assumed a demeanor of self-discipline: "I was not addicted to stealing in my youth," he said, "nor have [I] ever been." Nevertheless, he said, other slaves in the neighborhood would recruit him to plan any "roguery," so confident were they in his "superior judgment."[6] He continued to think of himself as exceptional.

The germ of rebellion, identified in these scenes, had formed by his twenty-first year. The memoir's account of its origin came to this: Turner once had believed that because of his unusual intelligence his masters might offer him special treatment, perhaps in the form of freedom, which would lead to some great purpose. In time, his masters proved disappointing.

Allegory

Events between 1821 and 1825 were not recorded in an orderly, exact sequence, making them difficult to pinpoint in time. The prisoner's mind may have jumped back and forth here, and Gray did not clarify. In sources outside the text, however, there is evidence connected to this period in Nat Turner's life, concerning contemporaneous, verifiable incidents in the lives of his masters. These other incidents, involving people Gray could not have known, unfolded in a parallel, independent chronology, helping to mark developments in time.

By 1831 Nat Turner had lived under the authority of as many as seven different adult slaveholders (not counting executors of his masters' estates), though he identified only the first and last of these. His chain of possession, confirmable in records at the county clerk's office, began with Benjamin Turner II, as reported in the memoir. (His first master's father was Benjamin I, also a slaveholder and dead many years by the time Nat Turner was born.) In about 1807, Benjamin II gave the boy to his son Samuel, who died in 1822.[7] Nat Turner then descended temporarily to Samuel's executors and indirectly to Samuel's widow, Elizabeth, in whose hands he remained for about a year.[8] From 1823 to 1827, he was the property of Thomas Moore and his wife, Sarah ("Sally"), the younger sister of Samuel G. Turner's deceased first wife. Moore, the third true, legal master, died in 1827. For about two years Nat Turner remained with Moore's widow, but legally he belonged to her minor son, Putnam.[9] During that time, he may have been among the slaves hired to a neighbor, Giles Reese.[10] Finally, in 1830, shortly after Sally Moore remarried, he became the servant of her new husband, Joseph Travis.[11] Travis thus became his final master, though Putnam Moore, still a minor, remained his true owner. The lives of these masters and mistresses intertwined with Turner's. His disappointment derived from their interests and motives, which increasingly conflicted with his own.

In the autumn of 1821, about five months before the death of his second master, Nat Turner arrived at what he called "man's estate." He did not specify the year, but it must have been 1821. Here was the moment in which he perceived the contradiction between his servitude and what he believed to be his destiny. This perception had its origin in religious meetings he had been attending in the neighborhood, meetings like those he had witnessed in childhood. He told Gray that at those meetings he had heard commentary on the scriptures and that he had been struck by a particular "passage," quoted in the *Confessions* as "Seek ye the kingdom of Heaven and all things shall be added unto you."[12] Though both men understood this passage to be biblical, neither identified its probable source as Luke, the Sermon on the Plain, or Matthew, the Sermon on the Mount. Nor did Gray note the variant wording in Turner's quotation.[13] Turner said he reflected much on this passage, indicating by his chronology that he began to do so around 1821. He prayed daily, he said, for light on its meaning. Then, probably in the spring of 1822, he heard a voice speaking that very passage. "As I was praying one day at my plough," he said, "the spirit spoke to me, saying 'Seek ye the kingdom of Heaven and all things shall be added unto you.'"[14] With this wording and without the preceding verses, the passage now lost its original tone of injunction and became a promise. Here, for the first time, Gray interrupted.

"Question—what do you mean by the Spirit."

"Ans. The Spirit that spoke to the prophets in former days."[15]

By this point, a design had appeared in the memoir: the significant age of thirty-one years, the birth in humble circumstances, the child's miraculous gifts, the amazement of the religious persons, and now the revelations. Detail by detail, the prisoner was piecing together an allegory.

Turner then recounted a succession of revelations and visions. Altogether, he told of ten supernatural appearances between 1822 and 1828, interspersed with memories of memories. In seven of the revelations, according to the text, Turner said specifically that the Spirit was present as a voice; it spoke always in biblical language, and on four occasions it quoted scripture. Two appearances involved visions of the Holy Ghost, and one, simply a vision and a voice. Finally, in 1831, he witnessed two signs that the Spirit had told him would appear in the heavens.

While the memoir's chronology for the years between 1821 and 1825 is confused, the beginning of that period coincided with the decline and death of Samuel G. Turner in January or February of 1822. Samuel, who knew he was dying, had enough time to write his will and settle his affairs. He gave his property to three heirs: his daughter, his widow, and his stepdaughter.[16] He freed none of his slaves. At about this time, according to the memoir, the Spirit made its first appearance. Then, after two years filled with prayer, Nat Turner experienced the second "revelation," identical to the first, confirming the impression that he was "ordained for some great purpose in the hands of the Almighty." This must have occurred late in 1823 or early in 1824. It must have been then that he also revisited in memory the childhood scene involving his first master, his grandmother, and the religious persons who had taught him to pray. Once again, he recalled their comment that he had too much sense to be brought up a slave; apparently he also revisited the episode in which his parents had foreseen his great purpose, the memory of which led him to ponder again what he saw as the irony of his life: "Now finding I had arrived to man's estate and was a slave, and these revelations being made known to me, I began to direct my attention to this great object, to fulfill the purpose for which, by this time, I felt assured I was intended." He told other servants about the Spirit's revelations, which led them to say that his wisdom came from God.[17]

The third revelation of the Spirit must have occurred shortly afterward, also in late 1823 or early 1824, during the first two years of Elizabeth Turner's tenure as widow at Samuel's farm. That was about the time, according to a detail revealed only in the memoir, when Nat Turner was placed under an overseer from whom, he said, he ran away. After remaining in the woods thirty days and being tempted by the desire to free himself, he returned, "to the astonishment of the negroes on the plantation, who thought I had made my escape to some other part of the country, as my father had done before." Other slaves criticized him, echoing words from the past, saying that "if they had my sense they would not serve any master in the world." He had returned in obedience to higher authority, however, for the Spirit had appeared to him again and chastised him (in terms drawn perhaps from 1 Corinthians) for directing his wishes "to the things of this world, and not to the kingdom of Heaven." It commanded him to return to the service of his "earthly master." Again, the Spirit quoted scripture: "For he who knoweth his Master's will, and doeth it not, shall be beaten with many stripes, and thus have I chastened you."[18] Here was another passage, almost verbatim, from Luke, though again neither Turner nor Gray identified it.[19] Gray apparently was taking the role of amanuensis literally, letting Turner quote and interpret scriptures at will. And since Gray apparently had neither time nor inclination to check biblical references, he missed the transforming literalism in Turner's quotation about seeking the kingdom of Heaven. He also missed the implication, subversive to its core, about one's duty to a higher, heavenly Master.[20]

Between 1821 and 1823, Turner had begun to take an open, public role at religious gatherings in the neighborhood, exhorting and singing—activities known to authorities before he was captured.[21] Among the slaves, at least, he became something of a religious teacher, a role implied in his early attitude toward stealing. Now he began to address other matters, condemning fellow slaves for such things as conjuring: "I always spoke of such things with contempt," he said in the memoir.[22] He cultivated a reputation for "austerity," which, he told Gray, became "the subject of remark by white and black."[23] (In fact, Gray already had heard about this austerity from other sources. "It is notorious," Gray observed in comments near the end of the pamphlet, "that he was never known to have a dollar in his life; to swear an oath, or drink a drop of spirits.")[24] To cultivate an aura of greatness, Turner said he "studiously avoided mixing in society," wrapped himself in "mystery," and devoted his time to "fasting and prayer."[25] (Gray did not remark at the words *austerity* and *mystery*, the first of which appears as the adjective *austere* in Luke, and the second in Ephesians.)[26]

By 1822 Turner was drifting into theological error. He had been "hearing the scriptures commented on at meetings," he told Gray; and if his language is evidence, he had gained some familiarity with the King James Bible, including the Gospel of Matthew and certainly the Gospel of Luke.[27] Some passages he had committed to memory. The memoir contains four attempts at scriptural quotation involving three different, brief passages of fourteen, twenty-three, and eighteen words. In Gray's rendering of them, each was in fact a misquotation. Each probably involved an authentic misquotation by Turner himself, a theory consistent with his having come to his beliefs through self-reflection and, as he said, "hearing the scriptures."[28] The direction of his thinking, moreover, suggests that he had studied scriptures without influences that might have kept him within the bounds of orthodoxy. His recollection of the first revelation, for example, indicates that by 1822 he already had been drawn to the notion that God was communicating directly with him through the Holy Spirit.

This line of thinking would lead to trouble. The austerity of his manners already implied a broad criticism of drunkenness, swearing, the love of money, and perhaps other failings, seeming to challenge things as they stood. Beyond that, his cultivated aura of mystery must have suggested a threat. That he understood the danger in this attitude, at least in retrospect, became evident in the account of his fourth revelation, which also occurred in 1823 or 1824, clearly after the episode of running away. This time, he said, he had a vision in which "white spirits and black spirits engaged in battle, and the sun was darkened—the thunder rolled in the Heavens, and blood flowed in streams." He heard a voice saying to him, "Such is your luck, such you are called to see, and let it come rough or smooth, you must surely bare it." Again, the imagery came from Luke.[29]

The fifth revelation, placed specifically in the year 1825, had reinforced the prisoner's belief that he possessed an extraordinary intelligence. The Spirit had reappeared and reminded him of past revelations; it had promised to reveal "knowledge of the elements, the revolution of the planets, the operation of tides, and changes of the seasons."[30] Again, the expression sounded biblical, though Turner at this point may not have been quoting either the Spirit or scripture.[31] The detail about the year provided a marker for subsequent events: after this revelation, Turner said, he was inspired to seek perfection: "I sought more than ever to obtain true holiness before the great day of judgment should appear, and then I began to receive the true knowledge of faith. And from the first steps of righteousness until the last, was I made perfect."[32] His mysticism and perfectionism would astonish residents of the parish and catch them theologically unprepared.

He did not keep his visions to himself. After each of the next four revelations, he described his experiences to people in the neighborhood, which explains how Thomas R. Gray learned of them weeks before the meetings in the jail. Gray would be puzzled and skeptical about what he had heard, however, so the interviews in November may have clarified his understanding.[33]

The sixth revelation must have come during the summer of 1826. The Spirit, identified as the Holy Ghost, was "with" Turner and said, "Behold me as I stand in the Heavens." Turner described what he saw: "And I looked and saw the forms of men in different attitudes—and there were lights in the sky to which the children of darkness gave other names than what they really were—for they were the lights of the Saviour's hands, stretched from east to west, even as they were extended on the cross on Calvary for the redemption of sinners."[34] Though Gray did not mention it, the Gospel of Matthew contains, after a warning about false Christs and false prophets, a similar passage about signs foretelling the coming of Christ: lightning east to west, the sun and moon darkening, and stars falling.[35] Turner prayed for understanding. Then, while laboring in the field, he discovered "drops of blood," like "dew from heaven," on leaves of corn. He related this vision to others, both black and white, and then found on leaves in the woods "hieroglyphic characters, and numbers, with the forms of men in different attitudes, portrayed in blood, and representing the figures I had seen before in the heavens."[36]

At the seventh revelation, also in 1826 apparently, the Holy Ghost made plain that these "miracles" were signs of a Second Coming: "For as the blood of Christ had been shed on this earth, and had ascended to heaven for the salvation of sinners, and was now returning to earth again in the form of dew—and as the leaves on the trees bore the impression of the figures I had seen in the heavens, it was plain to me that the Saviour was about to lay down the yoke he had borne for the sins of men, and the great day of judgment was at hand."[37] The image came from the passage in Luke concerning Christ in agony, in which his sweat falls to the ground like "great drops of blood."[38] In the memoir, it conveyed the message that someone must now prepare to take up the yoke.

At about this time, Turner said, he revealed his experiences to a white man, Etheldred T. Brantley, identified for the first time (by Gray, in a parenthetical note) in the memoir. Brantley, a landless young laborer, worked for neighborhood farmers with whom he lived probably until his marriage in 1840. He may have been the overseer from whom Turner had run away, though there is no evidence for that; but if the memoir can be trusted, Brantley certainly was living near Cross Keys in 1826.[39] Hearing about the revelations had a wonderful effect on this white man, Turner said, "and he ceased from his wickedness, and was attacked immediately with a cutaneous eruption, and blood oozed from the pores of his skin, and after praying and fasting nine days, he was healed." The Spirit then appeared in an eighth revelation commanding of the slave and the overseer that "as the Saviour had been baptised so should we be also."[40]

Turner announced a plan for their mutual baptism. Details about the attempt came to light in September 1831, weeks before Turner's capture, in an account by attorney William C. Parker. The incident, Parker learned, had occurred "more than four years" earlier, indicating that the year may indeed have been 1826. Soaked in skepticism, his account preserved the scriptural scene (from Luke 3:12–22) Turner had planned to enact at the pond. "Pretending to be divinely inspired, more than four years ago, he announced to the Blacks, that he should baptize himself on a particular day, and that whilst in the water, a dove would be seen to descend from Heaven and perch on his head,—thus endeavoring to collect a great crowd, perhaps with a similar design to that he afterwards effected."[41] Here, in silent allusion to the dove at the ancient baptism in the Jordan, Parker—perhaps unwittingly—became the first to document Nat Turner's knowledge of particular passages from scripture.[42] According to Parker, the "assemblage" was prevented, but Turner, "in company with a white man, did actually baptize himself."[43]

The account in Turner's confession omitted any reference to a dove, but it did provide some additional information. According to Gray, Turner recalled the following details: "And when the white people would not let us be baptised by the church, we went down into the water together, in the sight of many who reviled us, and were baptised by the Spirit—After this I rejoiced greatly, and gave thanks to God."[44] A crowd had been present and so had the Spirit—a ninth revelation. Later accounts identified the body of water as Persons Mill Pond, immediately west of Persons Methodist Church and about four miles west of the Moore farm by road.[45] Though neither Parker nor

Gray explained the refusal of the church to permit the ceremony, its authorities must have perceived a challenge in Turner's claim to a rite of the faith.

The immersion became an epiphany. In his memory of that moment, Turner saw church officials spurning his enthusiasm, as if they too were his masters. He granted them no indulgence for doing what ecclesiastical duty required. He saw himself entering the water with the white man, defiantly, and reenacting the scene in the Jordan. Perhaps juxtaposing another ancient scene—the one leading to the Cross—he remembered that the crowd had "reviled" them.[46] (Gray drew no attention to that unusual word.) Though Turner made no other comment, the reaction demonstrated that few in that crowd of 1826—the jubilee of the Revolution—were prepared to witness the transformation he had in mind.

Within a year, he was given a second, apparently pivotal demonstration of that lesson. The timing is corroborated by evidence outside the text of the memoir, some of it coming from the woman identified after the rebellion as Nat Turner's wife. Gray reported to the *Richmond Constitutional Whig* in September 1831 that this woman had given up papers proving Turner had been thinking closely about his mystical powers "for some time." Then, in the same report, Gray announced intelligence of even greater significance: "I have been credibly informed," he said, "that something like three years ago, Nat received a whipping from his master, for saying that blacks ought to be free, and that they would be free one day or other."[47]

Nothing about the whipping (or the wife) appeared in the memoir or in the entire *Confessions*, though Gray certainly knew about it before the interviews. Other evidence indicates that the master in the tale, also unnamed at the time, must have been Thomas Moore, Nat Turner's third master. Gray's informants must have included Mrs. Sarah Francis, Moore's mother-in-law, who had known Nat Turner since his birth, and her son Nathaniel. The incident probably occurred early in 1827, shortly before Moore's death (at age thirty-five). That would have been four years before the uprising, not three. Since Moore left no will, his widow, Sally (Francis) Moore, about twenty-six, became administrator of his estate and took over their farm.[48] Nat Turner, still a slave, then became the property of a six-year-old child and fell under the authority of a second widow. This transfer to yet another owner, coming after the reviling and the whipping, became a turning point, a confirmation that the chain of possession would continue into the future and that none of these people would free anyone for any purpose.

About one year later, according to the sequence of events in the memoir, "on the 12th of May, 1828," the Spirit made its final appearance, the tenth revelation. Turner heard a loud noise in the heavens, whereupon the Spirit revealed itself and told him that "the Serpent was loosened, and Christ had laid down the yoke he had borne for the sins of men, and that I should take it on and fight against the Serpent." Christ was abdicating, and Nat Turner must take up the work. This was necessary, said the Spirit, "for the time was fast approaching when the first should be last and the last should be first."[49] Gray made no attempt to identify the reference to the Serpent or the familiar quotation concerning the first and the last, but he did interrupt for the second and final time: "Do you not find yourself mistaken now?" he asked. To which the prisoner famously replied, "Was not Christ crucified."[50]

If at this point Gray understood the design, he restrained himself. Turner had completed the allegory: revelations, the mission to the lowly, healing the sick, baptism like that of the Savior, the man reviled by his enemies, taking up the yoke, the impending trial and execution at Jerusalem.

Signs

According to the memoir, the idea of an uprising may have occurred to Turner as early as 1823, or about the time he ran away from the overseer, and recurred around 1826, when he warned Brantley about a day of judgment. The idea became fixed in his mind at the time of the Spirit's final appearance on 12 May 1828. The Spirit had instructed him to conceal the plan for the "great work," Turner said, until signs appeared in the heavens. At the first such sign, he was told, "I should arise and prepare myself, and slay my enemies with their own weapons."[51]

He had been waiting nearly three years when, as promised, a sign appeared. Gray identified it (in parentheses) as the solar eclipse at midday on 12 February 1831. That annular eclipse (duration at Richmond of two hours and thirteen minutes) was observed across a wide section of central Virginia, including Southampton County, which lay in the penumbra on the eastern side of the shadow's path.[52] "And immediately on the sign appearing in the heavens," Turner was recorded as saying, "the seal was removed from my lips." Here the prisoner revealed that he had formed a conspiracy six months before the insurrection—much earlier than authorities in Jerusalem had thought. Names of the conspirators would appear for the first time in the

Confessions; those names, like more than a hundred other details, must have come directly from the prisoner.[53]

Then, Turner said, the sign appeared again. He referred no doubt to the unusual atmospheric conditions (attributed decades later to volcanic dust) observed from Albany, New York, to Savannah and Mobile between 12 and 15 August, one week before the rising. At Norfolk on the thirteenth and fourteenth, editors of the *Herald* reported, the sun rose in a "light but lively green" that turned to silver white, then pale yellow; at 5 P.M. it appeared "like a globe of silver through the thick haze," then assumed a "cerulean tint" before passing to light green. "A black spot near the center, was discernable by the naked eye, apparently the size of a walnut, and with a good spy glass two others were distinctly visible." An hour after sunset, the northwest horizon "exhibited a glare of ruddy light, bearing a strong resemblance to the red reflection of a large fire," the editors said. "We have heard no attempt to account for the singular phenomena."[54] Similar conditions in August were reported in the British Virgin Islands, in Bermuda, across Europe, and on the Mediterranean coast of Africa.[55] Nat Turner told Gray that upon observing these very phenomena in the heavens above Cross Keys, he determined "not to wait longer."[56]

Interpretations

Gray did not fabricate the account of Nat Turner's revelations and visions. Authorities in Jerusalem had known about them since August, and during the prisoner's first two days in custody he had spoken in identical terms before witnesses whose accounts Gray could not have seen.[57] "He is a shrewd, intelligent fellow," said Nathaniel Francis's neighbor, who heard Turner talking at the Edwards plantation; "he insists strongly upon the revelations which he received, as he understood them, urging him on, and pointing to this enterprize."[58] Within four days, editors at the *Norfolk Herald* had obtained similar details about the prisoner's statements through a letter from Southampton. "He still pretends that he is a prophet, and relates a number of revelations which he says he has had," the editors had heard, "from which he was induced to believe that he could succeed in conquering the *county of Southampton!*" (To which they responded, "What miserable ignorance!") They remarked at what they termed Turner's "profanity in comparing his pretended prophecies with passages in the Holy Scriptures" and thought that these prophesies afforded proof of his insanity.[59]

Whether Turner believed his own account or was merely pretending, Gray could not decide. In September he had assumed that the visions were fraudulent and that Turner was a calculating manipulator who had played upon the superstitions of his followers; but in November, after meeting the man, Gray seemed less certain. "He is a complete fanatic, or plays his part most admirably," he wrote in explanation of Turner's motives for rebellion. "On other subjects he possesses an uncommon share of intelligence, with a mind capable of attaining any thing; but warped and perverted by the influence of early impressions."[60] James Trezvant, after examining Turner on 31 October, thought him insane; and after witnessing the examination, so did Turner's court-appointed attorney, William C. Parker. Another analyst, the longtime neighbor of Nathaniel Francis, having heard Turner declare himself "in particular favor with Heaven," agreed. "He seems even now, to labor, under as perfect a state of fanatical delusion as ever wretched man suffered."[61]

Perhaps because Gray thought that readers could decide for themselves about the state of Turner's mind, he did not intrude (except to ask two questions) upon the content of the memoir proper, leaving undisturbed its account of visions, revelations, Spirit instructions, and signs. The prisoner's own explanation of his motives survived, therefore, and became a standard interpretation: moved by deeply held religious beliefs (*hallucinations*, some have said), Nat Turner had inspired a judgment against slavery, a rising to obtain freedom for his race.[62]

Perhaps because Gray was an outsider to the parish, he did not think to ask the prisoner for evidence about related motives that may have influenced the rebellion.[63] As an outsider, Gray knew little about the earliest of Turner's fellow conspirators, identified in the memoir by given names only: *Henry, Hark, Nelson, and Sam.* (The skeletal nature of this list would lead to confusion about the identities of Nelson and Sam in particular.) Gray knew nothing about relations between these four men and their masters: Richard Porter, Joseph Travis, Peter Edwards, and Nathaniel Francis. He did not know enough about the families involved to ask an antiquarian's questions about Samuel G. Turner's first wife, Esther (*Francis*); or his second wife and widow, the former Mrs. Elizabeth (*Reese*) Williamson; or Elizabeth's cousin John W. Reese; or Captain Moore; or slaves at the Reese farm, one of whom (as Gray did know) was Hark's wife. Turner's memoir says nothing about the connections between these people or about recent developments in their various households and quarters.

Gray could not have suspected, therefore, that soon after the February eclipse—as soon as the first four recruits had been drawn into a conspiracy—Nat Turner (regardless of what he later implied) must have known where the rising would begin, what route it would follow in its early stages, and which of the 339 slaveholding white households in St. Luke's Parish would be among the first involved.[64]

Lines of Descent

The Turners

> I Give and bequeath to my loving Son Samuel Turner the following negros: Sam, Nancy, Lidda, Natt, Drew, Chary, Miner, Elick which he has got in his procession to him and his heirs forever.
>
> —Benjamin Turner II, will, 1810

All of Nat Turner's masters belonged to a small circle of slaveholding families related to one another through a series of marriage alliances. The first of those alliances, not widely recalled at the time of the uprising, had connected the Turner and Francis families, longtime neighbors, in 1807. The second, in 1818, brought into the circle a nearby branch of the Reese family; and the third, in 1819, added the Moores. Finally, in 1829, Joseph Travis, a newcomer to Southampton, married into these families and early the next year began his brief tenure as master. By the time Travis arrived, most of the principals in the preceding alliances, including all three of Nat Turner's earliest masters, had long been dead.

Their exceptional slave could not have forgotten them. From his seventh or eighth year onward, they had passed him down a line of willing heirs and beneficiaries, assigning him as personal property in almost every conceivable way: the Turners had lent him, given him as patrimony, and conveyed him by will; the others had sold or transferred him, hired him out, and held him in trust. Whenever a vital event had taken place—a marriage, a death, or remarriage—his masters had been given an opportunity to consider anew his future, and at every such opportunity they had kept him in their holdings. Their decisions about dowries and patrimonies, gifts and loans, transfers and exchanges had determined the course of his life.

Motives for rebellion, as Turner implied in his confession, appeared long before the arrival of Joseph Travis. This final master, remembered as a kind and trusting man, inspired no complaints, but he arrived too late for any of his better qualities to matter. And in some respects, he and his predecessors were much alike. None of them were inclined toward reflection or the written word; their only recorded thoughts dealt with the property they transferred in occasional deeds and wills. All of them, including Travis, had ties to the Methodist Episcopal Church and therefore must have known about its troubles over slavery, but they did not seem troubled. On the contrary, their estate records indicate that, for reasons they clearly understood, they were determined to keep their slaves. Through the years, in fact, they allowed their holdings to grow and gradually surrounded themselves with people who, by August of 1831, did not wish them well. Had Travis known the history of their holdings from the earliest days, he might have suspected as much.

A reference to those distant days appeared in the opening sentences of Turner's memoir, in his account of the event that happened before he was born, something he claimed to have known as a child through clairvoyance. Thomas R. Gray wrote down the claim but declined to press for particulars. So, the world in 1831 learned nothing more about influences in the distant past, though Turner might have had a substantial store of such information. Having spent a significant part of his childhood in a slaveholding that included his grandmother and both of his parents, he must have inherited some factual lore about their earlier lives. In particular, he must have heard something about a series of events that took place between 1791 and 1793, involving his first master. Those events, nearly a decade before Nat Turner was born, had fixed his destiny.

The Turner Line

Benjamin Turner II belonged to the third generation of his family to hold slaves in Southampton County. His grandfather, William Turner Sr., headed the first generation. That patriarch, a pivotal figure in family history, died in 1766, having reached perhaps his eighty-second year. His grandson, Benjamin II, who was about six years old in 1766, must have known and remembered him. It was William Sr. who committed the Turners irrevocably to working their lands with slave labor. At his death William held twenty-one slaves, the family's first significant accumulation. Each of his children inherited at least two of those slaves and thereby carried forward his commitment.[1] It was William Sr., too, who moved the Turners away from the early settlements along the James River in Isle of Wight County onto new lands south and west of the Blackwater River. In 1714 he acquired the family's first property in what later became Southampton County, two hundred acres on Angelica Swamp. In 1728 he patented another 125 acres nearby. In 1749, when Southampton became a separate county, he was making his home there, not more than six miles north of what became the neighborhood of Cross Keys.[2]

William Turner Sr. also took the lead in adopting certain inheritance practices that were evolving among eighteenth-century Tidewater families like his own.[3] He was conscientious, for one thing, about making a will: he drew up his final instructions in 1763, almost three full years before he died. His descendants proved to be equally conscientious, recording by 1831 a remarkable chain of wills that remained unbroken through four generations. In making their wills, moreover, William Sr. and each of his successors followed form. They conveyed particular parcels of land to specific heirs and distributed items of personal property in similar, meticulous detail, giving greatest attention to the assignment of individual slaves. They were careful to deduct, sometimes explicitly, any gifts already settled upon older or married children. None of the Turners subscribed to primogeniture—none of them gave an entire estate to an eldest son, though they might have favored one son in particular now and then. On the whole, they divided their estates equitably, with a single restriction: they gave land to male heirs only. Slaves and other personal property, by contrast, they divided among all heirs, male and female. By the time Nat Turner was born, these practices had become implicit promises, engrained and handed down like patrimony itself. For a son, the paternal gift of land and slaves was an inducement to build his own estate near home, perhaps in association with his brothers. For a daughter, an inheritance of slaves was an endowment that might expand her options and enhance her influence in marriage. For the slaves involved, each division prompted a breaking of bonds and a scattering in as many directions as there were heirs and heiresses.

In planning his own estate, Benjamin Turner I, the son and executor of William Turner Sr., followed these practices to the letter. He wrote his will in 1777, at about age fifty-six, declaring himself "of Perfect mind and Memory" four full years before he died. All of his land went to his three sons, in unequal portions.[4] And he had plenty of land to give away, for he was the family's great expansionist in Southampton. Between 1762 and 1768, he bought almost fourteen hundred acres in the southern part of the county, including the tract that became the birthplace of Nat Turner.[5] Some of these properties he apparently soon traded or sold; tax records for 1782, the year after his death, indicate that he died owning 945 acres.[6]

His purchases suggest that Benjamin I was planning an enterprise beyond the physical capacity of his three sons and his modest slaveholding in

1781. Early death and the onset of the Revolution stopped him short: he died with fewer than half the number of slaves his father had held. In his will he listed only ten, distributed as follows among all of his heirs, male and female: Old Abram, Tom, and Lucy *(bequeathed to his son Benjamin II)*; Young Abram and Olive *(to son Henry)*; Dorcas, or "Darcus," a girl *(to daughter Ann)*; Nancy, a girl *(to grandsons Turner and James Newsum, children of his daughter Phoebe, or "Phebie," Turner Newsum)*; Aaron, Isaac, and Jude *(to son Nathan)*.[7] Following another form common in wills of the time, he identified these people by given name only, except for the four references to maturity or youth. His heirs needed no details about age, family, appearance, occupation, skill, or value. However cryptic the resulting list of slaves, it clearly included the names of at least six people who survived until 1815 or beyond and who must have been known to the young Nat Turner: Tom, Lucy, Young Abram, Olive, Dorcas ("Darcus"), and Aaron. Two of those six, Tom and Lucy, were given directly to Benjamin Turner II, the heir who would become Nat Turner's first master.

Heirs of Benjamin I

The three sons of Benjamin Turner I put their patrimonies to work in very different ways, with results that may explain why the youngest became the favored heir.

Nathan, the eldest, born about 1754, inherited a 120-acre tract seven miles distant from the home farm, on the south side of Flat Swamp, where his father had placed him when Nathan married around 1775; Benjamin I formally devised this property to Nathan in 1781. Ten years later Nathan still held the same small tract on the far side of the swamp, where, without ever adding another acre, he spent the rest of his life. The same inertia characterized his slaveholding. In 1781 he had inherited three slaves: Aaron, Isaac, and Jude. Ten years later he held just two slaves who were taxable (aged twelve or older); and when he died in 1817, he still had no more than two, one of whom was his patrimonial slave Aaron.[8] Content to subsist, Nathan withdrew from the expansionist enterprise of his father and grandfather.

Henry, the middle son, born about 1756, departed radically from expectations. He kept the land given to him in 1781 (four hundred acres, his portion of the tract shared with his younger brother, Benjamin II) but soon began to pursue other interests.[9] He apparently stopped growing field crops for the market—the accounts of his estate listed no tobacco, corn, or cotton. By 1791 he was operating two mills, was conducting a store at his farm, and had become a partner with his cousin William Turner in a second store, this one in Northampton County, just across the North Carolina line. He kept his two patrimonial slaves (Young Abram and Olive) and even saw his holding increase in size: by 1791 he held nine additional slaves, most of them acquired probably through his marriages in 1778 and 1783. The shift in Henry's interests, however, apparently affected his plans both for his slaves and for his children. By 1791 he was employing at least one slave, a man named Jack, in the operations of his Northampton store and had arranged for his eldest son, John—barely twelve years old—to enter the merchant's trade as an apprentice to Cousin William.[10] These measures, together with others he soon would announce, signaled a change: Henry Turner wanted to extricate himself and his household from an established way of life.

His purpose came to light in December 1791, ten years after the death of his father, in the first of two episodes that involved the Turners in decisions about slave keeping. In March 1791, the local tax collector had listed Henry Turner—alive and apparently well—as the owner of six slaves over the age of twelve.[11] Then, between March and early December, Henry fell mortally ill. On 13 December, being "Sick and Low of Body" but still in possession of "perfect senses," he made and signed a will. Oddly, he did not appoint as executor his brother Benjamin II, who lived next door, but chose instead his cousin William, a breach of custom suggesting some fraternal difference. He had his brother-in-law and two other neighbors witness the document, but he called in neither of his blood brothers for the signing. By early March 1792, at about age thirty-six, Henry was dead, leaving behind a widow, three young children, and a fourth child yet unborn on the day he signed his will. That document was unique in the annals of his family.[12]

Henry Turner's bequests resembled those of a merchant rather than a planter. Instead of assigning slaves to individual heirs, he gave equal cash legacies to each child, male and female: to his son John, daughter Elizabeth, son Benjamin, and his child unborn, £500 each, sums equivalent in value to his entire slaveholding, or to three hundred acres of good land.[13] In providing for his young second wife, the former Mildred Bittle, Henry had to make decisions almost without precedent among the Turners.[14] Down to the year 1791, only his grandfather, William Turner Sr., had anticipated leaving a widow (who predeceased him, however); Henry became the first in his line actually to leave a widow.[15] Mildred was to share with her children the use of one of his mills for ten years, and for the same period she was to have sole use of a second mill and all of his land. Son John was to work with Cousin William in the North Carolina store and was to have Henry's share of the goods there. Near the end of his instructions, Henry turned his attention to items of personal property, which he gave in equitable portions to the children and Cousin William. Finally, he came to the instructions concerning his slaves: "My negroes Peter, Abraham, Antony, Jesse, Isham, Tom, Venus, Olive, Jude, and Patt my will and desire is that they shall be free people in this our land, and my negroes [*sic*] Jack in Northampton he shall pay my Estate Sixty pounds with the discount of this years hire." His intention showed clearly through the troubled syntax: he meant to free these eleven people, who constituted probably his entire holding.[16] Henry was bolting. He placed no conditions on the manumissions, except in Jack's case: he required no other payments in return for emancipation, no periods of service, no qualifications of age, nothing. He offered neither legacies of cash or compensation, nor provisions for shelter or livelihood, nor words of sentiment, except perhaps in stipulating that the eleven should have their freedom in Virginia ("*this our land*"). His tone suggested an argument—perhaps with Thomas Jefferson, who had been airing a plan to emancipate all slaves born after a certain date and then to expatriate them at a certain age, hoping thereby to avoid "convulsions" between the races.[17] Henry was perhaps less ruthless than Jefferson, or more anxious to wash his hands quickly of slaves and slavery, or less fearful of vengeance and violence.

Most of what he ordered for his slaves came to pass. By the end of 1792, three of them (Abraham, Olive, and Jack) had gained their freedom.[18] At some point before 1798, a fourth (Tom) was freed.[19] As many as six others remained in some form of servitude between 1792 and 1799, three of them as part of the widow's dower.[20] Mildred Turner must have insisted on her right to their labor; she was, after all, a young widow with a young stepson and three of her own infant children to consider.[21] By 1800, however, nine of the eleven were free, and by 1806 the total had reached at least ten.[22] The widow and the executor of Henry's estate had followed his instructions.

If Henry Turner had expected his action to sway his family, he would have been disappointed, except in regard to his children. His efforts to disengage his children from slaveholding—the change of vocation, the accumulation of money, the legacies of cash—did seem to work, since none of the four became a significant holder of slaves in Southampton.[23] Only the second son ever paid tax on a slave in the county, and his payments covered just one slave in 1812 and 1813.[24] Henry's widow, who was listed in 1815 as coemancipator for one of his former slaves, Jesse Turner, must have accepted these manumissions, but no more.[25] Mildred Turner never gave up her own slaveholding. Each spring from 1793 through 1814, she paid tax on a few slaves, in numbers varying between two and eight, who may have been part of her patrimony. In 1820, the year she died, she paid tax on three slaves.[26] She gave no sign then of wanting to extend her husband's policy.

Some consequences of that policy, nonetheless, lasted for years. As late as 1831, forty years after his death, Henry Turner still ranked among the twelve leading emancipators whose slaves had remained in Southampton County as free people.[27] At least eight of his former slaves adopted his surname: first Olive, then Jack, Pat, Jesse, Peter, Anthony, Isham, and finally Abraham (or "Abram").[28] They stayed in Virginia, as Henry had wished, and from time to time found places to live near his old farm. In 1813, for example, Olive Turner and her daughter lived immediately west of that farm, on land belonging to Henry's nephew John Clark Turner, son of Benjamin II.[29] That same year and again in 1817, Abraham Turner took up residence with another nephew, Samuel G. Turner, at the very farm where Nat Turner was then a slave.[30] Also in 1817, at the old Henry Turner farm itself (still in Mildred's possession), Peter Turner settled for a time.[31] In 1823 another of the former slaves, Isham Turner (later to be acquitted on charges of conspiracy and making rebellion), became the first of the group to buy his own land, thirty-six acres on the northeast side of Flat Swamp, not far from Samuel G. Turner's house.[32] And by 1831 a namesake had come of age—a free black Henry Turner, who, like Olive Turner, lived on land owned by John Clark Turner.[33] The former slaves of Henry Turner, along with their descendants, were everywhere. From the days of Nat Turner's infancy, their presence was a reminder of 1791 and of the arbitrary workings of fate. They served, too, as precedents and a motive for his appropriation of the family name.[34]

Benjamin Turner II

The youngest son and namesake, Benjamin Turner II, proved to be the most accepting of the world and its gifts. He took possession of his inheritance in 1781 without hesitation and improved what he received. At one point, two years before he died, he owned almost a thousand acres.[35] At his death in 1810, his personal property tax bill ranked among the highest 8 percent of all such bills in St. Luke's Parish, thanks largely to his growing slaveholding.[36] He held twenty-nine slaves of all ages that year, most of whom he handed down to heirs in the fourth generation, as custom prescribed.[37] If, at one time, circumstances might have suggested a different option for his slaves, he had told himself to decline it. By standards implicit in the practices of his father and grandfather, he was a worthy heir.

On the death of his father in 1781, Benjamin II gained significant advantages. He was the favored heir, and while it is true that he had to share the estate with four other survivors (elder brothers Nathan and Henry; elder sister, Phoebe, already married; and younger sister, Ann), he got the largest portion. His father did not explain his distributions, but something more than partiality toward the youngest son must have been involved. The 425 acres Benjamin II received as patrimony constituted his family's largest single bequest of real property in the eighteenth century. The gift included the entire tract of 230 acres on which his father's house stood—the mansion farm—and about one-third of an adjacent, 595-acre tract on Cox's (sometimes "Cocke's") Swamp, a tract young Benjamin was to divide with his brother Henry. Benjamin's two parcels combined became his mansion farm and, in time, the place where Nat Turner first saw the light of day. Benjamin also inherited the biggest share of his father's farm animals (hogs, cattle, and sheep) and crops (tobacco and cotton). He got a bed and its bedding (or "furniture"), a table, a grindstone, a share of his father's iron pots, all of his hoes, axes, empty hogsheads and barrels, both of his horses, and the gift that singled him out: the best gun. He got three of his father's slaves: Old Abram, once the property of his grandfather, and Tom and Lucy, vigorous young adults in 1781 who would survive him thirty years later.[38]

His patrimony gave Benjamin Turner II the means for an independent existence, or competency, just as he came of age. He did not wait long to exercise his independence. In June 1781, at about the time his father was dying, he married a half-orphaned minor, Mary Griffin, whose stepfather consented to their union.[39] This was a good match. Mary must have brought with her as wedding gifts at least three slaves from her deceased father's estate, for in the following year Benjamin paid tax on six slaves, double the number in his patrimony.[40] In the next eight years, Mary gave birth to two of her four children who would survive infancy. By his thirtieth year, Benjamin was meeting expectations.

During the first ten years of his independence, Benjamin II confined his holdings to the 425 acres he had inherited and to the half-dozen slaves he had acquired in 1781 and 1782.[41] Then, in the months after his brother Henry died, he began purposely to enlarge his property holdings, starting with slaves. In this, the second family episode involving a decision about slave keeping, Benjamin II made his thinking plain. As if to emphasize his own views after Henry's death, Benjamin set about acquiring some of the dozen slaves belonging to the estates of his deceased father-in-law, Lemuel Griffin Sr., and deceased brother-in-law, Lemuel Griffin Jr. The negotiations were complicated, involving claims of Benjamin's wife, Mary; her brother, Wright Griffin; her mother, now Mary Holladay; her stepfather, Thomas Holladay; and her stepbrother, Thomas Holladay Jr. On 12 January 1793, barely a year after Henry's death, the parties reached a settlement, recorded in a deed giving Benjamin Turner II possession of four Griffin slaves: Lidia, Abraham, China, and Anne.[42] These people would remain as Benjamin's property until he died in 1810; their names would appear in his will, three of them with variant spelling or form—Lidia as "Lidda," China as "Chaney," and Anne as "Nancy."[43] While none of the four were ever listed with more than a given name or some indication of monetary value, their names did appear in patterns that marked their identities and outlined their lives.

Lydia, as her name came to be spelled, was the eldest of the four Griffin slaves. Born around 1757, she would have been in her midthirties and still of reproductive age in 1793, when she arrived at Benjamin Turner's farm. There she remained until she was about fifty; then, in about 1807, Benjamin transferred her and seven others (including Nat Turner) to his son Samuel's new farm. In his will in 1810, Benjamin gave her outright to Samuel, who kept her until he in turn died in 1822. Then, though she was legally the property of Samuel's minor daughter, Lydia fell under the authority of Samuel's executors. Those men persuaded the county court to declare her aged, infirm, and exempt from taxation, indicating that she had reached the age of sixty-five. Her name appeared for the last time in the inventory of Samuel G. Turner's estate taken on 4 March 1822, when her value was entered as zero.[44]

Abraham was the third man to bear that name among Turner family slaves. He was not the man referred to as Old Abraham in the 1777 will of Benjamin Turner I, nor was he the Young Abraham who got his freedom from Henry Turner in 1792. This third Abraham was born around 1776 and was about seventeen years old when he arrived with Lydia at the farm of Benjamin II. After 1807, when Benjamin II began to divide his slaveholding with his eldest son and daughter, Benjamin kept this man for himself at his mansion farm. Abraham, at about age thirty-one, thus became separated from the other Griffin slaves and never rejoined them. Three years later, in his will, Benjamin loaned Abraham to his widow and thereby kept him at the mansion farm. In the 1811 inventory of Benjamin's estate, Abraham was listed with a value of £120, the highest single amount in the inventory, an appraisal consistent with the value of a man aged thirty-five or thirty-six. By himself, Abraham was worth more than a tenth of the entire holding of eighteen slaves in Benjamin Turner's quarter. At some point shortly after the master's death, Abraham's name disappeared from the Turner family records, never to reappear.[45]

China arrived at the Turner farm near the beginning of her childbearing years, making her acquisition a promising one. She must have been born at about the same time as Abraham, or around 1776, and would have been about seventeen years old in 1793. In his will, Benjamin gave her to his daughter Susanna, along with Young Tom (China's infant son) and two other young slaves (also possibly her children). China's name appeared in the 1811 inventory of Benjamin's estate, her value (combined with that of her son Tom) put at £110, the second-highest figure in the account. After 1811 her name also disappeared from the Turner lists.[46]

Anne, the fourth addition in 1793, was probably the youngest member of the Griffin group. She was about sixteen when she arrived, or twenty years younger than Lydia and one year younger than Abraham and China. She was almost certainly the same slave Benjamin II referred to in 1810 as "Nancy," the pet form of her name preferred by the Turners. One clue to her identity was her consistent association in the records with Lydia: her name appeared only when Lydia's did, first in the deed of 1793 (as "Anne"), then in the will of 1810, and finally in the inventory of 1822. The ages of Lydia and Nancy, moreover, appear to have advanced together: in 1822, Nancy's value was put at $150, about right for a woman of forty-five, twenty years younger than Lydia. Her name disappeared after that point, but census and tax records indicate that a female fitting her description continued to live at Samuel G. Turner's farm, perhaps as a dower slave of Samuel's widow, through 1831.[47]

No one ever linked the Griffin slaves to Nat Turner or suggested they might have had some familial relationship to him; nor did Turner himself, in recalling his early years, name any of them as kin. In bare outline, however, the lives of three Griffin slaves suggest some connections: Lydia could have been the pious grandmother mentioned in the *Confessions*; Nancy, the discerning mother; and Abraham (who disappeared from the records after 1811), the fugitive father.[48] The evidence, while circumstantial, is particularly persuasive for Lydia and Nancy; on four different occasions—in 1793,

1807, 1810, and again in 1822—when the Turners could have separated these two women, they did not do so. It happened, therefore, that Lydia and Nancy were the only women significantly older than Nat Turner who were present with him in the same various quarters from the day of his birth through his twenty-second year. Related or not, they lived with him for years as if they were.[49]

Their arrival in 1793 was a sign that Benjamin Turner II had determined to remain a master of slaves, the role his father had in mind for him. Since Benjamin II knew by 1793 what his brother Henry had done, he must have made that determination deliberately. His new slaves were living proof that, unless he too was weighing a deathbed surprise, he had already ruled out a general emancipation of his slaves. That die was cast seven years before Nat Turner was born.

The odds in favor of surprise declined as Benjamin's accumulation of slave property doubled in size and value. He began farming in 1781 with just the three patrimonial slaves and perhaps three others (of unknown age, the presumed wedding gifts). From 1782 through 1793, he maintained a holding of almost constant size, averaging seven taxable slaves a year. The Griffin slaves, whose presence was evident in Benjamin's tax record for the first time in 1794, enlarged his taxable holding from eight to twelve, the most significant jump of his lifetime.[50]

To exploit and support the increase, he bought more land, starting in 1797 with a tract of 119 acres bordering his farm on the east; that purchase expanded his landholding by one-fourth, to 544 acres.[51] In November 1805, with a son approaching maturity, he bought still more land. From the estate of a deceased neighbor, he acquired an estimated 382.5 acres, paying just over £579 in cash—most of the money apparently borrowed from other neighbors. The accounts of Benjamin's own estate in 1811 disclosed that he still owed £439 in outstanding bonds and notes he had signed probably to make this purchase. The new property, which he called the Kindred tract, lay about two miles south-southwest of his mansion farm; it had a small house and a significant area in woodland. With this expansion, Benjamin Turner II reached the peak in his landholding, more than nine hundred acres.[52] Less than two years later, in the spring of 1807, he reached a similar peak in his slaveholding, with seventeen taxable slaves in a total holding approaching thirty, including all ages—more than any of his Turner predecessors had held in their final days.[53] Though he always owned far less land and far fewer slaves than the wealthiest individuals in St. Luke's Parish, his holdings had grown steadily until, between 1806 and 1808, he had risen into the top 10 percent of all taxpayers in the parish.[54] He had prospered.

His gains made it possible to plan generous patrimonies, given the modest number of his heirs. In 1801, after twenty years of marriage, he and his first wife, Mary Griffin Turner, had produced just four surviving children: Samuel G., born about 1786; Anne G. (or "Nancy," as the Turners called her), born about 1788; Susanna, born about 1796; and John Clark, born in 1801 (soon after Nat Turner).[55] The two long childless intervals—five years after their marriage, eight years after 1788—indicate that others were conceived who did not live. Here was evidence of a kind that Edmund Ruffin, the agricultural reformer from nearby Prince George County, would cite in arguing that eastern Virginia had declined after 1780 into a deep morbidity that he blamed in part on malarial mill ponds like the two on Henry Turner's farm.[56] Mary Griffin Turner herself died at some point after the birth of her last child in 1801, leaving her husband a widower in his early forties. At the completion of their marriage, Benjamin II had fewer heirs than his grandfather (who left eight) or his father (five) at the end of their lives. Still, the Turner line would continue, and so would its slaveholding.

In buying the Kindred tract, Benjamin II again tipped his hand. Had he been considering a general emancipation, he should have kept his farm at 544 acres and divided it with son Samuel, leaving each with 272 acres. (Benjamin's brother Nathan never farmed more than 120 acres and never held more than four slaves at one time, but he managed to support a family his entire life.) Instead, Benjamin chose to expand, apparently with borrowed money. His intention, doubly deliberate, must have been clear to every adult at his farm: he was going to keep his slaves.

Years later, Nat Turner would look back on this period and imagine that there had been some reason to hope for an exemption from bondage. His memories of the Turner place around the time of the Kindred purchase were infused with the dregs of that hope. His first mistress, Mary Griffin Turner, did not appear in those remembered scenes; she must have been dead. But the rest of the household, white and black, did appear: the "family," astonished that he could spell ("*one day, when a book was shewn to me to keep me from crying*"); the school children ("*getting their lessons*"); himself ("*looking at a book*"); his mother and father ("*saying in my presence, I was intended for some great purpose*"). The religious gatherings in the house had taken place then too, involving his grandmother ("*who was very religious, and to whom I was much attached*"), his master ("*who belonged to the church*"), and other persons ("*who visited the house, and whom I often saw at prayers*") from the families of Benjamin's brother Nathan, nephew Turner Newsom, neighbors Samuel and Sarah Francis, and John and Catherine Whitehead—Methodists all. From one such gathering came the unforgettable remarks about his intelligence ("*I had too much sense*") and manners ("*would never be of any service to any one as a slave*"), exchanged as if he had not been in the room. Even at the age of thirty-one, he detected no irony in their remarks. He still took them literally, still heard echoes of early Methodism, and believed to the end that there had been grounds for hope.

The decision to buy the Kindred tract affected everyone at the plantation and influenced all subsequent events there, beginning in September 1807, when eldest son Samuel married the neighbors' daughter, Esther Francis. Benjamin Turner II settled the couple at his new Kindred property and sent with them, on tentative assignment, a colony of eight slaves: Nat (or "Natt"), along with Lydia and Nancy, who remained together, and Sam, Drew, Cherry, Miner, and Elick. With promises of land and labor, Benjamin drew his son into slaveholding.[57]

At about the time Samuel married, Benjamin II himself began to consider a second marriage, turning his attention to Mrs. Elizabeth (nee Bynum) Boykin, a widow half his age whose husband had died in 1804, leaving her with a young daughter and dower rights to one-third of his 320 acres and one of his three taxable slaves.[58] To a second husband, Mrs. Boykin would offer this property (all of which she controlled) and more. Men found her attractive. She was married four times altogether (the fourth time in 1823, at forty-two) and widowed four times; with each marriage she improved her lot and enhanced her security. And though Benjamin II wanted a second marriage, he was cautious. He faced a dilemma common in his day among widowers tempted by younger women: chances were good that Elizabeth, not five years older than his eldest son, would survive Benjamin as his widow and stepmother to his children. She might lay claim to a significant portion of his estate, thereby reducing the legacies of his other heirs. With that in mind, on the day before he married her, he took the precaution of selling to Samuel most of the Kindred tract, asking a mere £50 (less than a tenth of the original purchase price) for 363 acres—in effect, a gift. Elizabeth could neither veto this arrangement nor claim a right to that property. The deed, sealed with Benjamin's mark on 9 January 1809, secured Samuel's patrimony, at least in its landed portion.[59]

The wedding took place the next day, conducted by the Reverend Benjamin Barnes, minister of the Methodist Episcopal Church. Within eighteen months, Elizabeth (now Elizabeth Turner I) bore her husband's third male heir, Benjamin Bynum Turner, born in time to be counted by the census taker in 1810. George Gurley, who made the enumeration in St. Luke's Parish starting in early August 1810, recorded the presence of four white females at the Turner farm (Elizabeth I, her daughter Sally, Benjamin's daughter Susanna, and one other female) and three white males (Benjamin II himself, the only individual listed by name, aged above forty-five, and his two younger sons). There were eighteen slaves, not counting the eleven assigned to son Samuel and daughter Nancy after their marriages. Immediately below the entry for Benjamin Turner's household, Gurley entered data for Olive Turner, then nearing the end of her second decade in freedom, a living reminder of emancipation.[60]

In the early autumn of 1810, during the season for fever spread by mosquitoes from the ponds and Cox's Swamp at the northern and western reaches of their home plantation, the Turners fell ill. On 9 October 1810, Benjamin and Elizabeth put their marks on a deed giving one acre to the local Methodist Church, stipulating that a meetinghouse be built to allow ministers of that church—and none other—to preach there. Elizabeth, apparently ill on that day, could not "conveniently travel" to the courthouse to acknowledge her consent.[61] Five days later, on 14 October, Benjamin II, now apparently ill himself, dictated a new will, affixing his mark at the end.[62]

The Estate

His instructions followed custom, for the most part. He handed down property exactly as his father and grandfather had handed down theirs, confirming a plan that had begun to form in his mind by 1805. He gave land exclusively to his three male heirs, in almost equal portions. Having deeded 363 acres to Samuel in 1809, he now divided his home plantation (563.5 acres) between his younger sons, John Clark and Benjamin Bynum. He distributed twenty-eight slaves (forgetting just one) among all of his heirs (including his widow and two daughters), but here again he favored his sons: the three male heirs got almost 60 percent of his slaveholding, both in numbers and in value. The paragraph in which he conveyed the eight slaves to Samuel is the earliest record of Nat Turner's existence: "I Give and bequeath to my loving Son Samuel Turner the following negros: Sam, Nancy, Lidda, Natt,

Drew, Chary, Miner, Elick which he has got in his procession to him and his heirs forever."[63] There, in Benjamin's dictation, was the line of legal descent, from father to son, from first master to second. And if Benjamin's clustering of the second, third, and fourth names is evidence, there too was Nat Turner's family—mother, grandmother, and son.

Benjamin II also confirmed the earlier assignment of three slaves to his daughter Nancy and then gave four slaves apiece to Susanna, John Clark, and Benjamin Bynum. To his widow he gave one elderly female slave (Nanny, probably Elizabeth's property before they married) and loaned her four others for the rest of her life; her portion of slaves, in terms of their number and value, amounted to less than a fifth of his holding. Finally, he gave to Elizabeth some tools that had belonged to her first husband, together with a grindstone, two feather beds, a pair of cart wheels, his horse Hard Money (or, depending on his meaning, one horse and some hard money), six cows and calves, two sows and shoats, fifteen fat hogs, and thirty barrels of corn—gifts amounting to just over 15 percent of his non-slave, personal estate. He freed no slaves, understandably making no exception for his most valuable man, Abraham, causing some disappointment perhaps, but no surprise for the adults. There was one other significant omission: he provided no land as dower to his widow, making her share of the whole estate significantly smaller than the customary widow's third.[64]

In devising his plan, Benjamin apparently thought he could take advantage of the range in his sons' ages, Samuel then being about twenty-four, John Clark, ten, and the infant Benjamin Bynum, the half-brother, about one. As executors Benjamin named son Samuel and an old friend, James Rogers, passing over Elizabeth.[65] In effect, he appointed Samuel to take his place as head of the family. Samuel could manage the estate. Samuel could oversee the lands and slaves of the younger boys until they came of age. In time, the legacies of the boys might link the three of them, like rungs on a ladder, into an alliance of brothers seated on adjoining properties with more than nine hundred acres altogether, their slaves near at hand, a pool of labor upon which each could draw. He must have thought too that in settling a generous amount of property on his wife's infant son, he was meeting her needs.

In less than two months he was dead, from causes never disclosed, at about age fifty. On 17 December 1810, the county court at Jerusalem noted that his will had been proved; one month later, on 21 January 1811, the court declared Samuel qualified as executor and ordered an appraisal of the estate.[66] On the next day, 22 January, a committee of three neighbors visited Benjamin's farm and executed that order. In making their inventory, they found not only the sources of his prosperity but traces of his life and character.

Items they listed from the farm's outbuildings and fields showed that in his planting Benjamin had stuck to a scheme his grandfather had followed, growing chiefly corn and tobacco, but introducing just enough cotton to keep up with his neighbors. He raised cattle and hogs in standard numbers and produced standard amounts of hard cider and pork, the latter being his most valuable commodity. At the end of his life, he owned seven more slaves than his grandfather had owned, six more hoes for grubbing and weeding, and seven more plow hoes. He had a fondness for horses: he had eight, compared to his grandfather's one, and his saddles—as many as ten in all—show that he liked to ride. His five plows (with no oxen or mules) might suggest that he had tried horses as draft animals, but in his collection of tools and implements there were few other signs of experimentation. Ten years into the nineteenth century, he did not yet own a cotton gin. He did have seven bushels of lime on hand, indicating perhaps that he was familiar with its ancient use as manure; but apparently he had not yet tried marl as a fertilizer, as some planters along the James already had begun to do. His crosscut saw and nine axes betrayed what must have been his basic idea about soil fertility: when he needed fresh fields, he would have them cleared. In short, Benjamin Turner had prospered because he had followed convention and because he was given almost thirty years to build his estate, more than twice the span granted to his brother Henry.

He had lived simply. The buildings at his farm, including the house he had inherited from his father, were modest.[67] So were their contents: at the end of his life, Benjamin held personal property worth about £1,800, of which household goods and furnishings accounted for less than £100.[68] The appraisers—still using British denominations in 1811—identified no rooms or buildings at the farm, but they did work their way in rough order through a series of different spaces, starting in what must have been a tool shed, proceeding next to a kitchen, and then into the house itself, before returning to the kitchen. From there they moved into an area for storage and spinning (perhaps off the kitchen itself), and then outside to a distillery, a barn, and a stable; finally, they addressed themselves to the occupants of the slave quarter and then made a second tour of the farm to find items overlooked.

The master's house could have had no more than six rooms: parlor, dining room, bedroom, and hall on its main floor, and perhaps two rooms for sleeping in a half story above. There were firedogs (andirons) for two fireplaces, seven walnut chairs with a walnut dining table, and eighteen additional "sitting chairs," corroborating Nat Turner's reference to the house as a meeting place. The appraisers counted five good beds (including a best bed worth £10 10*s*), one small bed, and a cradle. In the dining room they found a buffet worth £5, as well as a corner cupboard, a sideboard, two decanters (but no wine glasses), two mirrors, and, mixed with these items, an umbrella and a whip. In the parlor there was a desk worth £4 10*s*, presumably storing the accounts, bonds, and notes discovered later. The desk and its contents suggest that even though Benjamin Turner II always made his mark instead of signing his name (except perhaps on the 1793 deed for the Griffin slaves), he might have known how to read and write.[69] But there was nothing in the house anyone called a library—no collection of works by Wesley (1774) or Wilberforce (1797) touching on slavery, for example, or Hale (1758–59) or Bordley (1799) on husbandry, any of which might have stimulated new thought. The visitors did note a small parcel of books (titles not itemized) worth 12*s*, but these may have been books for children, perhaps the very books on which Nat Turner had glanced while the master's children were getting their lessons. Somewhere in the house, not far from the whip, they came across two guns, together worth £7 7*s*. In the kitchen or dining room they discovered ten silver spoons, worth altogether a pound or two, the only silver in the house. In the barn or stable they found a two-wheeled riding chair, or gig, worth £8 3*s*, but no four-wheeled coach or carriage.[70] At every turn, they found evidence of plain living.

One category of property listed in the inventory had contributed much to Benjamin Turner's prosperity. Over the course of twenty-eight years, his slaveholding had become a major asset, and although by 1811 his heirs had begun to remove some individual slaves, the eighteen who remained were by far the most valuable form of property in the estate, worth altogether £1,047.[71] After adding to that sum the value of other personal property and the market value of his land and then subtracting his debts and other liabilities, his entire estate had a net worth of £1,811. At the end of his life, slaves represented almost 60 percent of the value of his personal estate and his net worth (58.4 and 57.8 percent, respectively).[72]

How his holding grew must be deduced, since he preserved no record of births and deaths at his plantation.[73] The number of his slaves had increased from three to twenty-nine during his lifetime, a net gain of nearly one per year.[74] Some of the increase (perhaps eleven slaves at most) came to him through gifts and acquisitions from in-laws, first at his marriage in 1781 (three slaves) and then through the Griffin settlement in 1793 (four slaves). In 1807, when the number of his taxable slaves jumped briefly from thirteen to seventeen, it is possible that he made yet another acquisition, though his holding quickly declined to thirteen again by 1810. The pattern of small, steady increases (interrupted by one or two sharp jumps) suggests that the slaves themselves accounted for most of the increase. His holding in 1810 was large enough to have included four or five families. Its composition would have encouraged natural increase: among his mature slaves in 1810, the sex ratio stood at about four males to seven females.[75] At the time of his death he owned three women in their fifties, who had been of childbearing age between 1781 and 1800: Lucy (inherited from his father), Bridget (perhaps a wedding gift), and Lydia. He also owned three women in their thirties, old enough to have borne children between 1800 and 1810: Dorcas, China, and Nancy. If the older group had contributed nine surviving children by 1800 and the younger group half a dozen more by 1810, these six women together could have accounted for most of the increase. Slaves now represented the most valuable portion of Benjamin Turner's estate, the most significant source of his gains, and the crucial source of labor and support for his heirs. His decision to keep them all even as he was dying confirmed what always had been true: Nat Turner's destiny depended not on his own exceptional intelligence, but on the collective fortunes of a slaveholding.

If Benjamin Turner assumed that none of his heirs would refuse gifts of this kind, he was correct. But if he thought everyone would accept his plan, he was wrong. His estate wound up in a Dickensian chancery proceeding, a legal eclipse from which it emerged only in the spring of 1815. It is likely that Elizabeth challenged the will, since, while Virginia law did permit a husband to assign his widow personal estate "in lieu of" real estate, it also allowed a widow in such cases to "demand her dower."[76] It is also possible that the county court itself intervened sometime in 1812, after the death of little Benjamin Bynum, the infant beneficiary. In either case, by the time the estate began to reappear in county records in the spring of 1813, much had changed. Elizabeth had gained possession of the house and 208 acres "from Ben Turner Sr."[77] She would keep that property through two more marriages and two more decades, to the end of her life, and young Samuel would be dealing with her for the rest of his. In 1814 and 1815, the court divided the remaining portions of the estate in ways that differed from the original plan. Benjamin's land, excluding the part his widow occupied, was divided by lot and given in almost-equal shares to his four surviving children. The slaves he had assigned to his infant son were sold (all but one to members of the Turner family) and the proceeds divided into seven shares of $159.84 and 1/7 cents, with one share going to each of the four surviving children, two shares to the widow, and one share to the widow's daughter, Sarah Boykin. By terms of the division, Elizabeth secured a fair portion of dower land and slaves, taking her share in effect from the bequests intended for her deceased infant. The Turner daughters gained small portions of land and cash. Young John Clark, whose claims rested on his father's will, lost more than half the land intended for him but retained his assigned slaves. And Samuel, who had taken possession of his patrimony before Benjamin died, retained his original portion and actually gained a small piece of land.[78]

Members of the household dispersed within months. Soon, no Turners except the second Mrs. Turner lived in the house that had been the family seat since the middle of the eighteenth century. Mrs. Turner, or "Betsey," as she came to be called in the marriage register, remained there with her daughter until the end of 1816, when she took a third husband and began leasing her portion of the Turner farm to tenants, including at one point the family of Piety Reese, a significant figure in later events.[79] Benjamin's two youngest orphans, still minors, left their stepmother and went to live like servants with their older siblings—Susanna with Nancy, and John Clark with Samuel.[80] The Turner slaveholding, with a history reaching back thirty years and more, was broken into six different portions, and its members were scattered like the orphans to new masters. Those arrangements, at least, went according to plan.

Alliances

Turner, Francis, Reese

Now finding I had arrived to man's estate, and was a slave . . . , I began to direct my attention to this great object.

—Nat Turner, *The Confessions of Nat Turner*

The colony of eight slaves taken to the Kindred tract in 1807 by Samuel G. Turner represented the largest fragment ever taken from his father's holding. They were an odd lot, statistically. Lydia, in her early fifties, and Nancy, in her early thirties, both having lived with the Turners for fifteen years, were the colony's female elders, outranking in age and experience everyone at the new farm, including the master and mistress. (Samuel and his bride were barely twenty-one.) The rest of the slaves were children, aged about six to thirteen in 1807. The girl named Cherry ("Chary" in Benjamin Turner's will), perhaps eleven years old, was the only young female slave. The other five were young males: Sam, about thirteen; Drew, about ten; Elick (or "Ellic"), about eight; Miner, perhaps six; and finally, nearing seven, Nat Turner himself ("Natt"), whose home the Kindred tract would be for the next decade and a half.[1]

Through these selections, Benjamin Turner II may have been trying to keep intact some part of a family—Lydia with Nancy (always together), along with a grandson (or son), and perhaps one or two of the others. If that was Benjamin's idea, it remained undocumented, for in his will (the only record) he identified no one by family. For reasons of prudence, he might have hesitated to give particular individuals to his young daughters, which may explain why all eight of his juvenile males (aged nine through sixteen in 1810) went to his two eldest sons, Samuel and John Clark. In selecting Samuel's remarkable cluster of five such males, he must have been thinking of the future: Samuel would need a force to clear and work his fields for years to come. Miner would disappear before 1822 as would Cherry, but the others would remain. Between 1811 and 1822 the entire holding at the Kindred tract tripled in value and became an asset difficult to relinquish. Nat Turner tripled in value with the others.[2]

The new master resembled the old one in ways that became more apparent as time passed. Born in the house where his father had been born, schooled locally, and favored as an heir, he too would be faithful to an accommodating church; he too would be twice married, meticulous about his will, and dead before his time. And at key points in his short life, Samuel G. Turner, like his father, received, kept, and transferred slave property. But Samuel's life after 1807 differed from his father's in one important respect: his marriages would lead him into situations Benjamin II had never experienced. Those situations, in turn, would make the legal status of his patrimonial slaves ever more certain.

His father's two wives had been isolated figures, each having just one immediate blood relative in the county. Mary (Griffin) Turner, Samuel's mother, whose father had died by the time she married Benjamin II in 1781, was almost alone in the world. Her mother had remarried and moved away from Southampton by 1781, leaving Mary behind with her younger brother, Wright Griffin, who himself left the county before 1800.[3] Benjamin's second wife, Mrs. Elizabeth (Bynum) Boykin, was an equally solitary figure. She had arrived from Greensville County at the time of her first marriage (to Frederick Boykin) in 1798; by 1805 she was widowed and living with her young daughter, Sarah.[4] Only during the first twelve years of Benjamin Turner's adult life, therefore, did he find it necessary to negotiate with in-laws. After he acquired the Griffin slaves in 1793, he had no further experience in such diplomacy. By contrast, Samuel's wives came from thriving families with branches of every kind and degree. His marriages were true alliances, a fact his slaves would find significant.

Esther Francis

When Samuel G. Turner married Esther Francis in 1807, her father, mother, four sisters, and four brothers all were alive. Between 1807 and 1811, in fact, Esther's parents, Samuel and Sarah (Powell) Francis, brought forth yet another child, their sixth daughter. The Francis farm lay three-quarters of a mile north-northeast of Benjamin Turner's house and was comparatively healthful, its greater distance from the swamp and ponds providing some protection perhaps against malaria and typhoid. At their peak between 1812 and 1815, the Francis family counted twelve living members. In numbers alone, they mattered.[5]

They mattered also because Samuel Francis Sr. had accumulated significant amounts of property. In 1807 he owned 1,307 acres and ten taxable slaves.[6] His farm was larger than Benjamin Turner's, his slaveholding slightly smaller.[7] He managed his operations much as Benjamin Turner managed his, with comparable numbers of horses, cattle, and hogs; he produced more cotton, less tobacco, and similar amounts of corn, pork, and brandy. An inventory of Francis's personal estate taken in 1815, however, indicates that his household establishment was even more modest than Turner's.[8] The Francis house was small, having begun probably as an ordinary, commonly sized cabin, sixteen feet square. By 1815 it may have had two rooms on the main floor (a parlor/dining room and a bedroom), two additional areas for sleeping in an attic, and a detached kitchen.[9] The inventory listed seven beds, one cradle, two window curtains, and implements (two pairs of tongs, one shovel) for as many as two fireplaces.[10] In 1820, the buildings at the farm had an assessed value of $150, less than one-fourth the value of those at the Benjamin Turner II plantation and barely above the lowest third of building assessments in the county.[11] Samuel Francis had led a frugal existence. His slaveholding, though smaller than Benjamin Turner's, had grown in numbers through the years and become a significant asset, accounting in 1815 for 44.9 percent of his personal estate. In 1784, at his first appearance in the county's personal property tax rolls, he held no taxable slaves. By 1815 he owned sixteen slaves of all ages, not counting three he had given to married daughters.[12]

Francis died early in 1815, perhaps in a severe outbreak of influenza reported that winter in Southampton.[13] He was about fifty-three. His daughter Esther was still alive when he wrote his will on 10 February 1815, but not long after that date she too died. She was certainly dead by October 1816, leaving Samuel G. Turner a widower at age thirty with just one heir.[14] In nine years of marriage, Turner had fathered one surviving child, Mary C. ("Polly"), born in 1809; he now was in danger of becoming the first in his line in more than a century to die without male issue.[15] For his slaves, this circumstance raised a question of succession.

Samuel's ties to his dead wife's family survived to the end of his days. Starting in 1815, he administered his father-in-law's estate, though Samuel Francis actually had appointed his eldest son, William, and an older cousin to act as executors. Francis died before his son came of age, however, and his cousin declined to serve, so the court appointed the son-in-law.[16] At about age twenty-nine, while still settling his father's estate, Turner thus took charge of another. Combined, the two estates held almost seventeen hundred acres and nearly fifty slaves, all eventually to devolve upon the two widows, six male heirs (including the executor-son-in-law himself, eldest of the six), and eight female heirs. Samuel G. Turner now stood at the head of both families, embodying an old alliance that would continue to entangle everyone in its holdings.

His father-in-law's final instructions followed conventions of the day. Francis made permanent gifts of land to his four sons only, but he assigned particular slaves to both sons and daughters. To his widow he loaned for the duration of her life the "plantation" (as he called it) on which he lived (363 acres), together with specific, itemized personal property, including two horses, Ball and Bailey, and four slaves: Will, Edith, Dred ("Dread"), and Charlotte. At Mrs. Francis's death, their youngest son, Nathaniel, was to have the home farm and any of his mother's horses and slaves who might survive her. The rest of the land, at what Samuel Francis Sr. called his "quarter Plantation," was to be divided among his three older sons: William, Samuel Jr., and Salathiel. To his three married daughters he confirmed previous gifts, including a slave named Lucy given to Esther Turner at her marriage.[17] Lucy was the first slave to be exchanged between the Francis and Turner families, having been transferred informally as early as 1807, when she was about fourteen years old.[18] The rest of his slaves, Francis said, were to be divided equally among his seven unmarried children, all minors: Mary ("Polly"), William, Samuel, Sally, Salathiel, Nathaniel, and Martha Jane.[19] He set no one free. No one declined his bequests.

As executor, Samuel G. Turner was drawn into the affairs of the Francis family. It was he who kept all records of the estate, beginning with an inventory taken on 27 May 1815. It was he who wrote down the appraisals that day, noting among other items a parcel of old books (worth 9*s*), cash found in the house (£58 16*s*), a gun (18*s*), three axes (12*s* altogether), and sixteen slaves (including Benjamin, Peter, and Will, the three most valuable, each worth £120).[20] Starting in May 1815 and continuing for seventeen months, he kept a neat, accurate account of his payments and receipts, carefully documenting such items as doctor's bills, receipts from sales, debts paid and collected (including two debts owed by himself, one for the sizable sum of £25.10.10), and cash portions paid to the heirs. In November 1815 he assumed the role of defendant in a friendly suit filed by Mrs. Francis in chancery court to divide her husband's land and remaining slaves. In 1816 he oversaw two sales of personal property in the estate. By the time he settled accounts in October 1817, he knew more than anyone about the Francis family's financial affairs.[21]

His responsibilities as guardian, executor, and interim master kept him in place as head of the Turner and Francis families. Before his first wife died, he had brought his own younger brother and ward, John Clark Turner, into his household, along with that brother's four young, male slaves. By the spring of 1816, he also had taken in Samuel Francis Jr., Esther's brother, about eighteen years old, and probably also that brother's slave, drawn recently from the Francis estate. At about the same time, Turner acquired Peter, one of the three most highly prized men in his father-in-law's inventory, who joined Lucy, the wedding gift.[22] The two estates, with their heirs and holdings, now were mingling at Samuel's plantation, thanks to a connection that reached back to 1807.

Turner barely had closed his father-in-law's estate when William Francis, Esther's eldest brother, also chose him as executor. William wrote his will on 24 January 1819 and was dead within a month, the third member of the Francis family to die in four years. Unmarried at twenty-three, his estate was small and his instructions were simple. To his sister Martha Jane, then about eight years old, he assigned any cash proceeds that might come from the sale of his land. To his sister Sally (the future Mrs. Joseph Travis), then about eighteen years old and still single, he gave his two slaves: Anacka (or "Anarchy," as her name appeared in other Francis lists), a woman of about twenty-four acquired from his father's estate, and a boy named Moses, probably Anacka's son, born in 1818.[23] Turner administered these transfers, too.

As executor for his father-in-law, Samuel G. Turner dealt with a number of individuals later caught up in the events of 1831. Among the heirs Samuel Francis mentioned in his will in 1815, four were destined to become targets of the insurgents: his widow, Sarah; sons Nathaniel and Salathiel; and daughter Sally. Two of these—Salathiel and Sally—would be killed. Among the slaves Francis named, three were lost: Dred, Charlotte (the "wicked Charlotte" of historian William S. Drewry's later account), and Will (the "executioner" of Nat Turner's narrative). The two slaves of William Francis, Anacka and little Moses, would remain with William's sister Sally from 1819 through 1831, when Moses, at age thirteen, would witness almost the entire rising firsthand.

In Samuel G. Turner's own quarter, meanwhile, a cluster of young slaves with origins in four different estates was growing and maturing. The names of at least six Turner slaves between 1816 and 1822 would reappear in 1831: Hardy, Andrew, Jordan, Davy, Young Sam, and Nat. Nat Turner's memoir indicates that this was the period in which he began to spend time alone, praying and conducting experiments ("*attempting to make paper, gunpowder*"). He began to distance himself from his peers, disapproving of their stealing yet taking part ("*they would often carry me with them when they were going on any roguery, to plan for them*"). And he began to notice the impression he made ("*by the austerity of my life and manners*") on those around him.

Elizabeth (Reese) Williamson

The question of succession became moot for a time after June 1818, when Samuel G. Turner remarried, taking as his second wife Mrs. Elizabeth (Reese) Williamson, a young widow and the mother of a small child.[24] The new Mrs. Turner (or Elizabeth II, to distinguish her from Samuel's stepmother, Elizabeth I, or "Betsey") came from a family with substantial property in the Three Creeks neighborhood, near the western edge of the county. Her father, John Reese Sr., had owned 849 acres and as many as twenty-six slaves, accumulations comparable to those of the Turner and Francis families. In 1812, when Elizabeth was about eighteen, she had married a landless young man, Anselm Williamson, who came from the same part of the county, where he was living with his older brothers and sisters. Williamson owned two horses and two slaves, his only taxable property.[25] About one year later Elizabeth gave birth to a daughter, Rebecca Jane.[26] Then, before the end of February 1815, Elizabeth's father and husband both died, taken perhaps in the same outbreak of influenza that took Samuel Francis Sr. and his daughter Esther. Neither Reese nor Williamson wrote a will, so Elizabeth, who owned no taxable personal property, no land, and no house, was left to her own devices.

She acted quickly. She claimed at once her widow's right to a one-third, lifetime interest in Williamson's two slaves, Nathan and Peter (appraised in 1825 at $400 and $250, respectively); at the same time, she set about securing the remaining two-thirds interest in those slaves for her daughter, little Rebecca Jane.[27] Then, before the end of 1815, Elizabeth went to court, seeking a division of her father's estate. To that end, she filed a friendly chancery suit against her brother Edward, her sister Jane, and younger brothers Giles and Sampson (or "Samson").[28] In March 1817, the court gave her a parcel of 110 acres (worth $1,500 when sold in 1820) and six slaves (worth a total of $1,225 in 1817).[29] Her swift actions in court improved her fortunes.

The land and slaves Elizabeth gained from the two estates represented her only resources. She thought of her slaves not only as laborers and servants, but as assets that might help her secure a second marriage and, in the meantime, support her fatherless child. Her welfare depended on them; she could not let them go. She revealed her thinking on 11 June 1818, moments before she married Samuel G. Turner, when she executed a deed (as Elizabeth Williamson) transferring her one-third interest in Nathan and Peter to Rebecca Jane. She took that precaution, she said, for the sake of her child's "better support and maintenance."[30] Her new husband must have approved the arrangement and waived any right he might have claimed to Williamson's slaves. In return, Elizabeth apparently committed the remaining six slaves and 110 acres from her father's estate to the marriage settlement, a contribution that increased Samuel's net worth by about one-fourth.[31]

Samuel G. Turner's second marriage brought his family into a new alliance with blood relatives of Elizabeth II in the Reese family, a few of whose members had lived now and then near Cabin Pond. And since Samuel maintained his ties with his former Francis in-laws, he now became the link between all three families. By 1820 the expanded alliance encompassed five separate households: Samuel's, together with those of Mrs. Sarah Francis, Thomas and Sally Moore, Joseph and Piety Reese, and Giles Reese, all linked by Samuel's marriages to the former Esther Francis and Elizabeth Reese. All through the next decade, as the number of their households grew, members of the alliance maintained familial relations like those Samuel had established with his first marriage. Members continued the Methodist gatherings at the old Turner's meetinghouse (funded in 1810 by Benjamin II and Elizabeth I), occasionally took in one another's orphans, and helped to settle one another's estates. They exchanged property of all kinds through formal as well as informal transactions, including rents, loans, hires, gifts, trades, and sales. From time to time, as need arose, they exchanged slaves. Nat Turner, for example, was transferred at least twice between 1807 and 1830 from one household in the alliance to another.[32]

Through exchanges like these, individual slaveholdings of the Turner-Francis-Reese alliance were joined to a larger pool of servants and hands. Individually, the five holdings in the alliance in 1820 were modest; none stood among the largest thirty in the county (table 1). As a single, combined holding, however, theirs would have ranked fourth in the 1820 census

TABLE 1. Alliance slaveholdings, 1820 and 1830

Families and owners	1820	1830
Turner		
Samuel G. Turner	28	
Elizabeth Turner II		18
John Clark Turner		7
Francis		
Sarah Francis	10	
Salathiel Francis		7
Nathaniel Francis		15
Thomas Moore	9	
Joseph Travis		17
Reese		
Joseph Reese Sr.	13	
John W. Reese		21
Giles Reese	15	16
Total slaves	75	101
Total households	5	7

Sources: U.S. Census, 1820, 1830, Southampton County, manuscript returns.

Notes: The 1830 census recorded 7,756 slaves and 703 slaveholdings in Southampton. The largest holding (that of William Allen) was 179; the mean holding was 11. The holding of John W. Reese ranked 89th.

(seventy-five slaves) or fifth in the 1821 personal property tax list (forty-one taxable slaves).[33] And while they neither worked nor held their slaves in common, their holdings considered together did provide a convenient, flexible supply of labor, so they seldom had to buy or sell or hire on the market. There were other advantages as well. Their property was secured: if one master fell into debt or died without heirs, slaves could be transferred like orphans to others, reducing the pressure to sell. At the same time, these options countered the temptation to free anyone.

Through transfers and exchanges, alliance quarters became mixtures of people from the various member farms. By 1820, the slaves of Samuel G. Turner, for example, had been drawn together from at least six other holdings of the past and present; among the slaves at his plantation were people with ties to each of the four other holdings in the alliance. And gradually, some of the slaves formed their own family bonds, thereby linking the holdings in another way. At times, bonds between the slaves might have seemed to strengthen the alliance.

The most unusual of Samuel G. Turner's new relations were Elizabeth's uncle, Joseph Reese Sr., and the woman who lived with him, Piety Reese.

This pair had become a presence in the neighborhood in 1817, when they began renting the old plantation of Benjamin Turner II.[34] Joseph, a younger brother of Elizabeth's father, had been born in Southampton around 1768, around the time the Reese family was being drawn toward Methodism.[35] Piety (Vick) Reese was born about 1772 to Quaker parents, which may explain why neither her father nor her brothers had held slaves. After the death of her father in 1784, Piety Vick drifted away from her early moorings. In 1792 she married outside the Quakers, to Joseph Reese's cousin, Rivers Reese, with whom she had two daughters. Rivers died intestate in 1799, leaving 126 acres, two horses, and one slave.[36] Within two years Joseph, who had left the county for a time, returned. In 1802 and again in 1803, his name appeared immediately below Piety's on the personal property tax lists, suggesting that the two were paying their taxes together. Each was charged for one adult slave. In 1804, when their records were joined under Joseph's name, they paid tax on two adult slaves and three horses.[37] At some point between 1804 and 1811, Piety bore her third child, a son named John W. Reese; and by 1813, when she was about forty-one and had not yet remarried, she bore another, named Joseph William Henry Reese.[38]

From 1802 to 1817, Joseph and Piety Reese lived together in a cabin on land that had belonged to her dead husband, about one-third of which (or forty-five acres) she held as widow's dower; they did not bother to declare themselves in a common-law marriage, which the state of Virginia would not have recognized in any event.[39] Instead, they apparently adopted a pretense made possible by the fact that they shared the surname *Reese*: they *seemed* to be married. Nonetheless, any number of people, including the parish tax commissioners, Piety's daughters, and Joseph's niece, Elizabeth (Reese) Williamson Turner, knew they were not.

The Reeses, who were not known for their advanced social views, must have been led into this arrangement by self-interest. Possibly Joseph, on his return to Southampton, was not free to marry. Or, Piety may have feared she would lose her dower property if she married again; and indeed, in stages, her new partner did take possession of everything in her dead husband's estate. In 1804 he assumed the tax liability for Piety's dower slave. In 1817, through a formal deed, he purchased all eighty-one acres of the land allotted to her daughters. And in 1818, through a transaction involving no recorded deed, he took possession of the remaining forty-five acres Piety had been holding as dower.[40] Whatever their reasons, they maintained the pretense.

Their course entailed an occasional deception on their part and acquiescence by others, as in 1813, when Joseph wrote a new will. He was years away from dying, so he must have been moved to take this action by the birth of his namesake. He chose his words carefully: "I give and bequeath," he said, "Piety Reese['s] two sons John [and] Joseph W. Henry Reese all and every part of my estate real and personal." If either boy should die "without lawful heirs," as he put it, the survivor should have the whole of his estate. (In fact, at about age forty-five, Reese still owned no real estate, though he did have possession of four slaves and two horses.) In addition, he offered significant tokens to each boy: to young John, his "Gun and Cutrements," and to little Joseph, his "holsters and Pistols with all the equipage." For their mother, he made no provision, undoubtedly knowing that since Piety was not his wife, she would have no legal claim to dower. Five men witnessed the document, including Joseph's older brother John (father of Elizabeth II) and a young friend, John T. Vaughan.[41] It was Vaughan who later would betray Reese.

Early in 1817 Joseph Reese Sr. rented the old Benjamin Turner II plantation from Samuel G. Turner's stepmother (Elizabeth I), who had remarried in 1816 and vacated the house.[42] Reese must have been drawn there by Vaughan, his friend and witness, who had just purchased an adjoining farm.[43] His leases continued through the end of 1819. For about three years, therefore, he and his slaves worked the land at the old Turner place, two miles north-northeast of the Kindred tract. And since the master's residence at the old Turner place was more spacious than their cabin at Three Creeks, it is possible that Joseph and Piety actually occupied the house where Nat Turner once had astonished his elders with feats of spelling.[44] Joseph Reese was in midtenure at the old place when his niece married Samuel G. Turner.

Samuel and Elizabeth II established their household at the Kindred tract, on the eastern reaches of Flat Swamp, in June 1818. Samuel was about thirty-two at the time, Elizabeth about twenty-six. Their combined family included Samuel's daughter, Mary C. ("Polly"), about nine years old, and Elizabeth's daughter, Rebecca Jane Williamson, about five.

An image of their house and outbuildings has survived in a photograph taken around 1899 by William S. Drewy, the first historian after Thomas R. Gray to visit scenes of the uprising.[45] Drewry's camera caught seven structures, apparently from the northeast, on a day when the three tall trees (oaks, probably) in the yard were in full leaf. Another stood in the distance to the left; no others broke the horizon. A circular drive, invaded by tall, thin weeds and enclosed left and right by split-rail fencing, led up a low incline to the fenced yard. A horse, perhaps Drewry's, stood grazing, unsaddled, to the right in the drive. Here, Samuel and Elizabeth Turner had resided for the three and a half years of their marriage.

The master's house, centered in the photograph but partially obscured by overhanging branches, stood inside the yard, a few steps beyond the gate. It was a framed structure, one and a half stories high, about forty feet wide and perhaps a single room deep, with what must have been unpainted, clapboard siding. A porch, with its own roof and pediment about twelve feet wide, framed the central entry door. To the right and left of the door were single windows, indicating one room on each side of a central hall.[46] A chimney pierced the roof about a third of the distance from the left side, marking perhaps the extent of the original house.[47] There were no dormers, but the attic would have provided space for a pair of bedrooms. Toward the rear, on the left, outlined in shadow, appeared what must have been the kitchen wing.

In front of the house and to the left in the picture (toward the southeast?), about twenty-five feet from the front door but within the yard, stood a separate cabin, also unpainted, about sixteen feet square, once suitable for slaves or an overseer. Its only visible opening was a central door leading directly into the circular drive. To the right (northwest?) in Drewry's picture, opposite the cabin and perhaps forty feet from the master's front door, stood a small barn or stable. Behind that structure were four outbuildings in a row leading to the right, away from the master's house. The two in the middle, having no chimneys, must have been sheds or cribs; the other two, only partly visible, may have been cabins. Farther to the right, out of the picture, there once must have been two or three additional cabins. Altogether, the buildings at Samuel G. Turner's home plantation in 1821 had an assessed value of $1,000, exactly twice the value of those at his father's old place. These structures were modest compared to those owned by the wealthiest man in the parish, Francis Ridley, whose buildings were assessed at $6,000 that year. Still, Turner's structures ranked among the top 15 percent of all building complexes in St. Luke's Parish in terms of assessed value.[48]

Since Turner hired no overseer during the period of his second marriage, it is possible that he reserved the cabin in the yard for house slaves. Field hands he probably assigned to cabins or barracks behind the house or along the row to the right in Drewry's photograph. He preserved no plantation register and may never have kept a complete roster of his people, but partial lists bearing their names did appear from time to time in legal documents of the Turner, Francis, and Reese families—in their inventories, wills, deeds, and chancery reports, starting in 1810 and continuing through 1822. Those documents provide a bare minimum of detail: single, given names for individual slaves, together with market values for those listed in the inventories and chancery reports. Only a few people were identified by their family connections (mothers of infants, and perhaps the infants, too) or relative ages (young or old), and none by their dwellings.

The lists indicate that about thirty-three slaves altogether lived at the Turner plantation between 1815 and 1822. In 1818 Samuel's holding, combined with Elizabeth's, included two or three slaves left by her first husband, plus five of the six she had gained from her father's estate and at least twenty-three Samuel had gathered from his two grandfathers, his father, his first father-in-law, and through natural increase.[49] New individuals appeared occasionally and others disappeared, so the size of the slaveholding fluctuated, reaching a peak of perhaps thirty.[50] And for at least the tax year 1817, Abraham Turner, the former slave of Samuel's Uncle Henry and still a free man, lived on Samuel's land.[51]

Two of the oldest residents at the Turner place, Tom and Bridget, each about sixty years old in 1818, were now apparently a couple. They had a long history with the Turner family, Tom once having belonged to Samuel's grandfather, and Bridget, to his father. On the death of Samuel's father in 1810, this pair had been loaned to his stepmother; at her remarriage in 1816, they had been returned (without formal transfer) to Samuel.[52] When the Reeses took over Benjamin's old place in 1817, Samuel apparently brought Tom and Bridget to his home plantation for a brief time and then settled them on a tract he purchased in 1819 near the North Carolina border. The two other older women present at the home plantation throughout the period were Lydia, now in her early sixties, and Nancy, in her early forties. Also present at different times were fifteen children aged fifteen or younger and fourteen young adults between the ages of sixteen and forty. Nat Turner, who turned eighteen a few months after Samuel married Elizabeth, was among the young adults.[53]

Contrary to later accounts, Samuel G. Turner prospered in this period of his life, much as his father had prospered before him. He began to buy more land, perhaps planning to exploit the growing number of his slaves and to provide for any future male heirs produced by his union with Elizabeth. In January 1819, seven months after he remarried and just as the great financial panic was beginning, he added 129 acres to his holdings, paying nearly $900 for portions of his father's land that his two sisters had inherited.[54] In February he made another purchase of almost 330 acres south of Flat Swamp, for which he paid $1,318.50.[55] These additions brought his total acreage to 881 and by 1821 placed him in the top 15 percent of the 275 core taxpayers in St. Luke's Parish, a rank his father had reached briefly a decade earlier.[56] There is no evidence that his purchases put him in financial straits or forced him into debt.[57] In fact, he had sufficient cash in 1821 to make a loan of $890 to Elizabeth's brother Edward and another of $110 to his own brother, John Clark.[58]

Neighbors appointed by the court to make an inventory of Samuel G. Turner's personal property in 1822 found evidence of the same plain living and modest prosperity that had characterized his father's household. These were not planters of legend. In Samuel's house the assessors found six beds of good to ordinary quality (as in his father's house, which also had a cradle) and eight flag-bottomed chairs (compared to twenty-five chairs of all kinds at Benjamin's, where the Methodists once met). Each house had mirrors, but no pictures or paintings; each had two walnut tables, one cupboard, and one buffet, but no clocks. Samuel owned some china, Benjamin some silver spoons. Samuel had five decanters, his father two. (Neither was an abstainer.) Each had an umbrella, a shotgun, and a whip. Samuel alone had carpets (two, flowered, mentioned only in his will), tablecloths, and curtains. Like his father, he had only a small parcel of books, not itemized except for a large version of the New Testament. And while he had no desk, he did have an inkstand; he must have kept accounts at one of the walnut tables. At other locations around the plantation, the inventory takers found signs of the same sensible economy his father had exercised. Samuel had just a cart or two, a single gig, and no four-wheeled carriage or coach. He kept only three horses (including a bay named Fiddler, worth $120), far fewer than his father's eight; and he owned just three saddles, compared to Benjamin's ten. He operated a still, as did his father, and had all the apparatus for a distillery, including casks, barrels, apple mills, and cider presses. But nothing in his outbuildings suggested extravagance.[59]

Turner followed the farming practices of his day, just as his father had done. He planted corn as his chief field crop, but he abandoned tobacco altogether—his only innovation—in favor of cotton, a change he had effected by 1822.[60] He apparently had not heard Jefferson's call, issued in 1794, for the recovery of Virginia lands by finding substitutes for corn and bacon.[61]

Pork (including bacon) was his most valuable product, just as it had been for his father. His herd of cattle in 1822 was smaller than his father's in 1811 (seventeen head, compared to thirty-one), but he had almost as many hogs (forty-five to fifty-two). The assessors noted a parcel of oyster shells worth 38 cents, and an old kiln, worth about $2, suggesting that he was making lime and perhaps spreading it on his fields; but beyond that tried-and-true, progressive operation, there was little evidence of reform. He owned four ploughs, apparently of an ordinary type, but nothing like a threshing machine or cotton gin. His slaves worked chiefly with traditional hand tools: he had twenty-six hoes of all kinds, a scythe, and just one spade, suggesting that he had not begun to marl or drain land. The more basic task of clearing land still must have been under way, as indicated by other tools in the inventory—a saw, one hatchet, an iron wedge, and six axes.[62] He was following a familiar path, building his estate through patrimony, marriage settlements, and the practices of his father.

Samuel's experience with his slaveholding also was much like his father's. The number of his slaves grew—in part through gifts, but chiefly through natural increase—until by 1822 they represented the most valuable portion of his estate. This was true by any measure.

Taxable wealth. In 1809, at the start of his adult life, Turner held just four taxable slaves; in 1821, he held sixteen, each assessed at a rate of 53 cents. Within a dozen years, in other words, his slaveholding had become by far the largest portion of his taxable wealth. His total tax bill for all forms of property in 1821 came to $13.89, of which slaves accounted for $8.48, or 61 percent.[63]

Personal property. Slaves also accounted for most of his personal estate. In 1822, the value of all personal property in his inventory was placed at $6,187.13, of which his slaveholding accounted for $5,295, or 78 percent.[64]

Net worth. Slaves represented the most significant portion of his net worth. In 1822, his four tracts of land with their buildings were assessed at $4,494. That amount, added to his personal property, brought the total value of his estate to $11,511.13. Real property (at assessed value) accounted for 41 percent of his net worth, and other personal property (excluding slaves), 13 percent. Slaves accounted for the remaining 46 percent of his net worth.[65]

Once Samuel G. Turner's slaveholding had accumulated value on this scale, it became his most important resource for maintaining his family. The holding would cushion the effects of mortality. If he died and his heirs needed cash, slaves could be sold. If the heirs needed a stream of income, slaves could be hired out. Better yet—for everyone concerned—if all of his property could be kept together, the slaves might continue working his plantation without him, perhaps with an overseer to take his place. And they would continue to increase in number. Living when and where he did, Turner would have found it difficult to insure his buildings and impossible to insure his own life; but his slaveholding provided a kind of insurance, a form of financial security for his survivors.[66] His slaves had become assets of great importance to him and of great interest to his heirs and to the families he had brought into alliance. The notion of freeing people as his uncle Henry had done in 1792 must have seemed out of the question, just as it seemed to Jefferson near the end of his life.[67]

In the winter of 1821–22, Turner drew up a plan for distributing his estate. His circumstances were unprecedented. At thirty-six, he was younger by far than his father and grandfather had been when they wrote their wills, and younger perhaps even than his uncle Henry. He was the first in his line since 1700 to produce no male heir, a failure resulting in part from the brevity of his life and marriages. He wrote his will on 9 January 1822 knowing that his union with Elizabeth had not proved fruitful, that he would leave no child unborn, and that his only blood descendant would be Polly, about thirteen at the time, his daughter by his first wife. Including his stepdaughter, therefore, he would leave just three immediate survivors, all female, two of them minors. These circumstances shaped his plan in ways that affected everyone involved—heirs, relatives, and slaves.

He took pains to be fair. He returned to his wife and stepdaughter certain personal property Elizabeth had brought to their marriage. He gave outright to Elizabeth her spinning wheels and two of the slaves—Ephraim and Jordan—she had gained in 1817 from her father's estate. To his stepdaughter he gave three other slaves Elizabeth had owned—Davy and Young Sam, from the estate of Elizabeth's father, and Mary, probably from the estate of Elizabeth's first husband, all three of whom Samuel conveyed by deed to Rebecca Jane nine days after signing his will.[68]

He also was shrewd. From personal property that clearly had belonged to him, he made some outright gifts to his wife: two horses, including Fiddler ("Fidler"), a gig, one ladies' saddle, some plantation tools, a generous portion of other animals, crops, pork, household utensils, china, and furniture, including a bed, bedding, and all of his "sitting chairs." In addition, he loaned to Elizabeth for the period of her natural life his Kindred plantation, with its mansion house, outbuildings, and 363 acres. For the same period he also loaned her three slaves, identified as Nancy (still present), Molly, and Myrick. These gifts and loans, together with the property he was returning, were Samuel's means of insuring the maintenance of his household in Elizabeth's hands. Smaller gifts to the two girls strengthened his policy toward Elizabeth. Rebecca Jane (his "daughter-in-Law," as he called her) received a bed, bedding, and a walnut table, as did his daughter, Polly, who also received a walnut buffet (the girls' property to remain with Elizabeth or in his house until they married or became adults). To his brother John Clark, he gave his share of their father's dower land, still in the hands of their stepmother. With this consideration, which eventually amounted to about 37.5 acres, he created a small interest in his estate for his younger brother, thereby maintaining ties between branches of the Turner family.[69]

The remainder of his property he gave to his daughter. Turner executed this part of his plan in a carelessly drafted clause directing that if Polly died unmarried or before reaching eighteen, his estate should be divided equally among his nieces and nephews, the children of his brother and sisters. What he meant was clear: if Polly survived, she should inherit eventually his entire estate, excluding only the property he had given to other heirs. By implication, Turner meant for her to inherit all twenty-three slaves he considered as property of his estate. The remainder of his land, amounting to almost 518 acres, also would go to Polly Turner if she married or reached the age of eighteen. In addition, Elizabeth's dower land (the 363 acres at his home plantation) and his house and outbuildings would revert to Polly if she survived her stepmother. So would his slaves Nancy, Molly, and Myrick, if they too survived. Samuel's estate would support his daughter as long as she lived.[70]

Turner died in 1822, probably in late February, at about age thirty-six. He may have detected symptoms of mortal disease as early as December 1821, when he loaned the generous sum of money to his new brother-in-law. In January 1822, though he mentioned no illness, he put his affairs in order, writing his will and assigning the gifts to his stepdaughter. By March 4, the day the appraisers made the inventory of his personal estate, he was dead. He may have taken warning from the past, for the course of his decline resembled that of his father, who wrote his will in October of 1810 and died within two months. Between 1810 and 1820, at least six other relatives were taken before their time: his infant half-brother, Benjamin Bynum Turner (dead by 1814); first wife, Esther Francis (1815); father-in-law, Samuel Francis (1815); the man who would have been his second father-in-law, John Reese

Sr. (1815); uncle Nathan Turner (1817); and brother-in-law William Francis (1819). The two Francis men had experienced declines similar to his, with warning signs appearing in fall or early winter, followed by the writing of wills and then death a month or two later. Those who died in 1815 all may have been carried off by the influenza epidemic; living near ponds and swamps as most of them did, they must have suffered repeatedly from malaria, the common malady of the region, in league at times with dysentery and typhoid.[71] Turner's surroundings would have conditioned him to keep in mind the threat of an early death.

In the 1820s (three decades before the state began to collect vital statistics), parish tax records provided the only available evidence on local mortality, and that only for landholders like Turner. In the spring of 1821, when Turner paid his taxes for the last time, the St. Luke's revenue commissioner recorded the names of 295 resident, adult white men who owned real property in the parish.[72] One year later the commissioner noted that 9 of those 295 men, including Samuel G. Turner, had died (a crude death rate of 30.5 per thousand). In ten years' time, by the spring of 1831, more than a third of the 1821 cohort (123 of 295, or 41.7 percent) had died. Their deaths, confirmed in wills and court minutes, averaged more than a dozen each year, reaching a peak of nineteen in the tax year that ended in May 1828. Many were taken in their prime, as was Samuel Turner: of the 125 men in the cohort recorded as between ages twenty-six and forty-five in the 1820 census, more than a third (49, or 39.2 percent) died during the decade (table 2). Had officials known the dates and causes of death, they might have constructed bills of mortality like those that had been appearing in American cities for more than a century. Even a simple count of the dead would have confirmed suspicions that lower Virginia was morbid territory. Between 1822 and 1831, in fact, the average annual rate of mortality for all 295 male taxpayers in the 1821 cohort must have reached forty deaths per thousand, a high rate for any time and place.[73] The effects spread across the countryside: more than one-fourth of all land in the parish in 1831 belonged to the dead—either to their estates, to their widows in life tenure, or to their orphans under the care of guardians (table 3). For the slaves of landowners, the effects of death were magnified: of the 1,572 taxable slaves owned by resident, landowning white men in St. Luke's Parish in 1821, almost half (739, or 47 percent) experienced the death of a master by 1831.[74]

Samuel G. Turner's death had consequences for his slaves, whose initial distribution he determined through his will. Since he had produced just the

TABLE 2. Deaths reported, white male landowners, 1822–31

Ages	Alive in 1821	Deaths 1821–26	Deaths 1827–31	Total deaths	Percent who died
45+	106	30	24	54	50.9
26–45	125	22	27	49	39.2
16–26	11	1	0	1	9.1
Unknown	53	8	11	19	35.8
Total	295	61	62	123	41.7

Sources: St. Luke's Parish Land Books, 1821–31; Will Books 8 and 9; Court Minutes, June 1821–May 1831; U.S. Census, Southampton County, 1820, manuscript returns.

Notes: Figures include only resident white males of St. Luke's Parish. The years of account are tax years, extending from 1 June through 31 May of the next calendar year. Figures are based on the earliest reports of deaths in probate records, inventories, tax assessments, and court minutes. Richard Williamson, who was between 10 and 16 years of age in 1820, is assumed to have been between 16 and 26 when he died in 1824.

TABLE 3. Status of landholdings, St. Luke's Parish, 1831

Owners	Number	Percent	Acres	Percent
Owners alive				
White males	299	58.5	131,818	67.9
White females (fee simple)	47	9.2	7,768	4.0
Free black males	7	1.4	374	0.2
Free black females	4	0.8	157	0.1
Subtotal	357	69.9	140,117	72.1
Owners dead				
Estates	88	17.2	34,706	17.9
Widows (life tenure)	55	10.8	14,978	7.7
Orphans and heirs	11	2.2	4,402	2.3
Subtotal	154	30.1	54,086	27.9
Total	511		194,203	

Sources: Land Books, St. Luke's and Nottoway Parishes, 1831.

Notes: Figures include landholdings of nonresidents. Percentages may not add up because of rounding. According to the tax commissioner's figures, St. Luke's Parish had 193,890 taxed acres; St. Luke's Parish Land Book, 1831, p. 33.

one heir, he was able to keep his own slaves together in a single holding, which, however, he divided into three groups. Tom and Bridget ("my two old negroes," he called them) were to remain "on the Lot where they now are," a special provision allowing the elderly pair to continue living together, probably in a cabin on Samuel's new tract near the North Carolina border; with this gesture, he ventured as close as he could imagine to manumission.

The three slaves he loaned to Elizabeth were to be hers as long as she lived, but were to stay in his holding. The remaining eighteen would go to his daughter Polly when she married or came of age. He did not itemize these people in his will, but their names did appear in the inventory of his estate taken on 4 March 1822. Nat Turner's name ("Nat") came first, appraised at $450, making him one of the two most valuable slaves in the estate.[75] Other names followed, some of them familiar: Sam, Drew, and Ellick; and, on adjacent lines farther down the page, Lydia and Nancy. Of the slaves Samuel had received as patrimony, only Miner and Cherry were missing.

Most of his twenty-three slaves remained at the Kindred tract after his death, therefore, along with the five he assigned to his widow and stepdaughter.[76] Nat Turner must have been kept there for about a year, long enough perhaps to encounter the overseer from whom he briefly ran away. He and the other slaves assigned to young Polly fell initially under the control of two executors: John Spencer, second husband of Samuel's sister Nancy, and Lawrence Cook, a friend and neighbor, both of whom soon followed Turner to the grave, Spencer in 1825 and Cook in 1827, years before the estate was settled.[77]

Even before his executors died, however, Turner's former relatives had begun to assert their interests in the settlement of his affairs. In September 1823 the Francis family took custody of his orphaned daughter, Polly, who agreed to choose as guardian her uncle Thomas D. Browne, husband of her mother's older sister, Mary (Francis) Browne. At about the same time, Capt. Thomas Moore and his wife, Sally (Francis) Moore, the youngest sister of Polly's mother, took possession of Nat Turner. That transfer, never recorded, probably followed the episode of running away. Together, these actions by the Brownes and Moores demonstrated that the Turner-Francis marriage alliance of 1807 remained an influence, though both of its principals were dead. Thanks to the resilience of old connections, Nat Turner remained in the neighborhood. The executors had no need to sell him to the traders from New Orleans or Georgia, for Capt. Moore, a master with ties to the alliance of 1807, now stepped forward, prepared to bring any difficult property to heel.

Though he said nothing in 1831 about Samuel G. Turner, and though he spoke of Elizabeth Turner II only in recounting her killing, Nat Turner did refer to developments that must have taken place during that couple's marriage and around the time of Samuel's death. The high valuation placed on him in the 1822 inventory indicates that no one yet had expressed doubt about his attitude, but his memoir suggests that between 1821 and 1823 his behavior took an unusual, perhaps rebellious turn, as evidenced by his fasting and praying alone, his hearing the voice of a spirit, and his running away. By his own reckoning, it was at about this time that he began to view his life as an irony, finding he had "arrived to man's estate," he told Gray, "and was a slave." At this point, he recalled, he began to direct his attention to the "great object."[78]

Cherry

One other circumstance between 1818 and 1822 may have influenced Nat Turner's thinking. Accounts published in 1831 indicated that at some point—possibly during his second master's second marriage—Nat Turner also took a wife, or rather formed a slave's marriage. James Trezvant and Thomas R. Gray published the first reports mentioning his wife immediately after the uprising, while they were taking part in the trials at Jerusalem. In his letter to the *Raleigh Register* on 31 August, Trezvant referred to an admission by this woman that Turner had been "digesting" a plan of insurrection "for years."[79] Gray, writing to the *Richmond Constitutional Whig* on 17 September, claimed to have in his possession certain papers belonging to Nat Turner, "given up by his wife, under the lash."[80] Gray also must have been the source for the account published in New York City in October by pamphleteer Samuel Warner, who repeated earlier details about Turner's wife giving up his papers, including "something like a map, with figures inscribed in the margin." Warner then added this unique detail: "his wife was a slave, belonging to Mr. Reese."[81] Together, the three accounts indicate that the couple had known each other a long time, that they were roughly the same age, and that in 1831 they were living near one another, though apart, at different locations under different masters.

Neither Trezvant nor Gray doubted the existence of Nat Turner's wife or the authenticity of the evidence she surrendered to authorities. No other source in Southampton referred to her, however, either in court or in the press. The magistrates at Jerusalem summoned no witness identified as Turner's wife, and nothing the woman might have said about Turner came up in court, even at his trial. In Gray's rendering of the confession, Turner referred (though not by name) to his grandmother, mother, and father, but said nothing about a wife. Before the trials in Jerusalem were over, curiosity about this woman either faded, as if her identity had been merely of passing interest, or was suppressed for reasons never explained.

Nearly seventy years later, William S. Drewry, through personal interviews with elderly survivors and descendants, gathered testimony that Nat Turner's mother was indeed a woman named Nancy, and that Turner had fathered a son whose name Drewry rendered as "Redic."[82] Drewry published these findings in 1900. He apparently did not learn the names of the other relatives. Seventy years after Drewry, speculation about the identity of Turner's wife began to focus on a slave woman identified as Cherry, a name belonging to a number of women in the vicinity of Cross Keys.[83] The evidence is meager and circumstantial, but it may shed light on Turner's motives.

The name *Cherry* first appeared (spelled "Chary") in records of the alliance families in 1810, in the will of Benjamin Turner II, who gave a female bearing that name to his son Samuel G. Turner. She was one of the eight slaves already in Samuel's possession ("*in his procession*"), according to the will, which means she had been living at Samuel's plantation since about 1807.[84] No other evidence about her appears in the records of Benjamin's estate—nothing about her mother, family history, or age. Nor did any documents pertaining to Samuel's estate in 1822 contain a reference to her.[85] She must have been separated from his holding before Samuel died.

The name reappeared on 20 November 1826 in an inventory of personal property belonging to the estate of Joseph Reese Sr., the recently deceased former tenant at Benjamin Turner's old plantation.[86] The appraisers of Reese's property, John Clark Turner and Peter Edwards, had lived near Reese during his years at the old plantation and certainly had some acquaintance with his slaves; young John Clark, in particular, would have known any slave who once had belonged to his father or brother. He and Edwards identified fifteen of the sixteen slaves in Reese's inventory with the usual, minimal detail: first, a descriptive term (*Negro man, woman, boy, girl, child*), with repetitions of the terms indicated by the word *Ditto* or its nineteenth-century abbreviation, *Do*; then, the name, followed by market value in dollars. The list appeared in two columns in the will book, with entries proceeding down the left-hand column and then down the right (table 4).

In one of these entries the assessors linked a mother, Amy, to an infant, whom they did not name; they provided no information about the family connections of anyone else on the list. The careful arrangement of names, however (particularly those on lines seven through nine), suggests that the assessors knew more about their subjects than they were acknowledging. They grouped Reese's slaves according to gender and maturity, beginning

TABLE 4. Inventory of slaves, Joseph Reese Sr., 1826

Slave	Value (in $)	Slave	Value (in $)
1 Negro Man Sam	400	Do. Amy & child	300
Negro Man Moses	225	Girl Jinny	300
Do. Do. Richard	450	Do. Edith	250
Do. Ditto Tom	425	Negro Girl Harriet	200
Do. Boy Jack	275	Do. Do. Becky	70
Do. Ditto Jim	300	Ditto Ditto Hester	100
Do. Ditto Riddick	150	Ditto Ditto Manerva	75
Negro Woman Cherry	175		

Source: Inventory, Joseph Reese Sr., Will Book 10:180.

with the four men and proceeding down the list through the three boys, two women, and six girls. Thus, though they may not have known anyone's actual age, they certainly were aware of the relative ages of their subjects.

Cherry's name they entered on the eighth line, after the seven males, but ahead of the other females. They described her as a woman worth $175, or less than half of what Nat Turner had been worth in 1822, suggesting that she was older than he. In value, she ranked fifth among the seven females. Another indication of Cherry's maturity appeared in the entry immediately following hers, for Amy, the woman listed with her child. The assessors placed a combined value of $300 on this pair, suggesting that Amy alone was worth about $250 and that she was younger than Cherry. Finally, at the bottom of the list, Turner and Edwards entered the names of six girls, valued from $300 down to $70. In none of those six entries did they provide a mother's name, indicating that the girls were between four or five and sixteen—no longer infants, but not yet mothers themselves, and certainly much younger than Cherry.

Immediately above the entry for Cherry the assessors entered the name of the seventh and last male, the boy named Riddick. They said nothing about a blood relationship between Riddick and Cherry, and the placement of the two names may have been coincidental. Other details, however, suggest that the assessors knew of some link between the pair. The position of Riddick's name, his appraisal at $150, and his rank as the least valuable male all indicate that Turner and Edwards considered him the youngest of the three boys; by giving him his own entry and not identifying his mother, however, they indicated that he was no longer an infant. In 1826, in other words, Riddick must have been five or six years old, or about the right age for a first child of Nat Turner. And of the eight females listed, the one most likely to have been Riddick's mother was Cherry. None of the six girls was old enough to have been the mother of a child worth $150 that year; and Amy, who did have an infant, appeared two lines below Riddick. One other fact almost certainly never came to the attention of either assessor: the inventory of Joseph Reese's estate was the only record pertaining to the three alliance families between 1807 and 1831 in which a woman named *Cherry* was listed with a boy named *Riddick*. In other words, the inventory indicates that five years before the uprising a particular man named Reese, having close ties to the Turners, did hold a pair of slaves whose descriptions fit those of the woman and child linked by tradition to the insurgent leader.[87]

Two more pieces of evidence, highly circumstantial but possibly pertaining to this pair, came to light decades later in the census of 1870. At Boykins Depot in St. Luke's Parish, census marshals found a woman named Cherrie Turner, who was keeping house in a black household and who gave her age as sixty-five. Not far away, at Belfield, in neighboring Greensville County, a black man named Riddick Turner, aged fifty and therefore born about 1820, lived with a woman about his age and a small child. This man was making his living as a farm laborer. His census profile is consistent with the identification of the son made by Drewry in 1900.[88]

If the girl Samuel G. Turner inherited in 1810 was the same Cherry who belonged to the Reese estate in 1826, she would have known Nat Turner for many years indeed, having lived near him though at times apart, just as later accounts assumed. In his will of 1810, Benjamin Turner placed young Cherry at Samuel's farm, where she had been living since about 1807 as one of the original eight slave colonists. By 1822, she was gone. At some point between 1817 and 1819, while Joseph Reese Sr. was renting the old Benjamin Turner plantation, she may have been transferred from Samuel G. Turner to Reese through an informal transaction like the one that later sent Nat Turner to Capt. Moore. If she did take a husband and bear a child, she probably had done so by the spring of 1820, when Joseph Sr. gave up the Turner place and withdrew to his cabin and 126 acres at Three Creeks, seven miles north of Cabin Pond, taking his family and slaves with him.[89]

The Reeses left behind an atmosphere of ill will. Joseph's former friend, John T. Vaughan, went before the grand jury in November 1820 with information (recently discovered, he pretended) that Joseph had been "living in a state of fornication from the 15th September to the present time with Piety Reese."[90] The scandal subsided in the spring of 1821 after the couple, having been married theretofore only privately (as Dickens would have put it), then married officially before a minister, conceding a point to convention.[91] But hard feelings toward the family survived, thanks to the behavior of their nephew Giles Reese, a younger brother of Elizabeth Turner II. Between 1823 and 1825, young Giles came to trial four times on charges of creating disturbances in the parish, the first involving assault and battery upon none other than John T. Vaughan, who promptly complained again to the grand jury.[92] Joseph Sr. remained quietly at Three Creeks until he died in 1826, keeping his household and slaves a good distance from Cabin Pond.

Nat Turner said nothing in 1831 to indicate that separation from a wife and child had provoked him to rebellion, nothing to suggest a merely personal grievance fueled by sentiments about family. That vein of antislavery criticism, mined twenty years later in *Uncle Tom's Cabin*, remained unexploited in the *Confessions*. If Turner did voice such sentiments in the jail, Gray suppressed them. No one in the crowds who saw Nat Turner during his final days reported hearing him speak in those terms, however, and the subject of his family did not come up in court. If in fact a separation had occurred, it lay in the past and was obscured in 1831 by more recent motives. Gray did not have time in the summer and autumn of that year to dig deeply into the evidence linking Reese's Cherry to Joseph and Piety Reese, or to Samuel and Elizabeth Turner, or to the Francis family. He did not investigate those possible connections, even though sources in Cross Keys would have known about them and would have understood their significance. Gray settled for an easier, stock explanation of motives, one that rested on the confession and involved the chief insurgent's fanaticism.

Nat Turner's silence on the role of his second master meant that Samuel G. Turner, by dying in 1822, would be overlooked in the accounts of 1831. Yet, perhaps more than Elizabeth Turner II, he deserved to be remembered. If indeed a separation did occur in 1819 or 1820, Samuel had permitted it; and then, in his final hours, he had declined to free even his exceptional servant. The thoughtful provisions he made for his heirs in 1822 would perpetuate the condition of everyone in his quarter. The alliances he had established would continue to do their work down through the summer of 1831, securing his holding within a growing pool of laborers, drawing individuals from side to side and place to place, formally and informally, as need arose. Unlike his uncle Henry, Samuel G. Turner offered from his deathbed no gesture of gratitude or atonement. Samuel was no Henry.

Successors

Capt. Moore and Mr. Travis

He was once the Slave of Capt. Moore, whose widow married Mr. Travis, the first victim of these bloody cut throats!
—Samuel Warner, *Authentic and Impartial Narrative*

In the six years that followed the death of Samuel G. Turner, a new generation of masters took possession of property in the Turner, Francis, and Reese families. By 1828, all of the land and slaves held by those families had fallen into the hands of men about the age of Nat Turner. Some were even younger than he. Neighboring households belonging to the Moore, Whitehead, Porter, Barrow, and Harris families all were about to witness similar transitions. As anyone familiar with the new masters must have understood, their succession would have significant implications for slave property.

Nat Turner's first experience under the successors began in 1823 or 1824, when, probably just after his month as a runaway, he became the property of Capt. Thomas Moore, a man of about thirty years. Like Turner's previous master, this one had married (in 1819) into the Francis family, and thus had brought the Moores into the old alliance. The captain had an aura of authority. In 1814, at twenty-one, he had collected pay for riding with the local patrol. He knew the country and could ride. In 1816, at twenty-three, he had gained the rank of lieutenant in the county militia, and four years later he had been promoted to captain. He could command.[1]

He was born in about 1793, seven years before Nat Turner. The eldest of four sons of John and Temperance Moore (and the second of their seven surviving children), he spent his boyhood and youth a mile or two west of the Benjamin Turner II place.[2] He descended from a line of minor slaveholders, his maternal grandfather having held nine slaves when he died in 1771, and his father, eight when he died in 1803. Thomas inherited none of those slaves. His father's entire holding, along with the family's small farm, went to Temperance Moore for the remainder of her long life; Thomas received only a half share of his father's land in North Carolina.[3] Until he reached his late twenties, he acquired no slaves of his own.

John Moore's will, carefully prepared in 1801, bore the marks of a man not bred to planting. His sons, he said, were to be "bound out when they arrive to the age of Fifteen years," indicating he thought they might follow pursuits other than planting and slaveholding. The inventory of his estate in 1803 indicates that he once had pursued other callings: he owned the tools of a shoemaker and a brick layer, for example, and books worth twice as much as those in the 1811 inventory of Benjamin Turner II. He also had two desks (one of walnut), a pair of handcuffs, some "Jind Cotton," and the "Cotton Jin" itself—a simple, inexpensive model, but one of the earliest gins to appear in the records of Southampton County.[4]

From Thomas's tenth year until his marriage at the age of twenty-six, he lived most of the time with his mother and gradually became the head of her household. In 1809, when Thomas reached sixteen and Temperance paid a tax on his head for the first time, the number of her taxable slaves had declined to just three, the smallest holding she had known since her marriage in 1790. She came close to holding none at all, but then gradually regained ground. Early in 1818, when Thomas paid a personal property tax bill for the first time in his own name, he was charged for seven taxable slaves, all of whom belonged to his mother. In April 1819 he again paid her bill for seven slaves. He still had none of his own.[5]

His career as a slaveholder began early the next month, in May of 1819, when he married Sally Francis, younger sister of Esther (Francis) Turner (deceased, ca. 1815).[6] He was twenty-six, and Sally about eighteen. This marriage made him a master in his own right, for his bride owned three slaves: a valuable adult male named Ben, inherited from her father's estate in 1816, along with the young woman named Anacka and her infant son Moses, both of whom Sally had inherited in January 1819 from her brother William.[7] These three became Moore's first slaves. By the spring of 1820 Moore held four taxable slaves: Ben and Anacka, certainly, and two others—perhaps Maria and Lucy, two young women who may have come to him as wedding gifts from Sally's mother.[8] In 1820, at about the time of his promotion to captain, Moore was identified in the U.S. Census as head of his own household, with nine slaves of all ages. He still owned no land; slaves represented almost three-quarters of his taxable property.[9]

Through the Francis alliance, Moore soon acquired the land that became his farm, all of which once had belonged to the "quarter" plantation of Sally's deceased father. Starting early in 1822—just before Samuel G. Turner wrote his will—Moore took part in a series of land transactions with his new in-laws. He emerged with 429 acres in two parcels. The larger of these, containing 240 acres, he bought from Sally's mother. The smaller one, about 189 acres, he purchased from Sally's brother Salathiel; it came with buildings assessed at a total value of $50—nothing more than a few sheds and a cabin or two.[10] There, in 1822, at an isolated location two miles southwest of the old Francis and Turner home plantations, Moore settled with his wife, his infant son Putnam (born the previous year), and five slaves aged twelve and older.[11]

Thomas Moore kept an average of five taxable slaves all through the years between 1819 and 1827. His history of ownership was as consistent as his mother's: except for the temporary decline in 1809, Temperance Moore retained an average of six or seven taxable slaves from 1807 through 1830.[12] Neither he nor his mother ever attempted to part with slave property. Their record, like that of the Francis family, suggested a complacency of the kind Jefferson attributed in 1814 to "the quiet and monotonous course of colonial life," which, the former president noted, had been disturbed by no "alarm."[13]

Disaffection

The Moores and their neighbors apparently dismissed as trivial some evidence of growing, potentially violent disaffection among slaves that appeared in two sensational crimes in 1821.[14] In the first, a slave named Dread, twenty-eight years old, one of thirty-seven slaves belonging to St. Luke's resident John Underwood, became involved in a burglary. On the evening of 23 April, Dread and two other slaves, Sam and Sip, together with a white man, John E. Martin, broke into the store and counting room of David Vallance, the principal merchant in Jerusalem. They had waited that evening until around seven o'clock, when Vallance's two clerks went to supper at Gurley's tavern. Then they forced open the rear door.[15]

According to one estimate, they took "Bank notes, silver, goods and trunks containing bonds and notes, wearing apparel, two guns &c to the value of Eight thousand dollars."[16] They also stole a significant inventory of cloth, including "Broadcloths of the value of eighty dollars, cambricks, checks, calicoes, Black silk handkerchiefs &c. of the value of two hundred dollars." That done, they set what one clerk described as "a chunk of fire" at the front of the store and then ran out the back.[17]

They took away some merchandise on their persons, but they carried most of the plunder to a small boat tied to the bank of the Nottoway River behind the store. They rowed downstream to a swamp, where they divided the take. Martin took his share home and hid some of it under the covers of his bed. Sam and Sip, now runaways, made a "negro camp" and hid their share of the goods—cambrics, calicoes, and cash—in the swamp, in hollow trees and logs. Sam then sent out an appeal for anyone who could count money. Dread went home to his master's plantation, five miles west of town, and began looking for someone to help put his money to work. Within a month, he was brought to trial and his motive became clear.[18]

One of the clerks, John M. Gurley, testified that Dread had been in the store "a considerable time during the day on which the store was broken open at knight" and must have observed where money was kept.[19]

Patsey Scott, who had been standing within sight of the bridge leading out of town, said she had seen Dread leaving Jerusalem that evening, headed toward home, and that "he was at that time very well dressed, and in a short time saw him again returning to Jerusalem apparently in great haste and he was at [that] time very indifferently dressed."[20]

Another witness, Elizabeth Turner (no relative of the Cross Keys Turners), gave testimony indicating that Dread had something in mind beyond burglary. On Wednesday or Thursday following the break-in, she said, Dread "wrode in the yard" of the house in St. Luke's where she was staying. Addressing Miss Turner, about whom he may have heard some talk,[21] he told her that "he wished her to buy him." She refused his request, saying "she had not money sufficient." To this he replied that indeed "he had money sufficient or knew where it was, that he had two hundred and fifty dollars or three hundred dollars."[22] The terms of the offer suggested that, above all, Dread wanted out of Underwood's slaveholding, a motive whose modest scope may have played upon the court's sympathies. At his trial in May, the magistrates found him guilty of burglary and sentenced him to hang, but they recommended that the governor commute his sentence to transportation, which was granted. Sam was tried two months later, found guilty, and received no commutation. Sip apparently escaped.[23]

Further evidence of disaffection appeared that spring in the second, even more sensational crime. One month after Dread's trial, in the early morning hours of 14 June 1821, a young farmer of Nottoway Parish and his wife were murdered in bed. James and America Powell had married in 1817 and established a farm on 125 acres James had purchased four miles southeast of Jerusalem.[24] To help work their farm, the Powells had hired two young slaves, a girl named Celia, from an estate in Nansemond County, and Abel, described as a boy belonging to Sally Daughtry, a widow in Nottoway Parish. Both slaves were tried for murder on 28 June 1821.[25]

A neighbor, John Screws, testified he had heard Abel declare that if Powell whipped him "any more," he "would not live with him."[26]

A slave named Miles, who belonged to another neighbor, said that during fishing season Abel frequently had vowed that "if James Powell whipped him that he would be damn'd if he, the prisoner, did not kill him."[27]

Celia herself testified that on the night of the murders Abel had said that "he wanted her to kill them people, meaning Powell & wife, that he would give her . . . five dollars to do it," which she refused to do, "saying that they had done nothing to induce her to kill them and that she could not do it." Abel said again that she should kill them, or he would. Later in the night, Celia rose from her bed in the room where the Powells were sleeping and went to find drinking water in the room where Abel was lying. As she passed by his bed, he asked again if she meant to kill them. Again she refused "and went back and laid down, but did not go to sleep, neither could she rest." Finally, she returned to the room where Abel lay, "and got the axe and returned again in the room where Powell & wife slept & laid down, & then got up."[28]

She gave Powell one blow "on the breast" and two on the head. After the first blow, Powell said, "Don't," and Mrs. Powell asked "what was the matter." At that moment Celia "gave Mrs. Powell a blow in the breast and two on the head." While she was committing the murders, she said, Abel was restraining a slave boy (perhaps the property of the Powells) in the other room, and at the same time calling to her and telling her "to save them and spare them no life"—perhaps meaning, *Be thorough*. When Celia had finished, Abel set fire to the house while she began carrying furniture and trunks out to the yard.[29]

Abel told her that "it was best to save the infant of Mrs. Powell to prevent suspicion, which she accordingly did by taking it from its mother's side and carrying it out of doors."[30] The child, a newborn about the age of Putnam Moore, was found by neighbors in the garden, "laying on a potatoe ridge."[31]

Celia and Abel were found guilty; they were hanged on 15 August 1821.

Exchanges

Capt. Moore evidently saw nothing ominous in the episodes of 1821. In 1823, when he paid tax for the first time on land of his own, the number of his taxable slaves had climbed from four or five to six.[32] The increase probably resulted from two significant acquisitions: around 1823 he took possession of Nat Turner and Hark (later known as Hark Moore, and on one occasion as "Captain" Moore).

Nat Turner came to Thomas Moore—and thus to the Francis side of the related families—directly from the estate of Samuel G. Turner, a transfer of property that called to mind the original alliance of 1807.[33] Between 1820 and 1830, slaveholdings linked by the marriages of Samuel G. Turner grew from 75 slaves on five farms to 101 slaves on seven farms. In 1830 as in 1820, the alliance slaveholdings combined would have constituted the fourth-largest single holding in the county. Here was a resource for every member family. When death took a master, as it did in 1815, 1819, and 1822, slaves of the deceased were drawn into a pool of hands available for hire, for purchase, or for settling old accounts. Around 1823 or 1824, when Capt. Moore needed hands at his new farm, he found such a pool, from which (as luck would have it) he drew Nat Turner.

At Moore's farm a dozen slaves of all ages crowded together with his family into two or three cabins. The captain and his wife might have chosen to take up residence with either of their mothers, whose houses were nearby; but tax rolls and census returns indicate that early in their marriage they established their own household and lived alongside their slaves. Their buildings were assessed at just $50, one-third the value of those at the Powell farm, where, before the murders and fire of 1821, the master's family and slaves had shared a two-room house.[34]

Thomas Moore left no account of his life or property, nor did any of his former slaves mention his name in their statements in 1831. His place in Nat Turner's chain of possession became known at the time thanks probably to Thomas R. Gray, who apparently forwarded that detail to Samuel Warner, who published it in his pamphlet. "He was once the Slave of Capt. Moore," Warner wrote, "whose widow married Mr. Travis, the first victim of these bloody cut throats!"[35] A few other details concerning the captain's life after 1823 can be inferred from the memoir by his slave in *The Confessions of Nat Turner.* Two specific years cited in that document correspond roughly to Moore's years as Nat Turner's master: 1825, a year or so after Nat arrived, and 1828, the year after Moore died. Between 1824 and the end of 1826, Nat Turner experienced six revelations of the Spirit—seeing in the sky the "lights of the Saviour's hands" and finding in Moore's field the blood on the corn, developments he communicated "to many, both white and black, in the neighborhood."[36] By 1825, when the Spirit appeared for the fifth time and revealed knowledge of the elements, planets, tides, and seasons, Moore must have had second thoughts about this slave. Then, apparently in the following year, Nat Turner had healed the poor white man, Etheldred T. Brantley, and performed the baptism before the hostile crowd.[37] Moore must have been aware of his slave's disposition by 1826, the year in which Turner later said he had begun to act constantly from a "Divine impulse."[38]

Perhaps alarmed by that impulse, the captain apparently took corrective action, administering upon Nat's body the whipping ("*for saying that blacks ought to be free*") that Gray would mention in September 1831.[39] Gray's estimate of the timing would have placed the whipping in 1828, the year after Moore died. Probably his guess was off by a year. In all likelihood, it was Moore, not his successor, who held the whip and confronted the great issue of the day.[40]

Thomas Moore died in the late spring of 1827 at about the age of thirty-four. Even though he knew that his grandfather and father had left final instructions that had shaped his life, he did not leave a will, which suggests that he died suddenly, perhaps accidently, a fate common among men on farms—burns, a kick or a fall from a horse, wounds from an axe or a gunshot. The division of his estate fell to his court-appointed executrix, his widow, Sally.[41] Her task was not complicated, since, after eight years of marriage, the couple had produced just one surviving heir, their six-year-old son Putnam.

Nor was the estate large. In 1826, the last year Capt. Moore paid taxes, he still owned the same 429 acres and the same buildings, worth just $50. His taxable personal property included five horses, a gig, and five slaves over the age of twelve. His total tax bill in 1826 came to $5.25, which placed him in the top quarter of all core taxpayers in the parish. He paid $2.35 in tax on his slaves, who accounted for the largest portion (44.8 percent) of his total bill.[42] Nearly half of his taxable wealth, in other words, was invested in slaves. Mrs. Moore, a widow now at twenty-six, took possession for her lifetime of his 189-acre parcel and its buildings; the other parcel, with 240 acres, became the property of the estate until her son came of age.[43] In a sense, both of these properties were returning to Sally's family, to the Francis family. She also claimed for her use at least three dower slaves: Hark, Sam (a young boy), and Maria (or Mariah), who soon would become the mother of two children. Little Putnam took legal possession of six other slaves, including Nat Turner.[44]

Through the death of his third master, Nat Turner descended once again into the hands of a child (the first having been Polly Turner) and into a pool of slaves held by an estate, an experience common in St. Luke's at the time, as attested by the number of taxable slaves—nearly half of the total—who lost at least one master between 1821 and 1831 and thus found themselves subject to hire or sale by executors.[45] During the two years that followed Moore's death, the number of taxable slaves in his estate declined by just one; most in the holding must have remained at his farm after he died.[46] For a time, however, Nat Turner apparently did not.

Francis Connections

Once the court granted power of administration to Moore's widow, the entire slaveholding fell under the influence of the Francis family, whose male elder in 1827 was Sally's brother Salathiel, then about twenty-four years old. Salathiel had established a bachelor's household in a cabin across the road from Sally's house. Most of his farm (309 acres) had been drawn from his father's old quarter plantation, and as many as two of his four taxable slaves in 1827 had come from his father's estate.[47] In 1825 Salathiel made some improvements that raised the assessed value of his buildings from $50 to $175.[48] The house he occupied, a twin of the overseer's cabin at the Samuel G. Turner plantation, was still standing in 1899, when William S. Drewry found it in a cornfield and photographed it: perhaps sixteen feet square, one room, windowless in front, with unpainted clapboard siding, a central door, and a brick chimney on the left gable end. This house, like the one Salathiel's father had built, had a "jump" above the main floor and a door in back, according to Drewry.[49] Salathiel, though humble in possessions, was respectable enough to serve on grand juries in 1825, 1829, and 1830. He wrote and signed his own will in 1828—or, rather, the court accepted a document purporting to be his will in 1832.[50]

Drewry's sources told him that Sally Moore thought this brother "somewhat uncompromising, wild and reckless," a judgment substantiated by a pair of incidents that had brought Salathiel into court.[51] In 1825, a year or so before Nat's whipping, Salathiel—backed by Capt. Moore—accused a slave named Amos of stealing his saddle from a fence rail at a neighbor's farm. The court convicted Amos and ordered that he "be burnt in the [hand] and receive 30 lashes on his bare back."[52] In 1829 Salathiel was back in court, accusing a neighbor, Cordall Brantley (a relative of Etheldred T.), of attacking him with a knife.[53] Drewry's sources recalled yet another incident that must have occurred soon after Thomas Moore died, in which Salathiel, having become wary of Nat Turner, warned his sister against trusting this slave. Sally discounted the warning, detecting perhaps a hint of bad blood between the two men.[54]

Sally's youngest brother, Nathaniel Francis, about twenty-two years old in 1827, was still single and living with his widowed mother at the family's home plantation.[55] He had been the favored heir, chosen to take over the farm and care for his mother in her old age.[56] The family homestead, established in the eighteenth century by the senior Francis, stood in seclusion, surrounded by broad fields and woods, two miles northeast of the Moore farm.[57] The two farms were connected by footpaths so familiar they were cited as landmarks in deeds of the period.[58] From 1820 through 1836, the homestead's buildings, including the widow's house, were assessed at a modest $150.[59] Drewry photographed the house around 1899 and described how it must have appeared in 1831:

> The usual style of house for a farmer of small means consisted of one square room on the first floor, with what was called a "jump" above and a kitchen in the rear. This was the style of the Francis house. The "jump" was fashioned into a neat and serviceable room by lathing and plastering it in such a manner as to form a semi-cylindrical apartment with a window in each gable end. Thus there were considerable spaces between the roof and the plastering, which were called cuddies, and used for "plunder" rooms and were accessible by doors near the end.[60]

Its original section, clearly distinguishable, still was standing when Henry I. Tragle photographed it in 1971.[61]

In 1827 Nathaniel Francis already had a significant amount of property at his command. He and his mother together owned 548 acres, all of which he eventually would possess.[62] Mrs. Francis also owned seven taxable slaves, most of them destined to become Nathaniel's property.[63] The three Francis farms combined—Sally Moore's, Salathiel's, and the home farm—had a total of 1,286 acres and sixteen taxable slaves.[64] According to the 1830 census, together they had thirty-nine slaves of all ages.[65]

Nathaniel took charge of paying all the taxes for himself and his mother in 1828, thereby becoming head of the Francis family, master of slaves at the home farm, and arbiter over holdings at the other two farms. He was one of the youngest new masters in the neighborhood, but he quickly became a figure of authority; and since he had revealed not a trace of doubt about holding slaves, his ascent was an omen. In manner, he could seem as uncompromising as his brother, but no one ever thought him wild or reckless or accused him of disturbing the peace. He conducted himself in a controlled, disciplined manner. When he appeared in court, he did so as a juror or as a member of estate committees.[66] He took seriously his duties as head of the family, as in 1829, when he brought into his home the two orphaned sons of his sister Polly and her husband, Thomas Browne.[67] If females in his neighborhood needed assistance, Nathaniel would perform "acts of kindness," as he later described them, "which every man is in the habit of doing for his Neighbors as a matter of course."[68] If a relative or friend needed financial backing, Nathaniel might provide it, as he did in 1827, when he secured three bonds (of just under $777 each) for John W. Reese, Piety's elder son. With those bonds, Reese purchased the large property bordering (to the west-southwest) the farms of Sally Moore and Salathiel Francis. It was Nathaniel Francis, therefore, who sealed the return of the Reeses and their slaves to the neighborhood of Cabin Pond.[69]

Years later, Nathaniel's money lending would lead to complaints, as in 1843, when Harriet Whitehead, the only white resident to survive the attack at her mother's house in 1831, sued him for fraud and accused him of loving money.[70] The suit dragged on until 1852, when both parties were dead and their reputations tarnished. There were hints of bad blood also between Nathaniel and certain of his slaves, two of whom volunteered for the rising: Sam, a man probably in his thirties in 1831 who had come to Nathaniel in 1820 as a legacy from his cousin Mary ("Polly") Pope; and Will, also in his thirties, skilled with an axe, who was once the property of Nathaniel's father.[71] A third slave, Charlotte (Drewry's wicked Charlotte), would side openly with the insurgents during their stop at the Francis house.[72] The holdings of Nathaniel and his sister together would produce four of the seven original insurgents, including the leader, his chief lieutenant, and the "executioner." Yet, somehow Francis heard nothing of the conspiracy even as it infiltrated his own quarter.

Giles Reese

Sally Moore remained alone with her son and slaves for two and a half years after her first husband's death. During that period, when the number of taxable slaves at her farm declined briefly from five to four, it is likely that she hired out the most troublesome individual in her holding.[73] Nat Turner indicated in the *Confessions* that he was living elsewhere in October 1829, when his mistress brought home her second husband, Joseph Travis, and that he did not begin to live with Travis until "the commencement of 1830," or about three months after the wedding.[74]

One man who may have hired Nat Turner's time during the interval between masters was Giles Reese, the troubled, thirty-year-old brother-in-law of the late Samuel G. Turner. Reese, who was born around 1798, became a familiar figure in the Cross Keys area after 1820, when he sold his patrimonial land north of Three Creeks.[75] In 1823 and 1824 he came to trial twice for committing assaults—the first being the one against John T. Vaughan, the former friend and neighbor of Giles's uncle Joseph, the next involving two other adversaries at a country tavern.[76] By 1824 Giles had fallen into debt and secured a loan by offering as collateral five of his slaves, at least two of whom he eventually lost to creditors.[77] In 1825 he was back in court for breach of the peace. By that year, too, he was following in the steps of his uncle and aunt, renting land that belonged to the estates of dead men, near the home of his sister Elizabeth, the widow of Samuel G. Turner. In 1829 he appears to have leased the house and some part of the plantation belonging to the estate of Thomas Mason, which bordered properties of Sally Moore and Salathiel Francis.[78] By that time, Giles was hiring slaves from neighbors, including almost certainly some from the Moore farm, a practice he continued even after the arrival of Joseph Travis.[79]

If the hiring did occur, it would have brought Nat Turner under the authority of the third of the three families linked in the past by Samuel G. Turner's marriages. Reese would have engaged the slave's services around the time of the Spirit's momentous, still-secret, tenth appearance on 12 May 1828, when Nat Turner was charged to take up Christ's yoke ("*for the time was fast approaching when the first should be last and the last should be first*").[80] Giles Reese heard nothing of this, and neither did Joseph Travis, who a short time later summoned Nat Turner home.

Travis

Joseph Travis had arrived in St. Luke's Parish in 1829, a solitary figure from some distant place.[81] His name appeared in Southampton records for the first time on 5 October 1829, when he signed a marriage bond.[82] Until that day, he had no close relatives of his own in the county: the bride's family alone provided security and witnesses for the bond. The Reverend Benjamin Devany of neighboring Nottoway Parish conducted the ceremony, indicating that the groom shared the Francis family's Methodist faith. Five months later, on 15 March 1830, Travis paid his first personal property tax at the courthouse, the same day he acted as defendant in a friendly lawsuit settling Capt. Moore's estate. In September 1830 the court issued the order for his male slaves to perform road work, and at about that time the U.S. Census marshal listed him as head of his own household.[83] In 1831 he paid personal property tax again, served on a grand jury, and was listed for the first time as having possession (though not ownership) of his wife's dower land—160 of the now 411 acres in her first husband's estate.[84] This was the extent of his public record. He would leave no heirs, no will, and nothing in his own hand except his signature.[85] The only description of him came from Nat Turner, who said of Travis that he "was to me a kind master, and placed the greatest confidence in me; in fact, I had no cause to complain of his treatment to me."[86]

The new master may have tried through kindliness to compensate for being a greenhorn. From the start, Travis suffered in comparison with his predecessor. He ranked low in seniority at Moore's farm: not only was he a newcomer, but he was no older than its most significant slave—both men were approaching thirty in 1829, and Travis probably was the younger of the two. He lacked legitimacy: true possession of Nat Turner lay in the hands of the stepson, making Travis a pretender. And, like some itinerant laborer or overseer, Travis had arrived with little property of his own. Other than his clothing and perhaps some tools, he apparently brought nothing to his marriage: no land, no slaves, and perhaps not even the horse he owned in 1831 (a bay named Willis, worth $56).[87]

Marriage changed his fortunes. Travis set to work in a shop equipped probably by his predecessor with tools of a carpenter, cartwright, cooper, and blacksmith.[88] Meanwhile, agricultural operations at the farm continued, thanks to Capt. Moore's slaves, who tended the cattle and hogs and brought forth the usual productions of beef and bacon, fodder, corn, cotton, and cider. In the spring of 1831, when Travis paid $4.77 in taxes for both real and personal property, he ranked almost exactly where Moore had ranked five years earlier—near the bottom of the top quarter of core taxpayers in St. Luke's Parish, higher than either of his new brothers-in-law, Salathiel and Nathaniel Francis.[89] By that same spring, Mrs. Travis had conceived a child, to whom she would give birth before August.[90] By June 1831, the Travises had completed some improvements at their farm, increasing the value of its buildings from $50 (their value since 1823) to $200. These buildings, though modest compared to Samuel G. Turner's (worth $1,000 in 1831), had a higher assessment than those at the Powell farm before the fire of 1821 or at the Francis homestead in 1831 ($150 each).[91] Travis was making progress.

The improvements involved the master's house, which Travis either expanded from an existing cabin or built entirely new.[92] In 1971 historian Henry Irving Tragle reported that this house had been destroyed by the late 1890s, which may explain why William S. Drewry did not find it in 1899, when he photographed others in the neighborhood. Tragle, however, did publish a photograph of what he termed the "So-called Travis House," which he said occupied the approximate site of the original dwelling.[93] An even later photograph, included by county historians Gilbert Francis and Katherine Futrell in their film about the rebellion, showed the same house Tragle documented, though from a different angle and with different surrounding vegetation.[94] That structure resembled in many details the one described in 1831 in accounts of the uprising and inventories of the Travis estate.

The house of 1831 was a one-story, frame structure with two rooms, left and right.[95] A separate kitchen with its own roof stood behind the main part of the house, perhaps attached on the right side (as viewed from the front). Each end of the main house had a fireplace with an external chimney. There was a substantial front door (which, despite his trusting nature, Travis barred at night), flanked on each side by a single window. The house depicted in both the Tragle and Francis-Futrell images had a low front porch with four plain posts supporting a roof that covered the door but did not cover the windows on either side. In the left gable end of the main house, to the right of the chimney (or toward the front of the house) and about fifteen feet above the ground, was a small attic window, two feet wide by two-and-a-half feet high, large enough to climb through. The 1831 house must have had a similar window.

The front door probably opened directly into the room on the right, which apparently served as a hall, parlor, dining room, and sleeping area. Here Travis must have kept his weapons ("*four guns that would shoot, and several old muskets*"), all missing in December 1831.[96] That room, in turn, may have led through a door (also with a bar) back to the kitchen (with its own outside door), where at least one Travis slave, young Moses, slept.[97] The room to the left of the front door must have been the master's chamber, where Joseph, Sally, and their infant slept. From this room a stairway led up to the attic, which had a storage closet and "large Room," where on cool nights little Putnam and others may have slept.[98]

Most of the furnishings in the house, together with the other personal property at the farm, had belonged to Mrs. Travis and her first husband. When her second husband arrived, all of that property became his. The inventory and account of sales for his estate drawn in December 1831 show that Travis, who once had almost nothing to his name, had gained remarkably in the good things of life. His house had three feather beds (two of good quality, appraised at $30 each), one of which he shared with Sally; for privacy, there were bed curtains (two sets) and a window curtain.[99] His infant slept in a cradle, and others in the household (Moses, for one) could have lain on a mat, a cot, or a trundle bed. The master's chamber had a dressing table and a looking glass. There were three carpets in the house, a rocking chair, and two sets of sitting chairs, most of them probably in the parlor-dining room, along with a table, picture frames, buffet, and tea board with china. The family owned a hymn book and a Bible (worth $2 together), along with a small parcel of other books. Their only silver was a set of teaspoons (also worth $2). They had a bottle of castor oil. Mrs. Travis owned an umbrella, and Travis, a snuff bottle.[100]

Elsewhere, in or near the yard, there may have been two or three slave cabins (never mentioned), and certainly a small barn with a loft (noted) and places for a dairy and a still. The account of sales for the estate referred specifically to a smokehouse and a shop. There were more than fifty hogs, along with nineteen head of cattle, a yoke of oxen, and five horses. Moore's gig was still at the farm, and so was his whip. The fields were continuing to produce significant amounts of corn and cotton.[101] (In that corn field, three years before the arrival of Joseph Travis, Nat Turner had discovered signs, the "*drops of blood.*")[102] For cotton, a fresh field had been cleared, but Travis had neither purchased nor made a gin.[103] He had given no indication that he wanted to change anything about the culture or routine of the farm.

He must have spent most of his time in the shop. After the spring of 1830, he took on an apprentice from the neighborhood, Joel Westbrook, a boy of about sixteen whose father had died.[104] At the end of August 1831, Travis was assembling the wood for a wagon and was working on bodies and frames for three unfinished carts. He had 110 pounds of iron bar, together with a small inventory of iron hoops for barrels and three different lots of lumber for bedsteads.[105] His blacksmith accounts showed that fourteen different neighbors owed him a total of $117.70 for work completed.[106] Other accounts revealed that he had borrowed more than $1,500—all from local residents, none from blood relatives. His chief creditor, John Drewry of Three Creeks, had loaned him more than $1,100, a large part of which must have gone into the house. In August 1831 he had assets just sufficient to cover his debts: executors found a balance in his estate of $51.83.[107] His chief assets in 1831 were the slaves he had acquired upon his marriage.

In the federal census of 1830, which began less than a year after he married, Joseph Travis was listed as head of a household with twenty-two residents, five of whom were white. None of the whites had reached the age of thirty. Travis, the only individual named, was between twenty and thirty years of age, as was his wife; the three other white residents were a boy under ten (Putnam), a female between fifteen and twenty (never identified), and a male (never identified) the age of Travis. Of the seventeen slaves, six were male, eleven were female, and six were children younger than ten. No black adult was older than thirty-six.[108]

All but four of the slaves were identified in other documents of the day, ten of them by name and three specifically as children, making it possible to identify some individuals in the census numbers. Nat Turner and Hark, each about thirty years of age, were the male elders.[109] The four other males were youths or children: Moses, aged twelve in 1830; Sam, perhaps eleven; an unidentified boy described by Drewry as "simple and stammering," perhaps ten years old; and one other boy, never identified, under age ten. Three females, marked in the age category between ten and twenty-four (Louisa, Olive, and one never identified by name), all appear to have been about fifteen years old; five girls were under age ten. Just three women ranked with Nat Turner in age; these must have been Anacka, Maria, and Lucy, each between twenty-four and thirty-six.[110]

These three must have been mothers of the children present in 1830, including Moses, Samuel, and the six others under age ten. The three women must have found husbands at other farms, since the Travis farm had no adult male slaves other than Nat Turner and Hark, both of whom had wives elsewhere. All three women would survive the events of August. None would take part in the break-in; like the Travises, they must have been asleep. None would be arrested, brought to trial, or called before the court for testimony. From Nat Turner, who had distanced himself ("*I studiously avoided mixing in society, and wrapped myself in mystery*"), they appear to have kept their own distance.[111]

The slaveholding of which they were a part had a history reaching back a decade by the time Travis arrived, complicating his situation as master. The ten eldest slaves (those identifiable by name) had origins in four different holdings, now scattered; they had ties of marriage and personal history to at least four other holdings still in existence.[112] As property, the status of all seventeen had become mixed. Five now belonged to Travis by virtue of marriage and natural increase: Hark, Sam, Maria, and Maria's two infants. These five were by far Travis's most valuable property, accounting for half of his total assets.[113] His young stepson was heir to six others: Lucy, Olive, Louisa, Anacka, Moses, and Nat Turner.[114] The status of the remaining six is unknown, but they did not belong to Joseph Travis. In other words, for the majority of these people, including the eldest male, Travis was only nominally their master.

Travis could not have taken the one action that might have mollified his stepson's most disaffected slave, for while legally he could have emancipated Hark, Sam, and Maria and her infants, freeing Nat Turner was beyond his power.[115] And though Travis may have been a kind master, he gave no sign that he thought emancipation might be in the interest of his household or that his example might influence people around him. Had he been thinking in these terms (as Henry Turner once did), he might have adopted practices already in place at the nearby shops of Levi Waller and Solomon Parker, where artisans of both races were shoeing horses and working with metal and wood.[116] Elsewhere across the South, in shops not much larger than his, such artisans were working together at blacksmithing, making and repairing cotton gins, and developing other devices and tools.[117] Instead of taking on Joel Westbrook, Travis might have recruited an apprentice from his own farm and put him to work with the tools in his shop (the anvil and bellows, the bench and vice, lathe, foot adz, cooper's adz, augers and chisels, gouges, planes and saws, hammers and mallets, the screw cutter and screwdriver, rasps, brushes, and ruler) or at tasks involving materials found there (screws, leather, glue, sandpaper, paint, marble, iron, and wood).[118] There is no evidence that Nat Turner, who might have been a promising apprentice, ever worked in the shop; his appraised value in 1831 indicates that he never acquired shop skills.[119] He followed his master's plow, wielded his hoes, and on occasion, perhaps, handled his axes and hatchet.[120]

In any event, Travis had arrived too late for collaboration in the shop. By the time he arrived—more than a year after the Spirit's appearance on 12 May 1828—the appeal of the mundane skills he might have imparted as master cartwright or smith had been eclipsed by a great purpose, a vision sublime.

PART TWO

REBELLION

Levi Waller being summoned as a Witness states that on the morning of the 22d day of August last between 9 and 10 o'clock he heard that the negroes had risen and were murdering the whites and were coming.

—Court minutes, 5 November 1831

The Inner Circle

> I communicated the great work laid out for me to do, to four in whom I had the greatest confidence (Henry, Hark, Nelson, and Sam).
>
> —Nat Turner, *The Confessions of Nat Turner*

Only in November 1831, more than two months after the uprising, did authorities learn that in February of that year Nat Turner had gathered around himself a circle of four men in whom he said he had "the greatest confidence."[1] The existence of the inner circle more than six months before the rebellion was indisputable evidence of deliberation and purpose. Willingly, its members had joined a conspiracy to make an insurrection, a capital offense.[2] In the *Confessions*, Turner listed the men at least once and perhaps twice in his own voice: Henry, Hark, Nelson, and Sam.[3] Hark and Sam, who had survived the fighting and come to trial in early September, had said nothing to authorities about the group. Since all four men were dead by November, Gray apparently did not think to ask why Turner had trusted them in particular, or why they had joined his conspiracy, or why in the months between the eclipse and 22 August none had betrayed him. Turner had judged them well. Here is how he must have come to know them.

Conspirators

Little information came to light in 1831 about Henry (or Henry Porter). His name did not appear in court records, since he did not come to trial. No source identified his master. Newspapers of the day printed a few items noting his death in connection with that of Nelson (or Nelson Edwards), his companion in arms; the two men were shot separately near Cross Keys on 25 August, two days after the final skirmish, before they could be arrested.[4] On 26 August, a volunteer cavalryman from Norfolk wrote to the editors of the *American Beacon* that his company had brought in the head of "the celebrated Nelson, called by the blacks 'Gen. Nelson,'" and that he expected momentarily the head of "the Paymaster, Henry." A day or two later, when reports from the field were still confused, the *Beacon* editors offered a different summary: "*Nelson* killed and *Porter* (Gen. so called) in Jail."[5] Variations of these notices appeared in other newspapers, all mentioning "Henry" or "Porter," and all apparently referring to the same man.[6] Other slaves named Henry lived in the vicinity of Cross Keys, but none took part in the revolt and none could have been mistaken for the paymaster or general. The first reference to *Henry Porter*, linking his given name to that surname, did not appear until William S. Drewry published his account in 1900. Drewry, however, did not identify Henry's master.[7]

The surname *Porter* belonged to just one household in the neighborhood, that of Richard Porter, who lived two and a quarter miles east of the Travis farm, as the crow flies. In 1831 Porter paid tax on thirteen slaves; his younger brother Thomas, who lived with him, paid tax on two.[8] One of the Porter brothers must have been Henry's master, and the evidence points to Richard. That deduction gains weight from the fact that four other slaves of Richard Porter joined the rising at his plantation, recruited presumably by Henry.[9]

The presumption that Henry belonged to Richard Porter is consistent also with the history of slave property at the Porter plantation. The thirty slaves there in 1830 had origins in three different slaveholdings, portions of which were combined into a much larger holding in 1827, when Richard Porter married a young widow, his distant cousin, Mrs. Elizabeth (Porter) Barnes.[10]

One group came from the estate of Richard Porter's father, who died in the winter of 1815–16, leaving two slaves to Richard. The father's inventory listed thirteen slaves, among them the boy Jacob (shot in August 1831).[11] Henry was not one of these thirteen.

A second group, consisting of at least four men, came from the estate of Elizabeth Porter's father, also named Henry Porter. This white Henry, in fact, had owned the plantation where Richard, Elizabeth, and their slaves were living in 1831. At his death in 1824, the father's estate included slaves Aaron (also shot in August), Moses (shot), Daniel (executed), and Jim (case dismissed), but not Henry the paymaster.[12]

The third group came from the estate of Elizabeth's first husband, Bolling H. Barnes, a man at least ten years her senior whom she married in 1814. Barnes died in 1825 and left all of his slaves to his young widow.[13] His was a small holding, but it may have included the black Henry, the paymaster: in 1816 Barnes paid tax for the first time on a slave between twelve and sixteen years of age, who thus was born around 1804 and fit Henry's description.[14] In 1820, when the census taker counted ten slaves at Barnes's farm, Henry may have been the one male aged between fourteen and twenty-five.[15] At Barnes's death in 1825, Henry would have descended to Elizabeth Barnes, now a widow; and in 1827 he certainly would have fallen into the hands of her second husband, Richard Porter.

A plausible chain of possession, therefore, suggests that Henry the conspirator was born about 1804 at the farm of Henry Porter the slaveholder, near Cabin Pond; that by 1816 he had been transferred as a gift to Bolling H. Barnes, who married Porter's daughter Elizabeth in 1814 and settled on land about five miles north of the Porter farm; that the slave Henry then descended to Elizabeth at the death of Barnes in 1825; and that he was returned to the old Porter farm (which Elizabeth inherited in 1824) when she remarried in 1827.[16] In August 1831, Henry certainly was living there, two and a quarter miles east of the Travis farm.[17] Nat Turner would have known him since childhood. By 1831, both men had taken the measure of their new masters.

The Nelson who joined the conspiracy's inner circle belonged to Peter Edwards, whose home and slave quarter in 1831 lay two and a half miles northeast of the Travis place.[18] One of the men who shot and killed Nelson, Capt. Joseph Joiner of the county militia, described him as "uncommonly likely, and worth at least $400." In fact, Joiner said, "had he been mine, I would not have taken $500 for him."[19] Nelson was thirty-three years old in 1831, according to his master, whose certainty suggested that he remembered this slave's birth, in about 1798, six years after his own.[20]

Nelson probably was born the property of Peter Edwards's father, James Edwards, who was not a wealthy man and never had a large slaveholding. In 1811 James owned just five acres and two taxable slaves; in 1812 he joined his son's household, where he lived the rest of his life.[21] Through 1817, father and son shared a modest house on Peter's original tract of ninety-eight acres, three miles west of the Samuel G. Turner plantation; together, the Edwards men paid tax on three to five slaves each year.[22] In 1817, when he was twenty-six, Peter married Mrs. Nancy Bittle, whose first husband, William Bittle, had held fourteen taxable slaves when he died in 1815. It is possible that Nelson was one of those fourteen, and that Bittle, rather than James Edwards, was Nelson's first master.[23]

Peter Edwards appropriated most of the Bittle holding. In 1818 the number of his taxable slaves jumped from five to twelve, a sign of his ambitions;

in the 1820 census he registered a total of twenty-eight slaves, including six young males about Nelson's age.[24] One of the six must have been the future conspirator. Whatever his origins, by 1831 Nelson had lived for at least a decade with his current master and had spent his entire life near Cabin Pond, never more than three miles from the presence of Nat Turner.

The first reference to Sam, or Sam Francis, appeared in the will of Mary ("Polly") Pope, who died in 1820 and made a bequest of this slave to her cousin Nathaniel Francis.[25] In January 1821 appraisers of Polly's estate described Sam as a man worth $500, which suggests that he was about twenty-five years old, or about ten years older than his new master.[26] In 1830 Sam must have been one of four male slaves at the Francis farm who were between twenty-four and thirty-six years old, close in age to Nat Turner.[27] His enlistment gave the conspiracy an agent at the geographical center of the Edwards, Francis, and Porter plantations, which lay near one another in a tier that stretched two miles north to south. Sam was also a link between the Francis and Travis slave quarters, both of which had fallen under new masters in 1828 and 1829.

By 1831, after a decade at the Francis farm, Sam had become a familiar figure in St. Luke's Parish. On 22 August of that year, Levi Waller would recognize Sam at the Waller farm, five miles away, on Barrow Road—"for he saw him there," court minutes reported, "and has known him well for several years."[28] Nat Turner could have made the same claim.

Hark, whose role in the conspiracy made him second in importance only to Nat Turner, had the closest ties to the leader. In 1831 both men were living at the farm of Joseph Travis. Legally, Hark belonged to Travis that year, and Turner, to Travis's stepson, Putnam Moore. Court records identified Hark in comparatively rich detail, naming his owner, noting his current value ($450), and describing him as a man slave.[29] He was in fact about thirty years old.[30] One early account of the uprising identified him as "a young fellow, by the name of Moore," and as one of two insurgent leaders.[31] During the events in August he assumed the military title and surname of his previous master, calling himself "Captain Moore."[32] His early history is almost a blank, since there is no record of his acquisition by Thomas Moore. There is enough evidence, however, to establish a plausible chain of possession for him, and to prove that he did not originate in the slaveholdings of Benjamin or Samuel G. Turner, or in those of the Francis, Moore, or Reese families. His origins lay elsewhere. And he came to Moore neither through inheritance, nor marriage settlement, nor gift, but through Moore's picking and choosing.

The name *Hark* appeared in the 1821 inventory of personal property belonging to Edmund Turner Jr., a distant cousin and neighbor of Samuel G. Turner. That was the first-known probable reference to Hark Moore in the public record. His value, placed at $333.33 in 1821, indicated that he was a young man, perhaps slightly younger than Nat Turner.[33] One source in 1831 said his name was "the blacks' abbreviation of Hercules." Col. W. J. Worth, an army officer from Fortress Monroe near Norfolk, described Hark as "one of the most perfectly framed men he ever saw—a regular black Apollo."[34] As Edmund Turner's slave, Hark would have lived at a plantation bordering Samuel G. Turner's Kindred tract, where Nat Turner had spent much of his boyhood and youth.[35] When Edmund died (at about age thirty) in the winter of 1820–21, there were twenty-five slaves in his holding, most of whom his executors hired out for the benefit of his two orphans.[36]

Hark must have been assigned to the farm of Jarrell Turner, Edmund's first cousin, immediate neighbor, and executor. Evidently he remained long enough to form a lasting regard for Jarrell's younger sister, Sarah, who later became Mrs. James B. Newsom and was killed in the uprising.[37] Jarrell died (at about age thirty-five) in January 1823, two years after his cousin Edmund. The task of appraising his estate fell to four neighbors, including Thomas Moore (as luck again would have it), who must have appropriated Hark from Jarrell's holding.[38] It must have been Moore, then, who brought Hark under the daily influence of Nat Turner.

TABLE 5. Slaveholdings, St. Luke's Parish, 1830

	Households		Slaves	
Slaves in holding	Number	Percent	Number	Percent
101–79	2	0.4	324	7.2
51–100	6	1.1	434	9.6
31–50	18	3.3	708	15.7
11–30	117	21.5	2,119	46.9
1–10	203	37.3	929	20.6
Subtotal	346	63.6	4,514	100.0
No slaves	198	36.4	0	
Total	544	100.0	4,514	

Sources: U.S. Census, 1830, Southampton County, manuscript returns; author's data file on slaveholdings, 1830–31.

Notes: Figures do not include free-black households. In 1830 free blacks headed sixty-five households, one of which was recorded with one slave; two other free black men listed without slaves in the census paid tax on one slave each in 1831.

The core conspirators came from small to midsized holdings (fifteen to twenty-nine slaves) like those Nat Turner had known all his life, and so would all of the recruits they gathered along the way (from holdings of six to twenty-nine slaves), except perhaps the last four from Major Thomas Ridley's Buckhorn Quarter. Two-thirds (67.5 percent) of the slave population of St. Luke's Parish lived in comparable holdings of thirty or fewer slaves.[39] The rising would not be an affair of the great plantations (table 5).

Transfers and Connections

Capt. Thomas Moore died in the spring of 1827, aged about thirty-four.[40] Hark remained the property of Moore's widow until she married Joseph Travis in the autumn of 1829, when Travis took possession by right of marriage.[41] Hark, too, then outranked the new master in length of residence at the farm. In fact, because of high mortality among local white men, any number of slaves in the neighborhood found themselves in similar circumstances. For the same reason, many slaves in the neighborhood had family connections as extensive and enduring as those of their masters, given the standards of the time and place.

Hark Moore's most significant connections in 1831 dated from the winter of 1827–28, seven months after the death of Thomas Moore. That winter, after an absence of seven years, the Reeses returned to Cabin Pond from Three Creeks. In December 1827 John W. Reese, at age twenty-four, purchased in its entirety—and entirely on credit—the tract of 860 acres immediately west of the Moore farm.[42] That property had belonged to Benjamin Blunt Jr., now deceased, who had used it as one of his outlying plantations. Shaped on the surveyor's map like an italic figure *8*, with the upper half tilting to the right, its northeast section adjoined the farms of Salathiel Francis and Thomas Moore (and, later, of Joseph Travis). From the boundaries of those farms the plantation stretched perhaps two miles to the west-southwest.[43] A modest dwelling (probably an overseer's cabin) and outbuildings, worth altogether $300, stood in the southwest section, a mile or so from the Moore (later Travis) house.[44] By the spring of 1828, Reese had moved to his new property, bringing along his widowed mother, Piety Reese; his younger brother, Joseph William Henry Reese (called William); and sixteen slaves. Among the latter were Jack (or Jack Reese), whom Hark would recruit, and Jack's sister, who soon became Hark's wife. By 1829 another Reese, John's cousin Giles, had rented property a short walk north of the Travis place, beyond Cabin Pond.[45] The family again was becoming entangled in the web of local relations.

It is certain that Piety Reese or one of her sons owned the woman who became Hark Moore's wife. The identity of that woman never became a matter of record, but her name must have been one of those listed in the 1826 inventory of property belonging to Joseph Reese Sr., which included three young females described as girls: she must have been either Jinny (worth $300), Edith ($250), or Harriet ($200).[46] The evidence points to Edith. Her value and approximate age in 1826, together with her circumstances in 1831, are consistent with such a deduction. In a deed signed by John W. Reese on 5 February 1831, Edith was described no longer as a girl, but as the mother of a child named Tom.[47] The signing of that deed would have significant implications for Edith and her child.

The two slaves possibly tied to Nat Turner, Cherry and Riddick, also apparently returned to Cross Keys with the Reeses. These two were listed together as late as November 1826 (their names appearing on adjoining lines in the same inventory), just a year before John W. Reese bought the Blunt plantation. Cherry's whereabouts in 1831 remain uncertain, but she may have been living nearby: a woman bearing her name and matching her description was working at the farm of Nathaniel Francis that August.[48] Riddick certainly remained with John W. Reese through early February of that year.

Having provoked a scandal that had riled their neighbors in 1820, the Reeses now were about to disrupt the lives of their neighbors' slaves.

Creditors

The debt John W. Reese took upon himself to purchase the Blunt plantation in December 1827 led to difficulties. He had agreed to a purchase price of $2,330.60, not a penny of which did he have in his pocket. The seller, Blunt's executor, eager to be rid of the property, had accepted in payment three bonds, two for $776.87 and one for $776.86, the first of which Reese agreed to pay in 1828, the second in 1829, and the third in 1830.[49] The bonds were secured by the signature of Nathaniel Francis.[50] With those bonds, Reese and Francis joined the local network of debt and credit that tied neighbor to neighbor around Cross Keys, those with cash lending to those without, those with good (and not-so-good) credit securing loans for those who needed backing.[51]

Reese then failed to make the first payment. Blunt's executor did not demand the money; but in January 1829, one month after the due date, Francis, apparently worried, obtained Reese's signature on an indenture stipulating that if Reese did not make the payments and thus made Francis liable for the debt, Francis could demand a sale of the property—"on the premises."[52]

Payment continued to be a problem for Reese. In February 1830, after the second bond fell due, he borrowed money from neighbors ($300 from Richard Porter and $323.31 from Aubin Middleton), posting as collateral some farm animals, a man slave named Moses, and the girl Harriet.[53] He may have applied these loans to the second bond; if so, he was borrowing to cover debt. It is certain that he did not make the third payment, due on 19 December 1830. By New Year's Day 1831, apart from whatever amount he still owed for the land, he also owed a total of $1,781.56 in smaller personal loans ranging from $20 to $360, none of which could he repay.[54]

On 5 February 1831—a Saturday, seven days before the eclipse—a group of Reese's creditors assembled, almost certainly at his house ("*on the premises*"), to oversee the writing of three deeds that would settle his debts. Reese attended, of course, as party of the first part. Also present, as parties of the second and third parts, were three successors to members of the old Turner alliances: John Clark Turner (Samuel G. Turner's younger brother), Henry Moore (the captain's younger brother and executor), and Nathaniel Francis. Two other neighbors and creditors, Richard Porter and John R. Williams, were present, each to witness at least one document. Two outsiders also attended: Jesse Drewry, of Nottoway Parish, who would sign once as security and once as witness, and William A. Jones, from the far western corner of St. Luke's, who would sign once as witness.[55] Henry Bryant and Mildred Balmer, both of whom held bonds signed by Reese, may have attended as well. Mrs. Reese and her younger son also must have been present. Still others, including the wife of Hark Moore, must have observed the parties as they assembled.

First, the creditors disposed of the debts to neighbors. John Clark Turner agreed to stand as security for these obligations, guaranteeing payment if Reese defaulted. Jesse Drewry agreed to act as trustee for all funds and property involved. As collateral, Reese was to offer personal property; or, as the law writer in the room put it (in phrases that would have inspired Dickens), Reese promised the following: "at and before the ensealing and delivery of these presents the receipt whereof is this day acknowledged and him the said John W. Reese satisfied given granted and sold and by these presents do give grant bargain and sell unto the said Jesse Drewry his legal representative &c. the following property to wit." The items that followed, all of which Drewry could sell at public auction if Reese failed to pay, included corn, fodder, household and kitchen furniture, plantation utensils, a sorrel horse, and a shared interest in the slaves of Piety Reese. Also listed as collateral were three of Reese's own slaves: "one negro woman Edith, her child Tom, [and] one negro boy Riddick."[56]

Here Reese revealed his willingness to use his people as collateral with little or no regard for their connections. In fact, borrowing had left him little choice, for his slaves were assets his lenders would want as collateral.[57] The time to have avoided this conundrum, to have broken free and thought in different terms, had passed in 1827 when he assumed the original debt.[58]

After obtaining his signature on the first deed, the leading creditors made certain Reese would not default: they immediately drew up two additional deeds executing the sale of his land. With his second signature of the day, Reese agreed to sell 430 acres—the northeastern half of his plantation—for $800 (or $1.86 per acre) to Nathaniel Francis, who paid in cash.[59] And then, with the third, he agreed to sell the other half, including his house, for $950 ($2.21 per acre) to Henry Moore, the captain's brother, who paid only partly in cash.[60] Combined, the two transactions would net Reese almost exactly what he needed ($1,781.56) to cover the smaller sums he had borrowed. But, of course, he had given up his land, and the selling price fell considerably below the $2,330.60 ($2.71 per acre) he had agreed to pay in 1827. His creditors had driven a hard bargain. By sundown on 5 February, everyone between Cross Keys and Cabin Pond must have understood the significance of these transactions.

Reese would remain for a time as tenant at his lost plantation, sharing the house with his mother and brother. Apparently he did use the cash received for his land to pay off most of his small loans, though in March he signed another deed of trust acknowledging that he still owed money to his mother. She accepted as collateral some of the same property he had offered in February, including crops, tools, furniture, livestock, and his interest in her dower slaves. Piety Reese too could drive a hard bargain. On this deed she affixed her mark near the signatures of her younger son, William, and—again—Henry Moore and Jesse Drewry.[61]

Reese's circumstances had a familiar aspect, recalling difficulties his cousin Giles had encountered in 1827 that had resulted in the forfeiting of two or more slaves.[62] Everyone had observed the results of Giles's misfortunes; and once John had lost his land, everyone could have seen that all of his slaves were in jeopardy. His family's history gave a clear warning: debt trumped all other obligations. That Riddick was Nat Turner's son, that Edith was Hark Moore's wife, and that their peril moved the two men to vengeance—these are conjectures. But Reese's course of action and the ensuing loss of his land on 5 February must have confirmed suspicions concerning the new generation of masters. Barely a week after the meeting, Nat Turner and Hark Moore formed the conspiracy against them.

The Design

Turner imposed rules of secrecy and exclusiveness from the start, assuming that someone might betray him. Here he drew upon a sense of past events, recalling perhaps the failure of Gabriel in 1800.[63] That failure may have been what he had in mind when, according to Thomas R. Gray's sources, Turner told one of the conspirators "that the negroes had frequently attempted similar things, confided their purpose to several, and that it always leaked out." To prevent leaks, Gray reported, Turner had resolved that "their march of destruction and murder, should be the first news of the insurrection."[64] The inner circle would keep their silence from the middle of February to the evening of Saturday, 20 August.[65]

By design, Turner confined the conspiracy to a small number. At no point did he attempt to recruit a following like the one Gabriel gathered around Richmond in 1800. By design, Turner organized no clandestine communications, no chain of command, no codes, no cache of arms. The map of the county he drew in pokeberry juice, and the list he reportedly compiled of potential followers represented private notes and calculations, rather than records of an existing network.[66] In his judgment, preparation on a larger scale was impossible: preparation and training would alert the enemy. No one beyond the circle could be informed. The rising would be conceived in secret among the few he held in confidence.

Those rules were the initial elements of Nat Turner's developing theory of how to overturn slavery, a theory that would shape the rebellion to the end. Gray, always a skeptic, doubted at first that any theory or plan had existed, declaring in September that the affair had been a "momentary procedure."[67] Even in the *Confessions*, as contrary evidence mounted, Gray projected doubt, quoting Turner as saying that the purpose of the dinner at

Cabin Pond was "to concert a plan, as we had not yet determined on any." But Turner cannot have meant literally that the men had not *considered* a plan, or that the ensuing event had erupted spontaneously. "Many were the plans formed and rejected by us," he told Gray, "and it affected my mind to such a degree, that I fell sick." His own account indicates that indeed between February and late June the men had agreed on a general idea of the rising, if not on details of how it might begin. They saw themselves mounting a revolution, an assumption Turner revealed when he told Gray that they first planned to begin on "the 4th July last." They would be violent in tactics, confronting slaveholders through a "work of death."[68] That much was understood.

Some alternatives they either rejected or did not consider. They did not have in mind, for example, long-term resistance through concerted acts of terror. Such resistance would have been difficult to imagine in eastern Virginia and North Carolina, whose slave populations were restricted in movement, confined to local communications, and overwhelmingly illiterate.[69] Unlike Gabriel in Richmond, Turner and his followers expressed no interest in taking hostages whom they might have ransomed in exchange for freedom. The realities of their situation differed from Gabriel's: this was the countryside, not the capital. What hostage in Southampton might have compared in value to Governor James Monroe in 1800? And in addition to such realities, Turner and his men were disposed to confront rather than negotiate with enemies they did not trust.

Their secretiveness meant that they must take everyone by surprise, conquering suddenly or not at all. Turner assumed that his knowledge of the farms and slaves in St. Luke's Parish would guide the insurgents through the initial attacks, in which—as the Spirit had suggested—they would slay their enemies with the enemies' own weapons. He assumed also that the rising itself would inspire an ever-larger following from a slave population that did not need to be prepared.

Turner's remark about not having a plan meant simply that the group had not reached a final agreement on "how to commence," or how to proceed tactically, particularly at the start. They were still "forming new schemes and rejecting them," he said, "when the sign appeared again, which determined me not to wait longer."[70] That sign, a reminder from the Spirit, was the solar phenomenon of 13 August, when the sun assumed the greenish blue color that observers noted along the entire Atlantic seaboard.[71] One week later, on Saturday evening, 20 August, Turner agreed with Hark and

Henry to move forward. There was to be a dinner the next day, he said, "for the men we expected." Even at that late point, he apparently planned to assemble only the trusted four. Then, according to the understanding of Saturday evening, they were to settle upon (or as Gray put it, "*concert*") their plan.[72]

The Old Field Meeting

They began to assemble on Sunday morning, 21 August, according to a chronology implicit in the three surviving accounts of the dinner. Turner said that the dinner took place "in the woods," referring in all likelihood to a growth of young trees then reclaiming an old field near Cabin Pond and the Travis farm, not far from where Reese's creditors had met six and a half months earlier.[73] The day was dry and clear.[74] Turner recalled that Hark brought a pig for roasting and Henry brought brandy; Gray said they also had melons.[75] Sam and Nelson were present, summoned probably by Henry, and there were two new recruits: Will and Jack.[76]

Will Francis must have been recruited by Sam, the only other man present from the holding of Nathaniel Francis. (For reasons Turner would leave to suggest themselves, he had not drawn Will into the conspiracy in February.) Will was one of the two oldest men at the dinner. About thirty-five years of age, he had lived at the home farm of the Francis family probably from his birth around 1794. He and Nat Turner had lived near one another since 1807, the year Esther Francis married Samuel G. Turner, when the slaveholdings of the two white families had begun their gradual commingling. In 1815, on the death of Samuel Francis Sr., Will's first master, his name appeared in the estate inventory; he was described as an adult male and was one of the three most valuable slaves.[77] He was given first to Francis's widow, Sarah; when she gave up the farm in 1828, she turned Will over to her youngest son, Nathaniel.[78] As Nathaniel expanded his landholdings and cleared new fields, he could rely on Will and his axe.[79]

Jack, the other new recruit, was brought to the old field on Sunday morning by Hark, his sister's husband.[80] (Nat Turner would say, "Jack, I knew, was only a tool in the hands of Hark.")[81] About twenty-one years of age, Jack was the youngest man at the dinner. In the 1826 inventory of his first master, Joseph Reese Sr., he was listed as a boy slave worth $275.[82] He next became the property of Piety Reese's younger son, William, who was about his age or slightly younger.[83] Early in 1829 Jack had returned to the Cabin Pond neighborhood with the Reeses; and in the summer of 1831, probably because of John W. Reese's financial straits, he was hired to a neighbor, Jordan Barnes. He was living that summer at Barnes's farm but was given permission to go home to see his young master.[84] Through chance, he was drawn into the conspiracy.

The four lieutenants and two recruits passed the early afternoon together in the old field, waiting for their leader while the pig roasted. At three o'clock Turner appeared, staging a late entrance to enhance his aura of greatness and power.[85] With his arrival, the core group had formed. Though at least three of the men present would speak, it was Turner who directed the proceedings. In every detail, the plan would be his.

The seven men had much in common. They came from five farms and plantations with holdings of modest size (from fifteen to thirty slaves).[86] They knew their masters almost as well as they knew one another. They were familiar with the masters' houses (locks, keys, guns), barns (horses, saddles), and quarters (recruits). They knew the face of the countryside, its roads, trails, creeks, and swamps, from Cross Keys and Cabin Pond to Jerusalem. As they soon would demonstrate, all seven could ride and most could stay mounted at a gallop.[87] Six were in their early or middle thirties, the exception being Jack Reese, the youngest by a decade. All had spent their adult years in St. Luke's Parish, and all probably had been born there. All had lived near the Travis farm for at least six years except Jack, who had been returned to the neighborhood in 1828. Two were known to have wives and perhaps children but lived apart from them. Details about the familial relations of the others never entered the public record. Their only legal bonds, of course, were to their masters; with one exception, all were committed to dissolving those bonds.

Will's presence at the old field apparently took Nat Turner by surprise. "I saluted them on coming up," Turner later recalled, "and asked Will how came he there." Will responded, revealing his understanding of the purpose by declaring that "his life was worth no more than others, and his liberty as dear to him." "I asked him if he thought to obtain it?" Turner recalled. "He said he would, or lose his life. This was enough to put him in full confidence."[88] Of the two new recruits, Will was the more enthusiastic. His brief statement on liberty must have confirmed Turner's assumption that slaves everywhere were prepared to rise.

In the narrative Nat Turner gave to Thomas Gray, he recalled that the group "quickly agreed" on initial tactics and then "remained at the feast," waiting for darkness.[89] Two earlier accounts of the dinner, however, differed from that recollection. The first of these appeared in Jack Reese's confession, as recounted in court on 3 September by Thomas C. Jones, the town constable.[90] The second appeared in the letter Gray wrote on 17 September to the editor of the *Richmond Constitutional Whig*; Gray's account also was based chiefly on Jack's word. The two earlier accounts indicate that the agreement at the dinner fell short of unanimity.

Having heard Will's speech, Nat Turner took the men aside, "one at a time," according to Gray, and held "long conversations with them." After that, brandy was introduced, and the group together discussed the "affair."[91] Jack, who apparently had arrived in ignorance, later recalled others at the meeting explaining their intention "to rise and kill all the white people."[92] At that point an argument broke out. "Even then," as Gray put it, "one of the party, objected to the proposition, and denied the possibility of effecting it."[93] The dissenter was Jack, who soon alienated himself from the group. Though his subsequent behavior would suggest a deep disagreement, Jack's only recorded objection at the dinner was purely tactical in nature: he protested that "their number was too few." Hark answered that "as they went on and killed the whites the blacks would join them."[94] Turner responded in similar terms, arguing that despite the secrecy and consequent lack of preparation, "their numbers would increase as they went along."[95] Turner then introduced the demographic theory attributed to him by John Hampden Pleasants, editor of the *Constitutional Whig*, "that there were only 80,000 whites in the country, who, being exterminated, the blacks might take possession."[96] Jack's objections succeeded only in drawing suspicion. The four original confidants, Henry, Hark, Nelson and Sam, reaffirmed their commitment, apparently in silence. All four had supported the affair from the day Turner broached it; none had wavered.

The insurgents would clarify their ideas through action and, later, through statements some would give to authorities. Except perhaps Will Francis, they did not mean literally to kill all the white people they encountered. Turner understood the killing to be a temporary, qualified measure, later telling Gray that "until we had armed and equipped ourselves, and gathered sufficient force, neither age nor sex was to be spared."[97] As the pattern of their actions on 22 August would indicate, they did intend to be thorough wherever they attacked; but they would move neither randomly nor from door to door. The first four attacks—and six of the first nine—would follow a route through farms and plantations where at least one of the insurgents had been enslaved in the past, or remained so on that day. At each stop they meant to kill all whites with weapons seized along the way and to recruit followers among residents of each slave quarter. Gray understood by mid-September that they had intended to seize Jerusalem, though not to occupy it or simply to "massacre" its inhabitants as he first believed, but to seize its stores of arms and ammunition. With the slave population joining in the rising, Hark theorized (echoing Nat Turner), and the white population paralyzed by fear, the insurgents would move from Jerusalem across the countryside exactly as they would do on their way to the town. Their base of power would not be the town, but the guerrilla army itself. Through the momentum of a widening guerrilla movement, they would achieve their strategic objective, the overturning of slavery. By mid-September Gray understood this idea too, as he revealed when he said of Nat Turner, "His object was freedom." Later, Turner would allude to that object himself when he boasted that he had intended to conquer the whole of Southampton County, "as the white people did in the revolution."[98] *Revolution* must have been the word he had in mind in the first sentence of his confession, when he dismissed the term Gray had used ("*insurrection, as you call it*").[99]

With a plan in place, after nightfall the company of seven men (including the lone dissenter) left the old field. Even before departing, they had found it necessary to impose discipline within the ranks. Other measures, tactical in nature and of greater significance, they would develop along the way.

CHAPTER SIX

The Zigzag Course

It was quickly agreed we should commence at home.
—Nat Turner, *The Confessions of Nat Turner*

First, Turner and his men planned to attack thirteen households within a four-mile radius of Cabin Pond, each chosen or approved by the leader himself (map 2). In the days that followed 22 August, authorities in Jerusalem would fail to detect a design in those early attacks, even after they found the map, "said to have been drawn by Nat Turner" (in pokeberry ink), and a list of his men, who were said to have numbered "short of twenty."[1] Starting at the Travis farm, the insurgents would pursue an odd, "zigzag course," as Thomas R. Gray described it on 17 September. Gray also said they visited "every house" on their way from the Travis farm to the plantation of Newit Harris.[2] On that point he was wrong, for they neither stopped at every house nor attacked randomly. They followed a design conceived, as events would show, by their leader, involving specific households on a list committed to memory.[3] They would attack only people who held slaves in 1830 or 1831 and avoid anyone who did not, a pattern to the end. One other pattern would emerge in the early attacks: every master with a man at Cabin Pond was a target.

The men agreed, Nat Turner said, to "commence at home," a phrase Gray construed as a reference to the house of "Mr. J. Travis," but which developed a broader meaning as events unfolded.[4] They would indeed begin with Travis (master of both the leader and the chief lieutenant), but then would move directly to three other, related households south of the pond, those of Salathiel Francis (Travis's brother-in-law), John W. Reese (master of Hark's wife), and Elizabeth Turner II (widow of Turner's former master). In due time the insurgents also would visit three houses east of the pond, those of Richard Porter (master of Henry), Nathaniel Francis (master of Sam and Will), and Peter Edwards (master of Nelson). Turner chose these seven in part because they were at hand, but also because the men, being familiar

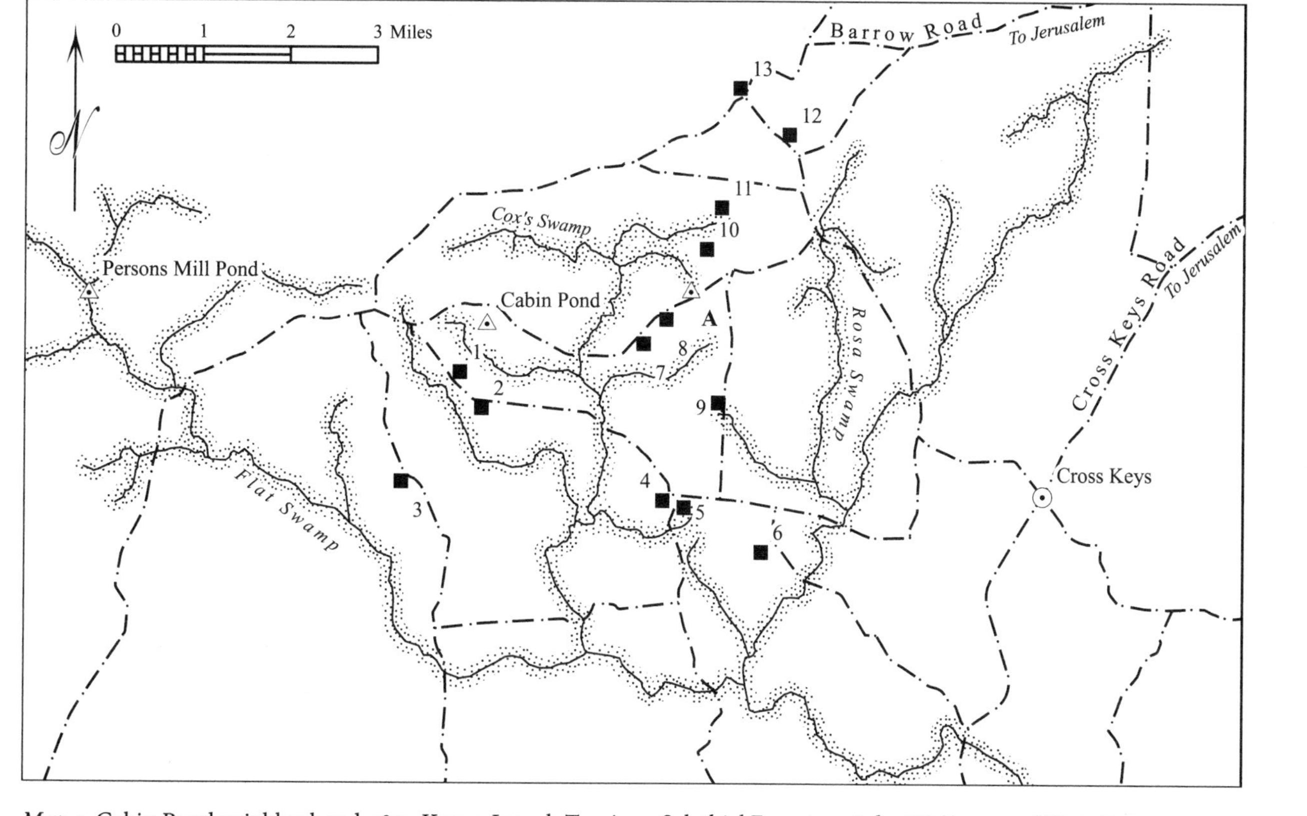

Map 2. Cabin Pond neighborhood, 1831. Key: 1, Joseph Travis; 2, Salathiel Francis; 3, John W. Reese and Piety Reese (conjectural); 4, Elizabeth Turner II (conjectural); 5, Henry Bryant (conjectural); 6, Catherine Whitehead; 7, Howell Harris (conjectural); 8, Augustus F. ("Trajan") Doyel (conjectural); 9, Richard Porter; 10, Nathaniel Francis; 11, Peter Edwards; 12, John T. Barrow; 13, Newit Harris; A, Benjamin Turner II plantation (conjectural)

with the grounds and buildings (not to mention the habits and whereabouts of the residents), would know where to look for guns, ammunition, horses, and recruits. But it was the connections of these particular households that placed them in jeopardy. Turner must have had all seven in mind long before he drew each man aside on Sunday and, after dinner and brandy, "developed his plans."[5]

The rising would begin, therefore, with opportunities to settle old scores. Where better to begin than at home, with the familiar faces of slavery's nearest agents? Recruiting as they advanced, revealing disaffection on a scale that would be difficult to deny, the men might travel miles before reaching the end of such motives.[6] The early attacks were intended to take a heavy toll especially on families linked by the marriages of Samuel G. Turner in 1807 and 1818. Nat Turner marked for removal every surviving branch of those old alliances—first (on the Francis side), Sarah ("Sally") Travis, her brothers Salathiel and Nathaniel, and their mother, Mrs. Sarah Francis; and second (on the Reese side), Elizabeth Turner II, her cousins John W. and Joseph William Henry Reese, and her aunt, Piety Reese. Salathiel Francis and Elizabeth Turner II, whose slaves took no part in the gathering on Sunday night, were marked chiefly because their paths had crossed Turner's in the past.

Turner intended also to attack six households having no connection—past or present, legal or familial—to anyone at the dinner in the old field. Three of those six were headed by young white men in modest circumstances: Henry Bryant, Augustus F. ("Trajan") Doyel, and Howell Harris. All three lived east-southeast of Cabin Pond, not far from Elizabeth Turner II; none held a significant number of slaves or owned much other property. The other three households in this group were headed by slaveholders of considerable wealth and influence: Catherine Whitehead, John Thomas ("Tom") Barrow, and Barrow's stepfather, Newit Harris. By including the Whitehead, Barrow, and Harris plantations, Turner indicated a purpose beyond the settling of scores.

Old Ties

The Travis house stood half a mile south of the pond. Nat Turner had known Sally Travis since their childhood years and had lived at her farm since about 1823. He knew the farm's buildings and may have worked on their recent improvements; he knew where Travis kept his weapons—the four guns and the old muskets, most of which must have been left by Travis's predecessor, Sally's late first husband. Turner would have known which of the five horses would be useful (the bay horse, Willis, and a bay mare) and where to find saddles. He could not have planned to recruit at this place, since he and Hark were the only adult males in its quarter; but he would take Moses, age thirteen, competent with horses, compliant, and a keen observer. And since Travis was the only adult male in the house, Turner must have known that resistance would be slight.[7]

Sally's brother Salathiel, whose cabin stood six hundred yards south and across the road from the Travis house, was still a bachelor at twenty-eight or twenty-nine but did not live alone.[8] Salathiel Francis headed a household that included one free black man, Emery Evans, and seven taxable slaves.[9] In 1831 he still owned the two lots (309 acres) that had been part of his father's land, with buildings still assessed at a modest $175. He had one bed, a few chairs, some kitchen utensils, and some farm tools, but no silver, no cash, no notes or bonds, and no books. He had a shotgun, three suitable horses (omitting his filly and colt), and four male slaves, at least two of whom were potential recruits. None of the four men, however, attended the dinner at Cabin Pond; and at least one of them, Red Nelson, apparently lived on good terms with his master, as did Emery Evans.[10] The insurgents certainly wanted Salathiel's shotgun, horses, and recruits, but his connections made him doubly vulnerable.

The three Reeses—John W., William, and Piety, the cousins and aunt of Elizabeth Turner II—were still occupying the house they had lost to creditors, a mile or so west-southwest of Salathiel Francis. Their new landlord, Henry Moore, brother of the late Thomas Moore, apparently had allowed them to remain as tenants.[11] John Reese, twenty-eight years old and not yet married, had listed himself in the 1830 census as head of the household, though Nat Turner still referred to the place as "Mrs. Reese's."[12] Together, the family owned eight horses and held twenty-one slaves; most of this property they had inherited at the death of Joseph Reese Sr. in 1826.[13] They would be drawn into peril through two of their slaves—Hark's wife (perhaps the woman named Edith) and Hark's brother-in-law (so to speak) Jack, who had permission to spend the weekend of 20–21 August at home. And if the boy Riddick and woman Cherry in fact had ties to Nat Turner, their presence would have drawn attention, though their whereabouts on 22 August are unknown.[14] Cherry almost certainly was the woman Samuel Warner mentioned in October 1831 in his sketch of Nat Turner ("*his wife was a slave, belonging to Mr. Reese*").[15]

Two widows, Elizabeth (Coggin) Harris and Sarah (Turner) Newsom, lived on small farms adjacent to one another about one mile east of the Reese plantation. The route to their houses (and to that of Elizabeth Turner II) involved a change of direction at the Reese house, a turn one would mark on a map as an acute angle, like the lower half of the letter *Z*. And though Mrs. Harris and Mrs. Newsom both held slaves, neither would be attacked; the men would pass through their properties.

Mrs. Harris, in her late fifties, shared her house with a widowed daughter and as many as seven young grandchildren. According to the deed by which she acquired her 158 acres in 1827, her property bordered land of Salathiel Francis and "Henry Turner's old mill pond"—a reference to the long-dead emancipator. She owned four horses (none taken) and fourteen slaves (seven taxable).[16] Apparently she lived on good terms with black people in the neighborhood.[17] In November 1831, after the uprising, Emery Evans, the free black man who had been living with Salathiel Francis, would seek her protection, agreeing to "sell and convey his freedom" and, for one dollar, "to be a servant slave during his life unto the said Elizabeth Harris."[18]

Mrs. Newsom, about thirty-six, lived next door in a house that belonged to the estate of her late brother, Jarrell Turner.[19] She too owned four horses, but held just three slaves, females she had acquired probably as patrimony. Her husband had died in about 1828. Before she married James B. Newsom in 1827, she had obtained his signature (affixed above her mark) on an unusual prenuptial agreement that prevented him as husband from claiming her land or slaves. The document was signed in the presence of neighbors, two as witnesses and two as witness-observers, one of whom was Elizabeth Harris. Its fifth clause stipulated that the property of neither party in the marriage could be "subject to the debts or contracts of the other."[20] In this way, Sarah Newsom had provided for her slaves some protection against uncertainties like those confronting Edith, Tom, and Riddick. Her exemption from attack apparently was to be a favor from Hark Moore, for the sake of old acquaintance.

Elizabeth Turner II still occupied the house at Samuel G. Turner's plantation, one mile east of the two neighboring widows. Now in her midthirties, she had remained there after Samuel's death in 1822, living by herself in the dwelling she had been granted for life (along with 363 surrounding acres) as widow's dower. Her daughter had married and moved away; Samuel's daughter, Polly, apparently had died. In 1831 Mrs. Turner hired an overseer, Hartwell Peebles, who no doubt occupied the cabin in her yard.

Her husband's property remained intact—936 acres including the dower land, with buildings worth $1,000.[21]

Some of Samuel's slaveholding also remained. In 1821 the number of his taxable slaves had stood at sixteen. In the spring of 1822, immediately following his death, the number declined to eleven; Samuel's executors obtained a tax exemption that year for two of the oldest slaves and must have sold or transferred or hired out three others. In 1823 Mrs. Turner paid tax on just seven slaves—another decline, almost certainly the result of sales or transfers by the executors.[22] By that year or the next, Nat Turner must have been sold to Capt. Moore. Over the next eight years, three older slaves apparently died: Tom and Bridget, the couple who were to live out their days at Samuel's property near the North Carolina border, and Lydia, the woman who probably was Nat Turner's grandmother.[23]

The number of Mrs. Turner's taxable slaves remained at seven through 1825 and then held steady at eight or nine. In 1830, she held eighteen slaves of all ages, nine of whom were old enough to remember when Nat Turner had been a resident at this plantation.[24] Those present in August 1831 included two young men, both promising recruits: Davy, about twenty-two (given to Elizabeth's daughter by Samuel just before he died), and Jordan, about twenty-one (acquired from the estate of Elizabeth's father in 1817 and regained from Samuel as a bequest in 1822).[25] Neither Davy nor Jordan knew on the morning of 22 August that the rising was in progress. Other survivors from Turner's holding, including no doubt the two mature women (between thirty-six and fifty-five) recorded there in 1830, must have been present that morning as well.[26] One of these may have been Nancy, now about fifty-four, who had been brought to Benjamin Turner's plantation in 1793 with Lydia.

Elizabeth Turner II had spent her life among slaveholders. Her grandfather, Edward Reese I, her father, John Reese Sr., and both of her husbands had owned slaves.[27] And at least three times within the previous fifteen years she had pressed claims to slave property, so her intentions could not have been mistaken: having preserved her holding, she did not mean to let it go. Yet none of the slaves in her possession in 1831 joined the rising before it reached her door. Her only significant encounter with any of the conspirators lay in the past, between 1818, when she joined Samuel G. Turner's household, and 1823 or 1824, when Nat Turner was sent to Moore's.

Richard Porter, Nathaniel Francis, and Peter Edwards, each of whom owned a member of the inner circle, lived roughly two and a quarter miles (as the crow flies) east of Cabin Pond. Their houses stood in an almost-straight line north-northeast from the Turner house, requiring another abrupt change of course, a turn of ninety degrees to the north, or left. After two intervening attacks and some complicated maneuvers east of the Turner house, the insurgents would turn decisively toward these three masters.

The Porter house stood a mile and a half by present-day roads from the Turner property. From some points near the Turner lane, it was visible three-quarters of a mile to the northeast across open fields. Given its location along the way to Barrow Road and Jerusalem, it might have been visited under any circumstances, but the presence of a Porter slave in the inner circle made a visit there certain.

Richard Porter, thirty-eight, had been born near Cabin Pond in 1793 and had spent most of his life in its vicinity.[28] In 1815 his father, Thomas Porter, though not a rich man, did own 385 acres and thirteen slaves. The father's house stood on land that bordered the old Henry Turner farm, which means that Richard grew up within sight of the Benjamin Turner II plantation and must have known Nat Turner—as well as some of the free black Turners—from childhood.[29] When Thomas Porter died in 1815, he left his land to two of Richard's younger brothers, both minors at the time, to be conveyed when the youngest became an adult, a strange decision at the time, since Richard, the eldest son, might have been considered a suitable replacement as head of the family.[30] Richard's fortunes suffered. He inherited no land and only a one-third share of his father's slaves. After his mother died in 1818, he had no permanent home. He lived for two years (1818 and 1819) with a non-slaveholding neighbor, presumably as a hired hand.[31] By 1822, when he became guardian for his brothers, he appears to have moved back to his parents' modest house, then legally the property of his brother Thomas Jr., still a minor.[32] In 1823 or 1824, Porter left for North Carolina, showing signs of becoming a rolling stone, but he was back by March 1827 (less than a year after the famous baptism at Person's Mill Pond). Still unmarried at thirty-four, Porter owned no land, no horse, and just one taxable slave.[33]

In April 1827, he married Eliza Barnes, thirty-one, the widow of his father's former neighbor, Bolling H. Barnes, who had preceded Richard as his brothers' guardian.[34] Like Joseph Travis, Richard Porter married advantageously. He now had a significant amount of property under his control, if not in his outright possession: by the spring of 1828, he was in charge of 1,310 acres, of which he controlled 809 acres through his wife (549 in her dower and 260 from her father's estate). The remaining 501 acres had fallen temporarily to him as guardian for his brothers.[35] That same spring, a year after returning to the county, he paid taxes on eight horses and seventeen slaves. Two years later, in 1830, he paid tax on ten horses and was listed in the census with thirty slaves.[36]

With his marriage, Porter also gained connections, for Eliza too had grown up near the Turner, Francis, and Reese plantations and, as a result of the prevailing rate of mortality in St. Luke's Parish, had ties to significant people. She herself was a Porter; her father and Richard's were distant cousins.[37] In 1819 her sister Martha had married Edward Reese, brother of Elizabeth Turner II, the second wife of Samuel G. Turner.[38] Then, in 1823, Eliza Porter's widowed father, Henry Porter, had become the fourth husband of Mrs. Elizabeth Prince, the second wife of Benjamin Turner II: Eliza's new stepmother (soon to be widowed a fourth time) was in fact Elizabeth Turner I, the former stepmother of Samuel G. Turner.[39] In 1828, three years after her father died, Eliza (Porter) Barnes inherited Henry Porter's land, along with his house and outbuildings at the home plantation, valued together at $600.[40] There, surrounded by neighbors Nat Turner would identify as enemies, Richard Porter settled into married life. His wife's home became his. By 1830 he too had become a major creditor of John W. Reese. In documents signed that year and at the meeting on 5 February 1831, in which Reese offered slaves as collateral for debts, Porter was named as a lender to be paid on demand.[41] Porter also witnessed the deeds in which Reese gave up his land to Henry Moore and Nathaniel Francis.[42]

A mile north of the Porter plantation lay the Francis farm, the home of conspirators Sam and Will Francis. This was the birthplace of Sarah ("Sally") Travis, her brother Salathiel, and Samuel G. Turner's first wife, Esther Francis, the second mistress of Nat Turner. In 1831 the Francis farm covered 548 acres, including portions still being cleared by Nathaniel, the youngest Francis brother, who also was born there and took over as master in 1828.[43] In 1829 Nathaniel had become the guardian of his two infant nephews, Samuel T. and John W. Browne, orphans of his sister Martha and her husband, who both died that year.[44] Nathaniel and his mother brought the boys into their home. In October 1830, at age twenty-five, Nathaniel married Lavinia Hart, aged seventeen, of North Carolina.[45] Later that year the census marshal counted twenty-seven people in Nathaniel's household, including six free blacks and fifteen slaves. Three of the slaves were males between the ages of ten and twenty-four; these must have been Nathan, Tom, and Davy, boys between thirteen and fourteen. Four others were between twenty-four and thirty-six years of age—prime recruits, including certainly Dred and perhaps a man named Reuben.[46] Sam and Will, the other two men in that bracket, would bring the insurgents to this farm.

The new master at the farm was one of the dozen or so young white men who had taken possession of land near Cabin Pond by 1828 and tied their fortunes to slavery. Nathaniel's intentions could be read in the history of his family's slaveholding, which had been scattered and reduced after his father died. Taxable slaves at the Francis home farm declined in number from fourteen in 1814 to just five in 1820, presenting an opportunity for Nathaniel and his mother to abandon that way of life.[47] But they recovered. Their taxable slaves rose in number to seven in 1827 and eleven in 1831. The census of 1830 recorded fifteen slaves at their farm, a gain of five over 1820 and just one fewer than in 1810.[48] Soon, as anyone could have observed, the entire holding would fall to Nathaniel, and he would not refuse it.

He made that clear in a series of financial transactions starting in 1827. While still in his early twenties, Francis had joined the local circle of creditors, offering security to other young white men who, unlike himself, needed credit to start their lives in planting; soon he was loaning actual money, backed by the patrimony he was about to inherit. His first transaction had enabled John W. Reese to purchase the Blunt plantation with a loan secured initially just by a signature, then by land.[49] In 1829 Nathaniel loaned $100 to Augustus F. ("Trajan") Doyel, a neighbor to the south, to fund the latter's farming operations on rented land. Doyel put up his crops, hogs, household goods, shotgun, mare, and saddle (but not his one slave) as collateral.[50] Then, in 1830, Nathaniel secured a bond of $423.78 for Drewry Bittle, a friend and neighbor to the east. As collateral, Bittle offered three of his slaves: "man Cain, boy Jacob and Girl Nancy."[51] Francis was accepting debt secured by slaves and slave children. The thought of repudiating the almost universal practice—a stance implicit in Sarah Newsom's marriage agreement of 1827—either had not occurred to him or had no appeal. With his expanding transactions, he thus signaled what he would do with regard to slaves, and what he would not. The conspirators with closest connections to Francis—Nat Turner, Hark Moore, Sam Francis, and Will Francis—had read his mind.

The Edwards plantation was situated on the northern bounds of the Francis farm; its house was a mile distant by dirt track through fields and around a swamp and woods. The stable there in 1831 had nine horses.[52] The quarter was the most promising for recruitment along the route to Jerusalem: in 1830 the number of male slaves there between ages ten and thirty-six stood at twelve.[53] Among those twelve in 1830 was Nelson Edwards.

Peter Edwards had lived in the parish all of his thirty-nine years. He was born in St. Luke's on 10 February 1792, during the month Henry Turner, the emancipator, was dying.[54] Peter's father, James Edwards, came from the lowest ranks of property holders; in 1810 he owned just five acres of land and two slaves, one of whom might have been Nelson. That same year, Peter had his first entry on the tax rolls, paying a tax on his own head but nothing for land or slaves.[55] In 1813, when Peter was twenty-one, an uncle gave him his first land, a tract of ninety-eight acres a short distance west of Samuel G. Turner. He and his father together were taxed that year for four slaves.[56] In 1816 their combined holding of five slaves represented 70.3 percent of their taxable wealth.[57]

The son then vaulted into the ranks of the planters. Upon his marriage in 1817 to Mrs. Nancy Bittle, the widow of a former neighbor, Peter Edwards became stepfather to three minor children, custodian of more than nine hundred acres in his predecessor's estate, and master of as many as twenty-one Bittle slaves.[58] A third of that slaveholding fell at once to Edwards, which explains the rise in the number of his taxable slaves to twelve the next year.[59] He took up residence at the Bittle plantation (the land north of the Francis place) and in 1827 bought outright from his stepdaughter the 688 acres that remained in her father's estate.[60] By 1831, in taxable wealth he ranked in the top 10 percent of 272 core taxpayers in the parish, holding 1,489 acres and seventeen taxable slaves.[61] Like Richard Porter and Joseph Travis, Edwards had married to advantage; and with his slaves providing labor, he rose in the world.

It was Nelson who brought the insurgents to the Edwards place. Peter Edwards had no record of having treated his slaves badly, no reputation for having committed outrages against them, as did James Powell (whipping), or perhaps Thomas Moore (whipping), or John W. Reese and Nathaniel Francis (collateralizing). In fact, in the aftermath of 22–23 August, Edwards would show a paternal concern for at least two of his men, James and Sam, who had been caught up in the violence.[62] But Nelson had not joined the conspiracy merely to gain personal satisfaction. Nor was his motive new-found; the affair for him was no spontaneous outburst, no *jacquerie*. For six months he had kept a disciplined silence. At some point in the previous fifteen years, Nelson must have realized that his master would not change course, that once this man held thirty slaves he would have fifty.

Minor Figures

The three young men who lived near Mrs. Turner and also became targets—Henry Bryant, Augustus Doyel, and Howell Harris—had no relatives in the other targeted households, nor did they have ties to the conspirators at Cabin Pond. They were minor figures, new in their places, with origins as humble as those of Peter Edwards. Together in 1830 they held just twelve slaves, including women and children.[63] But each was ambitious. Each had appeared for the first time in parish records between 1828 and 1830, joining the dozen other men in their late twenties and early thirties taking possession of properties in the Cabin Pond area. And each had become involved in the local circle of creditors and debtors.

Henry Bryant, at about twenty-five years of age, was the youngest of the three. If he was the grandson named in 1815 in the will of Nathan Bryant, he had spent his life within a mile or two of Nat Turner's home quarters.[64] If he was that Henry, his father was dead by early 1812 and apparently left no estate. In September 1812 his mother, Charlotte Bryant, married his grandfather's hired man, John Newton, who at that point owned neither land nor slaves.[65] Henry's name then disappeared from county records for a time; it is likely that he lived with his grandfather and then with his stepfather before himself becoming a hired man and a tenant.[66] In January 1830 Bryant married Elizabeth Balmer, about twenty-two, daughter of Mildred Balmer, a landless widow in her late fifties who since 1810 had maintained a household for her daughter and, at times, one female slave.[67] The Balmer women also belonged to their own circle of neighbors, one that included Elizabeth Harris and Sarah Newsom. In 1827 Mildred Balmer was an observer along with Elizabeth Harris at the signing of Sarah Newsom's prenuptial agreement.[68] Later that year, Mrs. Balmer still had in her hands most of the legacy of $500 left to her (apparently as an act of charity) by Sarah Newsom's brother, Jarrell Turner, when he died in 1823.[69] Mrs. Balmer had loaned $125.82 of that money to John W. Reese; on 5 February 1831 she was included, along with her new son-in-law, among the creditors demanding payment.[70] The balance of her legacy she may have given to her daughter and Bryant in 1830 as a marriage settlement.

For most of the year following his marriage, Henry Bryant made his living as a tenant farmer on land near Flat Swamp.[71] He paid tax in the spring of 1830 on one slave, probably the woman owned by his mother-in-law.[72] In the fall he appeared in the census as head of his own household, which included two white females (his wife and mother-in-law, no doubt) and two young female slaves (one a child).[73] Within the next twelve months, the Bryants produced a child of their own. Then, by 12 February 1831, both slaves had departed and were replaced by a free black man, Nat Day.[74] Bryant thus became the only man Nat Turner targeted who was not taxed for a slave in the year of the rising and whose farm could offer no recruits to the rising. Like many others in the parish, including his mother-in-law, Henry Bryant had drifted briefly into slaveholding and then out again. In time, he probably would have drifted in again.

Early in March 1831, for $350, Bryant bought 162 acres bordering lands of his stepfather and those of Elizabeth Turner II, Catherine Whitehead, and the heirs of Thomas Browne (the infant nephews of Nathaniel Francis).[75] He began at once to raise hogs and grow corn and cotton, much like his neighbors. In 1832, the buildings at his farm were assessed at $250—more than those of Nathaniel Francis by $100, and $50 more than those of Joseph Travis.[76] The house, according to Drewry's sources, stood several hundred yards northeast of Elizabeth Turner's.[77] Its furnishings included three beds and a cradle, five chairs, one mirror, a small collection of cooking and dining utensils, and andirons for one fireplace. Henry Bryant owned neither books nor desk, but he could read and write. (His mother-in-law could not write her own name, and there is no evidence that his wife could, either.) His personal property in 1831 was worth about $200, before deducting $26.60 he had borrowed from Sarah Newsom.[78] His one valuable possession was a $40 horse. The insurgents may have wanted that horse, but they singled out Bryant for other reasons, known at the time but since forgotten.

Augustus F. ("Trajan") Doyel, in his midthirties, was possibly the poorest of the intended victims. His name (also spelled "Doyle" and "Doyal") appeared for the first time in county records in 1828, about two years after the baptism at Persons Mill Pond (with which he almost certainly had nothing to do) and one year before the arrival of Joseph Travis. Like Travis, Trajan seems to have been an outsider drawn to St. Luke's in all likelihood by relatives, including a farmer named Joel Doyel and his son Allison, and one A. Doyle, overseer in 1831 for Nathaniel Francis.[79] Trajan Doyel, like Henry Bryant, may have worked for a time as a farm laborer and overseer before establishing his own household. On 17 March 1828, he appeared before the court and became the guardian for Margaret Simmons, an orphan half his age; later that day he obtained a bond to marry his ward.[80]

Doyel's bride had lived her entire fifteen or sixteen years near the Turner and Francis families. Her maternal grandfather was John Underwood, a prosperous St. Luke's planter, the owner in 1821 of 1,622 acres and of Dread, one of the men who burglarized the store of David Vallance that year. Underwood, credited in 1820 with thirty-seven slaves, reported in 1823 that he had bought three more people.[81] Margaret's mother, also named Margaret ("Peggy"), had married twice, neither time to great advantage; her first husband, Robert Bittle, died landless in 1809, leaving her with four children and three taxable slaves.[82] Her second husband, Cyer Simmons, with whom she had two more children—including Margaret Jr.—died in the morbid year of 1815.[83] Simmons, too, was landless at the time of his death and held just two taxable slaves, both of whom probably had belonged to Bittle.[84] Margaret Sr. kept her family together, thanks no doubt to aid from her father and from her first husband's family. In 1820 she was maintaining a household for three of her children and two slaves, apparently on Bittle family land that bordered the Francis plantation.[85] When John Underwood died in 1824, he provided a legacy of $1,000 (but no slaves) to his twice-widowed daughter; she in turn died in 1825 and left her minor daughter half of what remained of her legacy, along with a bed, pine chest, food safe, and half a share in two small bonds.[86] It is possible that she also left Margaret a share in a slave or two. Trajan Doyel must have sensed an opportunity.

In August 1831 Doyel appears to have been farming as a tenant on land owned by John Clark Turner and living in the small house John Clark had occupied until late 1830.[87] That house stood a mile or more north of Elizabeth Turner's house, apparently on the south side of Cabin Pond Road and considerably west of the direct route to Barrow Road and Jerusalem.[88] In December 1829, with Howell Harris acting as his security, Doyel had borrowed money from Nathaniel Francis to fund his operations, thereby linking himself to the local moneylenders. As collateral he offered his shotgun, his sorrel mare, saddle and bridle, two feather beds, household and kitchen furniture, his crops of corn and fodder, and his hogs.[89] Apparently he repaid that loan and survived. By the autumn of 1830, he had fathered a child.[90] In the spring of 1831, he paid taxes on one horse and one slave, a young male listed in the census as between ten and twenty-four years of age.[91] (Drewry later heard that this man's name was Hugh.)[92] Doyel still owned no land, however, and had accumulated almost $150 in new debt to neighbors, including Richard Porter and Howell Harris.[93] He had been able to settle down, but his gains were small. Certainly Nat Turner would not have sent his men more than a mile out of their way for a shotgun, a horse and saddle, and one possible recruit. Some other, unrecorded cause would lead to the attack on Doyel.

Howell Harris, the most important of the minor figures, had become the local constable in 1829, appointed by the county court as an officer of the law under the sheriff. Still single at twenty-six, Harris lived about five hundred yards west of Augustus Doyel in a small, new house he shared with his widowed mother, Lucy.[94] Also in residence was a young hired man, Edmund Stephenson, the son of a neighbor who had died in 1826.[95] The census of 1830 listed Harris with nine slaves—four females and five males. Two of the latter were between the ages of twenty-four and thirty-six; perhaps their presence was enough to draw a detachment of Turner's men far afield to visit the constable.[96]

Harris was born in St. Luke's Parish in 1805 and had spent most of his life on his father's farm, near lands of the Turner and Francis families.[97] His father, Joel Harris Sr., owned a modest 222 acres in 1821, along with six horses and nine taxable slaves, the latter accounting for 70 percent of the family's taxable wealth.[98] The father died intestate at about age fifty in 1821, leaving a widow and eight or nine surviving children, including five sons, of whom at least two already were adults.[99] The inventory of Joel Sr.'s personal property taken in November 1821 showed that he held fifteen slaves, who together represented the largest part of his family's assets.[100] For a man with five maturing, capable sons and just 222 acres, his was a large slaveholding.

The death of Joel Harris left Howell, at age sixteen, with no patrimonial land. A committee appointed by the court in 1821 to settle the estate elected not to divide the small farm into even smaller portions and gave most of it instead to an older brother, Joel Jr.[101] By the time Howell was twenty-one, however, his prospects had improved. In 1826, with his brother Lewis, he bought 248 acres on Cox's Swamp, bordering lands of John T. ("Tom") Barrow (another target) and the old plantation of Benjamin Turner II. Howell's half of the $950 purchase price must have come in part from funds he had inherited.[102] In the spring of 1828, at age twenty-three, Harris paid personal property taxes for the first time, charged for property that probably had been part of his mother's dower: six slaves, three horses, and a gig.[103] In 1829 he joined the circle of creditors and debtors in St. Luke's Parish, acting first as security for a loan from his brother Lewis to George Ivey, and then as security on another loan from Nathaniel Francis to Augustus Doyel (both targeted in 1831).[104] In 1830 he was party to at least three loans in which slaves were offered as collateral, including one from Joseph T. Claud to John R. ("Cherokee") Williams (whose family would be attacked inadvertently).[105] Harris also loaned money to young neighbors (one of whom borrowed the sizable sum of $344.47), thereby investing in the operations of slaveholders like himself.[106] Those funds may have derived in part from his father's estate, but there were signs that through his own efforts he was improving what little he had received. In January 1828 he bought from his brother Lewis the other half of the property on Cox's Swamp, paying $425 for 124 acres.[107] In 1830, for $100 he bought an outlying parcel of 115 acres, which brought his total landholding to 363 acres.[108] Later that year he completed some new buildings on his land, including what must have been the dwelling house for himself, his mother, and the hired man. In the spring of 1831, he paid taxes on one gig, three horses, and five slaves over the age of twelve. Though his holding was still modest, slaves accounted for 42.8 percent of his total tax bill and 64.7 percent of his personal property tax bill.[109] He seemed destined to rank among the planters.

A stimulus to Howell's gains may have been his appointment in 1829 (at age twenty-four) and reappointment in July 1831 to local office.[110] As constable, according to fees established in 1819, he received 50 cents for serving a warrant, 21 cents for summoning a witness, $3.15 for summoning a coroner's jury and witnesses, 21 cents for putting lawbreakers in the stocks, and 42 cents ("to be paid by the owner") for whipping a slave. He also made arrests and carried prisoners to jail.[111] To gain his appointment, Harris must have displayed a certain bearing—like Capt. Moore's, perhaps—and projected the authority necessary to call out citizenry, confront resistance, and preserve the peace. For such responsibilities, life had prepared him, giving him not only four brothers but a father who kept horses (six in 1821) and owned guns (two in his inventory). Howell, like Moore, could ride and shoot. Events on the morning of 22 August would suggest that his bearing and office, more than his slaveholding, horses, or friends, had made him a target. For tactical reasons, the constable was a man to remove early in the game.

Local Gentry

The remaining targets around Cabin Pond were households of the gentry, headed by Catherine Whitehead, John T. ("Tom") Barrow, and Capt. Newit Harris.[112] Though these three individuals together held nearly one hundred slaves in 1830, no one from their holdings had been present with the conspirators at Cabin Pond. None of the conspirators had lived in their quarters or had relatives in their holdings; none had a known grievance traceable to some intimate, old connection. These attacks in particular would leave the impression, difficult to repress, that Turner's men were taking aim at slavery itself.

Catherine Whitehead, a widow approaching sixty, lived one mile east-southeast of Elizabeth Turner II. In the 1830 census she was listed as the head of a household with eleven white family members (including possibly a daughter-in-law) and twenty-seven slaves. In August 1831 she was sharing her house with one son, Richard, a Methodist minister, unmarried, about thirty years of age, and five of her six daughters: Margaret, Harriet, Minerva, Mary Ann, and Mourning Ann, each also unmarried. An infant grandson was present that August but was never identified by name; he may have been the half-orphaned younger child of William Henry Whitehead, a son who died in 1830.[113]

Mrs. Whitehead was born in Southampton between 1772 and 1776, making her about the same age as Piety Reese. In the early 1790s her father, William Whitehead I, had owned a dozen slaves and six hundred acres in St. Luke's Parish.[114] Catherine was still a minor in March 1792 when, with her father's permission, she married a first cousin, John Whitehead.[115] (The wedding took place in the month Henry Turner died, and about one year before Benjamin Turner II acquired the Griffin slaves.) Two years later she gave birth to a daughter, Margaret, the first of her eleven children. In their probable order of birth, the children were as follows:

1. Margaret, born about 1794;
2. Harriet, born 1796;
3. Martha ("Patsy"), born about 1798;
4. William Henry, born about 1799;
5. Richard, born about 1801;
6. Edwin, born 1803;
7. Joseph Boswell, born 1804;
8. Minerva, born about 1806;
9. Mary Ann (or "Marion"), born about 1808;
10. John, born 1810; and
11. Mourning Ann (or "Mornan"), born about 1812.

It is possible that during the twenty-three years of her marriage, all of Catherine Whitehead's children survived infancy.[116] That record, remarkable in a malarial region before the introduction of metal window screens, may have been related to the location of the Whitehead house on relatively high ground half a mile from the nearest pond or swamp. Whatever the explanation, Catherine and her husband were dealt a difficult hand in providing portions for their hardy offspring.

The Whiteheads established their homestead in 1795 on a tract of land two and a half miles south-southeast of the Benjamin Turner II house. They were living at that homestead when Nat Turner was born. Neither they nor their slaves had relatives at the Turner plantation, but they did have social connections there. Like the Turners and Francises, the Whiteheads had joined the Methodist Church: in 1831 the Reverend George W. Powell (brother of Mrs. Sarah Francis) referred to "sister" Catherine Whitehead as "a shining light in the Methodist E. Church, for 40 years."[117] Mrs. Whitehead must have been among the religious persons the young Nat Turner had seen in prayer at his first master's house. The Whiteheads became immediate neighbors of Samuel G. Turner in 1808, when Samuel brought his new wife and slaves to the Kindred tract.[118] In 1810, when Benjamin Turner II and his wife gave the money to build the Methodist meetinghouse, they named John Whitehead a trustee for that project.[119] In 1813 Catherine's brother William registered as a Methodist minister in the parish, and in 1830 her son Richard ("Dick") followed suit.[120] Richard, whom Rev. Powell described as a "Methodist local preacher," may have been among the church members who had attempted to prohibit the baptism at Person's Mill Pond in 1826; he and Nat Turner must have crossed paths many times.[121]

At the start of their marriage, John and Catherine Whitehead held only modest amounts of real and personal property: in 1796 John paid taxes on just 260 acres and two slaves.[122] At the time of his death nineteen years later, his acreage had tripled and his slaveholding had increased six- or sevenfold. In 1815 he owned 740 acres, which, at $7 an acre, would have been worth $5,180.[123] In April of that year, when Catherine and four of her neighbors made an inventory of his personal property, the items they recorded were worth a total of $6,426.85, of which his fourteen slaves accounted for $3,665. Including land, the estate was worth about $11,600, of which slaves represented almost one-third.[124]

Whitehead died in his forties, in 1815, during the spring that carried off a number of his neighbors, including members of the Turner, Francis, and Reese families. He had written a will in May 1814, setting forth his final instructions in close detail. He loaned everything in the estate to his widow "during her natural Life or widowhood," he said, "for the purpose of raising and Schooling my children." (As many as eight of the children were under fifteen at the time; the youngest was just three.) He gave Catherine power to "Sell and dispose" of any part of the estate, and to lend portions to the children during her lifetime or widowhood. If she remarried, she was to keep one-third of the estate on loan for life. Any child under age fifteen at the time Catherine might die or remarry should have an additional allowance of $50 per year, again "for the purpose of raising and Schooling." At her death, he said, the remaining estate should be divided equally among sons (five) and daughters (six) alike: he listed their names twice, evidently in order of birth, underscoring his intention. He made no gifts of individual slaves to any heir, assuming that an equal division would necessitate a sale, with proceeds distributed in cash. (Had the division taken place in 1815, each heir would have received about $1,000—twice the legacy Jarrell Turner would give to poor Mildred Balmer in 1822, but a small patrimony considering the size of the Whitehead estate.) Finally, he named his executor. Since his sons were still minors and ineligible to serve (the eldest boy being not yet sixteen), he turned to Catherine.[125]

She proved a shrewd choice. She presented the will in court on 20 March 1815 and assumed the role she would play for the next sixteen years. Starting early in 1816 and continuing over the next three years, she purchased an additional 604 acres in five outlying parcels, probably using funds she collected in suits against John's debtors. By 1821 she had increased the landholdings under her control from 740 to 1,245 acres; in acreage that year, she ranked among the top 6 percent of 275 core taxpayers in the parish.[126] In the spring of 1831 she still owned all of that land and paid taxes on seven horses (one more than her husband in 1815) and fifteen slaves (seven more).[127] The twenty-seven slaves counted at her farm in the 1830 census represented an exact tripling of the number there in 1810.[128] Among the households visited by the insurgents, only those of Peter Edwards and Newit Harris ranked above hers in wealth (table 6).

Her rise, discernible to all, revealed what must have been her resolve from the day she became executor: she would not remarry, but would accept a long widowhood, the consequence of having produced eleven heirs. For the rest of her life, she would hold her husband's property. To provide decent patrimonies for his heirs, she would enlarge his estate (and its dividends) by purchasing land. To work an expanding plantation, she would keep his slaves and, in time, enjoy the fruits of their increase. Her

TABLE 6. Taxable wealth of targeted households, 1831

Taxpayer	Total tax (in $)	Rank in parish	Acres	Taxable slaves	Slaves in 1830 census
Newit Harris	17.86	10	1,969	31	49
Peter Edwards	10.50	27	1,489	17	29
Catherine Whitehead	10.36	28	1,245	15	27
Richard Porter	7.23	43	809	13	30
Elizabeth Turner II	7.22	44	936	8	18
James W. Parker	6.83	49	739	13	23
Levi Waller	5.99	62	587	10	18
John W. Reese (Piety)	5.66	65	860	9	21
Nathaniel Francis	5.18	71	548	10	15
Joseph Travis	4.77	77	411	8	17
John T. Barrow	4.19	87	521	5	13
Jacob Williams	3.53	113	613	4	6
Howell Harris	2.92	130	363	5	9
Rebecca Vaughan	2.74	141	0	8	9
Salathiel Francis	2.40	153	309	5	7
William Williams Jr.	1.40	234	145	3	4
Henry Bryant	0.69	317	162	0	2
Augustus F. Doyel	0.37	378	0	1	1

Sources: St. Luke's Parish Land Book, 1831; St. Luke's Parish Personal Tax List, 1831; U.S. Census, 1830, Southampton County, manuscript returns.

Notes: The mean total tax bill for all resident white heads of household in St. Luke's Parish was $3.21; the median was $1.48. "Rank in parish" refers to total taxes paid. These data pertain to 389 heads of household in the 1830 census who paid taxes on real or personal property in 1831; fifty-three census heads who paid no taxes in 1831 are not included. Figures for five of the targeted taxpayers represent combined totals for the head of household and at least one other related landowner belonging to the same household. They were as follows: Richard Porter (and wife), Elizabeth Turner II (and husband's estate), John W. Reese (and mother and brother), Nathaniel Francis (and mother), and Joseph Travis (and wife). Figures for Henry Bryant include the tax on land he bought in March 1831 but which was not assessed until 1832, when his estate was charged.

success—thanks particularly to that increase—became evident in 1830, when the census recorded exactly eleven slave children in her quarter, six boys and five girls under the age of ten.[129]

She had known long before she became executor that some of her Whitehead relatives had begun to have doubts about keeping slaves. She was aware that in 1790, two years before her marriage, John Whitehead's brother Arthur (who was also her first cousin) had freed at least three slaves (Nat, Judith, and Priss), and that before Arthur died in 1799, he had freed three more (Jordan, Abby, and Jacob). All six had taken the Whitehead surname and settled in the parish.[130] At Arthur's death, no slaves remained in his estate.[131] Then, not two years before her husband died, Catherine's own brother William had attempted, though feebly and without success, to emancipate his slaves by means of the will he signed in August 1813. Hesitantly, William had said that he wished his slaves "to be liberated at any time when my wife thinks proper, if the Law of the land will admit of their being liberated."[132] He made that gesture just two months after registering as a minister of the gospel, and not more than four months before he died. Catherine's husband would mention no such wish, and she would not raise the matter.

Though widowed, Mrs. Whitehead enjoyed a standard of living few of her neighbors could have matched. Her house and other structures were worth $1,250 in 1831, second in value only to those of Newit Harris among the households visited by the insurgents.[133] The Whitehead house survived, though in decay, into the late twentieth century, its plan almost as Catherine left it, with at least seven rooms devoted to specific functions: hall, parlor, dining room, kitchen, work room or storage room, and at least two bedrooms, including sleeping areas on the second floor shared by her daughters. According to the 1831 inventory of her estate, there were andirons for four fireplaces. Her parlor had one of the few pianos in Southampton, worth $100.[134] Her best bed was worth $75 (including bedding and seven coverlets), more than twice the value of the bed Newit Harris slept in. Nearby was a cradle for her grandchild. There were seven other beds, carpets in the hall and perhaps also in Catherine's bedroom, and curtains for at least four windows. She owned three looking glasses, including one of significant value ($17). The parlor had a small collection of books, including sermons by the English Methodist preacher Joseph Benson and an edition of Benson's Bible. She also owned a volume on medicine, probably either James Ewell's *The Planter's and Mariner's Medical Companion* (Philadelphia, 1807), a section of which addressed complaints of women and children, or an edition of Ewell's succeeding work, *The Medical Companion* (3rd ed., Philadelphia, 1816), which included instructions on "improving health and prolonging life." The appraisers mentioned no music for the piano—no Mozart, Beethoven, or Schubert, no book of hymns.

She owned a watch worth $5. She had two writing desks, including the secretary on which she probably drew up the inventory of her husband's estate in 1815. Her dining room was furnished with six new Windsor chairs, a buffet, a sideboard, another carpet, two sets of china, and a sizable collection of silver spoons. She had six goblets and, for a Methodist woman in 1831, a large number of wine glasses (a dozen of cut glass, and nineteen others "plain"). She had five decanters, a significant store of wine (sixteen gallons), brandy (342 gallons), and peaches for brandy (one keg). The wine, brandy, and peaches apparently were produced on the property.

There were seven horses in her stable, including one named Selim and a colt, Archie ("Archee"), at $75 her most prized animal, named no doubt for the famous thoroughbred still living at the time in neighboring Northampton County, North Carolina. Her livestock included forty-three head of cattle and, altogether, 135 hogs, sows, pigs, and shoats. Her chief field crop in 1831 was cotton, and there were smaller productions of corn, bacon, fodder, potatoes, plantains, and wheat, along with brandy. She owned thirty-two hoes of various kinds and a cotton gin, which, at $30, was by far her most valuable piece of farm equipment. She had a loom and eight spinning wheels of various kinds. And she owned two double gigs worth a combined total of $100—as much as her piano. Though her husband had owned at least one good shotgun in 1815, the appraisers in 1831 found no such weapon.[135] The Whiteheads could not have defended themselves.

During her widowhood, Mrs. Whitehead had depended increasingly on servants and laborers, in part because of developments in the lives of her sons, four of whom left her household between 1821 and 1830. William Henry, the eldest, married in 1821; and by the spring of 1831, Edwin and John (sons three and five) had married and departed.[136] Joseph, the fourth son, also had left home by 1831, perhaps to live with Rebecca Sweat, the free black woman with whom he would spend much of his adult life.[137] Joseph always would have difficulty supporting himself, though he did leave the nest.[138] By August 1831 the only adult white male remaining in the house was thirty-year-old Richard, the minister, the second son, still a dependent, but a prop to his mother's authority. And while Richard did oversee the work in his mother's fields, Catherine Whitehead relied on slaves to perform the actual plantation labor: in 1830, sixteen of her slaves were between ages ten and fifty-five—six males, ten females, all apparently fit for field work.[139] Slaves represented her most valuable personal property; in 1831, her fifteen taxable slaves accounted for 69.2 percent of her bill for personal property tax, and 36.2 percent of her total tax bill.[140] The Whitehead slaveholding in 1831 was worth perhaps three times its value in 1815 and promised returns greater than any contributions she might have expected from her sons.

Circumstances involving her daughters underscored the importance of her investment in slaves. By 1831 it was clear that three of the young women were not leading conventional lives and might require support from the estate and its holdings for years to come. Of the six Whitehead daughters, only Martha, two years younger than Harriet, had married (in 1816, at age eighteen, with her mother's permission).[141] The other five remained under Catherine's roof: Mourning Ann, about nineteen; Mary Ann, about twenty-three; Minerva, about twenty-five; Harriet, thirty-five; and Margaret, about thirty-seven. The eldest two already had become dependents for life, for reasons never brought to light, and Minerva seemed about to follow suit. Local suitors, overlooking evidence of skill and industry (the medical books, the desks, the eight spinning wheels), may have been put off by the air of gentility (the silver spoons, the piano). It is also possible that one daughter, Harriet, already was showing symptoms of the torment that would lead her to depend on house servants and hired substitutes for daily care. In the years between 1831 and 1843, Miss Whitehead would display other forms of dependency that she and her relatives would attribute to trauma suffered in the uprising. This daughter never would leave home.

The death of the eldest Whitehead son added to Catherine's burdens. William Henry Whitehead died suddenly in December 1829 without having written a will, leaving behind a young widow and at least one small child. He had married a neighbor girl, Mary Barnes, in 1821, when he was about twenty-two and she about seventeen. Her father, Bailey Barnes, owned a farm of 238.5 acres immediately north of the Whitehead plantation; in 1820 Barnes held sixteen slaves, seven of whom were taxable.[142] There is no record of where William Henry and his wife lived; probably they were tenants in a small house on an outlying parcel of Catherine's land near the Francis Ridley plantation. There, William Henry may have farmed that parcel's 319 acres with a few slaves borrowed from his mother and father-in-law.[143] Around 1825 Mary Barnes Whitehead gave birth to a son, William Augustus; and at about the same time, her father moved away from the county, leaving her dependent on the Whiteheads for support if trouble developed.[144] By 1829 William Henry—at age thirty—still had no land of his own and very little personal property. He did pay tax on slaves during most of the years between 1821 and 1829, their numbers increasing from two to five, but he probably did not own all of those people.[145] In hard times, he had made a slow start.

Within days of William Henry's death, his survivors and friends began to settle his affairs. On 21 December 1829 the court at Jerusalem appointed a neighbor, William Judkins, to administer his estate, "the widow refusing."[146] Mary Barnes Whitehead, who could not write, had stepped aside. Three weeks later, on 15 January 1830, Mary borrowed $218.35 from Judkins's son, Jarratt W. Judkins, offering as collateral "one negro girl named Cynthia, one sow, Ten Barrels of corn, one bed and furniture, one Walnut Table, one loom and chest, one woolen wheel, warping bars and boxes, and all my Earthen & Glassware and Kitchen furniture." At the bottom of the deed formalizing this debt, Mary affixed her mark; William Henry's brother John, barely twenty-one years old (if that), but fast becoming the family's rock and anchor, signed as witness.[147] One month later, on 15 February, the court appointed Catherine Whitehead as guardian of her grandson, William Augustus.[148] That summer, by the time the local census marshal made his inquiries at Catherine's door, she appears to have taken into her house both her grandson and daughter-in-law.[149] There, possibly in early September 1830, nearly nine months after William Henry's death, the young widow apparently gave birth to another son.

One arrangement for William Henry's survivors proved less than satisfactory. Near the end of October 1830, Mary Barnes Whitehead asked the court to summon her mother-in-law, "guardian to the orphans [*plural*] of William H. Whitehead decd.," and require her "to shew cause why she should not be displaced as Guardian aforesaid."[150] In December, the court appointed John Whitehead as the replacement guardian of William Augustus, its minutes making no reference to the initial appointee or to a second, younger orphan.[151] At that point, Mary and little William Augustus appear to have moved out of the Whitehead house.[152] Later evidence would indicate that the second grandson remained under Catherine's care, at least occasionally. The morning of 22 August 1831 would find an infant grandson there, along with the grandmother, the five aunts, and the uncle—a household of spinsters under the protection of a Methodist minister with access, perhaps, to one old shotgun.

The Whiteheads lived with no apparent fear for their safety, though they were outnumbered by their slaves twenty-seven to eight (counting the younger grandson), or by more than three to one. If Turner's men followed the order of attacks implicit in their plan, the Whitehead plantation would be the largest they would encounter to that point, the first with more than twenty-one slaves. Of the twelve male slaves present, six were boys under the age of ten: Gilbert, Curtis, Harrison, James, Lucy's child, and one other not identified. Two were as old as Catherine Whitehead herself: Hubbard (soon to become a family hero) and Wallace, both in their fifties. The remaining four, in their twenties or early thirties, would have been prime recruits: George, about thirty-five; Andrew, thirty-two; Tom, about twenty-five; and Jack, twenty-one.

Of the six mature male slaves, all but Jack had been present in 1815 when Catherine's husband died, and thus had lived under the Whiteheads for sixteen years or more; Jack, the youngest, may have been in the holding by 1820.[153] The reactions of these six on Monday morning, 22 August, would test the theory that country slaves on plantations of medium size were ready to rise on short notice. And since this attack would be the first against a household with no close ties to any of Nat Turner's men, it would produce the first evidence of motives beyond personal vengeance.

Four and a half miles north of the Whitehead plantation, by way of roads that passed through fields and woodlands of the Porter, Francis, and Edwards properties, stood the house of John Thomas ("Tom") Barrow, the twelfth target in chronological order. Barrow, scion of an old Southampton family, was about twenty-six years old, close in age to Nathaniel Francis.[154] In 1807 his grandfather, Capt. John Barrow, and father, Henry Barrow Sr., together owned eighteen taxable slaves and nearly 2,500 acres twelve miles west of Jerusalem. Henry Sr. also kept a store. The plantation lay at the western end of Barrow Road, which was named for the family in the eighteenth century.[155] In 1809 both grandfather and father died; their wills were recorded at the same court session. The grandfather departed first, before 16 September, leaving his four-year-old grandson John Thomas "one Negro Man Byrd, one Negro woman China, and one hundred pounds cash."[156] (Byrd was still living with the grandson twenty-two years later.) By December 1809 the father too had died, leaving instructions for only a portion of his estate and making no provision for his widow, Elizabeth (Turner) Barrow.[157] Henry's estate wound up in chancery court, where it remained unsettled and undivided for almost thirteen years. In early June of 1810, six months after becoming a widow, Elizabeth Barrow remarried, taking as her second husband a distant cousin, Newit Harris. Harris moved into the Barrow house and became both guardian and stepfather of Elizabeth's five children: Narcissa, Henry Jr., Richard, John Thomas, and Elizabeth Jr.[158]

Henry Barrow's estate was settled and divided finally in 1822 through friendly lawsuits initiated by the elder sister, Narcissa, and her first husband. After that husband died prematurely, Narcissa's second husband picked up the cause, surviving just long enough to see settlement. John Thomas, then about seventeen years of age, received 263 acres of his father's land and two slaves, Jacob and Amy, bringing his slaveholding to four.[159] In 1828 he began adding to his holdings of all kinds. By the time of the 1830 census, he held thirteen slaves altogether.[160] And by the spring of 1831, after a series of transactions with his surviving brothers and sister, he owned 516 acres, five taxable slaves, and five horses.[161] His patrimony had given him a good start.

Barrow also married well. By early 1828 he had taken as his wife Mary T. Vaughan, about twenty, daughter of the widow Rebecca Vaughan, whose house stood about six miles from the old Barrow plantation, near the eastern end of Barrow Road.[162] His bride's uncle and guardian, bachelor Henry B. Vaughan, was one of the wealthiest men in the county, the owner of Walnut Hill (eleven hundred acres and growing), master of twenty-one taxable slaves, and soon to be proprietor of the tavern in Jerusalem.[163] Mary Vaughan's sister, Martha Ann, had married the up-and-coming James W. Parker, who by 1824 had become—at age twenty-four—a magistrate of the county court and protégé of Congressman James Trezvant.[164] The gate to young Parker's plantation stood about two miles from the Vaughan house, toward Jerusalem, on the Cross Keys Road. The Barrow-Vaughan nuptials thus sealed an alliance of four powerful families from opposite ends of the main route to town: Barrow and Harris to the west, Vaughan and Parker to the east. Through that alliance, in turn, the four slaveholdings developed ties, starting when Mary T. Vaughan brought to her husband's farm two slaves from her mother's holding: Moses, about thirty-two years old in 1828, and Lucy, about seventeen. This pair, who may have become husband and wife, had been present in the Vaughan slaveholding when Mary's father died in 1816.[165] They maintained their connections in both the Vaughan and Parker quarters after 1828, and through the aging Byrd (the gift from Barrow's grandfather) they established relations with the Harris slaves. Events would prove, however, that Moses and Lucy felt no real attachment toward their new master, or his bride, or their families, or even toward Byrd.

By the spring of 1830 John T. Barrow had finished some new buildings at his farm, including a house for Mary and himself that stood less than a mile southeast of his stepfather's "mansion House" (as Newit Harris referred to the old Barrow house). The new buildings were assessed at $500 altogether, roughly half the value of those at the Turner and Whitehead plantations but about twice the value of buildings owned by the Travis, Francis, or Reese families.[166] Barrow's closest social ties appear to have been with his own brothers and new relatives—especially Mary's younger brothers George W. Vaughan (a foxhunter) and William A. Vaughan (known as Arthur).[167] By

September 1829, at about the time his house was completed, Barrow had joined the circle of borrowers and lenders around Cabin Pond, securing some debts for his brother Henry Jr., who owed more than $1,100 to various estates in the neighborhood. His co-securer was Salathiel Francis. As collateral, he and Salathiel accepted crops, furniture, and four slaves.[168] Unlike his two brothers, John T. managed to avoid significant debt, though by the summer of 1831 he did owe a local merchant, Gilbert M. Beale, $35.75, the seventh-largest balance among the fifty-six individual accounts in Beale's book, and certainly the largest owed by any of the Cabin Pond circle whose names appeared there: Barrow himself (listed as "Thomas"), John R. Williams, John W. Reese, John C. Turner, John W. Whitehead, Drewry ("Drury") Bittle, Jesse Porter (Richard's brother), Jarratt Judkins (and his father), Peter Edwards, and Howell Harris, the constable.[169]

Barrow's new house, though not a lavish affair, gave evidence that its occupants came from prosperous families. According to an inventory taken in 1832, it had a "Little room" (with a carpet worth $6 and best bed with curtains worth $45), where Mary and he must have slept; it also had a "large room," where they kept their second-best buffet (worth $8). These two rooms may have been above the main floor. There were andirons and shovels for two fireplaces, along with a single pair of tongs. Among other items of furniture, the house had four additional beds, another buffet (valued at $15), six Windsor chairs, two shuck-bottom chairs, curtains for six windows, two mirrors (one worth $4), and three walnut tables. The Barrows had five counterpanes, three tablecloths, two decanters, fifteen wine glasses (inexpensive), a China pitcher, eighteen deep blue plates (also inexpensive), eleven soup plates (the same), six large silver spoons, and five silver teaspoons (worth $23 altogether). They owned two gigs (including a double gig, valued at $50), three horses (Joe, worth $20; Jim, $40; and Grey, $60), and a yoke of steers.[170]

His personal possessions showed that Tom Barrow enjoyed having money and loved the pastimes of the country gentry: he had a fiddle, a backgammon set, fishing gear, a pair of goggles, a shotgun, a rifle, and one deer hide. He had two razors (one with a traveling case), a music box, three watches (one of gold, worth $60; one of silver, worth $40), a clock (worth $5), a valise, a desk, and an inkstand. He also owned a small collection of books, not itemized, worth less than $3.[171] His farm had begun to produce the conventional crops: corn, cotton, and fodder, but also peas, and no tobacco. It had the usual animals and fowl: thirty-seven hogs, thirteen head of cattle, thirty chickens, and six geese. In the tool shed were fifteen hoes of all kinds and seven plow frames. The inventory of 1832 recorded just eight slaves in Barrow's estate, down from thirteen counted in the 1830 census; those eight ranged in age from the superannuated Byrd to the four young children of Amy, now an adult. Neither Moses nor Lucy was named in the inventory, nor was a woman identified much later (by Drewry) as "Aunt" Easter.[172]

Apart from his few books, there was little in the inventory to suggest that Barrow was a reader or thinker. He may have traveled outside the county (the valise, the travel case for his razor), but he had not left home for any extended period of study or work. And yet, since he was a Barrow, he cannot have avoided the great question of the day. He must have heard about his father's cousin, David Barrow, the minister from Southampton who freed his slaves in 1784 and published a pamphlet (1798) calling on Baptists to end their involvement with slavery.[173] And he certainly knew that in 1828 his brother Richard had drawn up a deed of emancipation for a woman named Susan, one of Richard's last remaining slaves.[174]

The episode involving Susan's liberation sheds light on the Barrow brothers. Richard, at age twenty-seven, must have sensed death approaching. As a widower with an infant son, he needed help, so apparently he struck a bargain with this woman. "I Richard Barrow of Southampton County," he declared on 28 October 1828, "for and in consideration of the fidelity and good conduct of my negro woman slave named Susan otherwise called Sukey have manumitted emancipated and set free her the said negro woman slave and do by these presents manumit, emancipate and set her free." To this declaration he added a modifying clause, "reserving to myself the right of her services during our joint lives or so long as I shall live at the expiration of which said time I hereby declare her the said Susan to be entirely liberated from slavery and entitled to all the rights and privileges of a free person with which it is in my power to vest her." He closed with a description: "She the said Susan hereby liberated emancipated & manumitted is a woman of a light yellowish complexion about five or six feet high and about thirty or forty years of age."[175] Seven months later Richard was dead.[176]

Six months after that, John Thomas Barrow, the youngest brother (at twenty-four), wrote his will, cautioned perhaps by Richard's early demise. His last recorded words filled just three lines in the will book. They suited him: "I give to my wife Mary T. Barrow my land Negroes and property of Every description to do what she pleases with after paying my debts except two guns I give to Edwin Harris my half brother and my rifle to James

Turner my nephew." To the left of his signature, at the bottom, Mary T. Barrow and her brother George W. Vaughan signed as witnesses. Of the three signers, Mary alone was still alive when the will was recorded two and a half years later.[177]

All eight of the Barrow slaves who survived the uprising (Moses and Lucy would be executed) would descend as outright gifts to the young widow, who also inherited her husband's house and 521 acres. In the spring of 1831, Barrow's five taxable slaves had accounted for nearly a third (29.8 percent) of his total tax bill; in 1832, his eight surviving slaves would represent nearly half (45.9 percent) of his personal estate.[178] Though his holding was modest, its growth indicated the direction of his thinking. The attack on his farm, dictated only in part by its location and assets, would make a point about slave keeping.

The final objective within the four-mile radius was to be the former Barrow plantation, now the home of Newit Harris. The mansion house stood three-quarters of a mile from the stepson's farm, requiring a sharp, northwest turn, like the upper half of the letter *Z*, away from Jerusalem. Harris, now about fifty-nine, had been master of the household there since 1810, when he married the widow Barrow.[179] By 1831, all five of his stepchildren had departed, in one way or another. He had approved the relatively early marriages of Narcissa in 1817 (at age eighteen), Richard in 1822 (at about twenty), Henry in 1826 (at twenty-three), and John Thomas in 1827 or 1828 (at twenty-two or twenty-three). The fifth Barrow child, Elizabeth Jr., had died by 1820. Harris's first child with Elizabeth Sr., their daughter Charlotte, had married—with his permission—in 1829, in the Methodist Episcopal Church, at age eighteen. In August 1831 there remained in the household three Harris children: Edwin (age sixteen, who would inherit his half-brother's guns), Polly (fourteen), and Newit Jr., an infant.[180] The Harrises also had a housekeeper, identified in 1840 as Mary Weathers; she or someone like her was present in 1830 as well.[181] In the census of 1830, Harris was listed with forty-nine slaves, nearly twice the number in Catherine Whitehead's quarter. Twenty of the forty-nine were children under age ten (eight boys, twelve girls). Twenty-six were males, of whom eleven were between the ages of ten and twenty-six.[182] Only Peter Edwards held a larger number of males (twelve) in that prime recruitment category.

Newit Harris was born around 1772, at about the same time as Piety Reese and Catherine Whitehead. He was the eldest child of Nathan Harris, who in 1782 owned 560 acres in St. Luke's Parish, and Mary (Turner) Harris, a first cousin of Benjamin Turner I.[183] Newit Harris, therefore, was a second cousin of Benjamin Turner II (as was his wife); he may have remembered the day Nat Turner was born. Nathan Harris, Newit's father, died in 1785, when Newit was thirteen, leaving a widow, four sons, two daughters, and a child unborn, all remembered in a will. Newit was to inherit an equal share of slaves when he reached twenty-one; at his mother's death (which occurred in 1805 or 1806), he was to have the home farm.[184] Gradually, between 1793 and 1806, he gathered up the portions of his patrimony. In 1810, just before he married Elizabeth Barrow, he held 408 acres and ten taxable slaves, placing him in the wealthiest quarter of the 317 core taxpayers in St. Luke's Parish that year.[185] Then, with the Barrow estate under his control, he became wealthy, even after his stepchildren claimed their inheritances. His own acreage increased nearly five times between 1810 and 1831, to 1,969 acres, and his slaveholding tripled in size to thirty-one taxable slaves. By 1831 he had become the tenth-richest resident of the parish, holding the eighth-largest accumulation of land and the seventh-largest number of taxable slaves (table 7).[186]

TABLE 7. Wealthiest residents, St. Luke's Parish, 1831

Rank	Taxpayer	Total tax (in $)	Acres	Taxable slaves	Slaves in 1830 Census
1	Thomas Ridley	58.73	6,370	79	145
2	William B. Goodwyn	35.72	3,396	61	63
3	George B. Cary	29.22	2,254	47	90
4	Thomas Newsome	26.91	2,770	42	82
5	Lewis Worrell	22.21	2,512	34	70
6	Samuel Blunt	20.16	1,518	36	69
7	Henry B. Vaughan	19.13	1,899	25	33
8	James Trezvant	18.58	1,433	29	48
9	John A. Persons	18.54	1,094	20	28
10	Newit Harris	17.86	1,969	31	49

Sources: St. Luke's Parish Land Book, 1831; St. Luke's Parish Personal Tax List, 1831; U.S. Census, 1830, Southampton County, manuscript returns.

Notes: Rankings are drawn from data on 272 core taxpayers (adult white residents who paid taxes on both land and personal property). Three nonresidents and one estate paid more tax than Harris in 1831: William Allen, of Surry County (6,448 acres, $59.21 total tax, 111 taxable slaves, 179 census slaves); Absalom P. Smith, of North Carolina (2,103 acres, $20.43 total tax, 26 taxable slaves, 50 census slaves); John D. Maclin, of Greensville County, who rented land from resident Louisa R. Fields (256 acres, $18.49 total tax, 21 taxable slaves, 30 census slaves); and the estate of Lewis Fort, 1,963 acres, $18.14 total tax, 18 taxable slaves, no census listing). The wealthiest resident taxpayer in the county was John Urquhart Sr., of Nottoway Parish (11,150 acres, $87.00 total tax, 85 taxable slaves, 147 census slaves). Thomas Ridley was the second-richest resident taxpayer in the county.

After 1828 and the marriage of his youngest stepson, Newit Harris became the patriarch of the combined Harris, Barrow, Vaughan, and Parker families, linked now by alliances like those that had joined the Turner, Francis, and Reese families. Since Harris had kinship ties also to the Turners, he represented (along with his wife) the one genealogical connection between the two clusters of alliances. His importance grew as death removed, one by one, every other head of family in these clusters. The necrology (with Harris-Barrow connections in italic type, Turner connections in roman) included the following:

— 1808, *Frederick Parker, age about forty-six, father of James W. Parker*;
— 1809, *Henry Barrow, age about thirty-five, father of John T. Barrow*;
— 1810, Benjamin Turner II, age about fifty, father of Samuel G. Turner;
— 1815, John Reese, age about fifty-five, father of Elizabeth (Reese Williamson) Turner II;
— 1815, Samuel Francis Sr., age about fifty-five, husband of Sarah (Powell) Francis;
— 1816, *Thomas Vaughan Jr., age about thirty-two, husband of Rebecca (Foster) Vaughan*;
— 1822, Samuel G. Turner, age about thirty-six, husband of Elizabeth (Reese Williamson) Turner II; and
— 1826, Joseph Reese Sr., age about fifty-six, husband of Piety (Vick) Reese.

From Harris's point of view, the most significant death was that of Henry Barrow, whose widow he married. After that, with each departure his importance grew. By the end of 1826 he was the only survivor of his generation, the last elder.[187]

He became an influence also in county affairs. In August 1810, one month after his marriage, he qualified for appointment by the governor as justice of the peace, or magistrate of the court, a position he held over the next eighteen years. For a time during the War of 1812, he served as a captain in the Eighth Regiment of the Virginia militia, accompanied (according to one later account) by his slave Aaron, who acted as body servant. Harris probably served during the second half of 1814; he resigned his militia appointment in 1815. He extended his influence in the county, in part by loaning small sums of money in local credit exchanges, but chiefly by administering and appraising estates.[188] His prominence induced neighbors to name him as an executor and brought him frequent appointments to estate committees, including those for some of the wealthiest decedents in the parish. Harris helped settle the estates of Henry Barrow (his wife's first husband, 1810), Samuel Francis Sr. (Nathaniel's father, 1815), John Whitehead (Catherine's husband, 1815), William Whitehead II (Catherine's brother who attempted to free his slaves by will, 1816), William Francis (Nathaniel's brother, 1819), Edmund Turner Jr. (first husband of Harris's stepdaughter Narcissa, 1821), Francis Ridley and Stith Nicholson (the third-richest and sixth-richest residents of the parish, respectively, 1822 and 1826), and Benjamin Blunt Jr. (from whose estate John W. Reese purchased his land, 1827).[189] By 1831 Harris knew more than anyone about the financial affairs of his neighbors.

Harris devoted himself to personal business between 1821 and 1831, refusing in 1823 to be nominated for sheriff.[190] He added a thousand acres and eleven parcels of land to the west, south, and east of his mansion farm, and he began to create two additional, outlying properties, which he called his Flat Swamp and Lochhead's plantations, each eventually having its own house, furniture, and complement of livestock (including horses) and farm implements.[191] His slaveholding grew between 1820 and 1830 from twenty-two slaves to forty-nine, with most of the increase coming probably through natural reproduction, as indicated by the twenty slave children born in his holding after 1820. Four of his slaves were females between twenty-four and thirty-six, and as many as six other females may have entered or just passed beyond their prime reproductive years during that decade. He held a vigorous population.[192] In 1831, slaves accounted for 43.4 percent of his total tax bill (and 84.7 percent of his taxable personal property), including land and buildings.

His mansion house was the largest dwelling between Cabin Pond and Jerusalem. According to inventories taken by Peter Edwards in 1838 and Nathaniel Francis in 1840, the house had at least nine rooms and perhaps two full floors. There were andirons for four fireplaces. Upstairs, Edwards described a "hall room," with two or more beds, and a "small room" used for storage. Also upstairs, apparently, were a large closet and an area called the "potion room," which contained a bed and an old buffet. Edwards mentioned two other rooms specifically, both apparently downstairs: a "chamber," with a feather bed in which presumably the Harrises slept, and a "cook room," or kitchen. Francis mentioned a parlor, and there must have been a dining room and a large storage area or work room. Near the main house were a dairy (with north and south rooms), smokehouse, distillery, and other outbuildings.[193] In 1831 the parish tax commissioner placed the value of the mansion house and its complex at $1,500, nearly twice the value of buildings at Catherine Whitehead's home plantation ($800), and 50 percent more than those at the Samuel G. Turner homestead ($1,000).[194] Harris lived in a landmark.

In 1838 the house had eight beds, seven of which were feather beds; Mrs. Harris, in her 1840 will, referred to a "curtain bed."[195] There were two looking glasses, fifteen silver spoons, twenty-five chairs (fourteen Windsor and eleven others of walnut), six tables (two of walnut), a sideboard, a desk and desk clock, books (not itemized or assigned a precise value), and a bookcase. Edwards counted just two spinning wheels in the mansion house (compared to three at Flat Swamp), two flax wheels, and one loom; he found three guns (one an old shotgun). Near the books, Edwards found two unusual items, worth $5 for the pair: maps of the United States (with key).[196]

Harris owned a barouche, the most valuable carriage in the neighborhood, worth $225—more than twice the value of the Whitehead piano. At the three locations together he owned at least seventy hoes, eight saws, twenty-nine axes, and five barshare plows; and there were six carts, a wagon, and two old gigs, in addition to the barouche. He had not one but three cotton gins, two at the mansion farm worth about $20 each and one at Flat Swamp worth $50—the most valuable gin around. He grew the conventional crops of cotton (his most important), corn, and fodder, just as his neighbors did, but on a larger scale. He had 383 hogs in 1838, an enormous number compared to his neighbors' herds (almost three times the number at Catherine Whitehead's plantation). He had the most valuable stills and the most extensive store of distilled products, including one barrel of peach brandy and seven barrels of seven-year-old brandy, the latter worth $212.62. Harris had fifteen horses in 1831, and three from his stable in 1838—Robin, Red Bird, and Sally Hornet—were appraised at $75 each, equal in value to Mrs. Whitehead's colt Archie. Altogether, his horses were worth $775, accounting for about 15 percent of his personal estate excluding slaves.[197] He bore all the marks of a planter.

At every point in his adult life, Newit Harris had followed custom, accepting slaves as patrimony, taking advantage of their labor and increase, and distributing the gains as patrimony to his children and stepchildren. Individual acts of emancipation apparently did not move him: he betrayed no agreement with the manumissions ordered by his second cousin Henry Turner in 1791 (when Harris was nearly twenty years old) or with his stepson

Richard's freeing of Susan in 1828. Neither did the minor disorders that came to the attention of the court appear to worry him—neither the manslaughter of a slave in 1815, for which his own man Tom received thirty-nine lashes (on the bare back) and a burn (on the hand), nor the murders in 1821 at the Powell farm.[198] Infirm and outnumbered by his slaves, Harris remained resolute, predictable, and audacious. His influence must have dampened any thoughts of nonconformity in his family or among his neighbors, making all the more remarkable his stepson Richard's dying spark.

The attack on Harris would draw attention to a prevailing complacency in the parish, a frame of mind Gray later exhibited in harking back to the days before the uprising, a time when "every thing upon the surface of society wore a calm and peaceful aspect," as he put it, "whilst not one note of preparation was heard to warn the devoted inhabitants of woe and death."[199] Parish tax records document the complacency. In 1821, 219 resident white adults (including Harris) paid taxes on both land and slaves in St. Luke's Parish. Of those 219 taxpayers, 100 were still alive in June 1831, and 101 had died. (The status of 18 is unknown.) Of the 100 who survived, 83 (including Harris) continued to pay the tax on slaves in the spring of 1831, and at least 6 others, though paying no such tax, continued to live in slaveholding households.[200] The remaining 11 survivors withdrew from slaveholding either because of retirement or through attrition among their slaves (transfers, sales, old age, or death); none recorded an act of emancipation. As a group, the survivors were keeping their slaves.[201]

Of the 101 who died in those ten years, just four attempted to free slaves, three successfully. Catherine Barrett, a widow and grandmother who lived not far from Cabin Pond, accounted for nine of the nineteen individuals freed in the parish between 1821 and 1831.[202] Mrs. Barrett freed three children by deed in 1827, placing them in the care of their uncle, Dempsey Cosby (a free black man), specifying that they be taken to Ohio and that they bear their given names of Sidney, Harriet, and Jonas and the surname Cosby.[203] Three years later, Mrs. Barrett gave her remaining six slaves their freedom. "My will and desire is that at my death all my Black people should be free," she said in her will on 4 November 1830, "and named as follows, Dred, Venus, Peter, Miles, Jenny, and young Dread with all their increase if any."[204] All six took her surname when they registered as free blacks on 3 March 1831, nineteen days after the eclipse.[205] The idea of emancipation, always present in about half the population, flared briefly in the other half, now and then, under certain conditions.[206]

Of the ninety-eight decedents who freed no one, more than half (fifty-seven) wrote wills, which means they had had time to consider their legacies. They left instructions concerning slaves to be hired out, divided among heirs, sold (with proceeds divided or applied to debts), or given to enhance prospects of marriage. Most decedents leaving widows or minor children thought of their slaveholdings as sources of support and security for survivors, a form of insurance against risk in a setting of high mortality.[207] Among slaveholders high and low, that idea was fixed and prevailing.

At Cabin Pond a majority of the seven conspirators apparently accepted the view that isolated murders or assassinations—the solitary removal of Joseph Travis, for example, or Newit Harris—would make no impression. Six of the seven agreed to take part in a campaign planned to take them (whether all six knew it or not) across the parish to Jerusalem and have them introduce rebellion on a scale that might have been attempted once around Richmond, but which few had imagined deep in the Virginia countryside.[208] By the time the insurgents reached the Harris plantation, their leader expected to have (and in fact would have) more men in arms than anyone in Virginia had seen since the War of 1812, and of a kind no one there had seen since the Revolution. The image alone would serve a purpose.

Toward the Town

They show a great desire to cross the river.
—Witness near Jerusalem, letter, *Richmond Compiler*

From the gate at the Harris plantation, Turner intended to ride one mile northeast along a winding section of present-day Pinopolis Road and then strike eastward on Barrow Road, six and a half miles across the middle of the parish. At the end of Barrow Road, his men would bear left, or northeast, on the road from Cross Keys, toward the town (map 3). Half a mile farther, and roughly fifteen miles by road from the Travis house, they would arrive at James W. Parker's gate, almost within sight of Jerusalem.

Turner had planned to attack at least one house along this section of the route, and perhaps all five of those eventually visited. If he had planned all five stops—and each was clearly deliberate—then the original number of targets was eighteen.[1] He would continue to single out households with ties to slaveholding (though not all of these) and whose residents were familiar to individuals in his company; but he would change tactics, keeping his force together now, no longer sending out detachments to make multiple, simultaneous attacks. The track would be straighter, faster, less confusing. As the men moved away from Cabin Pond, they would have fewer personal scores to settle; gradually, the earliest motives would fall away. Then, by crossing the river with sixty men armed and mounted, he would make plain their purpose.

Waller and His Neighbors

They would stop first at Levi Waller's farmstead, a virtual hamlet about three miles east of the Harris plantation, on the north side of Barrow Road. Among the buildings there were the master's house, a blacksmith's shop, a wheelwright's shop or wood shop (where Waller made coffins for his neighbors), a distillery, other outbuildings, and four or five cabins. The complex was situated in an open, level area near the southern prong of Buckhorn

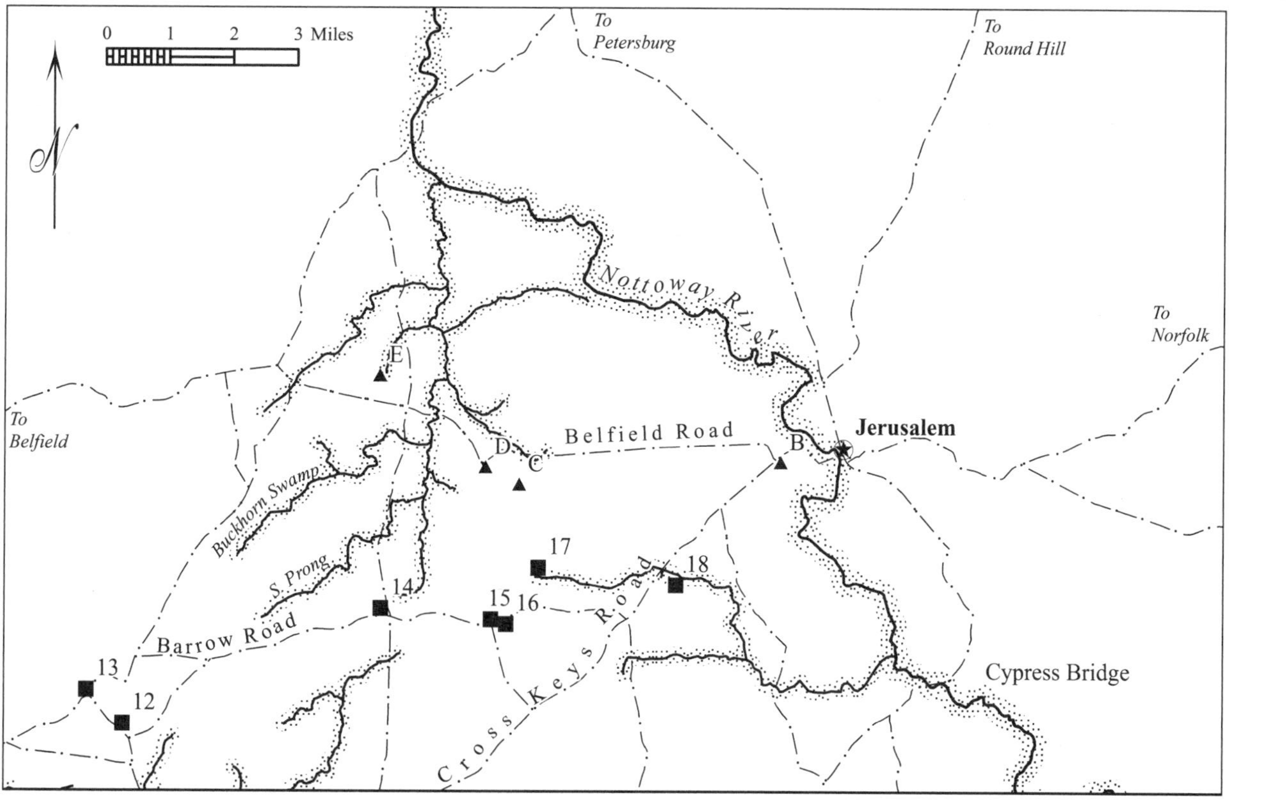

Map 3. Barrow Road neighborhood, 1831. Key: 12, John T. Barrow; 13, Newit Harris; 14, Levi Waller; 15, William Williams; 16, Jacob Williams and Caswell Worrell; 17, Rebecca Vaughan; 18, James W. Parker; B, James Trezvant; C, Henry B. Vaughan (Walnut Hill); D, Ridley's Buckhorn Quarter (conjectural); E, Samuel Blunt (Belmont)

Swamp.[2] A quarter mile away, but still on the property, stood a schoolhouse, where ten or so students, including some Waller children, were in attendance that August; some of the students were boarding with the Wallers.[3] In 1830 there were eighteen slaves in Waller's quarter, four of whom were males between the ages of twenty-four and thirty-six. One of the adult males, Alfred, worked alongside a white man in Waller's blacksmith shop, a progressive arrangement that Joseph Travis, among others, had yet to adopt. Waller's white household (the largest along the entire route to Jerusalem) included fourteen residents, five of whom were able-bodied males over the age of fifteen.[4] Anyone planning an assault on a settlement of that size must have considered the possibility of resistance.

Levi Waller had lived all of his fifty-two years around the northern fringe of the Cross Keys neighborhood. He was born in St. Luke's Parish around 1779, and like Peter Edwards, he began life in humble circumstances, his father having died by 1793 and his mother by 1804.[5] His name appeared in the land books for the first time in 1801, when he paid tax on 133.3 acres that probably constituted his patrimony.[6] Later that year he married Rebecca Jones, a minor, who died before the end of 1803.[7] From his paternal grandfather, Arthur Waller, who also died in 1803, Levi inherited four slaves (old Dick, Ben, Dave, and Jane), along with £20 in cash and a half share of the horses and plantation tools in the estate.[8] Early in 1804 he again married, again to a minor, and this time to advantage: his second wife, Martha, was the daughter of John Kindred, who owned 549 acres southeast of Cabin Pond. (Benjamin Barnes, the Methodist minister, performed the ceremony.)[9] Martha's father died the next year.[10] At that point, Waller must have accumulated a small surplus of cash drawn from three sources: his grandfather's estate, his first marriage settlement, and almost certainly from his second father-in-law. When John Kindred's executor sold 382.5 acres from his estate in 1805, it was Levi Waller who loaned almost a third of the price to the purchaser, Benjamin Turner II. This land became the Kindred tract, the patrimonial property of Samuel G. Turner and for fifteen years the home of Nat Turner. The bonds Waller accepted for the loan documented his earliest known association with the Turners.[11] Years later, he would recognize Nat Turner on sight.[12]

Waller had accumulated most of his property by 1821, his fortieth year. He owned 587 acres, exactly his holding ten years later. All through the 1820s, his buildings were valued at $1,000, equal in value to those of Elizabeth Turner II and $500 below those at the mansion farm of Newit Harris.[13] His slaveholding grew at a modest rate, from four taxable slaves in 1807, to seven in 1821, to ten in 1831.[14] Among the eighteen slaves of all ages at his farm in 1830, three were old enough to have been inherited from his grandfather in 1803.[15] None of Waller's slaves were among the conspirators, though two did become involved in the rising: Davy, perhaps a descendant of his grandfather's Dave, and Alfred, the blacksmith. By 1831 Waller had risen into the wealthiest quarter of the 272 resident white adults who paid taxes on land and slaves in the parish. Slaves represented 41.7 percent of his taxable wealth.

While he was neither rich nor influential, he had become comfortable: in 1831 he owned five horses, at least two guns, and four slaves who would have been seen as likely recruits.[16] An inventory taken at his farm in 1847 showed that his farm produced the customary hogs, fodder, corn, and cotton (he owned a gin worth $20). He owned the usual assortment of implements used by field hands, tools for his shops, and equipment for making cider and brandy. In the house, he had a two-part buffet, perhaps from his own wood shop (worth $31.50 including contents), and a sideboard; in one room of the house, the appraisers found a clock, two guns, a desk, and a collection of books (not itemized, but worth $21 altogether) rivaling in value those of Catherine Whitehead and Newit Harris. Other than these possessions, his rooms in 1847 were as plain as they must have been in 1831: he owned one looking glass (inexpensive), three tables (also inexpensive), fourteen chairs worth about 43 cents each, four others worth $5 altogether, and six beds (the best worth only $10). The inventory suggests that while Waller had not become one of the planter gentry (he never owned twenty slaves), he had prospered under the existing order.[17]

In twenty-seven years of marriage, Levi and Martha Waller (she was now about forty-five) had produced at least eight children who were alive in the year of the uprising. Their first child, born in 1804 or 1805, may have been the young woman of about twenty-six, never identified by name, who was living with them in August 1831. Their eldest son, Benjamin C. Waller, born in 1806, had married in 1827 and established his own household. Still present in 1831 were at least four younger sons, John K. (born about 1814), Levi C. (1815), Thomas (about 1818), and Peter (about 1820). And there were two very young children in 1831: Martha Jr., born in 1827, and a newborn daughter, described at the time as a nursing infant, who was born after the 1830 census.[18]

The presence of boarders made it difficult even at the time for outsiders to identify individuals in this large and complicated household. Four boys between the ages of five and ten were counted in the 1830 census but never identified by name; three of these may have been Waller offspring. All four apparently were attending the school in 1831, along with a fifth boy of about the same age, also never identified.[19] Two girls were present as students on 22 August 1831: Lucinda Jones, about fourteen, and her sister Clarinda, age twelve.[20] And, according to the census, two white men between forty and fifty years of age were living at the farm in 1830. One may have been a blacksmith. The other, though middle-aged, may have been the schoolmaster; in 1831 that post was filled by William Crocker.[21]

Waller's household was the last on Turner's list headed by a master whose history intersected his own, the last he certainly had singled out for attack. Later accounts of the assault (including Turner's own) indicate that he had targeted Waller before leaving the Harris plantation, perhaps even before leaving Cabin Pond. It is possible that he also had singled out each of the remaining four households his men would visit that afternoon, though the evidence in those cases is circumstantial. Two of the four were headed by members of the Williams family, and two by members of the intermarried Vaughan and Parker families.

The pattern of attacks along Barrow Road strengthens the case for premeditation. One mile east of the Waller farm, the insurgents would pass on their right the large farm of William H. Nicholson (767 acres, fourteen taxable slaves in 1831), whose house apparently stood well south of the road. They would not stop there. They would also pass without stopping at a cluster of four small properties—including, on their left, houses belonging to Mary Simmons (a widow between fifty and sixty years old) and Polly Johnson (a widow, probably between fifty and sixty), whose household apparently included Mills L. Gray (married, about twenty-five); and on their right, the house of Rebecca Knight (a widow between sixty and seventy), the only slaveholder (one slave) in this cluster of four, who shared her farm in 1830 with seven free black people (two women, four female children, and one young adult male).[22] Turner knew the residents of at least one of these houses; trial evidence later would indicate that he exempted them explicitly.[23]

Williams

A short distance east of the Johnson house and no more than six miles from Jerusalem, the men would arrive at three farms belonging to members of the Williams family—to Jacob Williams, to his nephew William Jr., and to Jacob's sister, Rhoda Worrell. The Williamses descended from people who had settled on Barrow Road in the eighteenth century.[24] In 1831 the first of their farms (heading toward the village), on the north side of the road, was occupied by William Jr., son of Jacob's brother Kinchen.[25] A quarter of a mile farther east and across the road to the south stood Jacob's house; and a short walk from there, but still on Jacob's property, near the road, stood his overseer's cabin, occupied by another nephew, Caswell Worrell (son of Jacob's sister). Rhoda Worrell, Caswell's mother, lived on her own plot of seventeen acres a short distance east of the cabin, but apparently well south of the road.[26] Of the four dwellings at these farms, the insurgents would ignore only Mrs. Worrell's.

The Williams attacks may have involved mere chance (women and children at home, nephews in the field, the uncle in distant woods measuring timber). No one in 1831 cited particular grievances against these families, who seem to have lived amicably with their neighbors, white and black.[27] They were indeed slaveholders, but on a small scale: their progenitor on Barrow Road in the 1780s died with no slaves in his estate.[28] In 1830 the three Williams holdings altogether amounted to just twelve slaves, half of whom belonged to Jacob.[29] Yet the pattern of attacks there and along the length of Barrow Road suggests they involved more than chance.

The original Williams settler, William Sr., owned 328 acres at this location in 1782 and may have built the house in which his son Jacob now lived.[30] That man died in 1783, leaving a young widow, Sarah, and four infants: daughter Rhoda ("Rhody") and sons Elisha, Jacob, and Kinchen, the youngest. In the will he wrote two months before he died, William Sr. divided his land into three roughly equal portions. To his widow he loaned the tract on which he had made his home, on the south side of Barrow Road; at her death or remarriage, this tract and its house were to be Jacob's—as indeed they were in 1831. The youngest son, Kinchen, was to inherit an adjacent tract, also on the south side of the road (and, William Sr. added, "also my Gun"). The eldest boy, Elisha, was to have the remaining land, farther south, on Blunt's Swamp (and also "my carpenters & Joyners tools"). To daughter Rhoda "& her heirs for ever," he left "One feather bed & furniture also 2 pewter dishes, & four plates."[31] Though he may have held a slave or two near the end of his life, neither he nor his executors mentioned them.

For the rest of her life, his widow, Sarah, maintained the farm as an undivided holding and kept her children close at hand. Like most of her neighbors, she was a Methodist, and so were her children, at least three of whom were married in that church.[32] The histories of her children can be told briefly.

Rhoda in 1800 married Joseph Worrell, who never owned land and who paid tax on a slave—a single slave—just three times in his life (in 1811, 1815, and 1822). In 1820, two years before Worrell died, he and Rhoda were maintaining a household with six children somewhere near the Williams homestead, on someone else's land.[33]

Kinchen, the youngest of the four children, married in 1804. He wandered farthest from home, selling his hundred-acre patrimony to brother Jacob in 1814, after settling on a small farm twenty miles west of Jerusalem. There, in 1820, Kinchen headed a household composed of his wife (the former Rebecca Ivy I), three boys, five girls, and one female slave.[34]

Elisha, the eldest son, retained a stake in his father's lands and then, just before he married in 1817, bought 145 acres of his own on the north side of Barrow Road, one mile west of his mother's house. There he settled with his wife, the former Elizabeth Newsum, a daughter of near neighbors; and there he remained until he died in 1829, childless.[35]

Jacob, the middle son, farmed his father's land and, as his father no doubt planned, shared the house with his mother until she died in 1827.[36]

By the summer of 1831 a third generation of Williams men had begun to take up land along Barrow Road. William Jr., son of the youngest son, Kinchen, took over his uncle Elisha's farm (west of the family homestead and across the road) as a legacy in 1830.[37] Young William was born between 1805 and 1810, probably at his parents' farm near the Sussex County line. During his boyhood, that farm had 118 acres; and though by 1831 it was still relatively small, it had nearly doubled in area to 219.5 acres. Its buildings, assessed at $100 in 1821, sheltered a household of eight children and one slave. William's father, who at no time before 1831 held more than two taxable slaves, could not have provided much in the way of patrimony.[38] Around 1819, Uncle Elisha, having no heirs of his own, apparently took this nephew into his household as a ward or apprentice.[39]

In 1821 Elisha and Elizabeth Williams drafted a deed promising that one day, out of love and affection for their nephew William Jr., they would give him their 145 acres and their three slaves, Jacob, Lydia, and Rosetta. Until they died, their property was to be held in trust by a neighbor, an arrangement that permitted Elisha "to make some provision" for young William, "and at the same time to retain a decent maintainancy [*sic*] for himself during his own life." Now in his forties, the uncle was to "occupy, enjoy, use, and receive the benefit of the said land and negroes" during his natural life; should the aunt survive her husband, she too would enjoy those benefits.[40] In these arrangements for a modest estate, there reappeared the familiar idea that land and slaves were security against old age and death. They were also endowments for the next generation.

Elisha died in 1829 (Elizabeth having predeceased him), leaving to his nephew, as promised, the tract on the north side of the road. Early in 1830, through the good offices of his uncle Jacob (the original trustee having died), the nephew took possession of the 145 acres and two slaves, Jacob and Rosetta (Lydia also having died).[41] Later that year William Jr. was listed in the census as head of a household with seven members, including himself (about twenty-five years old) and six others not named, but identifiable: his wife, the former Rebecca Ivy II (not yet twenty); a hired boy, Miles Johnson (not yet fifteen); and four slaves—Jacob (between thirty-six and fifty-five), Rosetta (over fifty-five), a female between ten and twenty-four, and a girl under ten.[42] By August 1831 a second hired boy, Miles Johnson's younger brother Henry, had joined the household.

The buildings at William's farm, though assessed at just $150, were worth more than those at his father's. And William now owned three horses, two saddles, a pistol (worth $8), and a shotgun ($2). Among his furnishings were a pine table (worth $1), four chairs, andirons for a single fireplace, one spinning wheel, a loom, six china plates, two beds with furnishings (one worth $10, the other $11), a pine bed frame, and a parcel of sheets and blankets. He owned a shaving kit, a boot-blacking kit, and two pairs of shoes, but no books. His entire stock of farm tools and household goods was worth less than $100.[43] But he had acquired new assets: land, accounting for more than a third of his taxable property, and slaves, accounting for more than half.[44] His uncle's gifts had placed William Jr. in what must have seemed a favorable position.

Jacob Williams, at the death of his older brother Elisha, became the patriarch of the family. He had lived all of his years (he was fifty-one in 1831) at his parents' farm, five miles southwest of Jerusalem. He had done well not through marriage, but by husbanding his patrimony and meeting his filial obligations. He did marry in 1826, at age forty-six; his bride was the former Nancy Pope, in her early thirties, daughter of John Pope, a farmer who lived a mile or so north of the Williams place.[45] The new couple made their home with Jacob's mother. Jacob did not gain materially through this alliance: John Pope died in 1828, leaving his entire estate (five taxable slaves and 155 acres) on loan to the widow Pope until her death, then as gifts in equal portions to his six children.[46] Also in 1828, having supported his mother through her old age, Jacob finally inherited—as his father's ancient will had prescribed—the dower property his mother had held for forty-four years: a small house, 219 acres, and four taxable slaves.[47] By August 1831 he was the father of three children, whose names never appeared in the public record.

In the spring of 1829 Jacob Williams recorded an improvement at his farm (the cabin, probably, set apart from the main house), which increased the value of his buildings from $150 to $200.[48] In August 1829, for $44.75, he and his wife sold to his sister Rhoda a plot of almost eighteen acres adjoining the eastern side of his house lot. There, before late summer in 1830, Rhoda built a small dwelling (never taxed) and established a household of three, including presumably a daughter and a son, but no slaves.[49] At about the same time, Jacob took into his household Rhoda's son Caswell, then eighteen or nineteen, much as Elisha had taken in William Jr., though without drafting a formal promissory document. In return, Caswell became Jacob's resident farmhand and overseer, the kind of position he had held the previous year under a distant cousin of the Reese family.[50] Jacob soon installed this nephew in the cabin a short walk from the master's house. At the end of summer in 1830, Caswell was living there with a young woman about his age, identified in accounts of the day only as Mrs. Caswell Worrell. A record of their union has not been found, suggesting they too may have married privately, in the manner of Joseph and Piety Reese.[51] By the end of that summer, Worrell had become the father of an infant child who, like the Williams infants, never was identified by sex or name.[52]

By 1831 Jacob Williams had increased his landholding to 613 acres, through inheritance of his patrimony and a series of land deals. His acreage, four times its size a decade earlier, ranked near the top fifth of landholdings in the parish.[53] He owned four horses, the same number he and his mother together had reported in 1821, and he had acquired a gig. He remained a slaveholder, though a minor one: in 1831 there were four taxable slaves at his farm, compared to five in 1821, when his mother was in charge.[54] In 1830 the census marshal counted six slaves in his household, compared to five in 1820.[55] The people he held in 1830 were identified by sex and age as follows:

— One female over fifty-five;
— One female between twenty-four and thirty-six;
— Two males between thirty-six and fifty-five;
— One male between twenty-four and thirty-six;
— One male between ten and twenty-four.

The youngest of these, a male, may have been too young to be taxed, and the oldest, a female too old. One of the two females must have been the cook,

Cynthia. And one of the three men (probably the one between twenty-four and thirty-six) must have been Nelson, soon to be suspected of betraying his master.

After 22 August, Jacob Williams and Caswell Worrell would conclude that Nelson had drawn the insurgents to their doors. Nelson's behavior in the days and hours before the attack would lead both uncle and nephew to conclude, upon reflection, that their man had known that the rising was in progress on Monday morning, that he had been waiting for the insurgents to arrive, and that he had tried to lure his master and overseer to their deaths. Underlying that deduction was the unstated certainty that Nelson and Turner knew each other on terms that would have allowed them to conspire together. Had the deduction proved true, the attacks on Williams and his nephews would have involved a wolf within the fold.

Later evidence in court would show that Nelson Williams could not have been among the conspirators and did not knowingly figure in planning the attacks where he lived, though Nat Turner may have intended to recruit him on the spot. Nor did any of the men who had met at Cabin Pond have connections—past, present, or familial—to Jacob Williams or his nephews. To the conspirators, Williams and his nephews were peripheral figures; there is no evidence that personal grievances prompted these attacks.[56] Turner must have planned them for reasons similar to those that had led him to single out the Whitehead plantation.

The motive, in other words, may have been the obvious one. William Williams Jr. clearly had set his course with regard to slavery. And while Jacob Williams had not gathered a large slaveholding, his position had become fixed: the total number of slaves at his farm had increased slowly over the years (four in 1810, six in 1830).[57] In 1831, when he paid tax on four slaves, his investment was still small enough to have made a change of course feasible. His most significant asset was land, which accounted for 51 percent of his total tax bill; slaves accounted for just 28 percent, the smallest portion among the seventeen slaveholders the insurgents would target or attack.[58] Yet Williams had shown no inclination to change. His entire life course—barely at its midpoint in 1831—suggests that he was not keeping his slaves merely because he was complacent, as Jefferson might have thought, but because he was hopeful of gains, as some have alleged of Jefferson, and could no longer imagine an alternative form of domestic economy.[59] Williams and Jefferson, at opposite ends of the social ladder, were sharers in a situation and a frame of mind.

Other, more tactical considerations also may have influenced the targeting of the Williams houses: each stood not far from the road, within striking distance of the town, and each afforded an opportunity to rehearse the long approach across the bridge into the town.

Vaughan

They would pass without stopping at the houses of Jacob Williams's sister (no slaves) and at least two near neighbors: Micajah ("Mike") Holleman (eight slaves), who lived on the north side of Barrow Road, and Sarah Carr (six slaves), who lived on the south side, just east of Jacob's farm.[60] But for Rebecca (Foster) Vaughan, whose killing would be described far and wide, there would be no exemption. Mrs. Vaughan lived just east of the Holleman farm. The location of her house, one-third of a mile north of the road and at the end of a long lane, might have provided her some security had Nat Turner determined not to stop there.[61]

Mrs. Vaughan was born about 1784 in the Barrow Road neighborhood and had spent all of her forty-seven years there.[62] She must have known Jacob Williams and Levi Waller from her childhood; and through her slaves and connections in the Vaughan family, she in turn was known to a number of people around Cabin Pond. In the 1780s and 1790s her grandfather, Moses Foster, had owned 450 acres near the Sussex County line, where he had farmed with half a dozen taxable slaves.[63] By the time Rebecca was born, her parents, Arthur and Martha Foster, had settled on land just west of her 1831 home. Most of their old farm belonged now to an estate and to Mike Holleman.[64] In 1810, near the end of her father's life, her parents had owned 453 acres and eighteen slaves, nine of whom were taxable.[65] Rebecca and her siblings, in other words, had followed a familiar path, becoming the third generation of Fosters after the Revolution to hold slaves. Widowed for fifteen years, she headed a household in 1831 that included her two sons, George (about twenty) and William Arthur (about sixteen); an orphaned niece, Ann Eliza Vaughan (about nineteen); and nine slaves.[66]

She had married in 1804. Her husband, Thomas Vaughan Jr., was one of six orphaned sons of William Vaughan (who died in 1794) and his wife, Ann (who died in 1803). Rebecca was a minor on her wedding day, her father giving permission for her to marry. Her groom, also a minor, married with permission from his guardian and uncle, Thomas Vaughan Sr. Three years later, in 1807, one of Rebecca's younger sisters, Martha N. Foster, married one of her husband's younger brothers, John T. Vaughan. Both ceremonies were conducted by Benjamin Barnes, the Methodist minister.[67] The Fosters and Vaughans thus were joined in a double alliance.

The ties between the two families proved vital to Rebecca Vaughan. She apparently began her married life at the farm of her husband's uncle Thomas, a near neighbor of her parents. The young couple may have spent two years at the uncle's farm under terms like those afforded the nephews in the Williams family, with Rebecca keeping house and Thomas Jr. overseeing the eight taxable slaves. They certainly were living with the uncle in the spring of 1805, when Thomas Jr. was taxed as a male member of his uncle's household.[68] In 1809, Uncle Thomas gave this nephew the section (estimated then at 250 acres) of his own plantation where Rebecca still lived in 1831.[69] There she had given birth to four children who survived infancy: Martha Ann (born in 1807), Mary Thomas (about 1808), George (about 1812), and William Arthur (about 1815).[70] In 1816 her husband died, at age thirty-two. Unlike his father, who foresaw his own early end, Thomas Jr. did not leave a will, though he could both read and write; death must have taken him by surprise.[71] Rebecca Vaughan thus became a widow in her early thirties, with four children between the ages of one and nine, and nothing more for support than the dower rights to her husband's property.

Unlike Catherine Whitehead and Sarah Francis (both widowed in 1815), Mrs. Vaughan did not assume the duties of settling her husband's affairs. She hired overseers in each of the first two years of her widowhood, and she apparently agreed at once, in December 1816, to have Henry B. Vaughan, her husband's youngest brother, administer the estate.[72] A bachelor for life, Henry at twenty-seven had yet to own a slave, an acre of land, or a house of his own. Since 1812 he had been living at the farm of his uncle Thomas, just as his brother and Rebecca had done a few years earlier.[73] In 1820, with Rebecca witnessing the deed, Henry bought the uncle's land, which he would call Walnut Hill. He thus became Rebecca's neighbor to the north; his gate opened on Belfield (also called "Crawford" or "Crafford's") Road, the northern route (parallel to Barrow Road) through the parish to the town of Belfield in Greensville County. That same year he became the guardian of Rebecca's children and assumed his role as head of the Vaughan family.[74]

In part because Mrs. Vaughan's husband left no debts, his estate was large enough to support a widow and four children. Rebecca would be permitted to occupy the farm's dwelling and land until her children came of age; at that point, she would have dower rights to a widow's third, or about eighty acres, and she could expect to have the house and outbuildings for life.[75] In 1821 those structures together had a tax value of $400, most of which must have been attributable to the house.[76] The plan of the house in 1816 would remain essentially unchanged over the next two centuries: four rooms, one and a half stories, and a foundation when completed of 18 by 32 feet, or a modest total of 1,152 square feet. Its southeastern front looked down the long, dusty lane toward Barrow Road. A high covered porch, at one time stretching nearly the full width of the structure, framed a central doorway leading into a hall. On each side of the hall were single rooms, each with a window in front and back, and each with a fireplace. The two chimneys, differing perceptibly in their placement, indicated that this house, like Samuel G. Turner's, had been built in sections at different times. The chimney at the left (or west) gable end stood outside the wall and rose to the peak of the roof; the one on the right stood inside the wall and pierced the front roof two feet from the east gable end. A kitchen, perhaps attached, may have stood to the rear. In the hall, a steep, curving stairway led immediately to the right, toward two sleeping rooms; upstairs there were three dormers in front (as in Belmont, the Blunt family home nearby), and two or three in back.[77]

The Vaughan house in 1816 had a full stock of furnishings, including four beds and a cradle, a dressing table and looking glass, twelve walnut chairs and six Windsor chairs, five tables (two of walnut), and a desk. There were andirons for two fireplaces, a loom, three spinning wheels, kitchen utensils, dinnerware in a buffet, five pewter plates, and six silver tablespoons (the only luxury items listed, worth $25 altogether). The family had a small parcel of books and two violins (with bows); one of the violins may have been the "fiddle" found later among the possessions of John T. Barrow, Mrs. Vaughan's future son-in-law. Thomas Vaughan had owned a good shotgun, a chaise, three carts, three horses and saddles, and two oxen. He had livestock (cattle, hogs, and sheep) in average numbers for a modest-sized farm, and he grew chiefly corn (by far his most valuable production). Altogether, his animals and material chattels were worth $1,063, or almost a quarter of his estate. His land, if valued at $5 an acre and surveyed at 250 acres, would have been worth $1,250, or another quarter of the estate. By far his most valuable property (appraised at $2,575 in 1817 and accounting for just over half of his net worth) was his slaveholding.[78] Upon this asset, chiefly, his widow and children were to fund their futures.

The appraisers listed the names of Vaughan's twelve slaves, along with brief descriptions and values for each: two women, Dilsy (or "Dilso") and

Rachel, worth $350 each; six girls, Clary, Charity, Nancy, Caroline, Lucy, and Silvy, worth between $75 and $250 each; one man, Moses, worth $400; and three boys, Sam, Davy, and Wright (or "Right"), worth between $75 and $250.[79] The court ordered eight of these to be held in common by the children; it assigned the remaining four (a widow's third) to Mrs. Vaughan as dower slaves: Rachel, Nancy, Moses, and Wright.[80] In fact, all twelve would remain with Mrs. Vaughan at least until 1822, when Martha Ann married; the whereabouts of all but one or two of these people can be traced through August of 1831. Names of six would appear in documents concerning the uprising, in which at least two—Lucy and Moses—would make plain their feelings toward the Vaughans and their relatives.

Mrs. Vaughan's involvement in slaveholding reached back twenty-seven years, to February 1804, when she was not quite twenty. In that month she inherited from her grandfather Foster a legacy of three female slaves, identified as Silvy (or "Sily," probably not the Silvy listed in 1816), Jenny ("Janny," or Jane), and Milly, all of whom she brought as dowry to her marriage in October of that year.[81] In 1811 she and her husband accepted another slave, Polly, as a gift to little Martha Ann (aged four) from the benevolent uncle, Thomas Vaughan Sr. Mrs. Vaughan must have played a role also in determining the assignments of her husband's slaves in 1817. And in 1820 she accepted three more gifts from Uncle Thomas on behalf of her three younger children: slave Betty for daughter Mary Thomas, Edmund for son George, and Tom for young William Arthur.[82] Again, in 1824, when James and Martha Ann Parker filed a friendly suit seeking distribution of the eight common slaves, Mrs. Vaughan must have had a hand in making the assignments. And sometime in late 1827 or early 1828, around the time daughter Mary Thomas married, she must have directed the transfer of Moses to her new son-in-law, scion of the Harris-Barrow families. In a final transaction, her brother-in-law Henry B. Vaughan (no doubt with her support) got permission from authorities in January 1830 to sell son George's slave Edmund, "it appearing to the Court that the said negro is of bad character."[83] Counting that sale, Mrs. Vaughan had played a role (receiving, witnessing, advising, approving) in conveying twenty-four individuals (by sale, gift, trade, distribution, loan, or hire), all in the interest of her family.

She appears not to have taken part in a single manumission, either as grantor or witness, though she certainly knew people who had freed slaves. She must have been aware that the uncle, Thomas Vaughan Sr., had gone through that process in 1806, signing a deed to "emancipate and set free two negroes, to wit, a negro man named Kit of the age of fifty years; also a negro Girl Fanny about nine years of age." In fact, Thomas Sr. had signed the deed in the clerk's office on 14 February 1806, possibly while Rebecca and her husband were living at his farm. He kept his motives to himself, saying only that he was acting "for divers good Causes me hereunto moving," but the form of the document required him to repeat certain operative words: "I do for my self, my heirs, executors and administrators," he had to say, "hereby emancipate and forever set free the aforesaid negroes, and I forever Quit Claim to all right which I have had or may hereafter have to the persons [of] the sd. negroes or any property they may hereafter have or acquire by any means whatever." He closed with the grantor's customary vow to defend "the right and title of the said negroes to their freedom free from the claim or claims of all, any, every person or persons whatsoever" (punctuation changed for clarity).[84] The purpose of the deed, if not the motive of the grantor, was clear.

The people Vaughan freed in 1806 were to be exceptions. He planned no general emancipation, a fact he made plain in giving Polly to Rebecca's daughter in 1811. Still, he executed the two manumissions. And while the girl Fanny vanished quickly from the record, Kit remained, a freed man known to every member of the Vaughan family. His name appeared (as "Kitt" Vaughan) in the personal property tax list for St. Luke's Parish in 1809, and in the county Register of Free Negroes in 1807, 1810, and 1814. As the years passed, officials entered his age as fifty-one, fifty-four, and sixty (making his birth year 1754 or 1756), his height as five feet seven or five feet eight inches, and his complexion as black. In 1807 and again in 1814, the registrar entered the name of Thomas Vaughan Sr. as his emancipator.[85]

Between the time of her husband's death and 1831, Rebecca Vaughan could not have freed anyone of her own volition, since she did not own a single slave outright.[86] The three females she had inherited from her grandfather in 1804 had either died or been transferred to other owners.[87] The initial division of her husband's slaveholding in 1817 had given her an interest for life in the four dower slaves, but those people were not hers to set free or to sell—at least not without the executor's approval, as in the case of the difficult Edmund.[88] In any event, her circumstances after January 1817 made it unlikely that she even considered manumission: at the beginning of her widowhood, slaves represented more than half of her assets and all of her workforce.

With Henry Vaughan's help, she succeeded in preserving much of her husband's estate. The number of slaves at the Vaughan farm declined by just one, from twelve in 1817 to eleven in August 1831, even after some slaves had been transferred to her new sons-in-law—Parker taking Davy and Silvy, and Barrow taking Charity, Lucy, and Moses.[89] She did relinquish the title to her husband's farm, but she retained its use, its size having been reduced only by a new survey in 1824, and then only by ten acres.[90] The house, though no longer hers legally, retained its value; and her personal property remained, though reduced somewhat in value: the four beds (but no cradle); five Windsor chairs (one less than in 1817) and eleven chairs of walnut (one less); books of greater value (but worth just $5); a trumpet (type not specified); three horses (including the sorrel colt of 1817, now mature); and similar herds of cattle and hogs and similar productions of corn and fodder, but much larger volumes of cider and brandy. Mrs. Vaughan continued to drive a fine gig (worth $45, compared to the $35 chaise in 1817), but by September 1831 the six silver tablespoons had disappeared and so had her husband's gun. Her son George may have lost the gun on his way to a foxhunt at John T. Barrow's, on 22 August. Someone else must have found the spoons.[91]

At her death in 1831, Mrs. Vaughan's dower and personal estate had a combined value of $2,347.02, which was more than enough to cover her obligations. She controlled nine dower slaves (worth a total of $1,575) named in her estate papers, though legally three of these belonged to her sons. Unlike her late husband, she had accumulated some debts: her liabilities totaled $644.46, one-sixth of which she owed to her principal creditor, her brother-in-law.[92] And since she owned no land, the nine slaves accounted for 92.5 percent of her household's net worth.

Her slaves were her fortune. They represented an accumulation of wealth as important as the work they performed. She could order them sold for cash (the executor and the court permitting) or hire them to neighbors for income. In time she could expect their value to increase, both through procreation and through market demand. In widowhood and old age she could draw upon this accumulation for income and for daily service, benefits sanctioned by the state. For material support, she need not depend on her children or the state, but could count on the required contributions—in lives and labor—of her slaves. For the sake of such benefits, she made slaveholding the basis of her domestic economy.[93]

The only uncertainty in this arrangement involved the behavior of certain individuals in her holding. But Mrs. Vaughan was no fool. She acted decisively when her son's slave Edmund revealed his "bad character." And if she could not rid herself of every individual who proved difficult, she could have one or two removed, as she appears to have done with Moses and perhaps Lucy, both sent to live under son-in-law Tom Barrow and both clearly disaffected by 1831.

Whenever there was trouble or whenever she needed assistance, Mrs. Vaughan could call upon her brother-in-law. As guardian, Henry B. Vaughan gave permission for his niece Martha Ann (at age fifteen) to marry James W. Parker in 1822.[94] He acted as counsel in *Parker v. Vaughan* in 1824; and to help settle that friendly litigation, he paid $800 to buy the widow's farm (newly surveyed at 240 acres) and distributed one-quarter of the proceeds to each niece and nephew.[95] At that point, he became Rebecca's landlord as well as her neighbor. As other relatives died, her dependence on Henry grew. Her grandfather and father had long been dead; her mother had died by the spring of 1822. Of her parents' six children, only Rebecca remained in Southampton in 1831. Her brothers all departed, one way or another: Nathaniel died in 1816, James Henry Collier Foster left the county in 1817, and Arthur Jr. disappeared from the record. Her sister Martha, the first wife of John T. Vaughan, was dead by 1818; and two other sisters, Lucy and Betty, disappeared from the record.[96] The ranks of her in-laws thinned as well. Her husband's parents had died before she married into the Vaughan family. Five of the parents' six sons had died by 1828: Howell in 1810, James in 1815, Maj. Thomas in 1816, William II around 1818, and John T. before 19 February 1828. Of the five deceased brothers, only John T. may have reached the age of forty.[97] With the death of John T. Vaughan, Henry (at thirty-eight) became the family elder, and Rebecca (at forty-three), its matriarch.

By taking Ann Eliza (her orphaned niece) into her home, Mrs. Vaughan renewed an old tie to the Cabin Pond neighborhood, where she and her husband once owned a parcel of fifty-six acres and where her niece had grown up. The Vaughans sold that parcel in 1816 to Ann Eliza's father, John T. Vaughan, the deed of sale noting that the property was bounded "by the lands formerly Henry Turner's deceased." At about the same time, John T. acquired three other adjoining parcels of land, thus piecing together a farm of 206 acres that also bordered the home farm of the Francis family.[98] By the spring of 1817, a year before his first wife died, John T. Vaughan had settled on this land with his family, including his daughter, then about five years old.[99] That was the spring Joseph and Piety Reese began renting the old Benjamin Turner II plantation, within sight of John T.'s house. Throughout Nat Turner's last five years under Samuel G. Turner, therefore, branches of the Vaughan, Reese, Francis, and Turner families (and their slaves) all were neighbors, and Ann Eliza had grown up among them.

The fortunes of Ann Eliza's father declined after 1820, the year he exposed the marital arrangements of Joseph and Piety Reese. In 1825 John T. Vaughan was humiliated and rebuked in his own right when the magistrates in Jerusalem determined (based on sources they did not reveal) that a poor child (named Rebecca) bound to him had been "miss treated." The court rescinded at once the child's indenture.[100] Other difficulties then became evident. The buildings at his farm never were worth more than $200, or half the value of those at Rebecca's farm.[101] By 1826 (about the time of Nat Turner's baptism and whipping) the number of John T.'s taxable slaves had dwindled to one, down from five in 1821.[102] In March 1826 he sold 137 acres (two-thirds of his farm) to Nathaniel Francis, leaving himself just sixty-nine acres.[103] He died intestate in the winter of 1827–28, at about the time Piety Reese and her sons returned to Cabin Pond. Upon his death, his second wife, Mary (formerly Newsom), took possession for life of his sixty-nine acres and one taxable slave, and Henry B. Vaughan of Walnut Hill became guardian for his two minor children, Ann Elizabeth and Charles.[104] Ann Eliza, at about the age of fifteen, was placed with her aunt Rebecca in the house on Barrow Road, where she was living in August 1831, a figure known around Cabin Pond from the days of her infancy. Her presence was a reminder of the need for property and patrimony, and of times and troubles past.[105]

Parker

To reach the bridge from the Vaughan house, Turner's men would retrace the lane, ride east a mile and a half to the end of Barrow Road, and then bear left, northeast, on the road from Cross Keys. In half a mile they would arrive at the gate of Mrs. Vaughan's son-in-law, James Williamson Parker, whose house stood out of sight to the east, beyond a broad field and some woods. Whether Turner planned to stop there, three miles from the courthouse, remains a question.

Parker had never lived near Cross Keys, but by 1831 his connections in that part of St. Luke's may have marked him. Born in 1800, he had grown up at his family's plantation in the northwest quarter of the parish, ten miles from Cabin Pond.[106] His father, Frederick Parker, died in 1808, leaving a widow, Temperance (nee Williamson), and three sons: James, the eldest, Solomon D., about five, and Joseph H., four. Frederick Parker described himself as in a "low state of health" when he wrote his will on 12 February 1808, about one week before he died. He instructed his executors to keep his estate "as it now is" until his eldest son turned twenty-one; then everything was to be divided equally among his widow and sons.[107] He ordered the executors not to appraise the estate, but a later listing of his personal possessions (with no monetary values attached) indicated significant wealth: forty-four slaves, eight feather beds, two desks, a cotton gin, eleven horses, andirons for three fireplaces, two guns, two wine glasses and a decanter, and a parcel of books, among many other possessions.[108] "My further desire," he added, thinking that his boys might find callings other than planting, "is that my Children be liberally educated out of my estate without touching any part or partacle of their estate individually."[109]

No record survives of the boys' education, but young James had talents that won attention even before he received his patrimony. Like Capt. Moore and Constable Harris, he could ride and handle a gun: the court paid him $2.34 in 1819 for patrolling.[110] And he could use his fists: the magistrates tried James in 1820 for taking part in an "affray" in the courthouse yard. To avoid jail, he had to post bond for $200 and find two men willing to put up additional security of $100 each. Two good friends came to his aid: Nathaniel Newsom, recently elected first scout of the local cavalry company, and Meriwether B. Brodnax, the future prosecuting attorney.[111] All through his fatherless youth, Parker enjoyed the assurance of knowing that a sizable patrimony awaited him. As late as 1820, at the age of twenty, he was still living in his mother's household, along with his two brothers and the family's forty-seven slaves.[112]

He was about to become a wealthy young man. In March 1822 he married Rebecca Vaughan's fifteen-year-old daughter Martha Ann, her uncle giving permission.[113] In November of that year, he and his bride filed their friendly lawsuit in chancery court against her siblings, seeking Martha Ann's share of her father's land and slaves.[114] Not quite one year later, in October 1823, James Parker filed a similar action against his own siblings and mother, seeking his quarter of his father's estate.[115] Both suits were settled on 21 June 1824. In the first, James and Martha Ann gained $190 in cash from the sale (to Henry B. Vaughan) of her father's land; they also acquired slaves Davy and Silvy. In the second, they got a good deal more.

The Parker estate was worth $20,952.35. It included 1,250 acres (worth $6,352), fifty-nine slaves ($12,570), and other personal property ($2,030.35). Slaves accounted for 60 percent of the total estate. Each of the four shares was worth just a quarter cent less than $5,238.09. James drew 325 acres of his father's land (with buildings worth $300) and sixteen slaves (worth $3,235, or 61.8 percent of his share).[116] At age twenty-four and in a single day, he had acquired a slaveholding almost large enough to place him in the South's planter class. On that same day, he took his seat as a magistrate of the county court.[117]

Parker's connections enhanced his prospects. In January 1825 his wife's uncle Henry handed him the plantation that would be his home for the next seven years: 739 acres on the Cross Keys road, three miles southwest of the courthouse. For this property, whose buildings alone were worth $450, Parker paid $1. In other words, he accepted nominal possession and, in return, freed Vaughan (the owner de facto) to pursue other interests at Walnut Hill and in the town.[118] In effect, Parker became a rich man's well-to-do tenant.

Within months he became the protégé of another influential man, Col. James Trezvant, seventeen years his senior and now his immediate neighbor two miles toward town.[119] Starting in 1815, Trezvant served as prosecuting attorney in Southampton, and beginning in 1816, as colonel of the county militia. In July 1825, shortly after Parker and his wife settled at their new home, Trezvant resigned those local positions to take a seat in Congress. In 1827, while still in Congress, he joined Parker on the county court, as did Thomas R. Gray.[120] Together, these three men entered (or reentered, in Trezvant's case) the circle of influence at the county seat, where events would find them in August 1831.

By the time of the 1830 census, Parker's household, in addition to his wife and three children, included twenty-three slaves. He had become a planter. Six of his slaves were males between the ages of ten and thirty-six, of whom at least three must have been prime candidates for recruitment by the insurgents.[121] In 1831 his thirteen taxable slaves represented almost half (47.6 percent) of his total tax bill. He owned seven horses. At age thirty-one he ranked—nominally, at least—among the wealthiest fifth of the 272 core taxpayers in the parish.[122] His course seemed set.

Combined, the six holdings that belonged to Parker, his brothers, and his in-laws formed a pool of 121 slaves in 1830. If theirs had been a single holding, it would have ranked fourth in size in the county, below those of William Allen (179 slaves), John Urquhart Sr. (147), and Thomas Ridley (145). By 1831, after nearly a decade of exchanges and transfers, the slaves in the Parker, Barrow, and Vaughan holdings had formed connections of their own. Moses and Lucy (transferred to the Barrows) would have known everyone, black or white, at Rebecca Vaughan's farm, where they had spent most of their lives. They would have known Edmund, sold for being troublesome in 1830. They also would have known at least three people at James W. Parker's plantation: Mrs. Parker (Martha Ann Vaughan), and Silvy and Davy (former slaves of Rebecca Vaughan). Through such connections, a significant number of individuals from these six holdings would be drawn into the events of 22 August: eleven would come before the court under suspicion of having taken part in the uprising; eight would be tried, three convicted, and two put to death.[123] Eight others would be summoned to testify for the prosecution, including Solomon Parker's girl Beck, whose statements would alarm the court.[124] Every adult in these slaveholdings must have known James W. Parker, and any of them recruited earlier in the day on 22 August might have wanted to stop at his gate.

If Parker's house figured in the original plan, it was the last on the list in St. Luke's Parish. The killing of Parker would have been the third political murder of the day, counting those planned for Howell Harris (the constable) and Newit Harris (the former magistrate). Parker's death would have removed every public official, past or present, living along the route to that point.[125] The attack would have fit the established pattern, making Parker one of ten targeted slaveholders whose households had ties of possession (in 1831 or in the past) to at least one individual riding with the insurgents. It would have tested Hark's theory ("*as they went on and killed the whites the blacks would join them*") of how the rising would proceed, at each stop gathering recruits who had connections down the road.[126]

That pattern would prevail in the Southampton rising because the route Turner had chosen for the first fifteen miles covered familiar ground.[127] If the insurgents had killed every white person at each of the eighteen households they targeted or visited through the Parker plantation, the dead would have numbered just over a hundred; in 1830 those households had 106 white residents (along with 298 slaves and 17 free blacks).[128] On a scale no greater than that, the killing of familiar people might have been dismissed as a mad, spontaneous settling of local grievances. Crossing the river would have established a different motive.

Jerusalem

After Parker's gate, the road from Cross Keys passed the fork with Belfield Road (on the left), descended into a marshy wetland half a mile wide, and traversed two small bridges before reaching the river bank.[129] There, heading a few degrees north of due east, it mounted a slight incline onto the planks of the bridge (map 4).

The new bridge, completed in 1824, spanned the Nottoway at a point where the channel was eight to ten feet deep and the stream surface about sixty yards wide—impossible to ford. It was a timber trestle bridge, much longer than the river's width at normal stage, with a deck probably of pine planks two inches thick.[130] It must have looked much like the next bridge downstream (five meandering miles south-southeast), the eight-spanned Cypress Bridge, which Drewry photographed at the end of the nineteenth century. Drewry also photographed the town bridge of 1900, looking across its narrow deck toward a horse and gig approaching at the far end from St. Luke's Parish.[131] It would be a long crossing. If the villagers were alerted, the insurgents would have to storm across, much as they would approach the houses along Barrow Road (but in files, not in ranks, owing to the narrowness of the deck).

At its western abutment the bridge stood on low land belonging to Col. Trezvant. At its eastern end it opened directly into the town, "immediately above the Jail," according to the bridge commissioners in 1824, "the road passing between the Jail and Samuel Nicholson's lot (where there is a space of fifty feet) to main street."[132] In 1831, the former Nicholson lot and house belonged to Mrs. Eliza W. Waddill (also Waddell), who bought the property in 1829 and apparently was renting it to her son-in-law, Theodore Trezvant, the storekeeper and postmaster.[133] On the original town plat of 1791, the Waddill property was designated as Lot 1; the town had twenty lots, each laid out to cover about half an acre.[134] Sixty yards into the town, the road from Cross Keys ended at a junction with Main Street, which (heading right, or southeast) passed alongside the public grounds, site of the jail, the 1803 courthouse, and the clerk's office (a brick repository housing nearly a century of records).[135] As recently as 1817 the court had overseen the construction of stocks and a whipping post on the public grounds.[136] Beyond the grounds, still on the right side of Main Street heading southeast, lay Lots 2 through 10.[137] Lot 5 and its house, at the southwest corner of Main and Cross Streets, belonged in 1831 to Thomas R. Gray, who recently had opened

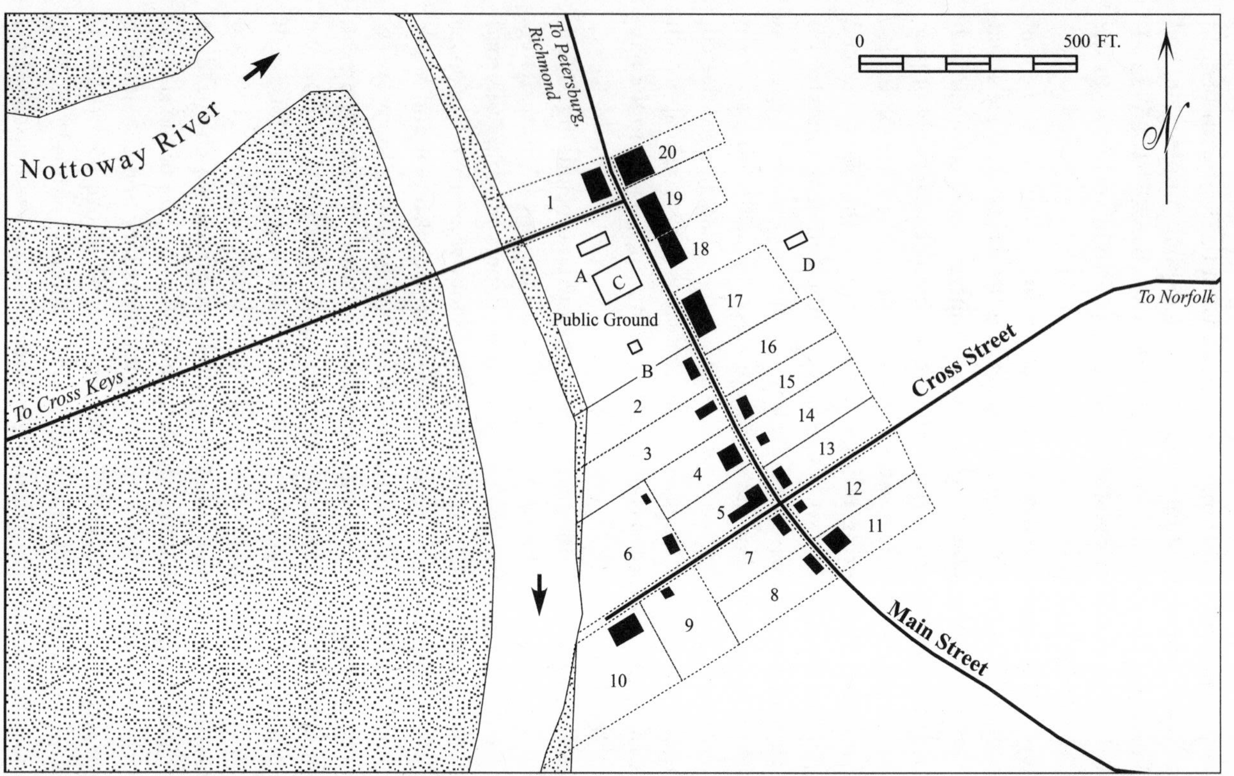

Map 4. Jerusalem, Virginia, 1831. Key: A, Jail; B, Clerk's Office; C, Courthouse; D, Stable; Lot 1, Theodore Trezvant's store; Lot 5, Thomas R. Gray's house and law office; Lot 15, James Rochelle's house; Lot 20, Vaughan's tavern (Henry B. Vaughan)

his law practice there.[138] This was the house once occupied by storekeeper David Vallance. Lots 11 through 20 lay on the opposite (or northeast) side of Main Street. The house of James Rochelle, the county clerk, stood on Lot 15, back toward the bridge from Gray's house. Rochelle owned six lots, five of which had buildings in 1831, making him the town's major landlord.[139] Two houses within the town limits had significant numbers of young adult male inhabitants in 1830, indicating the presence of boarders; the households of Nicholas F. Cox (or Cocke) and Albert Drewry, tavern keepers in 1830, had eight young men each.[140] On Lot 20, facing southwest toward Theodore Trezvant's house and the road from Cross Keys, stood the town's main tavern, a first-class inn under the proprietorship in 1831 of Henry B. Vaughan, Rebecca Vaughan's brother-in-law. The double house next door, situated on Lots 18 and 19, was used from time to time as part of the same establishment. Vaughan also was keeper of the jail opposite.[141]

In 1831 a Richmond newspaper editor, who referred to Jerusalem as a "village," estimated that it had "12 or 15 families in it," which was probably close to the actual number.[142] The census marshal in 1830 made no reference to the town or its bounds, but he did enter on a single page a loose cluster of fifteen names belonging to heads of households who almost certainly lived within its limits or just outside.[143] The names of at least four additional such residents appeared on other pages, which would have brought the total number of households in the greater community to nineteen.[144] In 1830 those households had 293 residents (103 whites, 8 free blacks, and 182 slaves), including slaves who lived at nearby plantations. Of the slaves, perhaps 140 lived permanently in or near the town.[145] The total population of Jerusalem in 1830 thus stood at about 251, making it the largest settlement in the county; the next largest, William Allen's slave quarter, had 191 inhabitants, of whom 179 were slaves.[146] Nat Turner might have found a large number of recruits among the town's slaves, about 33 of whom were males between the ages of seventeen and thirty-six.

The town in 1831 was less than a tenth the size of Richmond, the capital city, in 1800. No one in the village ever had ranked in importance with James Monroe, the governor in 1800, whom Gabriel had planned to hold hostage while demanding an end to slavery. Three Jerusalem residents, however, might have been prominent enough to attract attention: James Rochelle, James Trezvant, and Henry B. Vaughan.

Rochelle, the county clerk, was the richest man in town and, at forty-six, had become a village elder.[147] In addition to his six town lots, he owned a total of 1,435 acres in both parishes and had gained a reputation in the region as a breeder of fine horses.[148] In 1827 he made $800 worth of improvements on Lot 15 in the town, all of which probably went into his town house.[149] In 1830 he held forty-nine slaves, some of whom lived with him in town.[150] When he died in 1835, he had been clerk of the court for more than twenty years and had connections everywhere. During his tenure at the clerk's office, he had supervised the law studies of a number of deputy clerks, including James Gray (in 1813), son of former congressman Edwin Gray, and (in 1834–35) George H. Thomas Jr., Rochelle's nephew and a future Union Army general.[151] At the time of the uprising, Rochelle's brother, Clements, was both county sheriff and colonel of the militia.[152] And three years after the clerk's death, his connections still mattered: in 1838 his daughter Martha married John Tyler Jr., son of the future president.[153]

James Trezvant, the forty-eight-year-old congressman and magistrate, had developed a large plantation on the river, opposite the town, starting in 1817. His mansion stood a mile west-southwest of the courthouse, toward Parker's gate, but far back from the road to Cross Keys. In 1820 Trezvant completed $900 worth of improvements at this property, bringing the value of the buildings there to $1,900; his mansion was still standing in 1900.[154] Elected to Congress in 1824, Trezvant had just completed his third and final term in the U.S. House of Representatives.[155] According to the census of 1830, he held forty-eight slaves, all of whom lived near town.[156] In 1831 he owned 1,433 acres, twenty-nine taxable slaves, and nine horses.[157] Trezvant too had connections. Through his influence, no doubt, his brother Theodore had become the local postmaster in 1824.[158] And the congressman had recruited the town's new physician, his twenty-seven-year-old cousin from Savannah, Lewis Cruger Trezevant (who spelled the name with an extra *e*), a graduate of the medical college at the University of Pennsylvania.[159]

Henry B. Vaughan, the town's third eminent figure, had begun to develop his interests in Jerusalem only in 1830, when he bought the local tavern and became the innkeeper.[160] In 1830 he held thirty-three slaves of all ages.[161] In 1831 he owned 1,899 acres in the county; his largest single tract was his plantation at Walnut Hill, 585 acres on Belfield Road, three miles west of the courthouse. There, just north of his sister-in-law's residence, he kept twenty of his twenty-five taxable slaves and ten of his eleven horses. His other five taxable slaves and his other horse, assessed in Nottoway Parish in 1831, he apparently moved to town.[162]

The tavern had a history dating back thirty-five years under a succession of owners and proprietors.[163] It was a major local enterprise. An inventory drawn in 1826, when it occupied the large house on Lot 20 and the double house next door, shows that it had eight bedrooms on its second floor with more than enough beds (twenty-two, including one single) to accommodate overnight guests attending ordinary sessions of the court.[164] (An additional double bed was on the first floor, in a "passage" or hallway, perhaps between the two houses.) According to rates fixed by the court, lodging cost 12.5 cents a night.[165] The best room, number 3, had a fireplace (with andirons, bellows, shovel, and silver tongs), four beds, four carpets, six flag bottom chairs ("mahogany colored, with more gilt than usual"), a mahogany bureau, a dressing table with drawers and a mirror, a large mirror (mahogany) above the mantle, a folding table (mahogany), an inkstand, and a wafer box. It had a washstand (mahogany), washbowl, four chamber pots (one of Liverpool ware, with a top), a hairbrush and comb, a clothing brush, two pairs of slippers (deer leather), and two window curtains (calico). It also had a pair of large candlesticks (silver) with snuffers (silver), a sandbox and a spit box, five pitchers (two of Liverpool ware, two of blue Jasper, one of stone), a tea board, two decanters (cut glass), a dozen tumblers (cut glass), and a dozen wine glasses. The appointments in room 3 were such that when magistrate Robert Goodwin, the previous owner, turned the establishment over to a tenant-proprietor in 1826, he reserved that accommodation permanently for his own use when he came to town. Rooms 1, 2, and 6 offered comparable furnishings.

Downstairs, a "small front room" with a fireplace and eighteen black Windsor chairs served as a parlor. Near the parlor was a dining room, or "large room," with a fireplace, a set of mahogany dining tables, and twenty-two chairs. Here, guests could have dinner for 50 cents and "supper" or breakfast for 37.5 cents. A "back room," with a fireplace, round table, and twelve mahogany Windsor chairs, might have been suitable for gambling (but cards and dice were forbidden in taverns).[166] There was a well-equipped kitchen with a fireplace and five ovens, and near the kitchen was a "closet" for storing dinnerware and utensils. The bar, in a separate room, had ten pitchers, fifteen decanters, forty-two jugs, and three kegs. Per quart, wine cost $1.50; French brandy, $1; gin, 75 cents; toddy and apple brandy, each 50 cents; and "country" wine, 37.5 cents.

The entire establishment had andirons for eight fireplaces (four up and four down). It had 20 chamber pots (three of Liverpool ware, with tops),

84 chairs of all kinds, 151 glasses, 167 plates and dishes, 115 glasses and tumblers, 36 wine glasses, 80 cups, 70 saucers, 35 forks, 36 knives (with buck handles), 18 tablespoons (Britannia ware), and 24 teaspoons (also Britannia ware). At its tables, the tavern could have accommodated a fair-sized company of men.[167]

Nearby, behind Lot 17, stood a stable, where Vaughan must have kept his horse and those of his guests; for horse feed, he could charge 25 cents a day.[168] Tax records suggest that the town had as many as forty horses.[169] It also had a saddler, a milliner, and four resident attorneys, not counting the clerk and the congressman.[170] One of the attorneys, William C. Parker (not related to James Parker), aged thirty-nine, had distinguished himself in the War of 1812 as an army officer on the Canadian front.[171] The town had no public library and produced no newspaper of its own, but the lawyers had books: James Rochelle and T. R. Gray both kept libraries in their offices. Among the books on Gray's shelves in August 1831 were twenty-eight volumes on loan from Dr. Orris A. Browne, a magistrate and country doctor, chiefly law books (including four volumes of Hening and Munford's reports, and two of Hening's *Statutes at Large of Virginia*); Gray also had a volume of Shakespeare's plays. Those twenty-eight books alone were worth $73.50, almost as much as Catherine Whitehead's piano.[172]

At the northwest end of Main Street stood the Masonic Lodge (No. 34), and just beyond that, on the road to Petersburg, was the racetrack, maintained by the Jerusalem Jockey Club.[173] The club, formed in 1830, had attracted seventy-five members from six counties in Southside Virginia and North Carolina; virtually every male head of household in the town belonged, including the town's attorneys, all of whom could ride.[174] Apparently no scheduled stagecoaches passed through Jerusalem in 1831, but mail carriers from Richmond, Norfolk, and Raleigh stopped regularly at Theodore Trezvant's post office.[175]

What Nat Turner knew of Jerusalem he did not say. None of the town's principal figures (except perhaps Vaughan) knew him, and none could describe him from memory—not Gray, nor the Parkers, nor Rochelle, nor the Trezvants. The pokeberry juice map ("*descriptive of the county of Southampton*") might have revealed what Turner knew about the way to town, but that document, if it ever existed, quickly disappeared.[176] On horseback at an easy walk, the eighteen-mile trip from the Travis house took about three hours, so no one from Cross Keys went to town frequently. Still, Turner seems to have been familiar with the terrain. He had no difficulty plotting a course along the winding roads to Parker's gate, and he would make his way without hesitation to Cypress Bridge, below Jerusalem. From there, he knew the way to Buckhorn Quarter (on Belfield Road), one of the major slave quarters in the parish.

He may have come to town sometimes with Samuel G. Turner, who made several trips to the courthouse between 1815 and 1817 while administering the estate of Samuel Francis.[177] He could have waited outside, tended horses, and, like Moses Moore, observed. He may have accompanied Capt. Moore—before their falling out—when Moore served on juries (in 1823), administered estates (in 1824 and 1825), and appeared as a witness at the trial (in 1825) involving the saddle stolen from Salathiel Francis. (The defendant in that trial, a slave named Amos, was convicted and sentenced to be burned on the hand and given thirty lashes).[178] Or he might have been in Jerusalem as recently as 21 March 1831 (thirty-seven days after the eclipse), when his new master attended a meeting of the grand jury, though no one recalled Travis bringing along a slave.[179]

Authorities in 1831 did not press their sources concerning the extent of Turner's travels, though they did speculate. "Some allege that he had never left the vicinity of his master's dwelling," William C. Parker said, "whilst others think that he had even visited the Metropolis of the State in his character of Preacher and Prophet."[180] Gray scoffed at rumors of Turner "having been from home, many days at a time, preaching in Richmond, Petersburg, and Brunswick." "The truth is," he said, "I have never heard of his preaching any where."[181] Neither man mentioned trips to town. No one came forward who ever had seen Nat Turner there.

Both attorneys came to believe, however, that Turner had wanted to capture the town, a theory that began to form as early as Tuesday, 23 August, the second day of the uprising. A woman who lived five miles east of Jerusalem heard that day that the insurgents had attempted to "force their way" across Cary's Bridge, six miles upstream. "They show a great desire to cross the river," she observed.[182] By 31 August, Parker had concluded that capturing Jerusalem was "certainly their object had they considered themselves strong enough."[183] By mid-September, Gray was attributing the idea to Turner. "The seizure of Jerusalem, and the massacre of its inhabitants, was with him, a chief purpose, and seemed to be his *ultimatum*," he said. That success would have had little effect, he added, other than "supplying the band with arms, and ammunition."[184] Weeks later, Gray would quote the chief insurgent himself using similar words: "my object was to reach there as soon as possible," Turner says in the *Confessions*. "I had a great desire to get there to procure arms and ammunition."[185]

Jerusalem had no public arsenal, as Turner probably knew; in fact, complaints circulated that before the uprising the state of Virginia had withdrawn weapons from the county militia.[186] Residents did keep arms of their own, however. Gray had a gun, and so did Capt. Parker and Col. Trezvant.[187] The county clerk (the sheriff's brother) must have had weapons at his house, and so too James H. Sebrell (the sheriff's deputy). At the first word of trouble on 22 August, the town was able to send into St. Luke's Parish two companies of volunteers, all mounted and armed. Turner surely expected to find private stores of materiel in the town. There too his men might seize, if only for a time, a seat of law and authority, a place of trade, money, and comfort, a center of power and influence. One other consideration, widely understood but not discussed in print, must have made the town inviting: this county seat, unlike those around it (at Sussex Court House, Surry Court House, Isle of Wight Court House, Suffolk, Gatesville, Winton, Jackson, and Hicksford), would lend its captors an aura of allegorical significance.

The theory that Turner's strategy had involved the town would be put forth in some of the early trials at Jerusalem. The theory evolved slowly, however, and never gained complete acceptance. One of its key elements surfaced on 3 September in the thirdhand testimony of Thomas C. Jones. The town constable, while guarding prisoners in the jail, had heard the confession of Jack Reese; Jack had revealed Hark Moore's prediction at Cabin Pond ("*as they went on . . . the blacks would join them*"), with its clear implication that the insurgents had intended to move beyond familiar territory, beyond St. Luke's Parish.[188] Another element appeared the same day in a report by the editor of the *Richmond Constitutional Whig*, John Hampden Pleasants, fresh from the scene of the uprising, who doubted the feasibility of any insurrectionary effort to capture a town or territory. "A few lives they may indeed sacrifice," the editor conceded, referring to the tactic of massacre, "but possession of the country even for one week, is the most chimerical of notions."[189] But Pleasants did assume that a plan to control the countryside, chimerical or not, had existed. Two months later, at Turner's preliminary examination on 31 October, an almost-complete version of the theory emerged. Editors at the *Norfolk Herald* reported the prisoner's claim that he had intended to conquer the county ("*as the white people did in the revolution*").[190] And William C. Parker, who took part in the examination, heard from Turner's lips a version of the plan: "He says that indiscriminate massacre was not their intention after they obtained a foothold, and was resorted to in the first instance to strike terror and alarm. Women and children would afterwards have been spared, and men too who ceased to resist."[191] If Turner had been thinking in these extenuating terms, he must have intended to capture the town ("*a foothold*") and then move through the countryside, taking possession of territory (at least temporarily), gathering volunteers as he advanced, and, once terror had inhibited resistance, ending the policy of indiscriminate killing.[192] Crossing into Jerusalem would have signaled the existence of such a plan.

A campaign along these lines might have dampened speculation about fanaticism, old scores, and terror. A movement onto unfamiliar ground, beyond the scenes of personal grievance, might have established irrefutably the reason for the rising. Attacking only strangers who resisted might have demonstrated a purity of motive, while a policy of sparing the compliant might have softened the terror. Having learned of those intentions, only a skeptic, extenuating nothing, would have focused on what took place south and west of the river.

The Rising

She discerned a dust and wondered what it could mean.
—Dilsy Vaughan, recalling Rebecca Vaughan

Nat Turner told Gray that he and his men left the woods at "about two hours in the night," or at about ten o'clock Sunday night, 21 August, reckoning the hour by his senses, aided perhaps by a memory of the rising moon.[1] They had gathered during the day from points as distant as three miles northeast of Cabin Pond and two miles southwest: Turner and Hark Moore, from the nearby Travis farm; Jack Reese, from the plantation of Piety Reese and sons; Henry Porter, from Richard Porter's plantation; Will and Sam Francis, from the Nathaniel Francis farm; and Nelson Edwards, from the Peter Edwards plantation.[2] Since three o'clock that afternoon, Turner had been talking and giving instructions. He had heard Will Francis speak about his motives and Jack Reese raise his objections. The men had eaten Travis's pig, and all but Turner had drunk Richard Porter's brandy. The moon rose, nearly full, behind a line of trees at 5:53 P.M.; an hour later the sun set, and by half past seven twilight had ended.[3] Two hours later, in moonlight and under the cover of August crickets (cicadas quieting after dark), they started for the Travis house.[4]

Familiar Paths

They made their way three-quarters of a mile south along a familiar path, through brush and trees and across a field to the Travis yard, where they arrived at about quarter past ten.[5] There they found Austin, from Peter Edwards's quarter, waiting for them.[6] Moses Moore, the thirteen-year-old who belonged to Travis's stepson, first saw them apparently from the kitchen, behind the main house. He later said that his master's family had gone "abroad" on Sunday and had not returned "until it was dark." Undoubtedly they had heard a sermon by Sally Travis's uncle, George W. Powell, who besought his flock ("many that were afterwards murdered," Powell said) to "seek first the kingdom of God, and his righteousness, and all things else shall be added thereto."[7] Before retiring for the night, Travis had barred the doors; the house was quiet. Moses had not yet gone to bed when he noticed the presence of Jack, though he could not say exactly when Jack had arrived. He observed Jack sitting "with his head between his hands resting on his knees," complaining of being sick and wanting to go home. "Hark would not let him go," Moses said. As the boy went to sleep, he saw Jack in the kitchen; a few hours later (at about one in the morning), he awoke and saw Jack again, this time "in the yard sick."[8] Moses remained silent, watching.

At least three of the men carried weapons: Nat Turner, a hatchet; Hark, an ax; and Will, a broadax, the kind of implement once used in executions, this one no doubt having been used to fell trees at the Francis farm.[9] Hark, who had brought the pig to the fire, must have had a sharp knife. In the Travis kitchen and shop he could have found other knives, and in the tool shed at least two more axes.[10]

Between ten and one o'clock, all of the men except Nat Turner went to drink at Travis's cider press. When they returned, they must have wakened Moses, for it was he, along with Jack, who would give authorities the earliest evidence about the break-in at the Travis house—evidence consistent with the later account in *The Confessions of Nat Turner*. According to the *Confessions*, Hark, taking the initiative, stepped to the front door, and raised his ax. (He knew that Travis would have set the bar.) He paused, and the men conferred, realizing that forcible entry might rouse the neighborhood. (Salathiel Francis lived within earshot.) From the barn, Hark fetched a ladder (used in picking apples for the cider press, and, within the previous year, probably in siding and roofing the house), which he placed against the chimney at one end of the house. Nat Turner climbed up and, after "hoisting" the small window, stepped into the attic alone.[11]

He was familiar with the house. Two boys (Putnam Moore and Joel Westbrook, the apprentice) were sleeping that night in a feather bed apparently downstairs in the hall-parlor, while Joseph and Sally Travis lay in another feather bed in the master's chamber, their infant in a cradle nearby.[12] Turner came down the stairs, passed through his master's chamber (the only room darkened by curtains), and entered the hall-parlor, where he unbarred the door.[13] Then, according to the *Confessions*, he took the guns from their places (precluding Travis from gaining the upper hand) and stepped outside, once again in full view.[14] According to one later account, he then told his men "the work was now open to them."[15] At that point, at least one of the men demurred. "It was then observed that I must spill the first blood," Nat Turner recalled. "On which, armed with a hatchet, and accompanied by Will, I entered my master's chamber, it being dark, I could not give a death blow, the hatchet glanced from his head, he sprang from the bed and called his wife, it was his last word, Will laid him dead, with a blow of his axe, and Mrs. Travis shared the same fate, as she lay in bed."[16] The first four killings, he said, were "the work of a moment."[17] Thomas R. Gray, who viewed all five bodies there, believed each victim had been struck with a broadax. "One blow," he thought, "seems to have sufficed for two little boys, who were sleeping so close, that the same stroke nearly severed each neck."[18] Nat Turner, engaged in the master's chamber, apparently did not witness the boys' deaths, nor did he identify anyone responsible for them.

Outside, the men cleaned and loaded the family's firearms—"four guns that would shoot, and several old muskets," almost enough to go around—and saddled one or two horses.[19] Here Nat Turner may have appropriated the sword he was carrying when apprehended, in all likelihood the sword left behind by Capt. Moore. He then assembled the group at the barn, where they remained "some time," parading under the moon. "I formed them in a line as soldiers," he recalled, "and after carrying them through all the manoeuvres I was master of, marched them off to Mr. Salathul Francis', about six hundred yards distant."[20] During these exercises, according to one report, he assumed his first *nom de guerre*, "General Jackson." Hark became "Captain Moore."[21]

The addition of Austin Edwards brought the band's number to eight, and young Moses Moore, drafted to hold horses, made nine. Later, Moses would recall scenes he had witnessed along the route from positions near the horses, his testimony chiefly concerning other boys impressed to fill the ranks. Of the fifteen key slave witnesses who survived and testified, Moses would see more of the rising than anyone except Nat Turner and Hark Moore. It was Moses who would reveal the order of attacks and make it clear that, in starting, the band had proceeded "from Mr. Travis's to Salathiel Francis and Mrs. Reeses," a significant fact.[22] For the rest of the day, Moses would belong to the insurgents. He would obey orders, remain with the men through Parker's gate, and observe nearly every attack over the next thirteen hours.

At "some distance" from the Travis house, Turner said, along what is now White Meadow Road, the group paused and again conferred, one of the men having realized they had forgotten "a little infant sleeping in a cradle."[23] Of the four individuals present that night who later came to trial (Jack Reese, Hark Moore, Sam Francis, and Moses Moore), not one mentioned the pause, no doubt forgetting what no one wanted to remember. Turner alone mentioned it, in November, to Gray. He did not reveal who raised the matter, nor did he indicate what anyone said; but logic suggests that only the two who had entered the chamber could have known what they had left undone. One of the two, inhibited by scruple, must have wavered. The other, probably the stranger in the house, must have recounted and then insisted. No one objected. The *Confessions* has only this: "Henry and Will returned and killed it."[24] The description Gray wrote in September of the physical evidence he had observed on 23 August supports Turner's recollection: "a little infant with its head cut off," Gray wrote, "was forced to exchange its cradle for the fire place."[25] With that stroke, the insurgents yielded considerable moral advantage and put themselves at odds with bandits and rebels who, according to myth, kill only in self-defense or to avenge injustice, and who refrain from taking innocent life.[26]

The motive required no deep scrutiny. The killing of the infant had no bearing on the spread of warnings through the neighborhood and thus served no tactical purpose.[27] Sparing the child would not have slowed the march, as returning to the Travis house certainly did. The condition of the body (removed from the cradle, beheaded, and left in the fireplace) indicated that this was no accident and that the killer had not acted in rage. And while the deed may have served to initiate Henry Porter, neither Will nor Henry returned solely for that purpose. Nor did they intend merely to enforce a consistent policy, though that they certainly did. Primarily, they returned to leave a sign for those who later would enter the house, announcing that slaveholding was a capital crime that corrupted blood and for which there could be no plea of innocence. In time, after Turner gave his account of the incident, its purpose would be confirmed: to spread terror.

After the pause, the band moved a quarter of a mile farther south to the other side of the road, to the cabin of Salathiel Francis. They arrived at about quarter of four, when the moon would have been low on the southwest horizon but still casting shadows. Though all nine members of the party must have witnessed this second attack, the only account of it appeared in the *Confessions*.[28] Salathiel, the only white person in the household's "family," as Nat Turner called it, had barred his door for the night just as Travis had. Again, Will played a leading role, teamed this time with Sam, his fellow resident at the Francis quarter. They used an old ruse. "Sam and Will went to the door and knocked," Turner said. "Mr. Francis asked who was there, Sam replied it was him, and he had a letter for him, on which he got up and came to the door; they immediately seized him, and dragging him out a little from the door, he was dispatched by repeated blows on the head."[29] Salathiel's shotgun and horses were theirs for the taking, and one of his adult male slaves may have left with them. They did not recruit the man identified as Red Nelson, however; nor did they take Emery Evans, the free black man who had been living at Salathiel's farm that year.[30] The attackers departed at about 4:00 A.M.

They headed southwest, away from Jerusalem, to the Reese farm, one mile distant by straight line, the home plantation of Jack Reese, of Jack's sister (Hark's wife), and perhaps of Nat Turner's wife and child. The only account of this segment of the march does not indicate whether they kept to the roads or took a shorter path across Salathiel Francis's land, through woods and fields; Turner said only that they maintained "the most perfect silence."[31] They arrived just before the moon set (4:35 A.M.), or thirty minutes before morning twilight. Most of the party must have remained with the horses, quietly, at a distance. Turner did not say who went to the house, but he did know that they found the door unlocked.[32] Asleep inside were Piety Reese and her son William, Jack's eighteen-year-old master. The elder son, John W. Reese, was not in the house, having just left or not yet come home. "We entered," Turner said, according to the key account, "and murdered Mrs. Reese in her bed, while sleeping; her son awoke, but it was only to sleep the sleep of death, he had only time to say who is that, and he was no more."[33] Turner implicitly denied taking part in these killings.[34] Jack Reese, an unlikely killer, drew the suspicion of authorities, however, because he later was found wearing his master's shoes and socks, articles identified by the victim's cousin, Capt. Sampson C. Reese.[35] Other property taken by the band included some of the plantation's eight horses and perhaps a young man named Tom, who belonged to Piety Reese or one of her sons.[36] Here too they may have recruited Nathan Blunt, a man belonging to the estate of Benjamin Blunt Jr., previous owner of the Reese plantation.[37] (Later, Nathan would tell his captors that the blood on his breeches was cider.)[38] If others awakened during the attack, they made no attempt to alert the neighbors. When the band departed, they numbered at most twelve. Some were still on foot.

Changing direction again, they now headed east-southeast and, if they followed the most direct path, tracked the lower leg of the *Z*, or "zigzag," course that Gray would detect but never fully understand. They passed south of Salathiel Francis's cabin in early daylight and proceeded through the farms of Elizabeth (Coggin) Harris and Sarah (Turner) Newsom, attacking neither. Years later, Drewry heard that the white Harris household had slept undisturbed as the band passed, but that one of Mrs. Harris's slaves, Joe, joined them on condition that they spare his mistress. If that detail was true, it was Joe Harris, not the man who belonged to Salathiel Francis, who became the twelfth insurgent.[39]

A mile farther east, the men halted at the former Samuel G. Turner plantation, still occupied by Elizabeth Turner II. According to the confession, they arrived at "about sunrise, on Monday morning," or half past five.[40] Members of the household had started their daily routines. The overseer, Hartwell Peebles, had gone to the still, at the side of the lane leading to the house, where Henry Porter, Austin Edwards, and Sam Francis found him.[41] "Austin shot him," Nat Turner said (hunters, neighbors may have thought), "and the rest of us went to the house." On the porch near the front door they saw Mrs. Turner standing with—of all people—Sarah Newsom. As the men approached, "the family," Turner said, saw them coming, retreated, and shut the door. "Vain hope! Will, with one stroke of his axe, opened it, and we entered and found Mrs. Turner and Mrs. Newsome in the middle of a room, almost frightened to death. Will immediately killed Mrs. Turner, with one blow of his axe. I took Mrs. Newsome by the hand, and with the sword I had when I was apprehended, I struck her several blows over the head, but not being able to kill her, as the sword was dull. Will turning around and discovering it, despatched her also."[42] Will and his ax now had dispatched at least four of the seven dead. Only he and Nat Turner witnessed the killings inside this house; Moses, Jack, and the others apparently remained outside. Someone, perhaps Moses, did tell the prosecutor, Meriwether Brodnax, about an incident that took place outside the house, apparently after the two women had died. Brodnax documented the incident in a shorthand note, undated, written around the time of Hark's trial on 3 September: "Hark—Mrs. Newsome—shed tears—she the sister of his Master."[43] The note was ambiguous (Who shed tears? Who was watching?), but it documented the realization by Hark, or Mrs. Newsom, or both, that revolution is what it is.

A "general destruction" of property ensued, Turner told Gray, along with a search for money and ammunition.[44] Then, as if they were following a drill, the insurgents visited the slave quarter, a place familiar to Nat Turner, with as many as five residents who would have known him from his earliest days.[45] There the men found two willing recruits: Sam, in his twenties, and Jordan, about twenty-one. A third, Davy, also about twenty-one, had to be coerced. All three had lived at the Turner farm since 1818, when their mistress married Samuel G. Turner.[46] Moses Moore told the court that Davy (who either had ignored the gunfire at the still or had tried to hide) "took no part in murdering his mistress and family." The men forced Davy from his bed, Moses recalled, telling him that "if he did not join them he should die there," whereupon he "put on his clothes and went off with the insurgents."[47] The band now numbered fifteen, according to the *Confessions*, a figure confirmed by all other accounts; nine were mounted, six were on foot (appendix A).[48] Turner may have written most of their names on the list ("of a late date," Gray would report in September) found later and lost.[49]

A pattern had emerged, stemming from the decision to "commence at home," as Nat Turner would put it in the *Confessions*: the insurgents had attacked four households linked through their slaveholdings to Turner himself (since 1807) and to Hark Moore (since 1822). Eleven of the fifteen men in Mrs. Turner's yard were linked similarly to those four households, and a twelfth man, Nathan Blunt, appears to have been living at the plantation in the hands of the Reese family. Only three men in the yard—Henry Porter, Nelson Edwards, and Austin Edwards—had no such connections at the first four stops, and their home plantations lay just ahead.

Neighbors

In Elizabeth Turner's yard the men reassembled to hear assignments for the next two attacks, simultaneous assaults against people having no legal ties to anyone in the group. These would be the first attacks of their kind, the first to indicate motives beyond revenge, though each may have involved unforgotten grievances.

The six on foot separated and proceeded several hundred yards along a "by way," as Turner called it (a path or trail), to the house of Henry Bryant.[50] Hark Moore apparently led this detachment and took Jack Reese with him. Just one of these six was identified with certainty: Davy Turner, whose assignment was witnessed in the yard by Moses Moore and Nathan Blunt.[51] The main group, the nine on horseback, headed one mile east to the Whitehead plantation. Four of those nine were identified at the time: Nat Turner, Will Francis, Nathan Blunt, and Moses Moore (to hold horses).[52] The assignments of eight men—three on foot, five on horseback—never became known, in part because only one of the eight (Sam Francis) would survive and come to trial, and in part because no one in court ever asked Moses Moore about those particulars.

The detachment on foot killed all four members of the Bryant household: Henry Bryant; his wife, Elizabeth Balmer Bryant; their child (the second victim of infanticide, strictly defined); and Mrs. Bryant's mother, Mildred Balmer, longtime friend of Sarah Newsom and Elizabeth Harris. No one gave an account of what happened at the Bryant house or described evidence at the scene, which was discovered after a day or two; nor did anyone explain the motive for this attack.[53] It clearly was not random (a detachment was sent), nor did it fit the early pattern. Bryant's new land, 162 acres wedged between the Turner and Whitehead properties, had not made him a planter. Neither he nor his mother-in-law owned a slave in 1831. Their only known connection to any of the insurgents was the legal action they had joined in February demanding payment of the debts of John W. Reese, master of Edith, Tom, and Riddick.[54]

The main group, meanwhile, rode along White Meadow Road eastward toward the Whitehead plantation and approached the house on its lane, apparently from the north, at half past six. Harriet Whitehead, the second daughter, and at least one of her two younger sisters were still in their beds; their mother and Margaret, the eldest sister, must have been up and about, as were the house servants.[55] (Drewry's sources told him that Mrs. Whitehead was bathing a grandchild at the time.)[56] As the men rode up the lane, they saw Mrs. Whitehead's son Richard standing in the cotton patch near the fence. "We called him over into the lane," Nat Turner said.[57] Drewry heard that the men addressed the minister as "Dick" and that he complied.[58] "Will, the executioner, was near at hand with his fatal axe, to send him to an untimely grave," Turner said, according to Gray.[59] It must have been at this point that three of the Whiteheads' prime male field hands—Andrew, Jack, and Tom—fled.[60]

On reaching the house, Nat Turner saw a servant girl "run round the garden," fleeing; and mistaking her for a member of the white family, he said, he chased her down.[61] By the time he discovered his error, the attack at the house nearly had ended. "I returned to commence the work of death, but they whom I left, had not been idle; all the family were already murdered, but Mrs. Whitehead and her daughter Margaret. As I came round to the door I saw Will pulling Mrs. Whitehead out of the house, and at the step he nearly severed her head from her body, with his broad axe."[62] Turner, still carrying the sword he had used against Sarah Newsom, tracked Margaret to her hiding place at one end of the house. His was the only account of the incident: "Miss Margaret, when I discovered her, had concealed herself in the corner, formed by the projection of the cellar cap from the house; on my approach she fled, but was soon overtaken, and after repeated blows with a sword, I killed her by a blow on the head, with a fence rail."[63] He rejoined the band in the yard just as the detachment arrived from the Bryant house and reported.[64]

By chance, at that moment a pair of hunters appeared in the yard, carrying a raccoon. Hubbard, a house servant, gave the time as "about one hour by sun," or a short time after six thirty.[65] (Mrs. Whitehead owned a watch, but no clock.)[66] One of the hunters was Joe Turner, a thirty-year-old man belonging to John C. Turner (the surviving younger brother of Samuel G. Turner), whose old farmstead (now apparently rented to Trajan Doyel) lay a mile or so away. Joe was stopping to see his wife, a Whitehead slave.[67] There were other connections as well: Joe and Nat Turner had been born at about the same time and at the same place, the plantation of Benjamin Turner II.[68] The second hunter was another man named Nat, about thirty, who belonged to the estate of Edmund Turner, a distant cousin of Benjamin Turner II.[69] This young man, Nat Turner II, may have had a connection to Hark Moore: thirty years earlier, both apparently were born into the slaveholding of the distant cousin Edmund. And in 1830 Nat II had lived as a hired slave at the farm of John T. Barrow, brother of Edmund Turner's wife, Narcissa.[70] The hunters now found themselves conscripted as the sixteenth and seventeenth insurgents. Hubbard, watching from the house, thought Joe seemed "reluctant."[71] Nat Turner II apparently was not.

Again the men conferred and separated into two parties. A detachment of unknown size, led almost certainly by Hark, was to proceed northwest, probably on White Meadow Road and then along a byway toward the houses of Augustus F. ("Trajan") Doyel, presumed tenant of John C. Turner, and Howell Harris, the constable. Jack Reese and Joe Turner evidently were assigned to this detachment, along with Davy Turner.[72] The main group, under Nat Turner I, was to head north to the houses of Richard Porter and Nathaniel Francis, where the parties would reunite. Moses Moore and Nat Turner II certainly left with the main group, and so probably did Henry Porter, Will Francis, Sam Francis, Nelson Edwards, and Austin Edwards, whose masters lived at the next three stops. All of the insurgents were now mounted (though some may have been riding double), and more than half were carrying guns.[73] By a quarter past seven they had left the Whitehead place, taking no recruits (none) from the largest slaveholding on the route thus far.

Minutes later a neighbor, twenty-nine-year-old John R. ("Cherokee") Williams, arrived in the Whitehead yard. Williams (nicknamed for his long hair) kept a school and lived with his wife and infant in a tenant's house nearby. Having heard "cries" from the direction of the Whitehead house, he had come to investigate; his description of what he saw generated an early impression that the victims' wounds, inflicted with axes and blunt instruments, had resulted from deliberate mutilation. Williams found Mrs. Whitehead "butchered with an axe," and her son "with his head severed from his body." He stepped inside the house and saw "a young lady lying dead in the fire place of her chamber."[74] He left quickly for home, unaware that Harriet Whitehead had survived upstairs by "secreting herself between some beds," according to her later account, "whilst her sister and the entire remainder of the inmates of the house were murdered in a few feet of her."[75] George W. Powell, the minister from Northampton County, saw the bodies before they were moved. "I have been to sister Whitehead's, and beheld the most heart-rending scene that can be imagined," he reported. "They were killed in different places, where they were trying to escape."[76] Volunteers would find Mrs. Whitehead near the porch, Richard in the field, Margaret by the fence, and four in the house: daughters Minerva, Mary Ann, and Mourning Anne, and the grandson (the third victim of infanticide).[77] Shortly before nine o'clock, Jack and Andrew, two of the field hands who had fled, returned to the Whitehead yard and, as the prosecutor learned from Hubbard, "asked if the negroes were gone." "When they came up," the prosecutor understood Hubbard to say, "they were much grieved, neeled [*sic*] and prayed—but rode a horse off—whither he knows not."[78] They and half a dozen others like them from the neighborhood would spend the day wandering, ostensibly seeking but never finding the insurgents.

Warnings

The main group reached the Porter house, almost a mile and a half to the north, at about half past seven.[79] By then, Richard and Elizabeth Porter had gathered their white household (twelve members in 1830) and fled. "I understood there," Nat Turner recalled in the *Confessions*, "that the alarm had already spread."[80] The men spent no time searching for the Porters but turned their attention to the slave quarter, where thirty people lived in 1830, including eight males between ages ten and thirty-six.[81] This was the home of Henry Porter, the "General" and "Paymaster," who had brought brandy to the dinner.[82] Through Henry's influence, no doubt, the insurgents made four recruits here: Daniel and Aaron, each about forty-seven; Moses Porter, about twenty-five; and Jacob, eighteen. Another Porter slave, Jim, later would convince the court that he had not joined; but even without him, recruits from this plantation represented one of the three largest gains of the day.[83]

Aware now that warnings had gone out, Turner sent the main group north to the Francis farm while he returned alone to retrieve the detachment.[84] The latter group, at about half past seven, had encountered Augustus Doyel (on his way to Turner's mill, Drewry thought in 1900) and killed him in the road, just as the main group was arriving at the Porter house.[85] Doyel's wallet had found its way into Hark's pocket.[86] About fifteen minutes later, at a quarter to eight, Turner came upon the detachment somewhere near the entrance to Elizabeth Turner's lane. They had turned around before reaching the constable's house, having learned "from some who joined them," Turner said, that Harris too had been warned and was "from home."[87]

The number who joined (say, four) after the attack on Doyel was never established, but three other members of the detachment certainly defected at about that time. Jack Reese slipped away and took himself to the home of Jordan Barnes, the man who had hired his labor that summer. Barnes was working in his field that morning when he heard a rumor about murders in the neighborhood; he returned home and found Jack, who told him about the Whitehead killings, insisting he had been informed "by one of Mrs. Whitehead's negroes."[88] The two others who quit were Davy Turner, who had been forced from his bed, and Joe Turner, the hunter whose wife lived at the Whitehead plantation. Davy and Joe appeared with a third man (never identified) at the house of Elisha Atkins, a neighbor of the Porters, at "8 or 9 o'clock," according to Atkins's slave Christian. Davy was carrying a sword, Christian said, and "enquired if there was any gun or ammunition in the house & proposed to break in the house." Joe objected, saying (according to Brodnax's shorthand), "no we have enough ammun." The stragglers then departed, taking along an unidentified Atkins slave (who soon returned home), hinting that they intended to join the insurgents.[89]

Authorities showed little curiosity after the rebellion about the first alarm, its timing, its origin, or how it was spread. It must have reached Richard Porter at about half past six Monday morning and Constable Harris by seven. Both men left their houses immediately on hearing the news. Drewry asserted in 1900 that "a mulatto girl, Mary," had alerted both households and that a short time later a slave boy brought news of the Travis killings to Nathaniel Francis.[90] Then, from the Francis house, warnings apparently went out to John T. Barrow, Peter Edwards, Newit Harris, and finally to Levi Waller, the only resident on Barrow Road to be alerted.

Porter's warning had to have come from a credible witness who understood what was in progress. That witness probably was not white, since no one of that description had survived the first four attacks; and the only such survivor of the fifth, Harriet Whitehead, could not have reached the Porter house before the insurgents.[91] The timing and distance suggest that the first warning came from the farm of Elizabeth Turner II, where the men had arrived at sunrise (5:30 A.M.) and departed by quarter past six. Anyone at the Turner place who knew Henry Porter, Sam Francis, and Will Francis might have guessed the band's intentions, even without overhearing the assignments in the yard. The Porter house was about a fifteen-minute walk straight northeast across the intervening fields. If those fields were in cotton, grass, or low-standing grain that August, Porter's buildings would have been in view the entire way.

From the Porter place, the constable's house stood perhaps a mile and a half northwest, off Cabin Pond Road, a distance someone familiar with the paths could have covered on foot in twenty minutes. A messenger leaving the Turner house at a quarter past six could have warned Porter by half past six; the same messenger, or one sent by Porter, could have warned the constable by seven. In summary, events in this period must have taken place at about the following times:

— 6:15 A.M., insurgents leave the Turner house;
— 6:16 A.M., messenger leaves the Turner house;
— 6:30 A.M., insurgents approach the Whitehead house;
— 6:30 A.M., messenger warns Porter;
— 7:00 A.M., messenger warns Howell Harris;
— 7:15 A.M., insurgents divide and leave the Whitehead house.

In 1830 Elizabeth Turner II held three female slaves between the ages of ten and thirty-six, any one of whom might have carried a message some distance.[92] No slaves at the Turner farm had been identified by name in public records since 1822, but in that year—nine years before the rising—the Turner holding did include two young slaves named Mary, both of whom may have been present in August 1831.[93] One, possibly the younger of the two, must have descended (with Ephraim, young Sam, Jordan, and Davy) from slaves once held by Mrs. Turner's father and by her first husband. In 1822, shortly before he died, Samuel G. Turner gave this Mary (along with Davy and Sam) to his stepdaughter Rebecca Jane, reserving the "benefit and enjoyment" of the slave girl's service to his widow "during the term of her natural life."[94] The other Mary, about fifteen years of age in 1831, was known as "Molly," a pet name for Mary. In 1822, when Molly was about six, her name appeared in the will of Samuel G. Turner, who loaned her to his widow as a dower slave. At the same time, Samuel had loaned two other slaves to his widow: Myrick, a boy of about nine in 1822, and Nancy, then about forty-five, undoubtedly the woman believed by many to have been the mother of Nat Turner.[95] The dying master did not explain his grouping of these particular slaves, but he may have been trying to preserve a family: a daughter, a son, and their mother. Perhaps, too, he felt some obligation toward Nancy, who by 1822 had lived nearly thirty years with his family, having arrived at his father's plantation in 1793 along with Lydia (who died before 1830) and the other slaves acquired by Benjamin Turner II from the estates of his Griffin in-laws. Nancy and Nat Turner I, whatever their blood ties, had lived at the same plantations from 1800 through 1822, and young Molly would have known the chief insurgent since her childhood. In either case, whether Mary or Molly, Drewry's assertion about the role of the mulatto girl stands as the best guess.

The express rider, the man who carried the alarm to Jerusalem, has never been identified, but there was no more likely courier than Constable Howell Harris, the law's agent in the Cross Keys district. If Harris left his house at quarter past seven and rode fast, he might have reached James Trezvant's house (thirteen miles distant by Barrow Road) by half past eight and the courthouse (a mile farther on) by a quarter to nine.[96] Court was not in session that day, so the town was not crowded. At least three attorneys were in town, as were the clerk, the tavern keeper, and the deputy sheriff. The congressman apparently was at his home across the river until the rider from Cross Keys arrived. Within minutes a first group of volunteers, whose numbers would increase to eighteen by early afternoon, had assembled in town, taken arms, and headed across the bridge toward Cross Keys, ten miles straight to the southwest. Constable Harris, who would be seen among the volunteers at their camp on Tuesday morning, probably rode with them.[97] Key events in these hours took place at approximately the following times:

— 7:15 A.M., express rider departs from Cabin Pond neighborhood;
— 8:30 A.M., express rider arrives in Jerusalem;
— 9:00 A.M., first volunteers depart for Cross Keys.

While Nat Turner was retrieving the detachment, the main group of insurgents, numbering about fifteen, stopped first at the Nathaniel Francis farm, a mile and a half by road from the Porter place.[98] The Francis house and its outbuildings, in its broad clearing of two or three hundred acres, stood one-third of a mile west of the point where present-day Porter House Road meets Cabin Pond Road. The insurgents must have arrived within sight of the house at about eight o'clock. By then, Nathaniel Francis and his mother, Mrs. Sarah Francis, had gone to see for themselves what had happened at the Travis farm. Nathaniel apparently rode ahead while Mrs. Francis walked, taking the well-known paths.[99] Four members of the white household stayed behind: Lavinia Francis (Nathaniel's wife of ten months, now eight months pregnant); Samuel T. Browne (under ten years of age) and John L. Browne (under five), Nathaniel's two orphaned nephews; and the overseer, not identified at the time.[100] Few verifiable details about this attack ever came to light, in part because so few of those present remained after the uprising.[101] Lavinia Francis, the sole survivor among the four whites present, saw nothing from her hiding place in an upstairs attic next to her bedroom.[102] None of the Francis slaves testified about the attack, and Moses Moore gave only a partial account of what he observed.[103] Nat Turner saw none of it.

As they rode up the Francis lane, the band evidently overtook Louisa (Turner) Williams, about twenty, and her infant, not yet two—the wife and child of Cherokee Williams, the school keeper and neighbor of the Whiteheads. The first accurate list of attacks, compiled on 5 September by Theodore Trezvant, indicated that Mrs. Williams and her child (the fourth infant to die that morning) had been killed at the Francis farm. There, according to the postmaster, the dead included "1 man, 1 woman and 3 children." Trezvant must have included the two Williams victims in the count.[104] His list implicitly contradicted an earlier report from Winton, North Carolina, which placed the two killings at the Williams house, three miles to the south. The Winton author, writing on 24 August, had heard firsthand the school keeper's tale of hearing cries, walking to the Whitehead house, and finding the dead. "Mr. Williams immediately returned to his own dwelling," the Winton author said, "when he was met by one of his own negro boys with the horrible tidings that his wife and children had been murdered in his absence." The inference, which Williams himself may have drawn, was that the insurgents had attacked his house, too.[105]

The long narrative of the uprising cast in Nat Turner's voice, however, contains not a word about Louisa Williams or her child. In the entire twenty-three pages of *The Confessions of Nat Turner*, these two were mentioned just once, by Thomas R. Gray in his list of victims (as "Mrs. John K. Williams and child"), with no indication of their place of death.[106] That omission, together with the timing of the attacks in this neighborhood, suggests that Mrs. Williams was overtaken after the main insurgent group left the Porter house and after Nat Turner separated from them. In other words, the Williams killings probably did take place near the Francis house, and Nat Turner, who was not present, knew nothing about them. The omission supports a significant point about the narrative in the *Confessions*: by sustaining a point of view consistent with what Nat Turner could have observed, it provides additional evidence, if not proof, of authenticity.

Theodore Trezvant's list confirmed descriptions of the three other white victims at the Francis farm, who included the two nephews and the young overseer (identified years later as Henry Doyel, perhaps a relative of Augustus F. Doyel). No one in 1831 named the attackers here, but Drewry's informants told him years later that the overseer had been shot and the boys, bearing signature wounds, decapitated.[107] By November, Gray's sources in the Francis family had given him a few additional details: "Mrs. Nathaniel Francis, while concealed in a closet heard their blows, and the shrieks of the victims of these ruthless savages; they then entered the closet where she was concealed, and went out without discovering her. While in this hiding place, she heard two of her women in a quarrel about the division of her clothes."[108]

Moses Moore would testify that after the attacks he watched the insurgents impress three boys from the Francis slave quarters: Nathan, age fourteen (apparently the eldest, and, according to the court, "very badly grown"); Tom, also fourteen; and Davy, thirteen. The three were placed on horses, "one behind each of the company," Moses recalled, and went "unwillingly." They were "constantly guarded by negroes with guns," Moses said, "who were ordered to shoot them if they attempted to escape."[109] Moses did not testify concerning one other slave from the Francis farm, Dred, about thirty-five, who joined with no apparent hesitation. Counting Sam and Will, six of the fifteen slaves at the Francis farm now belonged to the rising.[110] At around half past eight, the company departed.

By a quarter to nine, they arrived at the house of Peter Edwards, half a mile north as the crow flies, or a mile and one quarter by a dirt track that skirted some woods and the upper branches of Cox's Swamp. No eyewitness described even a moment of the visit there, but circumstances suggest that it lasted no longer than fifteen minutes. Edwards and his family had fled; some of his slaves likewise may have taken to the woods. In 1830, the Edwards slave quarter had twenty-nine residents, including fifteen males. As many as eight of the males—those between ages sixteen and thirty-six—would have been viewed as prime recruits.[111] Nelson and Austin, aged thirty-three and twenty-two, respectively, already were riding with the insurgents, as their master probably suspected by the time he left the house. Two other Edwards slaves would leave with the band: Sam, about twenty-five, who proved to have no heart for the business; and James (or "Jim"), nineteen.[112] The rest kept their distance.

The main company numbered about twenty as they approached the farm of John T. ("Tom") Barrow, one and a third miles east-northeast of the Edwards place. Barrow, a lover of country sports, had planned to go hunting that morning with his brother-in-law, George Vaughan, who had not yet arrived. When he got word of the uprising, Barrow loaded his rifle and shotgun and, as the insurgents came into view, told his young wife, the former Mary T. Vaughan, to make her escape through the garden. At about quarter past nine, the attack began. Mary T. would testify later that one of the insurgents "fired off a gun in the yard and threw it down." She identified the shooter as Nat Turner II—the other Nat Turner, who had lived as a hired slave at her husband's farm in 1830 and who may have been denied one of Barrow's slaves as a wife.[113] Barrow returned fire, joining the first shootout of the day. "After firing his rifle," Gray said in his own afterword in the *Confessions*, "he discharged his gun at them, and then broke it over the villain who first approached him, but he was overpowered, and slain."[114] Drewry heard that one of the insurgents reached through a window, razor in hand, and cut Barrow's throat.[115] Barrow may have scored one significant hit, however: at about this point, the name of Will, the executioner, vanishes from the record. In the *Confessions* his name disappears after the account of Catherine Whitehead's death; and while physical evidence (the two small bodies) at the Francis farm suggests that he was present there, in none of the accounts of subsequent incidents did anyone refer to Will, Will Francis, or the executioner.[116]

The dozen slaves at the Barrow farm must have learned of the rising at about the time their master did and must have had the same number of minutes to consider their options. Of the four or five adults in the holding, just two—Lucy, about twenty years old in 1831, and Moses, about thirty-five—sided with the insurgents. Those two were the pair Rebecca Vaughan had transferred to Barrow, her new son-in-law, as gifts or pawns in 1828. Lucy aided the attackers openly, seizing and holding her mistress until another Barrow slave—probably Byrd ("Bird"), a man of at least fifty-five years—freed Mary T. from Lucy's clutches. Mary T. later would profess uncertainty about Lucy's intention, "but thought it was to detain her."[117] Moses Moore, the boy witness, would testify that he saw Lucy "in company with the insurgents" at the door of the Barrow house, "after the murder was committed." Moses Barrow, the man who shared a room with Lucy, may not have been home at the time of the attack (the evidence is unclear); but he certainly had enlisted by late Monday afternoon, when witnesses placed him at the home of his former mistress, Rebecca Vaughan.[118] On Tuesday morning he would prove his commitment to the rising.

Barrow's brother-in-law, George Vaughan, probably was caught in the gunfire as he approached the house along what is now Kindred Road, a shortcut from Barrow Road.[119] About this killing too, Nat Turner knew nothing.

From Barrow's house the insurgents could have proceeded directly to Jerusalem by taking George Vaughan's shortcut to Barrow Road. Instead, for the second time that morning they turned away from the town and headed three-quarters of a mile northwest on the present Clarksbury Road, a five-minute ride to the plantation of Newit Harris. Ben, one of two elders in the Harris slaveholding, caught sight of them at about ten o'clock.[120] (His master's house had at least one clock.) By that time, according to Drewry's sources, Ben had hidden his master ("old and feeble," as Drewry described him, though Harris was not yet sixty) in the branch of Angelica Swamp behind the house.[121] Ben saw Sam Edwards among the insurgents, holding "a gun or a stick," but riding "rather in the rear." Ben fled, pursued by Sam and others. Later, he was unable to say whether Sam could have left the band, "if he had been so disposed."[122]

At the same hour, near the Whitehead house, five miles to the south, the first group of volunteers from town picked up the insurgents' track; and, as Gray would recall, "pursuing them, we found the blood hardly congealed, in the houses they had left."[123] Gray later determined the relative positions of the two forces at that hour by using Ben's recollection of the time, one of the few references by anyone to a specific hour of that day. If Ben was right, the pursuit began at midmorning, as follows:

— 10:00 A.M., Ben sees the main group of insurgents arrive at the Harris plantation;
— 10:00 A.M., first volunteers arrive near the Whitehead plantation;
— 10:15 A.M., Nat Turner arrives at the Harris plantation.

Turner and the detachment reached the Harris plantation after passing the Francis farm at a distance, halting briefly at the Edwards and Barrow houses, and then turning northwest to meet the main body of men exactly where Turner assumed he would find them—further evidence of a plan. "The men now amounting to about forty, shouted and hurraed as I rode up," he recalled; "some were in the yard, loading their guns, others drinking." They had pillaged the house, taking "money and other valuables."[124] (In 1838 Harris still had valuables in the house, including fifteen silver spoons, the two maps of the United States, and his desk clock.)[125] Turner addressed the men: "I ordered them to mount and march instantly."[126]

Turner's estimate of forty men in the Harris yard would agree with that of Levi Waller at the next house, but it probably was too high. If four men joined the detachment near the scene of Doyel's killing (offsetting three defections), and if Moses Barrow joined at the Barrow farm, the total number of insurgents at that point would have been twenty-eight, of whom four were boys under guard. Their effective strength, in other words, stood at just over half the number claimed in the *Confessions*. They made no recruits among the Harris slaves, who must have fled into the swamp with Ben. Of the twenty-six males in the Harris quarter in 1830, as many as seven were between the ages of sixteen and thirty-six—"likely men," in the words of a witness at another farm.[127] As at the Whitehead plantation (twenty-seven slaves in 1830, three likely males, no recruits), none joined here. Men at two other large plantations along the route responded with similar reluctance: Henry B. Vaughan's Walnut Hill (about twenty-eight slaves, four or five likely, no recruits) and Blunt's Belmont (sixty-nine slaves, six likely, no recruits). At three others, however, the yield was larger: Porter's (thirty slaves, five likely, six recruits, including Henry, who brought the brandy to dinner), Edwards's (twenty-nine slaves, eight likely, four recruits, including Nelson and Austin), and Thomas Ridley's Buckhorn Quarter (number of residents unknown, four recruits). The recruiters Turner later would dispatch to the quarters of William Allen, the largest in the parish (179 slaves, thirty-three likely), and Thomas Newsom (eighty-two slaves, twelve likely) apparently failed to reach those plantations.[128] Gray would remark in mid-September at the lack of response from Allen's quarter.[129]

Tactics

Three miles from the Harris house, at around a quarter to eleven, the insurgent force came within sight of Levi Waller's farm. Had Nat Turner feared resistance, he might have avoided this place; but he confronted Waller in the open and in daylight. He halted within sight of the cluster of cabins and sheds and arranged his men in two ranks, a formation he must have devised before reaching that place. He had planned a classic cavalry charge, introducing a tactic he would employ at each stop along Barrow Road. Witnesses at three of the four farms visited on that road would corroborate his description of the charge.[130] "I took my station in the rear," he told Gray, "and as it 'twas my object to carry terror and devastation wherever we went, I placed fifteen or twenty of the best armed and most to be relied on, in front, who generally approached the houses as fast as their horses could run." In the following rank, under his own surveillance, he placed those he trusted least. "This was for two purposes," he said, "to prevent their escape and strike terror to the inhabitants."[131] (Gray left the pronoun *their* ambiguous in its reference.) From that point onward, he would conduct the attacks with no attempt at stealth. He meant them to be seen, to terrify, to discourage collective resistance, to frighten men into flight and into neglecting women and children. The assaults were to be remembered. The effects were apparent in Gray's early impression that Turner had employed the charge at every stop of the day. "The gait the negroes travelled, served to strike additional horror," Gray wrote in September. "For they never rode at less than full speed."[132]

Waller had received a timely warning. "On the morning of the 22d day of August last between 9 and 10 o'clock," the court secretary later wrote, "he heard that the negroes had risen and were murdering the whites and were *coming*." He sent his son Thomas, age thirteen, to the school (a quarter mile distant) to bring home the seven students and their teacher, William Crocker, all of whom were waiting now in the yard. Waller ordered Crocker to load the guns, while he himself remained at the still.[133] Altogether, seventeen white persons assembled near the house, ranging in age from infancy through fifty-two, including at least nine members of the Waller family, as many as seven boarding students, and the teacher. Four of the males present, all aged fifteen or older, might have put up a fusillade, had Waller organized one.[134]

Had there been a fusillade, Turner's most trusted lieutenants, the men riding in front, would have suffered; but in the absence of opposing fire, they must have had an easy ride and been able to observe the effects of their approach at close range. Their leader, watching from behind, must have had his view obstructed; Moses Moore, riding almost certainly toward the rear, left no account. Levi Waller, however, saw and said a great deal. "Before the guns were loaded," his testimony reads, "Mr. Crocker came to the still where witness was and said they were in Sight."[135] He thought he saw forty or fifty men, "mounted on horse back and armed with guns, swords, and other weapons." All of his family, he said, "attempted to make their escape," some running to the nearby prong of Buckhorn Swamp, others trying to hide near the house.[136] Waller himself "retreated" to tall weeds by a corner of the fence, on the lee side of the house, behind the garden. "Several negroes pursued him but he escaped them by falling among the Weeds over the fence," court minutes say. "One negro rode up and looked over, but did not observe him."[137] That was Dred Francis; Waller knew him well. Dred was mounted and armed with a shotgun or rifle—Waller did not know which.[138] Alfred, Waller's blacksmith, age thirty, distracted Dred, enabling his master to reach to the swamp.[139] Waller then crept back to within sixty yards of the house and hid "in the plumb orchard, behind the garden."[140] From there, he said, he could see "nearly all things that transpired at the house." He caught sight of Daniel Porter, Aaron Porter, and Sam Francis as they entered a "log house" in which Mrs. Waller and her daughter, four-year-old Martha Jr., had "attempted to secrete themselves," and he watched as the three men came out of the house, Daniel carrying Mrs. Waller's scissors (or scissors chain).[141] He spied James Edwards, Austin Edwards, and Nelson Edwards, and saw Nelson "knock one of the family's brains out with the but [*sic*] of his musket."[142]

The men began drinking, Dred Francis among them.[143] Waller recognized Hark Moore in the yard "with a gun in his hands" and heard the others call him "Capt. Moore."[144] As Waller lay watching, his own man Davy, about thirty years old, came up to the house, "dressed himself clean," drank with the men, and rode off "in good Spirits" on Waller's horse, seemingly "in great glee." One member of the company referred to the new recruit as "brother Clements."[145] Waller noticed Sam Edwards "at some distance wiping his eyes," seeming not to take part; he heard Nat Turner (who had come forward) order Sam to get on his horse, and observed that Sam seemed "not disposed to get up, but did get up and go off with them."[146] Nat Turner, whom Waller knew "very well," was riding a horse belonging to Dr. Robert Musgrave, son-in-law of Newit Harris. Turner "seemed to command the party." It was he who gave the order to "go ahead."[147] The blacksmith, Alfred, apparently departed with the men, the second of Waller's prime hands to join.[148] (Two others remained behind, somewhere.) Now numbering about thirty, the insurgents must have left at quarter past eleven.

Once they had gone, Waller ventured from the plum orchard and found some of the dead, including Mrs. Waller, daughter Martha, son Thomas, six other children under the age of fourteen, and the young woman never identified. The Waller infant, still alive, would die on Wednesday evening, the fifth victim of infanticide.[149] Its mortal wound, never described, could not have been inflicted by the blade of an ax. For a day or two no one realized that six others had survived: Waller and Crocker, three of Waller's boys (John K., seventeen; Levi C., sixteen; and Peter, about eleven), and one of the students, twelve-year-old Clarinda Jones, who had concealed herself first between the house and a chimney, then across the fence in weeds, then under Waller's old shop, and finally in the prong of Buckhorn Swamp, where she hid until the next morning.[150]

East of Waller's farm, on their left, the men passed woods surrounding the swamp, which lay about three hundred yards north of the road. On their right, they passed the house of William H. Nicholson (fourteen taxable slaves); then, on their left, the houses of Mary Simmons (no slaves) and the Johnson-Gray household (no slaves); then, on their right, that of Rebecca Knight (one slave, seven free blacks in 1830).[151] Along this stretch of road Davy Waller heard Nat Turner remark that he would not kill some "very poor people" whose house they were passing, because they "thought no better of themselves than they did of the negroes."[152]

In about a mile they arrived at the first of the three Williams family farms, this one on the north side of the road, recently inherited by William Williams Jr.[153] They surprised young Williams in his field, working with two hired boys ("two little boys," according to the *Confessions*), identified years later as Miles and Henry Johnson.[154] Nat Turner may have witnessed these killings, though he said nothing specific about his tactics here or how the three in the field died. He certainly witnessed the final moments of Rebecca (Ivy) Williams II, who apparently had been watching from the house. The account in the *Confessions* of her final moments suggests a growing boldness on the part of her assailants: "Mrs. Williams fled and got some distance from the house, but she was pursued, overtaken, and compelled to get up behind one of the company, who brought her back, and after showing her the mangled body of her lifeless husband, she was told to get down and lay by his side, where she was shot dead."[155] Another witness, a man named Jacob (one of William Williams's four slaves), later would testify only that he had seen Davy Waller at his master's farm that day. This Jacob, about forty years old, was the only male slave at the farm; he did not enlist.[156] The entire episode, lasting no more than twenty minutes, ended by a quarter to twelve.

The second Williams farm, that of the uncle, Jacob Williams, lay a quarter mile east and around a wooded bend to the right, on the south side of the road. The men arrived within sight around noon and again prepared to charge. Again, Turner observed from a distance. Nancy Williams, mistress of the house, in her twenties, was in the kitchen with her three small children (two infants) and the cook, Cynthia, a woman probably in her fifties or sixties.[157] Jacob Williams had gone to the woods to measure timber; his nephew, twenty-one-year-old Caswell Worrell, the overseer, was in a new (presumably distant) field with the hands.[158] Edmund (or Edwin) Drewry, the young overseer for James Bell of Nottoway Parish, had come to the farm with Bell's slave Stephen, about twenty-one, to pick up a cartload of corn. The two were "consulting" about which of them should fetch a corn measure when they heard horses approaching and Drewry exclaimed, "Lord who is that coming?"[159] He ran, but, according to Gray's rendering of the confession, he was "pursued, overtaken and shot."[160] Mrs. Williams and her children (including infants six and seven) were killed in the kitchen. Simultaneously, some of the attackers must have proceeded to the overseer's house and, while not in Turner's view, killed Worrell's wife and child (infant eight).

In the aftermath, Cynthia encountered Nelson, one of her master's four male slaves, perhaps thirty-five years old. She said later that Nelson "came home early in the morning seemingly very sick," but she did not explain where he had been. Court minutes summarized what she saw of him and heard him say: "Went to his house, dressed himself very clean, while the negroes were in the yard, came into the kitchen asked for some meat, took his Mistresses meat out of the pot. Cut a piece off. Said, 'Cynthia, you do not know me. I do not know when you will see me again.' Stepped over the dead bodies without any manifestation of grief."[161] Stephen Bell, the slave who had come to load corn, witnessed the impressment of Nelson, the only male slave of Jacob Williams who was near the house at the time. The insurgents "told Nelson to go with them," Stephen said, according to court minutes. "He seemed unwilling to go—but insisted upon dressing before he went—was forced to go with them—lagged behind when he was guarded." Stephen also left with the men—a gain of two for the insurgents, bringing their strength to about thirty-two.[162]

The company then rode half a mile east in the noonday heat, passing by the third Williams family farm, that of Rhoda Worrell (no slaves). At about half past twelve, they turned sharply left, off the road and into the long lane to Rebecca Vaughan's house. In the *Confessions*, Nat Turner said nothing about what took place at the house, suggesting he had remained at the road. No other member of the party left an account, but John Hampden Pleasants, the Richmond editor, later interviewed Mrs. Vaughan's house servant—a "venerable negro woman," he said—who described the scene "with great emphasis." That woman must have been Dilsy, the cook, about fifty. "It was near noon," Pleasants reported, "and her mistress was making some preparations in the porch for dinner, when happening to look towards the road she discerned a dust and wondered what it could mean."[163]

They approached at a gallop. "In a second," Pleasants wrote, "the negroes mounted and armed, came into view, and making an exclamation indicative of her horror and agony, Mrs. Vaughan ran into the house." They dismounted and surrounded the house, pointing guns at the doors and windows. "Mrs. Vaughan appeared at a window, and begged for her life, inviting them to take everything she had." Dilsy told Pleasants that one man fired at her mistress, "which was followed by another, and a fatal shot." Mrs. Vaughan's niece, Ann Eliza, who had been upstairs when the men arrived, was shot a few steps from the door.[164] Pleasants identified the man who may have been her killer only by the *nom de guerre* "Marmaduke."[165] Pleasants said Mrs. Vaughan's younger son, William Arthur, age sixteen, had been at the still; he was shot as he climbed over a fence on his way to the house.[166] "When the work was done," Pleasants reported, "they called for drink, and food, and becoming nice, damned the brandy as vile stuff."[167]

It was here that Stephen Bell (who was about to defect) noticed that Nelson Williams, who had taken no part in the killing, had joined in the drinking "and had his tickler filled by his own request."[168] Alfred Waller, the blacksmith, drank for a time before slipping away and heading for home.[169] When the men departed at around one o'clock, they apparently took along two slaves conscripted from Mrs. Vaughan's holding: Jim and Wright (aged about forty-five and sixteen, respectively), who remained only briefly with the band.[170] Those two, minus the one desertion, would have brought the company's roster to thirty-three. "Our number amounted now to fifty or sixty," Nat Turner says in the *Confessions*, "all mounted and armed with guns, axes, swords and clubs."[171] Gray let the claim stand without comment; if Turner's estimate was close to the mark, the identities of half the insurgents at that point would never be known.

Twelve hours and twenty miles into the day, the band had inflicted casualties at fourteen houses (counting those of Trajan Doyel and Caswell Worrell) and had visited or approached four others whose white residents all had fled. The behavior of the insurgents would lead some observers to think of them as bandits ("*Banditti*") and old-time rebels, neither raping nor burning, but drinking (as at the dinner in the old field and at the stills of Travis, Turner, Harris, Waller, and Mrs. Vaughan), pillaging (perhaps for a common purse), and exacting vengeance. With one exception, they had attacked only slaveholders, each of whom they knew. They had killed fifty-five people, and at midday they had not become jaded. But they had struck only at isolated homesteads whose residents had been caught unawares. They had yet to confront a fully prepared foe or gain an objective that might draw the slave population spontaneously to their side.

Their numbers had grown by more than four times, and their losses had been light—one casualty at most (Will Francis, perhaps) and four known defections or desertions to that point, excluding Will Francis and Stephen Bell (appendix B). But on at least three occasions—at the farm of Salathiel Francis and the plantations of Catherine Whitehead and Newit Harris—potential recruits had *fled*, surprised or fearful at the sudden appearance of the band, and reluctant to join. A quarter of the recruits, as shown in the formation at the Waller farm, had joined only through coercion and could not be trusted (appendix C). The failure to raise a broader following was a consequence of secrecy. To avoid the betrayal Gabriel had experienced in 1800, Turner had confined the plan to his inner circle down to the day it unfolded. He and his men thus took almost everyone, even willing recruits, by surprise. And in willingness to join on short notice, Turner found few that day who matched Will Francis.

The men rode back down the lane, regained the road, and headed east a mile and a half. At the end of Barrow Road, they made the turn to the left. Then, having introduced the tactic whose power to shock soon would be evident, Turner addressed the day's chief objective. The actions of his men had hinted for some time at a purpose beyond killing: they had tried to be thorough at each stop, but at the Whitehead, Francis, and Waller houses they had broken off—as if pressed for time—before tracking down all quarry. They had not searched for Porter, Edwards, Harris, or Jacob Williams. Now, on leaving the Vaughan lane, according to the *Confessions*, Turner committed his followers to a test: "I determined on starting for Jerusalem."

Parker's Field

A disagreement broke out half a mile along the road toward town, at the gate of James W. Parker. There, three miles from Jerusalem, the company halted. "Some of the men," Nat Turner said, had "relations" at Parker's plantation and wanted to "call and get his [Parker's] people."[172] (Moses Barrow, who had connections among the twenty-three Parker slaves, must have been present and must have insisted on stopping.) Turner objected, suspecting that Parker already had fled to town; but he yielded. He remained at the gate "with seven or eight" while the others rode to the house, half a mile distant, across its broad field and through the intervening woods. "After waiting some time for them," he told Gray, according to the *Confessions*, "I became impatient, and started to the house for them, and on our return we were met by a party of white men, who had pursued our blood-stained track."[173]

That party was the first sent out from Jerusalem on Monday morning. They had volunteered—perhaps according to law, under orders of a magistrate—to perform the duties of a patrol or *posse comitatus* (summoned in cases of resistance to law). The regular, compensated duties of patrolling, familiar to many young white men in the antebellum South, were defined in law as visiting "negro quarters and other places suspected of having therein unlawful assemblies," and detecting "such slaves as may stroll from one plantation to another without permission."[174] The first party, including Thomas R. Gray, after reaching the Whitehead plantation, had followed the track to the Waller farm and then to James W. Parker's gate. The second party, under William C. Parker, had left town before noon and apparently traveled west on the road to Belfield, but, not finding the track, turned back and reached the same gate minutes after the first volunteers.[175]

None of the white men wrote more than a few sentences about the pursuit, and only one—Alexander P. Peete—was identified by name at the time.[176] But three of those who rode from town in the first group can be identified: Gray himself, James Strange French, and Aubin Middleton.[177] Gray must have been at home, in his office, when the express arrived from the scene of the outbreak; he may have had to borrow a horse that morning.[178] French may have been at Vaughan's tavern, where he apparently was boarding. Now aged twenty-four, he had been practicing law in the town for about three years. According to one report, he too borrowed a horse, finding his at the tavern keeper's stable.[179] Neither Gray nor French owned a slave in 1831.[180] Middleton, about thirty-five, a captain in the militia, commanded the first party for a time.[181] He had been a figure of importance at the courthouse since his appointment as deputy clerk in 1816 and coroner in 1817; he must have been in town that morning, though his wife and four young children apparently were at the plantation he had purchased in February, a tract of 1,373 acres on Buckhorn Swamp, not far from the Waller farm.[182] In 1830 he held seventeen slaves.[183] Two men in the second party can be identified: Congressman James Trezvant, nearing fifty, the former colonel of the militia; and attorney William C. Parker, almost forty, the veteran of 1812 who had established his law practice in the town five years earlier.[184] Trezvant held forty-eight slaves in 1830, Parker four.[185] Trezvant outranked Parker, but Parker took command of the company and for two days would lead the suppression effort. The courthouse circle was taking the field.

If Howell Harris was in fact the man who warned the town, he must have returned to Cross Keys with the first party as its guide. As many as eight other volunteers from town went along: among the likely recruits were the deputy sheriff, Capt. James H. Sebrell, about twenty-five; Sebrell's two younger brothers, Nicholas and William; and the local saddler, Sugars Bryant, about twenty-five.[186] As many as twenty recruits could have been raised from the town's boarders alone: the eight young white men living at the tavern in 1830 (operated that year by Nicholas F. Cocke), the seven with stable keeper Albert Drewry (plus Drewry himself), and the four with Mrs. Cobb, one of the town's resident widows.[187]

The patrol (or posse) picked up recruits along the way, just as the rebels did. At Cross Keys they found Capt. Sampson C. Reese, twenty-five, brother of Elizabeth Turner II and nephew of Piety Reese. Reese had become a militia captain in 1829. That same year he bought two tracts of land, 855 acres known as the Cross Keys Plantation, ten miles southwest of the town and four miles east of the Whitehead house; in 1830 he held fourteen slaves.[188] In the same neighborhood the volunteers must have recruited James D. Bryant, twenty-eight, living at his parents' farm thirteen miles southwest of town and three miles beyond Cross Keys.[189] North of the Whitehead house they added Hardy ("Hartie") Joyner, about thirty, the third husband of Nancy Turner (sister of Samuel G. Turner). With his new wife's eight slaves, Joyner was farming her dower properties (475 acres), situated a mile or more east of the Porter and Barrow houses.[190] By the time the party reached the Waller farm, two men from the western edge of the county had joined: Newit Drew, about twenty-five, who held eight slaves in 1830 and lived on a small farm sixteen miles west of the courthouse; and Lt. Alexander P. Peete (soon to be captain) of the cavalry, aged about thirty-four, who held thirty-one slaves and owned 1,122 acres a mile farther west.[191] Drew and Peete must have learned of the uprising by late morning.

At about one o'clock (as the insurgents were leaving Rebecca Vaughan's lane), the first party of white men reached the Waller farm, where they dismounted and looked around. Bryant moved Waller's infant daughter—still alive, according to Drewry's later account—from direct sunlight into shade. Middleton determined at once to leave the company and attend to his own family, leaving Peete and Bryant in command.[192]

The first volunteers, eighteen in number, then mounted and proceeded eastward.[193] Along Barrow Road they met Waller's blacksmith, Alfred, heading home. "Not having an opportunity to secure him otherwise," Peete recalled in a December affidavit, "he was disabled by cutting the longer tendon just above the heel in each leg, in which situation I left him."[194] At about two o'clock they came upon the seven or eight sentries Nat Turner had posted at Parker's gate. Among the sentries, according to court minutes, Sampson C. Reese recognized Daniel Porter, "the first negro he saw after getting to Mr. Parker's gate." Reese shot at Daniel (now riding Dr. Musgrave's horse, he thought) and observed that Daniel seemed not to be armed.[195] The sentries scattered under fire.

The skirmish that followed in Parker's field, however small in scale, was only the second incident of its kind in the United States between the Revolution and the Civil War, pitting slaves in armed ranks under a black leader against a white force in similar array.[196] Not since 1775 and the Battle of Great Bridge, fifty miles to the east, had anyone in Virginia witnessed a comparable confrontation. Peete's men advanced toward Parker's house, which was screened from view by the woods. At the same time, Turner's men were starting back along the drive toward the gate, likewise screened, having recruited at most three men, who would have brought the band's strength to twenty-eight, not counting the seven or eight scattered sentries.[197] The new recruits remained with the insurgents no more than a few minutes, so Turner must have had about half the number of men claimed in the *Confessions* ("*fifty or sixty, all mounted and armed with guns, axes, swords and clubs*") and far fewer than William C. Parker would hear they had assembled later Monday night.[198] Gray's own count, which included recruits who separated along the way, suggested that the number of insurgents in the skirmish at Parker's field could not have exceeded thirty. "From the best evidence which I have been able to obtain," he told the *Whig* in September, "likewise from what I actually saw, the number of 40 will include every insurgent who was with them for the least time, throughout their whole route." Perceptions had been distorted. "The fact of their being mounted, and their irregular mode of riding, caused their number to appear much greater than it really was."[199]

On seeing the eighteen whites across the field and observing that his men "appeared to be alarmed," Turner ordered the band to "halt and form," much as he had done in front of the Waller farmstead. The whites advanced, Gray said (in his own, parenthetical voice), under orders from Peete "to reserve their fire until within thirty paces."[200] Just as they began their advance, according to one report circulating later in Richmond, a shower of rain began to fall.[201] At one hundred yards, a volunteer fired. One account holds that it was James Strange French who fired, accidentally, when his colt bolted; another that it was Hardy Joyner, also accidentally.[202] Nat Turner, observing half of the volunteers in sudden retreat, ordered his men to "fire and rush on them." As the insurgents closed to within fifty yards, the nine volunteers still in position fired. Then they joined the retreat. Turner's men pursued them for two hundred yards, overtook some, and left them for dead.[203]

The chase continued up a low hill, from the crest of which Turner saw the second party of volunteers (under Trezvant and Parker) arriving at the gate with perhaps as many men as the first.[204] The two white parties joined, regrouped, loaded, and counterattacked. The tide turned. "We arrested their progress," Trezvant reported, "and forced them to retreat—several were shot in this skirmish."[205] The veteran Parker recounted the incident with a coolness borne of the Canada campaigns. "The insurgents," he said, "after receiving a few raggling fires, retreated."[206] Nat Turner, now a target, told of riding under fire. "Hark had his horse shot under him, and I caught another for him as it was running by me," he said. Five or six insurgents, including several of his "bravest," were hit; and the rest became "panick struck and squandered over the field." Neither side left any dead on the field, though some riders fell and some went missing: Turner said he withdrew with just twenty men.[207] The three boys from the Francis farm separated and headed for home, apparently with Nathan Blunt; all were seen early the next morning at locations near the Francis house. Moses Moore separated probably with the Francis boys and saw nothing more of the rising.[208]

By half past two (i.e., within fifteen minutes), both sides had broken off.[209] The volunteers left the field before completing the rout (a "tell" in poker), behavior that belied Capt. Parker's later protestations of confidence. Parker returned with his party to Jerusalem, where he spent the night organizing defenses and planning the suppression—every inch a commander, doing everything right.[210] The other party, the first volunteers under A. P. Peete, spent the night south of the river, under the August moon, searching for the rebel force. Gray rode with them, eventually spending more than twenty-four hours in the field. "Though pursued the whole night," he wrote in September, "fortune seemed to sport with us, by bringing us nearer together, and yet, making us pursue separate routes."[211]

Weeks later, to Gray, Nat Turner would admit defeat at Parker's field, but his course after the skirmish indicates that on that day he had not yet given up. He and his remaining force withdrew to the east-southeast on what he (or Gray) called a "private way" toward Cypress Bridge, about five miles by road from Parker's field, thinking they might cross the Nottoway there and surprise the town from the rear. Along the way, they overtook "two or three" followers who had become separated and who said that the others had "dispersed in every direction." At Cypress Bridge white men were on guard, so Turner did not try to cross. He decided instead to recover stragglers. "After trying in vain to collect a sufficient force to proceed to Jerusalem," he told Gray, "I determined to return [to Cross Keys], as I was sure they would make [their way] back to their old neighborhood, where they would rejoin me, make new recruits, and come down again."[212] Still hopeful, he turned south and west, rode three miles to the plantation of Mrs. Elizabeth Thomas (a widow with twenty-eight slaves, her son a future Union general) and the farm of a woman Nat Turner referred to as "Mrs. Spencer" (now Mrs. Hardy Joyner, the former Nancy Turner Barrett Spencer, owner of eight slaves, the surviving sister of Samuel G. Turner).[213] Then, turning away from Cross

Keys and away from possible refuge in the swamps lying south and east, he headed north, passed within a mile of Parker's field, and moved into the heart of the parish, an odd course for a bandit on the run. Early that evening, according to Dilsy Vaughan, he and his men revisited the house of Rebecca Vaughan; there they found Moses Barrow.[214] By nightfall (twilight ended at 7:18 P.M.) they were camped just four miles west of Jerusalem, at Buckhorn Quarter, home in 1830 to a portion of Major Thomas Ridley's 145 slaves.[215] There, Turner again positioned himself to confront the town.

Places of Refuge

Along the route through the parish late Monday afternoon, the effects of terror were evident, as they would be for another week. The insurgents encountered no white people: Mrs. Thomas and Mrs. Joyner had fled by the time the men arrived, as had the overseer at Ridley's Quarter. The countryside lay abandoned and open to them. The next morning, in dispatching two recruiters to the Allen and Newsom quarters in the southeast corner of the parish, Turner assured the pair that "the white people were too much alarmed to interrupt them."[216] Others also observed the abandonment. Gray said that the houses he passed on Tuesday morning seemed "tenanted only by the dead" and claimed that even the slaves had taken refuge in the woods "through fear."[217] On Wednesday, one of the volunteers (James Strange French, almost certainly) described conditions in the parish. "For many miles around their track the country is deserted by the women and children," he said, according to a summary of his note; "but armed troops are in every mile in squads."[218] Theodore Trezvant saw the effects in town. "The oldest inhabitants of our county, have never experienced such a distressing time, as we have had since Sunday night last," he wrote on Wednesday afternoon. "Every house, room and corner in this place is full of women and children, driven from home, who had to take [to] the wood, until they could get to this place," he said. "We are worn out with fatigue."[219] John Hampden Pleasants, who arrived in Jerusalem Thursday morning, said that along the eighty miles from Petersburg the Richmond Dragoons had found "the whole country thoroughly alarmed; every man armed, the dwellings all deserted by the white inhabitants, and the farms most generally left in possession of the blacks." By the time the Dragoons arrived in Jerusalem, the town had filled with refugees, so Pleasants could not have found lodgings at Vaughan's tavern had he tried. "Jerusalem was never so crowded from its foundation," he said, "for besides a considerable military force assembled here, the ladies from the adjacent country, to the number of three or four hundred, have sought refuge from the appalling dangers by which they were surrounded."[220] To the east, abandonment was reported by a volunteer who made the sixty-mile journey from Norfolk. "The country we have passed through is completely deserted," he reported on Friday, 26 August, "and the inhabitants have absolutely left their doors even unbarred."[221] The white inhabitants, not waiting for official word, had reacted (another "tell") as if this were the hour Jefferson had warned would come, bringing emancipation not "by the generous energy of our own minds," as he once had put it, but by the alternative, "by the bloody process of St Domingo."[222]

By the time the insurgents encamped for the night at Buckhorn Quarter, Nat Turner said, they had doubled their numbers, once again reaching forty, including four men from Ridley's Buckhorn Quarter.[223] (The identities of just three of these late recruits became known to the court.) At 1:00 A.M., four miles away in the town, Capt. Parker received intelligence that the insurgents had stopped for the night at Buckhorn Quarter "with a force of about 200." At that hour, Parker said, he had about sixty men under his command. "Could I have been correctly informed of their numbers when they were at Ridley's quarter, we could have in all probability destroyed or taken the most of them." Even against odds of three or four to one, Parker thought his force would have been sufficient. "My first impulse was to have attacked them with 30 or 40 men, but those who had families here were strongly opposed to it, and as I might have missed them in my approach, I acceded to the suggestions of those who had so much at stake."[224] The odds had been more favorable than Parker had thought, since during the night the insurgent camp had scattered after a sentry raised a false alarm; their numbers were reduced again to twenty—not enough to force their way across the bridge and into the town (appendix D). "With this," Turner said, "I determined to attempt to recruit, and proceed on to rally in the neighborhood, I had left."[225]

Holding to that idea on Tuesday morning, he returned to tactics of the previous day, advancing to "the nearest house," that of Dr. Samuel Blunt, whose plantation, Belmont (1,518 acres and sixty-nine slaves in 1830), lay on the western side of Buckhorn Quarter.[226] The band arrived at Blunt's gate at first light, or at around five o'clock.[227] Blunt, fifty-five and suffering from gout, had fortified his house and was prepared to defend it with the aid of two neighbors (brothers Drewry and Thomas Fitzhugh, both in their twenties), his son Simon (fifteen), and his overseer, Shadrach Futrell (about twenty-five).[228] Between them, the five defenders had six guns.[229] They armed (with weapons unspecified) trusted slaves belonging to Blunt and the Fitzhughs and positioned them in front of the house.[230] Futrell, the overseer, was "standing at the portch" when, "a little after daybreak when it was light," he saw the insurgents at the gate. He put their number at twenty-five.[231] Turner and his men rode into the yard believing the white family had fled.[232] Futrell and Frank Blunt, a slave, later recalled seeing Moses Barrow riding "foremost," wearing a light-colored cap and light breeches; the other men wore dark breeches. Frank said Moses "held up his gun flashed it threw it down," and then dismounted to pursue a servant girl, Mary—she was holding her mistress's child—into the garden. There, fifteen minutes later, Frank took him prisoner; Moses was lame, Frank observed, and "could not run."[233] Nat Turner remembered seeing Hark fire his gun "to ascertain if any of the family were home," according to the *Confessions*. "We were immediately fired upon and retreated, leaving several of my men." Hark was shot from his horse, a casualty the leader did not notice.[234]

Turner and his remaining followers made their way back toward Cabin Pond, eleven miles distant via winding roads south and west of Belmont. At about seven o'clock Tuesday morning, six miles from Belmont, the insurgents again approached the lane to the plantation of Newit Harris. Shortly before they arrived, Turner dispatched Curtis and Stephen Ridley, each on a mule, to enlist recruits in the Newsom and Allen quarters, fifteen miles to the southeast.[235] Then, as the band came within sight of the Harris house, they saw a party of white men, a company of cavalry from Greensville County. Once again the band scattered, and this time all but two deserted: Jacob Porter (from Richard Porter's holding) remained, along with Nat Turner II.[236]

Together, the three men hid in the woods until nightfall on Tuesday, when Turner dispatched the other two with instructions to find his original lieutenants, Henry Porter, Sam Francis, Nelson Edwards, and Hark Moore. For all he knew, all four were still alive and at large. He ordered Jacob and Nat II, he said, to "rally all they could, at the place we had had our dinner the Sunday before, where they would find me, and I accordingly returned there as soon as it was dark."[237] Neither man rejoined him, nor did anyone else. Jacob went home to the Porter place, where a company of volunteers found him the next day.[238] Nat II (the other Nat) hid for almost a week before being apprehended.[239] On Wednesday, after seeing the white men (undoubtedly those who would capture Jacob) searching for someone, Turner concluded that his last two followers had been taken and forced to betray him. "On this," he told Gray in November, "I gave up all hope for the present." That evening, he abandoned his refuge near Cabin Pond.[240]

He would remain at large for another nine weeks and four days, hiding in woods and fields he had known since childhood, becoming the most sought-after fugitive of his time, a figure of legend. He would have all of September and October to review events, while marking the days on a stick.[241] On Wednesday afternoon, 24 August, minutes after he saw the white men searching for someone, he may have heard the gunfire at Peter Edwards's yard and orchard.[242] On Thursday night he moved to a more permanent location under a pile of fence rails in a field not more than a mile west of the old Benjamin Turner II house, the scene in 1805 or 1806 of his earliest triumph with words. There he would stay for as long as seven weeks before moving to his third and fourth hiding places.[243] During that period of seclusion, his thoughts apparently turned from deeds to words, from revolution to the idea of terror. Even as he sought refuge, he may have begun to anticipate another triumph like the one at the old Turner house, or like the one prophesied in Luke 21:12–28, following the verses on wars and commotions, fearful sights, and signs from heaven.

Suppression

The late events in this county have rendered us quite military.
—William C. Parker to Col. Bernard Peyton, 14 September 1831

Once dispersed, the insurgents became easy prey. Within a week, five of the seven men who had met at Cabin Pond had been captured or killed, one by one, not far from their homes. Jack Reese, the dissenter who broke away from the band soon after the Whitehead attack, sought out Jordan Barnes, who had been hiring Jack's labor that summer; Barnes must have taken him to the authorities. Jack at once began to give crucial information.[1] Hark Moore was shot and wounded on Tuesday morning at Belmont; Thomas Ridley witnessed his arrest the next morning and noted that in addition to Trajan Doyel's pocketbook, "the prisoner had powder and shot and some silver in his pockets."[2] Nelson Edwards had been shot to death. Volunteers had seen him in Peter Edwards's orchard on Wednesday, 24 August, but he got away; a party of local militiamen, commanded by Capt. Joseph Joiner, caught him the next day. "The negro retreated," Joiner testified, "and this affiant—and others fired on him, and he was . . . killed before he was arrested." Someone, observing an old custom, took Nelson's head to Cross Keys for display.[3] Henry Porter, the paymaster, was cornered and killed probably on Thursday; his head too was brought to Cross Keys.[4] Five days later, on Tuesday, 30 August, Sam Francis was brought to town by Nathaniel Francis and jailed.[5] Two others were still missing: Will Francis and Nat Turner I. Will, about whom authorities knew nothing and whose fate they never learned, may have died in the attack on John T. Barrow or in one of the other skirmishes; only in September did Thomas R. Gray begin to distinguish Will from Billy Artis, the free black man with whom the "executioner" often was confused. Turner, the seventh man at Cabin Pond, remained at large.[6]

Counts

By Wednesday, 31 August, authorities knew with certainty of twenty-five other individuals who had joined the original seven as the rising progressed. All were in custody or dead by that day.

Six of the twenty-five had separated from the band on Monday, 22 August, one of whom was killed the next day. Nathan Blunt and the four boys who held horses—Moses Moore, Nathan Francis, Tom Francis, and Davy Francis—all fled at Parker's gate or Parker's field. They were jailed by 27 August and began telling what they knew.[7] Alfred Waller, the blacksmith, left the band at the Vaughan house only to be caught and hamstrung by A. P. Peete and company; he fell into the hands of the Greensville cavalry on Tuesday, just after that unit had surprised Nat Turner's men at the Harris house. Richard Porter's brother Thomas described Alfred's second capture: "I saw Alfred a negro the property of Levi Waller tied to a tree by a party of the Greensville Dragoons . . . and shot by them."[8] Waller later maintained that Alfred was dying from his hamstring wounds but that the Greensville men "deemed that his immediate execution would operate as a beneficial example to the other Insurgents—many of whom were still in arms and unsubdued."[9]

Five were captured or killed on Tuesday, 23 August: Moses Barrow (taken alive in the garden at Belmont after the shootout there); Curtis and Stephen Ridley (taken alive on their way to Allen's quarter by John C. Turner); and James and Sam Edwards, slaves of Peter Edwards.[10] James surrendered to his master, who delivered him to Capt. Joseph Joiner at Cross Keys—"with a request," Joiner recalled, "that I would prevent his being shot if I could." Joiner could not. "I immediately tied him and placed him against the side of the house," he said, "when a party rushed up and shot him—he fell dead at my feet."[11] Sam Edwards was pulled from his hiding place under his mother's cabin Tuesday night by a search party that included Nathaniel Francis, who recalled going to the Edwards plantation at around ten o'clock that night and hearing a member of the party knocking at the cabin door, insisting that "some-body was there." Francis said he did not recall whether Sam's mother had denied that her son was present; but, according to trial records, "the next he saw they had the prisoner in custody, he being under the house."[12]

Five were caught and shot to death on Wednesday, 24 August: Jordan Turner, Austin Edwards, and three of Richard Porter's slaves, Aaron, Jacob, and Moses. Jordan's killing was witnessed by Sampson C. Reese and John H. Barnes.[13] Austin was caught by a search party who had stopped at the Edwards plantation to get dinner. John Womack, a member of that party, recalled first chasing and losing Nelson Edwards in the orchard, then seeing Austin, "standing in the yard by himself perfectly defenceless." One of the party, Womack said, "shot him down instantly"; inspection revealed that Austin had a powder gourd in his pocket.[14] Jacob Porter, one of Nat Turner's last two followers on Tuesday, must have gone straight home after taking his leave. He, Moses Porter, and probably Aaron Porter were taken prisoner near the Porter house Wednesday by the white men Nat Turner had seen from his hiding place near Cabin Pond—a detachment of a volunteer company from Murfreesboro, North Carolina, riding with Drewry Bittle and three other Southampton County men. Accounts of these three killings, inconsistent in some details, suggest that the three Porter men were shot in a field near the Whitehead plantation.[15] Col. Charles Spiers, who did not witness the killings, understood that all three prisoners were shot in that field and that the white men, observing yet another tradition, had divided the contents of the prisoners' pockets—$23 and a gold watch.[16] Drewry Bittle, an eyewitness, did not describe the shooting of Aaron, one of the two oldest insurgents, who may have died separately; but Bittle did say that Jacob and Moses "both confessed they had been engaged with the other insurgents, after which they were both shot by the company present."[17]

One other man also may have been taken on 24 August. That was Marmaduke, the prisoner John Hampden Pleasants saw at the jail on the next day. Marmaduke died on 26 August, before he could be tried; he was almost certainly the same man, terribly wounded and in the jail, referred to as "Tom" in the *Norfolk Beacon* of 29 August.[18]

Seven were identified, captured, or killed between 25 and 30 August. Six of these were taken alive and jailed: Davy Waller, Daniel Porter, Davy Turner, Nat Turner II, Nelson Williams, and Dred Francis. The seventh, Sam Turner, apparently was found on 30 August but not taken alive.[19]

One other man was brought to jail before 5 September. He was Joe Turner, the hunter who had stumbled onto the insurgent gathering in the Whitehead yard; authorities knew by 30 August that while he had accompanied the insurgents briefly, his involvement in the uprising had been minimal.[20]

By the time of the first trial on 31 August, authorities in Jerusalem had identified thirty-one men, including the leader, who at some point had accompanied the insurgent band. They had nineteen of the thirty-one in custody or knew their whereabouts; they also knew that eleven others were dead. They were not yet aware of Will Francis or his role, and they were still looking for Nat Turner.

Sixteen other individuals played minor roles in the uprising without actually joining the band. By 31 August the court had all of them in custody or knew their whereabouts.[21] Two of the sixteen, Matt Ridley (a slave of Thomas Ridley) and Stephen Bell, had ridden briefly with Turner's men before separating. Both apparently gave themselves up by 23 August, offered timely intelligence, and avoided serious trouble.[22] The other fourteen either had shown support openly for the rising or had expressed sympathy for the insurgents. Among these were Lucy Barrow and two free black men, Billy Artis and Berry Newsom. Artis's body was found lying near his pistol on 2 September; Newsom would be tried in superior court in 1832.[23] The remaining eleven all survived the rising, were arrested, and faced trial by early September.[24]

Finally, as many as six men were mentioned as insurgents in documents of the day but did not come to the attention of the court. The evidence on them is meager. No one ever established the identities of "some" men (say, four?) mentioned in the *Confessions* as having joined near Trajan Doyel's house.[25] Nor did anyone identify two other men said to have ridden with the band, one perhaps from the farm of Salathiel Francis, the other identified only as the fourth recruit from Thomas Ridley's Buckhorn Quarter.[26]

The number of insurgents became fairly well established, therefore, by the end of August. If the six unidentified men did take part, the total number who actually rode with Turner's band at various times came to forty—exactly the estimate Gray offered on 17 September ("*the number 40 will include every insurgent who was with them for the least time, throughout their whole route*").[27] Gray must have kept a list. The fourteen others observed aiding or sympathizing with the band (excluding Matt Ridley and Stephen Bell) would have brought the total number involved to fifty-four, one fewer than the number of white dead.

By 2 September, ten of the forty slave participants certainly had been killed without trial (appendix F). The presumed deaths of Will Francis and Sam Turner, had they been confirmed, and that of Billy Artis would have brought the total number of suspected insurgents who had died without trial to thirteen.[28]

Atrocities

During the five days that followed 22 August, reports of lawless violence against black people began to circulate, some suggesting that many more than thirteen had been put to death. George W. Powell (who owned five slaves in 1830), the Methodist minister and relative of the Francis family, wrote one of the earliest such reports, dated Saturday, 27 August, at his home in Northampton County, twelve miles south of Cabin Pond. "A number of negroes have already been killed," Powell said (with as little precision as anyone at that point), adding that "the exact number will never be ascertained." He said that "thousands" of troops were in arms, "searching in every direction," and that "many negroes" were being killed "every day." Powell had gathered his impressions while country people of all descriptions still were encamped in the town and at makeshift redoubts around the parish. His account rested on anecdotes he had heard between Tuesday and Saturday. "The alarm has been great in Virginia and North Carolina," he wrote; "almost every individual who can bear arms is on guard, and on scouting parties night and day."[29]

One day after Powell dated his account, Brig. Gen. Richard Eppes described the violence against black victims in similar terms. Eppes, who had taken command of all militia forces two days after the uprising began, issued an order through his aide, Francis M. Boykin, at Jerusalem on Sunday, 28 August.[30] In the official transcription, the general referred only to "acts of barbarity and cruelty" and declined to "specify all the instances that he is bound to believe have occurred." He alluded to just one such instance, no doubt the shooting and decapitation of Nelson Edwards: "One ample sacrifice," he said, "has been made to personal feeling and outraged humanity." But there should be no more, he implied, since the crisis had passed. All of the principal insurgents had been shot or arrested, including at that point, he hoped (but in vain), Nat Turner himself. So he issued the following somewhat garbled order: "Under such circumstances the commanding officer feels the most entire confidence in recommending to all descriptions of persons to abstain in future, from any acts of violence to any personal property whatever, for any cause whatever, unless the person by whom the violence is done, being in arms or otherwise refusing submission to the command of legally authorized and responsible individuals, under the authority of the commanding Officer, or of the Justice of the Peace, or other persons appointed by law for such duty."[31] He regretted that any "necessity" should have existed to justify "a single act of atrocity," he said, introducing that word. "But he feels himself bound to declare, and hereby announces to the troops and the citizens, that no excuse will be allowed for any similar acts of violence, after the promulgation of this order, and further to declare, in the most explicit terms, that any who may attempt the repetition of such act shall be punished, if necessary, by the rigors of the articles of war."[32]

John Hampden Pleasants, who returned to Richmond three days after the order was issued, had heard that many black people (between twenty-five and forty, he thought, or "possibly a yet larger number") had been put to death summarily, "by decapitation or shooting." The general had put a stop to such atrocities, Pleasants reported, "to his great honor."[33] William C. Parker, writing on 31 August, offered a similar estimate of the number of such killings. "I suppose not less than thirty have been slain, some of them no doubt innocent," he wrote to the editor of the *Richmond Compiler*.[34]

Gray, ever skeptical, acknowledged in mid-September that some killings of that kind had occurred, but he minimized the number. "Those who have been condemned to death and those actually shot, exceed the number attributed to the insurgents," he said. "It follows then, as a necessary consequence, that several innocent persons must have suffered."[35] He meant that on 17 September, the day he completed his letter to the *Whig*, the number of innocents shot was no greater than four or five. His lack of precision indicates that he did not know who those victims were, but he did not doubt they had been killed. He conceded that officials had made allowances for vengeance by aggrieved white relatives, but for others who violated the law he called for a "settlement." "They must bear in mind," he said, "that the matter has one day to be adjudicated before an impartial judge." He expected his views to be controversial.[36]

Gray was aware that by early September the suppression had given way to white reaction across the region—a persecution of the black population through false accusations, arrests, sham trials, intimidation by patrols, and violence (or its threat) at the hands of vigilantes. Accounts in the press and in later memoirs gave evidence, however impressionistic and anecdotal, of counterterror.[37] It is telling that Gray assumed that the danger of reaction was real: in September, in the *Whig*, he would attempt to allay fears and restrain persecution; and in November, in the *Confessions*, he still would have those purposes in mind.[38] At no point did he assume, however, that an ensuing counterterror in Southampton had added to the death toll, or that lawless killing had continued into September.

In time, historians came to mistrust Gray and accepted the notion that many more than "several" innocent black people had died in a wave of atrocious killings after 22 August.[39] "The truth is, it was a Reign of Terror," wrote Thomas Wentworth Higginson in 1861. "The number shot down at random must, by all accounts, have amounted to many hundreds, but it is past all human registration now."[40] Higginson's estimate clearly applied not to the entire South or to Virginia, but to the single parish of St. Luke's. Even William S. Drewry, who attempted to minimize the scale of atrocities, partially accepted the notion in 1900. Drewry, however, made no systematic inquiry into the matter.[41] In 1920 John W. Cromwell repeated Higginson's assertion and offered a statistic for the entire state. "A reign of terror followed in Virginia," he said. "In a little more than one day 120 Negroes were killed."[42] The notion reappeared in the 1937 master's thesis of Herbert Aptheker, published in 1966. "It appears safe to say," Aptheker wrote, "that at least as many Negroes were killed without a trial as whites had perished due to the Revolt and that probably the number in the former case was considerably more than in the latter." Since he had placed the number of white people killed at "more than fifty-five but less than sixty-five," Aptheker must have assumed that considerably more than fifty-five black people in the county had been put to death without trial, innocent or not.[43]

Had a wave of atrocities on such a scale occurred in St. Luke's Parish in 1831, its effects should have been evident in local tax records the following spring. In fact, those records suggest that not more than twenty-four people could have become victims of lawless killing that year, including participants in the uprising. The tax and court records suggest, moreover, that most of the unlawful violence took place in August and was directed against participants and their supporters, rather than against people who had not taken part—the *innocent*, as Gray understood the term.[44]

For free blacks in St. Luke's Parish, the personal property tax lists of 1831 (completed three months before the uprising) and 1832 (begun four months after) show no evidence of widespread, extraordinary loss of life. The taxed free black population survived virtually unchanged. Compared to 1830, its numbers already had fallen slightly in the spring of 1831 (before the uprising) from 195 to 193, and they fell again in 1832, from 193 to 192.[45] The suicide or murder of Billy Artis could have accounted for the entire net loss in 1832, as could the jailing of Berry Newsom, who was being held for trial and execution that spring.[46] And the percentage of taxed free blacks who persisted (whose names reappeared from year to year) remained almost constant, with 83 percent of those taxed in 1830 reappearing in 1831, and 81 percent of those taxed in 1831 reappearing in 1832.

For the slave population, tax records do indicate significant losses after the rising. Between 1822 and 1831, the number of taxable slaves (aged twelve and older) in the parish had remained almost constant, hovering around an average of 2,462. Then the recorded number fell from 2,444 in the spring of 1831 to 2,337 in 1832 (after the rebellion), a decrease of 107 slaves, or 4.4 percent.[47] Though county officials must have noticed the drop, they made no comment. In 1832, as in previous years, the parish tax commissioner drew up his list of assessments according to form, naming each taxpayer and entering (in column five of the original document) the number of slaves over age twelve in each holding. As in previous years, he did not note the names of individual slaves. Accounting for losses in the slave population, therefore, necessarily involves some conjecture.

More than a third of the net decrease in the number of taxable slaves recorded in 1832 resulted from confirmed losses in the rising, of which there were forty. The county court removed thirty taxable slaves (twelve through transportation and eighteen through execution). Skirmishes and other armed encounters led to ten of the confirmed slave fatalities, nine of which involved atrocities as defined by Eppes and Pleasants.[48]

Half of the decrease can be attributed to anomalies in the 1832 tax list. In other words, half of the decrease was apparent, not real. A quarter of the missing slaves, twenty-eight in number, belonged to three holdings whose owners did not declare them as taxable property in 1832. Another quarter, or as many as twenty-six slaves, belonged to the estates of people slain in the uprising and similarly were not declared as taxable property that year. All fifty-four of the unreported slaves appear to have been alive in 1832 and to have been returned to the tax list in 1833.

Combined, the sentences, fatalities, and anomalies would account for ninety-four missing slaves, just thirteen short of the entire decline recorded in the tax list.

The remainder of the decline can be attributed to the loss of about fourteen missing slaves whose identities, roles in the uprising, or deaths were not documented at the time. Scattered references appeared in 1831 to as many as eight insurgent slaves who never came to the attention of the court and were never listed among the dead. Just two of these were mentioned at the time by name: Sam Turner and Will Francis. No one sought compensation for any of the eight; their deaths remained unconfirmed, but may have involved atrocities as defined by Eppes and Pleasants. Finally, still another group of six missing slaves may have suffered atrocious deaths; three were mentioned at the time (perhaps the innocent victims Gray had in mind), and three others were identified in 1900 by William S. Drewry (appendix F, parts C and D).

Evidence in the St. Luke's Parish tax rolls casts doubt on the notion that a wave of atrocities carried off as many as forty people, or, as Pleasants speculated, "possibly a yet larger number."

Lessons

Suppression, effectively accomplished early on Tuesday, 23 August, had required no more than twenty-four hours, though the fact did not become widely accepted until nearly a week later. William C. Parker reported that on Wednesday night, as he sat down to draft his first communiqué for the press, he got word that the rebellious slaves were "still embodied in the upper part of the county, whither I repaired with a small number of mounted men."[49] This was a false alarm. As late as Friday night, 26 August, the intrepid Parker was still in the saddle, the *Compiler* reported, "at the head of a party of 20 or 30 mounted persons," in pursuit of fugitives near Cross Keys. Parker's party, the editor said, was keeping the town informed: "Tidings had been received from them on Friday evening, that they had probably surrounded Nat and his small band, and expected to take them. But as no accounts had arrived up to 11 o'clock on Saturday, some doubts were entertained of their immediate success."[50]

As the fact of suppression became more certain, it prompted some crowing. "Twelve armed and resolute men, were certainly competent to have quelled them at any time," Pleasants declared on 25 August (a few hours before Parker's foray into the upper part of the county).[51] Two days later, Gen. William Brodnax, who was stationed just over the line in Greensville County, insisted that "a force of 20 resolute men" could have put the rebels down.[52] Yet, witnesses remarked that the insurgents had been well mounted and well armed.[53] Apparently they had ridden well, despite the quantities of brandy and cider they had consumed; and they had handled weapons with greater skill than anyone might have expected. Gray, who saw them at around two o'clock on Monday afternoon, observed that by then "the practice of drinking had been entirely suppressed."[54] And throughout that day they had remained "flinty," as Gray put it, never wavering in their ruthlessness.[55] In truth, they were not defeated by the two parties of white men they had confronted in Parker's field—those white men whose horses had bolted, whose guns had discharged by accident, and many of whom had retreated to the safety of the town. The band saw neither of those parties again, despite all the talk at the courthouse about hard riding in hot pursuit.

Nonetheless, it is true that Nat Turner could not keep his men together. In the hours between Monday afternoon and Tuesday morning, the insurgents dispersed and retreated three times under fire and once in self-induced alarm. Their failure to cohere was a consequence of the essential secrecy at the heart of Turner's plan, which made it impossible for him to prepare anyone outside the conspiracy for the action to come. He did manage to conduct a few minutes' drill at the Travis barn, recalling maneuvers from 1812; but he did not have time to build the discipline necessary for guerrilla action or sufficient to storm the bridge, capture the town, and inspire the slave population to rise.

Authorities in Jerusalem, knowing nothing at first about the conspiracy, had assumed they were confronting the general uprising that had long been feared in Virginia. (This, they thought, was *it*.) Early impressions of the insurgents had been alarming, Gray conceded. ("*The fact of their being mounted, and their irregular mode of riding, caused their number to appear much greater than it really was.*")[56] The alarm at the courthouse was evident in the letter James Trezvant dispatched to Petersburg Monday morning by an express rider, later identified as the town constable, Thomas C. Jones.[57] Trezvant reported that "a large number of negroes" had been embodied in Southampton and that "many families" had been murdered; the number of insurgents, he said, was "too large to be put down without a considerable military force."[58] Those who saw the letter in Petersburg said that it appeared to have been written in "great haste." (Trezvant dated it 21 August by mistake.) "It required some little time to decypher it," the *Compiler* reported. "To remove any sort of doubt of its authenticity, Mr. Gilliam of Petersburg had certified that he knew Col. T's hand writing and that it was genuine."[59] The town recorder forwarded the message by fresh express to the capital, where it arrived at 3:00 A.M. Tuesday.[60] Later that day in Jerusalem, at around noon, Southampton officials—no doubt Trezvant, acting as magistrate, and the clerk, James Rochelle—dispatched Thomas R. Gray to Norfolk to enlist aid from U.S. forces stationed there. Gray arrived on the deck of the U.S.S. *Natchez* at 3:00 A.M. Wednesday, waking Com. Jesse D. Elliot with a report that "50 or 60 persons had been slaughtered," and that the local militia were unable to suppress the uprising.[61]

From all directions there began a gathering of forces estimated at over three thousand troops.[62] John Hampden Pleasants and his company came eighty-one miles on a "rapid, hot and most fatiguing march from Richmond."[63] Volunteers from Norfolk made a similar march from the east: "We are very much fatigued having rode 55 miles the first 16 hours," a Norfolk man reported. "Our horses worn out and ourselves completely knocked up."[64]

The Roanoke Blues, a cavalry company from Halifax, North Carolina, joined the campaign, departing for Southampton at four in the afternoon on Tuesday, 23 August, after express riders reported that insurgents had gathered in numbers reaching "2 or 300" or more. A spokesman for the Blues, Jesse H. Simmons, later gave an account of their march. At the Roanoke River crossing, Simmons said, they met another express, "from a highly respectable gentleman of Southampton," who informed them that rebel forces had increased in number to "about 1000 or 1500" and were continuing to grow in strength. The Blues proceeded "with a determination to reach the Virginia line by day break, so that no time might be lost." At about three o'clock Wednesday morning they reached the house of A. P. Smith, a mile or so south of the state line, where they found guards stationed. "They informed us that from circumstances and reports combined, it was probable that a party of negroes would or had crossed the Meherrin river near Haley's Bridge, and would come on to the road about that point." Thus informed, the Blues determined to rest until daylight, "being considerably fatigued, having rode all night." With the guards posted as sentinels, the men bedded down in Smith's house. Fearful of a surprise attack, however, the officers gave "strict orders" that each man should lie on his weapons. "About 4 o'clock," Simmons recalled, "one of the company had occasion to leave the room, and hearing the trampling of horses approaching, ran back into the house, and observed in a low tone of voice, that 'some one was coming.'" The men were wakened and prepared for an attack. Then, in a room lit by the moon, the Blues suffered their first and only casualty of the Southampton campaign: "One of the company awakening and mistaking the bustle for a surprise, seeing, by moonlight, a man not in uniform with his right hand raised as if in the act of stabbing one of the Blues, immediately fired his musket and lodged its contents in the leg of Mr. Shepard Lee. The wound caused his death in 35 hours."[65] Except for the cavalry from Greensville County and volunteers from Norfolk and Murfreesboro, all of the forces who reached the county, including the Blues, did so after dawn on Wednesday, 24 August. Later that day, Gen. Eppes declared the uprising suppressed.[66]

As the general discovered, however, the public had found a dire meaning in scenes like the one Mrs. Vaughan had discerned from her porch. Eppes confronted a panic, the effect of terror. On 28 August, seven days after the skirmish at Parker's field, he had to insist that people return to their homes. He assured citizens—"and *particularly* that portion of its citizens residing in the neighborhood where the violence has been done"—that there no longer existed "any cause of apprehension for the public safety or the security of individuals." Peace had been restored. "He desires, therefore," his aide announced, "that the citizens and their families, who have assembled at the Cross Keys, seeking the protection he has been called to afford, will return to their respective places of abode." Presumably, the order applied to people gathered in all places of refuge—the town, the swamps, Hick's Ford in Greensville County, the camp at Pate's Hill. It applied specifically to those at Cross Keys, including "all slaves, free negroes and mulattoes, at that place, who are not charged with the offence of rebellion or conspiracy to rebel." Slaves, free blacks, and mulattoes, Eppes insisted, should return "with written authority, if deserved, to their homes or masters."[67]

Anxiety was still evident in October, when a subscriber to the *Norfolk American Beacon* reported a remarkable series of deaths in Southampton, "within the period of a few weeks, and in the compass of a few miles." Names of the dead and their ages (all presented in numbers divisible by five) were as follows: "Capt. *Thos Gray*, aged 75; Mr. *Ro. Ricks*, aged 85; Mr. *Dixon Kitchen*, aged 80; Mr. *Andrews*, aged 75; *John Morris*, aged 90; Mrs. *Mary Boykin*, aged 80; Mrs. *Sarah Draper*, aged 90, and *Mrs. Mumford*, aged 90 years." All eight of the deceased had been active and in good health, the subscriber noted, "to the moment of the attack which brought them to their end." The arithmetical significance of their singular mortality did not go unnoticed: "The ages of the 8 individuals [make] an aggregate of 655 years, and an average of 83 1/8 years each."[68] This intelligence appeared immediately below the lead item in the news, "Emigrations to Liberia," which announced the chartering of "the fine ship James Perkins," 325 tons, capacity 300 passengers, "for the conveyance of Emigrants to the American Colony at Monrovia."[69]

Weeks after the crisis, local officials in southeastern Virginia were still pleading with Governor John Floyd to send them arms. "I had another application for arms from the town of Norfolk," Floyd complained to his diary on 17 October. "I am disgusted with the cowardly fears of that town." The pleas persisted into late November. "There are still demands for arms in the lower country," Floyd wrote in his entry on the twenty-first of that month. "I could not have believed there was half the fear amongst the people of the lower country in respect to their slaves."[70]

It was difficult, given that reaction, to dismiss the affair as insignificant, as one Southampton magistrate acknowledged on 4 September. "It came upon us as unexpectedly as anything possibly could, and produced a pretty general panic, especially among our females," he told the editors of the *Richmond Enquirer*. "In fact it was a desperate affair."[71] Two weeks later the same editors published a dark meditation by an anonymous subscriber whose thoughts had taken a significant turn. The circumstances of "the late murders in Southampton County," this subscriber said, were "too melancholy and too important a matter" for an intelligent community either to exaggerate or to blink. "As an insurrectionary movement," he said, "we can view this affair in no other light than one of very little moment." This, assuredly, was no Haitian Revolution. "But that a single neighborhood should have been the scene, in a thickly settled county, of such horrible murder—and that a few desperate villains should have had it in their power to destroy so many families before they were checked or routed, is a most serious matter—one that calls aloud for enquiry; and that the people and Government must hereafter guard against." The militia and its equipment, he said, had proved to be in "a most shameful condition."[72] (The white population, in this instance, had not really merited the reputation it later acquired as "one great militia.")[73] And the uprising had stirred an old fear. "I know what a panic can be produced, where attacks are made unexpectedly," the writer said, touching on the very thing that had drawn people to refuge in the town and Cross Keys. Inquiry must focus now on security, even in a thickly settled county. Here the author might have turned his thoughts to the ending of slavery (as indeed Governor Floyd would do, for a time), but he did not. Instead, he urged the General Assembly to call upon the state's "experienced officers" to devise a plan for distributing arms and organizing a militia suited, as he put it, "to our peculiar situation."[74]

In November, Gray's new friend in Richmond, Pleasants of the *Whig*, endorsed this line of thinking. The uprising, his paper said, had forced great questions upon the public and its legislature. "That which was esteemed too delicate to mention, before the occurrences in Southampton, is now freely and unreservedly canvassed," it said. Now, even slaveholders acknowledged the danger. "Every man feels the force of Mr. Jefferson's metaphor, that we have the wolf by the ears, and its increasing truth."[75] Someone at the *Whig* had seen at least a portion of Jefferson's confidential letter of 1820 to Congressman John Holmes, with its famous metaphor borrowed from Suetonius, biographer of Tiberius. But the *Whig* writer omitted that part of the passage in which Jefferson elaborated upon the dilemma within the image: "we can neither hold him, nor safely let him go."[76] Pleasants and his paper now were choosing the first of those two negative options. They too were drifting with the tide of opinion away from the notions of visionaries and fanatics. They now wanted the General Assembly to improve "the Patrole," as the writer called those units recently in action south of the James, so that local law enforcement would not promote "tyranny and exasperation" and thus provoke further uprisings. He thought that if legislators did "nothing else"—a discreet allusion to emancipation—they might undertake at least "the improvement of the Police."[77]

The courthouse circle in Jerusalem turned their thoughts similarly toward the police. Gray had moved cautiously in that direction by the third week of September, though he advised against keeping a permanent armed force in any section of the country, reasoning that such a policy would betray fear. Better to maintain—but only for "some time," he thought—"a regular patrol, always under the command of a discreet person, who will not by indiscriminate punishment, goad these miserable wretches into a state of desperation."[78] William C. Parker embraced the notion of suppression. By that same week in September, he had formed a volunteer corps of "the most respectable citizens," who at once elected him their captain. His men had adopted a uniform, "dark gray trimmed with black braid, gilt bullet buttons, etc.—Caps with *black* horse hair," he reported to Col. Bernard Peyton, an influential acquaintance in Richmond; "& we style ourselves the 'Southampton Greys.'" He had petitioned the governor to supply arms for seventy-five men and prevailed upon Peyton to lobby for the Greys. "We want carbines, swords, and pistols of the first order, such as the Richmond troop bore of the two latter," he wrote, recalling the gallant visitors from the capital. He also asked for a copy of the state's latest manual of cavalry tactics. "The late events in this county," he said, "have rendered us quite military."[79] So they had.

PART THREE

TELLING EVIDENCE

Can you not think the same ideas, and strange appearances about this time in the heaven's might prompt others, as well as myself, to this undertaking?

—Nat Turner, *The Confessions of Nat Turner*

The Inquiry

I have examined every source for authentic information.
—Thomas R. Gray, letter, *Richmond Constitutional Whig*

Gray must have returned from Norfolk on Thursday morning, 25 August, in company with the expedition he had been sent to recruit from Fortress Monroe and the U.S. ships *Warren* and *Natchez*. "The weather was oppressively warm," a member of the expedition wrote after their day-and-a-half trek, "and the men suffered exceedingly." They found Jerusalem crowded with country people and militia units from surrounding counties; Gen. Eppes, who had established headquarters in town the previous day, directed the Norfolk officers and men to make camp at the racetrack on the northwest side of the town.[1] So scarce was space that Eppes's quartermaster, Francis E. Rives of Prince George County, had to rent an office in Gray's house, five doors from the courthouse and six from the jail. In keeping with the military atmosphere, the quartermaster's assistant soon would be referring to the young attorney as "Major Gray."[2]

At nine o'clock that morning the Richmond Dragoons, between sixty and seventy cavalrymen under Capt. Randolph Harrison, rode into town, accompanied by Pleasants of the *Whig*, the only journalist to visit the county after the uprising. Pleasants, too, complained of the heat. For six full days, the Dragoons would make their headquarters at Henry B. Vaughan's tavern and take some meals there, though they bedded down elsewhere. Pleasants apparently introduced himself at once to the town's postmaster, Theodore Trezvant, whose store and house stood across Main Street from the tavern, a few steps north of the courthouse and the jail.[3] The postmaster, who was privy to details gathered at the courthouse by his older brother James (the magistrate and congressman), already had dispatched to Richmond two early reports, one of which Pleasants had cited in the *Whig*.[4]

From Trezvant's place, the journalist evidently made his way to the jail, where he found thirteen prisoners, "one or more of them severely wounded."

He then must have called on the man who in two months' time would write down Nat Turner's confession. That evening, by candlelight, perhaps in Gray's office, Pleasants drafted the opening section of a dispatch to the *Whig*. He knew by then that the insurgents had attacked the Travis farm first. He included details he must have obtained from Gray concerning the scene at the Waller farm; and Gray must have given him a fresh, if not yet final, list of white victims, naming twenty-three individuals (with some errors) and putting the number of whites killed at sixty-two. On Saturday, 27 August, Pleasants finished his dispatch and sent it along with the fresh list to Richmond, where both documents appeared on Monday, 29 August, in the *Whig*.[5]

That tabulation of victims and attacks was the sixth of fifteen such documents published between August and November, all compiled by members of the courthouse circle who took part in the unofficial inquiry into the rebellion. Word of the inquiry began to circulate within days of the uprising. "A judicial investigation will soon take place," the *Norfolk Herald* reported on Monday, 29 August, "when a correct history of this most extraordinary affair will be obtained."[6] Eppes noted the next day that "investigations" already had begun.[7] Seven men with ties to the court were involved, though their names were never announced: James Trezvant, the magistrate and recently retired congressman; his brother Theodore, the postmaster; James Rochelle, the county clerk; his brother Clements Rochelle, the sheriff and colonel of the local militia; and defense attorneys William C. Parker, James S. French, and Gray himself. The prosecuting attorney, Meriwether B. Brodnax (now of Greensville County, but formerly of Southampton), and Gen. Eppes (from Sussex County) also took part. Gray in particular seemed moved to explain what had happened.

T. R. Gray

Thomas R. Gray got his license to practice law in September 1830, less than a year before the uprising.[8] Like Nat Turner, he had been born in Southampton in 1800 and had lived there his entire life. He was the youngest of six children (four were sons) of Thomas and Ann Cocke Brewer Gray. His father's family had lived in Nottoway Parish for four generations, their first settler having been the young attorney's great-grandfather, Joseph Gray (1707–71), who arrived before the county separated from Isle of Wight. Gray's grandfather, Col. Edwin Gray (1743–90), held more than twenty slaves and nearly fifteen hundred acres by 1790.[9] Colonel Gray kept a diary in 1778 about his horses and their breeding, including a note about his stallion Damon covering a black mare in 1777.[10] At the grandfather's death in 1790, Gray's father, Capt. Thomas Gray (1771–1831), inherited five slaves and four hundred acres in Nottoway Parish near Round Hill; his land was about ten miles (by straight line) north-northeast of Jerusalem and twenty miles from Cabin Pond.[11] There, as the son of a slaveholder, T. R. Gray grew up. The family's home property bordered the plantation of a close family friend, Joseph Ruffin, a cousin of the father of Edmund Ruffin (1794–1865), the agricultural reformer.

Joseph Ruffin died in 1807, leaving a will that introduced the Gray children to the idea of emancipation and its antithesis. Ruffin freed one slave, Charles, who continued to live in the neighborhood and in 1816 petitioned the court for permission to remain in the county. In the same will, Ruffin bequeathed one slave to each child of Capt. Gray; to his young namesake, Thomas Ruffin Gray, he gave a boy named Hartwell.[12] In time Gray's father sold some of these legacy slaves (including Hartwell, evidently) and pocketed the proceeds. In his own will of 1831, Gray Sr. threatened to disinherit any child who filed a claim against his estate to recover losses "on account of the said negroes."[13] And yet, despite the captain's hard dealing and impetuous temperament, the younger Gray never broke openly with his father.

In 1821 Capt. Gray paid the second-highest total tax bill of any resident of Southampton County, falling below only John Urquhart Sr., his immediate neighbor to the north. The captain owned 2,408 acres and, according to the 1820 census, held fifty-seven slaves, the ninth-largest holding in the county.[14] Gray raised hogs and sheep and grew corn and cotton (in 1831 he owned a cotton gin worth $30); but, following family tradition, he chiefly bred fine horses. His stable (twenty-three horses in 1821, including two valuable studs) ranked third in size in the county.[15] His sons grew up on horseback.

Considering his wealth, Capt. Gray's house at Round Hill was an unpretentious affair. In 1821 the buildings on his land were assessed altogether at just $850 (compared, for example, to those at Catherine Whitehead's plantation, worth $1,250). The master's house cannot have been worth more than $300 (comparable in value to Rebecca Vaughan's), an indication perhaps of its age and condition.[16] In 1831 his residence had a kitchen, a cellar, and a main section of two stories with a hall on the main floor and passage on the second; it had a parlor, dining room, and as many as four bedchambers. His personal possessions placed him among the gentry, despite his being cash poor at the end of his life.[17] In 1815 he paid tax on a mahogany bookcase, six mahogany chairs, two looking glasses, a clothes press, and thirteen gilt-framed prints. (His brother, Edwin Sr., owned a portrait in crayon.) In 1821 Capt. Gray owned a four-wheeled carriage, one of just twelve in the parish.[18] Two inventories taken at Round Hill in 1831 listed among other items two gigs, two guns, a brace of pistols, three saddles, three barrels of wine, two stills, and 160 casks. His house had three pairs of andirons, six Windsor chairs, nine mahogany chairs, two carpets, eleven window curtains, two looking glasses (as in 1815), three tables, six tablecloths, eleven silver tablespoons, and eleven silver teaspoons. He owned a silver watch (worth $12), a backgammon game, and a map of the United States (worth 25 cents). He also had a bookcase (in the upstairs passage, worth $10, probably the one taxed in 1815) and a library (worth at least $30) that included works of Pope, Rousseau, and Shakespeare; at least one volume of the British satire collection *The Foundling Hospital for Wit*; and religious and other works not specified.[19] Some of the twenty-eight volumes young Gray had in his office in August 1831 probably came from his father's library, including Hening's *Statutes* (1819 and 1823) and Shakespeare's plays.

Gray claimed in 1834 that he had studied law—"in my youth," he said—though he left no record of having enrolled at a college or law school of any kind.[20] Between 1815 and 1820, he may have followed his cousin James as an apprentice to James Rochelle in the county clerk's office, which functioned at times as a school for lawyers.[21] He apparently put his knowledge of the law to use between 1819 and 1822, when he and his brother Edwin became involved in court proceedings after an affray (evidence of temper).[22] But law was not his first choice. He had wanted a life at Round Hill.

Ann Gray, his mother, died before 1820.[23] In the spring of 1821, his father began to distribute patrimonies; young Thomas, at age twenty-one, got four hundred acres at the Round Hill plantation, on which there stood a structure worth $50.[24] That spring, for the first time, Gray had his own entry in the Nottoway Parish personal property tax list, an assessment for two horses and fourteen slaves over age twelve.[25] By the spring of 1824 he apparently had built a house of his own, bringing the total value of his buildings to $500 (comparable in value to those of John T. Barrow in 1831).[26] At some point between 1823 and 1829 he married Mary A. Gray, whose family shared his surname and who may have been a sister of Julia Gray (wife of Edwin III, Gray's eldest brother); and he fathered a child, Ann Douglas Gray, an infant in 1831.[27]

His wealth and influence began to rise. In 1827 he held twenty-three taxable slaves, his peak holding.[28] In 1828 he became a justice of the peace and attended his first court meeting as a magistrate.[29] In 1829 he bought the patrimonial lands of his recently deceased brother Robert, bringing his holding of real property to a peak of eight hundred acres; he also took possession of Robert's property in town, one full lot (with a house) and three-quarters of another.[30] In 1830 he became a founding member of the Jerusalem Jockey Club.[31]

But even as he rose, his family's fortunes were sinking. Between 1822 and 1831, a period of hard times south of the James River, his brother Edwin fell into debt, and so did his father. By 1826 Edwin III owed sixteen creditors $3,737.61 (give or take a few dollars), or about as much as Edwin was worth.[32] By 1829 the brother was landless; in 1830 he held just two slaves, and in 1831 he paid tax on no personal property whatsoever—no gigs, no horses, no slaves.[33] Meanwhile, by 1828 Capt. Gray, the father, had accumulated a similar pile of debt. Thomas, the youngest son, assumed payment on an obligation of $1,900 his father had incurred to buy land, in return for which Thomas accepted Robert's real estate (including the house in town) and seven slaves.[34] In 1830 Gray's father, who no longer owned a carriage, turned to a new neighbor, Dr. Orris A. Browne, for security on loans of $2,745.37, offering as collateral 811 acres, ten horses, and eleven slaves.[35] In no time at all, the captain would lose most of his slaves. At the time of the 1830 census, he held just thirty-three, down by twenty-four from 1820; in October 1831 his estate held just eight, three of whom (Fed, Tom, and Peg) were too old to be taxed.[36]

T. R. Gray, as he now styled himself, sank with his family. He gathered some cash in March 1830 by selling five hundred acres to Dr. Browne, but two months later, still in trouble, he sought security for debts of $3,440 (including the one he had assumed for his father). He offered as collateral his gold watch, his gun, his right to a tract of land in North Carolina, his remaining 324 acres at Round Hill, and the house he had acquired from his father in Jerusalem.[37] On 4 February 1831 (one day before the creditors of John W. Reese met near Cross Keys) his trustee sold his remaining land at Round Hill for nonpayment.[38] In the spring of 1831, Gray, like his brother, held no taxable slaves and owned no horses; his father had been reduced to five of each.[39] The family had lost a large portion of their slaves almost certainly through forced sales. They left no record of having freed anyone.

Forced from the ranks of planters and slaveholders, young Gray moved to town and by March 1830 was living at his house on Main Street.[40] In October 1830 the magistrates certified his qualifications as an attorney and in December admitted him to practice in the court, whereupon he resigned as justice of the peace. He would look back on his change of vocation with a sense of loss. "Born and reared in the County of Southampton," he wrote in 1834, "having experienced every vicissitude of fortune, at the age of Thirty years, I found it necessary to resort to the practice of the Law."[41] He must have been near his desk on Monday morning, 22 August, when the express arrived from the neighborhood of Cabin Pond.

Reconnoitering

On Tuesday morning, 23 August, after the night pursuit across St. Luke's Parish, Gray took part in some reconnoitering. Before leaving for Norfolk, he joined other volunteers retracing, he said, "the route pursued by the banditti." What he saw shocked him. "My imagination was struck with more horror, than the most dreadful carnage in a field of battle could have produced," he said. "In visiting each house, the mind became sick, and its sensibilities destroyed." Inside the Travis house he viewed the bodies of the two little boys, "who were sleeping so close, that the same stroke nearly severed each neck," and, in the fireplace, the remains of the "little infant with its head cut off." He said nothing about the other sites near Cabin Pond, but he must have seen the corpse of John T. Barrow, "butchered" by the "savages."[42] (The previous day, along Barrow Road, Gray must have witnessed the hamstringing of Alfred, Levi Waller's blacksmith, though he did not mention that incident.)[43] He visited the Waller house a second time, before the burials there. "At Levi Waller's the spectacle was truly touching," he recalled. (That scene he described—as if viewed from the saddle or through a doorway—as "the massacre before me," principally of "helpless women and children.") An incident there remained in memory: he encountered a survivor, he said, a "little girl about 12 years of age, looking with an agonized countenance, on a heap of dead bodies lying before her." The child spoke to him. "She gave me a minute account of the tragedy there acted, having witnessed it from her place of concealment."[44] He had met Clarinda Jones, his first witness. It was Gray, apparently, who lifted the child to his saddle and carried her to her home. William C. Parker, who visited the Waller farm later on Tuesday morning with a different group of volunteers, did not mention her.[45]

Members of the unofficial inquiry began their labors as early as Tuesday evening, 23 August, while Gray was on his way to Norfolk and the *Natchez*. Their first task was to count the dead. A list of targeted families appeared in the *Norfolk Herald* on Friday, 26 August, three days after Gray's reconnaissance, and one day after the editor Pleasants arrived in Jerusalem. Its anonymous compiler, working just hours after the insurgents had been dispersed, put the total number of dead at fifty-eight. The compiler listed in tabular form the names of nine families and the number killed in each, in descending order, from fourteen dead at the Waller farm down to two in the "Barnes" family (a faulty transcription of *Barrow*). Those whose identities were still unknown, ten in number, came last. An express rider from Suffolk, Virginia, delivered this list to Norfolk on Wednesday, 24 August, after Gray had passed through the city.[46] Four versions of the list—each reporting the same number of dead, and each introducing corrections and new errors—appeared within four days: in the *Philadelphia National Gazette* and *Richmond Compiler* on 27 August, and in the *Richmond Enquirer* and Tarboro *North Carolina Free Press* three days later. A different, later list appeared in both Norfolk papers on 26 August, having been carried to Norfolk from Jerusalem by express rider. Compiled on the twenty-fourth (a day or so after the first list), it named eight families in no discernible order and introduced still more errors. It put the number killed, including "others not recollected," at sixty-four.[47]

Over the next two months, Theodore Trezvant and T. R. Gray became the chief compilers of such lists, their work distinguishable in form and content. Gray, for example, introduced the names of defendants. Their eight lists appeared in the following order:

1. [T. Trezvant], *Norfolk Herald*, 29 August, fifty-nine white victims;[48]
2. [Gray], *Richmond Constitutional Whig*, 29 August, sixty-two white victims;
3. [T. Trezvant], *Raleigh Register*, 1 September, fifty-nine white victims;
4. [Gray], *Norfolk American Beacon*, 14 September, fifty-five white victims, twenty-one slave defendants;
5. T. Trezvant, *Raleigh Register*, 15 September, fifty-five white victims;
6. [Gray], *Richmond Constitutional Whig*, 26 September, fifty-five white victims;
7. [Gray], in Warner, *Authentic and Impartial Narrative*, ca. 21 October, fifty-five white victims, nineteen slave defendants;
8. Gray, *Confessions*, ca. 22 November, fifty-five white victims, forty-eight slave and five free black defendants.

Trezvant apparently wrote down his first list of white victims on 24 August, drawing on information supplied by his contacts at the courthouse.

He must have sent a copy to his colleague John Wheeler, the postmaster in Murfreesboro, North Carolina, who forwarded the document on 25 August to the *Norfolk Herald*, adding that the colonel of the Southampton militia (Clements Rochelle, the sheriff) had confirmed its contents. This list appeared in the *Herald* on Monday, 29 August (one week after the uprising), and in the *Beacon* the next day. Trezvant put the number of dead at fifty-nine, mistakenly including the names of four survivors. He drew no attention to two significant details embedded in his list: he had named the family of Joseph Travis first and then listed others through the family of Rebecca Vaughan in correct chronological order.[49]

Gray must have produced his first list on Thursday, 25 August, the day he returned from Norfolk. He must have given it that afternoon to Pleasants; it appeared four days later without attribution in the *Whig*.[50] Gray named the Travis family first, as Trezvant had, revealing that he knew where the insurgents had started. He then proceeded through the other targeted families near Cabin Pond (but not in chronological order) and concluded with those along Barrow Road (in precise order). He noted that Levi Waller and one child—the first published reference to her—had escaped at the Waller house, "the child by getting up the chimney." Finally, he named two households (one of which in fact had not been attacked) from other locations and gave the total number of dead as sixty-two. Over the next four months, four different versions of this list would appear, organized in the same unique way but revised in content: in the *Norfolk American Beacon* on 14 September (without attribution); in the anonymous letter (from Gray) to Pleasants dated 17 September (published in the *Whig* on 26 September); in Samuel Warner's *Authentic and Impartial Narrative* (copyrighted in New York on 21 October); and finally—evidence that Gray was the compiler—in late November, in *The Confessions of Nat Turner*. In each of the four revisions, Gray put the number of white people killed at fifty-five and, starting with the second revision, provided the given names of eighteen white victims, more than any other authority (appendix E).

William C. Parker compiled his own list of victims, which he dispatched in a communiqué of 31 August to the Richmond *Compiler*. The work of a man in a hurry, Parker's complete list appeared as follows: "The names of the families slain were Travis's, Saluthrel's Francis', Whitehead's, Reese's, Waller's, Mrs. Vaughan's, Jacob William's, all but himself, and William Williams'."[51] He omitted the names of the Turner, Francis, Barrow, and Worrell families, all mentioned in earlier lists.

The lists revealed that within two or three days, thanks to observations from the field, participants in the inquiry had grasped the geographic scope of the uprising, if not of Turner's plan. They had sensed almost from the outset the general sequence of the attacks, beginning near Cross Keys and moving toward Jerusalem. They were able to make an almost-definitive count of the white victims, whittling the toll as survivors were found, though they never did compile a complete list of the dead by name. They also believed they knew who had led the insurgents. On Wednesday, 24 August, Richard Eppes named two suspects: "*General Nat Turner, (a preacher and a slave)* and Will Artist, a freeman of colour."[52] On the same day, independently, the volunteer (almost certainly James S. French) who wrote to his father in Petersburg said that the insurgents had been "led on by a fellow called Capt. Nat Turner."[53] Witnesses had difficulty identifying "Will," or "Will Artist," or the free man they thought they had seen, but all across the parish people had recognized Nat Turner on sight.

Informants

Of the thirteen prisoners John Hampden Pleasants said were in the jail on Thursday, he gave the name of just one, the young man he called "Marmaduke," aged about twenty-one, he said.[54] He did not mention three others who certainly were in jail and who knew a great deal about the origins and early hours of the insurrection: Hark Moore, Turner's original confidant, wounded at Samuel Blunt's house on Tuesday and arrested there on Wednesday; Jack Reese, present at the dinner in the old field, witness to the first six or seven attacks, and who separated from the band and surrendered early on Monday; and the boy Moses Moore, in custody probably by Wednesday.[55]

The jail, no more than three hundred yards from Gray's door, stood on public grounds near the courthouse and clerk's office, immediately to the right as one entered town from the bridge. It had been completed in 1824 under the supervision of Jeremiah Cobb, a local architect of some repute, a planter in Nottoway Parish, and the leading magistrate on the county court. The jail was surrounded by a wall of unrecorded height and material, also completed in 1824. The interior was divided into four cells, or "apartments," each enclosed by iron bars crossing at right angles and secured to the ceiling timbers. Each cell, according to state law, was required to have a stove, though a court committee in 1832 found just two of those conveniences, one of which was out of order. The apartments in 1832 were in good repair, "properly whitewashed & kept clean," and adequately ventilated for summer's heat, though they lacked shutters sufficient to protect against "the keen winds of winter."[56] In the jail, probably by Wednesday evening, Jack and Moses began talking to authorities; soon thereafter, Gray would act as counsel for both.

In Jack Reese's confession, Gray and his associates obtained the only account they would have until November of the dinner at Cabin Pond. Jack told them of Hark's role in recruiting him and described the plan ("*to rise and kill all the white people*"), the objection Jack had raised ("*their number was too few*"), and Hark's reply ("*as they went on and killed the whites the blacks would join them*").[57] Jack apparently kept to himself other details about the Travises, their infant, the Reeses, and anyone else he may have encountered while riding with the band.

Moses Moore gave the first account of the first attack, which he recalled from a vantage point outside the Travis house. Pleasants learned of this account before he returned to Richmond, either directly from Moses or through Gray and Theodore Trezvant. "According to the evidence of a negro boy whom they carried along to hold their horses," the journalist reported, "Nat commenced the scene of murder at the first house (Travis') with his own hand."[58] In many ways, Moses was the inquiry's most useful informant. A sheriff's deputy and guard at the jail, Jesse Drewry, said that on several occasions he heard the boy give evidence "freely and voluntarily" about other prisoners. Moses had insisted that "he had been compelled to go with the insergeants, that he continued with them untill after the insergeants were repulsed & forced to retreat from Parkers field," the deputy told the court.[59] In fact, Moses had observed all but two of the attacks, more than any witness, including Hark Moore or Nat Turner. His recollections enabled authorities to piece together a chronology of attacks like the one implied in the intricate sequence of names Theodore Trezvant constructed on Wednesday, 24 August, for his first list of victims. The same sequence appeared in the revised list Trezvant compiled on 5 September and sent to the editors of the *Raleigh Register*, explaining that he had "waited for correct information."[60] The Raleigh list established definitively the number of victims—fifty-five—and the order of attacks. Gray evidently concurred on the number, but not yet on the order. In none of the lists that bore Gray's stamp before November did he follow the order of events Trezvant posited.

Only in the *Confessions* would he do so, and there only in the narrative cast in the voice of Nat Turner.

Survivors along the insurgents' route began to give evidence by Thursday, 25 August. Theodore Trezvant heard some of their testimony: his first list of victims included a detail he may have gleaned from Mary T. Barrow about the attack on her husband, "who bravely fought between 20 and 30 negroes until his Wife escaped."[61] Pleasants apparently heard Dilsy Vaughan herself tell of the attack at the Vaughan house.[62] And Gray, after hearing an early account by Levi Waller, may have told Pleasants about Waller's retreat and return, together with other details Gray had observed with his own eyes—the "heap" of bodies at the house (both Gray and Pleasants used that word), and the discovery of the little survivor. "One small child in the house at the time," Pleasants reported, "escaped by concealing herself in the fire place, witnessing from the place of her concealment, the slaughter of the family, and her elder sisters [*sic*] among them."[63]

Authorities were given a windfall on 30 or 31 August, when a statement by Nat Turner's wife came to their attention, along with papers in her possession thought to have been written in Turner's hand. James Trezvant, the retiring congressman, had learned of the woman's statements before court convened (to hear charges against the first nine defendants) on the thirty-first; he knew that morning about her admission that Turner had been "digesting" the plan for the rebellion "for years." Reports concerning his papers began to circulate at the same time. Thomas Ritchie at the *Enquirer* in Richmond had heard about one document by Thursday, 1 September, when he wrote a summary of a dispatch from Gen. Eppes dated on the thirtieth. "It is reported," Ritchie said, "that a map was found and said to have been drawn by Nat Turner, with poke-berry juice, which was descriptive of the county of Southampton!"[64]

The Turner papers were in Gray's office as late as 17 September, when he described their contents for Pleasants. "They are filled with hieroglyphical characters, conveying no definite meaning." The oldest appeared to have been written in blood, he thought, "and on each paper, a crucifix and the sun, is distinctly visible; with the figures, 6,000, 30,000, 80,000, &c." The marks and numbers seemed inscrutable, but one document did make sense. "There is likewise a piece of paper, of a late date which all agree, is a list of his men; if so, they were short of twenty."[65] (In fact, Pleasants may have learned about the papers and odd figures before leaving Jerusalem on 31 August. On his return to Richmond he mentioned a theory circulating in Jerusalem that Nat Turner had deceived his followers into believing "there were only 80,000 whites in the country, who, being exterminated, the blacks might take possession.")[66] Around the time he was writing to Pleasants, Gray must have described the papers to Samuel Warner, the pamphleteer (and a stranger to him) in far-off New York City. Warner, in turn, described one of the documents in terms similar to Gray's: they had been found in the possession of Turner's wife ("*a slave belonging to Mr. Reese*") and included "something like a map, with figures inscribed on the margin."[67] The map and the list then disappeared and never again came to light.

Gray did not explain how the trove fell into his hands. Since official records of the uprising contain no references to Turner's papers, it seems unlikely that his wife was brought to town or into court to answer questions about them. Their discovery apparently resulted from a chain of events that started on 30 August, the day James Trezvant learned about the woman's existence.[68] On that day, Nathaniel Francis must have come to town from his farm, where the woman named Cherry (possibly the slave of John W. Reese) who later testified against Ben Blunt certainly was living at the time.[69] Cherry may have given up the papers at the Francis farm. It is certain that on 30 August Sam Francis, a slave of Nathaniel Francis and one of the original conspirators, was brought to town and delivered to the jail.[70] And early the next morning, Dred, another Francis slave, also was delivered to the jail. Notices of these captures did not reveal who brought the two prisoners to town, but Nathaniel Francis was involved directly in Dred's surrender and may have acted as a guard for both.[71] It is certain, moreover, that at about the time of Dred's incarceration on the morning of 31 August, Francis appeared in court and testified at the trial of Daniel Porter.[72] Four days later, on 3 September, Sam Francis came to trial; Gray was his counsel.[73] The chain of coincidence stretched from Cabin Pond to Jerusalem, linking the papers of Nat Turner to Cherry, to Nathaniel Francis, to T. R. Gray.

At midday Wednesday, 31 August, after six days in Southampton, the editor of the *Whig* departed for home with Capt. Harrison and the Dragoons. Three days later, from Richmond, the gallant Pleasants conveyed warm gratitude for the "unremitting kindness and attention" the men—cavaliers and knights, really—had received from the ladies of Southampton. "All that the troop regrets is, that some occasion had not offered, in which they could have manifested, by deeds, their zeal for the public safety, and their devotion to their hospitable and amiable countrymen of Southampton." He had but one sour word, concerning "one individual," Henry B. Vaughan, the tavern keeper and brother-in-law of the late Mrs. Vaughan. The proprietor was a wealthy man, the journalist said, who deserved exposure and chastisement. Under circumstances of the crisis, Vaughan should have charged "no more than would indemnify him" for serving the Dragoons during their time of duty; but a "base and sordid love of pelf" had prompted Vaughan to engage in profiteering. "We tended our own horses, with little aid from his servants; did not sleep in his house; were furnished with the coarsest and sometimes, stinking fare," Pleasants said. He added that "many" of the men neither ate nor drank at Vaughan's table and that on several occasions a number of the Dragoons had been absent, patrolling. The men left on Wednesday, he noted, "making the times less than five days." For this, Pleasants said, "the Landlord produced a bill exceeding $800!"[74]

Perhaps there was some misunderstanding. Pleasants did not say how many Dragoons, exactly, ate and drank elsewhere; nor did he explain how six days counted as five. The state's tavern rates (*dinner for 50 cents, "supper" or breakfast for 37.5 cents; horse feed for 25 cents*) allowed Vaughan to charge each customer $1.50 per day for meals and horse feed.[75] Thus, $1.50/day × 65 men × 5 days = $487.50 (accepting the guest's claim of five days). Pleasants did not mention alcohol (*per quart, wine $1.50; French brandy, $1.00; gin, 75 cents; toddy and apple brandy, each 50 cents; and "country" wine, 37.5 cents*). Thus, add $1.00/day × 65 men × 5 days = $325.00.[76] Did Dragoons pay in coin or expect drinks on the house? Pleasants did not say. In 1831 a gentleman of honor might seek satisfaction over such a misunderstanding, as the editor (who would be shot dead by his rival in Richmond in 1846) well knew. Some gentlemen in Jerusalem would have responded to the insult; Vaughan sought the amount due.

On that last morning in August as Pleasants prepared to leave town, James Trezvant reported that the jail held forty-eight prisoners; later that day, William C. Parker put the number at "about" forty.[77] Three of the prisoners had been present at Cabin Pond: Hark Moore, Sam Francis, and Jack Reese. Of the other four men at the Cabin Pond dinner, two were dead (Henry Porter and Nelson Edwards), and two were missing (Will Francis and Nat Turner). Neither Hark nor Sam revealed much about the origins of the plot, or the attack at the Travis house, or the assaults on Salathiel Francis and Trajan Doyel. Hark would testify soon as a witness for Moses Barrow, but he would undermine the defense in that case by saying that the defendant had joined the band voluntarily and had remained in their company for "some time."[78] Sam gave the inquiry very little information. Jack and Moses, both assigned to Gray for counsel, gave a great deal.

Findings

By 31 August, key figures in the inquiry had established what became the definitive number of white victims and the location of every attack, although they had yet to agree on the order of attacks or to see any significance in that order. They were close to agreement on the number of insurgents: James Trezvant put the number in Parker's field at forty, William C. Parker at "forty or fifty."[79] Gray, minimizing, soon offered an estimate of forty along the entire route, counting those who had separated.[80] Other information was emerging. Parker understood that "four or five" conspirators had attended the dinner in the "remote" field, that they had drunk spirits there until "11 or 12 o'clock on Sunday night," and that Nat Turner had entered the Travis house through an upstairs window. He had heard that Turner could read and write "with ease," and that he was a preacher and a cunning fellow who influenced superstitious followers by reading omens in the heavens like the blue-green-silver sun observed along the Atlantic seaboard on 13 and 14 August—"the late singular phenomenon of the Sun," Parker called it, repeating the cliché that had appeared in the *Norfolk Herald* on 15 August ("*the singular phenomena*"), in the *Raleigh Star* on 25 August ("*the late singular appearance of the sun*"), in a dispatch by Gen. Brodnax summarized in the *Richmond Compiler* on 29 August ("*the late singular appearance of the Sun*"), and eventually in Gray's letter to Pleasants on 17 September ("*the singular appearance of the sun in August*").[81]

As for the implications of what had happened, James Trezvant and William C. Parker were prepared to believe the worst. The congressman concluded that the plot had been a general one, "at least through many of our adjacent counties." Parker seemed to agree: "If my intelligence was confined to this place," he wrote, "I should say, that there was no general concert—but from examinations which have taken place in other counties, I fear the scheme embraced a wider sphere than I had at first supposed." Neither man was eager to address the motives behind the rebellion, though both had suspicions. Both called Nat Turner a fanatic—"a complete fanatic," Trezvant said, introducing another cliché that many observers, including Gray, quickly adopted. Parker hinted at one alarming, half-suppressed theory about motives: "Their *object* seems to have been, to produce unusual consternation and dismay, by indiscriminate massacre," he said. "In the language of the leader," he added, quoting Jack Reese (without attribution), "they determined to 'kill and slay as they went.'"[82]

On the central question concerning the extent of the conspiracy, Gray soon would express a dissenting opinion. There had been no general plot, he would argue, and never a threat of a general uprising ignited from a single source.[83]

Trial Evidence

Trials of the accused began in Jerusalem on 31 August, just nine days after the attack on the Travis house. The jailer, Henry B. Vaughan, brought nine defendants into the courthouse, where Meriwether Brodnax, the prosecutor (and brother of the general), charged them that morning with "feloniously consulting, advising & conspiring with each other and divers other slaves to rebel and make insurrection and making insurrection and taking the lives of divers free white persons of this Commonwealth." Brodnax had been taking depositions and had prepared notes for his presentations, a number of which found their way, word for word, into trial records. Five justices of the peace were present: Jeremiah Cobb, senior magistrate (and architect of the jail); Dr. Orris A. Browne, the Gray family's new neighbor at Round Hill (and young Gray's physician); James D. Massenburg, brother-in-law of Thomas C. Jones (the express rider); Capt. Alexander P. Peete, a former deputy sheriff (leader of the first volunteers at Parker's field); and James Trezvant, the retiring congressman (who had ridden with the second volunteers). Massenburg signed the minutes of the session. After Brodnax presented the charges, the court began at once to hear evidence against the first defendant, Daniel Porter, aged about forty-seven (with Aaron Porter, one of the two oldest insurgents), recruited at Richard Porter's plantation.[84]

Daniel's trial, which began and ended that day, followed procedures prescribed by state law. Statutes required that a slave charged with a felony be tried by the justices, not before a jury. The court had to be composed of at least five justices, none of whom could have an interest in the slave; and in a capital case, judges were required to reach a unanimous verdict. The county clerk was required to transmit to the governor trial records for all slaves found guilty of capital offenses. And finally, Virginia law required the magistrates to appoint an attorney for each defendant. For Daniel, they chose William C. Parker.[85]

Minutes of the entire Southampton proceedings filled the equivalent of thirty-five manuscript pages in the court minute book, providing about one page of evidence for each individual found guilty. Altogether, the names of fifty-one different witnesses appeared in the record. Most witnesses recounted what they had seen during single incidents; three-quarters testified for prosecution. The minutes represent a significant portion—but not all—of the evidence brought forth by the inquiry.

In Daniel Porter's case, the prosecutor called as first witness for the commonwealth Levi Waller, who testified that he had seen the defendant and two others enter a small house in which Mrs. Waller and a daughter had attempted to "secrete themselves," and that Daniel had emerged carrying Mrs. Waller's scissors (or scissors chain, according to the minutes). Waller said he later found his wife and daughter inside the house, murdered. Nathaniel Francis and Sampson C. Reese also testified for the state, Francis telling the court what it already knew—that "between 50 and 60 free white persons were murdered on Sunday night the 21st & Monday morning the 22d day of August 1831 by a number of negroes"—and Reese recalling that at James W. Parker's gate he had fired on the defendant, who had appeared to be unarmed. Richard Porter attempted to defend his slave, but Waller's testimony overwhelmed that effort. Daniel was found guilty and five days later, on 5 September, was hanged. In form, his trial presaged those to come.[86]

Between 31 August and 21 November, magistrates of the Southampton County Court considered evidence against fifty-five individuals, of whom fifty were slaves.[87] They dismissed charges against seven slaves and brought forty-three others to trial, all of whom pleaded not guilty.[88] The judges found thirty slaves guilty of capital crimes, and of that number recommended commutations (to transportation) for eleven others, one of whom (Jack Reese) the governor declined to spare. Two others received commutations for reasons the record does not make clear, bringing the total number actually transported to twelve.[89] For seventeen of those found guilty, the judges did not recommend commutations. Eighteen slaves were hanged, including the one (Jack Reese) whose commutation the governor and council rejected. County magistrates also examined five free black men, four of whom they recommended for trial before juries in superior court.[90] Of the four free men tried, one, Berry Newsom, was found guilty in 1832 and hanged; the other three were acquitted.[91]

Altogether, twenty white men, virtually the entire Southampton bench, sat as judges in the proceedings of 1831. All were slaveholders: fourteen held more than twenty slaves at the time of the 1830 census.[92] William B. Goodwyn, whose plantation lay at the western edge of St. Luke's Parish, held sixty-three; Jephthah Darden, son-in-law of Catherine Whitehead, held just one. As a group, the judges were wealthy: ten owned more than a thousand acres each. Goodwyn owned 3,396 acres; Benjamin Devany, the Methodist minister, had the smallest landholding at 160 acres. They were experienced. Four were in their fifties, seven in their forties, eight in their thirties, and just one in his twenties (the youngest was Dr. Richard Urquhart, scion of the wealthiest family in the county, a graduate in 1826 of the Jefferson Medical College in Philadelphia, and in his youth a neighbor of the Grays of Round Hill). Four had served in the Virginia House of Delegates, two had been sheriff, and two others deputy sheriff. Three had commanded the county militia as colonel. James Trezvant had been prosecutor, colonel, and legislator before he became a congressman.[93] Nine of the judges in 1831 had served more than a decade on the court; Jeremiah Cobb had been a magistrate since 1807. At least twelve had sat on murder trials in the past. All but one had been born in Virginia; at least thirteen had been born in Southampton. Six belonged to the Jockey Club; A. P. Peete was the club's secretary.[94] At least eight were Methodists, two were Baptists, and one, Thomas Pretlow (who soon would be aiding free blacks leaving for Liberia), came from a Quaker family. Devany had officiated at the weddings of five colleagues on the bench. As in colonial times, magistrates themselves controlled the court's composition. No one on the bench had been elected. Sitting justices recommended new justices to the governor, who appointed their nominees.[95] The court and its circle were the Establishment.

In trial procedure, the magistrates observed the letter of the law.[96] They kept records and transmitted them to the governor as required. At every session requiring the presence of five justices, five indeed were present—except on two occasions, one when six attended, and one other (the most important trial, in November) when ten were on the bench. Some attended far more frequently than others: James Trezvant, who lived one mile from the courthouse, was the most active judge, participating in twenty-six verdicts, twenty-one of which resulted in convictions. Jeremiah Cobb, who lived nine miles to the north (and presided at the most important trial), took part in seventeen verdicts, eleven of which resulted in convictions. Richard Urquhart, who lived twenty-three miles north, participated in just one verdict (at the most important trial). Every vote on the thirty verdicts for conviction was unanimous; on just one decision (concerning Jack Reese's sentence) was there disagreement. The judges were not required to record votes of individuals, nor did they do so. They did appoint counsel, as required, for each defendant. To members of the Jerusalem bar they assigned at least forty of the forty-three cases brought to trial.[97] James Strange French (of the first volunteers) was assigned twenty-one defendants (eight acquitted, eight convicted with commutation, and five executed), none involving the rebellion's leaders. William C. Parker drew fourteen defendants (four acquitted, two convicted with commutations, and eight executed) and was counsel in three of the most difficult cases: those of Hark Moore, Moses Barrow, and, in November, the chief insurgent himself.[98] Gray drew five defendants: Sam Francis, Davy Turner, Jack Reese, Moses Moore, and one of the boys from the Francis farm (all five convicted, one with commutation, one with commutation later denied, four executed). In what his defendants could tell, Gray drew the bonanza.

Forty-one of the slave defendants were tried individually and nine others in small groups. The trials took place in four periods separated by long recesses: twenty-seven trials between 31 August and 8 September, eleven in late September, three in mid-October, and two in November. Most yielded bits of information concerning isolated incidents recalled by witnesses at scattered locations. Only a few yielded evidence concerning the chief insurgent, his plan, or the scope of his cause.

Gray's first defendant, Davy Turner, came to trial on 2 September, the third day of proceedings, charged with conspiring to rebel and make insurrection, and with taking the lives of white persons.[99] He faced a panel of judges composed of James Trezvant (ever present), James W. Parker (Trezvant's protégé), Capt. A. P. Peete, and, in their first appearances at the trials, Thomas Pretlow (of the Quaker family) and Samuel B. Hine (a former colonel of the county militia). Davy, the young man taken from his bed at Elizabeth Turner's farm, had separated from the insurgents soon after they left the Whitehead house. Hubbard Whitehead testified as witness for the commonwealth, saying he had seen Davy with the band in the Whitehead yard. Moses Moore testified for the defendant, countering that Davy had been forced to join and had taken no part in the attacks on Mrs. Turner or the Whitehead family. Moses also recalled that the insurgents had divided their force at the Turner farm, and that Davy had been sent with the detachment to Henry Bryant's farm. Nelson Blunt, a second defense witness, largely corroborated Moses's testimony, but added unhelpful details about hearing Davy advise Joe Turner (in whose company Davy separated from the band) to join the insurgents. One witness in a later trial, Christian Atkins (a slave), would recall observing the defendant and Joe Turner at another location, seeming to act as a rump force (apparently hedging their bets).[100] The judges found the defendant guilty as charged and sentenced him to hang on 12 September. And though Davy had only a minor connection to the rising, the testimony at his trial about the division of forces and the detachment's movements would lead in time to a significant finding.

Sam Francis, Gray's second defendant, came to trial the next day, 3 September, charged with making insurrection and committing murder. Since Sam was one of the first conspirators, he could have told Gray about the origins of the plot in February, recruiting Will Francis, the dinner in the old field, the attack on Salathiel Francis, and the tactics at the Waller farm. Apparently he told Gray nothing. At the trial, James Trezvant again was on the bench, along with Dr. Carr Bowers (a former sheriff and former colonel of the militia), Dr. William B. Goodwyn (a former legislator and the wealthiest man on the court), Robert Goodwin (a former owner of the tavern, now a planter at his mother's dower lands), and Dr. Orris A. Browne (of Round Hill). Levi Waller again testified for the prosecution, recalling that he had seen Sam, along with Daniel and Aaron Porter, enter the small house where Mrs. Waller and her daughter were killed. The minutes do not indicate that Gray called a witness for Sam's defense. The defendant was found guilty and was hanged on 9 September, six days after his trial, taking what he knew to his grave.[101]

Jack Reese, on the other hand, told the court much of what he knew. Gray's third client had begun crafting a narrative the moment he surrendered to Jordan Barnes. He had confessed voluntarily, his guard said, about the dinner, the plan, and his objections. And he had given names. Gray apparently used his cooperativeness to advantage. Jack's trial (on the charge of making insurrection) began on 3 September, a Saturday, before magistrates Cobb, Devany, Goodwyn, Browne, and Trezvant. Moses Moore testified (for the prosecution, technically) about Jack's reluctance in the Travis yard, after which Thomas C. Jones told of hearing Jack's account of the meeting at Cabin Pond. At that point the judges suspended the proceedings in order to summon other witnesses they thought "necessary for the prisoner's defence." The trial resumed on Monday, 5 September, with Bowers (the former colonel) replacing Devany on the bench. Two witnesses from Cross Keys now came forward. Sampson C. Reese (of the first volunteers, nephew of the late Piety Reese and cousin of her late son William) confirmed the testimony given two days earlier by Jones, but added a detail that could not have helped the defense—"that the prisoner when arrested had on a pair of shoes and socks which the Witness believes to be William Reeses who has been murdered." Jordan Barnes, the other new witness, said that Jack came to him that morning with news of the Whitehead killings—news gained secondhand, Jack had claimed, from a Whitehead slave.[102]

There followed the only moment of uncertainty in the three months of proceedings. The magistrates agreed unanimously (as required) on the question of Jack's guilt but divided on his sentence, three favoring commutation to transportation, two insisting on death by hanging. The trial record gives no clue as to how the individual judges voted.[103] The majority's recommendation went forward to the governor, which provoked objections from judges (never identified) not present that day in court. "Two Magistrates not on the bench protest against the reprieve," Governor Floyd reported to Gen. Eppes. The governor's council in Richmond sided with those favoring execution, and Floyd acquiesced.[104] Jack was hanged with five other slaves as scheduled on 12 September.[105] His hanging followed by three days those of Hark Moore and Sam Francis, bringing the number of executions to thirteen. Within three weeks, the prisoners who knew most about the rising all had been put to death.

Jack's sentence clarified the thinking of the judges and the governor. They would offer commutations or even acquittals if the accused had been forced to join the band, had separated from it, had not come under suspicion of committing a crime, and had shown no sympathy for the insurgents. In time, Gray would argue that mere expressions of sympathy ought not to weigh against defendants, but his would be a dissenting view.[106]

Gray returned to court on 6 September, the day after Jack's conviction, to act as defense counsel alongside William C. Parker and James S. French in the combined trial of Nathan (age fourteen), Tom (fourteen), and Davy (thirteen), the boy slaves of Nathaniel Francis.[107] This would be Gray's final appearance in court until October. On the bench were justices Trezvant, Parker, Goodwyn, Peete, and Joseph T. Claud, the last a man of about thirty-five years and a resident of western St. Luke's Parish whose landholdings ranked second highest among the judges. Moses Moore again testified for the commonwealth, but again aided the defense. "The three prisoners were taken from Nathl. Francis's and placed one behind each of the company," Moses said, according to the minutes. "They went unwillingly but continued with them the whole of Monday—witnessed many of the murders but were constantly guarded by negroes with guns who were ordered to shoot them if they attempted to escape." Moses acknowledged one unhelpful fact: "They remained until the whole troop were dispersed," he said.[108] But the magistrates were merciful. "Questions being asked by the Court relative to the ages of the prisoners," the minutes said, "it appeared that the oldest was not more than 15 years—the other two much younger, the eldest very badly grown."[109] The court found the boys guilty of conspiring to make insurrection and to take the lives of white persons, but recommended a commutation for each. The governor concurred. Ten days later, the boys arrived at the penitentiary in Richmond; there they remained until 14 April 1833, when the state (slavery's sword and shield) sold them and banished them to parts unknown.[110] While in the Jerusalem jail, they served to verify Moses's account of incidents along the route from the Francis place to Parker's field. The evidence at their trial confirmed what Gray had heard about recruitment techniques and fed his growing skepticism about the degree of support for the insurgents. Their cases, together with those of Jack and Moses, deepened Gray's involvement in the inquiry, a task that now took hold of him.

What Gray Knew

Gray's preoccupation became apparent in the two weeks following the court's adjournment for the day on 6 September. His father had fallen ill shortly after the uprising; on the day Gray was in court with the Francis boys, the captain had written a will at Round Hill in the presence of neighbors, including Dr. Browne. The senior Gray died before 19 September (when his will was proved in court), leaving his heirs an uncertain fortune.[111] The younger Gray also had fallen ill. Over the nine days from 12 through 20 September, Dr. Browne charged him for daily visits (once in the rain on the sixteenth, prompting an extra charge) and for doses of "medicine" (on each of the first six days) in varying amounts. The dates of the visits, the known whereabouts of Browne, the season, and the patient's later medical history all indicate that Browne was attending the attorney, not the dying father. They indicate that the visits took place in town and that young Gray's malady was malaria.[112] Still, Gray worked.

During that week and a half, he composed the long letter to Pleasants at the *Whig*, his first account of the rebellion. He dated the letter on 17 September, the last day on which he received a dose of medicine, but three days before the doctor's last visit. He had notes and papers at hand, indicating that he was working near his desk. The editor in Richmond was forced to abridge (for "want of room") whole sections of his remarks, but said he omitted none of Gray's facts; the manuscript has not been seen since it was edited and set into type.[113] Argumentative, angry, and rambling as if written in a fever, the letter nonetheless became for a brief time the authoritative account. It would have remained so had it not been followed in November by the *Confessions.*

The *Whig* letter summarized the inquiry's findings through mid-September.[114] Gray rehearsed—as had William C. Parker at the end of August—Nat Turner's rise as a charismatic figure, adding details about Turner's knowledge of "the art of making gunpowder, and likewise that of making paper." He scotched Parker's claim that Turner was a preacher, but agreed that Turner had made himself a prophet by manipulating the superstitions of fellow slaves, citing specifically his interpreting of marks written in blood on leaves and pretending to have "conversations with the Holy Spirit." The Spirit, Gray supposed, had assured Turner that he was invulnerable, an encouragement to rebellion. "'Tis true," Gray said (displaying his fondness for archaic contractions), "that Nat has for some time thought closely on this subject." Anyone from the neighborhood around Cabin Pond might have confirmed those details; Gray probably obtained them in late August from Nathaniel Francis, from Turner's wife (indirectly), and, as he said, from Turner's papers.

Gray presented for the first time information obtained in August about Turner's men, based on the "credible testimony," he said, of "several negroes," referring to Jack and Moses. He now believed that no more than seven men had met in the old field on 21 August and that none (or so he thought) had known of a plan until the day before the attacks began. He drew up a list of those at the dinner, the first such list to appear in print: "Nat, Austin, Will, Hark, Sam, Henry, and Jack." (In November he would make one silent correction, removing Austin's name and adding Nelson's.) He knew about the food and rum, about Nat taking the men aside one at a time to hold "long conversations with them," and the objections raised by "one of the party." He knew they had begun "without a single firelock, and without the least particle of ammunition."

His account of the attack on the Travis family contained details that had been known at the courthouse for two or three weeks, some of which Gray now revealed, also for the first time. At "about one or two o'clock," he said,

Turner's men had applied the ladder to the window and entered the house. To Nat and Hark he gave "the credit of performing the first act," drawing, no doubt, on what Jack and Moses had seen from outside the house. Other details Gray had observed with his own eyes: evidence of blows delivered with a broadax, two little boys sharing a bed, and the infant ("*its head cut off*") in the fireplace.

Based on evidence provided by the boys who had held the horses, Gray concluded that along their entire route the insurgents had not made a dozen "efficient" recruits and that not more than ten individuals had performed all the "butchery." By mid-September he realized the significance of Moses's testimony in Davy Turner's trial—that the insurgents had divided ranks at the Whitehead house. "A division was there effected, for the purpose of extending their devastations," he said, "but they soon again united." A single body of men, advancing together, dividing briefly, and then reuniting and advancing again, had conducted every attack. The attacks had not been separate, simultaneous actions by slaves rising on command at scattered locations across the parish. There had been no broad conspiracy, no general insurrection.

Lulled, Gray drifted toward a view of the entire affair as merely a "momentary procedure," a spontaneous outburst that had posed only a minimal threat. Those who feared a general insurrection were "ignorant," he said, about the condition of the slaves. "Is it possible," he asked, "for men, debased [and] degraded as they are, ever to concert effective measures?"[115] He thought not. The trials of slaves in other counties were foolish.[116] Stationing armed forces in the countryside would be equally foolish. He called for a minimum of suppression—for keeping a regular patrol "for some time," always under the command of a discreet person, "who will not by indiscriminate punishment, goad these miserable wretches into a state of desperation."

Two pieces of fresh intelligence about Nat Turner, gathered early in September, appeared for the first time in the *Whig* letter. In that letter, Gray brought forth the details about the whipping Nat had received ("*for saying that blacks ought to be free, and that they would be free one day or other*") and thereby forced the public to acknowledge the dreaded motive, pushing aside for the moment naïve speculation about banditry and lunacy. To emphasize the point about motive, Gray repeated it twice. He also included in his letter a physical description of Nat Turner, which became the second such description to see print. "Nat in person is not remarkable," he reported. "His nose is flat, his stature rather small, and hair very thin, without any peculiarity of expression." Gray's text did not reveal the source of these new details.

Fresh intelligence fell also into the hands of William C. Parker during the court's week-long recess after 12 September. On Wednesday, 14 September, responding to an appeal from Governor Floyd, Parker composed his own description of "the contriver and leader of the late insurrection," as he put it. "I have been at some pains to procure an accurate one," he told the governor. "It has been improved and corrected by persons acquainted with him from his infancy."[117] Those persons must have included Nathaniel Francis and his mother, Sarah Francis, once the neighbor of Benjamin Turner II and, from 1807 to 1817, the mother-in-law of Samuel G. Turner. Parker, like Gray, described a man of small to medium stature ("5 feet six or 8 inches high, weighs between 150 & 160") with a "large flat nose" and "hair on the top of the head very thin." And he provided other, new details. The fugitive was between thirty and thirty-five years old, with a "rather bright" complexion (but was "not a mulatto"), broad shoulders, large eyes, and broad, flat feet. He was "rather knock kneed" and had a "brisk and active" walk. He wore no beard except on the upper lip and on the tip of his chin. He had a scar on one temple, "produced by the kick of a mule," and another "on the back of his neck by a bite." And he had "a large knot on one of the bones of his right arm near the wrist, produced by a blow." The governor sent out Parker's description almost word for word in the proclamation he issued on 17 September, offering a reward of $500 to any person or persons who might apprehend the fugitive and convey him to the jail of Southampton County.[118]

Four days after Gray wrote to the *Whig*, Parker gathered his own latest thoughts and sent them to Thomas Ritchie of the *Enquirer*, Pleasants's rival in Richmond.[119] The body of his letter, dated 21 September, indicates that a week or so earlier, at about the time he was working up the description, Parker had learned about Turner's baptism with the white man (whom he did not identify) at Persons Mill Pond. That incident, more than four years earlier, he now brought to the attention of the public.

On the central issue, Parker vacillated. Except for new evidence given by one witness, he said, "there has been nothing elicited, which goes to prove a concert, beyond the day before the insurrection broke out." Beck, the young female slave of Solomon Parker, had testified in Sussex County that she had been hearing talk about rebellion among her master's slaves for the preceding eighteen months; but still, Parker found "no sufficient reason to believe there had been a 'concert or general plan' among the Blacks." Then, wavering, he added, "I have no doubt, however, that the subject has been pretty generally discussed among them, and the minds of many prepared to cooperate in the design." Ritchie must have thought: *Parker is uncertain.*

Whatever the truth, Parker called for suppression, for "rigid enforcement" of laws governing slaves. Owners must keep them at home. There must be regular patrols, "composed of men of character and discretion." He agreed with Gray that proposals for a standing force in each county were foolish, but he urged the state to authorize "a greater number" of permanent volunteer corps, "who might frequently traverse every part, and produce an impression by the exhibition of a military force always prepared for prompt action." He would be more forceful than Gray, less tender about goading a large population. In a postscript, he put in a word for the Southampton Greys. "A volunteer company has been raised here," he reported to readers in Richmond, "composed of the most intelligent and respectable gentlemen."

In a second postscript, dated on the twenty-fourth, Parker seemed to withdraw his skepticism about a general insurrection. Court had reconvened in Jerusalem on the twenty-second and tried three slaves (two from Greensville County and another from the holding of Beck's master) for conspiring to rebel and make insurrection. All three were convicted on the strength of Beck's testimony concerning talk overheard in the quarter. "If her tale is true," Parker warned, "the plot was more extensive than we had previously believed." His differences with Gray were becoming apparent.

The anecdotes about the whipping and the baptism each implied a different motive, one having to do with freedom, the other, enthusiasm. Yet information about both may have come from the same source on the same day—from Nathaniel Francis on 12 September, the day Gray fell ill and Dred Francis was hanged. There is no record that Francis came to town to witness the execution of his slave, but it would have made sense for him to have done so. Nathaniel and his mother were familiar with the new details Gray and Parker were about to publish, and no one alive knew more about Nat Turner's appearance or his whipping. At some point around the twelfth of the month, Francis (who had lost a brother, a sister, a brother-in-law, four nephews, and six slaves to the prophet) must have come forward again to aid the inquiry. Two days later, on the fourteenth, Parker wrote the description for the governor.

If Gray knew about the incident at Persons Mill Pond, it was the only piece of new information he overlooked in his letter of 17 September to

Pleasants. He took pains in that letter to assure his readers that he was being thorough. "I have examined every source for authentic information," he said. "Every individual who was taken alive has been repeatedly questioned; many of them, when their stay in this world, was exceedingly brief."[120] He had been meticulous in assembling lists of white victims and had composed the only lists of defendants, updating them as the trials proceeded. He did not appear to be withholding evidence for later use; his interest in September lay in revealing quickly and widely what he knew. With the key figure still a fugitive and all the other conspirators dead or removed, Gray had reached the limits of the evidence at hand. And by the middle of September, he no longer expected that anyone in Southampton would see Nat Turner again. "My own impression is, he has left the State," he told Pleasants.[121]

There was much that he and his associates did not yet know. They had no direct way of knowing the history or motives of the leader. They had few accounts of what had happened during the attacks and none from inside the houses, no evidence permitting them to assign individual responsibility for any of the killings except those of Mrs. Waller and her daughter. They had only a few details—gleaned from sightings at the Turner and Whitehead houses and along Barrow Road—about the leader's actions and tactics. Gray wanted evidence in particular that the uprising had not been general and that prosecutions in distant counties were threatening innocent people—opinions he expected to bring "odium" down upon his head.

The Ultimate Source

Still ailing and under the care of Dr. Browne, Gray took no part in the court's proceedings on Monday, 19 September, when the magistrates proved his father's will and convicted Joe Turner and Lucy Barrow. Nor did he take part in the trials of nine other slaves in late September (three convicted but granted commutations; six acquitted or discharged). He did some writing, but after his letter of 17 September to Pleasants at the *Whig*, he fell silent. Parker too fell silent about the rebellion after writing to Ritchie at the *Enquirer* on 21 September (while continuing to promote the Greys). Lacking fresh evidence, the inquiry came to a standstill.

Gray did not return to court until 17 October, one week after the first great storm of the season blew across Norfolk and southeast Virginia, bringing the heavy winds and the "torrent of rain" reported in the *Beacon*.[122]

Gray acted as counsel on the seventeenth for Moses Moore, whose trial had been postponed twice so the court could continue calling the boy as a witness. By mid-October, Moses had depleted his store of information, his usefulness having ended with the conviction of Lucy Barrow, the last prisoner about whom he could offer testimony. The court, unable to postpone his trial legally any longer, finally proceeded, convicting him but recommending a commutation, which the governor granted.[123] Moses was removed from the jail probably on Friday, 28 October, and taken to the penitentiary in Richmond, where he was received on Sunday, 30 October, to be held until he could be sold and transported.[124]

On Saturday, 15 October, Red Nelson, now a slave of Nathaniel Francis, brought word to the town that he had seen Nat Turner in the woods that day. Twelve days later, Francis himself encountered the fugitive standing between the fodder stacks. Francis fired his pistol, sending the shot harmlessly through Turner's hat.[125] That confrontation occurred on 27 October—the day the weather turned cold and made the editors in Norfolk thankful for a fire. At the jail in Jerusalem, where Henry B. Vaughan was neglecting to light the fires, the number of prisoners had dwindled to about half a dozen, none of whom knew much about the uprising.[126] Then, at about nine o'clock Sunday night, 30 October, came the news that Nat Turner had surrendered willingly ("*Don't shoot, and I will give up*") at the Francis farm near Cabin Pond.[127] Word followed that he was talking, seemed prepared to make a confession, and would be brought to Jerusalem.

Confession

Without being questioned at all, he commenced his narrative.
—Thomas R. Gray, *The Confessions of Nat Turner*

Nat Turner spoke at every opportunity along the way to the jail, beginning no more than an hour or two after his surrender on Sunday afternoon, 30 October. By one o'clock he was talking to a crowd of one hundred ("a large concourse of people," one witness said), who had been attracted to the Peter Edwards plantation by celebratory gunfire. For more than an hour he told the crowd about his revelations and powers, his inspiration in the year 1826, and his motive and role in the rising. According to a neighbor of Edwards, he revealed that his fellow conspirators had numbered no more than "five or six," and that he had delivered the first blow to Travis. It must have been for this audience that he displayed his hat, with holes in the crown where the shot fired by Nathaniel Francis had passed through.[1]

He arrived ("well guarded," the postmaster said) in Jerusalem the next afternoon at quarter past one and was examined at the courthouse by magistrates James Trezvant and James W. Parker.[2] Some other members of the courthouse circle also were in the room: Attorney William C. Parker (captain of the Southampton Greys) certainly was present, along with the sheriff, his deputies, and the prisoner's guards. The jailer, Henry B. Vaughan, and the postmaster, Theodore Trezvant (brother of the magistrate), also may have been present. There is no evidence that the public was admitted or that other members of the inquiry—the prosecutor or the town's other attorneys—attended.

Examination

For nearly two hours Turner held forth, describing his interpretations of omens, recalling the healings he had performed, and giving what James Trezvant described as "a long account" of his motives and his communications with God (in which he once again referred to the year 1826). Trezvant said that the prisoner "pretended to have had intimations by signs and omens from God that he should embark in the desperate attempt."[3] According to William C. Parker, Turner gave, "apparently with great candour, a history of the operations of his mind for many years past; of the signs he saw; the spirits he conversed with; of his prayers, fastings and watchings, and of his supernatural powers and gifts, in curing diseases, controlling the weather, &c." Parker understood Turner to say that "the idea of emancipating the blacks" had not entered his mind "until rather more than a year ago." Here the prisoner addressed the question of all questions, but his testimony bewildered Parker. "How this idea came or in what manner it was connected with his signs, &c. I could not get him to explain in a manner at all satisfactory—notwithstanding I examined him closely upon this point, he always seemed to mystify."[4]

Some useful information did emerge, however. Turner confirmed that he had disclosed his plan to the "five or six" men who had "rendezvoused," Parker said, in the old field, and that he had entered the Travis house through an upstairs window. Turner revealed that he had passed through his master's chamber on his way to the front door and then, on returning to the chamber, had attempted to kill Travis. He gave other details that Parker did not mention, but which came to light in a report by an unidentified town resident (perhaps Gray) apparently not present at the examination, but who was a confidant of the "gentlemen" in the room. Turner, according to this source, had told his examiners that he first mentioned his plan to "two persons" in April or May, and that only those two knew of it until the day before the first attack. "He admits he struck his master with his hatchet first," the source said, "who called on his wife when he received the fatal blow from one of his associates."[5] (Here was the first reference in print to Will Francis.) According to James Trezvant, Turner also gave the inquiry its first information about the killing of Margaret ("Peggy") Whitehead, confessing that he himself was responsible.[6]

William C. Parker, on seeing the prisoner for the first time, thought he matched "exactly" the description (which Parker had written) in Governor Floyd's proclamation, "except that he is of a darker hue, and his eyes, though large, are not prominent." Turner's eyes in particular caught Parker's attention. "They are very long, deeply seated in his head, and have rather a sinister expression."[7] Gray, who may not have seen the prisoner until after three o'clock that afternoon, did not revise his own earlier description. "He is below the ordinary stature, though strong and active," he would write, "having the true negro face, every feature of which is strongly marked."[8]

The examination concluded at midafternoon, and Turner was escorted next door to the jail. There, according to a report from Littleton Barker, a resident of St. Luke's Parish, another crowd of one hundred people had gathered, "for the purpose of gratifying their curiosity." In the presence of the crowd, Turner answered the question about stolen money and made another comment about his motives.[9] Gray must have been among the crowd. By that evening Turner had appointed a time the next day for Gray to hear his confession in its final form.[10]

Interviews

According to Gray, the two men met in the jail on three successive days, Tuesday, Wednesday, and Thursday, 1, 2, and 3 November.[11] During their interviews, while Turner talked, Gray listened and took notes "as to particular circumstances," perhaps in a form of shorthand like the prosecutor's. Gray must have been seated face-to-face with Turner; he wrote unnoticed, he said, though he did not explain how he accomplished that. Neither man complained of feeling cold, though Vaughan had yet to light the fires. Gray described Turner as bearing bloodstains of his victims (of "helpless innocence," as Gray put it), dressed in rags, chained, his hands manacled.[12] The prisoner's voice must have been audible throughout the jail, though Gray gave no indication that anyone else was present. Others in the town confirmed that the interviews were taking place. Parker reported that "a gentleman" was taking down the prisoner's confession, "verbatim from his own lips." Another source (conceivably the note taker himself) identified that gentleman by name.[13]

Gray did not record the times of the interviews, except for the final session on Thursday, when the two met in the evening.[14] At their first meeting, "without being questioned at all," Gray observed, "he commenced his narrative."[15] The published text suggests that Turner devoted the Tuesday interview to events through early 1831, and that Gray then drafted this first section (the memoir, or autobiography), presumably at his office. On Wednesday, evidently, Turner gave his narrative of the rising, starting with its origins in 1830, at the beginning of the brief tenure of Joseph Travis. Later that day or on Thursday, Turner concluded his narrative with the account of his capture by Benjamin Phipps, after which Gray asked him about the extent of the conspiracy. Gray must have continued writing in his office on Wednesday night and Thursday. On Thursday evening he returned to the jail and, "having the advantage of his statement before me in writing," he said, "I began a cross examination." The young attorney, who now knew more about the uprising than any man alive except its leader, said he found the prisoner's statement "corroborated by every circumstance coming within my own knowledge or the confessions of others whom [*sic*] had been either killed or executed, and whom he had not seen nor had any knowledge since 22d of August last."[16]

The Text

Gray's notes have not been seen since November 1831, nor has the manuscript he delivered to the printer in Baltimore that month. Like Nat Turner's papers, they disappeared, perhaps in Baltimore, or perhaps into a trunk in an attic in Portsmouth (where Gray spent his last years), taking with them the physical evidence of their construction—ink, paper, numbers, crossovers, deletions, interlinings, insertions, marginalia, signatures, dates. The circumstances under which Gray conducted the interviews raised doubt—the jail, the manacles, the lack of witnesses or even a signature by the prisoner (who could read and write), the impossibility of verifying testimony. Gray's text opened the door immediately to questions about the voice in the *Confessions*. Thomas Ritchie of the *Richmond Enquirer* printed the first complaint on that score in a review published on 2 December. "The pamphlet has one defect—we mean its style," the reviewer (probably Ritchie himself) said. The language was "far superior to what Nat Turner could have employed." Portions were "even eloquently and classically expressed," he observed. "This is calculated to cast some shade of doubt over the authenticity of the narrative, and to give the Bandit a character for intelligence which he does not deserve, and ought not to have received."[17]

Ritchie saw the finished pamphlet as it came from the press in Baltimore, cleared of most, but not all, of the manuscript's construction debris. It had twenty-three printed pages and a total of 8,825 words, of which more than nine-tenths (8,299 words) was Gray's own writing. Its contents fell into eleven sections, as follows:

1. Title page (Gray), starting on page 1;
2. Copyright, page 2;

3. To the Public (Gray), page 3;
4. Court certificate, page 5;
5. Memoir (Gray, starting at "SIR," below the heading, "CONFESSIONS"), page 7;
6. Narrative of the rising (Gray), page 11;
7. Cross-examination (Gray), page 18;
8. Afterword (Gray), page 19;
9. Minutes, trial of Nat Turner (Gray), page 20;
10. List of persons murdered (Gray), page 22;
11. List of Negroes brought before the Court (Gray), pages 22–23.

Only the three middle sections derived from the interviews: sections 5 (the memoir of Turner's life), 6 (the narrative of the rising), and 7 (the cross-examination). Together, the middle sections composed two-thirds of the pamphlet; Gray evidently wrote them down in the order of their placement. The eighth section, Gray's own afterword concerning six white people who escaped death, could have been written before the prisoner was captured; all of section 10 (the list of white victims) and all but the last line of section 11 (the list of black defendants) already had appeared in print. A thoroughgoing skeptic might have suspected Gray of writing down the entire confession before the surrender.

Of all the sections, the memoir cast the darkest doubt. A long paragraph of sixty-eight sentences (roughly punctuated) and 2,055 words (excluding Gray's prefatory sentence), it began with the word *SIR* on page 5 of the original pamphlet and ended at the word *weapons* on page 11. Here, in seventeen or more episodes (roughly defined), Turner covered the period from 2 October 1800 through 13 August 1831. He recounted memories of childhood at the Benjamin Turner II plantation, including the astonishing feat of prenatal memory at age four and reactions to his exceptional intelligence. He told of his mental and spiritual life, of the Spirit that had appeared to him ten times (counting the one at the baptism) between 1821 and 1828, and of the signs he had seen in the heavens in 1831. He recalled memories (and memories of memories), visions, and voices he alone had perceived—experiences as difficult to verify as those of Joseph Smith (Turner's contemporary) or Joan of Arc, or other seers in the days of their common ancient source.[18]

Gray's difficulty in rendering Turner's voice became apparent in the third and fourth sentences of the memoir, in which he quoted the prisoner as follows: "In my childhood a circumstance occurred which made an indelible impression on my mind, and laid the ground work of that enthusiasm, which has terminated so fatally to many, both white and black, and for which I am about to atone at the gallows. It is here necessary to relate this circumstance—trifling as it may seem, it was the commencement of that belief which has grown with time, and even now, sir, in this dungeon, helpless and forsaken as I am, I cannot divest myself of."[19] Line after line of elevated diction came forth: the prisoner atoned, divested, experienced indelible impressions, and displayed singularity in manners and a fertility of imagination. He was inquisitive, was observant, and thought in terms of practicability. He alluded, studiously avoided, reverted, and spoke of cutaneous eruptions. Who but an attorney ever spoke like this? Gray was in deep water. Ritchie was right.

Yet no one beyond Southampton in 1831—and certainly not Thomas Ritchie—knew how Nat Turner spoke. As the memoir progressed, unobserved by Ritchie, a different voice emerged, less "classical" and more biblical, as in the exchange between Turner and Gray (in the eighth episode, a third of the way through the section) concerning the first appearance of the Spirit.[20] "As I was praying one day at my plough, the spirit spoke to me, saying 'Seek ye the kingdom of Heaven and all things shall be added unto you.' Question—what do you mean by the Spirit. Ans. The Spirit that spoke to the prophets in former days."[21] The ascending voice, more Lucan than lawyerly, spoke the next passage (concerning the ninth episode) in a changed cadence, starting with the scriptural *and*: "and I was greatly astonished, and for two years prayed continually, whenever my duty would permit—and then again I had the same revelation, which fully confirmed me in the impression that I was ordained for some great purpose in the hands of the Almighty."[22] That cadence and repetition of parallel clauses continued through the rest of the memoir:

— *and as it had been said of me in my childhood,*
— *And the negroes found fault,*
— *And about this time I had a vision—*
— *and I saw white spirits and black spirits engaged in battle,*
— *and the sun was darkened—*
— *and blood flowed in streams—*
— *and I heard a voice saying,*
— *and it appeared to me, and reminded me . . .*
— *And from the first steps of righteousness until the last,*

— *and the Holy Ghost was with me,*
— *and I looked and saw the forms of men in different attitudes—*
— *and there were lights in the sky . . .*
— *and shortly afterwards, while laboring in the field,*
— *And on the 12th of May, 1828,*
— *And by signs in the heavens . . .*
— *and until the first sign appeared,*
— *And on the appearance of the sign,*
— *And immediately on the sign appearing in the heavens, the seal was removed from my lips.*[23]

Other wording resembled Gray's in his letter of 17 September to the *Richmond Whig* and could have been imported knowingly into the *Confessions.* The two documents contained almost identical references to Turner's mind and imagination, to making gunpowder and paper, to influencing other slaves, to finding blood on leaves in the woods, to "hieroglyphical" characters, and to the appearance of the sun in August.

Most of the language and imagery of the memoir, however, came from the King James Bible, particularly from the gospels of Matthew and Luke. A list of references to Luke alone might have convinced readers about the origin of words like *austerity* (Luke 19:21–22); *Seek ye the kingdom* (12:31); *into the wilderness . . . forty days* (4:1–2); *his Master's will . . . beaten with many stripes* (12:47); *the sun was darkened* (23:45); *rough or smooth* (3:5); *the Holy Ghost was with me* (1:67); *drops of blood on the corn* (22:44); *laid down the yoke . . . , and that I should take it on* (9:23); and *slay my enemies with their own weapons* (19:27). Even Ritchie might have found authentic the allegory of the parallel lives, had he detected it.

Gray understood Turner's assumption about the revelation of 12 May 1828, when the spirit had instructed him to take up Christ's yoke.[24] ("*Ques. Do you not find yourself mistaken now? Ans. Was not Christ crucified.*") Since Gray's father had owned some "Religious Books" (as Gray Sr. had described them on giving them to his daughter), even young T. R., the son of a horse breeder, must have learned something about the Gospels.[25] But Gray displayed no scriptural fluency like that in the memoir. He neither identified the passages nor drew attention to the allegory. Those sections of the *Confessions* written in his own voice lack the religious sensibility of the memoir, as do Gray's two other published works, the *Whig* letter and the pamphlet of 1834 concerning his impending duel with Dr. Orris A. Browne.

If Gray invented the memoir's ascending voice, he was more gifted than Ritchie thought.

Turner's account of verifiable, real events raised no doubts at the time, though it might have done so, for Gray need not have gathered all of that material from the interviews. Informants in Cross Keys who had known Nat Turner ("*from his infancy*") and had provided Parker with the description (the scars, the knot) had been recalling details since August. One of those informants, Mrs. Sarah Francis, had lived at a neighboring farm on the day Nat Turner was born and had been among the religious visitors he had observed as a child. Nathaniel Francis, Sarah's youngest son, and John Clark Turner, second son of Benjamin II, were close in age to Nat Turner and must have been among the schoolchildren whose books he had glanced upon; both appeared as witnesses in court during the Jerusalem trials. Etheldred T. Brantley, the other man in the mill pond baptism, still lived in the neighborhood, as Gray knew. Nat Turner's wife (who had given up his list and map) was alive in Cross Keys, and his mother (prominent in early passages) may have survived there through 1831. Any of these six people might have given evidence for the memoir.

Gray had included in the *Whig* letter of 17 September information he might have gathered from sources in Cross Keys—specifically, the details about Turner's intelligence and literacy, his experiments, his fascination with numbers and hieroglyphics, his exhorting, and the whipping. Of these details, all but the last reappeared in the memoir.[26] Had Gray known about Turner's date of birth, his prenatal memory of 1803 (or 1804), the spelling demonstration of 1805, the marks on his head and breast, the favorite passage from Scripture, the revelation at the plough, and the significance of the year 1826, he might have included those particulars too for readers of the *Whig*. But he did not. They were fresh details, gained after 17 September and before 3 November. It seems unlikely that Gray learned about them before Turner's capture but withheld them from the public, planning to present them in his own voice, that of the relentless investigator of the *Whig* letter. By mid-September, Gray had formed the "impression" that Turner had escaped from Virginia. Having formed that impression, he had no reason to delay publication on the chance that more evidence would come his way. Had he completed a new account by the evening of 30 October, he certainly would have submitted it to the printers in Richmond or Baltimore. But he had not. Neither does it seem likely that he fabricated the accounts of the revelations or the allegory, or that he contrived the memoir in connivance with informants from Cross Keys. The most plausible conclusion is that the interviews took place as he claimed, that he captured the gist of Turner's statement, and that he did what he could with Turner's voice.

For readers in 1831, the question of authenticity mattered most in the middle section of the *Confessions*, the narrative of the rising. If authentic, this portion of the confession probably was dictated by the prisoner on Wednesday, 2 November, starting with plans for the dinner in the woods. Gray's transcription, 3,119 words covering seven full pages (more than a third of the pamphlet), immediately became the standard account. Like the preceding memoir, it presented events from the confessant's point of view. Except for parenthetical insertions (clearly marking Gray's comments), it imparted only what Turner could have known; it made no claim that he had witnessed everything. Even with those limitations, the narrative disclosed at least 116 factual details about the uprising that had never appeared in print.[27]

The narrative presented the first account of events inside the Travis house during the first attack. Nat Turner recalled entering his master's chamber with Will Francis, whose presence among the insurgents had not been mentioned in earlier accounts. When Turner failed to kill Joseph Travis with the hatchet, according to this account, Will had stepped forward. "Will laid him dead," the narrator says, "with a blow of his axe, and Mrs. Travis shared the same fate, as she lay in bed."[28] Turner did not identify the killer of the two boys, Putnam Moore and Joel Westbrook, but he did reveal that it had been Will who returned to the house with Henry Porter to kill the infant, "sleeping in a cradle," forgotten until the men had gone some distance from the house.[29] That information dispelled any notion that the child might have been struck accidentally in the mayhem.

Turner provided similar details concerning the assaults on the next four farms: Sam and Will luring Salathiel Francis to his door ("*Who is there?*"), dragging him from the house and dispatching him with repeated blows on the head; Piety Reese, asleep with her door unlocked, killed in her bed; her son William, wakened ("*Who is that?*") and put to death; Austin shooting Elizabeth Turner's overseer, Peebles, at sunrise; Mrs. Turner and Sarah Newsom ("*almost frightened to death*") seeking safety in the house ("*Vain hope!*"); Will breaking the door with his axe and dispatching Mrs. Turner; Nat grabbing Mrs. Newsom by the hand and striking her head with the sword; Will turning and dispatching her ("*the sword was dull*"); Richard Whitehead in his cotton patch, called to the lane, and Will ("*the execu-*

tioner") swinging his axe; Will pulling Mrs. Whitehead from the house, and again the axe ("*nearly severed her head from her body*"); the leader himself chasing Margaret Whitehead, his only victim, attacking her with the sword ("*repeated blows*") and killing her with a fence rail ("*a blow on the head*"); Will and his axe accounting for at least eight, and perhaps twelve, of the first thirteen.[30]

Revelation followed revelation. Turner recounted how, after dividing his forces, he had ridden alone to retrieve the detachment and then rejoined the main force at the Newit Harris house. (Here, in presenting a complicated series of movements, Gray maintained the insurgent leader's perspective flawlessly.) At the Waller farm, Turner had introduced the mounted charge (to "*strike terror to the inhabitants*"). From that point onward, Turner had positioned himself at the rear of the attackers; therefore, he had not witnessed any killings after leaving the Whitehead farm, "except in one case," certainly that of Rebecca (Ivy) Williams II, who nearly escaped but was caught, carried on horseback to the body of her husband, and shot.[31] At Parker's gate, Turner had argued against going to the house in favor of advancing directly on Jerusalem.[32] New details fit consistently into the pattern of old, known fragments.

The word *terror* appeared twice in the narrative, both times in the account of the assault on the Waller farm. In the first reference, Turner described the approach at full speed ("*and as it 'twas my object to carry terror and devastation wherever we went, I placed fifteen or twenty of the best armed . . . in front, who generally approached the houses as fast as their horses could run*"). In the second, he explained his purposes ("*to prevent their escape and strike terror to the inhabitants*").[33] In each case, he used the word in its oldest meaning—the state of being greatly frightened, or paralyzed with sudden fear.[34] That he had introduced this tactic at a specific place for a specific purpose had not occurred to Gray.

Turner's reference to the incident involving the Travis child indicated that from the beginning at least two of the insurgents had understood *terror* in a new way: Henry Porter and Will Francis, through the deed, had meant to instill a fear deeper than one that merely paralyzed immediate victims. They had intended to create an enduring dread in an entire population, an intention that reappeared in the seven infanticides that followed and in the killing of Rebecca Williams. The new understanding had gained adherents during that day in August, as the lists of the dead and the evolving roster of insurgents suggest. Gray's transcript does not indicate whether Turner himself endorsed the new meaning on that day, though he promoted it in the confession.

After the prisoner finished his statement, Gray asked him if he knew of any "extensive or concerted plan" of which the Southampton uprising may have been only a part. "His answer was, I do not," Gray wrote. When Gray asked him about an insurrection rumored at about the same time in North Carolina, he denied any knowledge of it. Gray looked him in the face, he said, "as though I would search his inmost thoughts." Turner then responds (as given in the *Confessions*), "I see sir, you doubt my word; but can you not think the same ideas, and strange appearances about this time in the heaven's might prompt others, as well as myself, to this undertaking?" At about that point, Gray went home to draft the day's account.[35]

He returned the next evening, Thursday, 3 November, with the statement in writing, to begin his "cross-examination," which became a section of 564 words almost entirely in Gray's voice, summarizing his own thoughts. Gray said Turner's responses that evening were consistent with the known evidence, and that the prisoner acknowledged the "impracticability" of his plan. That acknowledgment, at least, had a reassuring tone. Turner possessed a "natural intelligence" surpassed by few, Gray said. He had a decisive character, but a warped mind. He displayed a "calm, deliberate composure" when talking of his deeds and intentions, but a "fiend-like" expression "when excited by enthusiasm." In fact, he horrified Gray. "I looked on him," Gray said, "and my blood curdled in my veins."[36]

Gray had not intruded the previous day during Turner's account of the killing of the Travis infant, nor did he ask any questions about that incident during the cross-examination on Thursday evening. That new detail he chose not to emphasize. He included the new evidence about Henry and Will returning to the house, but let it pass without parenthetical comment or question, drawing no connection to evidence he had observed in the fireplace on 23 August. Since he could not have forgotten what he had seen in August and written in September, he must have decided to be reticent. For good reason, he must have chosen to put aside what he had seen, believing that the new evidence, if linked to the old, might further inflame a population whose fear it was his purpose to calm. As he constructed the record, only those readers who remembered his description in the *Whig* could have understood the meaning—the calculated terror—in the new revelation, had they chosen to do so. Parenthetically, too, only they could have understood what Gray must have realized the moment he heard Turner's account: that the leader had not seen everything (as he admitted) and that he must have known less about some particulars than Gray himself. Gray must have realized then that the inquiry had given him an advantage in dealing with this witness—if not in seeing the whole event, then certainly in being able to verify particulars. He did not intrude, however. His interest lay in *not* challenging the authority of the witness or the authenticity of his statement. At that point, therefore, Gray insinuated nothing beyond the ken of the witness and drew no attention to his own deep command of detail. For good reason, that too he put aside.

Minutes

The county court convened in Jerusalem for the trial of Nat Turner on Saturday morning, 5 November, probably at 9:00 A.M., its usual hour for a morning session. By then Gray had finished drafting the three main sections of the *Confessions*. Three other sections (the two lists and the afterword) he may have completed even before the capture. The proceedings took place in the 1803 courthouse, next to the site of the one that replaced it in 1834. Ten magistrates were on the bench, more than at any previous trial and twice the number required: Jeremiah Cobb (presiding), Samuel B. Hines, James D. Massenburg, James W. Parker, Robert Goodwin, James Trezvant, Orris A. Browne, Carr Bowers, Thomas Pretlow, and Richard A. Urquhart. Bowers, Pretlow, and Urquhart may have arrived after the court convened; in the court minutes, their names were grouped immediately below those of the other judges and after the collective title, *Gent.*, suggesting late entrances.[37] The court clerk, James Rochelle, was present to keep the official record. Gray also was present and wrote his own minutes in a form like those in the official book, but with differences in wording and detail. His version of what took place would appear as the ninth section of the *Confessions*, in his familiar style, complete with parenthetical intrusions and implausible speeches. It would arouse endless suspicion.

Before the proceedings began, according to Rochelle's record, the court ordered the sheriff to "summon a sufficient additional guard to repel any attempt that may be made to rescue Nat alias Nat Turner from the custody of the Sheriff."[38] The prisoner was brought into court in custody of the jailer, assigned William C. Parker as counsel, and arraigned by the prosecutor.[39] Brodnax read aloud the formal charges, written on a single sheet of paper dated 5 November.[40] According to both versions of the trial, Turner pleaded not guilty; Gray alone reported that the prisoner said explicitly, aloud to his counsel, "that he did not feel so."[41]

Brodnax called Levi Waller and James Trezvant as witnesses for the commonwealth and led the two men through statements he had heard beforehand, all the while referring to rough, undated notes he had made in his unmistakable scrawl during actual depositions a day or two earlier. Rochelle, the clerk, did not keep verbatim minutes. Following along with his pen in the court minute book, he too must have referred constantly to the prosecutor's notes, copying them almost word for word, making only minor changes as the testimony proceeded.[42]

According to the Rochelle minutes (and the Brodnax notes), Waller told of learning that the insurgents were headed his way, sending his son Tom to fetch the schoolchildren, and then ordering the schoolmaster to load the guns. (One detail in the notes, concerning Waller at the still, did not appear in the official minutes.) Waller told of seeing the prisoner, "whom he knew very well, mounted (he thought on Dr. Musgrave's horse)." He recalled that Turner "seemed to command the party" and had given the order to "go ahead" ("move" in the original notes) on departing.[43]

Trezvant testified about the prisoner's examination on Monday, 31 October, when Turner had acknowledged giving Travis and his wife "the first blow before they were dispatched" and admitted killing "Miss Peggy Whitehead." The prisoner had given a "long account of the motives which lead him" ("lead" in both versions) finally "to commence the bloody scenes" (changed from "scene") that had taken place. He also had detailed a "medley of incoherent and confused opinions" (corrected from "medly") that he had been entertaining since 1826.[44]

Brodnax introduced no other evidence. Gray then noted, as Rochelle did not, that the case was submitted to the court "without argument" from the defendant's counsel.[45] After announcing the unanimous verdict, the court—in the person of Cobb, certainly—asked the prisoner if he wished to speak. "He said he had nothing but what he had before said," Rochelle wrote, failing to specify whether Turner was referring to the examination after his capture, or to his jailhouse confession, or to both. The court then delivered its sentence: death by hanging in six days.[46] Before adjournment, as required by law, the clerk apparently read aloud the trial's two full pages of minutes for approval or correction.[47] Then, also as required, the presiding judge signed the minutes ("Jere. Cobb"), and the new deputy clerk, Littleton R.

Edwards, made a copy to send at once to the governor.[48] At no point did Rochelle refer to a reading in court of Nat Turner's confession.

Gray implied twice (or seemed to imply) in his minutes that a reading in court indeed had taken place. "Levi Waller was introduced," he wrote, "who being sworn, deposed as follows: (*agreeably to Nat's own Confession*)." He presented Trezvant's testimony in the same way. "Col. Trezvant was then introduced," he wrote, "who being sworn, narrated Nat's Confession to him, as follows: (*his Confession as given to Mr. Gray*)."[49] Here, in promoting his own work, Gray seemed to make claims that everyone in the courtroom would have known to be false, thereby darkening the shade of doubt.

He made similar claims in his long paragraph about the concluding moments of the trial. "Nat Turner! Stand up," Cobb says in that paragraph. "Have you anything to say why sentence of death should not be pronounced against you?" The defendant responds negatively ("*I have not*") and then explains, helpfully, "I have made a full confession to Mr. Gray, and I have nothing more to say." Cobb pronounces the sentence (the official minutes do not indicate that he did so) in 340 words. "Attend then to the sentence of the Court," he begins in Gray's minutes. Cobb reviews the defendant's arraignment, trial, and conviction for one of the "highest crimes" in the criminal code. Turner's hands, he says, are "imbrued in the blood of the innocent" and "stained with the blood of a master, in your own language, 'too indulgent.'" (Here Cobb refers to the passage about Travis in Gray's text.) He expresses pity for the defendant but says he is called upon to pass sentence, which he does in traditional form: hanging by the neck, on Friday, 11 November, between 10:00 A.M. and 2:00 P.M., "until you are dead! dead! dead and may the Lord have mercy upon your soul."[50] (The official minutes say simply, "until he be dead," and give the hours as 10:00 A.M. and 4:00 P.M.)[51] Gray did not note the hour of adjournment (neither did Rochelle), but since the magistrates reconvened that afternoon for other business, the Turner trial must have closed at midday.

A cursory reading of Gray's minutes might have given the very impression Gray intended to convey, that the confession had been introduced in court as evidence. A close, literal reading of what he wrote, however, ought to have raised doubt. Something nearer the truth appeared in the certificate Gray obtained after adjournment from individual members of the court, who agreed to affirm the following: "that the confessions of Nat, to Thomas R. Gray, was read to him in our presence, and that Nat acknowledged the same to be full, free, and voluntary; and that furthermore, when called upon by the presiding Magistrate of the Court, to state if he had any thing to say, why sentence of death should not be passed upon him, replied he had nothing further than he had communicated to Mr. Gray."[52] Six magistrates signed the certificate: Cobb himself, Pretlow, Parker, Bowers, Hines, and Browne. (Four did not: Trezvant, Massenburg, Goodwin, and Urquhart.) The signers certified that a reading of the document had taken place in their presence and that Nat Turner had acknowledged its authenticity, perhaps in their presence. Such a reading, if confined to the narrative of the uprising, would have required no more than half an hour and could have been accomplished on Friday night in Gray's office, or in Rochelle's parlor, or at the clerk's office, or in the tavern's back room (with its round walnut table and twelve Windsor chairs). But if Turner was present, it must have taken place in the jail.

Gray obtained a second certificate, this one from Rochelle, attesting that all six signers had been members of the court that conducted the trial.[53] Both certificates would appear in the pamphlet immediately after Gray's foreword. The full title Gray had in mind, as stated five days later on the copyright form, advanced his most brazen claim. The pamphlet presented, he would declare (in the District of Columbia), "*The Confessions of Nat Turner, the leader of the late insurrection in Southampton, Virginia, as fully and voluntarily made to Thomas R. Gray, in the prison where he was confined, and acknowledged by him to be such when read before the Court of Southampton.*"[54] True, literally. None of the six signers ever questioned the authenticity of the certificate they purportedly signed. If indeed Gray had fabricated his claims, no one betrayed him—not his colleagues at the bar, not the postmaster, not the judges (one of whom soon would want to shoot him), nor the clerk, the prosecutor, or the prisoner.

After the trial, finally, Gray wrote his foreword, "To the Public," a thousand words summarizing his thoughts. He dated this brief work at Jerusalem on 5 November 1831, signed it T. R. Gray, and placed it first in the pamphlet. His thinking had hardened since September. In writing to Pleasants at the *Whig* in September, he had taken pains to dispel fears of a general uprising and, with Gen. Eppes, had sought to prevent outrages upon innocents. He had argued against stationing a permanent armed force in the countryside, favoring instead a regular, local patrol ("*always under the command of a discreet person*") who would not goad the slave population ("*these miserable wretches*") to desperation. Similar concerns reappeared but briefly in the foreword of 5 November. There Gray noted again that the insurrection had led to "a thousand idle, exaggerated and mischievous reports" and reaffirmed that the outbreak had been "entirely local" in scope. He was submitting strong evidence that the affair had been the "offspring of gloomy fanaticism" in its chief contriver, whose mind, by "endeavoring to grapple with things beyond its reach," had become "bewildered and confounded, and finally corrupted." But Gray was drifting in the same tide of opinion that had caught John Hampden Pleasants. He put aside some of his earlier sentiments about repression and now drew a lesson on the necessity of "laws in restraint of this class of our population." Public officials and "citizens generally," he said, must insist that those laws be "strictly and rigidly enforced."[55] He, too, was turning to the state and its police.

The memoir and the narrative had led Gray to see danger lurking in an enslaved population. This "first instance" of open rebellion, as he put it, had left a deep impression, not only in Southampton, "but throughout every portion of our country, in which this population is to be found." The uprising, a product of deliberation and settled purpose of mind, would long be remembered, he predicted, "and many a mother as she presses her infant darling to her bosom, will shudder at the recollection."[56] He wanted the *Confessions* to preserve and promote that recollection.

Within two days Gray was in Richmond. He must have spoken to Ritchie at the *Enquirer* on Monday, 7 November. "We are informed by a gentleman from Southampton," Ritchie reported in Tuesday's paper, "that Nat Turner, the leader of the late insurrection in that county, was tried on Saturday last." Testimony at the trial had been "clear and conclusive."[57] On Thursday, 10 November, the day before Turner's execution, Gray was in Arlington County, in the District of Columbia, where he obtained from district clerk Edmund J. Lee the copyright noted inside the pamphlet's front cover. Between 14 and 18 November, he must have been in Baltimore, where Lucas & Deaver, printers, produced the first edition.[58] Notice of publication appeared on 22 November in Washington, in the *Globe*. The next day a book dealer in Norfolk was selling copies for 25 cents apiece; one dealer in Richmond offered "a liberal discount" for purchases by the hundred—a timely promotion, as preparations for the Virginia debates on the future of slavery got under way in the state capitol.[59] Gray did not take part in that debate except indirectly and addressed nothing further to the public about the subject.

Closing Scenes

His contrition was as sincere as its evidences were impressive.
—Editors, *Norfolk American Beacon*, 27 August 1845

Nat Turner died on the appointed day, Friday, 11 November 1831. Thomas R. Gray, already on his way to Baltimore, did not witness the execution. Reports in the press were brief, few in number, and contradictory. Editors at the *Petersburg Intelligencer* had learned through "a gentleman from Southampton" that the "fanatical murderer" was hanged in Jerusalem at about one o'clock that afternoon. "He exhibited the utmost composure throughout the whole ceremony," the editors understood, "and although assured that he might, if he thought proper, address the immense crowd assembled on the occasion, declined availing himself of the privilege, and told the sheriff in a firm voice, that he was ready." For the second time since hearing his sentence, Turner had declined to elaborate upon his statement. The execution proceeded. "Not a limb or a muscle was observed to move," the Southampton gentleman reported, providing a detail interesting to readers of that era. "His body after death, was given over to the surgeons for dissection."[1]

Editors at the *Norfolk Herald* had heard a different account. "Precisely at 12 o'clock he was launched into eternity," a source had told them. "There were but a few people to see him hanged." This account, while omitting any reference to Turner's refusing to speak, was consistent in its details about his last moments. He regretted nothing. "He betrayed no emotion, but appeared to be utterly reckless of the awful fate that awaited him," according to the source, "and even hurried the executioner in the performance of his duty!"[2] Gray's transcription of the confession thus became the prisoner's final word.

Those who survived the rising of 1831 changed as little as Nat Turner in their thinking or outward behavior. A single episode of violence lasting a few days, followed by threats of terror and counterterror, inspired neither the succession of outbreaks that Turner had anticipated nor the white flight from the county that some had feared. Both parishes in Southampton experienced declines in the numbers of taxable slaves, free blacks, and white males in 1832 and 1833, but all three populations showed signs of returning to stability in 1834 and 1835.[3] Over the remaining thirty years before the Civil War, long-term migration and the slave trade would influence the county's demographic history more powerfully than the rebellion of 1831. Turner's theory that the slave population would rise on short notice gained no lasting, official credence; Gray's ironic theory that the Virginia slave population was too degraded, too deprived of arms and letters to sustain an uprising, gained muted acceptance. Fear subsided. Old assumptions about the functions of slaveholding in the domestic arrangements of the white family resumed their sway, a significant aftereffect of the suppression, evidence that slavery would be uprooted only by some overwhelming, external force.

Heirs

For the rest of their lives, the surviving heirs of the three families who had held Nat Turner in slavery remained near Cross Keys and continued to hold slaves, apparently without fear or concern. Once they regained the currents of everyday life, they gave no sign of having heard a warning call to take some timely, conclusive action.

John Clark Turner, the second son of Benjamin Turner II, survived another twenty years in St. Luke's Parish. (His longtime slave Joe, who was impressed by the insurgents at the Whitehead plantation but left the company almost at once, was tried nonetheless for taking part, found guilty, and hanged on 26 September.) At the time of the rebellion, John Clark was thirty years old. He still owned part of his father's plantation, though he had moved to the home of his recently deceased mother-in-law near Monroe, half a dozen miles east of the insurgents' path.[4] Though never a planter like his father or older brother, John Clark did continue to hold a small number of slaves. In 1850, at age forty-nine, he held four (two men, ages sixty and thirty-five, and two women; ages sixty-three and forty-five). His household that year also included his wife (the former Nancy Knox, three years his junior), their five children (the eldest of whom, Franklin, was seventeen), and two free black children.[5] At his death in 1851 he left personal property worth a modest $1,363.05, barely one-sixth the value of his older brother's personal estate in 1822. He owned two horses (Larry and Boston, worth $90 together), seven head of cattle (including a cow named America, worth $8), and three slaves (Winney, probably in her forties, worth $125; Amos, in his sixties, worth $60; and Stephen, about thirty-six, worth $100).[6] Slaves represented just over one-fifth of his personal estate.

Nathaniel Francis, who lost seven slaves (including Will, the executioner) and seven family members in the uprising, acquired property from his dead brother and sister and thus quickly recouped most of his material losses. In 1833 he paid taxes on eleven slaves (a gain of one over his holding in 1831) and nearly seven hundred acres.[7] In 1835 he hired as his overseer none other than Etheldred T. Brantley, the man baptized with Nat Turner in Persons Mill Pond in 1826.[8] Early in 1836, after the death of his mother, Francis took possession of his father's modest house and 411 acres. In 1836 he built a new house (attached to the old one) and raised the value of his buildings from $150 to $1,000. By 1840 he owned more than sixteen hundred acres and held twenty-nine slaves of all ages. He died of pneumonia in the spring of 1849, aged about forty-three, leaving behind a widow, nine children, and an estate with almost thirty-five hundred acres and thirty-seven slaves.[9] He had prospered, undeterred. Nothing he saw that day in August inside his sister's house, or at his brother's, or at his own, had given him a prevision like the one Jefferson described in 1814 (and again in 1820) of how slavery might end.[10] Eighteen years after the rising and a dozen years before the war, Francis continued to display the same lack of concern that Jefferson had lamented.[11]

John W. Reese, who lost his land before the uprising (half going to Francis), managed to preserve most of the personal property that had belonged to his mother, Piety Reese, and younger brother, William; in the spring of 1832 he held seven taxable slaves.[12] Two years after the uprising, in the late spring of 1833, he married Martha T. Barham, the orphaned daughter of a well-to-do St. Luke's slaveholder; in December 1833 he and Martha gained four additional slaves through a friendly lawsuit involving her father's estate.[13] In 1838, with funds he must have borrowed, Reese bought at auction a farm of about 475 acres not far from Cabin Pond.[14] There he installed his slaves, whose total number by 1844 had reached seventeen and whose value represented nearly 60 percent of his assets. In that year he again went broke. This time, he lost nearly everything. At a public sale on 1 January 1844, neighbors were able to buy some of his slaves. Peter Edwards bought Henry and Richmond for a total of $478, and Nathaniel Francis (who now bought all of Reese's land) paid $122 for a female named Bridget. John Clark Turner bought Alfred (described as "unsound") for $12. Eleven of the Reese slaves (worth a total of $2,094) went to William T. Watkins, a trader with ties to the New Orleans market. Among those eleven were Jenny and her daughters Dorcas and Harriet, and Beck and her child Cherry.[15] Over the next sixteen years, Reese moved back and forth between Southampton and Greensville Counties. In 1850, at age thirty-nine, he was living in Greensville with his family and nine slaves; in 1860 he and his wife (listed in the census as head of their household) were still living just across the county line in Greensville with twenty slaves (all entered as the property of Martha T. Reese). Reese died before 1870.[16]

No one matching the description of Nat Turner's wife or her child appeared in the sale inventory of Reese's property in 1844 or in other documents of the Reese family after 1831. William S. Drewry, writing at the end of the nineteenth century, discovered nothing about the wife, but he did find a name for her child.[17] By Drewry's day, however, the trail of evidence leading to Cherry and Riddick had grown cold, the last possible traces having appeared just after the Civil War. According to the census of 1870, a black woman named Cherrie Turner, a housekeeper, was living with a black family not far from Cross Keys; she gave her age as sixty-five, perhaps too young to have been the woman in question. In that same census, a black man named Reddick Turner, a farm laborer aged fifty—exactly the right age—was listed as a resident of Belfield, just over the line in Greensville County. Both had been born in Virginia. Neither owned real property. Neither had been taught to read.[18]

Surviving Neighbors

Harriet Whitehead, the only white survivor in her mother's house, spent her remaining twenty-one years a single woman in that house, two miles west of Cross Keys. The final settlement of her mother's estate—through a friendly lawsuit involving Harriet, her four surviving siblings, and an infant nephew—gave her the family's mansion farm of 110 acres together with the house and four slaves; from a younger brother, Joseph B. Whitehead, she subsequently acquired her mother's slave Hubbard, who had saved her life.[19] For much of the decade after the insurrection, Miss Whitehead's brother Joseph managed her affairs; and for a time, he lived under her roof.[20] By 1838 she owned 461 acres; in 1840 the number of slaves at her farm had increased to nine.[21] The incident in 1831 had not led her to abandon slaveholding, although she did remain troubled by her memories. Sampson C. Reese, nephew of Piety Reese and, after the uprising, a storekeeper in Cross Keys, understood that for a "great portion" of the time between 1831 and 1835 Miss Whitehead was "Drunk and histerica [*sic*]."[22] Her attorney later would concede that the incident had left her depressed, weak, and hysterical and had led her to take "stimulating medicines, drinks and the like."[23] By 1843, according to Cuthbert D. Barham, a physician in Cross Keys, she no longer trusted her brother and was complaining that he had become impertinent and abusive. She disapproved of Joseph's association with "a mulatto family" (headed by the free black woman Rebecca Sweat), claiming he was supporting that family "out of her corn crib & smoke house, & would very soon bring her to want, if she did not take some steps to prevent it." Compounding her difficulties, she had accumulated between $600 and $800 in debts, which, she told Dr. Barham, she had no means of repaying without selling property. And, Barham recalled, she said she had "nothing to sell except some young negroes, and if she sold them, she should be left with old negroes, women, and children who could not support themselves & she must very soon come to poverty and want."[24]

She turned for aid to Nathaniel Francis, who still made it his policy to assist neighbors in managing their affairs. Francis agreed to meet Miss Whitehead on the morning of 13 November 1843 at the Porter house (halfway between their farms) and make arrangements for her support. He summoned Benjamin E. Pope, a young farmer from Cross Keys who often did legal writing for neighbors. The gathering was to be much like the one in 1831 at which Francis and other neighbors signed documents addressing the debts of John W. Reese. By chance, also on the thirteenth, Mrs. Porter had summoned Dr. Barham to attend to her overseer, Nathan Barnes, who lay ill in the Porter house. Pope and Barham rode together from Cross Keys. When they arrived, they found the sick man in one of the two main rooms and, in the other, Richard Porter. Miss Whitehead and Mrs. Porter must have been in the kitchen. In the sick room, while the doctor examined the patient, Pope and Francis drew up a deed of gift and a bond. Four years later, when asked why Miss Whitehead was not in the room while the documents were being written, Barham explained that a very sick man was in that room, rendering it "an improper place for a lady to be." "And in the other room," the doctor recalled, "we were so much annoyed by Mr. Porter that it was impossible to write." Asked to explain Porter's behavior, Barham said simply, "He was insane."[25]

With her signature on the deed, Miss Whitehead agreed to transfer all of her real and personal property to Francis—560 acres, the house, and eight slaves: Hubbard, now over fifty-five years old, and boys Curtis and George; Dinah and her children Jane and Wallace; and Winney and her child, Bob. The deed was witnessed by Barham, Pope, and John W. Reese.[26] In return, Francis offered his bond of $1,000 and a contract to furnish Miss Whitehead "a decent support" and to provide "clothing, medical attendance and all other necessary things during her life."[27] Essentially, by agreeing to provide equivalent financial security and assurance in Miss Whitehead's old age, Francis was taking the place of her slaves.

The arrangement worked for a year or two. Francis paid for repairs to the shingles and brickwork on the buildings at the Whitehead farm; he provided pork, sugar, coffee, and flour for the table; and he authorized Miss Whitehead to make purchases on his account at Sampson C. Reese's store.[28] In return, he took possession of her crops and her slaves, most of whom apparently remained at the Whitehead farm. According to Harriet's sister, Martha L. Darden (the only Whitehead daughter to marry), Dinah worked in the house; there she did weaving and spinning for the Francis family but cooked for and waited upon Miss Whitehead. When Dinah was sick, Martha recalled, Miss Whitehead was compelled to hire other "persons" to wait on her, or, in her topsy-turvy circumstances, to do the cooking herself and wait upon the servants.[29] According to Harriet's brother John, in late 1845 Francis sold one of the slaves, Winney, for $560 to "Mr. Watkins" (that is, to William T. Watkins, the trader with New Orleans connections).[30] Winney's son, Bob, according to other evidence, was kept at the farm near Cross Keys.[31]

In June 1847 Miss Whitehead told Dr. Barham that she had become dissatisfied with the arrangements and wished to take back her property, complaining that "Francis had not complied with his promise, in furnishing her all the necessaries of life, servants, &c."[32] A lawsuit in chancery court, *Whitehead v. Francis*, followed before the end of 1847, pitting the two families against each other through four years of accusations, depositions, bills of complaint, amendments, claims, and counterclaims. Through her attorney in Norfolk, Miss Whitehead alleged that Francis was "notorious for his love of money and the means used to get it." Having observed that this woman had considerable property and was suffering from an "unfortunate" state of mind (a condition her siblings no doubt had observed as well), Francis had determined, Miss Whitehead said, that she was "a fit subject for him to defraud of her estate."[33] The defendant, responding, insisted that the plaintiff had been “comfortably supported,” and he denied that he had tried to seize her estate or that he had sold more than “an inconsiderable part” of her property.[34] Francis barely outlived his own defense. He died suddenly, at forty-four, in the spring of 1849, four months after the superior court nullified the deed of 1843 and ordered all property returned to the plaintiff. Special commissioners were assigned to settle accounts between the parties, a task still in progress at the end of 1851.[35]

Harriet Whitehead and her siblings relieved Nathaniel Francis of responsibility for her support during her declining years and returned it to her servants, to whom they no doubt assumed it belonged. In August of 1850, at age fifty-four Miss Whitehead was living in her mother’s house in the company of just one other white person, twelve-year-old Martha Underwood, who probably was helping with the housework. Six slaves were present, the eldest a woman of thirty years, undoubtedly Dinah. Three young boys, ages ten, eight, and four, were present, along with two girls, both six years old.[36] Hubbard, Miss Whitehead’s protector, who had been listed as a grown man in her father’s estate in 1815, must have gone to his grave. Winney also was gone, probably to the lower South.

In the spring of 1852, at age fifty-six, Miss Whitehead died, leaving property worth $4,422.24, including her land (valued at $800, or less than one-fifth of her estate) and nine slaves. Her slaveholding in 1852 included just one adult, Dinah (her cook, spinster, and weaver, now thirty-two); Dinah’s three young children (not identified in the inventory by name); one unaffiliated minor girl (about six years old); and four valuable, unaffiliated young males (field workers, between the ages of ten and twenty), George, Curtis, Cal, and Bob (Winney’s son). Together, the nine slaves were worth $3,300, or three-quarters of the entire estate.[37] Whatever the cause of her anxiety after 1831, Miss Whitehead apparently did not fear her own servants, did not believe that Dinah would poison her or that her young males one day would invoke Luke and cut her throat. She did not share the suspicion voiced in 1832 by James McDowell Jr., the often-quoted antislavery delegate (and later governor) from Rockingham County, during a moment of hyperbole in the Virginia assembly’s debate on slavery, “that a Nat Turner might be in every family.”[38] But neither did she concern herself in succeeding years with the subject of that debate.

Miss Whitehead’s neighbors to the north who escaped death in 1831 resumed their lives with similar disregard for both physical danger and moral reform. Richard and Elizabeth Porter, who lost five of their thirty slaves in the uprising (including Henry, one of the two who returned for the Travis infant), remained at their plantation and in 1840 still held twenty-two slaves, though they never regained fully what they had lost.[39] In 1839 Richard Porter wrote his will, saying he was weak in body (but still of sound mind); and though he would live for another sixteen years, his existence became a troubled one.[40] His condition in November 1843, when Dr. Barham thought him annoying and insane, may explain the behavior of his rebellious slaves in 1831.[41] In the census of 1850, Porter was described as an "Idiot."[42] He died in 1855 at age sixty-two.

For Peter Edwards, the loss of four prime hands (three killed before trial, one executed) brought only a pause in his ascent into the middle ranks of the planter class. He found replacements almost at once, so that the number of his taxable slaves declined only briefly, by one slave, in 1832.[43] In 1834 he completed improvements worth $600 at his plantation north of the Francis farm, probably building the house there in the form it retained a century later.[44] In 1836, for $8,125 in cash, he bought a tract of 1,853 acres (with buildings worth $1,500) on the Meherrin River.[45] There, about five miles southwest of his old plantation, he apparently established a new residence. By 1838 he owned 3,362 acres and ranked among the top ten landholders in the county.[46] That year, after the death of his first wife, he married Mrs. Narcissa Newsom, thirty-seven, nine years his junior but already a widow three times, who held for life an additional 322.5 acres in dower land.[47] As a sister of the late John T. Barrow and stepdaughter of Newit Harris, Narcissa brought Edwards into the alliance of the Barrow, Harris, and Vaughan families.[48] The history of Edwards's slaveholding gives evidence of his long-term ascent: no slaves in 1810, twenty-eight slaves of all ages in 1820 (a combined holding with his father and brother), twenty-nine in 1830, forty in 1840, and fifty-three in 1850 (table 8), when his slaves outnumbered his white household by more than ten to one. His real property in 1850 was worth an estimated $11,000.[49]

TABLE 8. Slaveholdings of Peter Edwards and Jacob Williams, 1810–60

	Number of slaves					
Owner	1810	1820	1830	1840	1850	1860
Peter Edwards	0	28	29	40	53	—
Jacob Williams	4	5	6	8	13	12

Sources: U.S. Census, Southampton County, 1810–60, manuscript returns, slave schedules for 1850, 1860.

Note: The figure for Peter Edwards in 1820 represents the combined slaveholdings of Edwards, his father, and his brother.

Edwards died a wealthy man at age sixty-seven, in 1859. His investments in municipal and personal bonds in 1859 were worth about $50,000. In the will he drafted in 1855, he divided his estate into three portions. To his nephew John E. Briggs he gave the old plantation near Cabin Pond and fourteen slaves (plus an unspecified number of children in one family), asking only that John "support and take good care of his mother, Nancy Briggs," Edwards's sister, for the rest of her life. To his daughter Caroline Pope, wife of Benjamin E. Pope (the neighborhood deed writer of 1843), he gave six slaves (plus a similar, unspecified number of children in one family) and $30,000 in cash, to be raised from a sale of the "moneyed part" of his estate. The balance he gave to his widow for life, with a reversion at her death to his daughter.[50]

Narcissa Edwards renounced her husband's will, having determined at once that her portion might fall short of a widow's third.[51] On 15 August 1860, a chancery commissioner settled the estate, whose assets at that point totaled $73,893.12. The commissioner assigned to the widow a portion worth $24,631.04, or exactly one-third of the estate. Briggs, the nephew, received $5,650.84 (apparently in forgiven debt), and Pope and his wife, $43,611.24.[52] By August 1860, the time of the last census before the war, Narcissa Edwards had left the county and, at age fifty-nine, had taken up residence with just one young slave and a young white laborer on a farm property in the town of Petersburg. Her name did not appear in the census of 1870. In 1860 Briggs was living at the old Edwards plantation with his young family and a dozen of his own slaves. Ben and Caroline Pope were at their plantation near Cross Keys, with a household of four white persons (including a young housekeeper and the overseer) and eighty slaves.[53] All four heirs appear to have been satisfied with their legacies. Caroline Pope, Edwards's only surviving child, placed a headstone on her father's grave at the old plantation, bearing an epitaph she may have composed after 1865:

In Memory of
PETER EDWARDS
Born Feb. 10, 1792.
Died July 22, 1859.
Sleep on dear Father thy work is done.
The mortal pang is past;
Jesus has come and borne thee home
Beyond the stormy blast.

Mary T. Barrow, who had escaped from Lucy's clutches and fled to safety on 22 August, inherited almost all of her husband's estate, in accordance with provisions of John T. Barrow's will. (*"I give to my wife Mary T. Barrow my land, Negroes and property of Every description to do what she pleases with after paying my debts except two guns."*) The document was dated in 1829 and witnessed only by Mary's brother George (also killed) and the young widow herself.[54] Once the court accepted the will, Mrs. Barrow, at age twenty-three, took possession of her husband's 521 acres, his buildings worth $550, and as many as eleven of his surviving slaves, four of whom were of taxable age in 1833.[55] And in September 1831, through a friendly lawsuit against James W. Parker and his wife Martha (Mary Barrow's brother-in-law and sister), she acquired five of the nine slaves in the estate of her mother, Rebecca Vaughan.[56] During the ten months of Mary Barrow's widowhood, Newit Harris, her dead husband's stepfather, apparently supervised her slaves.[57] In June 1832 she married Capt. Fielding Rose, a militia officer in his forties with fifty-two slaves and a plantation in Sussex County, where the couple established residence.[58] By the end of 1838 the Roses had sold all of the land that had been John T. Barrow's farm; and the former Barrow and Vaughan slaveholdings, like those at four of the other most devastated households (Travis, Reese, Turner, and Whitehead), had been scattered beyond the powers of anyone to retrieve or trace.[59]

Newit Harris, after his hairsbreadth escape in 1831, maintained and expanded his holdings for another six years. He died in 1837, at about sixty-seven years of age, having added more than eight hundred acres to his three plantations after 1831 and having seen his taxable slaveholding increase from thirty-one to thirty-four.[60] The will Harris devised in October 1833, when memories of the uprising were still fresh, instructed his executors (one of whom was Peter Edwards) to distribute his estate among his widow and four children largely according to custom. He gave his Flat Swamp plantation to his son Edwin and some small tracts of land near the home plantation to his daughter Polly Hill Harris. All other land, including the home plantation, went to his widow on loan for her lifetime; at her death, this property was to be given to his youngest child, Newit Jr., born in 1831. Harris converted to gifts some earlier loans of slaves and money he had extended to his son-in-law, Dr. Robert T. Musgrave (husband of Charlotte), and gave absolute possession of any remaining money and bonds to his wife. Of the slaves still in his holding (about fifty in number), he loaned one-third to his widow for life and directed that at her death this group be divided equally among his surviving children. The remaining two-thirds of his slaves were to be divided at once among his children.[61] Each of the heirs accepted Harris's legacies. Nothing had changed.

Barrow Road Survivors

To the east, along Barrow Road, the few white survivors at targeted households displayed a similar persistence. Levi Waller, after great losses at age fifty-one, remained at his farm and worked in his blacksmith and wood shops for the rest of his life. In January 1833 he married a third time, to Nancy Rochelle of Surry County, about twenty years his junior.[62] In 1836 he held six taxable slaves, the same number he had held in 1831; and by 1838 he had added forty-five acres to his landholdings, making a total of 632 acres.[63] He did not abandon his former interests. In 1840 he held sixteen slaves of all ages, two fewer than in the previous census; altogether in 1840 there were eighteen black people in his household (including two free females) and five white people.[64] After 1840 he apparently began to distribute property to his sons, so that when he died in 1847, he held just two slaves, women named Ginny and Viney.[65] In the will he wrote in November 1847, he divided his estate much as Newit Harris had divided his. Waller gave his widow some furniture, animals, and crops, and he loaned her one-third of his remaining property for life, as required. To each of two favored sons, he gave one-third of his property and residual rights to their stepmother's dower. His two other surviving sons received token gifts, probably after having received property in the past.[66] At the sale of his personal estate in 1849, a neighbor bought Ginny for $200, and Mrs. Waller, the widow, bought Viney for $92.[67] Viney then disappeared from the records; Mrs. Waller held no slaves after 1850. Two of Waller's four surviving sons remained in the county in 1860 and kept a small number of slaves, two of whom were old enough to have belonged to their great-grandfather.[68]

Jacob Williams survived at his farm on Barrow Road into the centennial spring of 1876, his ninety-sixth year, still living with the woman he married in 1832 (Rachel Pope, his previous wife's sister, twenty years his junior).[69] He fathered five more children, the last being a boy, Shugars, born around 1845, when Jacob was sixty-five.[70] He must have known that his second family would want patrimony and the kind of security that derived from a holding in slaves. In fact, Williams's slaveholding, like that of Peter Edwards, grew significantly *after* the uprising. Between 1830 and 1850, it doubled in size and then remained stable through 1860, his eightieth year.[71] Nothing that happened in 1831 disposed him to give up his holding. His persistence and that of his like-minded neighbors evidently overcame any thought about the approaching *force majeure.*

Caswell Worrell, Williams's nephew, withdrew from the occupation of overseeing after the uprising and had only minor involvement thereafter with slaves and slavery. He remained in the parish until his death at age fifty-three, but he seems seldom to have crossed his uncle's path.[72] He never learned to sign his name. Though odd in character and never rich, he was a generous man and attractive to a series of women. In March 1832 he married, formally, an older woman, Jane Newsom, and took possession of her property: two taxable slaves, twelve acres, and a house worth $200.[73] In May 1835 he used two of his wife's young slaves, Sterling and Rose, as security for a small debt.[74] One month later, with no evident awareness of incongruity, he witnessed the marriage bond of Gilliam Artis and Caroline Newsom, free blacks.[75] In 1840 he headed a household that included three white females (none near his age, but one of whom was his second wife), four free black males, two free black females, and one slave (a young male, probably the property of Jane Newsom Worrell).[76]

After Jane's death in 1843, Worrell apparently stopped holding slaves, but his household remained different from others, as he continued to share his small farm with a mixture of people not always of his own family or race.[77] In April 1844 the court found evidence that Worrell had fathered a single woman's child, born in March (the second child of his to be born), and required him to pay support for seven years.[78] In 1850, when he was forty-one years old, one member of his household (all white now) was Dollie Simmons (listed as age twenty, but perhaps as old as twenty-six), whom he took as his third wife in 1854.[79] Finally, in 1857, he married a fourth time, to Beedy Furgason, a single woman of thirty-five who died the following year.[80] In 1860 Worrell was listed as head of a household of four white persons, none of whom had the same family name. One of the residents, Mary Drake, age twenty-three, would give birth to a daughter, Darthulia Drake, in March 1861, a year and a half before Worrell died.[81] In the will he dictated and marked with an *X* in May 1862, Worrell gave a servant girl in his household, Eveline Channel (then fourteen), a legacy of $100. He loaned his house and eight acres to Mary Drake for the rest of her life. The balance of his estate he gave to little Darthulia, instructing his executor to give the child "a tolerable good comon [*sic*] education and pay her expenses for board, clothing, tuition, books &c. out of her portion while going to school."[82] Worrell was attempting to devise for the women in his life a form of support and security grounded on their own efforts and on their ties to a household without slaves.

The Courthouse Circle

Thomas R. Gray had warned in September 1831 that the county might suffer a loss of population after the uprising. "Some of our citizens will leave us," he predicted in his letter to the *Whig*, "and all agree, that they never again can feel safe, never again, be happy."[83] He offered that gloomy assessment knowing that magistrates James W. Parker and James Trezvant, who had questioned Nat Turner at the pretrial examination on 31 October, were preparing to leave Virginia. Both men departed within six months for Tennessee.

Parker, who had fled to safety on 22 August only minutes before the insurgents reached his gate, determined within days to remove his wife and children from the county. He had lived all of his thirty-one years in Southampton and had been looking forward to a promising future; he later recalled that "he was making money as rapidly as he cared to," according to Drewry, "until the insurrection came along to interrupt him."[84] He had been named to the court in 1824. Between August and mid-November of 1831, he sat on the trials of nineteen rebellion defendants, including Nat Turner. On 3 September, twelve days after the skirmish in his cornfield, Parker sold all of his land and his sixteen slaves to Capt. A. P. Peete, commander of the first volunteers.[85] (At that point, three of the slaves Parker sold—Archer, Ferry, and Sam—had not yet been cleared of taking part in the rebellion.) Later in September, Parker gained four other slaves (including Dilsy, worth $100) from the estate of his late mother-in-law, Rebecca Vaughan; all four soon disappeared from local records.[86] On 19 March 1832, shortly before his departure, Parker resigned from the court.[87] He remained in the "western country" (as it was called in the tax lists) three years. By the spring of 1835 he had returned to Southampton and, with the help of his wife's uncle, Henry B. Vaughan, again began to buy land and slaves.[88]

Young Parker's neighbor and patron, James Trezvant, also decided without delay to move. Trezvant turned forty-eight in 1831. He had arrived in Jerusalem in 1807 and had risen quickly through a series of local, state, and national offices. As a justice of the peace in 1831, he sat on more than half of the rebellion trials (twenty-six, including Nat Turner's). Over the previous fifteen years he had developed his plantation across the river from the town, built his mansion there, and settled nearly fifty slaves.[89] He resigned from the court on 16 January 1832, two months before Parker.[90] By late spring he was in Nashville with his wife and family, preparing to look for land near Memphis. In June he wrote to his friend James Rochelle, the county clerk, one of whose slaves—"your man Harry," Trezvant called him—had accompanied the party to Tennessee. "After a journey of forty two days over bad roads and through bad weather, I arrived with my family at this place," he told Rochelle. Nothing in his letter suggested that he had been driven by physical fear. Rather, he was attracted by the prospect of keeping and improving his holding in slaves; he seemed to fear only that slavery in Virginia was destined now to decline. "The more I see of the West, the more I am pleased with my removal from Virginia," he said. "I have no doubt your negroes would make you more in the West than you will ever receive in Virginia from your whole estate including your office."[91]

In October 1832 Trezvant was still in Nashville, preparing to leave for western Tennessee, where he intended to "commence a plantation in the woods." By then, many of his slaves had arrived, though they were experiencing "much sickness."[92] By the spring of 1833, all of his hands were in Tennessee.[93] He predicted his force would clear "upwards of 200 acres of land by planting time, upon which I shall make more than a supply for my negroes and family the following year." In three years, he predicted, "with industry," he would clear enough land to employ all of his slaves in cultivating corn and cotton and raising livestock. A new neighbor from North Carolina, who owned about the same number of acres and hands, expected to gather two hundred thousand pounds of cotton in the seed. "You can easily estimate from this statement," he told Rochelle, "the difference between the value of slave labour in the Western District and Virginia."[94] Money, and the chance to make more of it with slaves, had attracted him. In 1840 he was living at his wilderness plantation with his white family of three (including Mrs. Trezvant) and sixty-four slaves.[95] There he died of natural causes in 1841, aged fifty-eight.[96]

Most of the other figures in the courthouse circle remained in Southampton the rest of their lives, contrary to Gray's expectations; and if they held slaves in 1831, they continued to do so. Magistrate Robert Goodwin died in the summer of 1832, leaving his slaves to his mother, Susanna Cobb (the widowed sister-in-law of the presiding judge).[97] Dr. Orris A. Browne (a rolling stone even before the uprising) departed in the spring of 1834 for

Norfolk and then Greensville County, where he held eight slaves in 1840.[98] The county clerk of twenty years, James Rochelle, died in 1835 at about fifty years of age, holding thirty-nine taxable slaves.[99] At least sixteen of the clerk's people were sold after his death, twelve of them in Richmond, probably at auction.[100] His brother Clements, the sheriff and the executioner of Nat Turner, remained in St. Luke's Parish until his death in 1846, when he was about seventy.[101] In 1840 Clements (or "Clem") headed a household that included six white people, one free black male, and seventy-nine slaves.[102] Jeremiah Cobb, the presiding judge, remained an influential figure in the county; in 1833 and 1834 he designed and helped to build the new courthouse (without its later portico).[103] He continued to be a slaveholder until April 1849 (a month before he died, at age seventy), when he sold his last seven slaves to his sons.[104]

The innkeeper and jailer, Henry B. Vaughan, abandoned his interests in the town and retreated to Walnut Hill. After the insult from John Hampden Pleasants, Vaughan suffered another humiliation when, in April 1832, the superior court summoned him to explain his failure to furnish recent prisoners, including Isham Turner (freed as a child by Henry Turner in 1791), Thomas Haithcock, and a slave, Daniel, "with wholesome and sufficient food, with sufficient fire when necessary and proper, and with cleanly and sufficient bed and bedding according to the season, and with the necessary clothing."[105] Vaughan retained his office for a time, but by the winter of 1833–34 he had sold the tavern and probably had given up his duties at the jail.[106] In June 1837, without explanation, he freed two of his slaves, Mary and Henrietta (a namesake, perhaps), signing deeds (much like the one his uncle Thomas signed in 1806 to free Kit and Fanny) stating his intention to "manumit, emancipate & set free" the pair, declaring each to be "entirely liberated from slavery, and entitled to all the rights and privileges of a free person." (Mary, he said, "is a woman of very bright or yellow complexion, or a mulatto, about five feet seven or eight inches high, and twenty eight years old," and Henrietta, he said, "is a woman of very bright or yellow complexion, or a mulatto, about five feet six or seven inches high, and will be seventeen years old on the 20th day of December next.")[107] The other people in his holding he would keep to the end. In 1840 his plantation household consisted of himself, two free blacks, and twenty-two slaves.[108] In 1850 he was living with a niece and seventeen slaves, still at Walnut Hill. There he died in 1852, aged sixty-three, still a bachelor and master of eighteen slaves, whom he divided by will among seven of his nieces and nephews.[109]

The postmaster in 1831, the literate and communicative Theodore Trezvant, remained in Jerusalem long after his brother James moved to Tennessee. At various times after 1815, Theodore had kept a store in town (in rented buildings), which he continued to do through 1840. In 1850, at age sixty or sixty-one, he was keeping a school.[110] Before the uprising, like many other white residents in modest circumstances, he had drifted in and out of slaveholding, paying tax on one or two slaves in 1823–25, then none in 1826–28, and then two again in 1829.[111] Though in 1830 he headed a household with fifteen slaves (one of the largest holdings in the town), he again paid no tax on slaves, indicating that at the time of the uprising he was living with people he did not own.[112] In 1840 his household had five slaves; in 1850, none.[113] His involvement with slaves did not change significantly after 1831. Sometimes he held them, sometimes not. No absolute philosophical or political line separated him from his more adventuresome, wealthier, older brother.

The leading attorney in the town, William C. Parker, basked in glory the rest of his days. He devoted himself to his profession, as he had from 1826, when he arrived and apparently rented a house for his family in or near the town.[114] He never became a planter—never owned land for more than a brief time, never held slaves in large numbers. In 1830, when he was thirty-eight, his household included just four slaves, two of whom were taxable—a family of domestic servants.[115] In the gloomy days after the rebellion, Parker boosted morale among his colleagues with his hardheaded talk favoring the "rigid enforcement" of laws and the creation of his volunteer military force, "always prepared for prompt action," measures he insisted would restore a sense of security and, as he said, "prevent the depopulation of our beloved Old Dominion."[116] The time for any other course of action had passed, he implied, and a single outbreak of terrorism only confirmed his views. His efforts during the suppression won him an appointment in 1832 as captain (and later as colonel) in the militia cavalry, and election (over T. R. Gray) in 1832 as commonwealth's attorney, replacing Meriwether Brodnax.[117] By 1840 he was living in Petersburg, still pursuing his profession and holding just seven slaves, none of whom worked in agriculture.[118] He died in 1847 at age fifty-five. His friends at the courthouse, grieving over his "sudden and melancholy" death, praised his merits "as prosecuting attorney, as a citizen and a man"—merits he displayed, they said, "in all the relations of life." They resolved to wear badges of mourning for thirty days.[119] To the magistrates, Parker remained the hero of '31.

James Strange French, the attorney for twenty-one defendants in the rebellion trials, continued to practice in the county through the 1840s. At the time of the uprising he had just turned twenty-four. He had been a student at the College of William and Mary in 1825 and at the University of Virginia in 1826, where, according to some accounts, he shared a room with Edgar Allan Poe.[120] French qualified as an attorney in Southampton in 1828 and began paying personal property tax (on two horses) in 1829; he held no slaves until 1832, when he was taxed for one.[121] A bachelor at the time of the uprising, he apparently rented rooms and boarded in town, though he briefly owned a house on a rented lot.[122] His name disappeared from the tax lists in 1833 but reappeared in 1835, when he again paid tax on one slave.[123]

French's sentiments about the Southampton rebellion apparently evolved after 1831, which made him an unusual figure. Evidence of his difference appeared in 1836, when he published the first volume of a novel, *Elkswatawa; or the Prophet of the West*, a tale about the Shawnee uprising of 1811.[124] The title character in the novel bears a striking resemblance to the narrator in *The Confessions of Nat Turner*. Seeking vengeance and aiming to inspire resistance to the white population, Elkswatawa persuades his reluctant brother, Tecumseh, to accept a plan for an uprising. By assuming a demeanor "shrouded in mystery," Elkswatawa gathers a following among superstitious members of the western tribes. He withdraws into his own thoughts, affects a "singularity" in manners, pretends to be a prophet, holds "daily converse with the Great Spirit," and tells his brother he needs recruits willing to "open the veins of a sleeping child." Wherever they go, he and his followers will spread "terror and desolation."[125]

While the novelist of 1836 did not condone terror, neither did he condemn it so emphatically as Parker and Gray in 1831. He and his white hero, Richard Rolfe (a young lawyer fresh from the College of William and Mary), had reached an understanding of what French termed "the causes of irritation" and "exasperation" among the tribes: encroachment, injustice, and prejudice on the part of whites.[126] In a preface dated at Jerusalem on 27 January 1836, French explained that he recently had resided in the West and had visited Indian tribes along the frontier.[127] "The more I saw of their peculiarities and traits of character," he wrote, "the more I found my feelings aroused, and my sympathies enlisted in their behalf."[128] It could be no matter for surprise, he suggested, that red people would "seek by bloody retaliation that redress, denied them by our courts, and the hostility of our people."[129] For Tecumseh especially, the author had developed a feeling of sympathy. "It seemed as if all the wrongs his race had suffered were glowing in him alone."[130] Young Rolfe (the character) has never believed in the justice of the war whites have waged against native people; "and there are moments," Rolfe confesses, sounding quite Jeffersonian, "when I cannot but think, Heaven will pay us off with a just retribution at last."[131] Rolfe's new understanding has led to ambivalence and thoughts of seeking forgiveness. Whether young French (the author) thought of his tale as an allegory, he did not quite say.

Last Words

T. R. Gray, unlike William C. Parker, saw his fortunes decline after his encounter in 1831 with the great and the sublime, though his later troubles had little to do with Nat Turner or the *Confessions* and much to do with his family and his alienation from certain white people in Southampton.

After a promising start in his twenties (eight hundred acres near Round Hill, twenty-three taxable slaves, the house in Jerusalem, the appointment as magistrate), he became entangled in his family's reverses and by the time of the rebellion was deeply in debt.[132] He gained nothing in 1831 from his father's much-reduced estate, whose remainders went to his sister Ann, his brother Edwin, and his own infant daughter, Ellen Douglas Gray.[133] Observers for decades have suspected that he undertook *The Confessions of Nat Turner* to make money and that it made him a fortune. The editor of the *Richmond Compiler* launched that balloon in November 1831 with a report that Gray planned a first printing of fifty thousand copies, a figure repeated in the *Philadelphia National Gazette*, the *Raleigh Star*, and thirty years later by Thomas Wentworth Higginson.[134] One historian has calculated that at the advertised price of 25 cents a copy and gross sales of $12,500, Gray must have collected a handsome royalty.[135] If so, the windfall did not save him. Three years later, on 16 February 1835, Gray appeared in court under arrest for debt and took the oath for the relief of insolvent debtors.[136] He was broke.

After his father's death in September 1831, Gray and his surviving brother Edwin attempted to hold together as much of the family's property as possible. Once again T. R. and Edwin became allies, as in their affray of 1819 and the legal difficulties that ensued. In 1831 they needed to act quickly, for Orris A. Browne, the executor chosen by their father, wanted to settle accounts at once. While Gray was still in Baltimore, in fact, Browne conducted a sale of personal property in the estate, some of which Edwin managed to buy, using funds borrowed from Browne.[137] (Edwin's bids may have rescued the books in Gray's office.) As security, Edwin offered Browne his own future interest in the captain's estate. And while T. R. was away, Edwin arranged to rent the home plantation at Round Hill from Browne for $50 a year (terms he neglected to mention to his brother).[138] Edwin also took charge of the slaves: old Davy (worth $50); young Davy ($225); Fed, Peg, and Tom (elderly, worth nothing); and Fanny and her two children ($200 altogether).[139] But Edwin had caught the same migration fever afflicting James Trezvant and James W. Parker; so, before taking his leave, in December he drew up an agreement giving power of attorney to T. R.[140] The alliance of the Gray brothers, with all of their intertwining interests, was about to break apart.

In February 1832, two of the elderly slaves at Round Hill, Tom and Peg, were found dead, and their deaths were subjected to an inquest by a jury of twelve Nottoway Parish neighbors headed by Dr. Browne. The panel found that Tom had died of natural causes at Indigo Field, an outlying Gray plantation. Peg, they said, had been murdered. Edwin and his hired man, John O'Donnelly, had assaulted Peg, the jury said, apparently at the home plantation,

> with two certain cowhides of the value of one shilling which they the said Edwin Gray and John O'Donnelly, then and there held in their right hands and inflicted divers mortal wounds and other injuries on the body of said Peg, of which the said mortal wounds and other injuries the said Peg at the place aforesaid and in the county aforesaid, languished and languishing until five o'clock in the afternoon of the day aforesaid, and that the said Peg on the day aforesaid at the time aforesaid at the place aforesaid in the said county of those mortal wounds and other injuries died.[141]

The jurymen attached to their findings brief inventories of the personal property of the two accused men; Edwin Gray's property included items he had retrieved at the November sale.[142] The magistrates in Jerusalem examined both of the accused on 20 March 1832 and discharged them.[143]

Edwin left the county within six months. On 17 September 1832, a court day in Jerusalem, a second auction took place at the demand of Dr. Browne, offering the property of Edwin Gray, "late of Southampton." This was a sale of Edwin's portion of his father's estate—the very portion he had posted as security the preceding November when buying (for $848.10) his father's goods and furnishings. The high bidder (offering a paltry $223) at the second sale was Thomas R. Gray, who borrowed funds to cover his bid.[144]

Relations between T. R. and his former physician deteriorated after November 1832. That month Gray gathered and stored a corn crop at his father's farm, on land Edwin had been renting from Dr. Browne. In May 1833 Browne (also in dire financial straits) filed a complaint against Gray, charging him with not paying the rent his brother owed. Gray denied the charge: Browne's claim that he, T. R. Gray, had agreed to pay the rent was a "Scandalous Falsehood." He had never agreed to pay the $50, had never heard of the debt, and did not believe it existed.[145] The two men began a public quarrel on 5 June 1833, when Gray insulted Browne. Browne responded on 6 June with the expected challenge, a reminder that in those days a man spoke his mind at some risk, regardless of the commonwealth's law against dueling.[146] Gray claimed that while he went about his legal duties the rest of that year, the doctor could be seen daily "in and near the town of Jerusalem," engaged in "shooting at a mark with a pistol."[147] In January 1834 Browne published a pamphlet detailing charges against Gray, which the latter answered in February—his second rhetorical blast in three years against a villain and scoundrel. "Dr. Brown [*sic*] came to the county of Southampton some eight or ten years past," Gray wrote, "a quack Doctor and needy adventurer, and succeeded in raising the wind by marriage." Five different individuals (Gray named four of them) had insulted Browne in that period without raising a response. Now the quack was airing suspicions about Gray that only a "coward soul" could conceive. Gray feared not, however, since the physician had a known preference for ink, rather than blood. "'Tis not in the Dr.'s nature," said he (employing a favorite contraction), "to treat any man's person thus harshly."[148]

On 17 March 1834, Dr. Browne and his wife abruptly sold their property in Southampton and soon thereafter moved to Norfolk.[149] On 21 April, Gray again was brought into court under arrest, this time charged with having shot (not fatally, it appears) John Vaughan, a nephew of the late Rebecca Vaughan, the same young man who had ridden and fought at Parker's field, according to Drewry, like "a perfect dare-devil."[150] Gray and Browne and their seconds must have met on some field of honor, though the official record says nothing about a duel. Gray's aim must have strayed. At his examination on 22 April, the magistrates heard testimony (not recorded) from seven witnesses and the defendant himself. They dismissed the charges and said no more.[151]

Gray remained in Jerusalem until November 1836, paying taxes on one horse and a gig (in 1833 and after), but no slaves.[152] By January 1835 he had lost his house in town and sold his last remnant of land.[153] The next month, he again was brought into court by the sheriff and, under suit by creditors, was declared insolvent.[154] With no land and no slaves, he was making little headway, no matter his merits as an attorney and pamphleteer. So he too left the county.[155]

Through connections in Washington he secured an appointment in August 1836 as consul for the port of Tabasco, Mexico. He departed in November for New Orleans and on 11 December was aboard the steamboat *Washita* on Lake Pontchartrain, bound for Pensacola, where he planned to seek passage to Tampa Bay or Mexico. At Pensacola he fell ill, suffering perhaps a recurrence of the autumnal fever that had felled him in September 1831. On 1 January 1837 he reported to the secretary of state that he was still in Pensacola, prevented from continuing to Mexico "by sickness and other causes beyond my control." He reached Tampa on the USS *St. Louis* but could not find passage to Tabasco, so he continued on the *St. Louis* to Havana, where he waited. Finally, he gave up and returned to the United States. He resigned the appointment in Tabasco, having "attempted in vain to reach that post," he said, "and other circumstances beyond my controul rendering this step indispensable."[156]

At some point between 1837 and 1839 he settled in Portsmouth and again took up his profession, though his name did not appear in the 1840 census as head of a household in that town, nor did he ever have a listing on the tax rolls of Portsmouth or Norfolk County.[157] Apparently he never owned real property in Portsmouth and never again held a slave. According to the *Norfolk American Beacon*, he died on Saturday evening, 23 August 1845, of bilious fever or congestive fever.[158] Malaria. His death notice and obituary prove that the town had come to know him well. "Whatever were his faults," the *Beacon* editors said, "there was in the character of the deceased much to admire and much that was worthy of esteem," including a "natural benevolence." He was neither malicious nor vindictive, they said, "and however the impetuosity of his temper might be misdirected, it proceeded from an independence and fearlessness of mind, which disdained alike concealment and restraint."[159] He spoke his mind.

One fault, "deeply painful to his friends," the editors could not overlook. Throughout his life, they noted, the deceased had spoken out boldly, fearlessly, and with "unhallowed lips" about "the sanctuary of religion." Perhaps the editors recalled the rude passages Gray had penned about the church and its authorities in his letter to the *Whig* in September 1831 ("*coloured preachers . . . haranging vast crowds*"; "*the misguided zeal of good men, preaching up equality*"; "*missionaries . . . bettering the condition of the world*"; ministers "*raving*" and playing "*the bloackhead*"). "Major Gray—let not the fact be concealed painful though it be—was a scoffer of religion."[160]

His friends had reason to hope, however, for the Reverend Vernon Eskridge of the Methodist Episcopal Church (and a holder of three slaves in 1840) had attended the major at the hour of his death.[161] And according to the pastor, Gray had made an astonishing confession. "I have been (said he to the Rev. Pastor)," the editors reported, "the vilest of sinners and nothing could have awakened me to a knowledge of my lost condition, but a blow like that which struck Saul of Tarsus to the earth." (The scoffer was familiar with Acts 9:3–9.) "O, that I could be permitted strength to go abroad but for an hour," Eskridge said Gray had lamented. "I would cover myself with dirt and ashes and cry aloud to sinners to repent and flee from the wrath to come" (Job 42:6; Matthew 3:7 and 11:21; Luke 3:7 and 10:13). While strength lasted, Gray (a prisoner now himself) had continued speaking, Eskridge said, revealing that his mind was absorbed by "reflection on a future state," his soul subdued to "penitence for his sins." Neither the parson nor the editors specified the sins, except for infidelity—of the kind that led to scoffing and, they hinted, perhaps to sensuality.[162] If Eskridge's account was complete, Gray said nothing on his deathbed about slavery or the rebellion of 1831. No one mentioned the *Confessions*.

Neither Eskridge nor the editors noted the ironies in this closing scene, this victory of sentiment over skepticism. In Gray's death they saw only a warning to "the infidel and sensualist" against a life like his. "His contrition was as sincere as its evidences were impressive," the editors opined.[163] A fitting epitaph, with the ring of literal truth and an air of authentic ambiguity, it might have been dictated by the scoffer himself.

Roster of Insurgents

With ages and households or slaveholdings in italics

1. On Leaving the House of Elizabeth Turner II

1. Nat Turner I *(31, Joseph Travis)*
2. Hark Moore *(ca. 30, Joseph Travis)*
3. Henry Porter *(ca. 27, Richard Porter)*
4. Sam Francis *(ca. 35, Nathaniel Francis)*
5. Nelson Edwards *(33, Peter Edwards)*
6. Will Francis *(ca. 35, Nathaniel Francis)*
7. Jack Reese *(ca. 21, William Reese)*
8. Austin Edwards *(22, Peter Edwards)*
9. Moses Moore *(13, Joseph Travis)*
10. Unidentified male *(ca. 30, Salathiel Francis)*
11. Nathan Blunt *(ca. 21, Benjamin Blunt Jr. estate)*
12. Tom ("Marmaduke") *(ca. 21, Piety Reese?)*
13. Sam Turner *(ca. 22, Elizabeth Turner II)*
14. Jordan Turner *(ca. 21, Elizabeth Turner II)*
15. Davy Turner *(ca. 21, Elizabeth Turner II)*

2. Recruited between the Whitehead House and the Newit Harris House

16. Joe Turner *(ca. 30, John C. Turner)*
17. Nat Turner II *(ca. 30, Edmund Turner estate)*
18. Daniel Porter *(ca. 47, Richard Porter)*
19. Aaron Porter *(ca. 47, Richard Porter)*
20. Moses Porter *(ca. 25, Richard Porter)*
21. Jacob Porter *(18, Richard Porter)*
22. Unidentified male 1 *(age unknown, near the Doyel house)*
23. Unidentified male 2 *(age unknown, near the Doyel house)*
24. Unidentified male 3 *(age unknown, near the Doyel house)*
25. Unidentified male 4 *(age unknown, near the Doyel house)*
26. Nathan Francis *(14, Nathaniel Francis)*

27. Tom Francis *(14, Nathaniel Francis)*
28. Davy Francis *(13, Nathaniel Francis)*
29. Dred Francis *(ca. 35, Nathaniel Francis)*
30. Sam Edwards *(ca. 25, Peter Edwards)*
31. Jim Edwards *(19, Peter Edwards)*
32. Moses Barrow *(ca. 35, John T. Barrow)*

3. Recruited along Barrow Road

33. Davy Waller *(ca. 30, Levi Waller)*
34. Alfred Waller *(ca. 30, Levi Waller)*
35. Nelson Williams *(ca. 35, Jacob Williams)*
36. Stephen Bell *(ca. 21, James W. Bell)*

4. Recruited at Ridley's Buckhorn Quarter

37. Curtis Ridley *(ca. 25, Thomas Ridley)*
38. Stephen Ridley *(ca. 25, Thomas Ridley)*
39. Matt Ridley *(ca. 25, Thomas Ridley)*
40. Unidentified male *(age unknown, Thomas Ridley)*

Sources: Gray, *Confessions*; County Court Minute Book, trial records, 1831; newspaper accounts; legislative petitions; and [Brodnax], prosecutor's notes, County Court Judgments, 1831.

Notes: Estimates of ages are based on household listings in U.S. census manuscript returns, and on descriptions and values of individuals cited in court minutes and estate inventories.

Part 1. The estimate of fifteen insurgents leaving the Turner house rests on the number claimed by Nat Turner (nine mounted, six on foot) in Gray, *Confessions*. Tom (of Piety Reese?) is included on the assumption that he was the man named Tom, dying in jail, mentioned in the *Norfolk American Beacon*, 30 Aug. 1831, and referred to as "Marmaduke" by Pleasants in the *Richmond Constitutional Whig*, 29 Aug. 1831. Two others might have been the twelfth man, however: a young male, nearly grown (perhaps Jim), belonging to Piety Reese; or Joe Harris, who belonged to Elizabeth (Coggin) Harris, identified by William S. Drewry. Nathan Blunt is included here on the assumption that he was recruited at the Reese farm. The unidentified male (number 10) is included on the assumption that he was recruited at the Salathiel Francis farm, as Theodore Trezvant suggested in the *Raleigh Register*, 15 Sept. 1831; the 1830 census included a male slave of about age thirty in the listing for Salathiel Francis.

Part 2. The inclusion of four unidentified males (numbers 22 through 25) represents an estimate based on Nat Turner's statement in the *Confessions* that "some" joined the insurgents after the killing of Augustus F. Doyel.

Part 3. Stephen Bell separated before the skirmish at Parker's field. Jim Vaughan and Wright Vaughan are excluded, although they were impressed at the Vaughan house and may have been present at the Parker house. Both were cleared of charges that they took part in the uprising.

Part 4. Curtis Ridley and Stephen Ridley, valued at $400 and $450, respectively, were tried and executed for their participation. Matt Ridley separated and gave information about the insurgent group. A fourth participant from Thomas Ridley's Buckhorn Quarter has not been identified.

Insurgents Who Separated before Parker's Field

With points of separation in italics

1. Jack Reese *(near the Doyel house)*
2. Davy Turner *(near the Doyel house)*
3. Joe Turner *(near the Doyel house)*
4. Will Francis *(Barrow house, conjectural)*
5. Alfred Waller *(Vaughan house)*
6. Stephen Bell *(Parker's gate)*

Sources: Gray, *Confessions*; County Court Minute Book, trial records, 1831; newspaper accounts; and [Brodnax], prosecutor's notes, County Court Judgments, 1831.

Coerced Participants

With witnesses to coercion in italics

1. Jack Reese *(Moses Moore)*
2. Moses Moore *(Moses Moore)*
3. Davy Turner *(Moses Moore, Nathan Blunt)*
4. Joe Turner *(Hubbard Whitehead)*
5. Nathan Francis *(Moses Moore)*
6. Tom Francis *(Moses Moore)*
7. Davy Francis *(Moses Moore)*
8. Sam Edwards *(Levi Waller)*
9. Nelson Williams *(Stephen Bell)*
10. Stephen Bell *("sundry witnesses")*

Sources: Gray, *Confessions*; County Court Minute Book, trial records, 1831; newspaper accounts.

Insurgents at Buckhorn Quarter

With households or slaveholdings in italics

1. Moses Barrow *(John T. Barrow)*
2. Nelson Edwards *(Peter Edwards)*
3. Austin Edwards *(Peter Edwards)*
4. James Edwards *(Peter Edwards)*
5. Sam Francis *(Nathaniel Francis)*
6. Hark Moore *(Joseph Travis)*
7. Aaron Porter *(Richard Porter)*
8. Daniel Porter *(Richard Porter)*
9. Henry Porter *(Richard Porter)*
10. Jacob Porter *(Richard Porter)*
11. Tom ("Marmaduke") *(Piety Reese?)*
12. Curtis Ridley *(Thomas Ridley)*
13. Matthew Ridley *(Thomas Ridley)*
14. Stephen Ridley *(Thomas Ridley)*
15. Fourth Ridley recruit *(Thomas Ridley)*
16. Jordan Turner *(Elizabeth Turner II)*
17. Nat Turner I *(Joseph Travis)*
18. Nat Turner II *(Edmund Turner Jr.)*
19. Davy Waller *(Levi Waller)*
20. Nelson Williams *(Jacob Williams)*

Sources: Gray, *Confessions*; County Court Minute Book, trial evidence, 1831; author's chronology of events; newspaper accounts, 1831.

Note: Nat Turner estimated the number of insurgents after the false alarm at about twenty; Gray, *Confessions*, 16.

White Victims

With approximate ages of victims and names of assailants in italics

1. Travis House

1. Joseph Travis* *(30, Will Francis, Nat Turner I)*
2. Sarah (Francis) Travis *(30, Will Francis)*
3. Putnam Moore *(10, unknown)*
4. Joel Westbrook *(16, unknown)*
5. Travis infant *(1, Will Francis, Henry Porter)*

2. Salathiel Francis House

6. Salathiel Francis* *(28, Will Francis, Sam Francis)*

3. Reese House

7. Piety (Vick) Reese* *(59, unknown)*
8. Joseph William H. Reese* *(18, unknown)*

4. Turner House

9. Hartwell Peebles* *(adult, age unknown, Austin Edwards)*
10. Elizabeth Turner II* *(37, Will Francis)*
11. Sarah (Turner) Newsom* *(36, Will Francis, Nat Turner I)*

5. Bryant House

12. Henry Bryant* *(25, unknown)*
13. Elizabeth (Balmer) Bryant *(22, unknown)*
14. Bryant infant *(1, unknown)*
15. Mildred Balmer *(60, unknown)*

6. Whitehead House

16. Richard Whitehead* *(30, Will Francis)*
17. Whitehead grandson *(2, unknown)*
18. Minerva Whitehead *(25, unknown)*
19. Mary Ann Whitehead *(23, unknown)*

20. Mourning Ann Whitehead *(19, unknown)*
21. Catherine Whitehead* *(59, Will Francis)*
22. Margaret Whitehead *(37, Nat Turner I)*

7. Doyel House (Near)

23. Augustus F. Doyel* *(35, Hark Moore)*

8. Nathaniel Francis House

24. Louisa (Turner) Williams *(20, unknown)*
25. Williams infant *(1, unknown)*
26. John L. Browne *(3, unknown)*
27. Samuel T. Browne *(7, unknown)*
28. A. (or Henry) Doyel *(21, unknown)*

9. Barrow House

29. John T. Barrow* *(26, unknown)*
30. George Vaughan* *(19, unknown)*

10. Waller House

31. Martha (Kindred) Waller *(45, Sam Francis, Daniel Porter, Aaron Porter)*
32. Martha Waller II *(4, Sam Francis, Daniel Porter, Aaron Porter)*
33. Waller daughter *(26, unknown)*
34. Waller infant daughter *(1, unknown)*
35. Thomas Waller *(13, unknown)*
36. Waller son *(9, unknown)*
37. Waller son *(7, unknown)*
38. Unidentified boy *(10, unknown)*
39. Unidentified boy *(10, unknown)*
40. Lucinda Jones *(14, unknown)*
41. Unidentified child *(10, unknown)*

11. William Williams House

42. William Williams* *(26, unknown)*
43. Miles Johnson *(14, unknown)*
44. Henry Johnson *(12, unknown)*
45. Rebecca (Ivy) Williams II *(18, unknown)*

12. Jacob Williams House

46. Edwin Drury* *(21, unknown)*
47. Nancy (Pope) Williams *(36, unknown)*
48. Williams child *(4, unknown)*
49. Williams child *(2, unknown)*
50. Williams child *(1, unknown)*

13. Worrell House

51. Mrs. Caswell Worrell *(21, unknown)*
52. Worrell infant *(1, unknown)*

14. Vaughan House

53. Rebecca Vaughan* *(47, unknown)*
54. Ann Eliza Vaughan* *(19, Tom, or "Marmaduke")*
55. William Arthur Vaughan* *(16, unknown)*

Sources: Gray, *Confessions*; U.S. Census, 1810–30, manuscript returns; Southampton County Marriage Register; Drewry, *Southampton Insurrection*; biographical and genealogical notes (author's research files).

Notes: Asterisks indicate victims for whom Gray found first names or initials. All ages listed are approximate. Spellings of Edwin Drury's names vary: "Edmund Drewry" in court minutes; "Edwin Drury" in Gray, *Confessions*; "Edwin Drewry" in William S. Drewry, *Southampton Insurrection*, 61. William S. Drewry identified the Francis overseer (number 28) as Henry Doyle; the personal tax list of 1831 listed an A. Doyle at the Francis house; Drewry, *Southampton Insurrection*, 47. Spellings of the name *Doyel* also vary.

Atrocities and the Tax Rolls

> We allude to the slaughter of many blacks, without trial, and under circumstances of great barbarity.
>
> —John Hampden Pleasants, *Richmond Constitutional Whig*

Prompted by the commentaries of John Hampden Pleasants in the *Richmond Constitutional Whig*, editors as far away as New England began to publish reports in early September 1831 about a wave of atrocities perpetrated against black people during the ten days that followed the uprising. Pleasants reported that in Southampton he and the Richmond Troop had witnessed with surprise a "sanguinary temper" in the white population, which seemed disposed to kill all prisoners immediately. "We allude to the slaughter of many blacks, without trial," he wrote, "and under circumstances of great barbarity."[1] His estimate that between twenty-five and forty ("*or possibly a yet larger number*") had died in such killings may have been suggested by Theodore Trezvant, who announced his own count on 5 September. "The scouting parties through the county," Trezvant said, "have killed 22, without law or justice, as they were determined to shew them no mercy."[2]

Readers north and south were shocked by the prediction Pleasants published on 3 September that another such rising would lead to the "extermination of the whole black population in the quarter of the state where it occurs."[3] In Boston on the same day, William Lloyd Garrison, using similar language, foresaw an inevitable "war of extermination" if slavery persisted.[4] Alexis de Tocqueville, touring in far-off Quebec on the day Pleasants arrived in Jerusalem, caught this strain of hyperbole in late September and October while passing through Boston, New York, and Philadelphia and carried it to France, where he in turn spread it, contemplating for America the most horrible of civil wars and perhaps *la ruine* ("extirpation," in Henry Reeve's translation) of one of the two races.[5]

Pleasants gave no verifiable details on the number of such crimes or their geographic extent, though he did offer a supportive anecdote or two gathered along the way to Jerusalem. "We met with one individual of intelligence, who stated that he himself had killed between 10 and 15," he reported, discreetly omitting the man's name. His source claimed that he nearly had lost his life in attempting to save a woman he thought innocent, "but who was shot by the multitude in despite of his exertions."[6] Evidence of a similar kind appeared in reports compiled by distant editors, who borrowed more than impressions from Pleasants. "Many of the negroes in the region of the insurrection were slaughtered under circumstances of great barbarity," wrote the editor of the *New York Daily Advertiser* in mid-September, whose text reappeared in Boston on 17 September, in the *Liberator*.[7] Samuel Warner, writing in New York City in October, put the number slain at "more than One Hundred," apparently referring to all fatalities from violence against black people throughout Southampton County.[8]

Authors in succeeding decades built upon these early impressions. Thomas Wentworth Higginson, writing in Massachusetts in 1861, raised the number of atrocities to "many" hundreds. "Petition after petition was subsequently presented to the Legislature," he said, "asking compensation for slaves thus assassinated without trial."[9] If Higginson was referring to petitions from Southampton County, he was exaggerating. Petitions have survived from six residents of the county who sought compensation for a total of ten slaves killed without trial, eight of whom certainly took part in the uprising: Peter Edwards sought compensation for the loss without trial of Nelson, James, and Austin; Richard Porter for Jacob, Moses, and Aaron; Levi Waller for Alfred; Thomas Fitzhugh's heirs for the young man shot by accident; heirs of Elizabeth Turner II for Jordan; and the heirs of Piety Reese for the boy nearly grown.[10] If other such petitions were submitted from Southampton or from any of the five surrounding Virginia counties, or from any place in Virginia in 1831 or 1832, they have yet to be retrieved from the archives.

Losses in St. Luke's Parish

Warner's estimate that more than one hundred black people had been slain in the county, though a mere guess, came close to the actual number of slaves missing from the St. Luke's Parish tax lists in 1832. The number of taxable slaves (aged twelve and older) in St. Luke's fell from 2,444 in 1831 to 2,337 in 1832, a loss of 107 (or 4.4 percent).[11] Of that decrease, the uprising and its aftermath removed as many as fifty-four slaves, of whom as many as forty-two had been killed in the fighting or put to death after trial. (In the lists that follow, households or slaveholdings to which individuals belonged are given in parentheses; asterisks denote documented atrocities.)

A. Slaves Sentenced by the Court

Altogether, thirty slaves were lost through the county court's sentences. Of that number, the governor agreed to commute the sentences of twelve to transportation from the United States; the eighteen other slaves were hanged. All of those losses, extraordinary in nature, were documented in court records. By the definitions of Eppes, Pleasants, and Theodore Trezvant, none involved an atrocity. The individuals lost were as follows:

Slaves transported: 12

1. Isaac Champion *(Samuel Champion)*
2. Jim Champion *(Samuel Champion)*
3. Isaac Charlton *(George H. Charlton)*
4. Hardy Edwards *(Benjamin Edwards)*
5. Isham Edwards *(Benjamin Edwards)*
6. Davy Francis *(Nathaniel Francis)*
7. Nathan Francis *(Nathaniel Francis)*

8. Tom Francis *(Nathaniel Francis)*
9. Moses Moore *(Joseph Travis)*
10. Frank Parker *(Solomon Parker)*
11. Andrew Whitehead *(Catherine Whitehead)*
12. Jack Whitehead *(Catherine Whitehead)*

SLAVES EXECUTED: 18

1. Lucy Barrow *(John T. Barrow)*
2. Moses Barrow *(John T. Barrow)*
3. Ben Blunt *(Benjamin Blunt estate)*
4. Nathan Blunt *(Benjamin Blunt estate)*
5. Sam Edwards *(Peter Edwards)*
6. Dred Francis *(Nathaniel Francis)*
7. Sam Francis *(Nathaniel Francis)*
8. Hark Moore *(Joseph Travis)*
9. Daniel Porter *(Richard Porter)*
10. Jack Reese *(John W. Reese, Joseph W. H. Reese)*
11. Curtis Ridley *(Thomas Ridley)*
12. Stephen Ridley *(Thomas Ridley)*
13. Davy Turner *(Elizabeth Turner II)*
14. Joe Turner *(John C. Turner)*
15. Nat Turner I *(Joseph Travis)*
16. Nat Turner II *(James Turner and Elizabeth Turner III)*
17. Davy Waller *(Levi Waller)*
18. Nelson Williams *(Jacob Williams)*

B. Confirmed Fatalities

Sources in 1831 documented the deaths of ten insurgent slaves fatally wounded during the uprising. At least three of these died of wounds they received before being captured—two died while being pursued and one in jail.[12] Those three were as follows:

SLAVES KILLED BEFORE CAPTURE: 2

1. Nelson Edwards* *(Peter Edwards)*
2. Henry Porter* *(Richard Porter)*

SLAVE WOUNDED, DIED IN JAIL: 1

3. Tom ("Marmaduke") *(Piety Reese?)*

Gen. Eppes apparently considered the deaths of Nelson Edwards and Henry Porter atrocities. Both men were shot before capture and their bodies decapitated. Each is included here among the confirmed deaths involving atrocities.

Records confirm that another seven insurgent slaves were killed at capture or soon after.[13] Each of these killings was an *atrocity*, as Eppes used the word: a cruel act of violence against an individual who had submitted to legal authority. In his order of 28 August, which introduced the word *atrocity*, the general was addressing primarily the treatment of individuals captured or arrested on suspicion of having taken part in the insurrection.[14] He considered even insurgent leaders to have been victims of atrocity if they were put to death outside the law, after surrender and without trial. The following slaves, whose deaths were well documented, were killed upon being captured, while defenseless or in submission:

Slaves killed upon capture: 7

1. Austin Edwards* *(Peter Edwards)*
2. James Edwards* *(Peter Edwards)*
3. Aaron Porter* *(Richard Porter)*
4. Jacob Porter* *(Richard Porter)*
5. Moses Porter* *(Richard Porter)*
6. Jordan Turner* *(Elizabeth Turner II)*
7. Alfred Waller* *(Levi Waller)*

C. Unconfirmed Fatalities

Reports in 1831 mentioned as many as eight insurgent slaves who may have died in the uprising but whose identities, roles, or circumstances at the time of death were not well documented. These included Will Francis and Sam Turner (the only individuals in this group identified by name in 1831), whose deaths were never described or recorded. Also included are the "several" men (perhaps four) who, according to the *Confessions*, joined the insurgents near the house of Augustus F. ("Trajan") Doyel. In addition, the unconfirmed fatalities may have included one slave recruited at the farm of Salathiel Francis (according to Theodore Trezvant, who was vague about the number) and one of the four men recruited from Ridley's Quarter, mentioned in the *Confessions*.[15] All eight may have died in atrocities, but only in the case of Sam Turner did any evidence appear about circumstances at the time of death.[16]

Slaves presumed killed: 8

1. Will Francis *(Nathaniel Francis)*
2. Unidentified male recruit *(Salathiel Francis)*
3. Fourth Ridley recruit *(Thomas Ridley)*
4. Sam Turner *(Elizabeth Turner II)*
5. Unidentified male 1 *(unknown, near the Doyel house)*
6. Unidentified male 2 *(unknown, near the Doyel house)*
7. Unidentified male 3 *(unknown, near the Doyel house)*
8. Unidentified male 4 *(unknown, near the Doyel house)*

D. Other Unconfirmed Fatalities

Finally, as many as six additional slaves may have been killed in atrocities for which the evidence is inconclusive. Even the skeptical Thomas R. Gray, who did not use the word *atrocity* in connection with the deaths of slaves or free blacks, believed nonetheless that "several innocent persons must have suffered" in the aftermath of the uprising.[17] He appears not to have considered the killing of any insurgent or overt supporter as an atrocity, but he probably would have applied the term to the killing of anyone, slave or free, who had not taken part in the insurrection. Since he believed that the uprising had been confined to Southampton, he assumed that individuals charged in other counties probably were innocent, regardless of any "superstitious remarks" they might have made about the rising. "Likewise," he wrote on 17 September, "if mere declarations made by slaves relative to what they would do if *Captain Nat* came that way, the insurrection, being at that time suppressed, *Nat's* party dispersed, and most of them shot, are to be construed into evidences of guilt, there can be no end to convictions."[18]

Gray's deduction that "several" innocent persons had suffered was based on calculations he did not reveal but which can be reconstructed. When he made that deduction, he had fixed the number of insurgents at thirty-nine slaves and one free black (*"the number of 40 will include every insurgent who was with them for the least time, throughout their whole route"*). On 17 September he also knew that the court had convicted twenty-one slaves.[19] That number added to the number of people shot (not given), he said, produced a sum greater than the number of insurgents (forty). Several innocents, therefore, must have been shot. Assuming that he understood the word *several* to mean more than three but not many more, Gray was suggesting that the total number of black people (slave and free) shot stood at twenty-three or twenty-four. (From the number forty he would have subtracted twenty-one, found a difference of nineteen, and then added four or five.) Thus, in September Gray believed that four or five innocent persons (all slaves) had been shot.

Gray never did identify the innocents, but he might have included the following cases (leaving one or two unaccounted for):

POSSIBLY INNOCENT SLAVES SHOT: 3

1. A "likely young man" *(Thomas Fitzhugh estate)*
2. A boy, "nearly grown" *(Piety Reese)*
3. Unidentified male *(unknown, at the Whitehead house)*

The young man belonging to the Fitzhugh estate was shot accidentally at Belmont; the boy nearly grown, never identified by name, was claimed as a loss by the heirs of Piety Reese; and the man who died at the Whitehead house was shot reportedly by a party that included residents of Southampton and Hertford County, North Carolina.[20]

The list of atrocities might be extended to include as many as three other slaves whose identities, roles in the uprising, and circumstances of death were not documented at the time but whose cases William S. Drewry brought forward in 1900. One of those was Charlotte Francis, a slave of Nathaniel Francis. Drewry heard that she had threatened to stab her mistress with a dirk after the insurgents left the Francis farm, and that she was shot to death later at the Cross Keys store by her master.[21] Drewry heard, too, that Joe Harris, after reluctantly joining the insurgents, had been hanged, though never brought to trial.[22] Sources also told Drewry that the son of Viney Musgrave, Robert T. Musgrave's cook, was compelled to join the band and that he "escaped" but was shot.[23] Gray might not have considered any of these three individuals innocent.

UNDOCUMENTED ATROCITIES: 3

1. Charlotte Francis *(Nathaniel Francis)*
2. Joe Harris *(Elizabeth Coggin Harris)*
3. Son of Viney Musgrave *(Robert T. Musgrave)*

Altogether, as many as twenty-four slaves may have been killed without coming to trial, including participants, sympathizers, and those who took no part. Of those twenty-four, as many as twenty-three could have been victims of atrocities, including the two killed before capture, the seven killed at or after capture, the eight presumed killed, the three meeting Gray's criterion of innocence, and the three cases opened years later by Drewry.[24]

E. Ordinary Gains and Losses

Tax and estate records do not indicate other significant losses in the slave population of St. Luke's Parish. Some gains and losses in the number of taxable slaves occurred every year as a matter of course, balancing one another. Masters transferred holdings, inherited property, or died; and slaves advanced through the life cycle, came of age, died, and at times were moved or sold out of the parish. In 1832, for example, the removal from the county of William H. Gee's holding of twenty-eight slaves was balanced roughly by a gain of thirty-one slaves belonging to the estate of the late William Allen, former owner (absentee) of Allen's Quarter.[25] Allen died in 1831, and his executors must have transferred some of his property into the parish from Surry County.[26] In addition to Gee, seven other individuals apparently removed their holdings—another twenty-eight slaves altogether—from the parish by the spring of 1832.[27] Removals thus accounted for a loss of fifty-six slaves. They were balanced evenly, however, by the addition of fifty-six slaves to the tax accounts of six nonresidents, including the estate of William Allen.[28]

F. Slaves Not Declared as Taxable Property

At least three slaveholdings belonging to St. Luke's taxpayers in 1831 did not appear on the personal property tax list of 1832, though in fact the slaves in those holdings were alive and present. One such holding was that of James W. Parker, the young magistrate who sold his land and thirteen slaves in March 1832 and moved to Tennessee; neither Parker nor his purchaser, A. P. Peete, paid tax on the thirteen slaves that year, but Peete did so in 1833.[29] Similarly, eight slaves belonging to Sampson C. Reese, brother of Elizabeth Turner II and nephew of Piety Reese, disappeared from the list in 1832 but reappeared in 1833.[30] The third instance involved a holding that had belonged to Rebecca Barham, a widow who died in December 1831. Seven of her fifteen slaves certainly disappeared from the 1832 list but were declared as taxable property again in 1833 by her eldest son, John L. Barham.[31] The short-term losses in these three holdings totaled twenty-eight.

G. Estate Slaves Not Declared

The insurgents killed the heads of ten slave-owning households, all of whom disappeared from the personal property tax rolls in 1832. Of the sixty-two slaves belonging to this group of households, thirteen were lost permanently in the uprising (and are included above in part A). The other forty-nine apparently survived and remained in the parish. As many as twenty-three of these survivors were declared as taxable property in 1832, including all of those in the Whitehead and Reese family holdings, and perhaps some belonging to the estates of Joseph Travis, Salathiel Francis, John T. Barrow, and William Williams. The remaining twenty-six survivors, belonging to estates then in various stages of settlement, apparently were not declared as taxable property in 1832; most appear to have been listed again in 1833 as the taxable property of heirs.

H. St. Luke's Losses: Slaves

The fifty-four slaves lost from all causes in the uprising, together with the twenty-eight undeclared slaves (of Parker, Reese, and Barham) and the estimated twenty-six estate slaves also not declared, would have amounted to 108 slaves, enough to account roughly for the net decrease in St. Luke's Parish in 1832. Dozens of other smaller, mutually offsetting gains and losses that year would have brought the final balance to a net loss of 107 slaves.

I. St. Luke's Losses: Free Blacks

Two free black men died in the aftermath of the uprising. They were as follows:

FREE BLACKS KILLED: 2

1. Billy Artis I
2. Berry Newsom *(Benjamin Edwards)*

Personal property tax lists, which did include the names of free black males, suggest that these two men were the only extraordinary losses by death among Southampton free blacks. The total number of taxed free black males in St. Luke's decreased from 193 in 1831 to 192 in 1832, a net loss of one.

In mid-September Thomas R. Gray did not consider Billy Artis I innocent, though he might have changed his mind in early November after learning about Will Francis and his axe. Whether Artis committed suicide remains a question. The earliest accounts indicated that he did not kill himself. Authorities in Jerusalem, who assumed initially that Artis had been a leader in the uprising, received the first report concerning his fate by 11:00 A.M. Saturday, 27 August. In Richmond the next evening, at "about candlelight," an express rider who had carried a dispatch from Gen. Eppes to Governor John Floyd gave the news to editors at the *Compiler*. On Monday the paper published its report, referring to Artis not by name but as the only free man of color involved in the uprising. "He had afterwards returned to his own house, and a party [was] sent there to apprehend him," the editors said. "He was accidently [*sic*] seen concealed in his yard and shot."[32] The editors assumed that Artis had been killed, but amended their story after receiving William C. Parker's letter of 31 August, with its long account of the uprising. "The free negro, Billy Artis, is wounded," Parker wrote, "and still lurking about the neighborhood."[33] Authorities found Artis's body on 2 September. A county magistrate (identified only by his residence at Cedardale) provided details. "One of the leaders, a free fellow," he wrote on 4 September, "was found shot two days ago; supposed by his own hand, as his hat was hung on a stake near him, and his pistol lying by him."[34] Theodore Trezvant, though doubting the theory of suicide, confirmed on 3 September that Artis's body had been found.[35] A newspaper report on 9 September, based on official dispatches, added a final detail supporting, it was thought, the theory of self-murder: not only had Artis been found with "a pistol lying at his side," but a ball, presumably from that pistol, had been "discovered in his body."[36] The earliest accounts by Eppes and Parker, however, together with Trezvant's skepticism and Gray's apparent reversal, weigh in favor of adding Artis's death to the list of possible atrocities.

In April 1832 a superior court jury found Berry Newsom guilty of conspiracy to make insurrection and sentenced him to death. Witnesses had reported that Newsom, who had remained at home during the rising, had said he would join the insurgents "if Capt. Nat came on" and vowed to become a "soldier," evidence of a kind Gray found worthy of ridicule.[37]

Losses in Nottoway Parish

The rising on 22 and 23 August 1831 did not involve directly the black population of Nottoway Parish. Just one slave from north of the Nottoway River came into contact with the insurgents—Stephen Bell, sent by his master to help pick up the cartload of corn at the Jacob Williams farm. Nonetheless, in 1832 Nottoway Parish experienced a decrease in its slave population comparable to that in St. Luke's. The total number of taxable slaves in Nottoway Parish declined from 1,701 in 1831 to 1,630, a net loss of 71 (or 4.2 percent).

This decrease north of the river can be attributed, as in St. Luke's, to causes other than death by atrocity. Nine Nottoway slaveholders died in 1831 (none directly as a result of the rebellion), placing the fifty-nine slaves in their estates in a legal status of transition to new owners, which explains the absence of both the dead and their slaves from the tax rolls in 1832.[38] At least two other Nottoway slaveholders removed their slaves (eleven in all) from the parish.[39] At least four others did not declare their slaves (nineteen in all) as taxable property in 1832 but returned them to the rolls in 1833.[40]

Unlike St. Luke's Parish, Nottoway Parish did experience a significant decline in its free black population in 1832. The number of taxed free black males in Nottoway decreased from 144 to 101, a net loss of 43 (or 29.9 percent). Among those lost were thirty-five males (some with families) who sailed from Norfolk on 5 December 1831 aboard the *James Perkins*, bound for Monrovia, Liberia, where the ship arrived on 14 January 1832.[41] Another twenty-one free black males disappeared temporarily from the rolls in 1832, only to return very much alive in subsequent tax years.

Southampton and the Rebellion Region

The documented, extraordinary losses through insurrection and emigration, together with the balance of ordinary losses and gains in the tax rolls (final entries against first entries, departures against arrivals, absences against returns), suggest that atrocities claimed as many as twenty-three slaves and one free black man in Southampton in 1831.[42] Those numbers are close to Theodore Trezvant's estimate of twenty-two ("*killed . . . without law or justice*").

Aggregate tax data from counties adjacent to Southampton show a pattern of comparable losses between 1821 and 1838. The number of taxable slaves in Southampton (the only county for which slaveholders listed on the tax rolls have been identified and linked through time) reached a peak in 1827 and then began to decline, deepening in 1832 and 1833, and then stabilizing. In the spring of 1832, Southampton tax lists recorded 178 fewer taxable slaves than in the preceding year, a decrease of 4.3 percent. Four of the five Virginia counties adjacent to Southampton also recorded losses in 1832: Greensville, a 2 percent loss; Isle of Wight, 1 percent; Surry, 5 percent; and Sussex, 3 percent. Nansemond County added two slaves. Combined, the five neighboring Virginia counties recorded 2.1 percent fewer taxable slaves in 1832 than in 1831. Slaves were not the only segment of the tax base to decline in 1832, however. Together, the five surrounding Virginia counties recorded an even larger decrease in 1832 in the number of horses (down 2.5 percent); Southampton itself lost 3 percent of its horses and 2 percent of its white males over age sixteen.[43]

If atrocities on the scale Higginson described were committed in any jurisdiction, they might have occurred in Northampton County, North Carolina, which borders Southampton to the southwest. Of the eight counties surrounding Southampton (five in Virginia, three in North Carolina), Northampton recorded by far the greatest loss of taxable slaves (or "black polls") after the uprising. The number of black polls in Northampton fell in 1832 by 253 (or 7.5 percent), the sharpest decrease there between 1823 and 1838. That loss was part of a long-term decline that began five years before the rebellion and continued in all but two years through 1838. Similar losses occurred in other segments of the Northampton tax base during that period; in 1828, for example, the county recorded a decrease of 7.9 percent in the number of free polls. In Gates County, North Carolina, which borders the southeast corner of Southampton for one-half mile, the number of taxable slaves declined in 1832 by thirty-eight (or 2.6 percent); the county recorded much larger declines in 1830 and 1834.[44]

The pattern in all nine counties of the rebellion region indicates a general downward trend in the tax base, attributable primarily to outward migration and the domestic slave trade rather than to a wave of atrocities. Since tax rolls did not include the names of individual slaves being taxed, however, doubters may always suspect that Higginson was right and that evidence of atrocities by the hundreds lies hidden in the aggregate data. For Higginson to have been right, however, hundreds of slaves must have been brought into Southampton in 1832 to replace those lost. The totals are inflexible. If 400 slaves were murdered atrociously in St. Luke's Parish, for example, 293 must have been found to replace all but 107 of the victims. The same arithmetical necessity applies to Nottoway Parish. Nothing in the tax lists, court records, or petitions indicates that replacements on such a scale took place, or that the number of individuals in Southampton County who suffered in atrocities was greater than twenty-four, which, at the time, was shocking enough.[45]

Notes

1. John Hampden Pleasants, "Southampton Affair," *Richmond Constitutional Whig*, 3 Sept. 1831, in *Norfolk American Beacon*, 6 Sept. 1831; *Norfolk Herald*, 16 Sept. 1831.
2. Theodore Trezvant, letter, 5 Sept. 1831, *Raleigh Register*, 15 Sept. 1831.
3. Pleasants, "Southampton Affair"; *Norfolk Herald*, 16 Sept. 1831.
4. *Liberator* (Boston), 3 Sept. 1831.
5. Alexis de Tocqueville, *Democracy in America*, 4th ed., trans. Henry Reeve (2 vols.; New York: J. & H. G. Langley, 1841), 1:410; Alexis de Tocqueville, *Alexis de Toqueville: Journey to America*, ed. J. P. Mayer (New Haven, CT: Yale University Press, 1959), 40–41.
6. Pleasants, "Southampton Affair"; *Norfolk Herald*, 16 Sept. 1831.
7. *New York Daily Advertiser*, in *Liberator*, 17 Sept. 1831.

8. Samuel Warner, *Authentic and Impartial Narrative of the Tragical Scene Which Was Witnessed in Southampton County* (New York: Warner & West, 1831), 15.

9. Thomas Wentworth Higginson, "Nat Turner's Insurrection," *Atlantic Monthly* 8 (1861): 173–87, in Higginson, *Travelers and Outlaws: Episodes in American History* (Boston: Lee & Shepard, 1888), 300.

10. Petitions of Peter Edwards, Richard Porter, and Levi Waller; petitions for estates of Thomas Fitzhugh, Piety Reese, and Elizabeth Turner II, 1831, Legislative Petitions, LVA.

11. St. Luke's Parish Personal Property Tax Lists, 1831, 1832, LVA.

12. John Womack, affidavit, 21 Nov. 1831, in Edwards, petition 9804-A, 12 Dec. 1831, Legislative Petitions; *Norfolk American Beacon*, 29 Aug. 1831. Tom ("Marmaduke") apparently died in the jail; he is assumed here to have belonged to the Reese family.

13. Womack and Joseph Joiner, affidavits, 21 Nov. 1831, in Edwards, petition 9804-A; Drewry Bittle and Peter Edwards, affidavits, 22 Nov. 1831, in Richard Porter, petition 9803, 12 Dec. 1831; Sampson C. Reese and John H. Barnes, affidavits, 19 Dec. 1831, in Elizabeth Turner II (estate), petition 9915-E; Thomas Porter, affidavit, 22 Nov. 1831, in Levi Waller, petition 9803-A, 12 Dec. 1831, Legislative Petitions.

14. Richard Eppes, order, 28 Aug. 1831, in *Norfolk American Beacon*, 31 Aug. 1831.

15. Thomas R. Gray, *The Confessions of Nat Turner* (Baltimore: Lucas & Deaver, 1831), 11–12, 14, 16; Theodore Trezvant, letter, *Raleigh Register*, 15 Sept. 1831.

16. [Meriwether B. Brodnax], information, 17 Oct. 1831, *Commonwealth v. Jack and Shadrach Simmons*, County Court Judgments, 1831, LVA.

17. [Thomas R. Gray], letter, 17 Sept. 1831, *Richmond Whig*, 26 Sept. 1831, in *Norfolk American Beacon*, 30 Sept. 1831.

18. Ibid.

19. Ibid.

20. Alexander P. Peete, affidavits, 20 Dec. 1831, 18 Jan. 1832, in Fitzhugh (estate), petition 9915-F, 29 Dec. 1831, Legislative Petitions; Reese (estate), petition 9915-D, Legislative Petitions; Charles Spiers and others, letter, 28 Sept. 1831, *Roanoke Advocate* (Halifax, NC), 13 Oct. 1831; letter, Winton, NC, *Norfolk Herald*, 29 Aug. 1831.

21. William S. Drewry, *The Southampton Insurrection* (1900; repr., Murfreesboro, NC: Johnson, 1968), 48, 85n2.

22. Ibid., 38–39.

23. Ibid., 94n1.

24. The total of twenty-three slave atrocity victims excludes Tom ("Marmaduke"), who died in the jail. The findings here agree generally with those in Patrick H. Breen, "Nat Turner's Revolt: Rebellion and Response in Southampton County, Virginia" (PhD diss., University of Georgia, 2005), 158–67.

25. St. Luke's Parish Personal Tax Lists, 1831, 1832, entries for William H. Gee and William Allen.

26. Allen family genealogy (author's research file).

27. The seven other individuals whose tax, land, and estate records indicate that they removed slaves were as follows: Henry Blow (6 to North Carolina); John T. Blow Jr. (4 to Georgia); Joseph Briggs (4 to Nottoway Parish); Charlotte Nicholson (3 to Nottoway Parish); Richard S. Nicholson (5 to Nottoway Parish); John Prince (4 to Sussex County); and Sarah Scarborough (2 to Sussex County).

28. The six nonresidents in 1831 who added slaves to the parish tax rolls in 1832 were as follows: William Allen's estate (31 from Surry County); Augustine C. Butts (3 from Petersburg); Peterson Goodwyn (8 from Greensville County); Henry Mason (1 from Sussex County); William Peters (3 from Sussex County); and Thomas Turner (10 from Nottoway Parish).

29. Deeds, James W. Parker and Martha Ann Parker to Alexander P. Peete, 3 Sept. 1831, Deed Book 22:78, 79, SCC; St. Luke's Parish Personal Tax List, 1833, entry for A. P. Peete.

30. St. Luke's Parish Personal Tax Lists, 1831, 1833, entries for Sampson C. Reese.

31. St. Luke's Parish Personal Tax List, 1831, entry for Rebecca Barham; 1833, entry for John L. Barham.

32. *Richmond Compiler*, 29 Aug. 1831, in "The Banditti," *Richmond Enquirer*, 30 Aug. 1831.

33. [William C. Parker], letter, 31 Aug. 1831, *Richmond Compiler*, 3 Sept. 1831, in *Richmond Enquirer*, 6 Sept. 1831. The editors issued the following correction in the introduction to Parker's letter: "It appears that the free man Billy Artis, [the only one proved to be concerned in the plot,] was not killed, as we stated on Monday, but is wounded and lurking about" (brackets in original).

34. Cedardale letter, 4 Sept. 1831, *Richmond Whig*, 8 Sept. 1831, in *Richmond Enquirer*, 9 Sept. 1831.

35. Theodore Trezvant, letter, 3 Sept. 1831, *Richmond Whig*, 6 Sept. 1831, in *Norfolk American Beacon*, 9 Sept. 1831.

36. *Richmond Compiler*, 6 Sept. 1831, summary in *Norfolk American Beacon*, 9 Sept. 1831.

37. County Circuit-Superior Court of Law and Chancery Minute Book, 4 Apr., 7 Apr. 1832, pp. 21, 28, SCC; [Meriwether B. Brodnax], prosecutor's notes, n.d., depositions of Henry Edwards and Harry Edwards, *Commonwealth v. Berry Newsom*, County Court Judgments, 1831.

38. The nine slaveholders who died were as follows: Robert Ricks Sr. (14 slaves), William Ricks (13), Brambly Bell (9), Benjamin Bradshaw Jr. (5), Thomas Gray Sr. (5), John Morris (5), David Whitney (4), Peter Booth (3), and Lawrence Abram (3).

39. The two who removed slaves were William T. Blow (7 slaves) and George H. Gray (4).

40. The four who did not declare slaves in 1832 were Burwell Williams (8 slaves), Hartwell Hart (4), Samuel James (4), and Benjamin Hines (3).

41. *Norfolk American Beacon*, 6 Dec. 1831. The names of the thirty-five Nottoway males who left on the *Perkins* appear in Tom W. Schick, *Emigrants to Liberia, 1820 to 1843, an Alphabetical Listing* (Newark: Department of Anthropology, University of Delaware, 1971), passim; their identities are confirmed in parish tax records. See also List of the Negroes removed from Thomas Pretlow, 22 Nov. 1831, American Colonization Society Manuscripts, VHS; and Thomas C. Parramore, *Southampton County, Virginia* (Charlottesville: University Press of Virginia, 1978), 114–15.

42. By Gray's narrow definition, as few as four innocent individuals may have been shot, including Billy Artis I. Altogether, Gray may have viewed as innocent eight slaves who were convicted by the court and transported, one slave convicted and executed (Ben Blunt), and one free black man convicted and executed (Berry Newsom).

43. Personal property tax lists for Southampton County (both parishes), 1822–35, and for Greensville, Isle of Wight, Nansemond, Surry, and Sussex Counties, 1831, 1832, LVA.

44. Lists of taxables, Northampton County, NC, 1823–38, and Gates County, NC, 1821–38, NCSA. Tax records of Hertford County, North Carolina, which lies between Northampton and Gates, do not survive for the period.

45. State records give some indication of the number of legal executions in counties other than Southampton. The Virginia state auditor's record listed ten slaves altogether as executed legally between the end of August and 19 Dec. 1831 in the Virginia counties of Sussex, Spottsylvania, Nansemond, Westmoreland, Prince George, and Loudon; "A Statement Shewing the Amount Paid from the Public Treasury Annually since 1819, for Slaves Executed, Transported and Escaped, &c.," *Journal of the House of Delegates*, 1831, in Henry I. Tragle, *The Southampton Slave Revolt of 1831: A Compilation of Source Material* (Amherst: University of Massachusetts Press, 1971), 452–53. Philip J. Schwarz lists five such executions; Philip J. Schwarz, *Twice Condemned: Slaves and the Criminal Laws of Virginia, 1705–1865* (Baton Rouge: Louisiana State University Press, 1988), 332–34. See also Philip J. Schwarz, *Slave Laws in Virginia* (Athens: University of Georgia Press, 1966), 68.

Rebellion and Local History

The biographies of slaves can hardly be individualized; they belong to the class.

—Thomas Wentworth Higginson, "Nat Turner's Insurrection"

When we inquire who the conspirators were, we are in essence asking about their motivation.

—Winthrop D. Jordan, *Tumult and Silence at Second Creek*

Fellow antiquaries will have recognized by now the kind of work represented in this account of the Southampton rising, a single incident in a particular place.[1] The central, consuming tasks have involved identifying individuals and reconstructing their lives from local records. More than a century and a half after the rising there existed no firm count of the insurgent slaves, no complete list of the dead by name. Those caught up directly in the rebellion had not been subjected to close study, as if their personal histories and connections had had little bearing upon the event or the evidence. Except for two key figures, Nat Turner and Thomas R. Gray (the latter identified as the wrong man in the three most-read modern works), writers and scholars had neglected individuals of all categories, perhaps for the reason Thomas Wentworth Higginson gave in 1861 to explain his lack of information about Nat Turner's wife: the biographies of slaves, he said, could "hardly be individualized."[2] At the time Higginson wrote, his dictum would have applied to almost every person involved in the affair, owing to the difficulties of getting to the evidence and analyzing its contents. With regard to those difficulties, much has changed.

Sources

Conventional biographical sources are meager indeed. No one who lived in the neighborhoods of the uprising left a sizable collection of letters, or a diary, plantation journal, or farm ledger. The Whitehead and Francis families, in their dispute of 1843–48, did generate twenty documents (including two letters by a survivor, Harriet Whitehead) with some details about the uprising; copies are deposited in the Kilby Papers at the David M. Rubenstein Rare Book and Manuscript Library, Duke University, and in Southampton County Court Records, Chancery Papers, in the Library of Virginia. Residents of the town of Jerusalem left some letters, including three by James Trezvant in the James Rochelle Collection, also at the Rubenstein Library. Three additional letters by William C. Parker and one by Alexander P. Peete survive in the Executive Papers of Governor John Floyd, Library of Virginia. And Thomas R. Gray's professional papers are scattered through the deeds and court records in the Southampton County courthouse, and in correspondence of the county's clerks at the Library of Virginia.

The true mine of information lies in the public records of Southampton County, some kept at the courthouse, others deposited at the Library of Virginia. Together, they constitute probably the richest collection on the history of a single locality in the South. The names of almost all of those involved in the remarkable episode of 1831 were entered at some point in the wills, deeds, inventories, court minutes, chancery records, marriage registers, free black registers, processioners' returns, tax lists, or poll books. Those records, linked to manuscript returns of the U.S. Census, have made it possible to trace individuals through time and to establish genealogies and family histories. Together, those records and the census are the sources of any statistical awareness in this work.

Southampton materials began to be widely accessible in 1946, when the National Archives microfilmed the local manuscript returns of the 1830 U.S. Census. Early the next year, the Genealogical Society of Utah, working in Courtland, microfilmed the county's marriage registers; and in 1949 the Society produced microfilm versions of the deed books, will books, and court minute books. In 1981 and 1993 the Library of Virginia (then called the Virginia State Library) microfilmed local tax records (the land books and personal property tax lists), sources rich in identifying detail and genealogical evidence.[3] The personal computer, useful in creating simple spreadsheets (for tax records of 1810, 1821, and 1831, and U.S. Censuses of 1820 and 1830), facilitated the retrieval and description of data in ways Higginson could not have imagined.[4] Now, digitized, indexed entries of the manuscript census returns are available online at Ancestry.com. And thanks to the Southampton Project, begun in 2009 by the Brantley Association of America, virtually all bound records in the courthouse—sixty thousand pages with more than one million name entries—are being digitized, indexed, and made available without charge or restriction on the Internet.[5]

Lacking access to such evidence, Higginson and those who followed him had to rely on newspaper reports and *The Confessions of Nat Turner*, even when they distrusted those sources. Most newspaper correspondents and reporters in 1831 remained anonymous (John Hampden Pleasants was an exception); attribution of their accounts has been a matter of guesswork. Most slaves were virtually anonymous, identified only as someone's property and by a single, given name. In the absence of identifying evidence, historians fell back on abstractions like "class," as Higginson used the term, or on guesswork and fiction. William S. Drewry, who lived in Southampton and was a graduate student at Johns Hopkins, relied on the same old news reports and the *Confessions* for his study (1900). Drewry did uncover new evidence, however, in local memories of the event: informants around Cross Keys identified Nat Turner's mother as Nancy (said to have been born in Africa) and his son as Redic (or Riddick). Mistrusted later because of his racial views, Drewry nonetheless gained a certain authority; many have accepted his theory about Nancy's origins in Africa, for example. F. Roy Johnson (1966 and 1970) followed Drewry in gathering local lore and cited him in all but two of the twenty chapters in his 1966 work.[6] But Johnson also went to the courthouse, where he opened the record books and found such nuggets as the will of Benjamin Turner II (1810) and the inventory of Samuel G. Turner (1822). It was Johnson, despite his faulty reading of manuscripts and his thoroughly flawed history of the Turner family, who plausibly identified Nat Turner's wife as a woman named Cherry.[7]

Inquiry reached a turning point in 1971 with the publication of Henry I. Tragle's *The Southampton Slave Revolt of 1831*, in which a complete (if not entirely accurate) transcript of the Jerusalem trials appeared in print for the first time. Tragle also published manuscripts he found in papers of the governor, governor's council, and state auditor, along with fifty-nine newspaper reports from 1831 and a wealth of other previously printed material. He included his own field photographs and offered an interpretation refuting novelist William Styron (1967) concerning the meagerness of the historical record.[8] Tragle did not venture far beyond the court minutes into other local records, some of which were too large in size and scale to consider for print.[9] Nor did he become familiar with individuals and their names: he followed Styron, for example, in identifying Thomas R. Gray as an old man.[10] And at times he did not recognize the names of other prominent personages when they appeared in court minutes: Alexander P. Peete (not Meriwether P., or Alexander L., or Abraham P.), James Trezvant (not Samuel, or Trezevant), Orris A. (not Ores) Browne, Carr Bowers (not Burress), William B. Goodwyn (or Goodwin, but never Goodyear), or Drewry (or Drew) Bittle (not Billes).[11] Perhaps because he confined himself to the trial evidence, Tragle was led to believe that nothing new could be learned in local sources, since, as he put it, "the essential historical facts became known within a relatively short period of time after the event was over." His task, he thought, involved simply "discarding the purely mythical" and resurrecting, assembling, and collating the evidence. "It seems most unlikely," he concluded, "that new and startling facts remain to be uncovered."[12]

Studies

Tragle reached that judgment—not quite a prediction or dictum—in the bibliographic essay he wrote for the final section of his volume. There he offered readings of sixteen works published between 1850 and 1970, beginning with the pamphlet by Henry Bibb and ending with books by Herbert Aptheker and F. Roy Johnson.[13] The sixteen authors had relied on the old printed accounts and had rehearsed familiar arguments concerning slaves and slavery, rebellion and motives. While Tragle's critical assessments of those works still stand, he underestimated the possibilities of discovery.

Stephen B. Oates drew upon the Tragle compilation in *Fires of Jubilee* (1975), which became the most popular nonfiction account of the uprising. Oates dipped into wills, deeds, and tax lists in preparing his brief profiles of Benjamin Turner II, Samuel G. Turner, Thomas and Sally Moore, Joseph Travis, and Levi Waller. He did not pursue the links between Cross Keys families, however; and his history of the Turner family was as flawed as Johnson's.[14] His narrative rested chiefly on printed sources, embellished with devices of fiction. In the end, Nat Turner's objectives remained unexplained, the route of the revolt unexamined, and the identities of key individuals unexplored: Oates was the last to cast Thomas R. Gray as an old man.[15]

New facts, dispelling Tragle's pessimism, appeared soon enough in Thomas C. Parramore's *Southampton County* (1978), which presented the author's findings about the Whitehead and Francis families, along with evidence complicating the recent identification of Nat Turner's wife.[16] Parramore saw in the rising a purposeful terror whose consequences he traced in the ensuing panic and free black diaspora, the latter documented in records of the American Colonization Society.[17] And though he later changed his mind, he was the first since Drewry to express doubt about the scale of atrocities during the white counterterror that followed the uprising.[18] Finally, Parramore uncovered the true identity of Thomas Ruffin Gray and provided the first account of the attorney's life, finding in him a character more complicated than that of the stereotyped Southern racist of old.[19] During the jailhouse interviews, Parramore thought, Gray had seen in Turner "the mirror image of his own ravaged soul" and had come to feel a "vein of compassion and identity" for the prisoner. In the jail, Parramore said, the two men had "conspired to create the most compelling document in the history of black resistance to slavery."[20]

The definitive case for the local study of slave resistance appeared in 1993, in Winthrop D. Jordan's *Tumult and Silence at Second Creek*, a book about an event in Adams County, Mississippi, in 1861. Though Jordan counted himself among "historians who do not 'quantify,'" he faulted historians of slavery for avoiding the task of gathering evidence on the "inarticulate" people who constitute their subject; he accused them of falling back on their own "ideological predispositions" to explain the motives behind conspiracies and rebellions, instead of seeking specific evidence about particular slaves and masters.[21] "It seems to me," he said, "that the people involved in these most particular events need to be taken seriously as individuals with their own agendas and concerns."[22] Hence derived the impetus to write *Second Creek*, in which local history would uncover a layer of new information. "When we inquire who the conspirators were," he said, "we are in essence asking about their motivation."[23]

In a similar spirit, the chapter on Jefferson in Philip J. Schwarz's *Slave Laws in Virginia* (1996) addressed the relationship between a particular slaveholder and particular African Americans, the author showing how Jefferson's reluctance to free his slaves had its roots in the way he lived.[24] By linking the holding of slaves to the domestic economy of a single white family, Schwarz pointed to yet another layer of new information about motives.

Evidence long buried in the Southampton rising's key text began to surface after controversy erupted in 1968 over Styron's novel.[25] In the first modern critical reading of the original *Confessions*, Seymour L. Gross and Eileen Bender (1971), defenders of the novelist, noted the presence of Gray's voice in the text and pointed to signs that Gray, not Turner, had dominated the account and had used it to dismiss the rising as the work of a fanatic. Gross and Bender expressed their "reservations" about the historicity of the original *Confessions* and asserted that its "relatively meager details" were surrounded by myth and folklore. Styron had merely followed tradition in using these fragments of a legend—"which is all there is," they concluded.[26]

Donald G. Mathews, in *Religion in the Old South* (1977), gave the key text a brief, old-fashioned reading, expressing no reservations about historicity or voice (though on one occasion he knowingly enclosed the word *confession* in quotation marks). The original text, Mathews said, revealed Turner (who had "terrorized southeastern Virginia") to have been a man of "profound religious sensibility" who thought of himself both as "a prophet in the Old Testament tradition" and as "the instrument of God's apocalyptic wrath." In this reading, which turned attention away from the novel and back to the original document, Mathews cited biblical sources he thought important in the text—Isaiah, Ezekiel, Mark, Matthew, Luke (12:31–32), and Revelation. Rather than fanaticism, he thought, the confession had revealed an "Apocalyptic anger," a motive of vengeance for enslavement.[27]

Interpretations of voice and motive in the *Confessions* were transformed in the long opening chapter of Eric J. Sundquist's *To Wake the Nations* (1993), the deepest reading of the text to date. Though profiting from Parramore's "detective work," Sundquist overruled the county historian's notion that Turner and Gray had "conspired" together to create the confession. Rather, the text revealed antagonism "between slave's voice and master's voice."[28] And despite Gray's efforts to suppress Turner's voice, the prisoner had gained command of his own narrative and thereby continued his insurrection in "the arena of terror and propaganda."[29] Motives of freedom and terror, disguised or masked as fanaticism, emerged from the text, thereby establishing internal evidence for the authenticity of Turner's "language and self-portrait."[30] In this reading, too, Turner seemed to have been inspired not by New Testament teachings, but by "Scriptures of prophecy and apocalypse" (though references to Luke 12:31 and 12:47 were duly noted); he seemed to have identified with an unforgiving Christ of Old Testament style.[31] The *Confessions*, riddled with "difficult problems of authenticity," had assumed a "scriptural quality" requiring the "highly speculative" piecing together (as in biblical scholarship, presumably) of corroborating evidence.[32]

Piecing together details about Turner, his scribe, the rising, and the great *Confessions* has involved a good deal of everyday fact-finding and plain detective work. The aim, no doubt quixotic, has been to limit speculation and avoid fiction.

Notes

1. Rosemary Sweet, *Antiquaries: The Discovery of the Past in Eighteenth-Century Britain* (London: Hambeldon & London, 2004), 4–6.
2. Thomas Wentworth Higginson, "Nat Turner's Insurrection," *Atlantic Monthly* 8 (1861): 173–87, in Higginson, *Travellers and Outlaws: Episodes in American History* (Boston: Lee & Shepard, 1888), 280.
3. Dates of microfilming appear in early frames of each reel.
4. Michael L. Nicholls, *Whispers of Rebellion: Narrating Gabriel's Conspiracy* (Charlottesville: University of Virginia Press, 2012), 11.
5. Brantley Association of America, Southampton Project, www.brantleyassociation.com.
6. F. Roy Johnson, *The Nat Turner Slave Insurrection* (Murfreesboro, NC: Johnson, 1966), 187–210.
7. F. Roy Johnson, *The Nat Turner Story: History of the South's Most Important Slave Revolt* (Murfreesboro, NC: Johnson), 48, 54.
8. William Styron, "Author's Note," in *The Confessions of Nat Turner* (New York: Random House, 1967), [ix].
9. Henry I. Tragle, *The Southampton Slave Revolt of 1831: A Compilation of Source Material* (Amherst: University of Massachusetts Press, 1971), 470–71.
10. Ibid., 402.
11. Ibid., 185, 186, 223, 405, 463. Tragle's transcriptions should be checked against the original trial records or the microfilm and Brantley images. He also was baffled occasionally by the print in nineteenth-century newspapers.
12. Ibid., 469.
13. Ibid., 469–89.
14. Stephen B. Oates, *The Fires of Jubilee: Nat Turner's Fierce Rebellion* (New York: Harper & Row, 1971), 158n2, 159n7, 163n23, 166n16, 170n12.
15. Ibid., 103, 168n5.

16. Thomas C. Parramore, *Southampton County, Virginia* (Charlottesville: University Press of Virginia, 1978), 78, 117–18, 243–44n43.

17. Ibid., 84, 97–99, 114–16.

18. Ibid., 99, 102–3; Thomas C. Parramore, "Covenant in Jerusalem," in *Nat Turner: A Slave Rebellion in History and Memory*, ed. Kenneth S. Greenberg (New York: Oxford University Press, 2003), 68–71. In his "Covenant" essay, Parramore appeared to say that Nathaniel Francis was the man Pleasants heard claiming to have killed between ten and fifteen black people, but the evidence he cited does not refer to Francis.

19. Parramore, *Southampton County*, 105–14, 119–21.

20. Ibid., 113, 121. In 2003 Parramore characterized the confession as a "joint enterprise" between the two men, "a covenant perhaps"; Parramore, "Covenant in Jerusalem," 76.

21. Winthrop Jordan, *Tumult and Silence at Second Creek: An Inquiry into a Civil War Conspiracy*, 2nd ed. (Baton Rouge: Louisiana State University Press, 1995), 6–7, 99.

22. Ibid., 7.

23. Ibid., 88–89, 99.

24. Philip J. Schwarz, *Slave Laws in Virginia* (Athens: University of Georgia Press, 1966), 35–62.

25. John Henrik Clarke, ed., *William Styron's Nat Turner: Ten Black Writers Respond* (Boston: Beacon Press, 1968).

26. Seymour L. Gross and Eileen Bender, "History, Politics and Literature: The Myth of Nat Turner," *American Quarterly* 23 (1971): 489–98, 506, 517–18.

27. Donald G. Mathews, *Religion in the Old South* (Chicago: University of Chicago Press, 1977), 231–36.

28. Eric J. Sundquist, *To Awake the Nations: Race in the Making of American Literature* (Cambridge, MA: Harvard University Press, 1993), 38–39.

29. Ibid., 43.

30. Ibid., 47–50.

31. Ibid., 57–59, 71–73. Walter L. Gordon, however, has noted the abundance of New Testament references in the *Confessions*, with Luke 12 being "the most frequently cited passage"; Walter L. Gordon, *The Nat Turner Insurrection Trials: A Mystic Chord Resonates Today* (Los Angeles: W. L. Gordon, 2009), 98.

32. Sundquist, *To Awake the Nations*, 80.

NOTES

For a complete list of sources on which this work builds, see "Works Cited in *Nat Turner and the Rising in Southampton County*," an online document at www.press.jhu.edu.

Citations of county records (e.g., "County Court Minute Book") refer to Southampton County unless otherwise indicated. The author's research files, mentioned in the notes, contain additional, minor details not cited.

Abbreviations have been used to locate sources in archival and manuscript collections, chiefly in the first references to those sources in each chapter.

CWM	Swem Library, College of William and Mary
LVA	Library of Virginia
NA	National Archives
NCSA	North Carolina State Archives
RDU	David M. Rubenstein Rare Book and Manuscript Library, Duke University
SCC	Southampton County Courthouse
UVA	University of Virginia Library
VHS	Virginia Historical Society

Introduction. The Key Account

1. *Richmond Compiler*, 27 Aug. 1831, in "The Banditti," *Richmond Enquirer*, 30 Aug. 1831.

2. Jesse D. Elliott to Levi Woodbury, 28 Aug. 1831, in *Richmond Enquirer*, 16 Sept. 1831; see also *Richmond Enquirer*, 26 Aug. 1831.

3. Turner was identified in [James Strange French?], letter to Petersburg, 24 Aug. 1831, summary in "The Banditti," *Richmond Enquirer*, 30 Aug. 1831.

4. Thomas R. Gray, *The Confessions of Nat Turner* (Baltimore: Lucas & Deaver, 1831), 15.

5. Ibid., 11.

6. David Walker, *David Walker's Appeal to the Coloured Citizens of the World*, ed. Peter P. Hinks (1829; repr., University Park: Pennsylvania State University Press, 2000), 5, 8, 18, 21, 32; Gray, *Confessions*, 11, 14; [Thomas R. Gray], letter, 17 Sept. 1831,

Richmond Constitutional Whig, 26 Sept. 1831, in *Norfolk American Beacon*, 30 Sept. 1831; [William C. Parker], letter, 1 Nov. 1831, *Richmond Enquirer*, 8 Nov. 1831. The similarities might bolster the view that Turner (or Gray) was familiar with Walker's pamphlet. Attributions of the Gray and Parker letters appear in David F. Allmendinger, "The Construction of *The Confessions of Nat Turner*," in *Nat Turner: A Slave Rebellion in History and Memory*, ed. Kenneth S. Greenberg (New York: Oxford University Press, 2003), 31–36.

7. Gray, *Confessions*, 17.

8. Elliott Whitehead, letter, n.d., *Norfolk Herald*, 7 Nov. 1831.

9. *Norfolk American Beacon*, 11 Oct. 1831.

10. *Norfolk Herald*, 28 Oct. 1831.

11. *Norfolk American Beacon*, 16 Sept. 1831; *Richmond Enquirer*, 4 Oct., 18 Oct. 1831; *Richmond Compiler*, 17 Oct. 1831, in *Norfolk American Beacon*, 19 Oct. 1831.

12. *Richmond Enquirer*, 25 Oct. 1831.

13. Alexander P. Peete to John Floyd, 20 Oct. 1831, Executive Papers, Gov. Floyd, LVA; *Raleigh Star*, 10 Nov. 1831.

14. *Norfolk Herald*, 4 Nov. 1831; *Norfolk American Beacon*, 3 Nov. 1831.

15. Letter, 31 Oct. 1831, *Richmond Whig*, 7 Nov. 1831, in *Nat Turner*, ed. Eric Foner (Englewood Cliffs, NJ: Prentice-Hall, 1971), 31–32.

16. *Norfolk Herald*, 4 Nov. 1831.

17. Isaac Pipkin, letter, 1 Nov. 1831, *Norfolk American Beacon*, 4 Nov. 1831; *Norfolk Herald*, 4 Nov. 1831.

18. *Norfolk Herald*, 4 Nov. 1831; Whitehead, letter, *Norfolk Herald*, 7 Nov. 1831; William S. Drewry, *The Southampton Insurrection* (1900; repr., Murfreesboro, NC: Johnson, 1968), 92–93; St. Luke's Parish Personal Property Tax List, 1831, entry for Benjamin Phipps, LVA; St. Luke's Parish Land Book, 1831, entry for Benjamin Phipps, LVA. Slaves twelve and older were taxable.

19. *Norfolk Herald*, 4 Nov. 1831.

20. Theodore Trezvant, letter, 31 Oct. 1831, *Norfolk American Beacon*, 5 Nov. 1831.

21. *Petersburg Intelligencer*, 4 Nov. 1831, in *Richmond Enquirer*, 8 Nov. 1831.

22. Gray, *Confessions*, 18.

23. Thomas C. Parramore, "Covenant in Jerusalem," in Greenberg, *Nat Turner*, 72; Eric J. Sundquist, *To Wake the Nations: Race in the Making of American Literature* (Cambridge, MA: Harvard University Press, 1993), 71–72.

24. Drewry, *Southampton Insurrection*, 92–93.

25. Letter, *Richmond Whig*, 7 Nov. 1831, in Foner, *Nat Turner*, 31.

26. *Petersburg Intelligencer*, 4 Nov. 1831, in *Richmond Enquirer*, 8 Nov. 1831.

27. Letter, *Richmond Whig*, 7 Nov. 1831, in Foner, *Nat Turner*, 31–32.

28. Pipkin, letter, *Norfolk American Beacon*, 4 Nov. 1831.

29. Theodore Trezvant, letter, *Norfolk American Beacon*, 5 Nov. 1831; *Norfolk Herald*, 2 Nov. 1831.

30. *Norfolk Herald*, 4 Nov. 1831.

31. *Petersburg Intelligencer*, 4 Nov. 1831, in *Richmond Enquirer*, 8 Nov. 1831.

32. John Wheeler, letter, 1 Nov. 1831, *Norfolk Herald*, 4 Nov. 1831.

33. *Norfolk Herald*, 4 Nov. 1831.

34. [Meriwether B. Brodnax], prosecutor's notes, deposition of James Trezvant, n.d., *Commonwealth v. Nat Turner I*, County Court Judgments, 1831, LVA; James Trezvant, testimony, trial of Nat Turner I, County Court Minute Book, 5 Nov. 1831, pp. 122–23, SCC.

35. Theodore Trezvant, letter, *Norfolk American Beacon*, 5 Nov. 1831.

36. [William C. Parker], letter, *Richmond Enquirer*, 8 Nov. 1831.

37. [Thomas R. Gray?], letter, [1 Nov. 1831], *Richmond Enquirer*, 8 Nov. 1831.

38. Gray, *Confessions*, 7. Gray said he first encountered Turner that "evening," meaning late afternoon or early evening.

39. Herbert Aptheker, *Nat Turner's Slave Rebellion* (1966; repr., Mineola, NY: Dover, 2006), 42–43; Daniel S. Fabricant, "Thomas R. Gray and William Styron: Finally, A Critical Look at the 1831 Confessions of Nat Turner," *American Journal of Legal History* 37 (1993): 333, 342; Tony Horwitz, "Untrue Confessions: Is Most of What We Know about Nat Turner Wrong?," *New Yorker*, 13 Dec. 1999, 80–89; Scot French, *The Rebellious Slave: Nat Turner in American Memory* (New York: Houghton Mifflin, 2004), 3.

40. Richmond Dragoon, letter, 23 Aug. 1831, *Richmond Enquirer*, 26 Aug. 1831.

41. Gray, *Confessions*, 18. Gray was counsel for three other defendants: Davy Turner, Sam Francis, and probably Nathan Francis. The court changed its record of Moses Moore's owner from Joseph Travis to Putnam Moore; County Court Minute Book, 19 Dec. 1831, p. 142.

Chapter 1. A History of Motives

1. Thomas R. Gray, *The Confessions of Nat Turner* (Baltimore: Lucas & Deaver, 1831), 3, 4, 7.

2. Ibid., 7, 9.

3. Ibid., 7.

4. Ibid., 7–8.

5. Ibid., 8.

6. Ibid. Gray revealed in a footnote that he questioned Turner about these experiments and found him "well informed." His aside appears to have been a fragment of an authentic exchange between the two men.

7. Will (original), Benjamin Turner II, 14 Oct. 1810, Wills and Inventories, 1749–2006, SCC (copy in Will Book 7:109); will, Samuel G. Turner, 9 Jan. 1822, Will Book 9:134, SCC. The transfer probably occurred informally at the time of Samuel's marriage in 1807; Marriage Register, p. 657, SCC.

8. Will, Samuel G. Turner, Will Book 9:134. Samuel was dead by 4 Mar. 1822, when an inventory of his estate was taken; inventory, Samuel G. Turner, 4 Mar, 1822, Will Book 9:254.

9. Account, Putnam Moore, 20 May 1833, Will Book 11:80–81. This account is the only evidence of Nat Turner's transfer to Thomas Moore. Tax records suggest that the year of transfer was 1823; St. Luke's Parish Personal Property Tax Lists, 1822, 1823, entries for Thomas Moore and Elizabeth Turner II, LVA. Sally Moore became administrator of her husband's estate in 1827; County Court Minute Book, 18 June 1827, p. 166, SCC.

10. In the fall of 1830, slaves identified as belonging to Joseph Travis (but not named) were working at the farm rented by Giles Reese; County Court Minute Book, 20 Sept. 1830, p. 355. Nat Turner told Gray that he had been living with Travis "since the commencement of 1830"; Gray, *Confessions*, 11.

11. Marriage Register, p. 402.

12. Gray, *Confessions*, 9.

13. In the King James Version, Luke 12:31 reads, "But rather seek ye the kingdom of God; and all these things shall be added unto you." See also Matt. 6:33.

14. Gray, *Confessions*, 9.

15. Ibid.

16. Will, Samuel G. Turner, Will Book 9:134; inventory, Samuel G. Turner, Will Book 9:254; deed, Samuel G. Turner to Rebecca Jane Williamson, 18 Jan. 1822, Deed Book 18:413, SCC.

17. Gray, *Confessions*, 9.

18. Ibid., 9–10.

19. Luke 12:47. "And that servant, which knew his lord's will, and prepared not *himself*, neither did according to his will, shall be beaten with many *stripes*."

20. Eric J. Sundquist, *To Wake the Nations: Race in the Making of American Literature* (Cambridge, MA: Harvard University Press, 1993), 59, 73; James Sidbury, "Reading, Revelation, and Rebellion: The Textual Communities of Gabriel, Denmark Vesey, and Nat Turner," in *Nat Turner: A Slave Rebellion in History and Memory*, ed. Kenneth S. Greenberg (New York: Oxford University Press, 2003), 128–29.

21. William C. Parker believed that Turner had "long been a preacher"; [William C. Parker], letter, 31 Aug. 1831, *Richmond Compiler*, 3 Sept. 1831, in *Richmond Enquirer*, 6 Sept. 1831. Gray disagreed. "He exhorted, and sung at neighborhood meetings, but no farther," Gray said. [Thomas R. Gray], letter, *Richmond Whig*, 26 Sept. 1831, in *Norfolk American Beacon*, 30 Sept. 1831. Turner did not refer to himself as a preacher in the *Confessions*.

22. Gray, *Confessions*, 9.

23. Ibid., 8.

24. Ibid., 18.

25. Ibid., 8–9. Gray used the expression "wrapt in mystery" in his introduction to the *Confessions*, 3.

26. Luke 19:21, Eph. 3:3–5.

27. Walter L. Gordon notes the importance of Luke for Turner in *The Nat Turner Insurrection Trials: A Mystic Chord Resonates Today* ([Los Angeles]: W. L. Gordon, 2009), 98–99.

28. Gray, *Confessions*, 9. Turner also quoted from memory at least twenty briefer quotations or allusions, leading Gray, a stranger to enthusiastic thinking, to record errors either man might have made.

29. Gray, *Confessions*, 10. Compare Luke 23:45 ("And the sun was darkened, and the veil of the temple was rent in the midst") and 3:5 ("Every valley shall be filled, and every mountain and hill shall be brought low; and the crooked shall be made straight, and the rough ways *shall be* made smooth").

30. Gray, *Confessions*, 10.

31. The passage is similar to Dan. 2:21–23.

32. Gray, *Confessions*, 10.

33. [Gray], letter, *Richmond Whig*, 26 Sept. 1831, in *Norfolk American Beacon*, 30 Sept. 1831. Gray said that Turner, like a "Roman Sybil," had "traced his divination in characters of blood, on leaves alone in the woods" and then sent "some ignorant black" to find them, "to whom he would interpret their meaning." Gray at this point suspected that Turner merely "pretended to have conversations with the Holy Spirit."

34. Gray, *Confessions*, 10.

35. Matt. 24:27–31. Paul refers to children of light and darkness in 1 Thess. 5:5.

36. Gray, *Confessions*, 10.

37. Ibid., 10–11.

38. Luke 22:44.

39. Brantley was listed in St. Luke's Parish Personal Tax Lists, 1830, 1831, 1832, 1833, entries for David Westbrook; and 1835, entry for Nathaniel Francis; Marriage Register, p. 500. Drewry identified Brantley as a "respectable overseer" who had to leave the county after his encounter with Nat Turner; the tax lists and marriage register contradict that story; William S. Drewry, *The Southampton Insurrection* (1900; repr., Murfreesboro, NC: Johnson, 1968), 33n1.

40. Gray, *Confessions*, 11.

41. [William C. Parker], letter, 21 Sept. 1831, *Richmond Enquirer*, 30 Sept. 1831.

42. Luke 3:22 has wording closest to that in Parker's account: "And the Holy Ghost descended in a bodily shape like a dove upon him, and a voice came from heaven, which said, Thou art my beloved Son; in thee I am well pleased." See also Matt. 3:16–17 and Mark 1:10–11.

43. [William C. Parker], letter, *Richmond Enquirer*, 30 Sept. 1831.

44. Gray, *Confessions*, 11.

45. Samuel Warner, writing in New York City between 22 September and 21 October 1831, said that the baptism took place in a mill pond, basing his account on a letter from an unnamed Southampton correspondent (probably Gray); Samuel Warner, *Authentic and Impartial Narrative of the Tragical Scene Which Was Witnessed in Southampton County* (New York: Warner & West, 1831), 31; Drewry, *Southampton Insurrection*, 33.

46. Matt 27:39, Mark 15:32, John 9:28. The word *mocked* conveys a similar meaning in Luke 18:32, 22:63, 23:11, and 23:36.

47. [Gray], letter, *Richmond Whig*, 26 Sept. 1831, in *Norfolk American Beacon*, 30 Sept. 1831.

48. County Court Minute Book, 18 June 1827, p. 166.

49. Gray, *Confessions*, 11.

50. Ibid. The source for the Serpent may have been Rev. 12:7–9; the passage about the first and the last appears in Matt. 19:30, Mark 10:31, and Luke 13:30.

51. Gray, *Confessions*, 11.

52. *Norfolk American Beacon*, 12 Feb. 1831; Fred Espenak, "Solar Eclipses of Historical Interest," NASA Eclipse Web Site (July 2008), eclipse.gsfc.nasa.gov/SEhistory/SEhistory.html; Louis P. Masur, *1831: Year of Eclipse* (New York: Hill & Wang, 2001), 2–8.

53. The memoir proper contains at least eighty-three details about Turner's life which had not appeared before the publication of the *Confessions*. Of these new

details, twenty-three pertained to events other witnesses might have observed. No witness ever disputed the details in public.

54. *Norfolk Herald*, 15, 19 Aug. 1831. Variations on the *Herald* catchphrase appeared widely in newspapers and communications referring to "the late singular appearance of the sun," or the "singular phenomenon of the sun." *Norfolk American Beacon*, 23 Aug. 1831; *Raleigh Star*, 18, 25 Aug. 1831; *Richmond Enquirer*, 23 Aug. 1831; Drewry, *Southampton Insurrection*, 34. See also Thomas C. Parramore, *Southampton County, Virginia* (Charlottesville: University of Virginia Press, 1978), 75.

55. The phenomena of 1831 were attributed decades later to volcanic eruptions in the Mediterranean, West Indies, and Pacific Ring of Fire; Francis A. Rollo Russell, "Previous Analogous Glow Phenomena, and Corresponding Eruptions," in Royal Society (Great Britain), Krakatoa Committee, *The Eruption of Krakatoa and Subsequent Phenomena* (London: Trubner, 1888), 396–99; John Milne, "Seismological Observations and Earth Physics," *Geographical Journal* 21 (1903): 12–15.

56. [Gray], letter, *Richmond Whig*, 26 Sept. 1831, in *Norfolk American Beacon*, 30 Sept. 1831; Gray, *Confessions*, 11.

57. [William C. Parker], letter, *Richmond Compiler*, 3 Sept. 1831, in *Richmond Enquirer*, 6 Sept. 1831; *Richmond Enquirer*, 30 Aug. 1831.

58. Letter, 31 Oct. 1831, *Richmond Whig*, 7 Nov. 1831, in *Nat Turner*, ed. Eric Foner (Englewood Cliffs, NJ: Prentice-Hall, 1971), 31.

59. *Norfolk Herald*, 4 Nov. 1831; Theodore Trezvant, letter, 31 Oct. 1831, *Norfolk American Beacon*, 5 Nov. 1831; Elliott Whitehead, letter, n.d., *Norfolk Herald*, Nov. 7, 1831; [William C. Parker], letter, 1 Nov. 1831, *Richmond Enquirer*, 8 Nov. 1831; [Theodore Trezvant?], letter, [1 Nov. 1831], *Richmond Enquirer*, 8 Nov. 1831; [Thomas R. Gray?], letter, [1 Nov. 1831], *Richmond Enquirer*, 8 Nov. 1831.

60. Gray, *Confessions*, 18–19.

61. Letter, 31 Oct. 1831, *Richmond Whig*, 7 Nov. 1831, in Foner, *Nat Turner*, 31–32.

62. Thomas Wentworth Higginson, "Nat Turner's Insurrection," *Atlantic Monthly* 8 (1861): 173–87, in Higginson, *Travellers and Outlaws: Episodes in American History* (Boston: Lee & Shepard, 1888), 284; Donald G. Mathews, *Religion in the Old South* (Chicago: University of Chicago Press, 1977), 232; Daniel S. Fabricant, "Thomas R. Gray and William Styron: Finally, A Critical Look at the 1831 Confessions of Nat Turner," *American Journal of Legal History* 37 (1993): 332; Sundquist, *To Wake the Nations*, 73, 81–82.

63. The memoir has encouraged the view that Turner's motives were not personal; Herbert Aptheker, *Nat Turner's Slave Rebellion* (1966; repr., Mineola, NY: Dover, 2006), 35. Anthony Santoro, while not ruling out the influence of personal or political motives, argues that in the confession Turner deliberately emphasized his religious motives; Anthony Santoro, "The Prophet in His Own Words: Nat Turner's Biblical Construction," *Virginia Magazine of History and Biography* 116 (2008): 115–49.

64. The 1830 census listed 339 white heads of household who can be identified as residents of St. Luke's Parish and whose households included slaves; an additional seven white nonresidents were recorded with slaves in the parish. In 1831, 334 parish residents (including three free black people) paid tax on slaves. U.S. Census, Southampton County, 1830, manuscript returns, NA; St. Luke's Parish Personal Tax List, 1831.

Chapter 2. Lines of Descent: The Turners

1. Will, William Turner Sr., 6 Sept. 1763, recorded 1766, Will Book 2:152, SCC; Blanche Adams Chapman, *Isle of Wight County Marriages, 1628–1800* (Smithfield, VA, 1933), 51; will, John Turner II, 25 Mar. 1705, Isle of Wight County Will and Deed Book 2:468, LVA; inventory, John Turner II, 1705, Isle of Wight Will and Deed Book 2:474.

2. Nell Marion Nugent, *Cavaliers and Pioneers: Abstracts of Virginia Land Patents and Grants*, 3 vols. (Richmond: Virginia State Library, 1979), 3:134, 379; deed, William Turner Sr. to John Turner, 20 Feb. 1753, Deed Book 1:468–69, SCC; deed, William Turner Sr. to Thomas Turner, 8 Mar. 1753, Deed Book 1:469–70.

3. James W. Deen, "Patterns of Testation: Four Tidewater Counties in Colonial Virginia," *American Journal of Legal History* 16 (1972): 158–62, 167.

4. Will, Benjamin Turner I, 26 May 1777, Will Book 3:333.

5. Deed, Francis Sharpe to Benjamin Turner I, 14 Jan. 1762, Deed Book 3:111; deed, Francis Sharpe and Joseph Scott to Benjamin Turner I, 26 Jan. 1765, Deed Book 3:333; deed, David Edmunds to Benjamin Turner I, 2 Sept. 1767, Deed Book 4:84; deed, Grover Sharpe to Benjamin Turner I, 9 July 1768, Deed Book 4:91.

6. This was the combined acreage inherited by the three sons of William Turner Sr. in 1782; St. Luke's Parish Land Book, 1782, entries for Benjamin Turner II (of Ben), Henry Turner (of Ben), and Nathan Turner, LVA.

7. Will, Benjamin Turner I, Will Book 3:333.

8. Ibid.; St. Luke's Parish Land Books, 1782–1817, entries for Nathan Turner; will, Nathan Turner, 22 May 1815, Will Book 8:296–97.

9. Will, Benjamin Turner I, Will Book 3:333; St. Luke's Parish Land Book, 1782, 1783, entries for Henry Turner.

10. Will, Henry Turner, 13 Dec. 1791, Will Book 4:472–73.

11. St. Luke's Parish Personal Property Tax List, 1791, entry for Henry Turner, LVA.

12. Will, Henry Turner, Will Book 4:471–73.

13. Ibid. Henry Turner's eleven slaves were valued at £455 in 1792; account, Henry Turner, recorded 1798, Will Book 5:63–64. In 1805 Benjamin Turner II paid £579 30*s* for 382.5 acres of comparable land; deed, Richard Blunt to Benjamin Turner II, 23 Nov. 1805, Deed Book 11:346–47.

14. Marriage Register, p. 36, SCC.

15. Will, William Turner Sr., Will Book 2:152. William's wife, Elizabeth, whose name does not appear among his survivors, must have died between 1763 and 1766; account, William Turner Sr., recorded 1774, Will Book 3:105a–b.

16. Will, Henry Turner, Will Book 4:471; Turner mentioned no other slaves in his will, though the name of a twelfth slave, Winny, appeared in his estate papers; account, Henry Turner, Will Book 5:63.

17. Thomas Jefferson, *Notes on the State of Virginia*, ed. William Peden (1787; repr., Chapel Hill: University of North Carolina Press, 1954), 137–38; the plan appears in Query 14.

18. Free Negro Register, vol. 1, 1794–1832, entries 93, 94, and 109, LVA. Abraham, Olive, and Jack gained their freedom in 1792. Abraham was listed as Young Abram in the will of Benjamin Turner I in 1777.

19. Tom, who may have been Olive's child, had no entry in the Free Negro Register but was listed elsewhere as free by 1797; account, Henry Turner, Will Book 5:63.

20. Account, Henry Turner, Will Book 5:63–64.

21. A widow could not be deprived of her dower right to one-third of her husband's slaves; *The Revised Code of the Laws of Virginia*, 2 vols. (Richmond: Thomas Ritchie, 1819), chap. 111, sec. 60.

22. There is no record of manumission for Venus, the eleventh member of this group.

23. Henry's son John died by 1807, when Benjamin IV sold the land he and John had inherited; deed, Benjamin Turner IV ("Jr.") to Thomas Porter, 27 Jan. 1807, Deed Book 11:476.

24. St. Luke's Parish Personal Tax Lists, 1812, 1813, entries for Benjamin Turner IV.

25. Free Negro Register, vol. 1, entry 962.

26. St. Luke's Parish Personal Tax Lists, 1793–1820, entries for Mildred Turner.

27. Free Negro Register, vol. 1, entries 1-1,875. The register includes multiple entries for many individuals; figures here exclude multiple entries.

28. Abraham, known as Young Abram in 1777, first took the surname Tow but changed that to Turner around 1809. His identity as Abraham Turner was noted in St. Luke's Parish Personal Tax Lists, 1809 and 1820, entries for Abram Turner (alias Tow).

29. St. Luke's Parish Personal Tax List, 1813, entry for Olive Turner.

30. St. Luke's Parish Personal Tax Lists, 1813, 1817, entries for Abraham (or Abram) Turner.

31. St. Luke's Parish Personal Tax List, 1817, entry for Peter Turner.

32. Deed, John and Amey Westbrook to Isham Turner, 22 Feb. 1823, Deed Book 19:133.

33. St. Luke's Parish Personal Tax List, 1831, entry for Henry Turner.

34. A differing theory about Nat Turner's name appears in Kenneth S. Greenberg, "Name, Face, Body," in *Nat Turner: A Slave Rebellion in History and Memory*, ed. Kenneth S. Greenberg (New York: Oxford University Press, 2003), 3–14.

35. St. Luke's Parish Land Books, 1807, 1810, entries for Benjamin Turner II. Benjamin's entries for land taxes in 1807 and 1810, together with deeds for his purchases and sales, indicate that he must have paid taxes on 926.5 acres in 1808, his peak holding. The land book for 1808 is missing.

36. Of the 563 individuals listed in the 1810 personal property tax list, 377 (67 percent) were slaveholders; St. Luke's Parish Personal Tax List, 1810. Benjamin Turner II held thirteen taxable slaves in 1810, which placed him among the top forty-one slaveholders on the tax rolls. He paid $7.30 in personal property taxes, which placed him among the top forty-two payers of personal property tax.

37. Will (original), Benjamin Turner II, 1810, Wills and Inventories, SCC; Turner listed all but one of his slaves, eleven of whom he already had transferred to his heirs.

38. Will, Benjamin Turner I, Will Book 3:333; St. Luke's Parish Land Book, 1782, entries for Benjamin Turner II, Henry Turner, and Nathan Turner.

39. Marriage Register, p. 30.

40. St. Luke's Parish Personal Tax List, 1782, entry for Benjamin Turner II.

41. St. Luke's Parish Land Books, 1782–92, and St. Luke's Parish Personal Tax Lists, 1782–92, entries for Benjamin Turner II.

42. Deed, Thomas Holladay to Benjamin Turner II and Wright Griffin, 12 Jan. 1793, Deed Book 7:823–24.

43. Will (original), Benjamin Turner II, 1810.

44. Sources on Lydia: deed, Holladay to Turner and Griffin, Deed Book 7:823; will (original), Benjamin Turner II, 1810; will, Samuel G. Turner, 9 Jan. 1822, Will Book 9:134; inventory, Samuel G. Turner, 4 Mar. 1822, Will Book 9:254; County Court Minute Book, 18 Mar. 1822, p. 242, SCC. Lydia was not mentioned in Samuel's will, indicating that he intended that she become the property of his daughter; her name did appear in his inventory.

45. Sources on Abraham: deed, Holladay to Turner and Griffin, Deed Book 7:823; will (original), Benjamin Turner II, 1810; inventory, Benjamin Turner II, 22 Jan. 1811, Will Book 7:168.

46. Sources on China: deed, Holladay to Turner and Griffin, Deed Book 7:823; will (original), Benjamin Turner II, 1810; inventory, Benjamin Turner II, Will Book 7:168.

47. Sources on Anne ("Nancy"): deed, Holladay to Turner and Griffin, Deed Book 7:823; will (original), Benjamin Turner II, 1810; will, Samuel G. Turner, Will Book 9:134; inventory, Samuel G. Turner, Will Book 9:254; U.S. Census, Southampton County, 1830, manuscript returns, p. 260, NA; St. Luke's Parish Personal Tax Lists, 1823–31, entries for Elizabeth Turner II. The female named Nancy given by Benjamin I to his Newsom grandsons in 1781 was a different individual. Yet another female of this name (a child of Dorcas) was listed in 1815 in estate records of Benjamin II; chancery report, estate of Benjamin Turner II, County Court Order Book, 17 Feb. 1815, p. 53, SCC.

48. Thomas R. Gray, *The Confessions of Nat Turner* (Baltimore: Lucas & Deaver, 1831), 9. William S. Drewry's sources at the end of the nineteenth century gave him information about Nat Turner's mother. Drewry became the first authority to identify her by the name *Nancy*. He accepted without question the stories about her African origins and her behavior at her son's birth. William S. Drewry, *The Southampton Insurrection* (1900; repr., Murfreesboro, NC: Johnson, 1968), 27.

49. Some authorities suggest that Bridget, a woman about Lydia's age, was Nat Turner's grandmother. In his will of 1810, however, Benjamin Turner II separated Bridget from Nat Turner and the former Griffin slaves, keeping her at his home plantation on loan to his widow for life. Bridget apparently remained at the old plantation until she was transferred informally to Samuel G. Turner before 1822.

50. St. Luke's Parish Personal Tax Lists, 1782–1810, entries for Benjamin Turner II. Data for 1792 and 1808 are missing.

51. Deed, Thomas and Lucy Porter to Benjamin Turner II, recorded 13 Oct. 1796, Deed Book 8:325; St. Luke's Parish Land Book, 1797, entry for Benjamin Turner II.

52. Deed, Richard Blunt, executor for John Kindred, to Benjamin Turner II, 23 Nov. 1805, Deed Book 11:346–47; account, Benjamin Turner II, 1811–15, Will Book 8:23–25; deed, Benjamin Turner II to Samuel G. Turner, 9 Jan. 1809, Deed Book 14:81–82.

53. The last three tax listings for Benjamin Turner II placed the number of his taxable slaves at seventeen (in 1807), thirteen (in 1809), and thirteen again (in 1810). His entry in the 1810 census, taken after he had transferred eleven slaves to his eldest son and daughter, listed him with eighteen slaves of all ages; U.S. Census, Southampton County, 1810, p. 852. In his will of 1810 he named twenty-eight slaves, apparently forgetting one, a female named Sukey, whose name did appear in the inventory of his estate.

54. In 1810, after Benjamin Turner II transferred the Kindred tract to Samuel, his holding fell to 552 acres; he ranked 88th among 599 landholders in acreage, still in the top 15 percent in that category. In tax paid for personal property in 1810, he remained in the top 10 percent, though the number of his taxable slaves declined to thirteen after his gifts to his son and daughter. St. Luke's Parish Land Book, 1810, and St. Luke's Parish Personal Tax List, 1810, entries for Benjamin Turner II.

55. Turner genealogy (author's research file); will (original), Benjamin Turner II, 1810; U.S. Census, Southampton County, 1810, pp. 126a–127; 1820, p. 120 (Samuel); 1850, p. 256a (John C.); deed, John C. and Nancy Turner to Nancy and Sally Vick, 22 Mar. 1826, Deed Book 20:53; bill of complaint, *Turner v. Barratt*, County Court Records, Chancery Papers, 1835, LVA.

56. Edmund Ruffin, "On the Sources of Malaria, or Autumnal Diseases, in Virginia, and the Means of Remedy and Prevention," *Farmers' Register* 6 (1838): 218, 222, in Ruffin, *Nature's Management: Writings on Landscape and Reform, 1822–1859: Edmund Ruffin*, ed. Jack Temple Kirby (Athens: University of Georgia Press, 2000), 104, 113–14; Darrett B. Rutman and Anita H. Rutman, "Of Agues and Fevers: Malaria in the Early Chesapeake," *William and Mary Quarterly*, 3d ser., 33 (1976): 33–38; Darrett B. Rutman and Anita H. Rutman, *A Place in Time: Middlesex County, Virginia, 1650–1750* (New York: W. W. Norton, 1984), 179.

57. Marriage Register, p. 657; will (original), Benjamin Turner II, 1810.

58. Elizabeth's first husband, Frederick Boykin, died in about 1804; she took his place in the personal property tax list in 1805. See also St. Luke's Parish Land Books, 1810, 1811, entries for Frederick Boykin; deed, Elizabeth Turner I to Ephraim Gee, 27 May 1811, Deed Book 12:407–8.

59. Deed, Benjamin Turner II to Samuel G. Turner, Deed Book 14:81.

60. U.S. Census, Southampton County, 1810, p. 852.

61. Deed, Benjamin Turner II and Elizabeth Turner I to Nathan Turner and trustees, 9 Oct. 1810, Deed Book 12:244–48.

62. Will (original), Benjamin Turner II, 1810.

63. Ibid. Punctuation added for clarity. The order of names in the original will differs from the version in the will book.

64. Will (original), Benjamin Turner II, 1810.

65. Ibid.

66. County Court Minute Book, 17 Dec. 1810, p. 161; 21 Jan. 1811, p. 167. One authority says that Benjamin II died of typhoid; Stephen B. Oates, *The Fires of Jubilee: Nat Turner's Fierce Rebellion* (New York: Harper & Row, 1971), 13.

67. In 1820 (when assessments of buildings first appeared in tax records) and 1821, structures at the former plantation of Benjamin Turner II were assessed at

$500, just below the average of $510 for payers of the land tax in the parish; St. Luke's Parish Land Books, 1820, 1821, entries for Elizabeth Turner I.

68. Inventory, Benjamin Turner II, Will Book 7:167–70; account, Benjamin Turner II, Will Book 8:23. The appraisers calculated the total value of Benjamin's personal estate at £1,689 14*s* 5*d*. Samuel G. Turner, Benjamin's executor, found additional sums owed to the estate in the account he filed with the court in 1815; those assets would have increased the value of Benjamin Turner's personal estate to £1,792.

69. His father and both brothers could sign their names; his sister, Phoebe, in witnessing his will, made her mark.

70. Inventory, Benjamin Turner II, Will Book 9:167–70.

71. Ibid. Dorcas gave birth to a daughter shortly after Benjamin Turner II died, bringing the holding to eighteen slaves in January 1811; the heirs had removed twelve others by that time. The daughter was listed with Dorcas in the inventory of 1811 and later identified as the child named Nancy.

72. In 1810 Benjamin's remaining eighteen slaves accounted for almost half (49.6 percent) of his taxable estate, or $5.72 of his total tax bill of $11.53; St. Luke's Parish Land Book, 1810, and St. Luke's Parish Personal Tax List, 1810, entries for Benjamin Turner II.

73. Deductions about the identities and ages of Benjamin's slaves can be drawn by comparing the list of slaves in the inventory of 1811 (which gave the value of individual slaves) with names appearing in his will of 1810 and the division of his estate in 1815.

74. The sequence of Turner's first acquisitions is not certain. He probably first acquired three patrimonial slaves assigned to him in the will his father (Benjamin I) wrote in 1777. Benjamin II married in June 1781; his father's will was proved in August 1781.

75. Benjamin Turner II paid tax on eleven slaves over age sixteen in 1810. The 4:7 ratio is based on inferences about which slaves remained at his farm in the spring of that year, after Samuel G. Turner and his sister Nancy had begun to remove their father's slaves. Samuel was taxed for four slaves over age sixteen in 1810; St. Luke's Parish Personal Tax List, 1810.

76. *Revised Code of Virginia* (1819), chap. 107, sec. 11, 12; *Code of Virginia* (Richmond: William F. Ritchie, 1849), chap. 110, sec. 4, 5.

77. St. Luke's Parish Land Book, 1813, entry for Elizabeth Turner I.

78. Chancery report, estate of Benjamin Turner II, County Court Order Book, 17 Feb. 1815, p. 53.

79. Marriage Register, p. 252; St. Luke's Parish Land Books, 1817–19, entries for Elizabeth Turner I.

80. On arrangements for Susanna Turner and John Clark Turner, see account, Benjamin Turner II, Will Book 8:25; St. Luke's Parish Personal Tax Lists, 1817, 1818, entries for Samuel G. Turner; 1819, entry for Nancy Barrett.

Chapter 3. Alliances: Turner, Francis, Reese

1. Will (original), Benjamin Turner II, 1810, Wills and Inventories, SCC. Estimates of the ages of the eight slaves are based on wills, inventories, and personal

property tax records for the Turner family, 1810–22, and on the entry for Samuel G. Turner in U.S. Census, Southampton County, 1820, manuscript returns, p. 126a, NA.

2. As the number of slaves in Samuel G. Turner's holding increased from eight to twenty-three between 1810 and 1822, the value of his holding rose from about $1,800 (in 1811) to $5,295. Nat Turner was appraised at £35 (about $135) in 1811 and $450 in 1822. Inventory, Benjamin Turner II, 22 Jan. 1811, Will Book 7:168, SCC; inventory, Samuel G. Turner, 4 Mar. 1822, Will Book 9:254.

3. Marriage Register, pp. 30, 112, SCC; deed, Thomas Holladay to Benjamin Turner II and Wright Griffin, 12 Jan. 1793, Deed Book 7:823–24, SCC; St. Luke's Parish Personal Property Tax Lists, 1790, 1791, 1795, entries for Benjamin Turner II; and 1784, entry for Thomas Holliday, LVA.

4. Ancestry.com, *Virginia Marriage Records, 1700–1850* [database online] (Provo, UT: Ancestry.com Operations, 2012); St. Luke's Parish Personal Tax Lists, 1805–7, entries for Elizabeth Boykin; chancery report, estate of Benjamin Turner II, County Court Order Book, 17 Feb. 1815, p. 53, SCC.

5. Francis genealogy (author's research file); F. N. Boney, "Nathaniel Francis, Representative Antebellum Southerner," *Proceedings of the American Philosophical Society* 118 (1974): 449–58; will, Samuel Francis Sr., 10 Feb. 1815, Will Book 7:447–48; U.S. Census, Southampton County, 1810, p. 875 (Samuel); 1820, p. 117 (Sarah ["Sally"]); 1830, pp. 259, 260 (Nathaniel, Salathiel ["Selathan"]); Marriage Register, p. 35.

6. St. Luke's Parish Land Book, 1807, entry for Samuel Francis Sr., LVA. The census of 1810 listed Samuel Francis Sr. with sixteen slaves of all ages; U.S. Census, Southampton County, 1820, p. 875.

7. In 1810 Samuel Francis Sr. ranked 10th in his landholding among 317 core taxpayers in the parish (defined as resident white adults who paid taxes on both land and personal property). Benjamin Turner II, with 552 acres, ranked 58th. Of the 317 core taxpayers, 252 (79.5 percent) paid tax on slaves, and 65 (20.5 percent) did not. Turner (with thirteen taxable slaves) ranked 27th among the slaveholders; Francis (ten taxable slaves) ranked 44th; St. Luke's Parish Land Book, 1810, and St. Luke's Parish Personal Tax List, 1810, entries for Samuel Francis Sr. and Benjamin Turner II. In 1821 there were 275 core taxpayers in St. Luke's, of whom 219 held slaves; in 1831 there were 272 core taxpayers, of whom 212 held slaves.

8. Inventory, Samuel Francis Sr., 27 May 1815, Will Book 8:379–80.

9. William S. Drewry, *The Southampton Insurrection* (1900; repr., Murfreesboro, NC: Johnson, 1968), 46, and photographs following p. 201.

10. Inventory, Samuel Francis Sr., Will Book 8:379–80.

11. Nathaniel Francis improved the structures at his father's farm in 1836 or 1837, giving them the form and size they maintained into the late nineteenth century; St. Luke's Parish Land Book, 1837, entry for Nathaniel Francis.

12. St. Luke's Parish Personal Tax List, 1784, entry for Samuel Francis Sr.; inventory, Samuel Francis Sr., Will Book 8:379–80.

13. Wyndham Bolling Blanton, *Medicine in Virginia in the Nineteenth Century* (Richmond: Garrett & Massie, 1933), 243–47.

14. Esther's name alone was missing from the list of Francis heirs in 1816; account, Samuel Francis Sr., 22 Oct. 1816, Will Book 8:311.

15. Polly Turner's year of birth can be deduced from the fact that in 1823 she chose her own guardian, which she could do legally at age fourteen; County Court Minute Book, 15 Sept. 1823, p. 340, SCC.

16. County Court Minute Book, 15 May 1815, p. 218.

17. Will, Samuel Francis Sr., Will Book 7:447. Only Samuel's eldest daughter, Rebecca Dupree, received no slaves. She received a cash legacy of £146.

18. A slave Lucy's age was added to Turner's tax record in 1809; St. Luke's Parish Personal Tax List, 1809, entry for Samuel G. Turner.

19. Will, Samuel Francis Sr., Will Book 7:447–48. The estimate of Lucy's age is based on her value ($300) in the inventory of Samuel G. Turner's estate, Will Book 9:254.

20. Inventory, Samuel Francis Sr., Will Book 8:379–80.

21. Account, Samuel Francis Sr., 1815–16, Will Book 8:309–11; *Francis v. Francis*, County Court Order Book, 21 Nov. 1815, p. 230, SCC; chancery report, estate of Samuel Francis Sr., County Court Order Book, 20 May 1816, p. 327.

22. Inferences about Moses and Peter are based on St. Luke's Parish Personal Tax Lists, 1815–20, entries for Samuel G. Turner and Sarah ("Sally") Francis. The slaveholding of Sarah Francis declined in size, indicating that the slaves distributed to her older children in 1816 scattered with those children to other farms. Moses (who was not the boy of that name involved in the rising) must have gone to Mississippi with his new master, Samuel Francis Jr., in about 1819. The identification of Peter is based on the inventories of Samuel Francis (1815) and Samuel G. Turner (1822). In the division of Samuel Francis's estate in 1816, Peter, one of the three most valuable slaves in the holding, was drawn by Mary (Polly) Francis, a minor; chancery report, estate of Samuel Francis Sr., County Court Order Book, 20 May 1816, p. 327. Peter's name reappeared in the 1822 inventory of Samuel G. Turner, in which he and Nat Turner were listed as the two most valuable slaves. The references to "Peter" suggest that they all involved the same man, and that he had been transferred informally from Mary Francis to Samuel G. Turner in 1816 or 1817, when Turner's tax records indicate that he added another slave.

23. Moses (later Moses Moore) was the boy recruited by the insurgents to tend horses. Anacka's name appeared (first as "Anarchy") in inventory, Samuel Francis Sr., Will Book 8:379. See also chancery report, estate of Samuel Francis Sr., County Court Order Book, 1816, p. 327; will, William Francis, 24 Jan. 1819, Will Book 9:09; account, Putnam Moore, 22 Dec. 1831, Will Book 11:80. Moses's name appeared in the will of William Francis and in account, Putnam Moore, Will Book 11:80. Moses's age was given in Auditor of Public Accounts, List of Slaves and Free persons of color received into the Penitentiary of Virginia, in Records, Condemned Blacks Executed or Transported, 1783–1864, LVA. It is possible that the boy Moses was the son and namesake of the Moses who was taken to Mississippi. Young Moses was allotted to Joseph Travis, "in right of his wife," in 1830; commissioners' papers, estate of Thomas Moore, 26 Feb. 1830, *Moore v. Travis*, Southampton County Chancery Causes, LVA. He was mistakenly identified as Travis's property until December 1831, when the court declared him the property of Putnam Moore's estate; County Court Minute Book, 19 Dec. 1831, p. 142.

24. Samuel G. Turner's new wife became the second Elizabeth to marry into the Turner family in less than a decade, the first having been his father's second wife, Elizabeth (Bynum) Boykin Turner. By 1818, the first Elizabeth had married a third time, to John Prince; and after December 1823, she married a fourth time, to Henry Porter, though she continued to be listed under the Turner surname in parish land books, holding dower lands from the estate of Benjamin Turner II.

25. Marriage Register, p. 223; St. Luke's Parish Personal Tax List, 1814, entry for Anselm Williamson.

26. Rebecca Jane Williamson's year of birth is deduced from the date of her parents' marriage and from that of her own marriage in 1829, when she would have been sixteen years old, her mother giving permission; Marriage Register, p. 398.

27. Deed, Elizabeth Williamson to Rebecca Jane Williamson, 11 June 1818, Deed Book 16:144.

28. *Williamson v. Reese*, County Court Order Book, 21 Nov. 1815, p. 231. Elizabeth Turner II filed suit on the day Sarah Francis filed a similar suit against Samuel G. Turner as executor of her husband's estate; Elizabeth and Samuel may have met that day in court; *Francis v. Francis*, County Court Order Book, 21 Nov. 1815, p. 230.

29. Chancery report, estate of John Reese Sr., County Court Order Book, 17 Mar. 1817, pp. 99–101; deed, Elizabeth Turner II to Alexander P. Peete, 2 June 1829, Deed Book 21:147. Elizabeth held the 110 acres in fee simple; St. Luke's Parish Land Book, 1818, entry for Eliza Williamson.

30. Deed, Williamson to Williamson, Deed Book 16:144; Marriage Register, p. 663.

31. The plot of 110 acres continued to be listed separately through 1820 under the name of Elizabeth Williamson. By 1821 Elizabeth II had sold the land to her eldest brother, Edward Reese, for $1,500; the proceeds probably went to Samuel G. Turner. The sale was not recorded until 1829; St. Luke's Parish Land Book, 1829, entry for estate of Edward Reese; deed, Elizabeth Turner II to Alexander P. Peete, Deed Book 21:147. In his will and in a deed of gift in 1822, Samuel G. Turner acknowledged the rights of Elizabeth and her daughter to slaves Elizabeth had gained from the estates of her first husband and from her father; will, Samuel G. Turner, 9 Jan. 1822, Will Book 9:134–35; deed, Samuel G. Turner to Rebecca Jane Williamson, 18 Jan. 1822, Deed Book 18:413.

32. Nat Turner was transferred legally to Putnam Moore after the death of Thomas Moore and may have been hired to Giles Reese in 1830, after the arrival of Joseph Travis at Moore's farm.

33. U.S. Census, Southampton County, 1820, pp. 117 (Sarah ["Sally"] Francis), 122 (Thomas Moore), 124a (Giles Reese, Joseph Reese Sr.), 126a (Samuel G. Turner); St. Luke's Parish Tax List, 1821, entries for Sarah ("Sally") Francis, Thomas Moore, Giles Reese, Joseph Reese Sr., and Samuel G. Turner. Thomas Urquhart of Nottoway Parish held the largest number of slaves in the county; he was listed with 236 slaves in the 1820 census, 120 in the 1821 personal property tax list.

34. St. Luke's Parish Land Book, 1817, entry for Elizabeth Turner I.

35. Reese genealogy (author's research file); inventory, Edward Reese (father of Joseph Reese Sr. and John Reese), 19 Dec. 1781, Will Book 3:404–5; will, Olive Reese (mother of Joseph Sr. and John), 15 May 1793, Will Book 4:578. Joseph Reese Sr. had left for parts unknown in 1793, when his mother, Olive Reese, wrote her will.

She bequeathed him a feather bed and furniture, "unless he should not return to receive it."

36. Will, William Vick, 15 May 1782, Will Book 4:80–82; Marriage Register, p. 86; County Court Minute Book, 20 Jan. 1800, p. 63; St. Luke's Parish Land Book, 1799, and St. Luke's Parish Personal Tax List, 1799, entries for Rivers Reese.

37. St. Luke's Parish Personal Tax Lists, 1802–4, entries for Joseph Reese Sr. and Piety Reese.

38. Reese genealogy (author's research file).

39. St. Luke's Parish Land Books, 1802–17, entries for Joseph Reese Sr. and Piety Reese.

40. St. Luke's Parish Personal Tax List, 1804, entry for Joseph Reese Sr.; deed, Arthur Vick and Nancy Reese to Joseph Reese Sr., 1 Sept. 1817, Deed Book 15:305; St. Luke's Parish Land Book, 1818, entry for Joseph Reese Sr.

41. Will, Joseph Reese Sr., 25 Oct. 1813 (recorded 17 July 1826), Will Book 9:359.

42. St. Luke's Parish Land Books, 1817–19, entries for Elizabeth Turner I.

43. Deed, Thomas and Rebecca Vaughan to John T. Vaughan, 16 May 1816, Deed Book 15:53.

44. St. Luke's Parish Land Book, 1820, entries for Elizabeth Turner I and Joseph Reese Sr.

45. Drewry, *Southampton Insurrection*, photograph following p. 201.

46. The Turner house did not match the house types ("hall and parlor house," "central-hall house," or "I-house") defined in Henry Glassie, *Pattern in the Material Folk Culture of the Eastern United States* (Philadelphia: University of Pennsylvania Press, 1968), 89, 96; or Henry Glassie, *Folk Housing in Middle Virginia* (Knoxville: University of Tennessee Press, 1975), 77, 93, 99, 100.

47. Benjamin Turner II referred to Charles Newton's house ("a house of Nooton") on the Kindred tract when he transferred the property to Samuel in 1809; deed, Turner to Turner, Deed Book 14:81.

48. The buildings at Samuel G. Turner's mansion farm ranked 56th in value among 398 farm complexes in the parish. In addition, Turner owned a structure worth $20 at the property he purchased in 1820, two miles to the south; St. Luke's Parish Land Book, 1821, entries for Samuel G. Turner and Francis Ridley.

49. St. Luke's Parish Personal Tax List, 1815, entry for estate of Anselm Williamson; chancery report, estate of John Reese, County Court Order Book, 17 Mar. 1817, p. 100; deed, Williamson to Williamson, Deed Book 16:144; inventory, Samuel G. Turner, Will Book 9:254; will, Benjamin Turner I, Will Book 3:333; will (original), Benjamin Turner II, 1810; inventory, Benjamin Turner II, Will Book 7:168; and deed, Holladay to Turner and Griffin, Deed Book 7:823.

50. Samuel G. Turner's household was recorded with twenty-eight slaves in U.S. Census, Southampton County, 1820, p. 127.

51. St. Luke's Parish Personal Tax List, 1817, entry for Abraham Turner.

52. Will (original), Benjamin Turner II, 1810.

53. Will, Samuel G. Turner, Will Book 9:134; inventory, Samuel G. Turner, Will Book 9:254; U.S. Census, Southampton County, 1820, p. 127a. Samuel's executors petitioned successfully to have Bridget and Lydia declared superannuated and tax-exempt in 1822; County Court Minute Book, 18 Mar. 1822, p. 242.

54. Deed, Nancy Barrett to Samuel G. Turner, 16 Jan. 1819, Deed Book 16:171; deed, Parker Barrett to Samuel G. Turner, 18 Jan. 1819, Deed Book 16:197.

55. Deed, James Kello to Samuel G. Turner, 5 Feb. 1819, Deed Book 16:291.

56. St. Luke's Parish Land Book, 1821, entry for Samuel G. Turner. In 1821 Turner ranked 40th among the 275 core taxpayers.

57. The inventory of Samuel G. Turner's personal estate was mistaken for a record of sale in F. Roy Johnson, *The Nat Turner Slave Insurrection* (Murfreesboro, NC: Johnson, 1966), 32–33; and in Stephen B. Oates, *The Fires of Jubilee: Nat Turner's Fierce Rebellion* (New York: Harper & Row, 1971), 29–30.

58. Deed, Turner to Williamson, Deed Book 18:413.

59. Inventory, Samuel G. Turner, Will Book 9:254; inventory, Benjamin Turner II, Will Book 7:167–70.

60. Inventory, Samuel G. Turner, Will Book 9:254.

61. Thomas Jefferson to John Taylor, 29 Dec. 1794, in Thomas Jefferson, *Thomas Jefferson: Writings*, ed. Merrill D. Peterson (New York: Literary Classics of the United States, 1984), 1,021.

62. Inventory, Samuel G. Turner, Will Book 9:254.

63. St. Luke's Parish Personal Tax Lists, 1809, 1821, entries for Samuel G. Turner; St. Luke's Parish Land Book, 1821, entry for Samuel G. Turner.

64. Inventory, Samuel G. Turner, Deed Book 9:254.

65. St. Luke's Parish Land Book, 1822, entry for Samuel G. Turner; inventory, Samuel G. Turner, Will Book 9:254.

66. Sharon Ann Murphy, *Investing in Life: Insurance in Antebellum America* (Baltimore: Johns Hopkins University Press, 2010), 33–37. By the time Turner died, the Mutual Assurance Company of Virginia no longer insured country properties.

67. Henry Wiencek, *Master of the Mountain: Thomas Jefferson and His Slaves* (New York: Farrar, Straus & Giroux, 2012), 89–90.

68. Will, Samuel G. Turner, Will Book 9:134; deed, Turner to Williamson, Deed Book 18:413.

69. Will, Samuel G. Turner, Will Book 9:134; St. Luke's Parish Land Book, 1836, entry for John C. Turner.

70. Will, Samuel G. Turner, Will Book 9:134–35.

71. John Duffy, *Epidemics in Colonial America* (Baton Rouge: Louisiana State University Press, 1953), 204–5, 214–15, 222–23.

72. Of the 295 resident white adult males who paid taxes on land in the parish in 1821, 256 (or 86.8 percent) left enough evidence about themselves and their land to permit a tracing of their holdings from year to year and to determine whether they survived through the spring of 1831. The remaining thirty-nine male landowners (13.2 percent) left no evidence on whether they survived in 1831; it is possible that all thirty-nine were still alive but had left the county or transferred their land to others through informal transactions. St. Luke's Parish Land Books, 1821–31.

73. Four tax years were exceptionally deadly for the group of 295 men: 1825 (fourteen deaths), 1826 (sixteen deaths), 1828 (nineteen deaths), and 1829 (fifteen deaths). Mortality in Southampton represented a continuation of conditions in the colonial South, documented in a large body of historical scholarship.

74. St. Luke's Parish Land Books and Personal Tax Lists, 1821–31.

75. Inventory, Samuel G. Turner, Will Book 9:254. The other top-ranking slave was Peter, perhaps six years older than Nat Turner. The inventory listed twenty-three slaves.

76. Tax records indicate that the number of slaves at the Turner farm did not decline greatly after Samuel's death. In 1822 Samuel paid taxes on eleven slaves; in 1831 Elizabeth II held eight taxable slaves. St. Luke's Parish Personal Tax Lists, 1822–31, entries for Samuel G. Turner and Elizabeth Turner II.

77. Will, John Spencer, 9 [Aug.] 1825, Will Book 9:269; account, Lawrence Cook, 18 June 1827, Will Book 10:246. Spencer, whose assumptions about the benefits of holding slaves were similar to those of Elizabeth Turner II, gave his widow two slaves "for the support of herself and my son Richard Carter Spencer."

78. Thomas R. Gray, *The Confessions of Nat Turner* (Baltimore: Lucas & Deaver, 1831), 9.

79. [James Trezvant], letter, 31 Aug. 1831, *Raleigh Register*, 3 Sept. 1831.

80. [Thomas R. Gray], letter, 17 Sept. 1831, *Richmond Constitutional Whig*, 26 Sept. 1831, in *Norfolk American Beacon*, 30 Sept. 1831.

81. Warner referred twice to a correspondent in Southampton who provided information about Turner's wife. Warner's lists of victims and insurgents, moreover, were almost identical to those Gray sent to the *Richmond Whig*, suggesting that Gray was the correspondent; Samuel Warner, *Authentic and Impartial Narrative of the Tragical Scene Which Was Witnessed in Southampton County* (New York: Warner & West, 1831), 9, 13–15, 31.

82. Drewry, *Southampton Insurrection*, 28.

83. F. Roy Johnson began the discussion about Cherry in *The Nat Turner Story: History of the South's Most Important Slave Revolt* (Murfreesboro, NC: Johnson), 54–55. Discussion continued in Henry I. Tragle, *The Southampton Slave Revolt of 1831: A Compilation of Source Material* (Amherst: University of Massachusetts Press, 1971), 327n2; Oates, *Fires of Jubilee*, 29, 162–63n21; and Thomas C. Parramore, *Southampton County, Virginia* (Charlottesville: University of Virginia Press, 1978), 104, 243–44n43. The Turner, Francis, and Reese families held at least three females named Cherry between 1826 and 1832. Cherry I, assumed here to have been the wife of Nat Turner, was mentioned in will (original), Benjamin Turner II, 1810. In 1826, two females listed in Reese family records bore the name *Cherry*, one owned by Joseph Reese Sr., the other by Reese's nephew Giles; inventory, Joseph Reese Sr., 20 Nov. 1826, Will Book 10:180; deed, Giles Reese to Alexander P. Peete, 22 Aug. 1826, Deed Book 20:64. Johnson, not knowing that Joseph Sr. had held a woman with this name, deduced that Nat Turner's wife was the woman who belonged to Giles. The evidence is stronger that in 1826 Cherry I (Turner's wife) belonged to Joseph Reese Sr., and Cherry II to Giles Reese. Cherry I probably was the woman who later testified at the trial of Ben Blunt, saying she was present at the house of Nathaniel Francis on 23 Aug. 1831; County Court Minute Book, 21 Nov. 1831, p. 130. Cherry II probably was the woman named in a deed, Giles Reese to Hardy Harris, 20 Mar. 1832, Deed Book 22:161. Cherry III, described as a girl in 1830, was named in an account of Thomas Moore's estate discovered by Parramore in 1976.

84. Will (original), Benjamin Turner II, 1810.

85. Johnson apparently misread as "Cherry" the name *Hannah* in the inventory of Samuel G. Turner's estate in Will Book 9:254; Johnson, *Nat Turner Story*, 54.

86. Inventory, Joseph Reese Sr., Will Book 10:180.

87. There is complicating evidence, however, confusing the identity of Cherry with that of another female, Jenny, in the report of commissioners, estate of Joseph Reese Sr., 29 Nov. 1826, *Reese v. Reese*, Southampton County Chancery Causes, LVA.

88. U.S. Census, Southampton County, 1870, p. 4; U.S. Census, Greensville County, 1870, manuscript returns, p. 68, NA; Drewry, *Southampton Insurrection*, 28.

89. Joseph Reese Sr. was listed in the 1820 census with thirteen slaves, including two females (their names were not given) who were about the age of Cherry; U.S. Census, Southampton County, 1820, p. 124a.

90. County Court Order Book, 20 Nov. 1820, p. 232.

91. Their marriage bond was dated 21 Mar. 1821, and their certificate of marriage was signed on 30 May 1821; Marriage Register, p. 301.

92. County Court Order Book, 18 Aug. 1823, p. 269.

Chapter 4. Successors: Capt. Moore and Mr. Travis

1. County Court Minute Book, 17 May 1814, p. 109; 19 Aug. 1816, p. 44; 20 Nov. 1820, p. 130, SCC.

2. Marriage Register, p. 65, SCC; St. Luke's Parish Personal Property Tax Lists, 1809–16, entries for Temperance Moore, LVA; U.S. Census, Southampton County, 1810, manuscript returns, p. 874, NA; St. Luke's Parish Land Book, 1821, entry for Temperance Moore, LVA.

3. Will, James Ramsey, 11 Feb. 1771, Will Book 2:399–400, SCC; will, John Moore, 15 Nov. 1801 (proved 21 Mar. 1803), Will Book 5:380–81; inventory, John Moore, 17 Feb. 1803, Will Book 5:541.

4. Will, John Moore, Will Book 5:380–81; inventory, John Moore, Will Book 5:540–41; inventory, Benjamin Turner II, 22 Jan. 1811, Will Book 7:167.

5. St. Luke's Parish Personal Tax Lists, 1809–18, entries for Temperance Moore; St. Luke's Parish Personal Tax Lists, 1818, 1819, entries for Thomas Moore.

6. Marriage Register, p. 281.

7. Will, William Francis, 24 Jan. 1819, Will Book 9:9; chancery report, estate of Samuel Francis Sr., County Court Order Book, 20 May 1816, p. 328, SCC.

8. Both Maria and Lucy were named in will, Samuel Francis Sr., 10 Feb. 1815, Will Book 7:447.

9. St. Luke's Parish Personal Tax List, 1820, entry for Thomas Moore; U.S. Census, Southampton County, 1820, p. 122.

10. Deeds, Sarah ("Sally") Francis to Thomas Moore, 2 Jan. and 5 Jan. 1822; Salathiel Francis to Thomas Moore, 1 June 1822; Thomas and Sally Moore to Salathiel Francis, 1 June 1822, Deed Book 19:29, 27, 6–7, 30, SCC. A map of the farm in 1830 appears in George H. Gray, plat, Joseph Travis farm, 26 Feb. 1830, *Moore v. Travis*, Southampton County Chancery Causes, LVA.

11. Putnam Moore's year of birth is deduced from the date of his parents' marriage (1 May 1819) and from the entry for Joseph Travis in U.S. Census, Southamp-

ton County, 1830, p. 260; St. Luke's Parish Personal Tax List, 1822, entry for Thomas Moore.

12. St. Luke's Parish Personal Tax Lists, 1807–30, entries for Temperance Moore; 1819–27, entries for Thomas Moore.

13. Thomas Jefferson to Edward Coles, 25 Aug. 1814, in Thomas Jefferson, *Thomas Jefferson: Writings*, ed. Merrill D. Peterson (New York: Literary Classics of the United States, 1984), 1,344.

14. Upward trends in violent crime by slaves in Virginia and Southampton are documented in Philip J. Schwarz, *Twice Condemned: Slaves and the Criminal Laws of Virginia, 1705–1865* (Baton Rouge: Louisiana State University Press, 1988), 231–37, 255, 259.

15. Examination of John E. Martin, County Court Order Book, 16 May 1821, pp. 303–4; trial of Dread, County Court Order Book, 16 May 1821, pp. 305–6; trial of Sam, County Court Order Book, 16 July 1821, pp. 332–33.

16. Trial of Dread, County Court Order Book, 16 May 1821, p. 305.

17. Trial of Sam, County Court Order Book, 16 July 1821, p. 332; trial of Dread, County Court Order Book, 16 May 1821, p. 306.

18. Trial of Dread, County Court Order Book, 16 May 1821, pp. 305–6; trial of Sam, County Court Order Book, 16 July 1821, pp. 332–33.

19. Trial of Dread, County Court Order Book, 16 May 1821, p. 306.

20. Ibid.

21. This Elizabeth Turner came before the court five days after Dread, charged with thefts committed in 1819 against three Southampton residents; County Court Minute Book, 21 May 1821, pp. 312–13.

22. Trial of Dread, County Court Order Book, 16 May 1821, p. 305.

23. Ibid., 306; examination of John E. Martin, County Court Order Book, 302; trial of Sam, County Court Order Book, 16 July 1821, p. 333.

24. Marriage Register, p. 259; deed, George Simmons to James Powell, 29 Sept. 1817, Deed Book 15:326–27.

25. Trial of Abel, County Court Order Book, 28 June 1821, pp. 321–24; trial of Celia, County Court Order Book, 28 June 1821, p. 325; Schwarz, *Twice Condemned*, 237.

26. Trial of Abel, County Court Order Book, 28 June 1821, p. 324.

27. Ibid.

28. Ibid., 322.

29. Ibid., 322–23.

30. Trial of Celia, County Court Order Book, 28 June 1821, p. 325.

31. Trial of Abel, County Court Order Book, 28 June 1821, p. 324.

32. St. Luke's Parish Land Book, 1823, and St. Luke's Parish Personal Tax List, 1823, entries for Thomas Moore.

33. The theory that the transfer took place in the tax year 1822–23 is consistent with a decline of four taxable slaves (from eleven to seven) that year at the farm of Samuel G. Turner's widow, Elizabeth II; St. Luke's Parish Personal Tax List, 1822, entry for estate of Samuel G. Turner; and St. Luke's Parish Personal Tax List, 1823, entry for Elizabeth Turner II. Exemptions for Lydia and Bridget in 1822 brought the real decline to just two; County Court Minute Book, 18 Mar. 1822, p. 242.

34. St. Luke's Parish Land Book, 1821, entry for Thomas Moore; U.S. Census, Southampton County, 1820, p. 122.

35. Samuel Warner, *Authentic and Impartial Narrative of the Tragical Scene Which Was Witnessed in Southampton County* (New York: Warner & West, 1831), 31.

36. Thomas R. Gray, *The Confessions of Nat Turner* (Baltimore: Lucas & Deaver, 1831), 10.

37. Ibid., 11; [William C. Parker], letter, 21 Sept. 1831, *Richmond Enquirer*, 30 Sept. 1831.

38. Isaac Pipkin, letter, 1 Nov. 1831, *Norfolk American Beacon*, 4 Nov. 1831.

39. [Thomas R. Gray], letter, 17 Sept. 1831, *Richmond Constitutional Whig*, 26 Sept. 1831, in *Norfolk American Beacon*, 30 Sept. 1831.

40. On the other hand, if Gray's estimate was correct, the "master" who administered the whipping might have been Giles Reese, who apparently hired Nat Turner after Moore's death. Drewry, in his account of a gallows encounter between the two men, said Turner referred to Reese as "Marse Giles." William S. Drewry, *The Southampton Insurrection* (1900; repr., Murfreesboro, NC: Johnson, 1968), 36n1. Gray clearly was estimating, however, and Moore had a motive for the whipping.

41. County Court Minute Book, 18 June 1827, p. 166.

42. St. Luke's Parish Land Book, 1826, and St. Luke's Parish Personal Tax List, 1826, entries for Thomas Moore. The estimate of Moore's rank is derived by comparing his total tax payments in 1826 with that of other core taxpayers in 1831. Among 272 resident white adults who paid taxes on both land and personal property in the parish in 1831, Moore would have ranked 70th, or among the wealthiest 26 percent.

43. St. Luke's Parish Land Books, 1823–30, entries for Thomas Moore and his estate.

44. Evidence that Sally Moore claimed these slaves lies in the fact that they later appeared in the estate of her second husband, Joseph Travis. The six other slaves appeared in the estate of Putnam Moore. Account of sales, estate of Joseph Travis, 22 Dec. 1831, Will Book 11:343; account, Putnam Moore, 1831–32, Will Book 11:80.

45. St. Luke's Parish Land Books and Personal Tax Lists, 1821–31.

46. St. Luke's Parish Personal Tax Lists, 1828, 1829, entries for estate of Thomas Moore.

47. U.S. Census, Southampton County, 1830, p. 260. His mother's tax assessment listed Salathiel's name for the first time in 1819, indicating he was born in about 1803; St. Luke's Parish Personal Tax List, 1819, entry for Sarah ("Sally") Francis; St. Luke's Parish Land Book, 1827, and St. Luke's Parish Personal Tax List, 1827, entries for Salathiel Francis. Slaves Nancy and Patt were given to Salathiel in the 1816 division of his father's estate; chancery report, estate of Samuel Francis, County Court Order Book, 20 May 1816, p. 328.

48. St. Luke's Parish Land Book, 1825, entry for Salathiel Francis.

49. St. Luke's Parish Land Book, 1831, entry for Salathiel Francis; Drewry, *Southampton Insurrection*, 38n1, and photographs following p. 201.

50. County Court Minute Book, 21 Nov. 1825, p. 90; 16 Nov. 1829, p. 295; 22 June 1830, p. 340; will, Salathiel Francis, 3 Sept. 1828 (proved 16 Jan. 1832), Will Book 10:355.

51. Drewry, *Southampton Insurrection*, 28.

52. Trial of Amos, County Court Minute Book, 21 Nov. 1825, p. 92.

53. Brantley was found not guilty; County Court Minute Book, 20 July 1829, p. 276.

54. Drewry, *Southampton Insurrection*, 28. Drewry did not discover the year of Salathiel's warning.

55. F. N. Boney, "Nathaniel Francis, Representative Antebellum Southerner," *Proceedings of the American Philosophical Society* 118 (1974): 449.

56. Will, Samuel Francis Sr., Will Book 7:447–48.

57. The 363-acre home plantation was listed in the name of Samuel Francis Sr. in St. Luke's Parish Land Book, 1792.

58. Deed, Temperance Moore, Henry Moore, and others to John Sykes, 4 Dec. 1833, Deed Book 23:192–93; deed, John Sykes to Robert T. Musgrave, 25 Mar. 1834, Deed Book 23:201–2; Drewry, *Southampton Insurrection*, 45.

59. St. Luke's Parish Land Books, 1820–36, entries for Sarah ("Sally") Francis.

60. Drewry, *Southampton Insurrection*, 46.

61. Henry I. Tragle, *The Southampton Slave Revolt of 1831: A Compilation of Source Material* (Amherst: University of Massachusetts Press, 1971), 162.

62. St. Luke's Parish Land Book, 1827, entries for Nathaniel Francis and Sarah ("Sally") Francis.

63. St. Luke's Parish Personal Tax List, 1827, entries for Nathaniel Francis and Sarah ("Sally") Francis.

64. Their 1,286 acres combined as a single plantation would have ranked 29th out of 507 landholdings in the parish in 1831. The largest landholding was William Allen's 6,448 acres; St. Luke's Parish Land Book, 1831.

65. U.S. Census, Southampton County, 1830, pp. 259, 260. In 1830 the former Moore household was listed under Joseph Travis.

66. County Court Minute Book, 17, 18 Mar. 1828, pp. 203, 207.

67. County Court Minute Book, 21 Sept. 1829, p. 288.

68. Answer to complaint (deposition, copy), Nathaniel Francis to Thomas Ridley, 17 July 1848, John Richardson Kilby Papers, RDU.

69. Deed, John W. Reese to Nathaniel Francis, 22 Jan. 1829, Deed Book 21:78; deed, John Thomas to John W. Reese, 19 Dec. 1827, Deed Book 20:329–30.

70. Harriet Whitehead, amended bill of complaint, County Court Records, Chancery Papers, 1851, LVA.

71. Will, Mary Pope, 29 June 1820, Will Book 9:69; will, Samuel Francis Sr., Will Book 7:447.

72. Drewry, *Southampton Insurrection*, 48.

73. St. Luke's Parish Personal Tax Lists, 1827, 1828, 1829, entries for Thomas Moore and Sarah Moore.

74. Gray, *Confessions*, 11.

75. St. Luke's Parish Personal Tax List, 1814, entry for John Reese Sr.; this was the first year Giles's name appeared, indicating that he was then about sixteen years old. Deed, Giles Reese and Nancy Reese to Edward Reese, 17 Apr. 1820, Deed Book 17:130–31.

76. County Court Order Book, 18 Aug. 1823, p. 269; 17 Nov. 1823, p. 330.

77. Deed, Giles Reese to Edwin B. Claud, 29 Nov. 1824, Deed Book 19:358; deed, Giles Reese to Robert Goodwyn, 21 May 1827, Deed Book 20:241–42.

78. Between 1825 and 1829 Giles Reese rented the plantation belonging to the estate of Edmund Turner Jr.; deed, Giles Reese to A. P. Peete, 1 Sept. 1826, Deed Book 20:116. (The deed copy refers mistakenly to Edwin Turner, a common confusion of first names.) Starting in 1830 Giles Reese also rented (with borrowed money) fifty acres belonging to the estate of John Birdsong, but apparently he did not reside at that farm until after the uprising; deed, Giles Reese to Hardy Harris, 20 Mar. 1832, Deed Book 22:161. No record of his lease on the Mason plantation has been found; the location of the plantation and its status as an estate appear in Land Books, St. Luke's Parish, 1821–31. Giles Reese was present on 7 Apr. 1830 when local processioners walked the bounds of the Mason estate; Processioners' Returns, 1830, Precinct 21, p. 2, LVA.

79. County Court Minute Book, 20 Sept. 1830, p. 355. The record reads as follows: "Ordered that the male labouring tythables of Joseph Travis, Robert T. Musgrave, [and] Thos. Mason at the residence of Giles Reese [and] Burwell Murfee do work on the road whereof Henry Moore is surveyor." Parramore found evidence in 1976 that Reese may have intended to purchase five of the Moore slaves in 1830, including Hark, Sam, a girl named "Charry," and Mariah and her child; Thomas C. Parramore, *Southampton County, Virginia* (Charlottesville: University of Virginia Press, 1978), 243–44n43. All of these slaves except the girl named Cherry remained in the estate of Joseph Travis in 1831, however.

80. Gray, *Confessions*, 11.

81. The origins of Joseph Travis remain undocumented. Drewry suggested he might have been related to the Travis family of Jamestown; Drewry, *Southampton Insurrection*, 27n1. One modern author has suggested that Travis had kin in Brunswick County, Virginia; Bill Bryant, *Tomorrow Jerusalem: The Story of Nat Turner and the Southampton Slave Insurrection* (Bloomington, IN: 1st Books, 2002), 351. One man in Brunswick, Joseph Hutchings Travis, might have been a relative, but he cannot have been the father of Joseph Travis of Southampton. In 1820, a man with Joseph Travis's name and fitting his description was living in Kentucky, but there is no proof that he was the man who settled at the Moore farm; U.S. Census, Shelby County, KY, 1820, manuscript returns, p. 148, NA. The genealogist of the Travis family found no information about its Southampton branches; Robert J. Travis, *The Travis (Travers) Family and Its Allies* (Savannah, GA, 1954).

82. Marriage Register, pp. 402, 679.

83. St. Luke's Parish Personal Tax List, 1830, entry for Joseph Travis; County Court Minute Book, 18 Jan. 1830, p. 309; 20 Sept. 1830, p. 355; U.S. Census, Southampton County, 1830, p. 260.

84. St. Luke's Parish Personal Tax List, 1831, entry for Joseph Travis; County Court Minute Book, 21 Mar. 1831, p. 29; St. Luke's Parish Land Book, 1831, entry for Sarah Moore (Joseph Travis).

85. Processioners' Returns, 1830, Precinct 21, p. 2.

86. Gray, *Confessions*, 11.

87. Travis never did own land in Southampton and apparently brought no slaves into the county. At the end of 1831 the only slaves in his estate (Hark, Sam, and

Maria and her two children) had belonged to his wife before their marriage or had been conveyed with Maria as her increase. The number of taxable slaves at the Moore-Travis farm did rise from four to eight between 1829 and 1831, but the increase could have resulted from the return of hired slaves. The number of horses at the farm, which stood at four in 1829 and 1830, did not rise to five until 1831, more than a year after Travis arrived. St. Luke's Parish Personal Tax Lists, 1829–31, entries for Joseph Travis; account of sales, Joseph Travis, Will Book 11:338–43.

88. The census of 1820 recorded two men in Moore's household engaged in manufacturing, suggesting that he operated a shop of some kind; U.S. Census, Southampton County, 1820, p. 122. Moore's tools probably were those listed in account of sales, Joseph Travis, Will Book 11:338–41.

89. St. Luke's Parish Land Book, 1831, combined entries for estate of Thomas Moore and Sarah Moore (Joseph Travis); St. Luke's Parish Personal Tax List, 1831, entry for Joseph Travis. Assuming that Travis also paid the taxes on the land in Moore's estate, he ranked 75th among 272 core taxpayers in 1831.

90. No contemporary source identified the Travis infant by name or sex. The child had not been born by the time the U.S. Census began in June 1830. Bill Bryant refers to a family tradition identifying the infant as "Joe" and contradicting previous accounts that he was killed in 1831; Bryant, *Tomorrow Jerusalem*, 105, 108, 351. All contemporary sources agreed that the Travis infant was killed.

91. St. Luke's Parish Land Book, 1831, entry for Sarah Moore (Joseph Travis); Nottoway Parish Land Book, 1821, entry for James Powell, LVA.

92. Descriptions of the house in 1831 indicate that it cannot have been the same one-room dwelling Moore had occupied until his death.

93. Tragle, *Southampton Slave Revolt*, 160.

94. Gilbert W. Francis and Katherine K. Futrell, *Nat Turner's Insurrection, 1831* (video recording, Southampton County Historical Society Living Library, 2000), disc 2. Francis and Futrell believed that the house they documented contained the core of the 1831 Travis house.

95. Details about the Travis house and homestead appeared in 1831 in the following sources: [William C. Parker], letter, 31 Aug. 1831, *Richmond Compiler*, 3 Sept. 1831, in *Richmond Enquirer*, 6 Sept. 1831; Moses Moore, testimony, trial of Jack Reese, County Court Minute Book, 3 Sept. 1831, p. 90; [Gray], letter, *Richmond Whig*, 26 Sept. 1831, in *Norfolk American Beacon*, 30 Sept. 1831; [William C. Parker], letter, 1 Nov. 1831, *Richmond Enquirer*, 8 Nov. 1831; Gray, *Confessions*, 12; inventory, Joseph Travis, 20 Dec. 1831, Will Book 11:353–54; account of sales, Joseph Travis, Will Book 11:338–43. Descriptions of the house in 1831 suggest that it conformed to the early hall and parlor type described in Henry Glassie, *Pattern in the Material Folk Culture of the Eastern United States* (Philadelphia: University of Pennsylvania Press, 1968), 65–68 and fig. 22-A.

96. Gray, *Confessions*, 12.

97. Moses's testimony placed him in or near the kitchen the night of 21–22 Aug. 1831; Moses Moore, testimony, trial of Jack Reese, County Court Minute Book, 3 Sept. 1831, p. 90.

98. References to the large room and closet upstairs appear in account of sales, Joseph Travis, Will Book 11:343.

99. Inventory, Joseph Travis, Will Book 11:353–54.

100. Ibid.; account of sales, Joseph Travis, Will Book 11:338–43.

101. Inventory, Joseph Travis, Will Book 11:353–54; account of sales, Joseph Travis, Will Book 11:338–43.

102. Gray, *Confessions*, 10.

103. Account of sales, Joseph Travis, Will Book 11:342.

104. Westbrook's name appeared in St. Luke's Parish Personal Tax List, 1831, entry for Joseph Travis.

105. Account of sales, Joseph Travis, Will Book 11:341.

106. Ibid., 343.

107. Account, Joseph Travis, 1831–34, Will Book 11:274–76.

108. U.S. Census, Southampton County, 1830, p. 260.

109. All five of the eldest male slaves at the Travis farm were recorded in the age category ten to twenty-four in the 1830 census, an apparent error.

110. U.S. Census, Southampton County, 1830, p. 260; Drewry, *Southampton Insurrection*, 45. Nat Turner was included mistakenly among the males aged ten to twenty-four, instead of twenty-four to thirty-six.

111. Gray, *Confessions*, 8–9.

112. The four slaveholdings of origin were those of Benjamin Turner II (Nat Turner I), Edmund Turner Jr. (Hark), Samuel Francis Sr. (Anacka, Maria, and Lucy), and William Francis (Moses). The four slaveholdings with connections of marriage and personal history were those of Joseph W. H. Reese (Nat Turner I and Hark through their wives), Elizabeth Turner II (Nat Turner I and Maria through personal history), Nathaniel Francis (Anacka and Moses through personal history), and Giles Reese (Nat Turner I, Hark, Maria and her two children, and Sam, through hiring). The three eldest women also may have had marriage ties within these holdings.

113. The assets credited to Travis in the 1831 account of sales for his estate totaled about $2,147, of which $1,064.75, or 49.6 percent, was attributed to the five dower slaves; account of sales, Joseph Travis, Will Book 11:343.

114. Account, Putnam Moore, Will Book 11:80.

115. The right to emancipate slaves was set forth in *The Revised Code of the Laws of Virginia*, 2 vols. (Richmond: Thomas Ritchie, 1819), chap. 111, sec. 53.

116. Alfred (of Levi Waller) and Frank (of Solomon Parker) were both employed in their masters' blacksmith shops; Alexander P. Peete and Thomas Porter, affidavits, 22 Nov. 1831, in Levi Waller, petition 9803-A, 12 Dec. 1831, Legislative Petitions, LVA; trial of Frank Parker, County Court Minute Book, 22 Sept. 1831, p. 113.

117. Angela Lakwete, *Inventing the Cotton Gin: Machine and Myth in Antebellum America* (Baltimore: Johns Hopkins University Press, 2003), 81–82, 97–121.

118. Inventory, Joseph Travis, Will Book 11:354; account of sales, Joseph Travis, Will Book 11:338–43.

119. Nat Turner's value in 1831 was placed at $375; trial of Nat Turner I, County Court Minute Book, 5 Nov. 1831, p. 123. Solomon Parker's blacksmith, Frank, was appraised at $600; trial of Frank Parker, County Court Minute Book, 22 Sept. 1831, p. 113. Levi Waller's blacksmith, Alfred, was not appraised in 1831.

120. Farm tools were listed in account of sales, Joseph Travis, Will Book 11:338.

Chapter 5. The Inner Circle

1. Thomas R. Gray, *The Confessions of Nat Turner* (Baltimore: Lucas & Deaver, 1831), 11.

2. *The Revised Code of the Laws of Virginia*, 2 vols. (Richmond: Thomas Ritchie, 1819), chap. 123, sec. 23; chap. 143; *Code of Virginia* (Richmond: William F. Ritchie, 1849), chap. 200, sec. 4.

3. Gray, *Confessions*, 11, 17. The first list, in parentheses, may indicate an insertion by Gray. The second list is in Turner's voice, without parentheses.

4. The death of Nelson Edwards is confirmed in Joseph Joiner, certificate, 21 Nov. 1831, in Peter Edwards, petition 9804-A, 12 Dec. 1831, Legislative Petitions, LVA.

5. *Norfolk American Beacon*, 29 Aug. 1831. Henry's title suggests he could read and count money.

6. *Richmond Enquirer*, 2 Sept. 1831; *Philadelphia National Gazette*, 31 Aug. 1831; *Raleigh Star*, 8 Sept. 1831; *Richmond Compiler*, 3 Sept. 1831, in *Richmond Enquirer*, 6 Sept. 1831.

7. William S. Drewry, *The Southampton Insurrection* (1900; repr., Murfreesboro, NC: Johnson, 1968), 33, 73.

8. St. Luke's Parish Personal Property Tax List, 1831, entries for Richard and Thomas Porter, LVA. One other slaveholder bearing the surname *Porter* lived in St. Luke's Parish ten miles northwest of the Porter farm; St. Luke's Parish Land Book, 1831, entry for Eliza Prince (Mrs. Porter), LVA; and St. Luke's Parish Personal Tax List, 1831, entry for Elizabeth Porter.

9. Three Porter slaves were shot to death at about the time Henry was killed: Jacob (aged eighteen), Moses (about twenty-three), and Aaron (about forty-seven). Another, Daniel (also about forty-seven), was tried, convicted, and executed; Richard Porter, petition 9803, 12 Dec. 1831, Legislative Petitions; County Court Minute Book, 31 Aug. 1831, pp. 72–73, SCC. Charges against a sixth Porter slave, Jim, were dropped; County Court Minute Book, 19 Sept. 1831, p. 105.

10. U.S. Census, Southampton County, 1830, manuscript returns, p. 256, NA; Marriage Register, p. 371, SCC; Porter genealogy (author's research file).

11. Will, Thomas Porter Sr., 30 July 1814, Will Book 8:79, SCC; inventory, Thomas Porter Sr., 9 Jan. 1816, Will Book 8:481.

12. Inventory, Henry Porter, 14 Dec. 1825, Will Book 10:24.

13. Marriage Register, p. 233; U.S. Census, Southampton County, 1820, p. 112. In his will, Barnes mentioned no slaves by name; will, Bolling H. Barnes, 4 Apr. 1823, Will Book 9:277.

14. St. Luke's Parish Personal Tax List, 1816, entry for Bolling H. Barnes. Henry Porter, the slave, had not belonged to Bolling H. Barnes's father, John Barnes, who died in 1820; inventory, John Barnes, 22 Aug. 1820, Will Book 9:114–15.

15. U.S. Census, Southampton County, 1820, p. 112. Henry and Daniel may have been the two male slaves between twenty-four and thirty-six years of age recorded in 1830 at the Porter plantation; U.S. Census, Southampton County, 1830, p. 256.

16. Bolling H. Barnes owned 654 acres in 1821; his home farm was ten miles southwest of the courthouse; St. Luke's Parish Land Book, 1821, entries for Bolling H. Barnes and Henry Porter.

17. St. Luke's Parish Land Book, 1828, entry for Elizabeth ("Eliza") Barnes.

18. Nelson Edwards often has been confused with Nelson Williams, who was not one of the early insurgents. Both Nelsons are correctly identified in Thomas C. Parramore, *Southampton County, Virginia* (Charlottesville: University of Virginia Press, 1978), 78, 91, 247n42.

19. Joseph Joiner, certificate, in Edwards, petition 9804-A, Legislative Petitions.

20. Edwards, Petition 9804-A, Legislative Petitions. Edwards's date of birth appeared on his tombstone, near the site of his 1831 residence. He was listed as fifty-nine years old in U.S. Census, Southampton County, 1850, p. 254.

21. St. Luke's Parish Land Book, 1811, and St. Luke's Parish Personal Tax Lists, 1811, 1812, entries for James Edwards.

22. St. Luke's Parish Land Books, 1812–17, and St. Luke's Parish Personal Tax Lists, 1812–17, entries for Peter Edwards.

23. Marriage Register, p. 258; St. Luke's Parish Personal Tax List, 1815, entry for estate of William Bittle. Bittle left no record of the names of his slaves; will, William Bittle, 31 Dec. 1814, Will Book 7:441.

24. U.S. Census, Southampton County, 1820, p. 117.

25. Will, Mary Pope, June 1820, Will Book 9:69.

26. The court placed Sam's value at $400; County Court Minute Book, 3 Sept. 1831, pp. 85–86. The *Richmond Enquirer*, quoting Gen. Richard Eppes, identified Sam as the slave of "Mr. Francis" on 2 Sept. 1831; Gray provided the master's full name in the *Confessions*, p. 22.

27. U.S. Census, Southampton County, 1830, p. 259. Francis had no slaves older than thirty-six, and those younger than twenty-four can be identified as other individuals.

28. Trial of Sam Francis, County Court Minute Book, 3 Sept. 1831, p. 86.

29. Trial of Hark Moore, County Court Minute Book, 3 Sept. 1831, pp. 86–87.

30. The estimate of Hark's age rests primarily on his description in inventory, Edmund Turner Jr., 13 Nov. 1821, Will Book 9:176.

31. *Richmond Compiler*, 29 Aug. 1831, in "The Banditti," *Richmond Enquirer*, 30 Aug. 1831.

32. Theodore Trezvant, letter, 5 Sept. 1831, *Raleigh Register*, 15 Sept. 1831; trial of Hark Moore, County Court Minute Book, 3 Sept. 1831, p. 86.

33. Inventory, Edmund Turner Jr., Will Book 9:176.

34. *Norfolk American Beacon*, 29 Aug. 1831; W. J. Worth, quoted in Drewry, *Southampton Insurrection*, 35n1.

35. St. Luke's Parish Land Book, 1821, entries for Samuel G. Turner and estate of Edmund Turner Jr.; deed, John T. and Mary F. Vaughan to Nathaniel Francis, 20 Mar. 1826, Deed Book 20:7, SCC; deed, Robert T. and Charlotte Musgrave to John Sykes, 25 Mar. 1834, Deed Book 23:200.

36. Inventory, Edmund Turner Jr., Will Book 9:176; chancery report, estate of Edmund Turner Jr., County Court Order Book, 17 June 1822, p. 76, SCC. A man named Nat (or Nathaniel) in Edmund Turner's holding joined the rising in progress and thus became the second insurgent of that name (Nat Turner II). He too was brought to trial and hanged.

37. The supposition that Jarrell Turner hired or acquired Hark rests in part on a note by Meriwether Brodnax, the commonwealth's attorney, identifying Sarah (Turner) Newsom as "the sister of his [Hark's] Master." (Brodnax should have said *former* master.) [Meriwether B. Brodnax], prosecutor's notes, *Commonwealth v. Daniel Porter and others*, County Court Judgments, 1831, LVA.

38. Will, Jarrell Turner, 1 Jan. 1823, Will Book 9:198; County Court Minute Book, 20 Jan. 1823, p. 297. The appraisal apparently was not recorded.

39. U.S. Census, Southampton County, 1830.

40. County Court Minute Book, 18 June 1827, p. 166.

41. Marriage Register, p. 679; Travis genealogy (author's research file); account of sale, Joseph Travis, Will Book 11:343.

42. Deed, John Thomas to John W. Reese, 19 Dec. 1827, Deed Book 20:329; deed, John W. Reese to Aubin Middleton and Nathaniel Francis, 22 Jan. 1829, Deed Book 21:78–79.

43. George H. Gray, plat, Travis farm, 1830, *Moore v. Travis*, Southampton County Chancery Causes, LVA.

44. Land records locate the Reese plantation west-southwest of the Moore-Travis farm, not southeast as Drewry indicated in *Southampton Insurrection* (map, frontispiece). The location is significant evidence concerning the route and intentions of the insurgents. The plantation's bounds are given in George H. Gray, survey, land of Benjamin Blunt, 13 Oct. 1826, Processioners' Plat Book, 1826–36, pp. 20–21, SCC; deed, Benjamin Peete and Ann Peete to Benjamin Blunt Jr., 12 Dec. 1817, Deed Book 16:55; deed, Thomas to Reese, Deed Book 20:329. The upper (or eastern) half of the farm lay immediately west of land that had belonged to Thomas Moore and Salathiel Francis; deed, John W. Reese to Nathaniel Francis, 5 Feb. 1831, Deed Book 21:495. The Reese house was situated in the lower (or western) half of the farm; deed, John W. Reese to Henry Moore, 5 Feb. 1831, Deed Book 21:495; St. Luke's Parish Land Book, 1831, entries for Salathiel Francis, Anthony Harris, James Harris, Thomas James, James Jackson, John W. Reese, and Thomas Moore.

45. Deed, Giles Reese to Edward Reese, 1 Sept. 1826, Deed Book 20:116; this deed documents Giles Reese's rental of the Edmund Turner farm from 1825 through 1829. Reese had no permanent listing in the St. Luke's land books between 1822 and 1831, though in 1831 he had a temporary listing for a transaction involving Nottoway Indian lands; St. Luke's Parish Land Book, 1831, entry for Giles Reese.

46. Inventory, Joseph Reese Sr., 20 Nov. 1826, Will Book 10:180.

47. Deed, John W. Reese to Jesse Drewry and John C. Turner, 5 Feb. 1831, Deed Book 21:474–75. Jinny's name did not appear in later Reese documents. Harriet was still described as a girl in 1830; deed, John W. Reese to Aubin Middleton and Drewry Bittle, 19 Apr. 1830, Deed Book 21:316.

48. Cherry (slave), testimony, trial of Ben Blunt, County Court Minute Book, 21 Nov. 1831, p. 130.

49. Deed, Thomas to John W. Reese, Deed Book 20:329–30.

50. Deed, John W. Reese to Middleton and Francis, Deed Book 21:78–79.

51. Herbert E. Sloan uses the term *network of debt and credit* in describing the "tens of thousands of such transactions" knitting Virginia society together between

1780 and 1830; Herbert E. Sloan, *Principle and Interest: Thomas Jefferson and the Problem of Debt* (New York: Oxford University Press, 1995; repr., Charlottesville: University of Virginia Press, 2001), 29.

52. Reese still owed the full amount of the bonds in January 1829; deed, John W. Reese to Middleton and Francis, Deed Book 21:78–79.

53. Deed, John W. Reese to Middleton and Bittle, 19 Apr. 1830, Deed Book 21:316.

54. Ibid.; deed, John W. Reese to Drewry and Turner, Deed Book 21:474–75; deed, John W. Reese and Piety Reese to Henry Moore, 15 Mar. 1831, Deed Book 21:539–40.

55. Deed, John W. Reese to Drewry, Deed Book 21:474–75.

56. Ibid.

57. No formal account of Reese's finances in 1831 exists, but deeds he signed after 1827 suggest that his liabilities exceeded his assets (other than slaves). His total debt, assuming he had paid two of the plantation bonds, was at least $2,500. His assets other than slaves amounted to about $2,300 (land, $1,750, and his share of his father's personal property other than slaves, about $550). His debts made it unlikely that he could avoid offering slaves as collateral. In 1831 he held six slaves worth an average of $200 each, based on their values in his father's 1826 inventory.

58. On a lesser scale, Reese's difficulties with debt typified those of the Virginia gentry in the early nineteenth century, the most prominent slaveholding debtor being Jefferson; Sloan, *Principle and Interest*, 29–34, 218–23. Critics suspect that Jefferson and slaveholders like Reese used debt as an excuse for not emancipating their slaves; Henry Wiencek, *Master of the Mountain: Thomas Jefferson and His Slaves* (New York: Farrar, Straus & Giroux, 2012), 4–9, 245–51.

59. Deed, John W. Reese to Francis, Deed Book 21:495.

60. Deed, John W. Reese to Moore, Deed Book 21:495.

61. Deed, John W. Reese and Piety Reese to Moore, Deed Book 21:539–40.

62. Between 1824 and 1827 Giles Reese negotiated at least four loans for which he offered slaves as collateral. The collateral for his first loan in 1824 included his men Sam, Will, Ben, Fed, and Lewis. He offered Fed and Lewis again to cover later debts that turned sour; he lost both men in a debtor's sale in 1827. Deed, Giles Reese to Jesse Holt and Edwin B. Claud, 29 Nov. 1824, Deed Book 19:358; deed, Giles Reese to James Rochelle and Robert Goodwin, 26 July 1826, Deed Book 20:41–42; deed, Giles Reese to Alexander P. Peete, 22 Aug. 1826, Deed Book 20:64; deed, Giles Reese and others to Robert Goodwin, 21 May 1827, Deed Book 20:242.

63. Michael L. Nicholls, *Whispers of Rebellion: Narrating Gabriel's Conspiracy* (Charlottesville: University of Virginia Press, 2012), 23–41.

64. [Thomas R. Gray], letter, 17 Sept. 1831, *Richmond Constitutional Whig*, 26 Sept. 1831, in *Norfolk American Beacon*, 30 Sept. 1831.

65. Three witnesses testified in county court that they had heard rumors about Turner's plan before Saturday, 20 August: Caswell Worrell, testimony, trial of Nelson Williams, County Court Minute Book, 3 Sept. 1831, p. 87; Henry Edwards, testimony, trials of Hardy Edwards and Isham Edwards, County Court Minute Book, 7 Sept. 1831, pp. 96–99; and Beck Parker, testimony, trials of Jim Champion and Frank Parker, County Court Minute Book, 22 Sept. 1831, pp. 110–13. None of the witnesses informed authorities before the uprising.

66. *Richmond Enquirer*, 2 Sept. 1831; [Gray], letter, *Richmond Whig*, 26 Sept. 1831, in *Norfolk American Beacon*, 30 Sept. 1831.

67. [Gray], letter, *Richmond Whig*, 26 Sept. 1831, in *Norfolk American Beacon*, 30 Sept. 1831.

68. Gray, *Confessions*, 11.

69. These obstacles were addressed in [Gray], letter, *Richmond Whig*, 26 Sept. 1831, in *Norfolk American Beacon*, 30 Sept. 1831.

70. Gray, *Confessions*, 11.

71. *Norfolk American Beacon*, 23 Aug. 1832; *Richmond Enquirer*, 23 Aug. 1831; Norfolk *Herald*, 31 Aug. 1831.

72. Gray, *Confessions*, 11.

73. Ibid., 12.

74. Three accounts alluded to weather conditions on 21–22 August. At the Vaughn house, Dilsy recalled that her mistress "discerned a dust" from the porch; John Hampden Pleasants, "Southampton Affair," *Richmond Whig*, 3 Sept. 1831, in *Norfolk American Beacon*, 6 Sept. 1831. At the Waller farm, a dying infant was "removed from the sun and placed under a tree"; Drewry, *Southampton Insurrection*, 64n1. And rumors reached Richmond on 23 August that a shower of rain had drenched the militia at Parker's field; *Philadelphia National Enquirer*, 27 Aug. 1831. No eyewitness mentioned rain, but local conditions may have produced an isolated shower.

75. Gray, *Confessions*, 11; [Gray], letter, *Richmond Whig*, 26 Sept. 1831, in *Norfolk American Beacon*, 30 Sept. 1831.

76. Gray, *Confessions*, 11–12.

77. Inventory, Samuel Francis Sr., 27 May 1815, Will Book 8:379.

78. Will, Samuel Francis Sr., 10 Feb. 1815, Will Book 7:447. Nathaniel Francis replaced his mother as taxpayer for the household in 1828; St. Luke's Parish Personal Tax List, 1828, entry for Nathaniel Francis.

79. Nat Turner I would surrender at the Francis farm in "a place where a number of pines had been cut down"; *Richmond Enquirer*, 8 Nov. 1831.

80. Trial of Jack Reese, County Court Minute Book, 3 Sept. 1831, p. 90. Moses Moore's testimony provided the only documentary evidence for this slave marriage.

81. Gray, *Confessions*, 12.

82. Inventory, Joseph Reese Sr., Will Book 10:180. Jack was described as a man slave in 1831; trial of Jack Reese, County Court Minute Book, 3 Sept. 1831, p. 89.

83. The court identified Jack as the property of William Reese's estate, correcting an earlier error; County Court Minute Book, 5 Sept. 1831, 21 Nov. 1831, pp. 91, 127.

84. Trial of Jack Reese, County Court Minute Book, 5 Sept. 1831, p. 91.

85. Gray, *Confessions*, 12.

86. According to the 1830 census, these were the five holdings: Nathaniel Francis, fifteen slaves; Joseph Travis, seventeen; John W. Reese, twenty-one; Peter Edwards, twenty-nine; and Richard Porter, thirty. The definition of *plantation* here is the conventional one: a landholding with twenty or more slaves.

87. Nine were mounted at the Whitehead farm, and at Parker's field all of the insurgents were mounted; Gray, *Confessions*, 13–15.

88. Gray, *Confessions*, 12.

89. Ibid.

90. Thomas C. Jones, testimony, trial of Jack Reese, County Court Minute Book, 3 Sept. 1831, p. 90; County Court Minute Book, 20 June 1831, p. 46.

91. [Gray], letter, *Richmond Whig*, 26 Sept. 1831, in *Norfolk American Beacon*, 30 Sept. 1831.

92. Trial of Jack Reese, County Court Minute Book, 3 Sept. 1831, p. 90.

93. [Gray], letter, *Richmond Whig*, 26 Sept. 1831, in *Norfolk American Beacon*, 30 Sept. 1831.

94. Trial of Jack Reese, County Court Minute Book, 3 Sept. 1831, p. 90. The court recorder first attributed the objection to "the prisoner," referring to Jack, but then crossed over that attribution and replaced it with "one of the company." The dissenter clearly was Jack.

95. [Gray], letter, *Richmond Whig*, 26 Sept. 1831, in *Norfolk American Beacon*, 30 Sept. 1831.

96. Pleasants, "Southampton Affair." Pleasants probably obtained this information directly from Gray, who was Jack Reese's attorney. Gray probably was the correspondent who two weeks later reported that in papers taken from Nat Turner's wife there appeared a series of figures, including "6,000, 30,000, 80,000 &c." [Gray], letter, *Richmond Whig*, 26 Sept. 1831, in *Norfolk American Beacon*, 30 Sept. 1831. Drewry maintained in 1900 that the slave Ben Harris had attributed the same demographic assumption to the rebel leaders; Drewry, *Southampton Insurrection*, 54.

97. Gray, *Confessions*, 12. Turner also softened the meaning of "killing all" in at least one statement immediately following his arrest; see [William C. Parker], letter, 1 Nov. 1831, *Richmond Enquirer*, 8 Nov. 1831.

98. *Norfolk Herald*, 4 Nov. 1831.

99. Gray, *Confessions*, 7. Authorities in 1831 generally used the words *insurrection* and *rebellion* to describe the event in Southampton. Nat Turner did not use the word *revolution* in any direct quotations ascribed to him, but some of his remarks quoted indirectly indicate that he thought in political and revolutionary terms. Other participants and observers, black as well as white, used forms of the words *rising* and *uprising*; Thomas C. Jones (quoting Jack Reese), testimony, trial of Jack Reese, County Court Minute Book, 3 Sept. 1831, p. 90; Henry Edwards, testimony, trials of Hardy and Isham Edwards, County Court Minute Book, 7 Sept. 1831, pp. 96, 98; Levi Waller, testimony, trial of Nat Turner I, County Court Minute Book, 5 Nov. 1831, p. 122; and letter, Halifax, NC, 24 Aug. 1831, *Richmond Compiler*, 29 Aug. 1831, in "The Banditti," *Richmond Enquirer*, 30 Aug. 1831.

Chapter 6. The Zigzag Course

1. *Richmond Enquirer*, 2 Sept. 1831; [Thomas R. Gray], letter, 17 Sept. 1831, *Richmond Constitutional Whig*, 26 Sept. 1831, in *Norfolk American Beacon*, 30 Sept. 1831.

2. [Gray], letter, *Richmond Whig*, 26 Sept. 1831, in *Norfolk American Beacon*, 30 Sept. 1831. Sites of targeted houses no longer standing can be located roughly through deeds, processioners' returns and maps, and parish land records; see also Gilbert Francis and Katherine K. Futrell, *Nat Turner's Insurrection, 1831* (video recording, Southampton County Historical Society Living Library, 2000), discs 2–4. The survey reports of O. Fred Cavin (1937), LVA, appear to have errors in mapping

the houses of Elizabeth Turner II and Levi Waller. Abandoned sites await archaeological investigation like that undertaken for the Rebecca Vaughan house.

3. Authorities had determined the order of attacks, if not the significance of the order, by 5 Sept. 1931; Theodore Trezvant, 5 Sept. 1831, letter, *Raleigh Register*, 15 Sept. 1831.

4. Thomas R. Gray, *The Confessions of Nat Turner* (Baltimore: Lucas & Deaver, 1831), 12.

5. [Gray], letter, *Richmond Whig*, 26 Sept. 1831, in *Norfolk American Beacon*, 30 Sept. 1831.

6. A similar interpretation of the motives of Turner's followers (if not Turner) appears in Patrick H. Breen, "A Prophet in His Own Land: Support for Nat Turner and His Rebellion within Southampton's Black Community," in *Nat Turner: A Slave Rebellion in History and Memory*, ed. Kenneth S. Greenberg (New York: Oxford University Press, 2003), 116–18; a differing view of neighborhood connections appears in Anthony E. Kaye, "Neighborhoods and Nat Turner: The Making of a Slave Rebel and the Unmaking of a Slave Rebellion," *Journal of the Early Republic* 27 (2007): 705–20.

7. U.S. Census, Southampton County, 1830, manuscript returns, p. 260, NA; St. Luke's Parish Personal Property Tax List, 1831, entry for Joseph Travis, LVA; account of sales, Joseph Travis, 22 Dec. 1831, Will Book 11:341, 343, SCC; inventory, Joseph Travis, 22 Dec. 1831, Will Book 11:354; account, Putnam Moore, 1831–32, Will Book 11:80. Nat Turner's age is given in Gray, *Confessions*, 7; Hark Moore's status as an adult appears in County Court Minute Book, 3 Sept. 1831, p. 86, SCC; Moses Moore's age appear's in Auditor of Public Accounts, List of slaves and Free Persons of color received into the Penitentiary, in Records, Condemned Blacks Executed or Transported, 1783–1864, LVA. Tax and estate records indicate that the 1830 census did not record accurately the ages of slaves at the Travis farm.

8. The distance is given in Gray, *Confessions*, 12.

9. U.S. Census, Southampton County, 1830, p. 260; St. Luke's Parish Personal Tax List, 1831, entry for Salathiel Francis.

10. Inventory, Salathiel Francis, 16 Dec. 1831, Will Book 11:65; U.S. Census, Southampton County, 1830, p. 260. In October, Red Nelson brought news to Jerusalem about his sighting of Nat Turner at the Francis farm; *Richmond Enquirer*, 25 Oct. 1831.

11. Deed, John W. Reese to Henry Moore, 5 Feb. 1831, Deed Book 21:495, SCC.

12. Reese genealogy (author's research file); U.S. Census, Southampton County, 1830, p. 257; Gray, *Confessions*, 13.

13. St. Luke's Parish Personal Tax List, 1831, entries for John W. Reese, Piety Reese, and William H. Reese; U.S. Census, Southampton County, 1830, p. 257.

14. Cherry may have been the woman who testified about events of 23 August at the Francis house; trial of Ben Blunt; County Court Minute Book, 21 Nov. 1831, p. 130.

15. Samuel Warner, *Authentic and Impartial Narrative of the Tragical Scene Which Was Witnessed in Southampton County* (New York: Warner & West, 1831), 31.

16. U.S. Census, Southampton County, 1830, p. 260; deed, James Powell Jr. and Sally Powell to Elizabeth Harris, 24 Aug. 1826, Deed Book 20:84; St. Luke's Parish Personal Tax Lists, 1831, 1832, entries for Elizabeth Harris.

17. According to Drewry, Joe Harris, a slave belonging to Mrs. Harris, agreed to join the insurgents only after the men agreed to spare the Harris family. A granddaughter of Elizabeth Harris, Bettie (Powell) Barnes, was Drewry's source; William S. Drewry, *The Southampton Insurrection* (1900; repr., Murfreesboro, NC: Johnson, 1968), 38–39n1.

18. Deed, Emery Evans to Elizabeth Harris, 8 Nov. 1831, Deed Book 22:110. In 1832 Evans was listed as a free black man living at Mrs. Harris's farm; St. Luke's Parish Personal Tax List, 1832, entry for Elizabeth Harris.

19. Jarrell Turner's house and land belonged to his estate in 1831; his land bordered properties of Salathiel Francis and Elizabeth Harris, according to Processioners' Report, 1830, Precinct 21, p. 3, LVA. He was a distant cousin of Samuel G. Turner.

20. Deed, James B. Newsom to Sally Turner, Apr. 1827, Deed Book 20:232.

21. St. Luke's Parish Land Book, 1831, entries for Elizabeth ("Eliza") Turner II and estate of Samuel G. Turner, LVA; St. Luke's Parish Personal Tax List, 1831, entries for Hartwell Peebles ("Peeples") and Elizabeth Turner II; Gray, *Confessions*, 13; Drewry, *Southampton Insurrection*, 39, 41.

22. St. Luke's Parish Personal Tax Lists, 1821–23, entries for Samuel Turner and his estate, and Elizabeth Turner II.

23. By 1830 the Turner holdings included no slaves of advanced age; U.S. Census, Southampton County, 1830, p. 260.

24. St. Luke's Parish Personal Tax Lists, 1824–31, entries for Elizabeth Turner II; U.S. Census, Southampton County, 1830, p. 260.

25. Will, Samuel G. Turner, 9 Jan. 1822, Will Book 9:134; deed, Samuel G. Turner to Rebecca Jane Williamson, 18 Jan. 1822, Deed Book 18:413; chancery report, estate of Joseph Reese Sr., 12 Dec. 1816, County Court Order Book, 17 Mar. 1817, pp. 99–100, SCC.

26. U.S. Census, Southampton County, 1830, p. 260. The number of taxable slaves in the holding of Elizabeth Turner II stood at eight in both 1830 and 1831, indicating that all of her slaves of middle age survived in 1831; St. Luke's Parish Personal Tax Lists, 1830, 1831, entries for Elizabeth Turner II.

27. Reese genealogy (author's research file).

28. Porter genealogy (author's research file); U.S. Census, Southampton County, 1850, p. 252a.

29. St. Luke's Parish Land Book, 1813, entry for Thomas Porter.

30. Will, Thomas Porter, 30 July 1800, Will Book 8:79.

31. St. Luke's Parish Personal Tax Lists, 1818, 1819, entries for Joseph M. Faircloth.

32. County Court Minute Book, 21 Oct. 1822, p. 281.

33. St. Luke's Parish Personal Tax Lists, 1824, 1827, entries for Richard Porter.

34. Marriage Register, p. 371, SCC; County Court Order Book, 16 Dec. 1816, p. 67.

35. St. Luke's Parish Land Book, 1828, entries for Elizabeth Barnes, Thomas Porter, and Jesse Porter.

36. St. Luke's Parish Personal Tax Lists, 1828, 1830, entries for Richard Porter; U.S. Census, Southampton County, 1830, p. 256.

37. Porter genealogy (author's research file).
38. Marriage Register, p. 286.
39. Marriage Register, p. 329.
40. St. Luke's Parish Land Book, 1828, entries for Elizabeth ("Eliza") Barnes.
41. Deed, John W. Reese to Aubin Middleton and Drewry Bittle, 19 Apr. 1830, Deed Book 21:316; deed, John W. Reese to Jesse Drewry and John C. Turner, 5 Feb. 1831, Deed Book 21:474–75.
42. Deeds, John W. Reese to Nathaniel Francis; deed, John W. Reese to Henry Moore, Deed Book 21:495.
43. Francis genealogy (author's research file); St. Luke's Parish Land Book, 1831, entries for Nathaniel Francis and Sarah ("Sally") Francis.
44. County Court Minute Book, 21 Sept. 1829, p. 288.
45. F. N. Boney, "Nathaniel Francis, Representative Antebellum Southerner," *Proceedings of the American Philosophical Society* 118 (1974): 450n10.
46. U.S. Census, Southampton County, 1810, p. 259.
47. St. Luke's Parish Personal Tax Lists, 1814–20, entries for Samuel Francis Sr. and Sarah ("Sally") Francis.
48. St. Luke's Parish Personal Tax Lists, 1827–31, entries for Sarah ("Sally") Francis and Nathaniel Francis; U.S. Census, Southampton County, 1820, p. 117; 1830, p. 259.
49. Deed, John W. Reese to Nathaniel Francis and Aubin Middleton, 22 Jan. 1829, Deed Book 21:78–79.
50. Deed, Augustus F. Doyel to Howell Harris and Nathaniel Francis, 5 Dec. 1829, Deed Book 21:236.
51. Deed, Drewry Bittle to Nathaniel Francis and Aubin Middleton, 20 Aug. 1830, Deed Book 21:373–74.
52. St. Luke's Parish Personal Tax List, 1831, entry for Peter Edwards.
53. U.S. Census, Southampton County, 1830, p. 259.
54. Inscription, tombstone of Peter Edwards at his 1831 residence.
55. St. Luke's Parish Land Book, 1810, and St. Luke's Parish Personal Tax List, 1810, entries for James Edwards and Peter Edwards.
56. St. Luke's Parish Land Book, 1813, entry for Peter Edwards; there is no record of this transfer in the deed book. St. Luke's Parish Personal Tax List, 1813, entries for James Edwards and Peter Edwards.
57. St. Luke's Parish Land Book, 1816, and St. Luke's Parish Personal Tax List, 1816, entries for Peter Edwards.
58. In 1810 Bittle was listed with twenty-one slaves of all ages. In 1815 he held fourteen slaves over the age of twelve. U.S. Census, Southampton County, 1810, p. 866; St. Luke's Parish Personal Tax List, 1815, entry for estate of William Bittle.
59. St. Luke's Parish Personal Tax List, 1818, entry for Peter Edwards.
60. Deed, Samuel Drewry and Mary Ann Drewry to Peter Edwards, 15 Dec. 1827, Deed Book 20:325–26.
61. St. Luke's Parish Land Book, 1831, and St. Luke's Parish Personal Tax List, 1831, entries for Peter Edwards. Edwards ranked 28th among 272 resident white adults who paid taxes on both land and personal property in 1831. In the 1830 census Edwards was listed with twenty-nine slaves. Of the 272 core taxpayers in 1831,

212 (78 percent) paid tax on slaves and 60 (22 percent) did not. Figures exclude James Rochelle Sr., then a resident of Nottoway Parish.

62. Joseph Joiner, certificate, in Peter Edwards, petition 9804-A, 12 Dec. 1831, Legislative Petitions, LVA; trial of Sam Edwards, County Court Minute Book, 17 Oct. 1831, p. 118. At one point Edwards apparently was held in some regard by at least one free black man. In 1819 and 1820, Bill Artis, probably the same man ("Billy") who styled himself an insurgent in 1831, made his home at the Edwards farm; St. Luke's Parish Personal Tax Lists, 1819, 1820, entries for Peter Edwards.

63. U.S. Census, Southampton County, 1830, pp. 245, 257, 264.

64. Will, Nathan Bryant, 23 Apr. 1815, Will Book 9:14.

65. Marriage Register, p. 220; St. Luke's Parish Personal Tax List, 1812, entry for Nathan Bryant and John Newton.

66. In 1831 Henry Bryant was renting land belonging to Turner Newsom (nephew of Benjamin Turner II), an arrangement probably in effect the previous year; St. Luke's Parish Land Book, 1831, entry for Turner Newsom.

67. Marriage Register, p. 406; Balmer genealogy (author's research file).

68. Deed, James B. Newsom to Sally Turner, Deed Book 20:232.

69. Will, Jarrell Turner, 1 Jan. 1823, Will Book 9:198; will, Mildred Balmer, 26 July 1827, Will Book 10:335.

70. Deed, John W. Reese to Drewry and Turner, Deed Book 21:474.

71. St. Luke's Parish Land Book, 1831, entry for Turner Newsom.

72. St. Luke's Parish Personal Tax List, 1830, entry for Henry Bryant.

73. U.S. Census, Southampton County, 1830, p. 257.

74. St. Luke's Parish Personal Tax List, 1831, entries for Henry Bryant and Nat Day.

75. Deed, William H. Gee to Henry Bryant, 1 Mar. 1831, Deed Book 21:522.

76. St. Luke's Parish Land Book, 1832, entry for estate of Henry Bryant.

77. Drewry, *Southampton Insurrection*, 42.

78. Inventory, Henry Bryant, 6 Oct. 1831, Will Book 10:409; account, Sarah ("Sally") Newsom, 1831–35, Will Book 11:366–67. Bryant's signature appears on the will of Nathaniel Newsom, 29 Mar. 1830, Will Book 10:236. Mildred Balmer made her mark; will, Mildred Balmer, Will Book 10:355.

79. St. Luke's Parish Personal Tax List, 1831, entry for Nathaniel Francis and A. Doyle (probably Alfred Doyel); the latter may have been the Francis overseer killed in the uprising. Drewry identified the overseer as Henry Doyle; Drewry, *Southampton Insurrection*, 47.

80. County Court Minute Book, 17 Mar. 1828, p. 203; Marriage Register, p. 384. The groom's name was given as "Augustus F. Doyle" in the marriage register. His name appears as "Trajan Doyle" in James Rochelle, summons to Amos Stephenson, 23 July 1831, *Underwood v. Whitehead*, Southampton County Chancery Causes, LVA.

81. St. Luke's Parish Land Book, 1821, entry for John Underwood; U.S. Census, Southampton County, 1820, p. 127; will, John Underwood, 1 June 1821, with codicil, 6 Feb. 1823, Will Book 9:235–36.

82. Marriage Register, p. 115; St. Luke's Parish Personal Tax List, 1809, entry for Robert Bittle; 1810, entry for Margaret ("Peggy") Bittle; inventory, estate of Robert

Bittle, 12 Jan. 1810, Will Book 7:190–91; will, Margaret ("Peggy") Simmons, 19 Jan. 1825, Will Book 9:251–52.

83. Marriage Register, p. 207; account, Cyer Simmons, 1815–17, Will Book 8:340–42.

84. Will, Margaret ("Peggy") Simmons, Will Book 9:250; St. Luke's Parish Personal Tax List, 1815, entry for Cyer ("Sire") Simmons.

85. U.S. Census, Southampton County, 1820, p. 125a; deed, Henry Bittle to Aubin Middleton, 15 June 1825, Deed Book 19:418–19.

86. Will, John Underwood, Will Book 9:235–36; will, Margaret ("Peggy") Simmons, Will Book 9:251–52.

87. Doyel owned no land in 1831. John C. Turner continued to own his patrimonial land near Cabin Pond but apparently had moved his residence to the farm he acquired from his deceased mother-in-law, Sally Knox, near Monroe; St. Luke's Parish Land Book, 1831, entries for John C. Turner.

88. Drewry located Doyel's house one mile west of the Whitehead house; Drewry, *Southampton Insurrection*, 44. Hubbard Whitehead, a slave of Catherine Whitehead, testified that John C. Turner's slave Joe lived "about a mile" from the Whitehead plantation; Hubbard Whitehead, testimony, trial of Joe Turner, County Court Minute Book, 19 Sept. 1831, p. 102. Joe must have been living at his master's old homestead. A photograph of a house identified as the home of Trajan Doyel (or Doyle) appears in "A Guide to a Speech and Photographs Relating to Nat Turner's Insurrection" (2007), Special Collections Department, UVA; and ead.lib.virginia.edu.

89. Deed, Doyel to Harris and Francis, Deed Book 21:236.

90. U.S. Census, Southampton County, 1830, p. 264.

91. St. Luke's Parish Personal Tax List, 1831, entry for Augustus F. Doyel ("Doyle").

92. Drewry, *Southampton Insurrection*, 45.

93. Account, Augustus F. Doyel ("Doyle"), 21 July 1834, Will Book 11:401.

94. U.S. Census, Southampton County, 1830, p. 245. Drewry said the distance between the Doyel and Harris houses was "a few hundred yards." Drewry also reported that the land on which the houses stood was sometimes called "the J.C. Turner place." Drewry, *Southampton Insurrection*, 44, 45n1.

95. St. Luke's Parish Personal Tax Lists, 1829–31, entries for Howell Harris and Edmund Stephenson.

96. U.S. Census, Southampton County, 1830, p. 245.

97. Harris was forty-five years old in 1850; U.S. Census, Southampton County, 1850, p. 248a.

98. St. Luke's Land Book, 1821, and St. Luke's Parish Personal Tax List, 1821, entries for Joel Harris.

99. Harris genealogy (author's research file).

100. Inventory, Joel Harris Sr., 12 Nov. 1821, Will Book 9:226–27.

101. County Court Minute Book, 16 Feb. 1824, p. 361; St. Luke's Parish Land Books, 1823–26, entries for Joel Harris Jr.; St. Luke's Parish Land Book, 1827, entries for Joel Harris Jr. and Lucy Harris.

102. Deed, John and Sally Foster to Lewis Harris and Howell Harris, 26 Feb. 1826, Deed Book 20:6.

103. St. Luke's Parish Personal Tax List, 1828, entry for Howell Harris.

104. Deed, George Ivey to Howell Harris, 15 Apr. 1829, Deed Book 21:119–20; deed, Doyel to Harris and Francis, Deed Book 21:236.

105. Deed, John R. Williams to Howell Harris and Joseph T. Claud, 17 May 1830, Deed Book 21:330; deed, William L. Everitt to Stephen Murdaugh, Lewis Harris, and Howell Harris, 1 June 1830, Deed Book 21:365–66; deed, Peter Pope to Joseph T. Claud and Howell Harris, 18 Oct. 1830, Deed Book 21:420.

106. Deed, James Stephenson to Howell Harris, 14 Apr. 1830, Deed Book 21:325–26; deed, James Harrison to Lewis Harris and Howell Harris, 27 Apr. 1830, Deed Book 21:228; deed, Everitt to Murdaugh, Harris, and Harris, Deed Book 21:365–66.

107. Deed, Lewis Harris to Howell Harris, 21 Jan. 1828, Deed Book 20:331.

108. Deed, Edmund Stephenson to Howell Harris, 19 June 1830, Deed Book 21:358.

109. St. Luke's Parish Land Book, 1831, and St. Luke's Parish Personal Tax List, 1831, entries for Howell Harris.

110. County Court Minute Book, 18 July 1831, p. 65.

111. *The Revised Code of the Laws of Virginia*, 2 vols. (Richmond: Thomas Ritchie, 1819), chap. 84; chap. 85, sec. 12; *Code of Virginia* (Richmond: William F. Ritchie, 1849), chap. 184, sec. 12.

112. Newit Harris was not a close relative of this Elizabeth Harris, whose property the insurgents would pass through, or of Howell Harris, the constable.

113. Whitehead genealogy (author's research file); U.S. Census, Southampton County, 1830, p. 260.

114. St. Luke's Parish Land Books, 1792–95, entries for William Whitehead I; inventory, William Whitehead I, 20 Sept. 1797, Will Book 5:34.

115. Marriage Register, p. 81.

116. Whitehead genealogy (author's file); will, John Whitehead, 22 May 1814, Will Book 7:438–39. Years of birth for four of the children (Harriet, Edwin, Joseph, and John) can be determined by their entries in the 1850 census. Those data are consistent with the order of the eleven names as cited in John Whitehead's will, which apparently followed birth order. Estimates for the years of birth of the other seven children rest on the assumption that Catherine Whitehead did not give birth to twins and that a two-year interval between births was her norm.

117. George W. Powell, letter, 27 Aug. 1831, *Christian Advocate and Journal and Zion's Herald*, 9 Sept. 1831.

118. The common bounds of the Whitehead and Turner plantations are described in Processioners' Report, 1830, Precinct 11.

119. Deed, Benjamin Turner II and Elizabeth Turner I to Nathan Turner, 9 Oct. 1810, Deed Book 12:244–48.

120. County Court Minute Book, 29 Aug. 1813, p. 5; 15 Mar. 1830, p. 315.

121. Powell, letter, *Christian Advocate*, 9 Sept. 1831.

122. St. Luke's Parish Land Book, 1796, and St. Luke's Parish Personal Tax List, 1796, entries for John Whitehead.

123. St. Luke's Parish Land Book, 1815, entry for John Whitehead. Whitehead's 740 acres had an appraised value of $1,151.30 for tax purposes in 1815. In 1808, when

he made his most recent purchase, he paid $7 an acre for 100.6 acres; deed, Richard Blunt et al. to John Whitehead, 21 Dec. 1808, Deed Book 12:40–41.

124. Inventory, John Whitehead, 5 Apr. 1815, Will Book 8:14–15.

125. Will, John Whitehead, Will Book 7:438.

126. St. Luke's Parish Land Books, 1816–21, entries for Catherine Whitehead.

127. St. Luke's Parish Personal Tax List, 1815, entry for John Whitehead; St. Luke's Parish Personal Tax List, 1831, entry for Catherine Whitehead.

128. U.S. Census, Southampton County, 1810, p. 159; 1830, p. 260.

129. U.S. Census, Southampton County, 1830, p. 260.

130. Free Negro Register, vol. 1, 1794–1832, entries 75, 76, 77, 124, 376, and 468, LVA. At various times between 1800 and 1815, all six were listed in the register of free blacks; the men's names appeared in personal property tax lists for St. Luke's during that period.

131. Inventory, Arthur Whitehead, 26 Dec. 1799, Will Book 5:198–99.

132. Will, William Whitehead II, 29 Aug. 1813 (proved 15 Jan. 1827), Will Book 10:6. William Whitehead II was listed in the 1810 census with three children under the age of ten and eight slaves of all ages; U.S. Census, Southampton County, 1810, p. 155. His estate held six slaves; inventory, William Whitehead II, 23 Feb. 1814, Will Book 7:363.

133. St. Luke's Parish Land Book, 1831, entry for Catherine Whitehead.

134. In 1815 tax commissioners found just two pianofortes in St. Luke's Parish and none in Nottoway Parish; St. Luke's Parish Personal Tax List, 1815, data summary, printed form near the end of the list.

135. Inventory, Catherine Whitehead, 3 Jan. 1832, Will Book 11:40–41.

136. Whitehead genealogy (author's research file).

137. Rebecca Sweat (also spelled "Sweatt" and "Swett") was born in 1802; Free Negro Register, vol. 1, entry 1,976; Sweat biography (author's research file). In 1833 she was living with three children on Samuel G. Turner's land, which bordered the Whitehead plantation. The relationship between Sweat and Joseph Whitehead certainly had begun by November 1843, when Harriet Whitehead complained about it to a neighbor. In 1850 Rebecca Sweat and Joseph Whitehead were sharing a household; U.S. Census, Southampton County, 1850, p. 254a. State law forbade marriage between the races; *Code of Virginia* (1849), chap. 196, sec. 8.

138. In the 1850 census, Joseph's occupation was listed as "None."

139. U.S. Census, Southampton County, 1830, p. 260.

140. St. Luke's Parish Personal Tax List, 1831, entry for Catherine Whitehead.

141. Marriage Register, p. 251.

142. County Court Minute Book, 21 Dec. 1829, p. 306; Marriage Register, p. 301; St. Luke's Parish Land Book, 1821, entry for Bailey Barnes; U.S. Census, Southampton County, 1820, p. 113; St. Luke's Parish Personal Tax List, 1820, entry for Bailey Barnes.

143. St. Luke's Parish Land Books, 1821–29, entries for Catherine Whitehead.

144. Deed, Bailey Barnes to Thomas E. Holliday, 20 June 1825, Deed Book 19:438.

145. St. Luke's Parish Personal Tax Lists, 1821–29, entries for William H. Whitehead.

146. County Court Minute Book, 21 Dec. 1829, p. 306.

147. Deed, Mary Whitehead to Jarrett W. Judkins and William Judkins, 15 Jan. 1830, Deed Book 21:323–24.

148. County Court Minute Book, 15 Feb. 1830, p. 313.

149. The census marshal recorded the presence of one white male under five years of age (who must have been William Augustus) and three white females between the ages of twenty and thirty (one of whom probably was Mary B. Whitehead). The census began on 1 June; returns were certified on 18 Oct. 1830. U.S. Census, Southampton County, 1830, pp. 260, 290.

150. County Court Minute Book, 18 Oct. 1830, p. 357. The reference to Mary B. Whitehead's motion in the minute book index also uses the plural, "orphs."

151. County Court Minute Book, 20 Dec. 1830, p. 20.

152. William Augustus Whitehead survived the uprising, according to a reference to him (with his father's middle initial, however) in will, Harriet Whitehead, 1 June 1842 (recorded 5 May 1852), Will Book 11A:36.

153. Inventory, John Whitehead, Will Book 8:14–15; Whitehead family slaveholding (author's research file).

154. Barrow genealogy (author's research file).

155. St. Luke's Parish Land Book, 1807, and St. Luke's Parish Personal Tax List, 1807, entries for John Barrow and Henry Barrow Sr. A reference to Barrow Road appears in the will of William Williams, 1 Dec. 1782, Will Book 4:2.

156. Will, Capt. John Barrow, 22 Mar. 1806, Will Book 6:703–4.

157. Will, Henry Barrow Sr., 19 Sept. 1809, Will Book 6:703.

158. Barrow genealogy (author's research file); Marriage Register, p. 201.

159. *Goodwyn v. Harris et al.*, County Court Order Book, 21 Jan. 1822, p. 422; *Turner v. Barrow infants*, County Court Order Book, 18 Mar. 1822, pp. 10–14; *Goodwyn v. Harris and Barrow*, County Court Order Book, 15 Apr. 1822, pp. 45–46.

160. U.S. Census, Southampton County, 1830, p. 259.

161. St. Luke's Parish Land Book, 1831, and St. Luke's Parish Personal Tax List, 1831, entries for John T. Barrow; Deed Books 20 and 22 have a series of deeds in 1828 and 1830 between John T. Barrow, Henry Barrow Jr., Richard Barrow, William B. Goodwyn, and Newit Harris.

162. Vaughan genealogy (author's research file). The marriage was not recorded in the Southampton register, but it had taken place by the end of February 1828; deed, John T. Barrow and Mary Barrow to Henry Barrow Jr., 27 Feb. 1828, Deed Book 20:342.

163. St. Luke's Parish Land Book, 1828, and St. Luke's Parish Personal Tax List, 1828, entries for Henry B. Vaughan.

164. Parker took his seat as justice of the peace in 1824; County Court Minute Book, 21 June 1824, p. 10.

165. Inventory, Thomas Vaughan, 2 Jan. 1817, Will Book 8:407; Byrd Barrow, testimony, trial of Lucy Barrow, County Court Minute Book, 19 Sept. 1831, p. 103.

166. St. Luke's Parish Land Book, 1830, entry for John T. Barrow; will, Newit Harris, 17 Oct. 1833 (proved 19 Dec. 1837), Will Book 12:5.

167. Drewry, *Southampton Insurrection*, 51, 61.

168. Deed, Henry Barrow Jr. to Salathiel Francis, John Thomas Barrow, and Robert T. Musgrave, 19 Sept. 1829, Deed Book 21:202.

169. Deed, Gilbert M. Beale to William B. Whitehead, 23 Jan. 1833, Deed Book 22:273.

170. Inventory, John T. Barrow, recorded 15 Oct. 1832, Will Book 11:18–20.

171. Ibid.

172. Ibid.

173. Carlos R. Allen Jr., ed., "Notes and Documents: David Barrow's *Circular Letter* of 1798," *William and Mary Quarterly*, 3d ser., 20 (1963): 440–51.

174. St. Luke's Parish Personal Tax Lists, 1827, 1829, entries for Richard Barrow.

175. Deed, Richard Barrow to Susan, 20 Oct. 1828, Deed Book 20:474; deed, Richard Barrow to Theophilus T. Barrow, 22 Jan. 1827, Deed Book 20:150; deed, Richard Barrow to Joseph T. Claud, 24 Dec. 1827, Deed Book 20:299.

176. County Court Minute Book, 17 May 1829, p. 266.

177. Will, John T. Barrow, 8 Mar. 1829, Will Book 10:347.

178. The eight slaves included Byrd, who had no monetary value in 1831; St. Luke's Parish Land Book, 1831, and St. Luke's Parish Personal Tax List, 1831, entries for John T. Barrow; inventory, John T. Barrow, Will Book 11:18–20. With Moses (worth $400) and Lucy (worth $275) included, slaves would have accounted for 60.7 percent of Barrow's estate; County Court Minute Book, 1 Sept., 19 Sept. 1831, pp. 78, 104.

179. Marriage Register, p. 201.

180. Harris genealogy (author's research file).

181. Will, Elizabeth (Turner Barrow) Harris, 26 Mar. 1840, Will Book 12:389–90.

182. U.S. Census, Southampton County, 1830, p. 263.

183. Harris genealogy (author's research file); St. Luke's Parish Land Book, 1782, entry for Nathan Harris.

184. Will, Nathan Harris, 15 Sept. 1785, Will Book 4:147–49. Nathan Harris's land was transferred to his widow in 1786; St. Luke's Parish Land Book, alterations, 1786, p. 65.

185. St. Luke's Parish Land Book, 1810, and St. Luke's Parish Personal Tax List, 1810, entries for Newit Harris.

186. St. Luke's Parish Land Book, 1831, and St. Luke's Parish Personal Tax List, 1831, entries for Newit Harris. Thomas Ridley and his sons held seventy-nine taxable slaves in 1831, the largest holding among resident white slaveholders. In the 1830 census Ridley was listed with 145 slaves of all ages. William Allen, of Surry County, held the largest number of slaves in St. Luke's Parish and in the county: 111 taxable slaves and 179 slaves of all ages. U.S. Census, Southampton County, 1830, p. 243, entries for Thomas Ridley and John R. Kelley (overseer for Allen).

187. This list does not include deaths among near neighbors (John Whitehead in 1815; Bolling Barnes and Henry Porter in 1825) or younger masters connected to the alliances (Jarrell Turner in 1823, Thomas Moore in 1827). Years of death for all of these individuals can be found in land books, will books, and minutes of the county court.

188. Harris appears as a creditor in account, Joshua Johnson, 1829–32, Will Book 10:379.

189. Will, Henry Barrow Sr., Will Book 6:703; County Court Minute Book, 15 May, 1815, p. 218; 18 Dec. 1815, p. 307; 15 July 1816, p. 32; 19 July 1819, p. 28; 13 Oct. 1819, p. 44; 15 Oct. 1821, p. 219; 21 Oct. 1822, p. 280; 17 July 1826, p. 126; 21 May 1827, p. 161. The rankings of Ridley and Nicholson are based on their tax bills in 1821 for land and personal property.

190. County Court Minute Book, 16 June 1823, p. 318.

191. St. Luke's Parish Land Books, 1821–31, and St. Luke's Parish Personal Tax Lists, 1821–31, entries for Newit Harris; inventories, Newit Harris, Lochhead's, mansion house, and Flat Swamp plantations, 16 Dec. 1837–8 Jan. 1838, Will Book 12:228–32.

192. U.S. Census, Southampton County, 1820, p. 119; 1830, p. 263.

193. Inventory, Newit Harris, mansion house, Will Book 12:228–30.

194. St. Luke's Parish Land Book, 1831, entry for Newit Harris.

195. Inventory, Newit Harris, mansion house, Will Book 12:229; will, Elizabeth (Turner Barrow) Harris, Will Book 12:390.

196. Inventory, Newit Harris, mansion house, Will Book 12:228–30.

197. Inventories, Newit Harris, Lochhead's, mansion house, and Flat Swamp plantations, Will Book 12:228–32.

198. Trial of Tom, County Court Minute Book, 18 Sept. 1815, p. 278.

199. Gray, *Confessions*, 4; [Gray], letter, *Richmond Whig*, 26 Sept. 1831, in *Norfolk American Beacon*, 30 Sept. 1831.

200. One of the eighty-three was James Rochelle Sr., the county clerk, who paid his personal property tax in Nottoway Parish in 1831.

201. St. Luke's Parish Land Books, 1821–31; County Court Minute Book, 1821–31; Will Books 9–11. Two surviving slaveholders, acting in official roles, freed a total of five slaves by court order between 1821 and 1831; Free Negro Register, vol. 1, entry 1,601; deed, Samuel Blunt (executor) to William [Irwin], 21 June 1826, Deed Book 20:61; deeds, Thomas Ridley (sheriff) to Mingo, Esther, Mary, and Nicodemus, 19 Dec. 1826, Deed Book 20:193–95.

202. The number of emancipations recorded in wills and deeds agrees with the number recorded in the Free Negro Register for these years. Altogether, seven individuals were freed by will in this period and twelve by deed; St. Luke's Parish Will Books 9 and 10, and Deed Books 18–22, 1821–31.

203. Deed, Catherine Barrett to Sidney, Harriet, and Jonas [Cosby], 23 Apr. 1827, Deed Book 20:237.

204. Will, Catherine Barrett, 4 Nov. 1830, Will Book 10:280–81. Benjamin Blunt Sr. gave one of his forty-nine slaves, his "trusty and faithful old servant Anthony," his "liberty as a free man"; will, Benjamin Blunt Sr., 18 Dec. 1825, Will Book 9:302; inventory, 7 Apr. 1826, Will Book 10:25. The third emancipator among the decedents was Richard Barrow. The fourth, William Hill, made a tentative effort to free six slaves, but his manumissions were never executed; will, William Hill, 4 Aug. 1825, Will Book 9:285.

205. Free Negro Register, vol. 1, entries 1,829–34.

206. According to the U.S. Census in 1830, the county had a slave population of 7,756; the free black population stood at 1,745, the white population at 6,573. Tax

lists, which make it possible to determine approximately where heads of household lived, suggest that about 4,532 of those slaves (58.4 percent of the county total) lived in St. Luke's Parish and 3,224 (41.6 percent) lived in Nottoway Parish. The same sources suggest that St. Luke's had a white population of 2,911 (44.3 percent of the county total) and a free black population of 907 (52.0 percent of the county total). A check of the addition in the manuscript returns for 1830 found a discrepancy only in the total for white men (two fewer than the official result of 3,191 for the county).

207. The fifty-seven wills were recorded in Will Books 9 and 10. The total includes the will of William Hill, who failed in his effort to free six slaves. The idea that slaveholdings were assets for the support and security of survivors appeared in the following wills: Benjamin Barham, 8 May 1816, Will Book 9:169–70; Richard Williamson, 14 Oct. 1823, Will Book 9:215; Joel McGlemore, 10 Nov. 1823, Will Book 9:223; Joel Westbrook, 14 Jan. 1825, Will Book 9:259; James Wright, 4 Oct. 1825, Will Book 9:297–98; Lewis Ford, 21 Aug. 1826, Will Book 10:2; Benjamin Blunt Jr., 1 Jan. 1827, Will Book 10:19–20; David Newsom, 30 Jan. 1827, Will Book 10:35; Thomas Fitzhugh, 19 May 1827, Will Book 10:73–74; and Richard P. Clements, 16 July 1826, Will Book 10:74.

208. Michael L. Nicholls discusses the number of Gabriel's recruits in *Whispers of Rebellion: Narrating Gabriel's Conspiracy* (Charlottesville: University of Virginia Press, 2012), 40–43.

Chapter 7. Toward the Town

1. The total of eighteen targets excludes the dwelling of Caswell Worrell, whose family was part of the Jacob Williams household. It includes the houses of Augustus F. Doyel and Howell Harris, both of which the insurgents planned to attack but did not reach.

2. Waller's land is described in the following documents: deed, commissioners to Levi Waller, 2 Jan. 181[6], Deed Book 14:405–6, SCC; deed, Charles E. C. Brittle to Newit Harris, recorded 21 Mar. 1831, Deed Book 21:494; deed, Newit Johnson to Mills L. Gray, 14 Feb. 1835, Deed Book 23:362. See also Gilbert W. Francis and Katherine K. Futrell, *Nat Turner's Insurrection, 1831* (video recording, Southampton County Historical Society Living Library, 2000), disc 3; William S. Drewry, *The Southampton Insurrection* (1900; repr., Murfreesboro, NC: Johnson, 1968), 56; inventory, Levi Waller, 24 Nov. 1847, Will Book 14:133–34, SCC; account, Arthur Foster, 1810–12, Will Book 7:156; account, Robert Williams and Elizabeth Williams, 22 May 1816, Will Book 8:219; account, John Pope, 1828–32, Will Book 10:376.

3. Levi Waller, testimony, trial of Nat Turner I, County Court Minute Book, 5 Nov. 1831, p. 122, SCC. The estimate of the number of children at the Waller farm is based on Gray's list of white victims in the *Confessions*, Waller's entry in the census of 1830, and Waller genealogy (author's research file).

4. U.S. Census, Southampton County, 1830, manuscript returns, p. 263, NA; Alexander P. Peete and Thomas Porter, affidavits, 22 Nov. 1831, in Waller, petition 9803-A, 12 Dec. 1831, Legislative Petitions, LVA.

5. Waller genealogy (author's research file).

6. St. Luke's Parish Land Book, 1801, entry for Levi Waller, LVA.

7. Marriage Register, p.148, SCC.

8. Will, Arthur Waller, 18 Dec. 1800, Will Book 5:412–13. Dick may have been the man recorded as one hundred years old in the 1860 census, a slave of Waller's son Levi C. Waller.

9. Marriage Register, pp. 159, 656; St. Luke's Parish Land Book, 1804, entry for John Kindred.

10. Inventory, John Kindred, 7 July 1804, Will Book 6:517.

11. Account, Benjamin Turner II, 1811–15, Will Book 8:23–25.

12. Waller, testimony, trial of Nat Turner I, County Court Minute Book, 5 Nov. 1831, p.122.

13. St. Luke's Parish Land Books, 1821–31, entries for Levi Waller.

14. St. Luke's Parish Personal Property Tax Lists, 1807, 1821, 1831, entries for Levi Waller, LVA.

15. U.S. Census, Southampton County, 1830, p. 263.

16. St. Luke's Parish Personal Tax List, 1831, entry for Levi Waller; Waller, testimony, trial of Nat Turner I, County Court Minute Book, 5 Nov. 1831, p. 122.

17. Inventory, Levi Waller, Will Book 14:133–34. Waller's largest recorded slaveholding was eighteen in 1830.

18. Waller genealogy (author's research file). The infant is identified as a girl in Drewry, *Southampton Insurrection*, 64n1.

19. Waller genealogy (author's research file).

20. Drewry, *Southampton Insurrection*, 57.

21. Ibid.; U.S. Census, Southampton County, 1830, p. 263.

22. Family histories of William H. Nicholson, Mary Simmons, Polly Johnson, Sarah Johnson, Mills L. Gray, and Rebecca Knight (author's research files); U.S. Census, Southampton County, 1830, p. 259.

23. Jarratt W. Judkins, testimony, trial of Davy Waller, County Court Minute Book, 3 Sept. 1831, p. 89.

24. Williams genealogy (author's research file).

25. Deed, Elisha Williams and Elizabeth Williams to William Williams Jr., 22 Mar. 1821, Deed Book 18:80.

26. St. Luke's Parish Land Book, 1831, entries for Jacob Williams and Rhoda Worrell; U.S. Census, Southampton County, 1830, p. 259; Caswell Worrell, testimony, trial of Nelson Williams, County Court Minute Book, 3 Sept. 1831, p. 87.

27. In 1830, eight free black people (one man over fifty-five, six women over fifty-five, and a female child under ten) lived at the Jacob Williams farm; U.S. Census, Southampton, 1830, p. 259. Personal property tax lists do not confirm their presence.

28. Will, William Williams Sr., 1 Dec. 1782, Will Book 4:1–2; inventory, William Williams Sr., 7 Mar. 1783, Will Book 4:18.

29. U.S. Census, Southampton County, 1830, pp. 259 (Jacob Williams, William Williams Jr., and Rhoda "Rody" Worrell), 262 (Kinchen Williams).

30. St. Luke's Parish Land Book, 1782, entry for William Williams Sr.

31. Will, William Williams Sr., Will Book 4:1–2.

32. Marriage Register, pp. 360, 655, 656, 662, 702. Rhoda, Kinchen, and Elisha were married by Benjamin Barnes, minister of the Methodist Episcopal Church. Jacob's first marriage may have been in the same church.

33. St. Luke's Parish Land Books, 1810–22, and St. Luke's Parish Personal Tax Lists, 1807–22, entries for Joseph Worrell; U.S. Census, Southampton County, 1820, p. 130.

34. Deed, Kinchen Williams and Rebecca Williams to Jacob Williams, 19 Aug. 1814, Deed Book 14:230; St. Luke's Parish Land Book, 1818, entries for Jacob Williams, Sarah Williams, and Kinchen Williams; U.S. Census, Southampton County, 1820, p. 128 (Kinchen Williams the younger). Rebecca Ivy II and William Williams were married in 1829 with her father's consent; Marriage Register, p. 395. Rebecca (Ivy) Williams II was between fifteen and twenty years old in 1830. U.S. Census, Southampton, 1830, p. 259.

35. Deed, Benjamin Johnson to Elisha Williams, 22 Feb. 1817, Deed Book 15:198; St. Luke's Parish Land Books, 1829, 1830, entries for Elisha Williams and estate of Elisha Williams.

36. St. Luke's Parish Land Book, 1828, entries for Jacob Williams and estate of Sarah Williams.

37. St. Luke's Parish Land Book, 1831, entry for William Williams Jr.

38. St. Luke's Parish Land Books, 1810–31, and St. Luke's Parish Personal Tax Lists, 1810–31, entries for Kinchen Williams. In 1830 William Williams Jr. was between twenty and thirty years of age; U.S. Census, Southampton County, 1830, p. 259.

39. William Williams Jr. was listed for the first time in the St. Luke's Parish Personal Tax List of 1819, immediately below the entry for his uncle Elisha; both were credited with payments on 2 February. In the 1820 census, Elisha Williams's household included one white male under the age of ten, who probably was William Jr.

40. Deed, Elisha and Elizabeth Williams to William Williams Jr., Deed Book 18:80–81.

41. Deed, Jacob Williams to William Williams Jr., 16 Apr. 1830, Deed Book 21:310.

42. U.S. Census, Southampton County, 1830, p. 259.

43. Inventory, William Williams Jr., 31 Mar. 1832, Will Book 12:232–33.

44. Land accounted for 33.6 percent of William Williams's total tax bill in 1831, slaves for 53.6 percent.

45. Marriage Register, p. 360.

46. Will, John Pope, 8 Dec. 1827, Will Book 10:84.

47. St. Luke's Parish Land Book, 1828, and St. Luke's Parish Personal Tax List, 1828, entries for Jacob Williams.

48. St. Luke's Parish Land Book, 1829, entry for Jacob Williams.

49. Deed, Jacob and Nancy Williams to Rhoda Worrell, 17 Aug. 1829, Deed Book 21:178; U.S. Census, Southampton County, 1830, p. 259.

50. Worrell, testimony, trial of Nelson Williams, County Court Minute Book, 3 Sept. 1831, p. 87; St. Luke's Parish Personal Tax List, 1830, entry for Joseph Reese Jr. and C. Worrell.

51. Seven months after the uprising Worrell signed a marriage bond with Jane Newsom; his mother gave permission, an indication that he was not legally married in 1831; Marriage Register, p. 429.

52. U.S. Census, Southampton County, 1830, p. 259, entry for Jacob Williams. The census marshal recorded four children under age five (two boys and two girls) in the Jacob Williams household, combining the two families into one household.

53. Jacob Williams ranked 57th in acreage among 272 core taxpayers in 1831, three places above Levi Waller.

54. St. Luke's Parish Personal Tax List, 1821, entries for Jacob Williams and Sarah ("Sally") Williams; St. Luke's Parish Personal Tax List, 1831, entry for Jacob Williams.

55. U.S. Census, Southampton County, 1830, p. 259.

56. Jacob Williams was twenty years older than Nat Turner I and lived nine miles from the Travis house, a three-hour walk. He had exchanged no loans or slaves with the Turner, Francis, or Reese households; he had no entries in the estate accounts of Benjamin Turner II in 1811 or of Samuel Francis in 1815; account, Benjamin Turner II, Will Book 8:24; account, Samuel Francis Sr., 1815–16, Will Book 8:309.

57. U.S. Census, Southampton County, 1810, p. 160; 1830, p. 259.

58. St. Luke's Parish Land Book, 1831, and St. Luke's Parish Personal Tax List, 1831, entries for Jacob Williams. The seventeen slaveholders did not include Henry Bryant or Caswell Worrell, neither of whom owned slaves in 1831.

59. Philip J. Schwarz, *Slave Laws in Virginia* (Athens: University of Georgia Press, 1966), 58–62; Henry Wiencek, *Master of the Mountain: Thomas Jefferson and His Slaves* (New York: Farrar, Straus & Giroux, 2012), 242–45.

60. Deed, Micajah Holleman and Rebecca Holleman to Jacob Williams, 17 Aug. 1829, Deed Book 21:177; St. Luke's Parish Land Book, 1831, entries for Micajah Holleman ("Holliman") and John Carr's estate; U.S. Census, Southampton County, 1830, pp. 259, 263; St. Luke's Parish Personal Tax List, 1831, entries for Micajah Holleman and Sarah ("Sally") Carr; deed, John Carr and Sally Carr to Jacob Williams, 14 June 1823, Deed Book 19:176.

61. St. Luke's Parish Land Book, 1824, entry for estate of Thomas Vaughan (Rebecca); and St. Luke's Parish Land Books, 1825, 1831, entries for Henry B. Vaughan.

62. Vaughan genealogy (author's research file).

63. St. Luke's Parish Land Books, 1782–92, and St. Luke's Parish Personal Tax Lists, 1796–1805, entries for Moses Foster; deed, James C. H. Foster and Polly F. Foster to John Browne, 27 Feb. 1826, Deed Book 19:522–23.

64. Deed, Nathan Pope and Nancy Pope to Matthew R. Pope, 16 Oct. 1837, Deed Book 24:142; deed, Arthur T. Foster to Nathan Pope, 29 Mar. 1830, Deed Book 22:245.

65. St. Luke's Parish Land Book, 1810, and St. Luke's Parish Personal Tax List, 1810, entries for Arthur Foster; U.S. Census, Southampton County, 1810, p. 874 (Martha Foster).

66. U.S. Census, Southampton County, 1830, p. 259; St. Luke's Parish Personal Tax List, 1831, entry for Rebecca Vaughan and two sons.

67. Vaughan genealogy (author's research file); Marriage Register, pp. 162, 656, 657.

68. St. Luke's Parish Personal Tax List, 1805, entry for Thomas Vaughan Sr. and Thomas Vaughan Jr.

69. Deed, Thomas Vaughan Sr. to Thomas Vaughan Jr., 13 Feb. 1809, Deed Book 11:584.

70. St. Luke's Parish Land Book, 1810, entry for Thomas Vaughan Jr.; Vaughan genealogy (author's research file).

71. County Court Minute Book, 16 Dec. 1816, p. 73.

72. Ibid.; St. Luke's Parish Personal Tax Lists, 1817, 1818, entries for Rebecca Vaughan.

73. Vaughan gave his age as sixty-one in 1850, making his birth year 1789; U.S. Census, Southampton County, 1850, p. 282a; St. Luke's Parish Personal Tax List, 1812, entry for Thomas Vaughan Sr., Henry B. Vaughan, and Howell Vaughan.

74. Deed, Thomas Vaughan Sr. to Henry B. Vaughan, 13 May 1820, Deed Book 17:283–84; Drewry, *Southampton Insurrection*, 69; County Court Minute Book, 15 May 1820, p. 84.

75. *Parker v. Vaughan*, County Court Order Book, 19 Nov. 1822, p. 154, SCC.

76. St. Luke's Parish Land Book, 1821, entry for estate of Thomas Vaughan Jr.

77. Henry I. Tragle, *The Southampton Slave Revolt of 1831: A Compilation of Source Material* (Amherst: University of Massachusetts Press, 1971), 164 (photograph); Archaeological Consultants of the Carolinas, Inc., "The Rebecca Vaughan House: Archaeological Evaluation of the Original Site of the Rebecca Vaughan House, Southampton County, Virginia," http://Archcon.org/investigations/the-rebecca-vaughan-house/.

78. Inventory, Thomas Vaughan Jr., 2 Jan. 1817, Will Book 8:407–9. The percentages were as follows: animals and material chattels, 21.7 percent; land, 25.6 percent; slaves, 52.7 percent.

79. Inventory, Thomas Vaughan Jr., Will Book 8:408.

80. *Parker v. Vaughan*, County Court Order Book, 19 Nov. 1822, p. 154; chancery report, estate of Thomas Vaughan Jr., County Court Order Book, 21 June 1824, p. 16.

81. Will, Moses Foster, 25 May 1803, Will Book 5:471–72.

82. Deed, Thomas Vaughan Sr. to Martha Ann Vaughan, 15 Dec. 1811, Deed Book 12:415–16; deeds, Thomas Vaughan Sr. to George Vaughan, Mary Thomas Vaughan, and William A. Vaughan, 13 May 1820, Deed Book 17:241, 242, 262. For each of these gifts, the children each were to compensate their uncle with a modest payment of $100, an arrangement their mother must have approved.

83. County Court Minute Book, 8 Jan. 1830, p. 309.

84. Deed, Thomas Vaughan Sr. to Kit and Fanny, 14 Feb. 1806, Deed Book 11:48.

85. Free Negro Register, vol. 1, entries 417, 805, 943, LVA; St. Luke's Parish Personal Tax List, 1809, entry for Kit Vaughan.

86. Court minutes in 1831 identified Rebecca Vaughan as the owner of Wright, assigned to her for life in 1817; County Court Minute Book, 7 Sept. 1831, p. 99.

87. If the Silvy named in 1804 was the same Silvy listed in the inventory of Thomas Vaughan Jr. in 1817 (still described as a girl after thirteen years), she no longer belonged to Rebecca Vaughan.

88. *The Revised Code of the Laws of Virginia*, 2 vols. (Richmond: Thomas Ritchie, 1819), chap. 103, sec. 29; *Code of Virginia* (Richmond: William F. Ritchie, 1849), chap. 123, sec. 10. In 1849 the state law read as follows: "If the intestate leave a widow, and issue by her, the widow . . . shall have only the use for her life of such slaves as may be in her share."

89. St. Luke's Parish Personal Tax List, 1817 and 1831, entries for Rebecca Vaughan; chancery report, estate of Thomas Vaughan Jr., County Court Order Book, 21 June 1824, p. 16. No record has been found for the transfer of Moses Barrow, though he

was living at the Barrow farm in 1831 and was identified in trial records as the property of John T. Barrow.

90. St. Luke's Parish Land Book, 1825, entry for Henry B. Vaughan.

91. Inventory, Rebecca Vaughan, 26 Sept. 1831, Will Book 10:336–35; Drewry, *Southampton Insurrection*, 51, 61.

92. Inventory, Rebecca Vaughan, Will Book 10:336–35; report of commissioners, estate of Rebecca Vaughan, Sept. 1831, County Court Records, Chancery Papers, 1831, LVA; account, Rebecca Vaughan, recorded 20 Feb. 1832, Will Book 10:358.

93. On the role of slaveholdings in the domestic economy of other Virginians, see Michael L. Nicholls, *Whispers of Rebellion: Narrating Gabriel's Conspiracy* (Charlottesville: University of Virginia Press, 2012), 147–48 (for Thomas Henry Prosser); and Wiencek, *Master of the Mountain*, 8, 68–69, 89–90, 172 (for Thomas Jefferson).

94. Marriage Register, p. 311.

95. Chancery report, estate of Thomas Vaughan Jr., County Court Order Book, 21 June 1824, p. 16.

96. Foster genealogy (author's research file).

97. Vaughan genealogy (author's research file).

98. Deed, Thomas Vaughan Jr. and Rebecca Vaughan to John T. Vaughan, 16 May 1816, Deed Book 15:53; deed, Henry B. Vaughan to John T. Vaughan, 3 June 1816, Deed Book 15:74; St. Luke's Parish Land Book, 1817, entry for John T. Vaughan; St. Luke's Parish Land Book, 1821, entries for Sarah ("Sally") Francis and John T. Vaughan.

99. Vaughan genealogy (author's research file).

100. County Court Minute Book, 15 Aug. 1825, p. 80.

101. St. Luke's Parish Land Books, 1820–26, entries for John T. Vaughan.

102. St. Luke's Parish Personal Tax Lists, 1821–26, entries for John T. Vaughan.

103. Deed, John T. Vaughan to Nathaniel Francis, 20 Mar. 1826, Deed Book 20:7.

104. County Court Minute Book, 19 Feb. 1828, p. 301; 17 Mar. 1828, p. 204; St. Luke's Parish Land Book, 1828, entry for estate of John T. Vaughan; Vaughan genealogy (author's research file).

105. Samuel Warner heard about the impending marriage of "the beautiful Miss Vaughn [*sic*]" through his correspondent in Southampton. Drewry said that Ann Eliza at eighteen had become "the beauty of the county," and that she was paying her aunt a visit in August 1831; later accounts elaborated upon the legend, adding that Ann Eliza was dressing upstairs, preparing for male guests on 22 August. Samuel Warner, *Authentic and Impartial Narrative of the Tragical Scene Which Was Witnessed in Southampton County* (New York: Warner & West, 1831), 8, 14; Drewry, *Southampton Insurrection*, 61–62.

106. U.S. Census, Southampton County, 1850, p. 257; St. Luke's Parish Land Book, 1821, entries for estate of Frederick Parker and for Joseph, Solomon, and James W. Parker.

107. Will, Frederick Parker, 12 Feb. 1808, Will Book 6:551–52. Frederick was dead by 19 February 1808; will, Lucy Deloach, 19 Feb. 1808, Will Book 6:552.

108. Inventory, Frederick Parker, recorded 1813, Will Book 7:205–7.

109. Will, Frederick Parker, Will Book 6:551.

110. County Court Minute Book, 21 June 1819, p. 27.

111. County Court Minute Book, 20 Nov. 1820, pp. 130–32.

112. U.S. Census, Southampton County, 1820, p. 124.

113. Marriage Register, p. 674.

114. *Parker v. Vaughan*, County Court Order Book, 19 Nov. 1822, p. 154.

115. *Parker v. Parker*, County Court Order Book, 20 Oct. 1823, p. 321.

116. Report of commissioners, *Parker v. Vaughan*, County Court Order Book, 21 June 1824, p. 16; report of commissioners, *Parker v. Parker*, County Court Order Book, 21 June 1824, pp. 22–24. Temperance Parker and her sons paid taxes on only a fraction of this property from 1810 through 1824; the extent of the estate became apparent in the settlement of 1824 and in tax records of 1825. St. Luke's Parish Land Books, 1810–24, and St. Luke's Parish Personal Tax Lists, 1810–24, entries for estate of Frederick Parker.

117. County Court Order Book, 21 June 1824, p. 10.

118. Deed, Henry B. Vaughan to James W. Parker, 7 Jan. 1825, Deed Book 19:377; St. Luke's Parish Land Book, 1826, entry for James W. Parker. Tax commissioners consistently estimated the distance from the courthouse to Parker's house lot at four miles.

119. St. Luke's Parish Land Book, 1828, entry for James Trezvant.

120. County Court Minute Book, 20 June 1815, p. 230; 18 Mar. 1816, p. 330; 16 May, 1825, p. 62; 20 June 1825, p. 65; 17 Sept. 1827, p. 178.

121. U.S. Census, Southampton County, 1830, p. 259.

122. St. Luke's Parish Land Book, 1831, and St. Luke's Parish Personal Tax List, 1831, entries for James W. Parker. Parker ranked 48th in taxable wealth out of 272 core taxpayers, five places below Richard Porter and thirteen above Levi Waller.

123. According to court minutes, the eleven who appeared in examinations or trials were as follows: Lucy and Moses Barrow (executed); Archer, Bob, Daniel, Davy, Ferry, Frank, and Sam Parker (all dismissed or acquitted except Frank, who was convicted and transported); and Jim and Wright Vaughan (dismissed or acquitted).

124. According to court warrants, the eight summoned as witnesses were Beck, Charles, Meggy, Moll, and Franky Parker; and Rachel, Dilsy, and Nanny Vaughan; warrants summoning justices for the trials of Sam, Ferry, Jim, Archer, and Wright (slaves of James W. Parker, William A. Vaughan, and Rebecca Vaughan), 2 Sept. 1831, Southampton County Court Judgments, 1831, LVA.

125. Harris no longer attended court regularly in the 1820s, though he still performed minor official duties as late as 1830; certificate of relinquishment of dower, Mary T. Barrow, 4 Dec. 1830, Deed Book 21:464. He took no part in the trials in 1831.

126. The ten with ties were as follows: Travis, Salathiel Francis, Reese, Turner, Porter, Nathaniel Francis, Edwards, Barrow, Vaughan, and Parker. This assumes that Moses Barrow joined the insurgents at the farm of his master, John T. Barrow, and that he took part in the attacks on the Harris, Vaughan, and Parker households.

127. See Anthony E. Kaye, "Neighborhoods and Nat Turner: The Making of a Slave Rebel and the Unmaking of a Slave Rebellion," *Journal of the Early Republic* 27 (2007): 705–10.

128. U.S. Census, Southampton County, 1830, pp. 245, 256, 257, 259, 260, 263, 264. The total of eighteen households targeted or visited includes those of Augustus

F. Doyel and Howell Harris; Caswell Worrell and his family were counted in the household of Jacob Williams.

129. County Court Minute Book, 21 June 1831, p. 53.

130. Reports of bridge commissioners, County Court Order Book, 19 Aug. 1822, p. 101; 21 June 1824, pp. 12–13; 20 Dec. 1824, p. 114. Deck specifications are based on those for the new bridge at Three Creeks in 1822; County Court Order Book, 21 Oct. 1822, p. 136.

131. Drewry, *Southampton Insurrection*, photographs following p. 201.

132. County Court Order Book, 21 Jun 1824, p. 12.

133. Deed, Lewis C. Trezvant and Rebecca Trezvant to Eliza W. Waddill, 23 Oct. 1828, Deed Book 21:47; Marriage Register, p. 379; Trezvant genealogy (author's research file).

134. Deed, Jerusalem trustees to John Crichlow, 14 Oct. 1796, Deed Book 8:349–51; Thomas C. Parramore, *Southampton County, Virginia* (Charlottesville: University of Virginia Press, 1978), 47. A map of the town, differing in minor details from map 4 in the present work, appears in Bill Bryant, *Tomorrow Jerusalem: The Story of Nat Turner and the Southampton Slave Insurrection* (Bloomington, IN: 1st Books, 2002), xv.

135. A photograph of the clerk's office appears in "A Guide to a Speech and Photographs," Special Collections Department, UVA; and ead.lib.virginia.edu.

136. County Court Minute Book, 20 June 1815, p. 229; 18 Mar. 1816, p. 327; Southampton County Court Order Book, 17 June 1817, p. 181.

137. Jerusalem deeds, 1796–1830 (author's research file).

138. Deed, Thomas Gray Sr. to Thomas R. Gray, 15 Mar. 1828, Deed Book 20:344.

139. Jerusalem deeds (author's research file).

140. U.S. Census, Southampton County, 1830, p. 272.

141. Deed, Robert Goodwin to Henry B. Vaughan, 4 Oct. 1830, Deed Book 21:412–13; County Court Minute Book, 16 May 1831, p. 39; 18 July 1831, p. 67; Nottoway Parish Personal Property Tax List, 1831, list of ordinary licenses, entry for Henry B. Vaughan, LVA.

142. *Richmond Compiler*, 27 Aug. 1831, in "The Banditti," *Richmond Enquirer*, 30 Aug. 1831. In 1835, according to one description, the village had "about 25 dwelling houses, 4 mercantile stores, 1 saddler, 1 carriage maker, 2 hotels, 1 masonic hall, and 2 houses of public entertainment"; Joseph Martin, *A Comprehensive Description of Virginia, and the District of Columbia* (Richmond: J. W. Randolph, [1835]), 279. Martin estimated the population at 175, "of whom 4 are resident attorneys, and 4 regular physicians."

143. U.S. Census, Southampton County, 1830, p. 272.

144. The four residents listed on other pages were William C. Parker, James Rochelle Sr., James Trezvant, and Dr. Lewis C. Trezvant; U.S. Census, Southampton County, 1830, pp. 259, 277, 286, 289.

145. U.S. Census, Southampton County, 1830, pp. 259, 272, 277, 286, 289; figures include residents who lived within the bounds of the town's twenty lots, or on properties adjacent to the town, or within a mile of the courthouse (including a small portion of St. Luke's Parish). People listed on p. 272 of the manuscript census who owned land and buildings elsewhere in the county are assumed not to have been

residing in the town in 1830. The fifteen town residents on p. 272 of the census were Archibald Johnson, Everett Edwards, Lucy Doyle, Nicholas F. Cox (Cocke), Stephen Skinner, William S. Wells, Mary Daughtry, Albert Drewry, William Poole, Elizabeth Cosby, Theodore Trezvant, J. (Josiah) Joyner, Eliza Best (Betts?), Mrs. (Martha) Milliken, and Martha Madera. The four listed on other pages but residing in town brought the total number of households to nineteen. See also Nottoway Parish Land Book, 1830, LVA; Nottoway Parish Personal Tax List, 1830; St. Luke's Parish Land Book, 1830; and St. Luke's Parish Personal Tax List, 1830, entries for all nineteen individuals.

146. U.S. Census, Southampton County, 1830, p. 243 (entry for John R. Kelly, overseer for William Allen).

147. Rochelle family genealogy (author's research file).

148. Nottoway Parish Land Book, 1831, and Nottoway Parish Personal Tax List, 1831, entries for James Rochelle; St. Luke's Parish Land Book, 1831, and St. Luke's Parish Personal Tax List, 1831, entries for James Rochelle. On Rochelle and his horses, see John Y. Mason to James Rochelle, 1 Mar. 1826; and Richard E. Parker to James Rochelle, 20 Jan. 1829, Rochelle Papers, RDU.

149. Nottoway Parish Land Book, 1827, list of town lots, entries for James Rochelle.

150. U.S. Census, Southampton County, 1830, p. 289.

151. Edwin Gray to James Rochelle, 12 June 1813, Rochelle Papers; Francis F. McKinney, *Education in Violence: Life of George H. Thomas and the History of the Army of the Cumberland* (Chicago: Americana House, 1991), 6–7; Parramore, *Southampton County*, 152; Thomas R. Gray, *To the Public* [Jerusalem, 1834], 8.

152. County Court Minute Book, 20 Dec. 1830, p. 21; 17 Jan. 1831, p. 22.

153. Marriage Register, p. 485; John Tyler to Martha Rochelle, 20 Oct. 1838, 22 Oct. 1843, Rochelle Papers.

154. St. Luke's Parish Land Books, 1817–31, entries for James Trezvant; Drewry, *Southampton Insurrection*, photograph following p. 201.

155. *Biographical Directory of the American Congress, 1774–1996* (Alexandria, VA: CQ Staff Directories, 1997), 1,961.

156. U.S. Census, Southampton County, 1830, p. 259.

157. St. Luke's Parish Land Book, 1831, and St. Luke's Parish Personal Tax List, 1831, entries for James Trezvant.

158. U.S. Census, Southampton County, 1830, p. 272; 1850, p. 297a; Nottoway Parish Personal Tax Lists, 1815, 1830, 1831, lists of licenses, entries for Theodore Trezvant; Edith F. Axelson, *Virginia Postmasters and Post Offices, 1789–1832* (Athens, GA: Iberian, 1991), 175.

159. John Timothee Trezevant, *The Trezevant Family in the United States* (Columbia, SC: State Company, 1914), 31; W. J. Maxwell, comp., *General Alumni Catalogue of the University of Pennsylvania, 1922* [Philadelphia, 1922], 495. Lewis Cruger Trezevant (spelled with two *e*'s), the cousin, and Lewis Crouch Trezvant, the middle brother between James and Theodore, both lived in Nottoway Parish, a source of confusion at the time.

160. Deed, Goodwin to Vaughan, Deed Book 21:412–13; Nottoway Parish Personal Tax List, 1831, list of licenses, entry for Henry B. Vaughan.

161. U.S. Census, Southampton County, 1830, p. 243.

162. Nottoway Parish Land Book, 1831, and Nottoway Parish Personal Tax List, 1831, entries for Henry B. Vaughan; St. Luke's Parish Land Book, 1831, and St. Luke's Parish Personal Tax List, 1831, entries for Henry B. Vaughan.

163. Deeds, Jerusalem Trustees to William Crichlow, 14 Oct. 1796, Deed Book 8:340–41, 343–44; deed, Jerusalem Trustees to John Crichlow, 14 Oct. 1796, Deed Book 8:347–51; deed, Exum Scott and Ann Scott to Thomas Hunt, 9 Dec. 1796, Deed Book 8:577–78.

164. The county had twenty active magistrates in 1831, half of whom lived within nine miles of the courthouse.

165. County Court Minute Book, 21 May 1827, p. 160.

166. *Revised Code of Virginia* (1819), chap. 147, sec. 5; *Code of Virginia* (1849), chap. 198, sec. 1–8. Bowls, chess, backgammon, and draughts were permitted.

167. Deed (lease), Robert Goodwin to William L. Everitt, 20 July 1826, Deed Book 20:57–58; inventory of furniture belonging to the tavern, 5 Sept. 1826, Deed Book 20:62–63; O. Fred Cavin, Survey report, Fielding J. Mahone home (Jerusalem tavern), 19 July 1937, LVA.

168. Deed, Henry B. Vaughan to Thomas C. Jones and James H. Sebrell, 1 Jan. 1839, Deed Book 24:306–7; deed, Sebrell's trustee to William I. Sebrell and Nicholas M. Sebrell, 24 Aug. 1839, Deed Book 24:391; County Court Minute Book, 21 Aug. 1826, p. 127.

169. Nottoway Parish Personal Tax List, 1831, entries for town residents.

170. The saddler was Sugars Bryant; the milliner was Martha Madera. For Bryant, see articles of agreement, Robert Goodwin and George E. Hines, 15 Dec. 1828, Deed Book 21:363; for Madera, see Nottoway Parish Personal Tax List, 1831, list of licenses, entry for Martha Madera. In addition to William C. Parker and Thomas R. Gray, the resident attorneys in 1831 included James S. French and William D. Boyle. Boyle left town soon after the rebellion trials. A fifth attorney, Robert Birchett, may have lived part-time in the village; he was counsel for Ben Blunt.

171. "The Parker Family of Essex, the Northern Neck, &c.," *Virginia Magazine of History and Biography* 6 (1898): 195; *Richmond Compiler*, 2 Sept. 1831, in *Richmond Enquirer*, 6 Sept. 1831.

172. Gray had borrowed the books from Browne, his father's physician, neighbor, and executor; see List 1, Books Loaned to T. R. Gray, August 1831; and List 2, Books Borrowed by T. R. Gray from O. A. Browne, August 1831, *Browne v. Gray*, County Court Records, Chancery Papers, 1835.

173. Deed, James Rochelle and Martha Rochelle to Alexander P. Peete and members of the Benevolent Lodge No. 34, 19 Dec. 1831, Deed Book 22:147–48; and Robert Goodwin to Henry B. Vaughan, Deed Book 21:412.

174. List of members, Jerusalem Jockey Club, [1830?], *Nicholson v. Garrison*, County Circuit Superior Court of Law and Chancery, in Box 13, Blow Family Papers, CWM; Parramore, *Southampton County*, 51.

175. The Southern Mail Stage between Norfolk and Petersburg followed a route that passed twenty miles north of Jerusalem; see "The Traveller's Guide," *Norfolk Herald*, 18 Jan. 1830.

176. *Richmond Enquirer*, 2 Sept. 1831.

177. County Court Minute Book, 15 May, 1815, p. 218; County Court Order Book, 17 Feb. 1815, pp. 133–34; 20 Oct. 1817, pp. 217, 221.

178. County Court Minute Book, 17 Mar. 1823, p. 303; 16 June 1823, p. 317; 17 Nov. 1823, p. 348; 20 Dec. 1824, pp. 44, 46; 21 Feb. 1825, p. 50; 21 Nov. 1825, p. 92.

179. County Court Minute Book, 21 Mar. 1831, p. 29. State law prohibited slaves from going at large without proof of permission from a master; *Revised Code of Virginia* (1819), chap. 111, sec. 6; *Code of Virginia* (1849), chap. 104, sec. 6. William C. Parker and Thomas R. Gray both assumed that the prohibition was not rigorously enforced. In one of his final actions as magistrate (on the day he qualified for his attorney's license), Gray brought before the court judgments against two masters for violating this law; County Court Minute Book, 18 Oct. 1830, p. 357.

180. [William C. Parker], letter, 21 Sept. 1831, *Richmond Enquirer*, 30 Sept. 1831.

181. [Thomas R. Gray], letter, 17 Sept. 1831, *Richmond Constitutional Whig*, 26 Sept. 1831, in *Norfolk American Beacon*, 30 Sept. 1831.

182. Letter, [23 Aug. 1831], *Richmond Compiler*, 27 Aug. 1831, in "The Banditti," *Richmond Enquirer*, 30 Aug. 1831.

183. [William C. Parker], letter, 31 Aug. 1831, *Richmond Compiler*, 3 Sept. 1831, in *Richmond Enquirer*, 6 Sept. 1831. By the time John Hampden Pleasants returned to Richmond, he too believed that the village had been "the immediate object of their movement." John Hampden Pleasants, "Southampton Affair," *Richmond Whig*, 3 Sept. 1831, in *Norfolk American Beacon*, 6 Sept. 1831.

184. [Gray], letter, *Richmond Whig*, 26 Sept. 1831, in *Norfolk American Beacon*, 30 Sept. 1831.

185. Thomas R. Gray, *The Confessions of Nat Turner* (Baltimore: Lucas & Deaver, 1831), 15, 16.

186. One correspondent complained that in Southampton action "many persons have to use fowling pieces and bird-shot." On the lack of arms, see the letter from a gentleman from Smithfield, 24 Aug. 1831, *Richmond Compiler*, 27 Aug. 1831, in "The Banditti," *Richmond Enquirer*, 30 Aug. 1831; *Norfolk Herald*, 26 Aug. 1831.

187. The volunteers with whom Gray, Parker, and Trezvant rode at Parker's field were armed; Gray, *Confessions*, 15–16. Gray's father owned two shotguns and a brace of pistols; inventory, Thomas Gray Sr., 26 Oct 1831, Will Book 10:386, 387.

188. Thomas C. Jones, testimony, trial of Jack Reese, County Court Minute Book, 3 Sept. 1831, p. 90. Jones had been tried in 1819 for the murder of a slave; County Court Minute Book, 27 Aug. 1819, p. 36. In 1831 he was a constable for lower Nottoway Parish, the area surrounding Jerusalem; County Court Minute Book, 20 June 1831, p. 46.

189. Pleasants, "Southampton Affair."

190. *Norfolk Herald*, 4 Nov. 1831.

191. [William C. Parker], letter, 1 Nov. 1831, *Richmond Enquirer*, 8 Nov. 1831.

192. Parker's report was consistent with Nat Turner's statement that "until we had armed and equipped ourselves, and gathered sufficient force, neither age nor sex was to be spared"; Gray, *Confessions*, 12.

Chapter 8. The Rising

1. Thomas R. Gray, *The Confessions of Nat Turner* (Baltimore: Lucas & Deaver, 1831), 12.

2. In a list of seven conspirators Gray compiled in September, he omitted Nelson's name and mistakenly included that of Austin, another Edwards slave; [Thomas R. Gray], letter, 17 Sept. 1831, *Richmond Constitutional Whig*, 26 Sept. 1831, in *Norfolk American Beacon*, 30 Sept. 1831. Gray silently corrected this list in November; Gray, *Confessions*, 11–12.

3. U.S. Naval Observatory, Astronomical Applications Department, "Complete Sun and Moon Data for One Day," www.usno.navy.mil/USNO/astronomical-applications/data-services.

4. Nat Turner said that the men remained in the field "until about two hours in the night"; Gray, *Confessions*, 12. William C. Parker put their time of departure at "11 or 12 o'clock"; [William C. Parker], letter, 31 Aug. 1831, *Richmond Compiler*, 3 Sept. 1831, in *Richmond Enquirer*, 6 Sept. 1831. Drewry said "ten o'clock in the night"; William S. Drewry, *The Southampton Insurrection* (1900; repr., Murfreesboro, NC: Johnson, 1968), 35. They had no need for the fictive torch mentioned in Stephen B. Oates, *The Fires of Jubilee: Nat Turner's Fierce Rebellion* (New York: Harper & Row, 1971), 69.

5. The path is mentioned in George H. Gray, plat, Travis farm, 1830, *Moore v. Travis*, Southampton County Chancery Causes, LVA.

6. Gray, *Confessions*, 12.

7. George W. Powell, letter, 27 Aug. 1831, *Christian Advocate*, 9 Sept. 1831.

8. Moses Moore, testimony, trial of Jack Reese, County Court Minute Book, 3 Sept. 1831, p. 90, SCC.

9. Gray, *Confessions*, 12.

10. Inventory, Joseph Travis, 20 Dec. 1831, Will Book 11:353–54, SCC.

11. Gray, *Confessions*, 12; Moses Moore and Thomas C. Jones, testimony, trial of Jack Reese, County Court Minute Book, 3 Sept. 1831, p. 90; [William C. Parker], letter, *Richmond Compiler*, 3 Sept. 1831, in *Richmond Enquirer*, 6 Sept. 1831; [Gray] letter, *Richmond Whig*, 26 Sept. 1831, in *Norfolk American Beacon*, 30 Sept. 1831.

12. [Gray], letter, *Richmond Whig*, 26 Sept. 1831, in *Norfolk American Beacon*, 30 Sept. 1831; [William C. Parker], 1 Nov. 1831, letter, *Richmond Enquirer*, 8 Nov. 1831. Parramore believed that all five occupants of the house were sleeping upstairs; Thomas C. Parramore, *Southampton County, Virginia* (Charlottesville: University of Virginia Press, 1978), 82; Thomas C. Parramore, "Covenant in Jerusalem," in *Nat Turner: A Slave Rebellion in History and Memory*, ed. Kenneth S. Greenberg (New York: Oxford University Press, 2003), 59. Parker's letter in the *Enquirer* and inventories taken at the Travis house suggest that all were sleeping downstairs.

13. [William C. Parker], letter, *Richmond Enquirer*, 8 Nov. 1831; inventory, Joseph Travis, Will Book 11:354; Gray, *Confessions*, 12.

14. Gray, *Confessions*, 12.

15. [William C. Parker], letter, *Richmond Enquirer*, 8 Nov. 1831.

16. Ibid.

17. Ibid.

18. [Gray] letter, *Richmond Whig*, 26 Sept. 1831, in *Norfolk American Beacon*, 30 Sept. 1831.

19. Gray, *Confessions*, 12. Travis's inventory listed one saddle and five horses (two prime); inventory, Joseph Travis, Will Book 11:354.

20. Gray, *Confessions*, 12.

21. Theodore Trezvant, letter, 5 Sept. 1831, *Raleigh Register*, 15 Sept. 1831.

22. Moses Moore, testimony, trial of Jack Reese, County Court Minute Book, 3 Sept. 1831, p. 90.

23. Gray, *Confessions*, 12.

24. Ibid.

25. [Gray] letter, *Richmond Whig*, 26 Sept. 1831, in *Norfolk American Beacon*, 30 Sept. 1831.

26. In November Gray referred to Turner as a "great Bandit," attempting to allay fear with irony. As late as December a few white observers were still referring to Turner as a bandit in the literal sense, denying his significance as an insurgent; see *Richmond Enquirer*, 8 Nov., 2 Dec. 1831. On the significance of the distinction, see Philip J. Schwarz, *Twice Condemned: Slaves and the Criminal Laws of Virginia, 1705–1865* (Baton Rouge: Louisiana State University Press, 1988), 269. Eric Hobsbawm revived legends of the noble robber and social bandits in *Bandits* (New York: New Press, 2000), 47–48, 63–64, and *Primitive Rebels: Studies in Archaic Forms of Social Movement in the 19th and 20th Centuries* (New York: W. W. Norton, 1965), 19–20.

27. Eugene Genovese suggested that in the "desperate warfare" confronting Nat Turner, "compassion for women and children equaled a death warrant for the compassionate." Eugene Genovese, *From Rebellion to Revolution: Afro-American Slave Revolts in the Making of the Modern World* (Baton Rouge: Louisiana State University Press, 1979), 105–6.

28. Gray, *Confessions*, 12–13.

29. Ibid.

30. Drewry, *Southampton Insurrection*, 38; inventory, Salathiel Francis, 16 Dec. 1831, Will Book 11:65; Theodore Trezvant, letter, *Raleigh Register*, 15 Sept. 1831.

31. Gray, *Confessions*, 13. Apparently neither Gray nor William C. Parker found the way to the Reese house.

32. Gray, *Confessions*, 13.

33. Ibid.

34. Turner later said that he killed Margaret Whitehead, the only killing he attributed to himself; Gray, *Confessions*, 13–14.

35. Sampson C. Reese, testimony, trial of Jack Reese, County Court Minute Book, 5 Sept. 1831, p. 91.

36. A slave named Tom was listed in the 1826 inventory of Joseph Reese Sr., 20 Nov. 1826, Will Book 10:180. He may have been the man for whom the estate of Piety Reese sought compensation after the uprising; Piety Reese (estate), petition 9915-D, 29 Dec. 1831, Legislative Petitions, LVA. He is assumed here to have been the wounded prisoner of that name in the Jerusalem jail on 25 August; *Norfolk American Beacon*, 29 Aug. 1831. He also is assumed to have been the man Pleasants saw in the jail on 25 August and referred to as "Marmaduke," the killer of Ann Eliza

Vaughan; John Hampden Pleasants, letter, 25–27 Aug. 1831, *Richmond Whig*, 29 Aug. 1831, in *Richmond Religious Herald*, 2 Sept. 1831.

37. Nathan Blunt was present during the attack on Elizabeth Turner II and later testified about the division into detachments that occurred at her house; Nathan Blunt, testimony, trial of Davy Turner, County Court Minute Book, 2 Sept. 1831, p. 80.

38. Daniel (slave), testimony, trial of Nathan Blunt, County Court Minute Book, 6 Sept. 1831, p. 94.

39. Drewry, *Southampton Insurrection*, 38–39n1. Mrs. Harris's granddaughter, who was present that morning, was Drewry's source for both details. Joe's name appeared (as Joseph) in the estate papers of Mrs. Harris's husband; inventory, Matthew Harris, 14 June 1814, Will Book 8:241. There is no contemporaneous evidence that he joined the rising, however; he may have been a victim of atrocity during the suppression of the uprising (appendixes A and F).

40. Gray, *Confessions*, 13. The distance between the Reese and Turner houses is given as one mile (not two) in the *Confessions*.

41. Ibid., 13; Drewry, *Southampton Insurrection*, 41.

42. Gray, *Confessions*, 13.

43. [Meriwether B. Brodnax], prosecutor's notes, n.d., *Commonwealth v. Daniel Porter and others*, County Court Judgments, 1831, LVA. The stray note pertaining to Hark Moore is filed with trial documents of Daniel Porter and others. Brodnax was unaware that Mrs. Newsom was the sister of Jarrell Turner, who for a short time after 1822 apparently hired Hark.

44. Gray, *Confessions*, 13.

45. Three slaves in the holding of Elizabeth Turner II in 1830 were between the ages of twenty-four and thirty-six; two were between thirty-six and fifty; U.S. Census, Southampton County, 1830, p. 260, NA.

46. Chancery report, estate of John Reese Sr., 12 Dec. 1816, County Court Order Book, 17 Mar. 1817, pp. 99–100, SCC; deed, Samuel G. Turner to Rebecca Jane Williamson, 18 Jan. 1822, Deed Book 18:413, SCC; slaves of Elizabeth Turner II (author's research file).

47. Moses Moore, testimony, trial of Davy Turner, County Court Minute Book, 2 Sept. 1831, p. 80.

48. Gray, *Confessions*, 13.

49. [Gray], letter, *Richmond Whig*, 26 Sept. 1831, in *Norfolk American Beacon*, 30 Sept. 1831.

50. Gray, *Confessions*, 13.

51. Moses Moore and Nathan Blunt, testimony, trial of Davy Turner, County Court Minute Book, 2 Sept. 1831, p. 80.

52. Ibid.

53. News of the Bryant killings reached Norfolk on 24 August and was forwarded that day to Philadelphia; editors of the *Norfolk Herald*, letter to "Lyford," 24 Aug. 1831, *Philadelphia National Gazette*, 27 Aug. 1831. Thomas R. Gray, who had ridden through the Cabin Pond neighborhood on 22–23 August and passed through Norfolk in the early morning hours on 24 August, may have brought the news; Jesse D. Elliott to Levi Woodbury, 28 Aug. 1831, in *Richmond Enquirer*, 16 Sept. 1831.

54. Bittle and Balmer were named as creditors in deed, John W. Reese to Jesse Drewry and John C. Turner, 5 Feb. 1831, Deed Book 21:474–75.

55. Gray, *Confessions*, 13; Turner's account suggests that Catherine and Margaret Whitehead had dressed for the day. Another account of the attack appears in Harriet Whitehead, amended bill of complaint, *Whitehead v. Francis*, County Court Records, Chancery Papers, 1851, LVA.

56. Drewry, *Southampton Insurrection*, 43.

57. Gray, *Confessions*, 13.

58. Drewry, *Southampton Insurrection*, 43.

59. Gray, *Confessions*, 13.

60. Hubbard Whitehead and Wallace Whitehead, testimony, trials of Jack Whitehead and Andrew Whitehead, County Court Minute Book, 1 Sept. 1831, pp. 74–76.

61. The servant girl may have been Dinah Whitehead, who still lived in the Whitehead house with her three children twenty years later; inventory, Harriet Whitehead, 27 Apr. 1852, Will Book 11A:42–43; John Whitehead, Joseph B. Whitehead, and Martha Darden, depositions, 16 Sept. 1851, *Whitehead v. Francis*, County Court Records, Chancery Papers, 1851.

62. Gray, *Confessions*, 13.

63. Ibid., 13–14.

64. Ibid., 14; Moses Moore and Nathan Blunt, testimony, trial of Davy Turner, County Court Minute Book, 2 Sept. 1831, pp. 79–80.

65. Hubbard Whitehead, testimony, trial of Joe Turner, County Court Minute Book, 19 Sept. 1831, p. 103. Hubbard was suggesting that the time was about an hour after sunrise or daylight.

66. Inventory, Catherine Whitehead, 3 Jan. 1832, Will Book 11:41.

67. Hubbard Whitehead, testimony, trial of Joe Turner, County Court Minute Book, 19 Sept. 1831, p. 102.

68. Will, Benjamin Turner II, 14 Oct. 1810, Will Book 7:109; inventory, 22 Jan. 1811, Benjamin Turner II, Will Book 7:168.

69. Turner genealogy (author's research file).

70. Report of commissioners, estate of Henry Barrow Sr., Nov. 1818, County Court Order Book, 18 Mar. 1822, p. 14; inventory, Edmund Turner Jr., 13 Nov. 1821, Will Book 9:176–77; Mary T. Barrow, testimony, trial of Nat Turner II, County Court Minute Book, 3 Sept. 1831, pp. 90–91.

71. Hubbard Whitehead, testimony, trial of Joe Turner, County Court Minute Book, 19 Sept. 1831, p. 102.

72. Gray, *Confessions*, 14. Inferences about assignments to the detachment are based on circumstantial evidence concerning Doyel's pocketbook, found later in Hark's possession, and the points at which Jack Reese, Joe Turner, and Davy Turner separated from the insurgents; Thomas Ridley, testimony, trial of Hark Moore, County Court Minute Book, 3 Sept. 1831, p. 87; appendix B.

73. Gray, *Confessions*, 14. Combined, the first six targeted households had thirty horses in 1831; St. Luke's Parish Personal Property Tax List, 1831, entries for Joseph Travis, Salathiel Francis, J. W. Reese, Elizabeth Turner II, Henry Bryant, and Catherine Whitehead, LVA.

74. Letter, Winton, NC, 24 Aug. 1831, *Norfolk Herald*, 27 Aug. 1831. The chamber and fireplace may have been those shown in Gilbert W. Francis and Katherine K. Futrell, *Nat Turner's Insurrection, 1831* (video recording, Southampton County Historical Society Living Library, 2000), disc 3. General Eppes reported that bodies of some victims had been "horribly mangled"; *Richmond Compiler*, 27 Aug. 1831, in "The Banditti," *Richmond Enquirer*, 30 Aug. 1831.

75. Harriet Whitehead, amended bill of complaint, *Whitehead v. Francis*, County Court Records, Chancery Papers, 1851; Jepthah Darden to John R. Kilby, 29 Sept. 1847, *Whitehead v. Francis*, Kilby Papers, RDU; Drewry, *Southampton Insurrection*, 43–44.

76. Powell, letter, *Christian Advocate*, 9 Sept. 1831.

77. The grandson was identified as Harriet Whitehead's nephew in Darden to Kilby, 29 Sept. 1847, Kilby Papers.

78. [Meriwether B. Brodnax], notes, deposition of Hubbard Whitehead, *Commonwealth v. Daniel Porter and others*, County Court Judgments, 1831.

79. Venus Porter, testimony, trials of Jack and Andrew Whitehead, County Court Minute Book, 1 Sept. 1831, pp. 74, 75. Venus testified that the band had left the Porter place before Jack and Andrew Whitehead arrived, riding a mule, "about 9 o'clock in the morning."

80. Gray, *Confessions*, 14.

81. U.S. Census, Southampton County, 1830, p. 256.

82. Norfolk gentleman, letter, 26 Aug. 1827, *Norfolk American Beacon*, 29 Aug. 1831.

83. Trials of Daniel Porter and Jim Porter, County Court Minute Book, 31 Aug. 1831, p. 72; 19 Sept. 1831, p. 105; Richard Porter, petition 9803, 12 Dec. 1831, Legislative Petitions.

84. Gray, *Confessions*, 14.

85. Drewry, *Southampton Insurrection*, 44–45.

86. Thomas Ridley, testimony, trial of Hark Moore, County Court Minute Book, 3 Sept. 1831, pp. 86–87.

87. Gray, *Confessions*, 14. Nat Turner identified none of the insurgents he said joined the detachment and did not give their number. No slaves from the neighborhood, other than those known to authorities, were charged with enlisting at that point; and no slave owners from the neighborhood, other than those who petitioned for compensation, reported losses of such property.

88. Jordan Barnes, testimony, trial of Jack Reese, County Court Minute Book, 5 Sept. 1831, p. 92.

89. Christian Atkins, testimony, trial of Joe Turner, County Court Minute Book, 19 Sept. 1831, p. 102; [Meriwether B. Brodnax], notes, deposition of Christian Atkins, *Commonwealth v. Joe Turner*, County Court Judgments, 1831.

90. Drewry, *Southampton Insurrection*, 45, 50. Hearsay evidence supporting Drewry's account of the warning to Porter appears in L. Minor Blackford, *Mine Eyes Have Seen the Glory: The Story of a Virginia Lady, Mary Berkeley Minor Blackford, 1802–1896* (Cambridge, MA: Harvard University Press, 1954), 27–28.

91. Harriet remained in hiding near the Whitehead house until the next day; Drewry, *Southampton Insurrection*, 43–44.

92. U.S. Census, Southampton County, 1830, p. 260.

93. Personal property tax lists and the U.S. Census recorded the presence of slaves at the Turner farm who matched the descriptions of the two young women; St. Luke's Parish Personal Tax Lists, 1823–31, entries for Elizabeth Turner II; U.S. Census, Southampton County, 1830, p. 260.

94. Deed, Samuel G. Turner to Rebecca Jane Williamson, Deed Book 18:413.

95. Will, Samuel G. Turner, 9 Jan. 1822, Will Book 9:134.

96. [James Trezvant], letter, 31 Aug. 1831, *Raleigh Register*, 3 Sept. 1831. The route to town by Barrow Road would have taken Howell Harris past the Waller household, which did not receive its warning until after the express had reached Jerusalem. Trezvant did not report the rider's time of arrival at the town, which must be inferred from the known timing of later events.

97. Two accounts placed Howell Harris with Peete's volunteers on Tuesday, 23 August; Alexander P. Peete, affidavit, 18 Jan. 1832, in Thomas Fitzhugh (estate), petition 9915-F, Dec. 1831, Legislative Petitions; Drewry, *Southampton Insurrection*, 85n1.

98. Gray, *Confessions*, 14.

99. Drewry, *Southampton Insurrection*, 45.

100. F. N. Boney, "Nathaniel Francis, Representative Antebellum Southerner," *Proceedings of the American Philosophical Society* 118 (1974): 450–51; Gray, *Confessions*, 22; Drewry, *Southampton Insurrection*, 45–47; Francis genealogy (author's research file).

101. In 1830 the Francis farm had six white residents of all ages (including the two orphans) and fifteen slaves (including four adult males and two young adult females); U.S. Census, Southampton County, 1830, p. 259. Three white residents were killed in the uprising; among the slave residents, three adult males also died (two by execution), as did one adult female, possibly a victim of atrocity (appendixes E and F).

102. Gray, *Confessions*, 19–20, 22; Drewry, *Southampton Insurrection*, 46.

103. Moses Moore, testimony, trial of Nathan, Tom, and Davy Francis, County Court Minute Book, 6 Sept. 1831, pp. 94–95.

104. Theodore Trezvant, letter, *Raleigh Register*, 15 Sept. 1831.

105. Letter, Winton, NC, *Norfolk Herald*, 27 Aug. 1831.

106. Gray, *Confessions*, 22.

107. Drewry presented a detailed account of the attack at the Francis farm. His sources included Mrs. Lavinia Francis (who died in 1885, when Drewry was fourteen) and William S. Francis (born in September 1831); Drewry, *Southampton Insurrection*, 45–48, 197. The account, based on memory and tradition, contains both valuable information and a number of inconsistencies.

108. Gray, *Confessions*, 19–20.

109. Moses Moore, testimony, trial of Nathan, Tom, and Davy Francis, County Court Minute Book, 6 Sept. 1831, pp. 94–95; Auditor of Public Accounts, List of Slaves and Free persons of color received into the Penitentiary, in Records, Condemned Blacks Executed or Transported, 1783–1864, LVA.

110. In 1830 nine Francis slaves were aged ten or older, and seven of the nine were males; U.S. Census, Southampton County, 1830, p. 259.

111. In 1830 the Edwards plantation registered twelve male slaves between ages ten and thirty-six; U.S. Census, Southampton County, 1830, p. 259.

112. Peter Edwards to members of the General Assembly of Virginia, [Dec. 1831], in Edwards, petition 9804-A, 12 Dec. 1831, Legislative Petitions; Nathaniel Francis, Peter Edwards, and Levi Waller, testimony, trial of Sam Edwards, County Court Minute Book, 17 Oct. 1831, pp. 117–18. Sam's approximate age is based on entries for the Edwards slaves in U.S. Census, Southampton County, 1830, p. 259.

113. Mary T. Barrow, testimony, trial of Nat Turner II, County Court Minute Book, 3 Sept. 1831, pp. 90–91; *Richmond Compiler*, 27 Aug. 1831, in "The Banditti," *Richmond Enquirer*, 30 Aug. 1831.

114. Gray, *Confessions*, 20.

115. Drewry, *Southampton Insurrection*, 51. Barrow owned at least one rifle and a shotgun; inventory, John T. Barrow, 1832, Will Book 11:18.

116. Drewry asserted that Will Francis was shot to death on Tuesday morning, 23 August, in an encounter with the Greensville cavalry at Newit Harris's plantation, but he offered no evidence; Drewry, *Southampton Insurrection*, 73. George W. Powell said that one insurgent had been killed Tuesday morning at Samuel Blunt's house, but he did not identify the dead man; Powell, letter, *Christian Advocate*, 9 Sept. 1831. It is also possible that at some point Will Francis separated from the insurgents.

117. Mary T. Barrow, testimony, trial of Lucy Barrow, County Court Minute Book, 19 Sept. 1831, p. 103. Byrd had been a slave of Barrow's grandfather; will, Capt. John Barrow, 22 Mar. 1806, Will Book 6:704.

118. Witnesses at the Barrow house did not mention Moses Barrow in their trial testimony, and six other witnesses who encountered him elsewhere could not have known his whereabouts during that attack; trials of Lucy Barrow and Moses Barrow, County Court Minute Book, 1 Sept. 1831, pp. 76–78; 19 Sept. 1831, p. 103.

119. In his list of 5 September, Theodore Trezvant said that two white men died at the Barrow Farm; Trezvant, letter, *Raleigh Register*, 15 Sept. 1831.

120. Ben Harris, testimony, trial of Sam Edwards, County Court Minute Book, 17 Oct. 1831, p. 117.

121. Drewry's sources told him that in 1831 Newit Harris (who recently had fathered a child) was an invalid and had to be carried to safety; Drewry, *Southampton Insurrection*, 52.

122. Ben Harris, testimony, trial of Sam Edwards, County Court Minute Book, 17 Oct. 1831, p. 117.

123. [Gray], letter, *Richmond Whig*, 26 Sept. 1831, in *Norfolk American Beacon*, 30 Sept. 1831.

124. Gray, *Confessions*, 14.

125. Inventory, Newit Harris, mansion house, 2 Jan. 1838, Will Book 12:229.

126. Gray, *Confessions*, 14. Nat Turner estimated the time at "about nine or ten o'clock."

127. U.S. Census, Southampton County, 1830, p. 263; Henry Edwards, testimony, trial of Isham Edwards, County Court Minute Book, 7 Sept. 1831, p. 98.

128. U.S. Census, Southampton County, 1830, pp. 243, 244, 256, 259, 260, 264. On the reluctance of slaves to join the rising, see Patrick H. Breen, "Nat Turner's

Revolt: Rebellion and Response in Southampton County, Virginia" (PhD diss., University of Georgia, 2005), 89–92, 115–16.

129. [Gray], letter, *Richmond Whig*, 26 Sept. 1831, in *Norfolk American Beacon*, 30 Sept. 1831. Gray referred to Allen's quarter as "the chief settlement" among the plantations Nat Turner visited. In fact, Turner did not visit Allen's, but sent others to recruit there.

130. The three witnesses were Levi Waller, Stephen Bell, and Dilsy Vaughan.

131. Gray, *Confessions*, 14.

132. [Gray], letter, *Richmond Whig*, 26 Sept. 1831, in *Norfolk American Beacon*, 30 Sept. 1831.

133. Waller, testimony, trial of Nat Turner I, County Court Minute Book, 5 Nov. 1831, p. 122.

134. Waller genealogy (author's research file); U.S. Census, Southampton County, 1830, p. 263; Drewry, *Southampton Insurrection*, 56–57; Gray, *Confessions*, 19.

135. Waller, testimony, trial of Nat Turner I, County Court Minute Book, 5 Nov. 1831, p. 122.

136. Waller, testimony, trial of Daniel Porter, County Court Minute Book, 31 Aug. 1831, p. 72.

137. Waller, testimony, trial of Nat Turner I, County Court Minute Book, 5 Nov. 1831, p. 122.

138. Waller, testimony, trial of Dred Francis, County Court Minute Book, 5 Sept. 1831, p. 92.

139. Waller, testimony, trial of Nat Turner I, County Court Minute Book, 5 Nov. 1831, p. 122. Alfred's age was estimated in Alexander P. Peete, affidavit, 22 Nov. 1831, in Waller, petition 9803-A, 12 Dec. 1831, Legislative Petitions.

140. Waller, testimony, trials of Dred Francis and Nat Turner I, County Court Minute Book, 5 Sept. 1831, p. 93; 5 Nov. 1831, p. 122.

141. Waller, testimony, trial of Daniel Porter, County Court Minute Book, 31 Aug. 1831, p. 72; [Meriwether B. Brodnax], notes, deposition of Levi Waller, *Commonwealth v. Daniel Porter*, County Court Judgments, 1831.

142. Waller, affidavit, 21 Nov. 1831, in Peter Edwards, petition 9804-A, 12 Dec. 1831, Legislative Petitions.

143. Waller, testimony, trial of Dred Francis, County Court Minute Book, 5 Sept. 1831, p. 93.

144. Waller, testimony, trial of Hark Moore, County Court Minute Book, 3 Sept. 1831, p. 86.

145. Waller, testimony, trial of Davy Waller, County Court Minute Book, 3 Sept. 1831, pp. 88–89. The estimate of Davy's age is based in part on the value assigned him ($300) by the court.

146. Waller, testimony, trial of Sam Edwards, County Court Minute Book, 17 Oct. 1831, p. 118. Waller's reference to Nat Turner I was consistent with movements Turner must have made at the Waller farm, corroborating the account in the *Confessions*.

147. Waller, testimony, trial of Nat Turner I, County Court Minute Book, 5 Nov. 1831, p. 121.

148. A. P. Peete and Thomas Porter, affidavits, 22 Nov. 1831, in Levi Waller, petition 9803-A, 12 Dec. 1831, Legislative Petitions. Waller's eighteen slaves included four males between the ages of twenty-four and thirty-six; U.S. Census, Southampton County, 1830, p. 263.

149. Waller, testimony, trial of Daniel Porter, County Court Minute Book, 31 Aug. 1831, p. 72; Waller genealogy (author's research file).

150. Drewry, *Southampton Insurrection*, 57, 58. Drewry interviewed Burrell J. Wall and Lucinda Hill, descendants of Clarinda Jones; ibid., 197. Ages of Levi C. Waller and John K. Waller were given in U.S. Census, Southampton County, 1850, pp. 242a, 252.

151. Will, John Nicholson, 18 Aug. 1828, Will Book 10:127; U.S. Census, Southampton County, 1830, p. 258; St. Luke's Parish Land Book, 1831, entries for William B. Pope and Peter Pope, LVA; will, Nathan Pope Sr., 24 May 1828, Will Book 10:255; deed, Peter Pope and Mary Pope to Thomas D. Knight, 28 Mar. 1836, Deed Book 23:613–14.

152. Jarratt W. Judkins, testimony, trial of Davy Waller, County Court Minute Book, 3 Sept. 1831, p. 88.

153. U.S. Census, Southampton County, 1830, p. 259; Williams genealogy (author's research file).

154. Gray, *Confessions*, 14; Drewry, *Southampton Insurrection*, 59.

155. Gray, *Confessions*, 14–15.

156. Jacob Williams (slave), testimony, trial of Davy Waller, County Court Minute Book, 3 Sept. 1831, p. 89; U.S. Census, Southampton County, 1830, p. 259.

157. U.S. Census, Southampton County, 1830, p. 259; Cynthia Williams, testimony, trial of Nelson Williams, County Court Minute Book, 3 Sept. 1831, p. 88.

158. [Meriwether B. Brodnax], notes, depositions of Jacob Williams (master) and Caswell Worrell, *Commonwealth v. Nelson Williams*, Southampton County Court Judgments, 1831.

159. Stephen Bell, testimony, trial of Nelson Williams, County Court Minute Book, 3 Sept. 1831, p. 88. Stephen was described as a "man slave" in ibid., 21 Sept. 1831, p. 109.

160. Gray, *Confessions*, p. 15. The account of Edmund Drewry's killing in the *Confessions* is not consistent with the statement attributed to Turner that he witnessed only one killing after leaving the Whitehead house; the account is based on what Gray, not Turner, knew about Drewry's identity, his business at the farm that day, and his death. The *Confessions* has no account of the Worrell attack, an omission consistent with Nat Turner's point of view.

161. Cynthia Williams, testimony, trial of Nelson Williams, County Court Minute Book, 3 Sept. 1831, p. 88.

162. U.S. Census, Southampton County, 1830, p. 259; Stephen Bell, testimony, trial of Nelson Williams, County Court Minute Book, 3 Sept. 1831, p. 88.

163. John Hampden Pleasants, "Southampton Affair," *Richmond Whig*, 3 Sept. 1831, in *Norfolk American Beacon*, 6 Sept. 1831. Theodore Trezvant said they arrived at the Vaughan house at about 3:00 P.M., but he gave no evidence for his estimate; [Theodore Trezvant], letter, *Raleigh Register*, 15 Sept. 1831.

164. Pleasants, "Southampton Affair."

165. Pleasants, letter, *Richmond Whig*, 29 Aug. 1831, in *Richmond Religious Herald*, 2 Sept. 1831.

166. Pleasants gave the son's age as fifteen; Pleasants, "Southampton Affair."

167. Ibid.

168. Stephen Bell, testimony, trial of Nelson Williams, County Court Minute Book, 3 Sept. 1831, p. 88.

169. Drewry, *Southampton Insurrection*, 44n2; A. P. Peete and Thomas Porter, affidavits, in Waller, petition 9803-A, 1831, Legislative Petitions.

170. Wright Vaughan was brought into court but not tried, and Jim Vaughan was found not guilty; trial of Jim Vaughan, County Court Minute Book, 7 Sept. 1831, p. 99.

171. Gray, *Confessions*, 15.

172. Ibid.

173. Ibid.

174. *The Revised Code of the Laws of Virginia*, 2 vols. (Richmond: Thomas Ritchie, 1819), chap. 242, sec. 1; *Code of Virginia* (Richmond: William F. Ritchie, 1849), chap. 49, sec. 25; chap. 98, sec. 1–7.

175. Routes of the two volunteer parties are reconstructed from the accounts in [Gray], letter, *Richmond Whig*, 26 Sept. 1831, in *Norfolk American Beacon*, 30 Sept. 1831; [William C. Parker], letter, *Richmond Compiler*, 3 Sept. 1831, in *Richmond Enquirer*, 6 Sept. 1831; and Gray, *Confessions*, 15–16.

176. Gray, *Confessions*, 15.

177. Later historians identified French and Middleton as members of the first volunteers; Drewry, *Southampton Insurrection*, 63–64; Parramore, *Southampton County*, 92–93, 248n47. French must have been the volunteer whose letter to his father in Petersburg was summarized in another letter, dated Petersburg, VA, Thursday, 25 Aug. 1831, *Richmond Compiler*, 27 Aug. 1831, in "The Banditti," *Richmond Enquirer*, 30 Aug. 1831.

178. Gray paid no tax for a horse that year; Nottoway Parish Personal Property Tax List, 1831, entry for Thomas R. Gray, LVA.

179. County Court Minute Book, 21 Apr. 1828, p. 209; Parramore, *Southampton County*, 92. French in 1830 had no listing in the census and owned no real property in the county.

180. Nottoway Parish Personal Tax List, 1831, entries for Thomas R. Gray and James S. French. Unlike Gray, French did own a taxable horse in 1831.

181. U.S. Census, Southampton County, 1830, p. 243; Drewry, *Southampton Insurrection*, 63–64.

182. County Court Minute Book, 20 May 1816, p. 354; County Court Order Book, 17 June 1817, p. 178; deed, Thomas Ridley and others to Aubin Middleton, 28 Feb. 1831, Deed Book 22:66–67.

183. St. Luke's Parish Personal Tax List, 1831, entry for Aubin Middleton.

184. [James Trezvant], letter, *Raleigh Register*, 3 Sept. 1831; [William C. Parker], letter, *Richmond Compiler*, 3 Sept. 1831, in *Richmond Enquirer*, 6 Sept. 1831; County Court Minute Book, 21 Aug. 1826, p. 128.

185. U.S. Census, Southampton County, 1830, pp. 259, 277.

186. Jerusalem residents, 1831 (author's research file).

187. U.S. Census, Southampton County, 1830, p. 272.

188. Sampson C. Reese, testimony, trial of Daniel Porter, County Court Minute Book, 31 Aug. 1831, p. 73; Reese genealogy (author's research file); County Court Minute Book, 20 Apr. 1829, p. 264; deed, Thomas J. and Mary J. Harper to Sampson C. Reese, 19 Mar. 1829, Deed Book 21:105; U.S. Census, Southampton County, 1830, p. 264.

189. Drewry, *Southampton Insurrection*, 64, 198; U.S. Census, Southampton County, 1850, p. 310a; will, Charles Bryant, 12 May 1829, Will Book 10:177; St. Luke's Parish Land Book, 1831, entry for estate of Charles Bryant; St. Luke's Parish Land Book, 1832, entry for James D. and John R. Bryant. Drewry's source was Bryant's widow, Elizabeth S. Bryant. Drewry referred to Bryant as "Captain." Bryant's militia record has not been found.

190. Drewry, *Southampton Insurrection*, 65; Turner genealogy (author's research file); Marriage Register, p. 417, SCC; U.S. Census, Southampton County, 1830, p. 255 (Nancy S. Spencer); St. Luke's Parish Land Book, 1831, entry for estate of John Spencer.

191. On Drew, see Newit Drew, testimony, trial of Moses Barrow, County Court Minute Book, 1 Sept. 1831, p. 77; U.S. Census, Southampton County, 1830, p. 263; St. Luke's Parish Land Book, 1831, entry for Newit Drew. On Peete, see U.S. Census, Southampton County, 1830, p. 257; County Court Minute Book, 21 Feb. 1831, p. 27; 19 Sept. 1831, p. 106; A. P. Peete, affidavit, in Levi Waller, petition 9803-A, 1831, Legislative Petitions.

192. Drewry, *Southampton Insurrection*, 64n1. Waller testified that the child died Wednesday evening; Waller, testimony, trial of Daniel Porter, County Court Minute Book, 31 Aug. 1831, p. 72.

193. Gray, *Confessions*, 15. William C. Parker put the number of first volunteers at sixteen; [William C. Parker], letter, *Richmond Compiler*, 3 Sept. 1831, in *Richmond Enquirer*, 6 Sept. 1831.

194. A. P. Peete, affidavit, in Waller, petition 9803-A, Legislative Petitions. Drewry said that the cutting was performed by Sampson C. Reese; Drewry, *Southampton Insurrection*, 64n2.

195. Sampson C. Reese, testimony, trial of Daniel Porter, County Court Minute Book, 31 Aug. 1831, p. 73.

196. An uprising in Louisiana in 1811 was suppressed after a confrontation west of New Orleans; Daniel Rasmussen, *American Uprising: The Untold Story of America's Largest Slave Revolt* (New York: HarperCollins, 2011), 135–44.

197. [William C. Parker], letter, *Richmond Compiler*, 3 Sept. 1831, in *Richmond Enquirer*, 6 Sept. 1831; Reese, testimony, trial of Daniel Porter, County Court Minute Book, 31 Aug. 1831, p. 73; Gray, *Confessions*, 15–16. George W. Powell said that the insurgents numbered "about 30" at Parker's field; Powell, letter, *Christian Advocate*, 9 Sept. 1831.

198. Three slaves of James W. Parker came before the court on suspicion of taking part in the uprising, but charges against all three were dismissed; trial of Sam Parker, County Court Minute Book, 7 Sept. 1831, p. 99; Gray, *Confessions*, 15; [William C. Parker], letter, *Richmond Compiler*, 3 Sept. 1831, in *Richmond Enquirer*, 6 Sept. 1831.

199. [Gray], letter, *Richmond Whig*, 26 Sept. 1831, in *Norfolk American Beacon*, 30 Sept. 1831. Gray did not comment on Turner's estimate in the *Confessions*, though he must have been skeptical of the higher number. His restraint adds another note of authenticity to the *Confessions*. The woman who wrote from a location five miles east of Jerusalem had heard an estimate of thirty insurgents at Parker's field; letter, [23 Aug. 1831], *Richmond Compiler*, 27 Aug. 1831, in "The Banditti," *Richmond Enquirer*, 30 Aug. 1831. James Trezvant, who took part in the skirmish, put their number at forty; [James Trezvant], letter, *Raleigh Register*, 3 Sept. 1831. William C. Parker did not hazard an estimate.

200. Gray, *Confessions*, 15.

201. Letter, 23 Aug. 1831, *Richmond Compiler*, 27 Aug. 1831, in "The Banditti," *Richmond Enquirer*, 30 Aug. 1831. This was the reported shower that no eyewitness mentioned.

202. Parramore, *Southampton County*, 92, 248n47; Drewry, *Southampton Insurrection*, 65.

203. Gray, *Confessions*, 15.

204. Ibid., 15–16.

205. [James Trezvant], letter, *Raleigh Register*, 3 Sept. 1831. Trezvant said only that he volunteered with "several others," and Parker gave no indication of the number in the second party. John Vaughan, brother of Ann Eliza Vaughan and nephew of Rebecca Vaughan, was a member of this party; Drewry, *Southampton Insurrection*, 66n1.

206. [William C. Parker], letter, *Richmond Compiler*, 3 Sept. 1831, in *Richmond Enquirer*, 6 Sept. 1831.

207. Gray, *Confessions*, 16. Drewry's sources told him that Stephen Bell, the slave of James Bell, defected during the skirmish and rode to town, "hallooing at the top of his voice who he was and why he was riding so rapidly"; Drewry, *Southampton Insurrection*, 61.

208. Moses Moore, testimony, trials of Nathan Blunt and Nathan, Tom, and Davy Francis, County Court Minute Book, 6 Sept. 1831, pp. 94–95; Jesse Drewry, testimony, trial of Moses Moore, County Court Minute Book, 18 Oct. 1831, p. 120; Luke Bittle, Charlotte Edwards, and Cherry (slave), testimony, trial of Ben Blunt, County Court Minute Book, 21 Nov. 1831, p. 130.

209. Pleasants said they separated "early in the afternoon"; Pleasants, "Southampton Affair."

210. [William C. Parker], letter, *Richmond Compiler*, 3 Sept. 1831, in *Richmond Enquirer*, 6 Sept. 1831.

211. [Gray], letter, *Richmond Whig*, 26 Sept. 1831, in *Norfolk American Beacon*, 30 Sept. 1831.

212. Gray, *Confessions*, 16.

213. Ibid.

214. Dilsy Vaughan, testimony, trial of Moses Barrow, County Court Minute Book, 1 Sept. 1831, pp. 77–78.

215. Gray, *Confessions*, 16; U.S. Census, Southampton County, 1830, p. 243. In 1830 Ridley held a total of 145 slaves, divided (in numbers not recorded) between his home plantation and Buckhorn Quarter.

216. John C. Turner, testimony, trial of Curtis Ridley, County Court Minute Book, 2 Sept. 1831, p. 81.

217. [Gray], letter, *Richmond Whig*, 26 Sept. 1831, in *Norfolk American Beacon*, 30 Sept. 1831.

218. [James Strange French?], letter to Petersburg, 27 Aug. 1831, summary in "The Banditti," *Richmond Enquirer*, 30 Aug. 1831.

219. Theodore Trezvant, letter, 24 Aug. 1831, *Richmond Compiler*, 27 Aug. 1831, in "The Banditti," *Richmond Enquirer*, 30 Aug. 1831.

220. Pleasants, letter, *Richmond Whig*, 29 Aug. 1831, in *Richmond Religious Herald*, 2 Sept. 1831.

221. Norfolk gentleman, letter, *Norfolk American Beacon*, 29 Aug. 1831.

222. Jefferson to Coles, 25 Aug. 1814, in Thomas Jefferson, *Thomas Jefferson: Writings*, ed. Merrill D. Peterson (New York: Literary Classics of the United States, 1984), 1,345.

223. Gray, *Confessions*, 16. Turner suggested that as many as twenty recruits joined the insurgents after Parker's field, but he referred only to the four from Buckhorn Quarter.

224. [William C. Parker], letter, *Richmond Compiler*, 3 Sept. 1831, in *Richmond Enquirer*, 6 Sept. 1831.

225. Gray, *Confessions*, 16.

226. Ibid.; St. Luke's Parish Land Book, 1831, entry for Samuel Blunt; U.S. Census, Southampton County, 1830, p. 264.

227. Gray, *Confessions*, 16.

228. Pleasants, "Southampton Affair"; Drewry, *Southampton Insurrection*, 70–72; Dragoon express, report, in "The Banditti," *Richmond Enquirer*, 30 Aug. 1831; U.S. Census, Southampton County, 1830, pp. 243 (Fitzhugh), 264 (Blunt).

229. Pleasants, "Southampton Affair."

230. A. P. Peete, affidavit, in Thomas Fitzhugh (estate), petition 9915-F, Legislative Petitions. Peete said that on the following night loyal slaves were positioned near the front door and, he implied, were armed with guns.

231. Shadrach Futrell, testimony, trial of Moses Barrow, County Court Minute Book, 1 Sept. 1831, p. 76.

232. Gray, *Confessions*, 16.

233. Shadrach Futrell, Frank Blunt, and Mary Blunt, testimony, trial of Moses Barrow, County Court Minute Book, 1 Sept. 1831, pp. 76–77.

234. Gray, *Confessions*, 16–17; Hark Moore, testimony, trial of Moses Barrow, County Court Minute Book, 1 Sept. 1831, pp. 76–77; Pleasants, "Southampton Affair"; Drewry, *Southampton Insurrection*, 72.

235. John C. Turner, testimony, trials of Stephen Ridley and Curtis Ridley, County Court Minute Book, 2 Sept. 1831, pp. 81, 82.

236. Gray, *Confessions*, 17; Drewry, *Southampton Insurrection*, 73. Drewry's sources told him that a skirmish took place during the second visit at the Harris plantation and that the cavalry charged the insurgents "and killed nearly all of them" in woods near the house. "For months," Drewry was told, "skeletons could be seen in these woods." Among the dead, according to Drewry, was Will Francis, "the savage executioner." Nat Turner did not mention such a skirmish.

237. Gray, *Confessions*, 17.

238. Drewry Bittle, affidavit, 22 Nov. 1831, in Richard Porter, petition 9803, 12 Dec. 1831, Legislative Petitions.

239. Nat Turner II was committed to jail on 30 August; Alexander Myrick, warrant, 30 Aug. 1831, *Commonwealth v. Nat Turner II*, County Court Judgments, 1831, LVA.

240. Gray, *Confessions*, 17.

241. Elliott Whitehead, letter, n.d., *Norfolk Herald*, 7 Nov. 1831.

242. John Womack, affidavit, 21 Nov. 1831, in Peter Edwards, petition 9804-A, 12 Dec. 1831, Legislative Petitions.

243. Elliott Whitehead said Turner remained in this hiding place five weeks and six days; Whitehead, letter, *Norfolk Herald*, 7 Nov. 1831. Turner said he remained at this location six weeks; Gray, *Confessions*, 17. Another account implied that the period was closer to seven weeks; Alexander P. Peete to Gov. John Floyd, 20 Oct. 1831, Executive Papers of Gov. John Floyd, LVA.

Chapter 9. Suppression

1. Jordan Barnes, testimony, trial of Jack Reese, County Court Minute Book, 5 Sept. 1831, pp. 91–92, SCC.

2. Thomas Ridley, testimony, trial of Hark Moore, County Court Minute Book, 3 Sept. 1831, pp. 86–87.

3. Joseph Joiner, certificate, 21 Nov. 1831, in Peter Edwards, petition 9804-A, 12 Dec. 1831, Legislative Petitions, LVA; Norfolk gentleman, letter, *Norfolk American Beacon*, 29 Aug. 1831.

4. Norfolk gentleman, letter, *Norfolk American Beacon*, 29 Aug. 1831.

5. *Richmond Enquirer*, 2 Sept. 1831.

6. On the identity of Will, see "A Note on the Executioner," www.press.jhu.edu.

7. Henry Edwards, testimony, trial of Isham Edwards, County Court Minute Book, 7 Sept. 1831, p. 98; James Trezvant, warrant, 27 Aug. 1831, *Commonwealth v. Nathan Blunt*, County Court Judgments, 1831, LVA; John Hampden Pleasants, "Southampton Affair," *Richmond Constitutional Whig*, 3 Sept. 1831, in *Norfolk American Beacon*, 6 Sept. 1831; *Norfolk Herald*, 16 Sept. 1831.

8. Alexander P. Peete and Thomas Porter, affidavits, 22 Nov. 1831, in Levi Waller, petition 9803-A, 12 Dec. 1831, Legislative Petitions.

9. Levi Waller to the Senate and House of Delegates, [Dec. 1831], in Waller, petition 9803-A, Legislative Petitions.

10. Frank Blunt, testimony, trial of Moses Barrow, County Court Minute Book, 1 Sept. 1831, pp. 76–77; John C. Turner, testimony, trials of Curtis Ridley and Stephen Ridley, County Court Minute Book, 2 Sept. 1831, pp. 81–82.

11. Joiner, certificate, in Edwards, petition 9804-A, Legislative Petitions.

12. Nathaniel Francis, testimony, trial of Sam Edwards, County Court Minute Book, 17 Oct. 1831, p. 118.

13. Sampson C. Reese and John H. Barnes, affidavits, 19 Dec. 1831, in Elizabeth Turner II (estate), petition 9915-E, 29 Dec. 1831, Legislative Petitions.

14. John Womack, affidavit, 21 Nov. 1831, in Edwards, petition 9804-A, Legislative Petitions.

15. According to two different accounts, this search party shot to death a fourth man at the Whitehead house. In both accounts the victim (never named) was described as an adult male insurgent who belonged to Catherine Whitehead; no slave matching his description has been identified. See Charles Spiers and others, letter, 28 Sept. 1831, *Roanoke Advocate* (Halifax, NC), 13 Oct. 1831; letter, Winton, NC, *Norfolk Herald*, 29 Aug. 1831.

16. Spiers, letter, *Roanoke Advocate* (Halifax, NC), 13 Oct. 1831.

17. Drewry Bittle, affidavit, 22 Nov. 1831, in Richard Porter, petition 9803, 12 Dec. 1831, Legislative Petitions.

18. John Hampden Pleasants, letter, 25–27 Aug. 1831, *Richmond Whig*, 29 Aug. 1831, in *Richmond Religious Herald*, 2 Sept. 1831; Piety Reese (estate), petition 9915-D, 29 Dec. 1831, Legislative Petitions; *Norfolk American Beacon*, 29 Aug. 1831.

19. Jarratt W. Judkins, testimony, trial of Davy Waller, County Court Minute Book, 3 Sept. 1831, p. 89; trial of Daniel Porter, County Court Minute Book, 31 Aug. 1831, pp. 72–73; J. D. Massenburg, warrant, 29 Aug. 1831, and [Meriwether B. Brodnax], information, 17 Oct. 1831, *Commonwealth v. Jack and Shadrach Simmons*, County Court Judgments, 1831 (for Davy Turner and Sam Turner); Alexander Myrick, warrant, 30 Aug. 1831, *Commonwealth v. Nat Turner II*, County Court Judgments, 1831; James W. Parker, warrant, 31 Aug. 1831, *Commonwealth v. Dred Francis*, County Court Judgments, 1831. The date of Nelson Williams's capture and jailing is a deduction based on the date of his trial; Hark Moore, Moses Barrow, and Davy Waller were tried the same day; [Meriwether B. Brodnax], information, 3 Sept. 1831, *Commonwealth v. Hark Moore, Moses Barrow, Davy Waller, and Jacob Williams*, County Court Judgments, 1831.

20. James W. Parker, warrant, 5 Sept. 1831, *Commonwealth v. Joe Turner*, County Court Judgments, 1831.

21. See warrants and summonses for trials of these defendants, County Court Judgments, 1831.

22. Trial of Matt Ridley, County Court Minute Book, 19 Sept. 1831, p. 204; Alexander P. Peete, affidavit, 18 Jan. 1832, in Thomas Fitzhugh (estate), petition 9915-F, 29 Dec. 1831, Legislative Petitions; trial of Stephen Bell, County Court Minute Book, 21 Sept. 1831, p. 109; William S. Drewry, *The Southampton Insurrection* (1900; repr., Murfreesboro, NC: Johnson, 1968), 61.

23. Theodore Trezvant, letter, 3 Sept. 1831, *Richmond Whig*, 6 Sept. 1831, in *Norfolk American Beacon*, 9 Sept. 1831; Cedardale letter, 4 Sept. 1831, *Richmond Whig*, 8 Sept. 1831, in *Richmond Enquirer*, 9 Sept. 1831.

24. The eleven others who played minor roles were as follows: Ben Blunt, Isaac Champion, Jim Champion, Isaac Charlton, Hardy Edwards, Isham Edwards, Frank Parker, Jack Simmons, Shadrach Simmons, Andrew Whitehead, and Jack Whitehead. See warrants, summonses, and court minutes for their trials.

25. Thomas R. Gray, *The Confessions of Nat Turner* (Baltimore: Lucas & Deaver, 1831), 14.

26. Theodore Trezvant, letter, 5 Sept. 1831, *Raleigh Register*, 15 Sept. 1831; Drewry, *Southampton Insurrection*, 69–70.

27. [Thomas R. Gray], letter, 17 Sept. 1831, *Richmond Whig*, 26 Sept. 1831, in *Norfolk American Beacon*, 30 Sept. 1831. The estimate of forty includes Stephen Bell and

Matthew Ridley, who rode briefly with the insurgents; it excludes Viney Musgrave's son (not identified by name), Joe Harris, and any of the Vaughan or Parker slaves who might have been recruited by the band but who separated almost at once (appendix A).

28. The ten slaves who certainly had died by 2 September without being tried were Austin Edwards, James Edwards, Nelson Edwards, Aaron Porter, Henry Porter, Jacob Porter, Moses Porter, Jordan Turner, Alfred Waller, and Tom ("Marmaduke"), the man who died in jail.

29. George W. Powell, letter, 27 Aug. 1831, *Christian Advocate*, 9 Sept. 1831; U.S. Census, Northampton County, NC, 1830, p. 110, NA; O. M. Smith, letter, 29 August 1831, *New Hampshire Post*, 14 Sept. 1831, quoted in Thomas C. Parramore, *Southampton County, Virginia* (Charlottesville: University of Virginia Press, 1978), 99–100.

30. Eppes arrived in Jerusalem and took command on Wednesday, 24 August; Richard Eppes, dispatch, 24 Aug. 1831, summary in *Richmond Compiler*, 27 Aug. 1831, in "The Banditti," *Richmond Enquirer*, 30 Aug. 1831; Richard Eppes, order, 28 Aug. 1831, in *Norfolk American Beacon*, 31 Aug. 1831. In 1830 Eppes held sixty-two slaves at Palestine, his plantation in neighboring Sussex County; U.S. Census, Sussex County, VA, 1830, p. 28, NA. The general fell ill while in Southampton and died in July 1832, aged about forty-one; Gov. John Floyd to Gen. Richard Eppes, 6 Sept. 1831, and Eppes to Floyd, 8 Nov. 1831, in Henry I. Tragle, *The Southampton Slave Revolt of 1831: A Compilation of Source Material* (Amherst: University of Massachusetts Press, 1971), 272–73, 428–29; death notice in *Virginia Free Press* (Charles Town, WV), 16 Aug. 1832.

31. Eppes, order, *Norfolk American Beacon*, 31 Aug. 1831. Eppes meant that he would allow forceful action against any person committing unauthorized violence by arms or refusing to submit to lawful authority.

32. Ibid.

33. Pleasants, "Southampton Affair."

34. [William C. Parker], letter, 31 Aug. 1831, *Richmond Compiler*, 3 Sept. 1831, in *Richmond Enquirer*, 6 Sept. 1831.

35. [Gray], letter, *Richmond Whig*, 26 Sept. 1831, in *Norfolk American Beacon*, 30 Sept. 1831.

36. Ibid.

37. Accounts in Eric Foner, ed., *Nat Turner* (Englewood Cliffs, NJ: Prentice-Hall, 1971), 61–67; Tragle, *Southampton Slave Revolt*, 104–16; Henry Box Brown, *Narrative of the Life of Henry Box Brown*, ed. Richard Newman (1849; repr., New York: Oxford University Press, 2002), 30–31; Harriet A. Jacobs, *Incidents in the Life of a Slave Girl, Written by Herself*, ed. Jean Fagan Yellin (1861; repr., Cambridge, MA: Harvard University Press, 1987), 63–67.

38. [Gray], letter, *Richmond Whig*, 26 Sept. 1831, in *Norfolk American Beacon*, 30 Sept. 1831 (final paragraph). In November, Gray would try to minimize Turner's radical intentions, which may explain his reticent account of the killing of the Travis child; Gray *Confessions*, 12.

39. F. Roy Johnson retold the tale of massive bloodletting in 1966, in *The Nat Turner Slave Insurrection* (Murfreesboro, NC: Johnson, 1966), 109–16; Stephen B. Oates

repeated it in *The Fires of Jubilee: Nat Turner's Fierce Rebellion* (New York: Harper & Row, 1971), 97–101.

40. Thomas Wentworth Higginson, "Nat Turner's Insurrection," *Atlantic Monthly* 8 (1861): 173–87, in Higginson, *Travellers and Outlaws: Episodes in American History* (Boston: Lee & Shepard, 1888), 299, 304.

41. Drewry, *Southampton Insurrection*, 86–88.

42. John W. Cromwell, "The Aftermath of Nat Turner's Insurrection," *Journal of Negro History* 5 (1920): 212.

43. Herbert Aptheker, *Nat Turner's Slave Rebellion* (1966; repr., Mineola, NY: Dover, 2006), 50, 62.

44. Parramore treated the evidence on atrocities with skepticism in 1978. He suggested that reports of "massive homicide" were exaggerated and that the total number of black people killed in the suppression "in all likelihood" fell below fifty, apparently including those killed in skirmishes; Parramore, *Southampton County*, 102–3. In 2003 he revised the toll upward again, estimating that "at least 100 blacks, and possibly several times that figure, were killed"; Thomas C. Parramore, "Covenant in Jerusalem," in *Nat Turner: A Slave Rebellion in History and Memory*, ed. Kenneth S. Greenberg (New York: Oxford University Press, 2003), 70. Other historians have cast new doubt on the scale of white reaction. One recent estimate, based in part on personal property tax lists of 1831 and 1832, has put the number of slaves killed without trial in Southampton at between 16 and 148 (with the latter figure thought to be too high); Patrick H. Breen, "Nat Turner's Revolt: Rebellion and Response in Southampton County, Virginia" (PhD diss., University of Georgia, 2005), 158–62. See also Patrick H. Breen, "Contested Communion: The Limits of White Solidarity in Nat Turner's Virginia," *Journal of the Early Republic* 27 (2007): 702–3n28; and Melvin Patrick Ely, *Israel on the Appomattox: A Southern Experiment in Black Freedom from the 1780s through the Civil War* (New York: Alfred A. Knopf, 2004), 178–86.

45. St. Luke's Parish Personal Property Tax Lists, 1830, 1831, 1832, entries for free black taxpayers, LVA.

46. Three other free black men who came to trial were acquitted and then reappeared in the tax rolls of 1832; all three remained in the parish at least through 1833. See St. Luke's Parish Personal Tax Lists, 1830–33; trials of Exum Artis, Isham Turner, and Thomas Haithcock, County Circuit-Superior Court of Law and Chancery Minute Book, 5 Apr. 1832, p. 22; 4 Apr. 1832, p. 21; 6 Apr. 1832, p. 24, SCC. One free black man, Arnold Artis, was arrested, cleared of charges, and released without trial on 5 September 1831; examination of Arnold Artis, County Court Minute Book, 5 Sept. 1831, p. 93. Another was tried and found guilty of taking part in the conspiracy; trial of Berry Newsom, County Circuit-Superior Court of Law and Chancery Minute Book, 7 Apr. 1832, pp. 21, 28.

47. St. Luke's Parish Personal Tax Lists, 1821–32.

48. The nine cases include Nelson Edwards and Henry Porter, both killed before being captured and whose bodies were decapitated. They also include Austin Edwards, James Edwards, Aaron Porter, Jacob Porter, Moses Porter, Jordan Turner, and Alfred Waller. They exclude Tom (Marmaduke) and Billy Artis I.

49. [William C. Parker], letter, *Richmond Compiler*, 3 Sept. 1831, in *Richmond Enquirer*, 6 Sept. 1831.

50. *Richmond Compiler*, 29 Aug. 1831, in "The Banditti," *Richmond Enquirer*, 30 Aug. 1831.

51. Pleasants, letter, *Richmond Whig*, 29 Aug. 1831, in *Richmond Religious Herald*, 2 Sept. 1831.

52. William Brodnax quoted in *Norfolk Herald*, 31 Aug. 1831.

53. Letter, [23 Aug. 1831], *Richmond Compiler*, 27 Aug. 1831, in "The Banditti," *Richmond Enquirer*, 30 Aug. 1831; Belfield militiaman, letter, 24 Aug. 1831, *Petersburg Intelligencer*, 26 Aug. 1831, in *Norfolk American Beacon*, 30 Aug. 1831; [James Trezvant], letter, 31 Aug. 1831, *Raleigh Register*, 3 Sept. 1831; Levi Waller, testimony, trial of Daniel Porter, County Court Minute Book, 31 Aug. 1831, p. 72; Frank Blunt, testimony, trial of Moses Barrow, County Court Minute Book, 1 Sept. 1831, pp. 76–77.

54. [Gray], letter, *Richmond Whig*, 26 Sept. 1831, in *Norfolk American Beacon*, 30 Sept. 1831.

55. Gray, *Confessions*, 4.

56. [Gray], letter, *Richmond Whig*, 26 Sept. 1831, in *Norfolk American Beacon*, 30 Sept. 1831.

57. Drewry identified Jones in 1900 as the rider who carried the letter "to the Governor" (meaning to Petersburg); Drewry, *Southampton Insurrection*, 77n1.

58. Journal, Governor's Council, 23 Aug. 1831, in Tragle, *Southampton Slave Revolt*, 419.

59. *Richmond Compiler*, 24 Aug. 1831, in *Norfolk American Beacon*, 26 Aug. 1831.

60. Ibid.

61. Jesse D. Elliott to Levi Woodbury, 28 Aug. 1831, in *Richmond Enquirer*, 16 Sept. 1831. Com. Elliott described the messenger ("Mr. Gray") as "a highly respectable gentleman . . . who came direct from the scene of the disturbance."

62. *Norfolk Herald*, 26 Aug. 1831.

63. Pleasants, letter, *Richmond Whig*, 29 Aug. 1831, in *Richmond Religious Herald*, 2 Sept. 1831. Mileage from Richmond to Jerusalem was given in Joseph Martin, *A Comprehensive Description of Virginia, and the District of Columbia* (Richmond: J. W. Randolph, [1835]), 279.

64. Norfolk gentleman, letter, *Norfolk American Beacon*, 29 Aug. 1831.

65. Jesse H. Simmons, letter, [n.d.], *Roanoke Advocate* (Halifax, NC), 8 Sept. 1831.

66. Richard Eppes, letter to Lt. Colonel, Isle of Wight County militia, 24 Aug. 1831, *Richmond Compiler*, 27 Aug. 1831, in "The Banditti," *Richmond Enquirer*, 30 Aug. 1831.

67. Eppes, order, *Norfolk American Beacon*, 31 Aug. 1831.

68. *Norfolk American Beacon*, 28 Oct. 1831. Capt. Thomas Gray, father of Thomas R. Gray, was sixty years old, not seventy-five; he was dead by 19 Sept. 1831, when his will was proved.

69. The editors printed a correction the next day, noting that the *Perkins* carried a burden of 385 tons, not 325; *Norfolk American Beacon*, 29 Oct. 1831.

70. John Floyd, *Life and Diary of John Floyd*, ed. Charles H. Ambler (Richmond: Richmond Press, 1918), 165, 170 (diary entries for 17 Oct., 21 Nov. 1831).

71. Cedardale letter, *Richmond Whig*, 8 Sept. 1831, in *Richmond Enquirer*, 9 Sept. 1831. The author said he had been "engaged three or four days, trying those scoundrels."

72. Letter, "To the Editors," *Richmond Enquirer*, 20 Sept. 1831.

73. Eugene Genovese, *From Rebellion to Revolution: Afro-American Slave Revolts in the Making of the Modern World* (Baton Rouge: Louisiana State University Press, 1979), 17.

74. Letter, "To the Editors," *Richmond Enquirer*, 20 Sept. 1831; Floyd, *Life and Diary of John Floyd*, 170 (diary entry for 21 Nov. 1831).

75. Editorial, *Richmond Whig*, in *Philadelphia National Gazette*, 22 Nov. 1831.

76. Thomas Jefferson to John Holmes, 22 Apr. 1820, in Thomas Jefferson, *Thomas Jefferson: Writings*, ed. Merrill D. Peterson (New York: Literary Classics of the United States, 1984), 1,434.

77. Editorial, *Richmond Whig*, in *Philadelphia National Gazette*, 22 Nov. 1831.

78. [Gray], letter, *Richmond Whig*, 26 Sept. 1831, in *Norfolk American Beacon*, 30 Sept. 1831.

79. William C. Parker to Col. Bernard Peyton, 14 Sept. 1831; Parker to Gov. John Floyd, 14 Sept. 1831, 1 Oct. 1831, Executive Papers of Gov. John Floyd, LVA.

Chapter 10. The Inquiry

1. Letter, "The Late Expedition against the Insurgents," *Norfolk American Beacon*, 29 Aug. 1831; Jesse D. Elliott to Levi Woodbury, 28 Aug. 1831, *Richmond Enquirer*, 16 Sept. 1831.

2. Samuel Blunt, certificate, 12 Sept. 1831, Auditor of Public Accounts, Insurrections, Records, 1831–33, Southampton Insurrection, Military Papers, LVA.

3. Trezvant indicated that he had met Pleasants that week in Jerusalem; Theodore Trezvant, letter, 3 Sept. 1831, *Richmond Constitutional Whig*, 6 Sept. 1831, in *Norfolk American Beacon*, 9 Sept. 1831. Trezvant still occupied the house owned by his mother-in-law, Eliza W. Waddill; deed, Lewis C. Trezvant and Rebecca Trezvant to Eliza W. Waddill, 23 Oct. 1828, Deed Book 21:47, SCC; U.S. Census, Southampton County, 1830, manuscript returns, p. 272, NA; deed, Theodore Trezvant to James S. French, 18 Dec. 1837, Deed Book 24:480–81.

4. *Richmond Whig*, 30 Aug. 1831, in *Philadelphia National Gazette*, 27 Aug. 1831.

5. John Hampden Pleasants, letter, 25–27 Aug. 1831, *Richmond Whig*, 29 Aug. 1831, in *Richmond Religious Herald*, 2 Sept. 1831.

6. *Norfolk Herald*, 29 Aug. 1831.

7. *Richmond Enquirer*, 2 Sept. 1831.

8. Gray gave his age in his pamphlet on dueling; Thomas R. Gray, *To the Public* [Jerusalem, 1834], 8. His death notice in 1845 gave his age as forty-five; *Norfolk American Beacon*, 26 Aug. 1845.

9. John Bennett Boddie, *Virginia Historical Genealogies* (Redwood City, CA: Pacific Coast, 1954), 315–16; Gray genealogy (author's research file); Nottoway Parish Land Book, 1786, and Nottoway Parish Personal Property Tax List, 1782, entries for Col. Edwin Gray, LVA.

10. Edwin Gray, diary, 1778, passim, VHS.

11. Will, Col. Edwin Gray, 3 Sept. 1788, Will Book 4:380, SCC.

12. Will, Joseph Ruffin, 26 Jan. 1806, Will Book 6:405–7; deed, John Urquhart to Charles Ruffin, 24 Feb. 1810, Deed Book 19:132. Charles Ruffin, aged fifty, was registered as a free black man in 1823; Free Negro Register, vol. 1, entry 1,413, LVA.

13. Will, Thomas Gray Sr., 6 Sept. 1831, Will Book 10:343.

14. Nottoway Parish Land Book, 1821, and Nottoway Parish Personal Tax List, 1821, entries for Thomas Gray Sr.; U.S. Census, Southampton County, 1830, p. 118. In 1821 Thomas Gray Sr. and his sons Robert and Thomas R. (both still living under his roof) together held forty-four taxable slaves; as a single holding, theirs would have been the fourth largest in the county.

15. Nottoway Parish Personal Tax List, 1821, entry for Thomas Gray Sr.; Thomas C. Parramore, *Southampton County, Virginia* (Charlottesville: University of Virginia Press, 1978), 51.

16. Nottoway Parish Land Book, 1821, entry for Thomas Gray Sr.

17. Inventory, Thomas Gray Sr., 26 Oct. 1831, Will Book 10:386–87. The men who appraised his estate found just 69 cents in his house.

18. Nottoway Parish Personal Tax List, 1815, entries for Thomas Gray Sr. and Edwin Gray Sr.; Nottoway Parish Personal Tax List, 1821, entry for Thomas Gray Sr.

19. Inventory, Thomas Gray Sr., Will Book 10:386–87; deed, Thomas Gray Sr. to Ann Gray, 6 Sept. 1831, Deed Book 22:93; deed, Edwin Gray to Jesse Drewry and Orris A. Browne, 19 Nov. 1831, Deed Book 22:123.

20. Gray, *To the Public*, 8.

21. Edwin Gray Sr. to James Rochelle, 12 June 1813, Rochelle Papers, RDU.

22. County Court Minute Book, 15 Nov. 1819, p. 49, SCC; 21 Mar. 1820, p. 78; 19–20 Mar. 1822, pp. 244–46; *Gray v. Jeremiah Wistra executors*, 1 Oct. 1829, Southampton County Court Judgments, 1829, LVA.

23. No white woman of Ann Gray's age was listed in Capt. Gray's household in 1820; U.S. Census, Southampton County, 1820, p. 118.

24. Deed, Thomas Gray Sr. to Thomas R. Gray, 10 Apr. 1821, Deed Book 18:134.

25. Nottoway Parish Personal Tax List, 1821, entry for Thomas R. Gray.

26. Nottoway Parish Land Book, 1824, entry for Thomas R. Gray.

27. A record of the marriage has yet to be found. Mary A. Gray witnessed a deed with her father-in-law in 1827; deed, William West and Lucretia West to Thomas R. Gray, 8 Dec. 1827, Deed Book 20:361. The name of Thomas R. Gray's daughter appears in will, Thomas Gray Sr., Will Book 10:343.

28. Nottoway Parish Personal Tax List, 1827, entry for Thomas R. Gray.

29. County Court Minute Book, 19 Feb. 1828, p. 201.

30. Deed, Thomas Gray Sr. to Thomas R. Gray, 15 Mar. 1828, Deed Book 20:344.

31. List of members, Jerusalem Jockey Club, [1830?], *Nicholson v. Garrison*, County Circuit Superior Court of Law and Chancery, in Box 13, Blow Papers, CWM.

32. Deed, Edwin Gray III to William Blow, trustee, 23 Nov. 1826, Deed Book 20:100–101.

33. Nottoway Parish Land Book, 1829, and Nottoway Parish Personal Tax Lists, 1830, 1831, entries for Edwin Gray III.

34. Deed, Thomas Gray Sr. to Thomas R. Gray, Deed Book 20:344.

35. Deed, Thomas Gray Sr. to James Rochelle and Orris A. Browne, 9 Aug. 1830, Deed Book 21:427–28.

36. U.S. Census, Southampton County, 1830, p. 287; inventory, Thomas Gray Sr., Will Book 10:386–87.

37. Deed, Thomas R. Gray to Orris A. Browne, 24 Mar. 1830, Deed Book 21:306; deed, Thomas R. Gray to Richard A. Urquhart, 17 May 1830, Deed Book 21:339–40.

38. Deed, Richard A. Urquhart, trustee, to Richard Williams, 4 Feb. 1831, Deed Book 21:525.

39. Nottoway Parish Personal Tax List, 1831, entries for Thomas Gray Sr. and Thomas R. Gray.

40. Deed, Thomas R. Gray to Richard Urquhart and others, 17 May 1830, Deed Book 21:339–40.

41. Gray, *To the Public*, 8.

42. [Thomas R. Gray], letter, 17 Sept. 1831, *Richmond Whig*, 26 Sept. 1831, in *Norfolk American Beacon*, 30 Sept. 1831.

43. The first group of volunteers encountered Alfred on Barrow Road; Alexander P. Peete, affidavit, 22 Nov. 1831, in Levi Waller, petition 9803-A, 12 Dec. 1831, Legislative Petitions, LVA.

44. [Gray], letter, *Richmond Whig*, 26 Sept. 1831, in *Norfolk American Beacon*, 30 Sept. 1831.

45. [William C. Parker], letter, 31 Aug. 1831, *Richmond Compiler*, 3 Sept. 1831, in *Richmond Enquirer*, 6 Sept. 1831.

46. *Norfolk Herald*, 26 Aug. 1831.

47. Ibid.; *Norfolk American Beacon*, 26 Aug. 1831.

48. Brackets indicate anonymous publication.

49. Trezvant's first list appeared in the *Norfolk Herald* on 29 August, in the *Norfolk American Beacon* on 30 August, and in the *Raleigh Register* on 1 September.

50. Pleasants said on Thursday, 25 August, that he had the list in his possession; it was published with his addendum of Saturday, 27 August, in Pleasants, letter, *Richmond Whig*, 29 Aug. 1831, in *Richmond Religious Herald*, 2 Sept. 1831.

51. [William C. Parker], letter, *Richmond Compiler*, 3 Sept. 1831, in *Richmond Enquirer*, 6 Sept. 1831.

52. Richard Eppes, dispatch, 24 Aug. 1831, summary in *Richmond Compiler*, 27 Aug. 1831, in "The Banditti," *Richmond Enquirer*, 30 Aug. 1831.

53. [James Strange French?], letter to Petersburg, 24 Aug 1831, summarized in letter, *Richmond Compiler*, 27 Aug. 1831, in "The Banditti," *Richmond Enquirer*, 30 Aug. 1831.

54. Pleasants, letter, *Richmond Whig*, 29 Aug. 1831, in *Richmond Religious Herald*, 2 Sept. 1831.

55. Trials of Hark Moore, Jack Reese, and Moses Moore, County Court Minute Book, 2 Sept. 1831, pp. 86–87; 3, 5 Sept. 1831, pp. 89, 91–92; 18 Oct. 1831, p. 120.

56. County Court Order Book, 1 Jan. 1824, p. 363; 21 June 1824, p. 19, SCC; Report, Committee to inspect the Jail, Aug. 1832, *Commonwealth v. Henry B. Vaughan*, County Court Records, Superior Court of Law and Chancery, Judgments, 1832–33, LVA.

57. Thomas C. Jones, testimony, trial of Jack Reese, County Court Minute Book, 3 Sept. 1831, p. 90.

58. John Hampden Pleasants, "Southampton Affair," *Richmond Whig*, 3 Sept. 1831, in *Norfolk American Beacon*, 6 Sept. 1831.

59. Drewry, testimony, trial of Moses Moore, County Court Minute Book, 18 Oct. 1831, p. 120.

60. Theodore Trezvant, letter, 5 Sept. 1831, *Raleigh Register*, 15 Sept. 1831.

61. [Theodore Trezvant], "List of persons ascertained to have been killed," *Norfolk Herald*, 29 Aug. 1831.

62. Pleasants, "Southampton Affair."

63. [Gray], letter, *Richmond Whig*, 26 Sept. 1831, in *Norfolk American Beacon*, 30 Sept. 1831; Pleasants, letter, *Richmond Whig*, 29 Aug. 1831, in *Richmond Religious Herald*, 2 Sept. 1831.

64. *Richmond Enquirer*, 2 Sept. 1831.

65. [Gray], letter, *Richmond Whig*, 26 Sept. 1831, in *Norfolk American Beacon*, 30 Sept. 1831.

66. Pleasants, "Southampton Affair."

67. Samuel Warner, *Authentic and Impartial Narrative of the Tragical Scene Which Was Witnessed in Southampton County* (New York: Warner & West, 1831), 31.

68. [James Trezvant], letter, 31 Aug. 1831, *Raleigh Register*, 3 Sept. 1831.

69. Cherry (slave), testimony, trial of Ben Blunt, County Court Minute Book, 21 Nov. 1831, p. 130.

70. *Richmond Enquirer*, 2 Sept. 1831.

71. Pleasants, "Southampton Affair."

72. Nathaniel Francis, testimony, trial of Daniel Porter, County Court Minute Book, 31 Aug. 1831, p. 72.

73. Trial of Sam Francis, County Court Minute Book, 3 Sept. 1831, p. 85.

74. Pleasants, "Southampton Affair."

75. County Court Minute Book, 21 May 1827, p. 160.

76. Ibid.

77. [James Trezvant], letter, *Raleigh Register*, 3 Sept. 1831; [William C. Parker], letter, *Richmond Compiler*, 3 Sept. 1831, in *Richmond Enquirer*, 6 Sept. 1831.

78. Hark Moore, testimony, trial of Moses Barrow, County Court Minute Book, 1 Sept. 1831, p. 77. Hark probably did not witness the attack at the Barrow farm.

79. [James Trezvant], letter, *Raleigh Register*, 3 Sept. 1831; [William C. Parker], letter, *Richmond Compiler*, 3 Sept. 1831, in *Richmond Enquirer*, 6 Sept. 1831. George W. Powell heard that there were thirty insurgents at Parker's field; Powell, letter, 27 Aug. 1831, *Christian Advocate*, 9 Sept. 1831.

80. [Gray], letter, *Richmond Whig*, 26 Sept. 1831, in *Norfolk American Beacon*, 30 Sept. 1831.

81. [William C. Parker], letter, *Richmond Compiler*, 3 Sept. 1831, in *Richmond Enquirer*, 6 Sept. 1831.

82. [James Trezvant], letter, *Raleigh Register*, 3 Sept. 1831; [William C. Parker], letter, *Richmond Compiler*, 3 Sept. 1831, in *Richmond Enquirer*, 6 Sept. 1831.

83. [Gray], letter, *Richmond Whig*, 26 Sept. 1831, in *Norfolk American Beacon*, 30 Sept. 1831.

84. County Court Minute Book, 31 Aug. 1831, pp. 72–74.

85. *The Revised Code of the Laws of Virginia*, 2 vols. (Richmond: Thomas Ritchie, 1819), chap. 111, sec. 32, 40, 43; *Code of Virginia* (Richmond: William F. Ritchie, 1849), chap. 212, sec. 2–8.

86. Trial of Daniel Porter, County Court Minute Book, 31 Aug. 1831, pp. 72–73; "Trial of the Insurgents," *Norfolk Herald*, 16 Sept. 1831.

87. County Court Minute Book, 31 Aug.–21 Nov. 1831, pp. 72–100, 102–14, 117–23, 129–31.

88. Tragle's transcription of Davy Turner's plea omits the word *not* in "not guilty"; Henry I. Tragle, *The Southampton Slave Revolt of 1831: A Compilation of Source Material* (Amherst: University of Massachusetts Press, 1971), 185.

89. Jim and Isaac Champion were transported; Auditor of Public Accounts, List of Slaves and Free persons of color received into the Penitentiary, 1816–42, in Records, Condemned Blacks Executed or Transported, 1783–1864, LVA. One slave, Joe Briggs, was jailed and brought to court twice but was never tried or formally dismissed. He is included here among the seven whose cases were dismissed; County Court Minute Book, 19 Sept. 1831, p. 106; 20 Sept. 1831, p. 109.

90. Examinations of Arnold Artis, Thomas Haithcock, Berry Newsom, Exum Artist, and Isham Turner, County Court Minute Book, 5 Sept. 1831, p. 93; 19 Sept. 1831, p. 105; 20 Sept. 1831, pp. 107–8; 18 Oct. 1831, p. 120.

91. Trials of Thomas Haithcock, Isham Turner, Exum Artist, and Berry Newsom, County Circuit-Superior Court of Law and Chancery Minute Book, 3–7 Apr. 1832, pp. 17, 19, 21–22, 24, 28, SCC.

92. Magistrate profiles (author's research file); Walter L. Gordon, *The Nat Turner Insurrection Trials: A Mystic Chord Resonates Today* ([Los Angeles]: W. L. Gordon, 2009), 130–32.

93. *Biographical Directory of the American Congress, 1774–1996* (Alexandria, VA: CQ Staff Directories, 1997), 1,961.

94. List of members, Jerusalem Jockey Club, Box 13, Blow Papers.

95. *Revised Code of Virginia* (1819), chap. 71, sec. 2; *Code of Virginia* (1849), chap. 48, sec. 2; Robert Brugger, *Beverley Tucker: Heart over Head in the Old South* (Baltimore: Johns Hopkins University Press, 1978), 35.

96. This paragraph and the next rest on magistrate profiles (author's research file) and trial records in the court minute book.

97. Robert Birchett of Petersburg and William D. Boyle, who may have resided briefly in Nottoway Parish, were assigned one defendant each. Court minutes do not give the name of the attorney for Stephen Bell, who was acquitted.

98. William C. Parker was assigned to defend Joe Briggs, whose case did not come to trial.

99. Trial of Davy Turner, County Court Minute Book, 2 Sept. 1831, pp. 79–81.

100. Christian Atkins, testimony, trial of Joe Turner, County Court Minute Book, 19 Sept. 1831, p. 102.

101. Trial of Sam Francis, County Court Minute Book, 3 Sept. 1831, pp. 85–86; magistrate profiles (author's research file).

102. Trial of Jack Reese, County Court Minute Book, 3, 5 Sept. 1831, pp. 89–90, 91–92.

103. Ibid., 92.

104. Floyd to Eppes, 10 Sept. 1831, in Tragle, *Southampton Slave Revolt*, 273.

105. Warner, *Authentic and Impartial Narrative*, 15.

106. [Gray], letter, *Richmond Whig*, 26 Sept. 1831, in *Norfolk American Beacon*, 30 Sept. 1831.

107. Trial of Nathan, Tom, and Davy Francis, County Court Minute Book, 6 Sept. 1831, pp. 94–95.

108. Moses Moore, testimony, trial of Nathan, Tom, and Davy Francis, County Court Minute Book, 6 Sept. 1831, pp. 94–95.

109. County Court Minute Book, 6 Sept. 1831, p. 95.

110. Auditor of Public Accounts, List of Slaves received into the Penitentiary.

111. Will, Thomas Gray Sr., Will Book 10:343–44.

112. Orris A. Browne, medical account of T. R. Gray, Sept. 1831, *Browne v. Gray*, County Court Records, Chancery Papers, 1835, LVA. Capt. Thomas Gray was attended by Dr. Robert Murray; account, estate of Thomas Gray Sr., 1831–33, Will Book 11:199.

113. Editor's remarks, *Richmond Whig*, 26 Sept. 1831, in Tragle, *Southampton Slave Revolt*, 90.

114. This paragraph and the five following are based on evidence in [Gray], letter, *Richmond Whig*, 26 Sept. 1831, in *Norfolk American Beacon*, 30 Sept. 1831.

115. Jefferson used similar terms to describe the "degraded condition" and "degradation" of the slave population; Jefferson to Coles, 25 Aug. 1814, in Thomas Jefferson, *Thomas Jefferson: Writings*, ed. Merrill D. Peterson (New York: Literary Classics of the United States, 1984), 1,344.

116. Names of twenty-seven slaves and one free black charged with conspiracy and insurrection in other Virginia counties in 1831 are listed in Philip J. Schwarz, *Twice Condemned: Slaves and the Criminal Laws of Virginia, 1705–1865* (Baton Rouge: Louisiana State University Press, 1988), 332–34.

117. Letter, William C. Parker to Gov. John Floyd, 14 Sept. 1831, Executive Papers of Gov. John Floyd, LVA.

118. John Floyd, proclamation, 17 Sept. 1831, Executive Papers of Gov. John Floyd.

119. This paragraph and the three following rest on [William C. Parker], letter, 21 Sept. 1831, *Richmond Enquirer*, 30 Sept. 1831.

120. [Gray], letter, *Richmond Whig*, 26 Sept. 1831, in *Norfolk American Beacon*, 30 Sept. 1831.

121. Ibid.

122. *Norfolk American Beacon*, 11 Oct. 1831.

123. Statutes limited to three the number of continuations in cases involving slaves; *Revised Code of Virginia* (1819), chap. 111, sec. 35; *Code of Virginia* (1849), chap. 212, sec. 7.

124. Auditor of Public Accounts, List of Slaves received into the Penitentiary. Moses was sold on 14 April 1833, the same day Nathan, Tom, and Davy Francis were sold.

125. *Richmond Enquirer*, 25 Oct. 1831; letter, *Richmond Whig*, 7 Nov. 1831, in *Nat Turner*, ed. Eric Foner (Englewood Cliffs, NJ: Prentice-Hall, 1971), 31.

126. Names of the other prisoners in November and December appear in *Commonwealth v. Henry B. Vaughan*, Aug. 1832, County Court Records, Superior Court of Law and Chancery, Judgments, 1832–33; County Circuit-Superior Court of Law and Chancery Minute Book, 7 Apr. 1832, p. 28.

127. Theodore Trezvant, letter, *Norfolk American Beacon*, 5 Nov. 1831.

Chapter 11. Confession

1. Isaac Pipkin, letter, 1 Nov. 1831, *Norfolk American Beacon*, 4 Nov. 1831; letter, 31 Oct. 1831, *Richmond Whig*, 7 Nov. 1831, in *Nat Turner*, ed. Eric Foner (Englewood Cliffs, NJ: Prentice-Hall, 1971), 31–32; *Norfolk Herald*, 4 Nov. 1831.

2. Theodore Trezvant, letter, 31 Oct. 1831, *Norfolk American Beacon*, 5 Nov. 1831.

3. [Meriwether B. Brodnax], prosecutor's notes, deposition of James Trezvant, n.d., *Commonwealth v. Nat Turner I*, County Court Judgments, 1831, LVA; James Trezvant, testimony, trial of Nat Turner I, County Court Minute Book, 5 Nov. 1831, pp. 122–23, SCC.

4. [William C. Parker], letter, 1 Nov. 1831, *Richmond Enquirer*, 8 Nov. 1831.

5. [Thomas R. Gray?], letter, 1 Nov. 1831, *Richmond Enquirer*, 8 Nov. 1831.

6. [Meriwether B. Brodnax], notes, deposition of James Trezvant, *Commonwealth v. Nat Turner I*, County Court Judgments, 1831; James Trezvant, testimony, trial of Nat Turner I, County Court Minute Book, 5 Nov. 1831, pp. 122–23; Elliott Whitehead, letter, n.d., *Norfolk Herald*, 7 Nov. 1831.

7. [William C. Parker], letter, *Richmond Enquirer*, 8 Nov. 1831.

8. Thomas R. Gray, *The Confessions of Nat Turner* (Baltimore: Lucas & Deaver, 1831), 19.

9. Letter, Sussex, VA, 31 Oct. 1831, *Richmond Enquirer*, 4 Nov. 1831.

10. Gray, *Confessions*, 7.

11. Ibid., 7, 18.

12. Ibid., 18–19.

13. [William C. Parker], letter, *Richmond Enquirer*, 8 Nov. 1831; [Gray?], letter, *Richmond Enquirer*, 8 Nov. 1831.

14. Gray, *Confessions*, 18.

15. Ibid., 7.

16. Ibid., 18.

17. *Richmond Enquirer*, 2 Dec. 1831.

18. Accounts published before Turner's capture, together with reports of statements he made after being captured, indicate the sincerity of his belief in his visions; see also Eric J. Sundquist, *To Wake the Nations: Race in the Making of American Literature* (Cambridge, MA: Harvard University Press, 1993), 59–60.

19. Gray, *Confessions*, 7.

20. The two voices are analyzed in Sundquist, *To Wake the Nations*, 36–56.

21. Gray, *Confessions*, 9.

22. Ibid.

23. Ibid., 9–11.

24. Ibid., 11.

25. Deed, Thomas Gray Sr. to Ann Gray, 6 Sept. 1831, Deed Book 22:93, SCC.

26. Turner's account of the baptism in the *Confessions* (p. 11) has no reference to the predicted dove. Either Turner failed to mention it, or Gray neglected to record it. If Gray knew of this detail through William C. Parker's account (which seems likely), he may not have appreciated its significance.

27. The narrative begins in the final paragraph of Turner's recollections, on page 11 of the original pamphlet, where Turner says, "And immediately on the sign

appearing in the heavens . . . ," and concludes on page 18, where he says, "I am here loaded with chains, and willing to suffer the fate that awaits me." The count includes only new details presented from the perspective of Nat Turner. The number might vary with different definitions and methods, but probably would not fall below 100 or rise above 125.

28. Gray, *Confessions*, 12.

29. Ibid.

30. Ibid., 12–14.

31. Ibid., 14–15. From a distance, Turner also may have witnessed the other three killings at the farm of William Williams Jr.

32. Ibid., 15.

33. Ibid., 14.

34. *Oxford English Dictionary*, 2nd ed., s.v. "terror."

35. Gray, *Confessions*, 18.

36. Ibid., 18–19.

37. Trial of Nat Turner I, County Court Minute Book, 5 Nov. 1831, p. 121. The clerk customarily recorded the names of judges as they arrived and departed.

38. Tragle transcribed the word *rescue* as "remove"; Henry I. Tragle, *The Southampton Slave Revolt of 1831: A Compilation of Source Material* (Amherst: University of Massachusetts Press, 1971), 221.

39. Trial of Nat Turner I, County Court Minute Book, 5 Nov. 1831, p. 121.

40. [Meriwether B. Brodnax], information, *Commonwealth v. Nat Turner I*, County Court Judgments, 1831.

41. Gray, *Confessions*, 20.

42. [Meriwether B. Brodnax], notes, depositions of Levi Waller and James Trezvant, *Commonwealth v. Nat Turner I*, County Court Judgments, 1831; Levi Waller and James Trezvant, testimony, trial of Nat Turner I, County Court Minute Book, 5 Nov. 1831, pp. 122–23.

43. [Meriwether B. Brodnax], notes, depositions of Levi Waller and James Trezvant, *Commonwealth v. Nat Turner I*, County Court Judgments, 1831; Levi Waller and James Trezvant, testimony, trial of Nat Turner I, County Court Minute Book, 5 Nov. 1831, pp. 122–23.

44. [Meriwether B. Brodnax], notes, depositions of Levi Waller and James Trezvant, *Commonwealth v. Nat Turner I*, County Court Judgments, 1831; Levi Waller and James Trezvant, testimony, trial of Nat Turner I, County Court Minute Book, 5 Nov. 1831, pp. 122–23.

45. Gray, *Confessions*, 20.

46. Trial of Nat Turner I, County Court Minute Book, 5 Nov. 1831, p. 123.

47. *The Revised Code of the Laws of Virginia*, 2 vols. (Richmond: Thomas Ritchie, 1819), chap. 71, sec. 19; *Code of Virginia* (Richmond: William F. Ritchie, 1849), chap. 161, sec. 5.

48. *Revised Code of Virginia* (1819), chap. 111, sec. 40; *Code of Virginia* (1849), chap. 212, sec. 6; L. R. Edwards, minutes (copy), trial of Nat Turner I, County Court Judgments, 1831.

49. Gray, *Confessions*, 20.

50. Ibid., 20–21.

51. Trial of Nat Turner I, County Court Minute Book, 5 Nov. 1831, p. 123.

52. Gray, *Confessions*, 5.

53. Ibid., 5–6.

54. Edmund J. Lee, copyright, Arlington County, VA, District Court Copyrights Secured, 1803–45, LVA.

55. Gray, *Confessions*, 3–5.

56. Ibid.

57. *Richmond Enquirer*, 8 Nov. 1831.

58. The *Philadelphia National Gazette*, relying on the *Richmond Compiler*, reported on 16 November that Gray was carrying the manuscript to Baltimore. "It will make a pamphlet of about sixteen octavo pages and it is intended to print 50,000 copies." The same report appeared in the *Raleigh Star*, 17 Nov. 1831.

59. C. Hall advertisement, *Norfolk American Beacon*, 23 Nov. 1831; John H. Nash advertisement, *Richmond Enquirer*, 20 Dec. 1831.

Chapter 12. Closing Scenes

1. *Petersburg Intelligencer*, n.d., in *Philadelphia National Gazette*, 17 Nov. 1831; *Norfolk American Beacon*, 18 Nov. 1831; *Richmond Enquirer*, 22 Nov. 1831. The *Enquirer* put the time at "about 10 o'clock."

2. *Norfolk Herald*, 14 Nov. 1831.

3. Nottoway Parish and St. Luke's Parish Personal Property Tax Lists, 1831–36, LVA.

4. Turner genealogy (author's research file); Sally Knox's property is described in deed, Alfred Strong and Disey Strong to Josiah Vick, 21 Aug. 1822, Deed Book 18:522, SCC.

5. U.S. Census, Southampton County, 1850, p. 256b, NA.

6. Inventory, John C. Turner, 20 Dec. 1851, Will Book 14:634–36, SCC.

7. St. Luke's Parish Land Books, 1831, 1833, LVA; St. Luke's Parish Personal Tax Lists, 1831, 1833, entries for Nathaniel Francis; F. N. Boney, "Nathaniel Francis, Representative Antebellum Southerner," *Proceedings of the American Philosophical Society* 118 (1974): 454.

8. St. Luke's Parish Personal Tax List, 1835, entry for Nathaniel Francis and Etheldred T. Brantley.

9. Boney, "Nathaniel Francis," 455–56.

10. Jefferson to Coles, 25 Aug. 1814; Jefferson to Holmes, 22 Apr. 1820, in Thomas Jefferson, *Thomas Jefferson: Writings*, ed. Merrill D. Peterson (New York: Literary Classics of the United States, 1984), 1,343–46, 1,433–35.

11. Dumas Malone, *Jefferson and His Time: The Sage of Monticello* (Boston: Little, Brown, 1981), 320–27, 334–38.

12. St. Luke's Parish Personal Tax List, 1832, entry for John W. Reese.

13. Marriage Register, p. 440, SCC; report of commissioners, *Parker v. Barham*, 23 Dec. 1833, County Court Order Book, 15 Jan. 1838, p. 385, SCC.

14. Deed, Robert Ridley to John W. Reese, 9 Nov. 1838, Deed Book 24:282–83.

15. Account of sales, John W. Reese, 1 Jan. 1844, Deed Book 26:183–87; account of sales, John W. Reese, 2 Jan. 1844, Deed Book 26:188–90; Jonathan B. Pritchett,

"The Interregional Slave Trade and the Selection of Slaves for the New Orleans Market," *Journal of Interdisciplinary History* 28 (1997): 77.

16. U.S. Census, Greensville County, VA, 1850, p. 373a, NA; slave schedules, Greensville County, 1850, entries for J. W. Reese, NA; U.S. Census, Greensville County, 1860, p. 573; slave schedules, Greensville County, 1860, p. 284.

17. William S. Drewry, *The Southampton Insurrection* (1900; repr., Murfreesboro, NC: Johnson, 1968), 28.

18. U.S. Census, Southampton County, 1870, Boykins Depot Township, p. 150b; U.S. Census, Greensville County, 1870, Belfield, p. 346b.

19. Commissioners' report, division of the land and slaves of John and Catherine Whitehead, 28 Mar. 1832, *Whitehead v. Whitehead*, Southampton County Chancery Causes, LVA.

20. Harriet Whitehead's brother John said he also attended to her affairs; John Whitehead, deposition, 16 Sept. 1851, *Whitehead v. Francis*, County Court Records, Chancery Papers, 1851, LVA.

21. St. Luke's Parish Land Book, 1838, entry for Harriet Whitehead; U.S. Census, Southampton County, 1840, p. 103.

22. Sampson C. Reese, deposition, 8 Nov. 1848, *Whitehead v. Francis*, County Court Records, Chancery Papers, 1851.

23. John R. Kilby, Amended Bill of Complaint, [1851], *Whitehead v. Francis*, County Court Records, Chancery Papers, 1851.

24. Cuthbert D. Barham, deposition, 12 Jan. 1848, *Whitehead v. Francis*, County Court Records, Chancery Papers, 1851.

25. Ibid.

26. Deed, Harriet Whitehead to Nathaniel Francis, 13 Nov. 1843, Deed Book 26:97. Hubbard probably was the senior male slave counted at the Whitehead farm in the 1840 census. Barham estimated the value of the property conveyed to Francis at $3,600.

27. Bond, Nathaniel Francis and John Drewry to Harriet Whitehead, 13 Nov. 1843, Deed Book 26:98.

28. Joseph B. Whitehead, deposition, 16 Sept. 1851; Nathan Thomas, deposition, 6 Oct. 1851; Sampson C. Reese, deposition, 8 Nov. 1848; Barham, deposition, 12 Jan. 1848, all in *Whitehead v. Francis*, County Court Records, Chancery Papers, 1851.

29. Martha L. Darden, depositions, 17 Feb. 1849, 16 Sept. 1851, *Whitehead v. Francis*, County Court Records, Chancery Papers, 1851.

30. John Whitehead, deposition, 16 Sept. 1851, *Whitehead v. Francis*, County Court Records, Chancery Papers, 1851.

31. Inventory, Harriet Whitehead, 27 Apr. 1852, Will Book 11A:43.

32. Barham, deposition, 12 Jan. 1848, *Whitehead v. Francis*, County Court Records, Chancery Papers, 1851.

33. Kilby, Amended Bill of Complaint, *Whitehead v. Francis*, County Court Records, Chancery Papers, 1851.

34. Nathaniel Francis, Answer to Amended Bill of Complaint, 17 July 1848, *Whitehead v. Francis*, Kilby Papers, RDU.

35. Decree (copy), *Whitehead v. Francis*, Nov. 1848, Circuit Superior Court, Kilby Papers; will, Nathaniel Francis, 18 Mar. 1849, Will Book 14:180.

36. U.S. Census, Southampton County, 1850, p. 256b; slave schedules, Southampton County, 1850, entries for Harriet Whitehead, NA.

37. Inventory, Harriet Whitehead, Will Book 11A:42–43. Harriet Whitehead's nine slaves represented 74.6 percent of her entire estate in 1852, including land; they accounted for 91.1 percent of her personal estate. Her father's thirteen slaves in 1815 represented 56.9 percent of his personal estate; inventory, John Whitehead, 5 Apr. 1815, Will Book 8:14–15.

38. James McDowell, *Speech of James McDowell, Jr. (of Rockbridge) in the House of Delegates of Virginia on the Slave Question* (Richmond: Thomas W. White, 1832), 29.

39. U.S. Census, Southampton County, 1840, p. 99.

40. Will, Richard Porter, 18 Oct. 1839 (proved 21 May 1855), Will Book 15:387–88.

41. Barham, deposition, 12 Jan. 1848, *Whitehead v. Francis*, Southampton County Court Records, Chancery Papers, 1851.

42. U.S. Census, Southampton County, 1850, p. 252b.

43. St. Luke's Parish Personal Tax List, 1832, entry for Peter Edwards.

44. St. Luke's Parish Land Book, 1834, entry for Peter Edwards; Henry I. Tragle, *The Southampton Slave Revolt of 1831: A Compilation of Source Material* (Amherst: University of Massachusetts Press, 1971), 163 (photograph).

45. Deed, Richard Mason and Mary Louisa Mason to Peter Edwards, 9 Nov. 1836, Deed Book 24:22; St. Luke's Parish Land Book, 1837, entry for Peter Edwards.

46. St. Luke's Parish Land Book, 1838, entry for Peter Edwards.

47. Marriage Register, p. 707; St. Luke's Parish Land Book, 1838, entry for Peter Edwards; Barrow genealogy (author's research file).

48. Narcissa Edwards's first husband, Edmund Turner Jr., probably was master of Hark Moore until 1821; his children, James and Elizabeth Turner, inherited Nat Turner II; Barrow genealogy (author's research file).

49. U.S. Census, Southampton County, 1820, p. 116; 1830, p. 259; 1840, p. 93; 1850, p. 253b; U.S. Census, slave schedules, Southampton County, 1850, entries for Peter Edwards.

50. Will, Peter Edwards, 16 Apr. 1855 (recorded 15 Aug. 1859), Will Book 16:555.

51. Renunciation, Narcissa Edwards, 13 Aug. 1859, Will Book 16:555–56.

52. Account, estate of Peter Edwards, 1859–60, Will Book 17:200–204.

53. U.S. Census, Dinwiddie County, VA, 1860, p. 63, NA; slave schedules, Dinwiddie County, 1860, city of Petersburg, entry for Narcissa Edwards, NA; U.S. Census, Southampton County, 1860, pp. 135, 142 ("Brigg"); slave schedules, Southampton County, 1860, pp. 285a–b ("Brigg"), 283a–b.

54. Will, John T. Barrow, 8 Nov. 1829, Will Book 10:347.

55. St. Luke's Parish Land Book, 1831, and St. Luke's Parish Personal Tax List, 1831, entries for John T. Barrow; U.S. Census, Southampton County, 1830, p. 259 ("Thos."). Mary T. Barrow's second husband paid tax on the four slaves in St. Luke's in 1833; St. Luke's Parish Personal Tax List, 1833, entry for Fielding Rose.

56. Report of commissioners, estate of Rebecca Vaughan, Sept. 1831, County Court Records, Chancery Papers, 1831.

57. The number of Harris's taxable slaves increased by four in 1832; St. Luke's Parish Personal Tax List, 1832, entry for Newit Harris.

58. Marriage Register, p. 433; U.S. Census, Sussex County, 1830, p. 34, NA.

59. Deed, Fielding Rose and Mary T. Rose to Henry B. Vaughan, 8 July 1833, Deed Book 23:65–66; deed, Rose and Rose to Nathaniel Francis and others, 9 Sept. 1838, Deed Book 24:273–74; deed, Rose and Rose to James Maclamore, 29 Dec. 1838, Deed Book 24:301–2.

60. St. Luke's Parish Land Book, 1831, 1837; and St. Luke's Parish Personal Tax List, 1831, 1836, entries for Newit Harris.

61. Will, Newit Harris, 17 Oct. 1833, Will Book 12:5.

62. Waller genealogy (author's research file).

63. St. Luke's Parish Personal Tax List, 1836; and St. Luke's Parish Land Book, 1838, entries for Levi Waller.

64. U.S. Census, Southampton County, 1840, p. 104.

65. Inventory, Levi Waller, 24 Nov. 1847, Will Book 14:134.

66. Will, Levi Waller, 11 Oct. 1847, Will Book 14:53–54.

67. Account of sales, estate of Levi Waller, 24 Nov. 1847, Will Book 14:218.

68. U.S. Census, slave schedules, Southampton County, 1860, pp. 288b, 279a. The two remaining in 1860 were Benjamin C. Waller, the eldest son, and Levi C. Waller, the third son. They were the favored heirs in 1847. Benjamin C. held thirteen slaves in 1860, and Levi C., three.

69. Marriage Register, p. 428.

70. U.S. Census, Southampton County, 1850, p. 256a.

71. U.S. Census, Southampton County, 1830, p. 259; 1840, p. 103; U.S. Census, slave schedules, Southampton County, 1850, entries for Jacob Williams; slave schedules, Southampton County, 1860, p. 280b.

72. Death Records, 1853–90, 23 Sept. 1862, p. 454, SCC.

73. Marriage Register, p. 429; St. Luke's Parish Land Book, 1832, entry for Jane Newsom; St. Luke's Parish Land Book, 1833, entry for Caswell Worrell; St. Luke's Parish Personal Tax List, 1831, entry for Jane Newsom; St. Luke's Parish Personal Tax List, 1832, entry for Caswell Worrell.

74. Deed, Caswell Worrell to John R. Williams, 11 May 1835, Deed Book 23:419–20.

75. Marriage Register, p. 456.

76. U.S. Census, Southampton County, 1840, p. 103.

77. Account, estate of Jane Worrell, 1843–46, Will Book 14:76–77.

78. County Court Minute Book, 15 Apr. 1844, p. 148, SCC.

79. U.S. Census, 1850, Southampton County, 1850, p. 281b; Marriage Book 1, 18 Dec. 1854, p. 17, SCC.

80. Marriage Book 1, 21 Dec. 1857, p. 50; Death Records, 5 Sept. 1858, p. 454.

81. U.S. Census, 1860, Southampton County, pp. 144–45; Birth Records, 29 Mar. 1853, p. 51, SCC.

82. Will, Caswell Worrell, 23 May 1862, Will Book 17:544–45.

83. [Thomas R. Gray], letter, 17 Sept. 1831, *Richmond Constitutional Whig*, 26 Sept. 1831, in *Norfolk American Beacon*, 30 Sept. 1831.

84. Drewry, *Southampton Insurrection*, 21, 63n1; Drewry is the source for Parker's moving to Tennessee.

85. Deeds, James W. and Martha Ann Parker to Alexander P. Peete, 3 Sept. 1831, Deed Book 22:78, 79.

86. Report of commissioners, estate of Rebecca Vaughan, Sept. 1831, County Court Records, Chancery Papers, 1831.

87. County Court Minute Book, 19 Mar. 1832, p. 157.

88. St. Luke's Parish Personal Tax List, 1835, entry for James W. Parker; deed, Henry B. Vaughan to James W. Parker, 1834, Deed Book 23:530.

89. St. Luke's Parish Land Books, 1816–31, and St. Luke's Parish Personal Tax Lists, 1816–31, entries for James Trezvant; U.S. Census, Southampton County, 1830, p. 259.

90. County Court Minute Book, 16 Jan. 1832, p. 145.

91. James Trezvant to James Rochelle, 11 June 1832, Rochelle Papers, RDU.

92. James Trezvant to James Rochelle, 5 Oct. 1832, Rochelle Papers.

93. James Trezvant's final entry in local tax records appeared in the St. Luke's Parish Personal Tax List of 1832.

94. Trezvant to Rochelle, 5 Oct. 1832, Rochelle Papers.

95. U.S. Census, Shelby County, TN, 1840, p. 223, NA.

96. John Timothee Trezevant, *The Trezevant Family in the United States* (Columbia, SC: State Company, 1914), 24.

97. Will, Robert Goodwin, 30 July 1832, Will Book 11:37; will, Benjamin Cobb, 15 Feb. 1823, Will Book 10:1.

98. St. Luke's Parish Land Book, 1834, entry for Orris A. Browne; U.S. Census, Greensville County, 1840, p. 421.

99. Rochelle genealogy (author's research file); Nottoway Parish Personal Tax List, 1835, and St. Luke's Parish Personal Tax List, 1835, entries for James Rochelle.

100. Account, estate of James Rochelle, 1835–39, Will Book 12:86, 88.

101. Account, estate of Clements Rochelle, 1846–47, Will Book 14:67–68.

102. U.S. Census, Southampton County, 1840, p. 99.

103. County Court Order Book, 18 Jan. 1803, p. 128; 21 May 1804, p. 231. John O. Peters and Margaret T. Peters, *Virginia's Historic Courthouses* (Charlottesville: University of Virginia Press, 1995), 102–3; Carl R. Lounsbury, *Courthouses of Early Virginia: An Architectural History* (Charlottesville: University of Virginia Press, 2005), 376–77; Bruce Montgomery Edwards, *The Cobbs of the Tidewater* (Knoxville, TN: Montgomery, 1976), 93.

104. Edwards, *Cobbs of the Tidewater*, 95.

105. County Circuit-Superior Court of Law and Chancery Minute Book, 7 Apr. 1832, p. 28, SCC.

106. Deed, Henry B. Vaughan to Thomas C. Jones, 17 Dec. 1833, Deed Book 23:136–37.

107. Deed, Henry B. Vaughan to Mary, 15 June 1837; deed, Henry B. Vaughan to Henrietta, 15 June 1837, Deed Book 24:97–98.

108. U.S. Census, Southampton County, 1840, p. 102; U.S. Census, Southampton County, 1850, p. 282b.

109. Henry B. Vaughan, will, 10 July 1851, Will Book 15:28–30; inventory, Henry B. Vaughan, 18 Aug. 1852, Will Book 15:76.

110. U.S. Census, Southampton County, 1850, p. 297b.

111. Nottoway Parish Personal Tax Lists, 1823–29, entries for Theodore Trezvant.

112. U.S. Census, Southampton County, 1830, p. 272; Nottoway Parish Personal Tax Lists, 1830–31, entries for Theodore Trezvant.

113. U.S. Census, Southampton County, 1840, p. 84; Trezvant had no entry in the 1850 slave schedules.

114. County Court Minute Book, 21 Aug. 1826, p. 128.

115. Nottoway Parish Personal Tax Lists, 1826–31, entries for William C. Parker; U.S. Census, Southampton County, 1830, p. 277.

116. [William C. Parker], letter, 21 Sept. 1831, *Richmond Enquirer*, 30 Sept. 1831.

117. County Court Minute Book, 16 Jan. 1832, p. 148; 17 Sept. 1832, p. 202; County Circuit-Superior Court of Law and Chancery Minute Book, 1 Sept. 1831, p. 3.

118. U.S. Census, Dinwiddie County, 1840, Petersburg East Ward, p. 93.

119. "The Parker Family of Essex, the Northern Neck, &c.," *Virginia Magazine of History and Biography* 6 (1898): 592; County Court Order Book, 20 Sept. 1847, p. 552.

120. *A Provisional List of Alumni . . . of the College of William and Mary in Virginia, from 1693 to 1888* (Richmond: Division of Purchase and Printing, 1941), 18; *A Catalogue of the Officers and Students of the University of Virginia, Second Session, Commencing February 1st, 1826* (Charlottesville, VA: Chronicle Steam Book Printing House, 1880), 7; Thomas C. Parramore, *Southampton County, Virginia* (Charlottesville: University of Virginia Press, 1978), 137–43; French genealogy (author's research file).

121. County Court Minute Book, 21 Apr. 1828, p. 209; Nottoway Parish Personal Tax Lists, 1828–32, entries for James S. French; Parramore, *Southampton County*, 92.

122. Deed, Robert Goodwin to James S. French, 10 Apr. 1829, Deed Book 21:96.

123. Nottoway Parish Personal Tax Lists, 1834 and 1835, entries for James S. French.

124. Parramore, *Southampton County*, 139–43.

125. James Strange French, *Elkswatawa; or, the Prophet of the West: A Tale of the Frontier* (New York: Harper & Brothers, 1836), 21–22, 192–203, 206–10, 225, 230–32, 237.

126. Ibid., 19–20.

127. Ibid., x.

128. Ibid., v.

129. Ibid., 20.

130. Ibid., 73.

131. Ibid., 142.

132. Deed, Thomas Gray Sr. to Thomas R. Gray, 15 Mar. 1828, Deed Book 20:344; deed, Thomas R. Gray to Richard A. Urquhart, 17 May 1830, Deed Book 21:339–40. Evidence in the deeds and estate documents does not support the theory that father

and son were thoroughly estranged in 1831. Rather than disinheriting T. R. in his will, Gray Sr. appears to have taken into account gifts already bestowed on this son.

133. Will, Thomas Gray Sr., 6 Sept. 1831, Will Book 10:343; deed, Thomas Gray Sr. to Ann Gray, 6 Sept. 1831, Deed Book 22:93.

134. *Richmond Compiler*, quoted in *Philadelphia National Gazette*, 16 Nov. 1831; *Raleigh Star*, 17 Nov. 1831; Thomas Wentworth Higginson, "Nat Turner's Insurrection," *Atlantic Monthly* 8 (1861): 173–87, in Higginson, *Travellers and Outlaws: Episodes in American History* (Boston: Lee & Shepard, 1888), 319.

135. Parramore, *Southampton County*, 112.

136. County Court Minute Book, 16 Feb. 1835, p. 377.

137. Deed, Edwin Gray to Orris A. Browne, 19 Nov. 1831, Deed Book 22:123.

138. Invoice, *Orris A. Browne v. Thomas R. Gray*, 22 May 1833, County Court Records, Chancery Papers, 1833.

139. Inventory, Thomas Gray Sr., 26 Oct. 1831, Will Book 10:386–87.

140. Deed, Edwin Gray to Thomas R. Gray, 5 Dec. 1831, Deed Book 22:240.

141. Inquisition upon the body of Tom, slave, 6 Mar. 1832, and Inquisition upon the body of Peg, slave, 6 Mar. 1832, Southampton County Inquisitions, 1823–35, LVA.

142. Ibid.

143. County Court Minute Book, 20 Mar. 1832, p. 162.

144. Deed, Jesse Drewry to Thomas R. Gray, 17 Sept. 1832, Deed Book 22:335–36; deed, Thomas R. Gray to Littleton R. Edwards and John Urquhart, 17 Sept. 1832, Deed Book 22:337.

145. Bill of complaint, *Orris A. Browne v. Thomas R. Gray*, 21 Aug. 1833; Answer of T. R. Gray, 14 Jan. 1844, both in *Browne v. Gray*, County Court Records, Chancery Papers, 1835.

146. Thomas R. Gray, *To the Public* [Jerusalem, 1834], 1.

147. Ibid., 4.

148. Ibid., 7–9.

149. Deed, Orris A. and Susan J. Browne to Edwin B. Claud, 17 Mar. 1834, Deed Book 23:196–97; St. Luke's Parish Land Book, 1834, entry for Orris A. Browne.

150. Drewry, *Southampton Insurrection*, 66n1.

151. County Court Minute Book, 21–22 Apr. 1834, pp. 326, 328.

152. Nottoway Parish Personal Tax Lists, 1832–36, entries for Thomas R. Gray.

153. Deed, Samuel and Elizabeth Polkinhorn to Thomas R. Gray and John Urquhart, 25 Dec. 1833, Deed Book 23:165–67; deed, Thomas R. Gray to Richard Williams, 15 Jan. 1835, Deed Book 23:351.

154. County Court Minute Book, 16 Feb. 1835, p. 377.

155. Deed, Thomas R. Gray to William D. Hodges, 21 Sept. 1836, Deed Book 23:683–84.

156. Letters, Thomas R. Gray to John Forsyth, 1 Jan. 1837; John Young Mason to Forsyth, 21 Jan. 1837; Gray to Forsyth, 1 Feb. 1837; Gray to Forsyth, 12 Apr. 1837, Consular Despatches, Tabasco, 1832–74, General Records of the Department of State, NA.

157. Parramore, *Southampton County*, 254n63.

158. *Norfolk American Beacon*, 26 Aug. 1845, 27 Aug. 1845.

159. Ibid., 27 Aug. 1845.

160. Ibid.; [Gray], letter, *Richmond Whig*, 26 Sept. 1831, in *Norfolk American Beacon*, 30 Sept. 1831.

161. U.S. Census, Norfolk County, VA, 1840, p. 117, NA.

162. *Norfolk American Beacon*, 27 Aug. 1845.

163. Ibid.

INDEX